Economists studying environmental collective action and green governance have paid little attention to gender. Research on gender and green governance in other disciplines has focused mainly on women's near absence from forestry institutions. This interdisciplinary book turns that focus on its head to ask: what if women were present in these institutions? What difference would *that* make?

Would women's inclusion in forest governance—undeniably important for equity—also affect decisions on forest use and outcomes for conservation and subsistence? Are women's interests in forests different from men's? Would women's presence lead to better forests and more equitable access? Does it matter which class of women governs? And how large a presence of women would make an impact? Answers to these questions can prove foundational for effective environmental governance, yet they have been subject to little empirical investigation.

In an analysis that is conceptually sophisticated and statistically rigorous, using primary data on community forestry institutions in India and Nepal, this book is the first major study to comprehensively address these wide-ranging issues. It traces women's history of exclusion from public institutions, the factors which constrain their effective participation, and how those constraints can be overcome. It outlines how strategic partnerships between forestry groups and other civil society institutions could strengthen rural women's bargaining power with community and government. And it examines the complexities of eliciting government accountability in addressing poor rural women's needs, such as for clean domestic fuel and access to the commons.

Located in the interface of environmental studies, political economy and gender analysis, the volume makes significant original contributions to current debates on gender and governance, forest conservation, clean energy policy, critical mass, and social inclusion. Traversing uncharted territory with rare analytical rigor, this lucidly written book will be of interest to scholars and students as well as to policy makers and practitioners.

BINA AGARWAL is Director and Professor of Economics at the Institute of Economic Growth, Delhi University. She has held distinguished positions at many leading universities, including at Harvard, Minnesota, Princeton, Michigan, and New York. She has been Vice-President of the International Economic Association; President of the International Association for Feminist Economics; and on the Board of the Global Development Network. Agarwal is also the first woman President-elect of the International Society for Ecological Economics. In addition she serves on the UN Committee for Development Policy and on the editorial boards of several international academic journals. An original thinker with many professional papers and eight books, including the multiple award-winning, *A Field of One's Own*, she has contributed to broadening the frontiers of economic thought both theoretically and empirically. An economist with a keen interest in interdisciplinary and inter-country explorations, her pioneering work on gender inequality in property and land, and on environmental issues, has had global impact among academics and policymakers. In 2008 the President of India honoured her with a Padma Shri, and in 2010 she was awarded the Leontief prize by Tufts University.

Praise for *Gender and Green Governance*

It is hard to write a short endorsement, given how important this book is. Based on years of intensive field research in India and Nepal, using diverse empirical methods, and drawing on a deep understanding of the significance of gender representation in governance, Bina Agarwal has crafted a book of central importance in today's world. Both women and their connections with forests have been under-represented in the field, in academic research, and in policy. With analytical rigour and originality, Agarwal bridges these major gaps in our understanding of the difference women can make, when they are actively involved in forest governance.

Elinor Ostrom, Nobel Laureate in Economics 2009

Beautifully written and soundly argued, this book makes an outstanding contribution to the fields of both environmental economics and governance. Drawing on over a decade of fieldwork in India and Nepal, and eschewing easy generalizations, Bina Agarwal offers a richly layered and insightful treatment of the effects of women's presence in local bodies governing village forests. Given its mix of quantitative and qualitative evidence, this work will be accessible to scholars and practitioners of many hues. It should be mandatory reading for anyone interested in the impact of heterogeneity on village collective action, effective versus nominal participation of marginalized groups, and environmental conservation.

Jean-Philippe Platteau, University of Namur and co-author of *Halting Degradation of Natural Resources*

GENDER AND GREEN GOVERNANCE

GENDER AND GREEN GOVERNANCE

The Political Economy of Women's Presence Within and Beyond Community Forestry

BINA AGARWAL

OXFORD
UNIVERSITY PRESS

OXFORD
UNIVERSITY PRESS

Great Clarendon Street, Oxford OX2 6DP

Oxford University Press is a department of the University of Oxford.
It furthers the University's objective of excellence in research, scholarship,
and education by publishing worldwide in

Oxford New York

Auckland Cape Town Dar es Salaam Hong Kong Karachi
Kuala Lumpur Madrid Melbourne Mexico City Nairobi
New Delhi Shanghai Taipei Toronto

With offices in

Argentina Austria Brazil Chile Czech Republic France Greece
Guatemala Hungary Italy Japan Poland Portugal Singapore
South Korea Switzerland Thailand Turkey Ukraine Vietnam

Oxford is a registered trade mark of Oxford University Press
in the UK and in certain other countries

Published in the United States
by Oxford University Press Inc., New York

First published 2010

British Library Cataloguing in Publication Data
Data available

Library of Congress Cataloging in Publication Data
Data available

Typeset by SPI Publisher Services, Pondicherry, India
Printed in Great Britain
on acid-free paper by
MPG Books Group, Bodmin and King's Lynn

ISBN 978–0–19–956968–7

3 5 7 9 10 8 6 4 2

In memory of my mother
An indomitable spirit
(1923–2006)

Contents

List of Figures

List of Tables

Abbreviations

AKRSP(I)	Agha Khan Rural Support Programme (India)
CF	Community Forest
CFI	Community Forestry Institution
CPR	Common Pool Resource
DFO	District Forest Officer
EC	Executive Committee
FAO	Food and Agriculture Organization
FECOFUN	Federation of Community Forest Users, Nepal
GB	Governing Body
GoI	Government of India
GoN	Government of Nepal
JFM	Joint Forest Management
ME	Marginal Effects
MP	Member of Parliament
NGO	Non-governmental Organization
NWFP	Non-Wood Forest Products
OLS(r)	Ordinary Least Squares regression (with robust standard errors)
PRI	Panchayati Raj Institutions
SARTHI	Social Action for Rural and Tribal Inhabitants of India
SHG	Self-Help Group
VIKSAT	Vikram Sarabhai Centre for Development Interaction

Preface

I was about 11 years old, as I recall, when hearing the sound of an axe I ran to the inner walled garden of our bungalow in Delhi, located on what was then called Electric Lane. Two men were heavily lopping a tree in the neighbouring house that was occupied by a member of parliament. The branches and blossoms of the tree overhung our shared wall. I called out to the men that it was forbidden to cut trees in Delhi without permission. Startled to see my earnest little face, the men assured me that they were only cutting a dry branch, but seeing my disbelief and realizing that I would not budge until they ceased, they climbed down. The tree still stands, albeit armless, as does another which sprouted from a mango seed I had planted. Long years later, I discovered that numerous other people were also seeking to protect their green spaces, not least the women in South Asia's villages, many of whom had formed informal patrol groups to guard their local forests.

Although my interest in trees and women's causes goes back to childhood, this book brings to these concerns the significant aspect of governance, carrying forward my earlier research. Academically, I first explored the interconnections between forests, institutions, and gender inequality in 1980, when writing a monograph on the woodfuel crisis and social forestry at the Science Policy Research Unit of the University of Sussex. In the 1970s, long before forests were valued as carbon sinks, and far away from the global clamour following the oil crisis, vast numbers in developing countries, dependent primarily on woodfuels for their domestic energy, were facing a less-noticed crisis—one that stemmed from the everyday consequences of depleting forests and shrinking supplies of firewood and charcoal. Women of poor households—the main gatherers of firewood for cooking and heating—were the most adversely affected. Attempts to promote afforestation and improved wood-burning stoves as solutions by governments and international agencies, including the FAO and the World Bank, had had rather limited success. In particular, few of these initiatives had involved or benefited the rural poor. My monograph (later a book, Agarwal 1986a) critiqued the top-down methods of planning and implementing social forestry and improved stove programmes, and made a strong case for following a more democratic and participatory approach that would include the rural poor and especially women. It also stressed the importance of entrusting communities with forest management and ensuring an equitable distribution of benefits.

Throughout the 1980s, in fact, there was an intense debate, both in India and globally, as to who could most effectively manage local forests—the State, village communities, or individual owners. Widespread State failure and emerging stories of community success in forest protection also fuelled the debate. Many argued that communities living near forests and dependent on them for their daily needs would be the best custodians and conservators. Theoretically, there was a growing recognition that Hardin's (1968) model of 'the tragedy of the commons' had been overextended, as had the idea that free riding would necessarily undermine collective action within communities. Administrative decentralization was also moving apace. These and related factors created a favourable climate for experimenting with community management of natural resources in many parts of the world.

In 1988, India formulated a 'people-friendly' forest policy, which shifted the earlier emphasis on forests for commercial gain to forests for fulfilling local subsistence needs and conserving the environment. The involvement of villagers (including women) was integral to the new approach. The Joint Forest Management (JFM) programme, launched by the government of India in 1990, was founded on this new policy. Similar shifts in thinking and policy took place in Nepal, where the 1993 Forest Act laid the foundation for its community forestry programme.

Since such a change in approach was precisely what many of us had advocated, I decided to see for myself, at first hand, how it was working on the ground—in particular to what extent community forestry provided scope for women and the poor to participate. My field visit to India's Gujarat state in 1995 revealed that despite an impressive improvement in forest canopies under JFM, there had hardly been a dent in the firewood problem; and although women were informally active in forest protection, they were little seen or heard in the formal decision-making bodies. Subsequently, in 1998–99, when I travelled across six states of India and two districts of Nepal, conducting unstructured interviews in some ninety-four villages and community forestry institutions, I found that women's exclusions from decision-making were widespread, as were their complaints (sharper in some regions than others) about firewood shortages. These exclusions meant that the new institutions of forest governance, which had enormous potential for challenging entrenched gender inequalities, were in fact creating new ones. And women who had enjoyed rights as citizens over the commons, prior to the launch of community forestry, now had rather little say in their use.

In an earlier book, *A Field of One's Own* (Agarwal 1994), I had drawn attention to the adverse implications of women's lack of effective rights in agricultural land—a largely private resource—for their economic and social well-being and productivity. My exploratory fieldwork in community forestry indicated that now women were being excluded even from public resources. In the current book I therefore move from field back to forest, to focus on the gender effects of the new institutions of governance. I do so, however, from a rather different angle than that found in the literature so far.

Much of the existing research on gender and local forest governance has focused on women's near *absence* from governance institutions. In this book I invert that focus to ask—what difference would it make if women were *present* in these institutions? And how much presence do women need for making a difference? Although there is a considerable body of work on the difference women's numbers make to governance, almost all of it is concentrated on women in legislatures, especially in western democracies. Yet questions such as the above are equally relevant for local governance and for women in developing countries. In addition, there are unaddressed dimensions, such as the impact of women's presence on policy implementation, as opposed to simply policy formulation.

In the book I address many of the issues raised in the gender and politics literature, but in the rather different context of forest governance. I also address questions which have been neglected in both contexts. And I deviate from emerging studies on village councils in India, which have focused on the impact of women chairpersons and not on women's proportions in the council. In particular, I empirically test a number of propositions. Some of these have acquired the status of truisms without much verification, such as the idea that women need at least one-third presence to be effective. Others are assumed to be true by default, such as the presumption by many that once women enter governance various benefits will follow automatically. I believe empirical testing—based on a healthy scepticism—is especially important where there are strong stakes in particular arguments, such as those arising from gender, race, religion, or ethnic considerations.

By this approach (which also builds on qualitative and historical evidence), I hope to draw into the discussion several constituencies: environmental and governance analysts who have not gendered their analysis; gender analysts who have neglected environmental concerns; scholars of gender and the environment who have drawn rather little on quantitative evidence; and those studying gender and governance in other contexts (including legislatures in western democracies) who might find in the results some interesting contrasts, or a confirmation of their own insights.

The empirical analysis was, in fact, the most challenging part of this book. In the absence of an appropriate data set, I collected my own, focusing on selected regions of India and Nepal. None of the Indian states, however, had baseline information on the gender composition of community forestry groups from which I could draw a sample. My efforts to persuade the forest departments in several states to field a simple questionnaire for obtaining such data, also proved largely unsuccessful. Three NGOs in Gujarat, however, did have this crucial information. I therefore located my India-related analysis in Gujarat, a region with which I was also familiar through prior visits. In Nepal, the forest department does collect country-wide information on the gender composition of forestry groups on which I could base my sample selection, although subject to the security constraints imposed by the Maoist insurgency, which put several regions out of bounds.

My survey began at a point when community forestry was high on the agenda of several funding agencies, especially the Ford Foundation, and my 2000–01 research was funded by a generous grant from the Foundation's Delhi office. I am immensely grateful to the Foundation for the opportunity to explore this topic in depth, and thank Doris Capistrano, Gowher Rizwi, Vasant Saberwal, Ganesan Balachander, and Jeffery Campbell for their support at various stages of the project's life. Doris, in particular, with her keen interest in India's JFM programme, always found time for a discussion and I value her intellectual enthusiasm for this research. I am also grateful to the Foundation for a small grant to cover my 1998–99 fieldwork in India. A similar visit to two districts of Nepal in 1999 was sponsored by the International Centre for Integrated Mountain Development (ICIMOD). Anupam Bhatia (then at ICIMOD) encouraged me to undertake the trip, and provided invaluable help in making local contacts and organizing my visit. He and his wife, Kiran Bhatia, also sustained me through many a long hotel stay in Kathmandu with their warm hospitality, home food, and conversation. Egbert Pelinck was then Director-General of ICIMOD and Gabriel Campbell succeeded him. I thank them both for extending ICIMOD's support during my many visits and offering me the position of honorary scientist and an office where I could meet my research team.

The success of my field visits in 1998–99 depended greatly on the generous help of many civil society organizations working on community forestry. They provided me with contacts and information, helped chart out my itinerary, took me to their fieldsites, debated their experiences, and even spared a staff member to accompany me as translator and guide. Several forest officials and researchers also generously shared their insights and facilitated my visits. In earlier papers (e.g. Agarwal 2000a) I have named many of the organizations and individuals that helped me, and I thank them all again. I also recall with pleasure my conversations with the Divisional Forest Officer in Harda district of Madhya Pradesh who late one night regaled me with accounts of how he had tackled illegal logging. He had a secret informer, reminiscent of Watergate's 'deep throat', who would tell him on which day and at what time bullock cart loads of illegal logs would pass along the road; and he and his men would wait to nab the culprits, sometimes hiding in the bushes for long hours in the dark.

My 2000–01 survey was more structured, and here again local support was critical. In Gujarat, as noted, my sample was based on the fieldsites of three major NGOs: AKRSP(I), SARTHI, and VIKSAT. I am immensely grateful to Apoorva Oza, Giriraj Singh, and Srinivas Mudrakartha, who headed these NGOs respectively, and to their senior staff, for their unstinting help throughout the survey. They provided me their baseline data for sample selection, introductions to the villagers where needed, and answers to my innumerable background questions before, during, and after the survey. I owe special thanks to Dhansinghbhai Rathore, senior staff member of SARTHI, who shared many insights, helped organize additional data gathering and map making, and unfailingly responded to my follow-up queries. I am also grateful for valuable inputs from Rughabhai and Kishore Bhai at SARTHI, Vijay Kaushal, Jhalabhai, Hena Bhen, Sujit Kumar and Ramesh Patel at VIKSAT; and Ashok Gupta, Mahendra Bhai, Natwar Singh, and Thakursi Bhai Rathore at AKRSP(I). Nirmal Bhen's warm hospitality sustained me during several field trips to Panchmahals, and I thank her too for sharing her understanding of women's associations in the area.

In Nepal, I am immensely grateful to FECOFUN (the Federation of Community Forest Users, Nepal), which delegated staff members to accompany my research teams, and provided the researchers with background information and introductions where needed. In particular, I thank Hari Prasad Neupane, Ram Bahadur Kesi, Bhola Bhattari, and the district-level heads of FECOFUN in the regions of my research. I also thank Clare Sakya and Peter Neil of the Nepal UK forestry programme, Krishna Shrestha, Deputy Director General of Community Forestry in Nepal's forest department, and Bhumi Raman Nepali for their help. To Bharat Pokharel (now Project Director with the Nepal Swiss Community Forestry Project) I owe an immense debt of gratitude. As a resource person on the project from the very beginning, he provided me invaluable help, both when I was pilot-testing the questionnaires and later, in tackling any problems the researchers faced, contacting members of the forest department and FECOFUN, locating supplementary data, and with amazing cheerfulness answering my numerous technical and other queries that continued till the book was completed. In Gujarat, I warmly thank Rajesh Kapoor who served as a resource person during the data gathering process.

The quality of any research, however, depends critically on the research team and mine gave of their best in meticulous data collection and documentation. For the Gujarat fieldwork, Ruchi Malhotra, Ramesh Patel, Purvi Vyas, and Umesh Rathod stayed for the full length of the project, while Bina Srinivasan and Mustak Ali Masi participated for a part of the time. In Nepal, Bidya Bhurtel, Bhola Bhattarai, Shambhu Kattel, Radhika Pokharel, and Shyamu Thapa again worked for the full period, while Lok Prasad Bhattarai, Sujata Thapa, and Chuda Mani filled in for shorter spells. I thank all of them for their dedication, hard work, enthusiasm, and the many subtle skills they brought to bear for drawing out the villagers in a free-flowing discussion. Fieldwork in Nepal was especially difficult, both because of the hard physical terrain of the middle hills and the security threat posed by the Maoist insurgency. It is to the courage and credit of my Nepali researchers that they stayed and completed the work, despite personal risks. Most members of my research teams in both Gujarat and Nepal remain in touch with me, and I was pleased to hear from several of them that their association with the project helped in advancing their careers and interests. Several are teaching or working with development NGOs. Bhola Bhattari is now General Secretary of FECOFUN. And Ramesh Patel, who was farming when I met him, is now one of VIKSAT's principal researchers, while Purvi Vyas has moved in the reverse direction—from research to organic farming in Gujarat.

Three people who played a particularly important role in data analysis and served as research analysts at various stages are Manoj Pandey, Ram Ashish Yadav, and Bidya Bhurtel. Manoj and Ram Ashish, in particular, worked with me for an extended period, on diverse aspects of the analysis, continuing to provide valuable assistance even while I was away at Harvard in 2006–07. I thank them for their dedication and excellent work, and for devoting many precious weekends and evenings to see the project through its critical stages. Bidya Bhurtel, who was part of the data gathering team, came to Delhi to help with the coding and initial analysis, leaving the cool Pokhra mountains for Delhi's hot summer. Others who provided valuable inputs in various capacities include Sevinc Rende, Swati Virmani,

Manoranjan Pattnaik, Rajnish Kumar, Advaita Marathe, Vikas Batra, and creative designer Bindia Thapar.

As the book progressed, many friends, colleagues, and associates gave me valuable comments and critical feedback. I am immensely grateful to Jim Boyce, Caroline Elliot, Paul Seabright, Sharad Lele, Vikram Dayal, and OUP's anonymous referee for their detailed comments on the full draft manuscript in one or other of its incarnations. For insightful feedback on individual chapters, I warmly thank Elizabeth Anderson, Amrita Basu, Amita Baviskar, S. Charusheela, William Clark, Ashwini Chhatre, Nancy Fraser, Raghav Gaiha, Arti Garg, Vegard Iversen, Robert Jensen, Sunil Kanwar, K. L. Krishna, Jane Mansbridge, Kay Mansfield, Pratap Bhanu Mehta, Puran Mongia, Pauline Peters, Karen Polenske, Sanjay Reddy, Kay Schlozman, Janet Seiz, Sanjay Srivastava, Patricia Uberoi, and Eliza Willis.

To Robert Jensen and Paul Seabright I owe very special thanks for sparing the time from their crowded academic schedules to painstakingly brainstorm with me on aspects of my econometric analysis, offering suggestions to address particular concerns and responding to my queries on others, although I alone am responsible for the end result. I am also most grateful to Vikram Dayal and Sunil Kanwar for their thoughtful engagement with aspects of the statistical analysis. On specific issues I gained a great deal from discussions with Arun Agrawal, Mani Shankar Aiyar, V. K. Bahuguna, Jean-Marie Baland, Pranab Bardhan, Kaushik Basu, Nina Bhatt, Prabhakar Bhatt, Bhola Bhattarai, Haimanthi Biswas, Sam Bowles, Gabriel Campbell, Jeffrey Campbell, Elizabeth Cecelski, Ram Chhetri, Dilli Dahal, Purnamita Dasgupta, A. P. Dubey, V. B. Eshwaran, Jana Everett, Anne Marie Goetz, Bishwanath Goldar, R. Gopalakrishnan, Ashok Gupta, Indrani Gupta, Shireen Hassim, N. S. Jodha, Jorrit de Jong, Kenneth Keniston, Michael Kollmair, Arup Mitra, Peter Neil, Hemant Ojha, Nabaghan Ojha, Elinor Ostrom, S. N. Pandey, S. C. Pant, Jyoti Parikh, Kirith Parikh, Kedar Paudel, Shirin Rai, Jairam Ramesh, N. H. Ravindranath, Sushil Saigal, Madhu Sarin, N. C. Saxena, Janet Seeley, Govinda Shrestha, Gay Siedman, Wendy Singer, K. Sivaramakrishnan, Kathleen Staudt, C. P. Sujaya, Nandini Sundar, George Verguhese, and Barry Underwood.

Stimulating conversations with many other friends and colleagues over the years, on several of the ideas presented here, enriched the process of my writing and I thank Andrew Barnett, Rajeev Bhargava, Judith Bruce, Kavita Chakravarty, Amrita Chhachhi, Ester Duflo, Diane Elson, Nancy Folbre, Madhav Gadgil, Ann Gold, Ramachander Guha, Anil Gupta, Geoffrey Hawthorn, Ronald Herring, Gail Hershatter, Jane Humphries, Mani Shankar Iyer, Jean Jackson, Sheila Jasanoff, Niraja Jayal, Kumari Jayawardena, Roger Jeffreys, Raphie Kaplinsky, Ashish Kothari, Shiv Kumar, Ranjana Kumari, Pareena Lawrance, Primila Lewis, Rod Macfarquhar, T. N. Madan, Renuka Mishra, Mark Moore, Rukmini Bhayya Nair, Martha Nussbaum, Mahesh Rangarajan, Vijayendra Rao, Ingrid Robeyns, Jeffrey Sachs, Anthony Saich, Ashwani Saith, Amartya Sen, Vikram Seth, the late Anil Shah, Nicolas Stern, Diana Strassmann, Norman Uphoff, and Margaret Woo. To Amartya Sen I owe particular thanks for sparing the time for many challenging discussions around the issues of cooperative conflict, capabilities, adaptive preferences and public deliberation.

I have presented aspects of my findings at several institutions and events, and I thank the participants for their engaged responses at the School for Natural Resources and Environment (University of Michigan, Ann Arbor); the Center for International Development, Kennedy School of Government (Harvard University); the Santa Fe Institute; the Political Economy Research Institute (University of Massachusetts at Amherst); the University of Minnesota; Michigan State University; The South Asia Program and the Polson Institute (Cornell University); the Environmental Studies Program (University of Chicago); and the Turin conference of the International Association for Feminist Economics. In addition, I held a two-day workshop in Ahmedabad (Gujarat) to present my initial findings to the NGOs in whose field areas I had done the survey. Feedback from the workshop participants, which also included forest officials, researchers, and members of my research team, proved most valuable. Some of the analysis in this book has also appeared in several papers (see e.g. Agarwal 2006, 2009a, 2009b, 2010).

I undertook a part of my analysis at Harvard University at two points in time. First, in 1999, I analysed my 1998–99 fieldwork notes while based there as the first Daniel Ingalls Visiting Professor, affiliated simultaneously with the Harvard Yenching Institute, the Asian Center, the Department of Government, and the Department of Indian and Sanskrit Studies. I especially thank Roderick Macfarquhar and Leonard W. J. van der Kuijp for the invitation. Second, during 2006–07, I spent several months as a research fellow of the Ash Institute for Democratic Governance and Innovation at the Kennedy School of Government. I am most grateful to Gowher Rizwi, then Director of the Ash Institute, for inviting me; to him and his wife, Agnese Borolo, for their warm hospitality and friendship; to the staff of the Institute for its support; and to the Center for Population and Development Studies at Harvard for providing me a most congenial office and work environment.

To my home institution—the Institute of Economic Growth—I owe a substantial debt. Without IEG's administrative support this project could not have been undertaken. In particular, I thank Kanchan Chopra, B. B. Bhattacharya, and the late Pravin Visaria (all of whom served as Directors of the IEG during the project's tenure); Sushil Kumar Sen, our efficient academic programmes officer; P. K. Jain and his excellent team of library staff, especially Shampa Paul, Jasvinder Kaur, and R. Vishwanathan; the hardworking staff (past and current) of the computer unit, in particular K. Lal, Vinod Tyagi, Parag Sharma (who put in many painstaking hours on the maps and sketches), and S. Sreedharan; the former and current finance officers, Shankar Dhar and D. D. Kandpal; Mr Trivedi and his staff in the accounts office; Mr Sher Singh Bisht, now administrative officer; Vikram Chauhan, my personal secretary; Sudha from the photocopying unit; and not least my able and feisty administrative assistant Neeta Bakhru, who is the only person I know who remembers my birthday not just with flowers but also with a flower vase to hold them!

Throughout this long journey from data collection to final completion, the one constant and sustaining feature has been my wide-ranging conversations with my father, S. M. Agarwal, on many ideas in this book, but especially around public participation, democracy, and women's rights. His responses—both critical and appreciative, both conceptual and practical—were invaluable.

While working on this book, when I was still at Harvard, my mother passed away in November 2006. As I write this preface I imagine her as she was when I last saw her, sitting in her armchair, reminiscing about her childhood spent rebelling against the strictures of a conservative Rajasthani family by climbing trees and swimming in the village stepwell, emboldened by the quiet indulgence of a loving father. Throughout her life she insisted on the importance of women having a voice, both within the home and outside it. Although increasingly fragile in frame, she remained, till the end, a woman of indomitable spirit. This book is dedicated to her and to my father who remains a continuing source of inspiration and strength.

Part I

The Potential of Presence

1

Presence and Representation

> It is green issues that will most crucially shape our lives in the current century and life for humans and other living things on the planet far into the future.
>
> (Lorey 2002: p. xi)

> I know a lot about the forest and I would speak if I was not afraid. I am scared to speak in front of so many men. If we were in a majority we would speak in the meeting.
>
> (Group discussion with women in Bhagwati Chisapani community forest, Baglung, Nepal, author's survey, 2000–01)

> We go to the forest in the morning and only return in the evening. Since the end of the rainy season, we have been going every day. I go myself as does my daughter. Earlier too there was a [firewood] shortage but not as acute.
>
> (Woman to author, Kangod village, Karnataka, 1998)

In the late 1990s, as I travelled for many months across six states of India and parts of Nepal, interviewing rural communities that were protecting their local forests, two stories surfaced repeatedly. One was the story of women's near-exclusion from decision-making within local institutions of forest governance, although they were the principal users of forests and knew a great deal about them. The other was the story of firewood—the single most important cooking fuel in South Asia—which had become even more scarce for many after protection began, despite growing availability. Underlying each story was a paradox. In the one case it lay in the exclusion of precisely the group with substantial stake in and knowledge of the forest. In the other case it lay in persisting shortages amidst growing plenty. Usually I heard the stories from women of both well-off and poor households, and sometimes only from the poor. But I heard them almost entirely from women. Most village men brushed aside the issue of firewood shortages, saying women had enough fuel through cropwaste. And their response to women's sparse presence in the governing institutions ranged from the dismissive ('there is no need for women to attend meetings—they don't know what to do') to the narrowly functional ('if we give women responsibility, violations will decrease'). The men recognized the potential usefulness of involving women to reduce rule violations by other women, but seldom to draw on women's knowledge of local ecology.

These stories constitute the centrepiece of the mosaic of pulls and pressures, of cooperation and conflict within communities that lie beneath the green canopies emerging from the protection efforts. In particular, they beg the key questions driving this book: would women's inclusion in governance—undeniably important for gender equity—also make a difference to the process of decision-making and to the outcomes for conservation and subsistence? Are women's interests in forests different from men's? Will decisions be different in groups where there are more women decision-makers? Will women's presence lead to better forest conservation or more equitable benefit distribution? Does it matter which class of women represents other women? And what proportion of women is needed to make a difference?

Answers to these questions can prove to be foundational for effective environmental governance, which in turn is an imperative as we find ourselves in the throes of an ecological crisis. Locally we see the crisis in disappearing forests, depleting water sources, and degrading soils. Globally we see it in the portents of global warming. The scale and form that institutions of environmental governance should take, however, can vary by resource context. Forests, in particular, are widely recognized as global public goods, serving as sources of biodiversity and carbon sinks, with a notable impact on climate change. But forests are also crucial for the everyday needs and livelihoods of millions of communities living in their vicinity. This makes conservation and sustainable extraction simultaneously important goals—the latter as a welfare necessity as well as an incentive for local communities that are potentially key figures in protection efforts. Indeed our ability to save forests as well as sustain livelihoods can depend, in critical ways, on the local collective action of innumerable communities scattered across the globe. This was recognized as early as 1987 by the World Commission on Environment and Development in its *Brundtland Report*, which specifically emphasized the link between conservation and community resource management.[1]

Communities are, however, far from homogeneous units.[2] Broadly defined here in spatial terms, they can embody a range of social and economic differences and inequalities, predicated especially on the gender, class, and caste/ethnicity of those that constitute it.[3] The men and women, the landed and landless, the low caste and high caste that form a community can differ in their dependence on local forests according to their economic endowments, their needs and preferences, prevailing social norms, and most particularly the gender division of labour which places particular responsibility on women for procuring firewood and fodder. The relationship of a community to its local forest can thus be characterized by multiple interests, which can differ not just by socio-economic class but especially by gender,

[1] This confidence in the ability of people to cooperate was in sharp contrast to the pessimism on this count underlined in Hardin's (1968) 'tragedy of the commons' (see also Chapter 3).

[2] On this see also Agrawal and Gibson (2001).

[3] Caste divisions refer broadly to the system of social stratification followed by Hindus in South Asia and elsewhere, which historically related to occupational categories but also overlapped with systems of endogamy and other social practices. A number of social and ethnic groups, such as tribal communities in India, however, fall outside Hindu caste categories and typically follow distinct religious and social customs. Both caste and tribe are contested and evolving categories.

and the intersectionality of class and gender. How these interests play out can make a critical difference to the effectiveness and sustainability of institutions of forest governance, since these institutions require community members to cooperate and act collectively in relation to a common pool resource.

Yet in the burgeoning body of work on collective action for natural resource management there are some striking lacunae from a gender perspective. These lacunae stem on the one hand from the virtual absence of such a perspective in the general environmental governance literature, especially, but not only, that by economists.[4] On the other hand, they stem from an overarching focus in the gender and green governance literature on questions of equity and women's limited participation, to the neglect of other aspects.[5] Although the goal of gender equality provides strong a priori grounds for enhancing women's presence in institutions of green governance,[6] we know rather little about the impact of their presence on outcomes (e.g. the regeneration of forests, or the sharing of benefits), or even on their effective—as versus nominal—participation in governance. Many argue that women tend to be more conservationist than men. But this is based more on belief than on verification. In particular there is rather little rigorous empirical examination of the difference women can make to green governance and why.

I explore this, focusing on communities managing their local forests—one of the fastest spreading forms of collective action around natural resources in South Asia, and possibly anywhere—to assess how women's presence in these initiatives can contribute both to conservation and to subsistence. Empirically I examine what difference women's presence makes to the decisions and outcomes of these community forestry institutions. In particular, does the gender composition of the executive committee—their principal decision-making body—affect the way the committee functions, the rules it makes for forest use, how it deals with rule violators, and what impact it has on the efficiency of forest regeneration and the equity of benefit distribution?[7] If women's presence does make a difference, how large a proportion of women is effective and how can their presence be enhanced to reach effective proportions? Moreover, can village women transcend the

[4] As a sample, see Baland and Platteau's (1996) review of an extensive literature. See also Bromley (1992), Ostrom (1990), Poffenberger and McGean (1996), Wade (1988), Baland et al. (2006), and Lam (1998).

[5] See details and discussion in section 4 below.

[6] Broadly, 'green issues' relate to natural resources and biodiversity in the rural context, and 'brown issues' to industrial waste, pollution, and other externalities stemming from industrial and urban development (see e.g. Lorey 2002). The term 'green governance', as used here, relates to green issues, especially forest resources.

[7] I use the term 'efficiency' not to imply the economists' concept of Pareto efficiency, but to mean both productive efficiency (e.g. better forest regeneration) and efficiency in the more general sense of the ability to produce a desired product or achieve institutional goals, with a minimum of effort, expense, or waste. Hence, sustainability of community forestry institutions and improvement in forest condition through biomass regeneration, could both be termed the efficiency effects of community forest management.

limitations of the local to build extra-local pro-women, pro-green links? And can institutions of government be made more accountable to them?

My initial fieldwork in the late 1990s provided some pointers to the directions in which answers to these questions may lie.[8] More definitive answers required a systematic survey of community forestry institutions with varying gender composition. I undertook such a survey in 2000–01, in selected regions of India and Nepal, the two South Asian countries with country-wide community forestry programmes. This unique data set has enabled me to test propositions about the impact of women's presence in local governance which have not been tested so far, either in the environmental governance literature or in the gender and politics literature.

1. THE QUESTION OF PRESENCE

Of course the idea that a group's social composition, especially its gender composition, can make a difference to how individuals within the group respond and what decisions they take, is not new. Research on other types of institutions, such as legislatures and village councils, points to notable differences between men's and women's policy priorities. There is a substantial literature, for instance, on the effect of women's enhanced presence in legislatures on the laws passed and policy initiatives taken.[9] There is also an emerging literature on the impact of women's presence in local village councils, especially in South Asia. Indeed, gender quotas instituted in legislatures and village councils in many countries have catalysed research interest in the difference women's presence might make.

Studies of legislators—mostly focused on western democracies with a few on developing regions—point to substantial gender differences in the kind of legislation women and men introduce in parliament. Women are found to give significantly greater priority than their male colleagues to laws and policies that promote women's equality and empowerment,[10] or that improve family welfare through health, education, childcare, housing, and other human services.[11] In some countries female legislators have helped prioritize women's economic interests through gender budgets.[12] They are also found to be more committed

[8] The results of this fieldwork are published in Agarwal (1997a, 1997b, 1998a, 2000a, 2000b, 2001).

[9] As a sample, see Andersen (1975), Barry (1990), Bergqvist (2004), Berkman and O'Conner (1993), Bratton and Haynie (1999), Brill (1995), Britton (2002), Carroll (2001), Dahlerup (1988), Darcy et al. (1994), Franceschet (2001), High-Pippert and Comer (1998), Lovenduski (1997), Mansbridge (2003), Norris and Inglehart (2001), Norris and Lovenduski (1989, 1995), Reingold (2008), Saint-Germain (1989), Schwindt-Bayer (2006), Studlar and McAllister (2002), Swers (2001), Thomas (1994), Thomas and Welch (2001), Vallance (1988), and Wängnerud (2000).

[10] See Berqvist (2004), Berkman and O'Connor (1993), Darcy et al. (1994), Saint-Germain (1989), Thomas (1994), and Vallance (1988).

[11] See Carroll (2001), Darcy et al. (1994), Norris and Lovenduski (1995), Schwindt-Buyer (2006), Thomas (1994), Thomas and Welch (2001), and Wängnerud (2000).

[12] See Darcy et al. (1994) on Australia.

than men to seeing their bills through.[13] Similarly, there is emerging evidence that women heads of local councils are more likely than male heads to prioritize village infrastructure for improving health care, drinking water, and sanitation.[14]

The nature of decisions apart, there is a widespread perception and frequent assertion that women by their presence can transform the culture and values of public bodies. Women are perceived to be more cooperative, less competitive, and less corrupt.[15] Many also see them as likely to bring more caring, sharing, and moral values to the public domain,[16] and to encourage less aggressive modes of discussion (Dahlerup 1988). Most of these studies do not discuss *why* women might prioritize a particular set of issues, or behave differently from men, but some correctly emphasize structural factors, such as an entrenched gender division of labour and other social norms, and caution against essentializing women as being different or more moral qua women.

Studies in experimental psychology provide additional insights. Although unlinked to governance, they indicate that the gender composition of a group can affect the extent to which men and women cooperate with their group members.[17] Women, for instance, are found to cooperate more in all-female groups than as a minority in a mixed group. Men, by contrast, cooperate more when they are a minority in a mixed group than in all-male groups (Sell 1997). Women also display solidarity with female partners, and female dyads rarely fail to reach an agreement, in contrast to all-male or mixed dyads (Eckel and Grossman 1998). Female majority groups tend to be more generous and egalitarian as well, in decisions involving monetary divisions (Dufwenberg and Muren 2006); and women, in general, are found in a wide range of studies to be more cooperative and egalitarian than men and to display greater altruism and trust.[18]

This varied body of research, although quite diverse in its context and methodology, converges in suggesting that a group's gender composition can significantly affect decision-making, and lead to choices that are more other-regarding and public-goods promoting. For our purposes, however, such research at best provides pointers. A gender perspective on local green governance requires us to

[13] For instance, Thomas (1994: 104, 142) found that female officeholders were more thorough and detail-oriented in preparing, advocating, and opposing legislation than men, and were willing to work harder to see a piece of legislation through. Saint-Germain (1989) found that US women legislators were successful in enacting 40 per cent of *all* bills they initiated, while men were successful in enacting 30 per cent of those they initiated.

[14] See Gandhi and Shah (1991), Vijaylakshmi (2003), and Chattopadhyay and Duflo (2004). See also Ban and Rao (2008) who find gender differences in preferences among councillors, although not in actual public good choices due to limited budgetary discretion.

[15] See e.g. Anand et al. (2001), Flammang (1985), Htun (2002), and Vijaylakshmi (2008).

[16] See e.g. Bonder and Nari (1995), Flammang (1985), Phillips (1995), and Thomas (1994).

[17] See e.g. Sell (1997), Eckel and Grossman (1998), and Stockard et al. (1988). Sell examines how a group's gender composition might affect cooperation in public goods settings, using undergraduates in American universities as subjects.

[18] See Innocenti and Pazienza (2006), Croson et al. (2008), Kamas et al. (2008), Eckel et al. (2008), and Eckel's (2008) overview, based on a review of a large body of work in this field.

address a much wider range of questions, to grapple with the specificity of a natural resource and the local context, and begs empirical testing.

For a start, we would like to know whether women in a forest management group are likely to participate more actively by attending meetings and speaking up at them if there are more women in the group. Active participation in the decision-making process is a necessary intermediate step for women to influence institutional decisions and outcomes. Studies of western societies often implicitly assume that women once inducted into decision-making will attend meetings and voice their views. They therefore concentrate on the impact of women's numerical strength on policy changes, rather than on their ability to participate better in the *very process* of decision-making. In practice, such participation cannot be taken for granted even in western contexts, and even less so in non-western cultures where gendered social norms and perceptions can seriously constrain women. It is therefore relevant to ask: would the presence of other women enable individual women to transcend social norms and personal hesitations and be more effective participants? Similarly, would women's presence lead to different decisions from those made by male-dominated committees?

Some aspects of decision-making in forestry institutions, such as rule formulation, are superficially akin to legislators introducing bills in parliament, but in substance there are important differences. To begin with, forest management committees make *group* decisions and not individual decisions, and women's influence over such decisions is revealed indirectly, say in the forest use rules the group makes or the kind of tree species it plants. This is unlike the question addressed by the bulk of the gender and politics literature in which the priorities of *individual* legislators or individual village council heads are compared across the genders.[19] Moreover the 'local' nature of local forest governance means that decision-makers can be affected directly by the decisions they take, since they are governing resources on which they themselves depend. Hence when a group is deciding whether or not to extract forest products and how much, self-interest might suggest high extraction while conservation interest may suggest low extraction. Parliamentarians are unlikely to be affected similarly or immediately by the laws they pass. The possible direct impact on forest committee members of their own policies thus gives a greater immediacy to resource management at the local level and allows a more direct play of personal interest in processes and outcomes. Village councils as wings of local government are closer to forestry groups than to legislators in this respect: for instance, they too can be conflicted between self-interest and community interest, in terms of the public goods they favour.

Most importantly, we would like to know whether groups with greater female presence—through the management decisions they take, the personal commitments they show, and the knowledge they bring to bear—have better forest conservation and equity outcomes. In other words, we are interested not only

[19] This difference will be less where bills are typically sponsored by parties rather than by individual legislators.

in what kinds of rules are formulated for forest use but also how they are implemented, and in the end results on forest condition and benefit sharing. Indeed, the real testing ground of public policy, even that framed at the highest level of decision-making, is the local—the communities that are affected by or that have responsibility for actual policy implementation. Unlike at the level of legislators or upper-level bureaucrats, where there can be a disjuncture between framing policy and implementing it, in local forest governance the lines between policy-making, implementation, and impact are less distinct insofar as the same set of people are involved and responsible at each stage. The full sequence of processes can thus be observed. This also offers scope for exploring a wider range of issues in relation to gender and governance than possible in more macro contexts, but which have relevance for those contexts.

Below I present, in broad brushstrokes, why on a priori grounds we might expect women's presence in institutions of green governance to make a difference (these dimensions are further explored in specific chapters). I then discuss the complexities that can restrict the impact of mere presence, such as inadequacy of numbers, or heterogeneity among women, or the limitations imposed by the local. Finally, I outline the book's expected contributions and its overall structure.

2. POTENTIAL IMPACT OF PRESENCE

Why would we expect women to respond differently from men within institutions of green governance? The answer lies especially in differences between women and men in the extent and nature of their dependence on forests. Rural women's dependence on community resources is greater than men's because they have lesser access to private resources. And their dependence is of an everyday nature and for a somewhat different set of products due to the pre-existing gender division of labour. Firewood, for example, constitutes one of the most important sources of rural domestic fuel in developing countries (Modi et al. 2005), and the numbers dependent on it and other traditional biofuels are likely to increase over time (IEA 2004).[20] Especially in rural South Asia firewood is largely gathered, mostly from local forests and commons, and women and girls are mainly responsible for its procurement.[21] Similarly, men are mainly responsible for procuring timber for home use. However, women need to collect firewood for subsistence almost every day while men need timber for subsistence only occasionally. And while much of the firewood used in villages is non-monetized, timber can also be purchased. Women's dependence cuts across class lines but is substantially greater if they are poor and landless and so have

[20] Firewood and other traditional biofuels such as cattle dung and cropwaste are not always separated in the global figures, but individual country figures for India and Nepal show the dominance of firewood (see Chapter 2).

[21] For details see Chapter 2.

few alternatives to community resources. Hence, although in the long-term we would expect both men and women, and women across classes, to have a shared interest in conservation, in the short-term interests can diverge since women in relation to men and the poor in relation to the better-off are less able to defer current consumption for future benefit. In other words, gender differences in responses within governance institutions can arise especially from the everyday nature of rural women's need and responsibility for forest products such as firewood, and the sporadic nature of rural men's need and responsibility for products such as timber. Class differences in responses arise from the substantially greater dependence of landless women on local forests, relative to landed women.

These gender/class commonalities and differences can affect institutions of forest governance in complex ways through interactions which can be conceptualized analytically as cooperative conflicts.[22] Community members, for instance, may cooperate out of a shared interest in regenerating the forest for its conservation value or for increasing the availability of products they are interested in extracting, but they can be in conflict over forest use or what forest products to extract, when to extract, and how frequently to extract, due to differences in their holding capacities and priorities. These cooperative conflicts are likely to play out both among the members of a village community and among the representatives (men and women, the landed and landless) that constitute the institution's decision-making bodies. To illustrate how these and other dimensions of the gender and social composition of green governance institutions could make a difference to decisions and outcomes, I outline some propositions below. These are empirically examined in later chapters.

Empirically I focus on India and Nepal where the last decade and a half has seen the formation of thousands of community forestry institutions (CFIs) for the management of State-owned forests.[23] Most of these have emerged under the Joint Forest Management (JFM) Programme launched in India in 1990, and a somewhat similar community forestry initiative in Nepal in 1993.[24] The participating communities have rights to extract non-timber products and to a share of any

[22] Cooperative conflict implies the simultaneity of cooperation and conflict. Two or more parties may cooperate, for instance, because it adds to the total availability of a product, but they may be in conflict over the sharing of what becomes available. Or cooperation might be over a non-material objective, such as women's organizations negotiating with the State for changing a law, but there could be conflict between the cooperating organizations over particular clauses in the legislation. For elaboration, see Sen (1990) and Agarwal (1997c). Sen (1990) uses the concept in the context of intra-household interactions, but Agarwal (1997c) extends it to extra-household arenas. See also the discussion in Chapter 2 of this volume.

[23] The term 'State' is used here, and throughout the book, in the political economy sense of the word and implies government, while the term 'state', as used in the book, is specific to India and relates to administrative divisions within the country.

[24] See Chapter 3 and 4 for more details on the origins and features of these institutions in India and Nepal, and differences therein. For useful comparative perspectives on these counts, see also, Hobley (1996), and Springate-Baginski and Blaikie (2007).

mature timber harvested—the latter in conjunction with the forest department. By the early 2000s, India had around 84,000 JFM groups involving 8.4 million households and 22.4 per cent of its forest land, and Nepal had around 9,100 community forestry groups involving about 1 million households and 11.4 per cent of its forest land.[25] The forests that these groups are managing are government owned but given over to local communities to govern, with a sharing of responsibilities and benefits. This represents a significant shift away from the earlier top-down approach to forest management to a decentralized approach. The communities manage the forests broadly through a two-tier organizational structure, consisting of a general body (GB) with members drawn from the whole village and an executive committee (EC) of nine to fifteen members. The EC is the core decision-making body which interacts with the GB (and in varying degree with the forest department) to define rules for forest use and benefit sharing, penalties for rule violation, methods of protection, and so on.

Improving the condition of a degraded forest requires forest closure (restricting forest use), and the strictness of closure can range from a complete ban on entry to allowing limited entry for a regulated extraction of selected items such as firewood, fodder, and seasonal products such as fruits, wild vegetables, berries, herbs, and so on. If the rootstock is intact, simply disallowing entry can lead to forest regeneration; otherwise selected planting may be done to fill the gaps. Either way, committed protection and knowledge of forest species could make a substantial difference to effective regeneration. Similarly, benefits from protection depend critically on what kinds of rules the EC makes for forest use and product extraction. If a section of people are excluded from representation in the decision-making bodies of forest management groups, they would be excluded effectively from having a say in the formulation of forest use rules as well as from directly contributing to forest improvement. These 'participatory exclusions' as I term them (that is, exclusions within seemingly participatory institutions) can, in turn, unfavourably affect both institutional efficiency and equity (see also Agarwal 2001). In particular, who is represented on or has voice in the EC can have a crucial bearing on how well the institution functions, and who gains or loses from it.

The gender composition of ECs can range from no women to only women, with varying degrees of mixed-gender groups in between. In both India and Nepal, the EC composition is heavily skewed in favour of men. Even mixed-gender groups seldom include more than two women.[26] The key question, however, is: what might we expect if the ECs did include more women? *Potentially,* women's presence on the EC can have an impact on at least five aspects of institutional functioning: representation and participation, rule-making, forest conservation, empowerment, and welfare. Let us first consider these potential

[25] For India, see Bahuguna (2004). Nepal's figures are computed from its forest department data (GoN 2000).

[26] This has changed in some regions in recent years (see also Chapter 3, this volume).

effects before examining the complexities posed by concerns such as how much presence would be effective, and of which women.

2.1 Representation and Participation

When a community is protecting its forest, it is important that the concerns of all the community members (and especially of the most vulnerable) are taken into account and represented in decision-making. Effective representation, however, is a complicated issue. At one extreme, it can be argued, as Phillips (1995: 6) points out, that 'one person may easily stand for another'... as long as there is 'a congruity in political beliefs and ideals'. Hence if a set of ideas has wide prevalence a person need not be present in decision-making herself for her interests to be represented.[27] In this case, no disadvantaged group need personally be in a decision-making body, since those already there would be conversant with such a group's ideas and interests, or would be acting on an agreed set of policies and programmes. At the other extreme it could be argued that none can be represented by another, since no two people's experience is identical; hence each person must be present directly in decision-making. Both extremes are clearly untenable. We need some balance between the two, which could lie in a person being represented by someone who shares their selected identity (based on gender, caste, ethnicity, etc.).[28] For a variety of reasons, village women's concerns regarding forests are likely to be better represented if there are women in the management committees of community forestry groups.

To begin with, channels of information are usually gendered. In most societies women tend to be more accessible to other women, and men to other men, but this is especially so in village communities that follow female seclusionary practices and segregate public space by gender.[29] Hence, in the context of community forestry, without women on the main decision-making body—the EC—there will be limited institutional understanding of the priorities, needs, or wants of a large section of the community. Moreover, given that men and women have rather divergent interests in forests due to their noted differences in dependence on forest products, women EC members are more likely than men to represent women's interests effectively in EC meetings (setting aside, for the moment, the issue of socio-economic differences between women).

We would also expect institutions that are demonstrably inclusive and fair to perform better by motivating those affected and giving them voice. Women's lack

[27] Of course the terms 'interests' and 'representation' are themselves contested, as discussed further below, but see especially Pitkin (1967) on the complexities underlying attempts to define 'representation'.

[28] I say 'selected' identity, since each person has multiple identities, of which gender is but one; others could stem from nationality, caste, religion, profession, and so on, or several of these together (see also Sen 2006, Chhachhi 1991, and Menon 2000).

[29] In large parts of northern South Asia, for example, village women are expected to avoid places where men commonly congregate, such as the marketplace.

of involvement in framing rules and policies which centrally affect them carries the risk that the decisions made will grossly disadvantage women, qua women, as historical experience in many contexts and countries bears out.[30] Women's presence in decision-making may not guarantee outcomes in their favour but it could guarantee them representative voice, and this has both intrinsic worth and instrumental value. Intrinsically it can be seen as a form of empowerment, a recognition of women's citizenship claims, and an indication that the local institution is inclusive and democratic. The existence of democratic institutions is also found to be positively correlated to individual perceptions of well-being (Owen et al. 2008). Instrumentally, women's presence can impinge on the potential effect of women in CFIs on key dimensions: rules, efficiency, empowerment, and welfare.

2.2 Rule-Making

Women EC members, if they participate effectively in meetings, could influence the kinds of rules made for forest use. These rules define what forest products can be extracted, how frequently and in what quantities, and how they are to be distributed. In other words, they determine benefits derived from forest protection. We would expect these extraction rules to be different if ECs have more women members, given gender differences in abilities to defer current consumption. This could play out in diverse ways. On the one hand, the substantial and daily nature of women's dependence on local forests would make it more difficult for them to forgo current use for future benefits. With forest closure, it is women who bear the immediate burden of finding alternative sources for gathered items. Conversely, since women more often than men tend to place family needs over personal needs (see e.g. Dwyer and Bruce 1988), they might be more willing to endure the current costs of conserving forests for their children. Or there could be group characteristics associated with gender—for instance, if the forest department perceives women as less capable it might give smaller and more degraded areas to women's groups to protect. This would disadvantage such groups from the start and reduce their ability to extract items of daily use even if they wished to, and could even compel them to place more restrictions on forest use than men.

Basically, forest use rules need to be both ecologically and socially appropriate. Overly strict rules can cause resentment, and increase tendencies to break them.[31] Since it is women who regularly collect firewood, grasses, and various other non-timber forest products, we would expect the rules to be more workable if women participated in framing them. But here the economic situation of women committee members—whether they come from rich or poor households—could also make a difference. Women of poor landless households who have limited options

[30] For South Asia, see Agarwal (1994).

[31] See Shah and Shah (1995), Singh and Kumar (1993), Agarwal (1997a, 2001), and Chapter 7 in this volume.

are likely to favour rules that allow more extraction of forest products than those from landed households. Hence it could matter not only whether women are included in the EC but also *which* women are included (a point I will return to). A group's gender composition could thus play out in complex ways in the formulation of forest use rules, the end result depending (among other factors) not only on the motivations, capabilities, and resources of individual women representatives, but also on how gender bias affects the kind of forests they receive.

More generally, as is well recognized in the substantial (albeit ungendered) literature on institutions governing common pool resources, the rules made and the process by which they are made (e.g. who participates in formulating them) can prove key to institutional sustainability,[32] given their potential impact on the commitment and incentive to protect, and the equity and conservation outcomes.

2.3 Conservation

A forest managing body brings to governance not only the interests, preferences, and priorities of its members, but also their knowledge, skills, and commitments. These can have an impact on the efficiency of governance, both in terms of institutional sustainability (as noted above) and in terms of forest condition. For a start, the better the representation of all socio-economic sections in village institutions, the more likely it is that these disparate sections will comply with the rules of forest use, even if they are strict. Women's inclusion in the decision-making body can thus enhance their commitment to protect the forest, even if they disagree with the rules the group finally formulates.

Equally, given the noted gendered nature of information flows, information about forest use rules, or about changes in membership eligibility conditions, does not always or automatically filter down to village women. Women's presence in local decision-making bodies would enhance information flows not only, as noted above, from village women to EC women, but also from EC women to village women, especially through informal channels. Even men appreciate this and their responses are characteristically similar across regions: 'We inform men in our phalia [hamlet] and our women at home. *They then inform other village women*'; or 'we discuss things with our wives *who inform other women*'. Women on the EC are also socially in a better position to persuade other women (from within or outside the village) to follow the rules and apprehend those who fail to do so. As a result, forest protection is likely to improve and violations decline, with potential gains for conservation.

Moreover, any institution that includes women can draw on a wider pool of talent, commitment, skills, intellectual resources, experience, and knowledge than one constituted only of men. A good example is gender-differentiated knowledge of local natural resources. Although it is important not to over-generalize,

32 See, among others, Ostrom (1990), Ostrom et al. (1997), Wade (1988), and Baland and Platteau (1999).

women and men are often privy to different types of knowledge.[33] Rural women, as the main fuel and fodder collectors, can often better explain the attributes of trees (growth rates, quality of fuelwood, medicinal and other uses, etc.) than men (Pandey 1990). They are also better informed about the local environment—the trees, shrubs, and grasses growing in nearby fields and pastures where they gather and collect—while men know more about the species *they* use, or that are found in distant areas (Gaul 1994, Chen 1993). Knowledge of medicinal herbs is similarly use-related and gender-specific.[34] The systematic exclusion of one gender from consultation, decision-making, and management of forests can thus have negative efficiency implications, by failing to tap either women's knowledge of diverse species that could enrich forest regeneration and biodiversity, or their understanding of traditional silviculture practices. More gender-inclusive approaches, in contrast, could significantly improve conservation.

Men and women can also have different understandings of what constitutes a 'green' forest. For instance, men may view forests that regenerate firewood and fodder species (women's domain) less favourably than forests which regenerate mainly timber species (men's domain), while women may have the opposite view.[35] This can influence decisions on which species to plant if new plantations are undertaken in the protected area, or which species to privilege in silviculture operations, with far-reaching effects on the type of forest that emerges from the community's efforts. Hence, here again the gender balance of the decision-making body could make an important difference, both to the use value of the regenerated forest and to biodiversity. There could also be associated implications for gender equity. We can thus expect women-inclusive CFIs to have superior outcomes to those which limit their pool of members to only half the population.[36]

2.4 Empowerment

Participation in public decision-making is both a form of empowerment for the women involved and a basis for empowering other village women. Membership in public bodies can enhance village women's self-confidence, help them overcome their shyness and reticence, and give them an opportunity to express themselves in public which they might not have had otherwise. In addition, if

[33] Gender-*differentiated* knowledge does not imply that women are the main repositories of knowledge about the environment, as some scholars, such as Shiva (1988), argue.

[34] See Gaul (1994), Daniggelis (1997), Kelkar and Nathan (1991), Sarin and Khanna (1993), and Agarwal (1994). For caution against over-generalization, see Corbridge and Jewitt (1997) on Jharkhand (India).

[35] Similarly, there could be differences along caste/occupational lines (see also Lele 1994).

[36] See also a brief discussion in Agarwal (1994) and Thomas (1994: 146–7). This is a general argument that applies not only to public decision-making but to most fields, including the labour market, agriculture, education, health care, and so on. See also Anderson (2006) who suggests that women's presence will bring in a more universalist perspective.

women constitute a sufficiently large presence in these bodies, it can enhance their bargaining power and influence, and generate a sense of collective empowerment.[37]

In turn, women representatives can empower other women by the fact that they are more socially approachable than men, and can better represent women's problems and perspectives to the EC. In village councils, for instance, women are found more likely to participate in gram sabhas (village meetings where all voters can participate) and be more involved in the affairs of the council, if the head of their council is a woman (Chattopadhyay and Duflo 2004). Women in positions of authority can also serve as role models for other women, giving them the courage to step into the public sphere.[38] Moreover, women's presence in decision-making positions has an important demonstration effect, indicating to male community members that women are capable of functioning effectively in public positions. This would especially be the case in village communities where women have few other chances of demonstrating such abilities. Even after the one-third reservation of seats for women in India's village councils and city municipalities, for instance, there continues to be speculation about their capability to serve in office, and their ability and willingness to exercise autonomy. It is frequently argued that women will be mere figureheads, while their husbands or male relatives will be the real decision-makers. What is likely to be context specific and time bound is given a universal characterization. The chance to actually participate in governance provides women the opportunity to undermine the basis of such perceptions and prove them false, as women gain self-confidence, governance skills, and familiarity with the public domain. Human capabilities, as Amartya Sen has so forcefully argued, are a constituent measure of human development, and he correctly places great weight on public debate and political voice (Sen 2006, 2009). In any capability list, participating freely in public decision-making must surely figure, as it does, for example, in Nussbaum's (2006: 81) capability list, under 'political empowerment', which she defines as 'being able to participate in and have a fair chance of [having an] influence on political decision-making'.

Hence even though the community forestry programmes in India and Nepal do not flag women's empowerment as a specific goal, women's participation in these programmes which give communities control over significant resources have that potential. A woman EC member in Gujarat put it to me eloquently: 'If we step out of the house, we become more aware, we become more vocal, we get more information, we gain more exposure, we get more respect . . .'

[37] Some of these elements may be more important in southern societies where women have long been excluded from the public domain, but they are not entirely absent in western cultures (see e.g. Thomas 1994, Witt et al. 1995, and Chapter 5, this volume).

[38] Moreover, if one institution inducts more women into decision-making, others might follow, thus opening up more space for women all round, as noted in the context of political parties (see e.g. Kaiser 2001, who studied twenty-three OECD countries, and Britton 2002 on the South African experience).

2.5 Welfare

Welfare benefits to women, their families, and their communities may be expected to follow from women's effective presence in decision-making and associated empowerment. For example, insofar as women's participation improves their status and bargaining power, they could negotiate a fairer allocation of forest products, leading to more equitable outcomes within green governance institutions. Through their presence on the EC, they could better persuade male EC members to take measures for alleviating cooking energy poverty,[39] such as by opening the forest for a longer period for firewood extraction, or using community funds for establishing firewood plantations or acquiring clean fuel technology. This can have substantial welfare enhancing effects. Cooking energy is a quintessential human need. Fuel shortages impact negatively on family nutrition and rural women's already heavy work burdens. Unclean fuel is not only environmentally polluting,[40] it can have life-threatening health effects that are gender and age related: in developing countries, women and children relative to men face substantially higher morbidity and mortality risks from indoor air pollution caused by smoky fuels.[41] Alleviating cooking energy poverty, by enhancing access to clean fuel, would thus bring substantial improvement both in women's health and family health, apart from reducing the costs associated with smoke-blackened clothes, utensils, and home interiors.

Indirect welfare benefits could also result if women who gain voice in forestry groups can persuade women councillors in local government to invest in low-cost green technologies for cooking, or use community land for firewood plantations. This could reinforce any proclivity women councillors may themselves have to invest in particular pubic goods and bring welfare gains to communities.

* * *

A priori, therefore, we can argue that women's presence in forest governance could matter on a range of counts. It could enhance prospects of women's public participation and effective representation, help formulate more socially acceptable forest use rules, improve efficiency in institutional functioning and forest conservation, lead to better welfare/equity outcomes, and empower women. These effects could be both stand-alone and interactive. Equality in representation and benefit-sharing, for instance, could enhance women's incentive and commitment to protect forests and their willingness to forgo immediate needs in the interests of conservation. Intermediate steps, such as women's involvement

[39] Defined here as shortages of clean fuel. The lower the emission of particulate matter and harmful gases, the cleaner the fuel.

[40] There is emerging evidence of greenhouse gas emissions linked with the use of unprocessed biofuels for cooking, with negative implications for climate change (see e.g. Smith et al. 2000; EPA 2000).

[41] Women's mortality risk from indoor air pollution caused by kitchen smoke is found to be substantially higher than for men (Goldemberg et al. 2004), and thousands of infants die annually from this cause (Misra et al. 2005b). For figures and further discussion see Chapters 2 and 9, this volume.

in the formulation of forest use rules and forest protection, could enhance prospects of sustainable extraction and improve institutional workability. All these effects—better representation, improved forest conservation, and a fair distribution of gains, however—constitute the *potential* benefits of women's participation in forest management groups. Whether they are realized in practice requires empirical testing—the central project of this book. There are also a number of complexities that can impinge on potential outcomes.

3. SOME COMPLEXITIES OF REPRESENTATION

At least three complexities can limit the potential gains from women's presence on conservation and subsistence: inadequate presence, heterogeneity of interests among those present, and the confines of the local.

3.1 Effectiveness: Critical Mass

> If there are more women in the Samiti [executive committee] we can encourage and support each other.
>
> (Women EC members, Urleni CFI, Baglung, Nepal, author's survey 2000–01)

We have noted that to be effective in a group you need, for a start, to be active in the group, by attending meetings and speaking up at them. Even in western contexts women unused to public speaking take encouragement from the presence of other women. Flammang (1985) found, for instance, that the presence of other women made women county supervisors in the USA less reticent in speaking up in public; and Thomas (1994) noted that in states where the proportion of women legislators was highest, conformity pressures on women were low, and they felt most able to raise issues of particular interest to themselves. We would expect the comfort of numbers to have an even stronger effect in non-western cultures. Greater numbers can help women be more effective in pushing through women-friendly policies or legislation by adding to voting strength and providing opportunities to collude and act collectively (see also Witt et al. 1995). Numbers can also mellow the culture of aggressive male interaction noted in public institutions—be it village CFIs or western legislatures—which many women find alienating.[42]

But how much presence constitutes an effective presence? Many have argued that we need a 'threshold representation' (Kymlicka 1995: 147), or a 'critical mass'.[43]

[42] See Chapter 5 for elaboration on CFIs, and Dahlerup (1988) on legislators in Scandinavian countries.

[43] The terms threshold effect and critical mass are used interchangeably in the book.

Crossing this threshold, it is argued, will make women's presence effective.[44] Kanter (1977a, 1977b), one of the earliest to broach this issue (without actually using the term), notes, in the context of industrial corporations, that different minority ratios (ranging from a token minority of 15 per cent or less, to a substantial minority of 40 per cent or more) can have different degrees of effectiveness: she argues that 15 per cent would constitute merely a nominal presence while 40–50 per cent would provide a balanced and effective presence. She does not, however, specify any single percentage as *the* effective one. Many others similarly emphasize the idea of critical mass without giving a figure. Indeed, many writers—most of them focusing on western democratic institutions—support the concept of critical mass without specifying exact figures, while some mention percentages ranging from 15 to 50. Rather few, however, statistically verify what proportions make a difference, and even fewer test for a threshold effect.[45] The question of critical mass thus remains contested. Meanwhile, globally, the figure of one-third has gained popularity as *the* magic proportion, and forms the basis for legislating or lobbying for gender quotas in diverse institutions—from parliaments to village councils—in most countries.[46]

A related question is whether the wide range of percentages suggested by different studies is due to differences in the context studied, or in the data used,[47] or in structural and cultural factors. Some authors suggest that a formal women's caucus which provides political clout can substitute for numbers (e.g. Thomas 1994). Or women in cultures which have enabling social norms or an ideology of gender equality, as found in Nordic countries, might need a lower proportion to participate effectively in public forums than women in cultures with disabling social norms and ideologies, such as in northern South Asia. The effect of such differences is not easy to capture empirically, but will be explored qualitatively in the observed cultural differences between India and Nepal in the book.

[44] On critical mass see, among others, Kanter (1977a, 1977b), Agarwal (1997a, 2001), Bratton (2005), Bratton and Ray (2002), Carroll and Taylor (1989), Dahlerup (1988), Lovenduski (1997), Saint-Germain (1989), Studlar and McAllister (2002), Swers (2001), Thomas (1994), and Wängnerud (2000).

[45] Among these few are Bratton and Ray (2002) and Studlar and McAllister (2002). The latter find no critical mass effect, however.

[46] Most Latin American countries with political party quotas (e.g. Brazil, Chile, Mexico, Nicaragua, and El Salvador) specify 30–35 per cent (Htun 2002). India and Pakistan reserve one-third seats for women in village councils. Women's groups in many countries have also been demanding one-third in legislatures (see e.g. Stevenson 1999, Norris and Inglehart 2001, Singer 2007, and Goetz 2009). Progress on this front has been gradual. In 2007 only nineteen countries had one-third or more women in their national parliaments (Goetz 2009).

[47] Thomas (1994: 101), for instance, found no US legislature with over 31 per cent women, and because of this data constraint could not test for the potential impact of higher levels of women's presence (see also Goetz 2008). Studlar and McAllister (2002) could undertake such tests using cross-country data.

3.2 Heterogeneity and Women's Interests

Apart from inadequate numbers, the effectiveness of women's presence can be confounded by social and economic heterogeneity among women. Indeed an important criticism against expecting a great deal from simply increasing women's numbers in decision-making has been that such heterogeneity could prove divisive, since women could have conflicting interests, depending on their social and economic situation. Others emphasize, however, that women have common interests which can cut across difference.

In this context, two sets of distinctions can prove useful: one is that between heterogeneity per se and *hierarchical* heterogeneity; the other is that between an *implicit* commonality of interest between women and their *explicit* recognition of those commonalities. Consider first the issue of hierarchy. A village A which has three caste groups would be more heterogeneous than a village B with two caste groups. But if the three castes in the former are all upper castes the heterogeneity would not be especially divisive, while if the two castes in village B are Brahmin (highest caste) and scheduled caste (lowest caste category)[48] the social grouping would be hierarchical and could prove divisive. It is hierarchy and not heterogeneity per se which is likely to matter. Differences in economic class are by definition hierarchical, although here again the degree of difference rather than difference per se would be important. Such hierarchies could undermine the ability of one set of women to represent another set of women. Rich or upper-caste women, for instance, may have a different set of interests (or needs) from poor women, and may not be able to represent the latter's interests effectively. If, however, women share common interests, then even hierarchical heterogeneity may not be much of a problem, as detailed below.

Common interests and hierarchical heterogeneity

Whether or not women qua women have common interests will depend on where interests derive from and how universal we seek to make the argument for commonality. An argument frequently found in the feminist literature is that women have common interests based on common experiences that cut across class privilege or deprivation.[49] This common experience can stem from one or more of several factors: a system of norms that makes it women's responsibility to attend to housework, childcare, and, increasingly, elder care (even if in practice not every woman might do the work herself—some could afford helpers or have supportive

[48] 'Scheduled castes' (SCs) and 'Scheduled tribes' (STs) are groups listed in a special schedule of the Indian Constitution. In recognition of their history of being socially oppressed (scheduled castes were historically considered 'untouchables') they are eligible in India for affirmative action measures in education, employment, and political office. In South Asia (including Nepal) many scheduled castes also self-designate themselves as 'dalits', literally meaning oppressed.

[49] See e.g. discussion in Agarwal (1994), Phillips (1995), and Sapiro (1981), among others.

husbands, or be childless, and so on);[50] their responsibility for particular tasks, such as fetching firewood and water especially in rural societies; their limited access to assets such as land and homesteads; the risk of marital breakdown that all women face—even women born in rich households can be left destitute and forced to seek wage work if they have no personal property, reflecting their economic vulnerability *as women*. In other words there is an ambiguous character to women's class position (see also Agarwal 1994). These shared vulnerabilities can define areas of common gender interests, and public policies that address them would benefit all women. Childcare support, access to forest products and clean cooking fuel, and legal equality in property rights are some among many policy issues in which women, irrespective of their social or economic position, would have a common interest.

A second argument emphasizing the commonality of women's interest, even while recognizing potential variations among women, is that *inter*-gender differences count for more than *intra*-gender differences. As Phillips (1995: 68) notes: 'The argument from interest does not depend on establishing a unified interest of all women; it depends rather on establishing a difference between the interests of women and men.' The fact that interests might vary among women does not negate the claim that interests are gendered. Hence even if women occupy different positions in the occupational hierarchy, their interests might still differ from those of men of the same class. Sapiro (1981) similarly argues that women and men might both have an interest in something but from different standpoints.

A third argument is that whatever be women's class, caste, or race, their ability to gain effective rights in economic resources, or participate in public forums, or contest women-unfriendly State policies, can depend on whether they can challenge conservative social norms, traditional notions about women's roles, and negative ideas about women's capabilities. Such ideas can affect women of all socio-economic categories. Indeed, in South Asia, the upper-caste, rich peasant women are often the most constrained by social strictures on their roles and behaviour. All women would thus have an interest in challenging disabling social norms and attitudes (Agarwal 1994). Ideological contestation against existing social constructions of gender thus offers potential benefits to a broad range of women.

A fourth argument is that people can have interests on behalf of others. Mothers, for instance, can have an interest in ecologically safe environments for their children's well-being.[51] Most might also be willing to forgo self-interest for environmental conservation, where sacrifice of individual self-interest is necessary to conserve resources for future generations.[52] Or people may define their

[50] It is important to identify the system of norms embodied in a gender division of labour, wherein women as a gender are *expected* to perform or be responsible for certain tasks, even if not every woman might end up doing all those tasks. Even childless women, for example, often take on care responsibilities for nephews and nieces or elderly relatives (see e.g. Basu 1999).

[51] There are several examples of green activism propelled by mothers, including the Love Canal movement started in 1978 in New York against toxic waste dumping.

[52] A caveat to this might be poor women who are likely to have short time horizons, stemming precisely from their children's immediate needs.

interests in terms of another's benefit out of altruism or a sense of fairness or moral responsibility, as the affluent might on behalf of the poor.[53] Other-regarding motivations could also bridge potential differences and create convergence between different categories of women.

On several counts, therefore, factors rooted in women's material or ideological circumstances could make for an implicit commonality of interests between them, despite socio-economic hierarchy. On some counts, however, there can still be an implicit conflict of interest between women which is structural, again predicated on economic circumstance (e.g. women's class) and social identity (e.g. women's caste, race, etc.). This conflict could be manifest in at least two ways: a weak conflict if women of different socio-economic circumstances are interested in the same thing but in different degree, and a strong conflict where they have mutually exclusive goals. In forest governance, for instance, we might have a weak conflict where women of landless and landed households both need firewood from the forest, but those from landed households need it much less since they can also draw upon their private land. They would thus be less resistant to strict forest closure than those from landless households. A strong conflict could arise where, say, landless women encroach on a part of the forest land for agricultural cultivation because they have no other source of livelihood, but landed women want the encroached land reintegrated into the protected forest for future needs.

Conceptually, therefore, there can be arguments both for and against women having common interests across economic and social hierarchy. In practice, these implicit commonalities and conflicts could play out in various ways, depending on context. We would expect intra-gender conflicts of interest to impinge less on policy decisions made by women in public office where the policies have no direct impact on them personally, and to impinge more on policy decisions which can affect them personally. We had noted earlier, for example, that a piece of parliamentary legislation is unlikely to affect women MPs individually (although it may affect them as a class), so individual self-interest would not impinge much on their approach to that legislation. In contrast, for a woman village councillor or woman EC member of a CFI, any decision relating to the village she resides in could affect her personally and create a potential conflict of interest between personal gain and others' needs. Hence, if an upper-caste woman head of a village council prioritizes a drinking water well, the well's location could be determined by self-interest (locating it near her own home, or her caste hamlet) rather than by considerations of equity and public need (locating it in a low-caste, underserved neighbourhood). Similarly, when village communities formulate use rights for the forests they are protecting, women EC members from well-off households might have less interest in pushing for lenient forest closure rules

[53] See e.g. Agarwal and Vercelli (2005), for some recent work by economists on the multiple motivations that can drive people's responses in the family, the workplace, and the community. See also Mansbridge's (1980) study of a small New England town and the concern of its citizens for 'the common good'.

than poor women. Here the class of the woman representative could matter, and not simply the fact that she is a woman.[54]

What about commonalities of women's 'needs'? Some writers, such as Diamond and Hartsock (1981), favour replacing 'interest' with 'needs', and reject a focus on women's interests, especially on the grounds that people are not driven solely by self-interest and that all women do not have the same interests. These authors argue that what women have in common are needs. It is debatable, however, whether needs and interests can be separated neatly. Much of Diamond and Hartsock's argument appears to stem from their narrow interpretation of interest to mean mainly self-interest and their assuming that needs have more universal scope. In fact, replacing 'interests' by 'needs' does not solve the problem of heterogeneity. Just as there can be a heterogeneity of interests so there can be a heterogeneity of needs. Indeed both interests and needs are interlinked. Interests can derive from many things, of which need is a central one. Rural women in South Asia, for instance, have an interest in greater access to firewood, fodder, and various non-wood forest products, because these constitute basic subsistence needs. Moreover, needs themselves constitute an arena of contestation (Fraser 1989: 10). Women need easier access to firewood since it is *their* time that is spent collecting it and they need clean cooking fuel because smoky fuels adversely affect their health. But often their husbands deny that women have any such need, arguing that the firewood and cropwaste they use is perfectly adequate. Here for women to even have their need recognized by the family and community, so that community resources could be allocated for clean fuel, is an issue of struggle. A focus on interests helps underline the possibility of conflict between people better than a focus only on needs.[55]

Summing up this part of the argument, hierarchical heterogeneity among women could limit the potential of a positive impact of women's presence, if we are depending simply on women's numbers in decision-making bodies, irrespective of their socio-economic background or context. One way of addressing this issue could be to ensure that women from disadvantaged backgrounds are also represented in decision-making bodies. The case for this already exists on grounds of justice, but here it can also be argued on grounds of effectiveness in decision-making. Another way of overcoming this constraint is through less universalistic and more context-specific approaches, by recognizing, for instance, that despite hierarchy women can benefit from forging a *strategic* commonality of interests among themselves on some counts (based, say, on shared social norms and constraints), even if not on every count. I emphasize strategic not just to distinguish it from essentialist notions of shared interests among women but also to highlight a pragmatic way of dealing with inequality and difference. Given the

[54] Moreover, if women representatives see themselves as representing constituencies defined by other than gender, such as by caste or ethnicity, then whether they are MPs or village councillors or CFI members, there can be divisions between women along caste or ethnic lines.

[55] See Phillips (1995), and also Jonasdottir (1988) who too takes the middle ground, arguing that needs cannot fully replace interests.

substantial gaps in interests predicated on gender, such alliances between women could prove important to further the interests of all women.

Explicit recognition of implicit interests

Implicitly sharing a common interest—strategic or otherwise—does not mean, however, that women will automatically recognize themselves as sharing that interest, or be in a position to forge strategic alliances. To develop a sense of shared identity for the promotion of common interests, women will need to move from being 'women in themselves' (a biological description) to 'women *for* themselves' (as a collective entity).[56] As Sapiro (1981) also emphasizes, 'Political systems are not likely to represent previously un-represented groups until those groups develop a sense of their own interests and place demands on the system.' In others words, political consciousness and activism would matter, although this still leaves open the question—what kinds of institutional mechanisms might be needed for this purpose? Toward the end of the book I explore the directions in which answers might lie and discuss potential mechanisms at some length. Important among these, I suggest, would be forums of deliberative space within which women might discuss their differences and seek to forge common understandings and to arrive at a broad congruity of priorities. Imaginative institutional solutions could also lie in women within forestry institutions forging alliances with local women's groups, especially those that have vertically federated structures, such as self-help groups in India.

3.3 The Extra-local Dimension

A third limitation of focusing on women's presence alone can arise from the level of institutional decision-making. Having women on the EC may well be sufficient for women in forestry groups to promote their interests at the local level, but as we move beyond the local all the contestations around representation can surface, including who might represent the interests of poor women. Moreover, local institutions alone cannot solve local problems. Most public policy issues have both local and extra-local dimensions. Policies relating to common pool resources, such as forests and water bodies, or to cooking energy security may be implemented locally but are often framed nationally. Where the solution to a given problem extends beyond the local, women in local bodies can have only a limited influence. At the same time, establishing extra-local links and influencing institutions at higher levels is likely to prove no mean task.

[56] This is similar but not quite analogous to the distinction made in Marxist literature between 'class in itself' and 'class for itself' (see e.g. Lukács 1971). The Marxist distinction, however, carries with it the idea that the main obstacle to move from 'in itself' to 'for itself' is false consciousness, a notion that I have eschewed in relation to women (see e.g. Agarwal 1994: 437 n. 27, and pp. 57–8), focusing rather on the structural and ideological constraints women face in asserting their claims.

4. EXPECTED CONTRIBUTIONS

In addressing the issues concerning gender and governance raised above, this book seeks to throw light on many of the questions which remain unaddressed, even unasked, despite the substantial literature on women's representation in public decision-making, as well as the growing research on local green governance. Indeed, each of the three bodies of work relevant to our discussion has gaps on one or more counts—the issues examined, the analytical perspective, or the empirical verification.

For a start, the considerable general research on environmental governance pays little or no attention to gender. Economists studying environmental collective action who focus on what makes for successful cooperation among people managing a common pool resource, for instance, while paying considerable attention to group heterogeneity stemming from class or caste/ethnicity seldom cover gender.[57] At the same time, a substantial body of work on gender and environmental governance—most of it relating to forests—focuses predominantly on women's limited participation in management bodies and some gender equity effects, to the neglect of other aspects of institutional functioning or outcomes.[58] There is an implicit assumption (rather than verification) that once women are included in decision-making, other benefits will follow. Hence although many existing studies have provided valuable insights on the constraints women face in public participation and some gave early warnings of women's lengthening firewood collection time amidst regenerating forests,[59] we know rather little about the likely impact of women's presence on aspects such as rule formulation, rule violation, forest condition, or product distribution. The dominant focus on women's relative absence from management also misses asking the question: what effect would women's greater presence have, and how large a presence would make a difference? Moreover, even for the issues covered, barring a few exceptions there is little testing of propositions based on careful statistical analysis that controls for factors other than gender.[60]

[57] See, among others, Bardhan (1993, 2001), Seabright (1997a, 1997b), Baland and Platteau (1999), and several articles in Baland et al. (2006).

[58] In an extensive literature, see, as a sample, Ahmed (1994), Bingeman (2001), Britt (1993), Buchy and Subba (2003), Correa (1997), Dahal (1994), Davidson-Hunt (1995), Ghimire-Bastakoti and Bastokoti (2006), Guhathakurta and Bhatia (1992), Gururani (1996), Hobley (1990, 1996), ISO/Swedfest (1993), Kant et al. (1991), Lama and Buchy (2002), Mansingh (1991), Moffatt (1998), Mukerjee and Roy (1993), Pandey (1990), Roy et al. (*c.*1992, 1993), Sarin (1995a, 1998), Sarin and Khanna (1993), Seeley (1996), Shah and Shah (1995), Sharma and Sinha (1993), Singh and Kumar (1993), TERI (1995), Venkateshwaran (1992), and Viegas and Menon (1993).

[59] See especially Sarin (1998) for India, and Hobley (1996) for Nepal. Sarin was amongst the earliest to point out that forest protection efforts were worsening women's firewood problems.

[60] Apart from the studies mentioned in n. 58 above, see also references in Agarwal (2000a, 2000b, 2001, 2006) and recent papers under the Capri/CGIAR project (http://www.capri.cgiar.org/pubs.asp), most of which too are largely descriptive. The exceptions, namely the studies which undertake statistical testing, are few, and include my paper—Agarwal (2006)—a prelude to my current analysis;

The third body of work—broadly falling within the domain of gender and politics—opened up the field of gender and governance in many ways and (as noted earlier) raised a number of questions that have relevance for studying gender and green governance. At the same time, notwithstanding its richness, this literature too falls short in the limited range of issues addressed and their empirical verification. In part this is due to the level at which most such analysis is undertaken, namely parliament and state legislatures, with relatively little on community institutions, interest in which is fairly recent and confined to a few developing countries. Insofar as governance is a continuum, simply increasing women's presence in parliament or even the top bureaucracy would have limited impact beyond macro-policy formulation, without women's effective presence in local institutions where these policies are implemented. Similarly, much has been said on the difference women make, but rather less on whether the observed differences are important for women's well-being. A study may, for instance, show that women legislators prioritize laws on family welfare, but can we presume that this will benefit women themselves?[61] Also, as is now beginning to be recognized,[62] much more work is needed to statistically test propositions concerning the impact of women's presence.[63] This would include more testing for a critical mass effect and the ways in which this might make women's participation more effective (such as in attending and speaking up at meetings or in holding office), although lack of appropriate data could prove to be a constraint. Finally, there is rather little focus on some significant aspects of public policy which have important gender implications, a crucial one being environmental management.

Some of these lacunae are overcome in studies of *local* government, but others persist. A spate of research, for example, sparked especially by gender quotas in village councils and municipalities in India, throws interesting light on the gendered nature of community decision-making. Rather like the studies of parliament they show gendered differences in policy priorities or preferences. They also provide rich qualitative information on the constraints that women councillors face from being embedded in societies with traditional social norms and perceptions. But on the downside, these studies mostly fail to exploit the potential offered by community institutions for examining conflicts between

Prokopy's (2004) study, although on water management; and Agrawal and Chhatre (2006) who test the effect of several variables (including gender) on forest condition in Himachal Pradesh, but neither of their gender variables are linked with forest governance, nor is gender the focus of their study (see Chapter 8 n. 3 for elaboration).

[61] On this, see also Dodson (2006) who correctly argues that it is not simply gender difference that matters but whether the difference women make enhances gender goals.

[62] See e.g. Dodson (2006), Reingold (2008), and Schwindt-Bayer and Mishler (2005).

[63] Studies that have undertaken statistical testing are still rather few (although growing) and include Carroll (2008), Bratton and Ray (2002), Heath et al. (2005), High-Pippert and Comer (1998), Norris and Lovenduski (1995), Studlar and McAllister (2002), and Schwindt-Bayer and Mishler (2005). Bratton and Ray are also exceptional in focusing on policy outcomes in local government, namely municipalities in Norway.

individual self-interest and group interest, and the impact of women's socio-economic circumstances on the decisions they take when in public office. We might ask, for instance: do landless or low-caste women councillors differ from affluent ones in the policies they favour? Most studies on local government, with some exceptions, also fail to empirically test for gender differences in decision-making or outcomes, after accounting for the effect of other factors.[64] In fact, since in nominal terms quotas prefix the gender composition of the village councils to one-third women members, and one-third of the councils have female heads, the data base is not conducive to testing the impact of variations in council composition, and serves better for testing whether the gender of the council head makes a difference to policy priorities.[65] There is also no specific focus on green issues, or indeed on any particular natural resource (except tangentially in relation to clean drinking water). In other words, although existing research provides many insights, it also leaves challenging gaps in the issues covered, the contexts in which they are covered, and the depth and care of empirical probing.

The present study takes up this challenge in the context of green governance, focusing on some key issues that have been little addressed so far. Methodologically it uses both quantitative and qualitative data for understanding processes as well as outcomes. Qualitative information itself has been used here in two ways—one for constructing discrete variables for empirical testing, the other for illustrating processes which are often difficult to capture through numbers. Conversations with villagers can be especially revealing. And the data on gender composition (described in detail in Chapter 4) covers a wide range of women's proportions in CFIs.

Local institutions of green governance can also throw light on the gendered nature of public decision-making in ways that get obscured in studies of macro-level bodies like the parliament, such as differences that can arise because of gender/class intersections of CFI composition. Moreover, CFIs open up the space for examining a variety of decisions, such as on forms of protection, forest use rules, product distribution methods, and rule enforcement mechanisms. Few other contexts provide a lens for examining public decision-making in such detail and depth. An understanding of community-level issues is also necessary for framing socially relevant policies. Programmes formulated at the national level with little adaptation to local needs can fail miserably, as demonstrated by the experience of many developing countries in the 1970s when they sought unsuccessfully to promote social forestry schemes top down (Agarwal 1986a).

Moreover, CFIs encompass aspects of both local government and voluntary groups—an institutional form that is growing in importance globally, as State and market failures and high transaction costs push governments to seek the involvement of non-governmental organizations (NGOs) in policy framing and

[64] The main exceptions are Chattopadhyay and Duflo (2004), Duflo and Topalova (2004), and Ban and Rao (2008), but see also Lama-Rewal (2001), and Vijaylakshmi (2003).

[65] The present study does not face these constraints since the sample includes groups with considerable variation in gender proportions.

implementation.[66] CFIs have features of local government in that most are in co-management arrangements with the government over a State-owned resource. They have features of voluntary groups in that they function largely as self-organizing community collectivities. They can therefore hold lessons for both types of institutions.

Empirically the book is based largely on primary data on community forestry governance, collected by me and my research team in 2000–01 from parts of India and Nepal, often under difficult field conditions. Nine types of questionnaires were fielded at various levels (through focus group discussions and key informant interviews) on a sample of 135 CFIs with varying gender composition, selected through stratified random sampling (see Chapter 4). These data are supplemented by my 1998–99 fieldwork in ninety-four villages in the two countries, and related literature. Most of the CFIs studied have emerged over the past fifteen years or so, although there are also cases of forest management that claim a history of protection going back several decades.

The results demonstrate the importance of women's presence in local institutions of green governance for improving both efficiency and equity, for enhancing both justice and welfare, as well as for empowering women. But the qualitative evidence also reveals the difficulties women face in balancing the needs of conservation alongside those of subsistence, and in confronting conservative social norms and perceptions. And it highlights the need for CFI women to form networks with women in other local institutions, to overcome social constraints and to go beyond the local in building linkages within civil society. These would help CFI women strengthen their bargaining power within patriarchal communities as well as with the upper tiers of government, where rights over forest use and energy policies are framed.[67] I examine whether such alliances are possible, given the heterogeneity of women's interests across economic and social difference and rural/urban divides, and what institutional innovations could serve as bridges. I also reflect on how government representatives at different levels could be brought to engage more with rural women's concerns.

Overall, the basic questions of presence and representation, of interests, effectiveness, and accountability, that are examined here, cut across countries and contexts and would be central to any gendered analysis of politics, governance, and public policy today. At the same time, the context of this study—communities managing local forests in South Asia—is of particular importance given the imperatives of ensuring sustainable livelihoods, protecting biodiversity, and mitigating climate change.

Analytically situated in the interfaces of environmental studies, political economy, and gender analysis, the book covers uncharted territory within each. It

[66] In 1999, over fifty countries were pursing partnerships with local communities to better protect their forests (Agrawal and Gibson 2001).

[67] On some counts, similar concerns could be raised for poor men, but gendered representation has particularities, especially due to women's historic exclusion from public forums, as discussed in Chapter 3.

grounds its exploration not just in institutions of community forestry but also their links (or lack thereof) with other civil society institutions, as well as national bodies of government. Hence many of the lessons it foregrounds would have relevance beyond governing the local commons.

5. STRUCTURE OF THE BOOK

The book is divided into three uneven parts. Part I, which consists of three chapters (1–3), including this introduction, focuses on *The Potential of Presence* and outlines the possible implications of including women in governance. It also spells out conceptual and historical aspects. Part II, which contains Chapters 4 to 9, empirically examines *The Impact of Presence.* And Part III—*Beyond Presence*—discusses in the two concluding chapters how we might move beyond nominal to effective presence, and look beyond the local to forge extra-local alliances, as well as engage with government to increase its accountability toward poor women.

Chapter 2, which follows, focuses on the complex and ambiguous nature of women's relationship with the environment, problematizing the typical linear narrative. It outlines the interests women might have in environmental resources and explores whether women are likely to be more conservationist and cooperative than men. Chapter 3 then examines the history of South Asian women's absence from public decision-making in general and from environmental institutions in particular, and the factors which underlie recent shifts toward gender inclusiveness. It notes that the invisibility of women in institutions of green governance lies not just in their practice, but also within environmental history itself which has focused rather little on local governance and even less on gender. Equally, the history of women's presence in institutions of green governance in South Asia is closely intertwined with that of women's entry into local government in general, necessitating an understanding of the latter for insights into the former.

The six subsequent chapters (Chapters 4 to 9) which constitute Part II—*The Impact of Presence*—are the empirical core of this book, and are based in most part on my primary data on community forestry institutions. Here I examine how far simply increasing women's numbers in local institutions will take us, in terms of influencing participation, rule-making, conservation, and distribution. In particular, I outline a series of hypotheses and test them statistically to answer whether the percentage of women in the CFI's executive committee makes a difference to several key aspects of gender and forest governance, such as women's effective participation in the process of decision-making and any critical mass effect; the nature of decisions taken regarding forest use; and the outcomes in terms of forest condition and women's access to forest products (especially firewood and fodder) that are of particular interest to them.

Chapter 10, the first of the two concluding chapters which form Part III, *Beyond Presence*, returns to the themes and dilemmas posed in this introduction. It examines how women's presence can be enhanced in CFIs and argues for creating what I term 'a web of strategic alliances' between CFIs and local women's groups (such as India's self-help groups), and their federations, as ways forward. At the same time it recognizes that there are limits to how far simply increasing women's numbers in local institutions can take us for alleviating key problems that poor women face, such as problems of cooking energy poverty. This leads into the final Chapter 11, which highlights the importance of engaging with different levels of government where energy and forest policies are framed and implemented, and the difficulties posed by the limited interest that most women councillors, bureaucrats, and politicians show in what get defined as 'women's issues'. In particular, it reveals the inadequacy of existing mechanisms for identifying poor women's needs and for bridging gaps arising from socio-economic heterogeneity and rural/urban divides among women. It concludes by seeking an answer to a question of wide relevance: what kinds of forums for public deliberation and what forms of institutions can help overcome these limitations?

2

Gendered Interests and the Environment

> Of course it pains me to cut a green branch, but it also pains me when my children's stomachs hurt if there is no firewood to cook them a meal.
>
> (Near-landless woman in Uttarakhand, India, to author, 1993)

> What do men care whether or not there is firewood? They want cooked food, that is all. Men don't go to fetch firewood. If they did go they would take a bullock cart—unlike women who bring headloads.
>
> (Women in group discussion to author, Sakwa village, Narmada, Panchmahals, Gujarat, 1999)

Women's relationship with the environment in general, and with forest resources in particular, is complex and ambiguous. It reflects, especially, three interrelated dualities that play out in differing ways across gender and class lines: one, the opposing pull of conservation interests and survival needs; two, the scope for both cooperation and conflict between men and women, and between women of different socio-economic groups; and three a potential gap between a person's interests in conservation and her freedom to pursue those interests. These dualities are rather little recognized in the linear narratives about gender and the environment that dominate the literature. Recognizing the dualities can prove to be a useful way of conceptualizing the variability of women's responses in environmental governance; and they constitute a running thread in the empirical analysis presented in Part II of the book. Here I consider in more conceptual terms what might constitute women's interest in environmental governance, and what special features women might bring to bear on it.

1. GENDERED STAKES IN FORESTS

Do women and men have different stakes in and hence different interests in forest conservation? If so, what is the nature of these differences and what underlies them?

Forests have both intrinsic and instrumental worth. There appears little reason to expect gender differences in intrinsic worth, but instrumentally differences can arise between women and men in the use value of forests. For a variety of reasons outlined below, women differ from men both in the nature of their dependence on community forests and its extent. Hence they are also likely to be affected more adversely by forest degradation. These gender differences in dependencies and effects can make for gender differences in stakes in forest conservation, as elaborated below.

1.1 Dependence on Forests

Women's dependence on forests is different from, greater, and more everyday than men's. This distinctiveness stems especially from the gender division of labour on the one hand, and the gender division of economic resources on the other. The former affects the *nature* of women's dependence on non-privatized local natural resources, and the latter affects the *extent* of that dependence.

The *nature* of women's dependence on communal resources is predicated on their specific responsibilities within the household stemming from a given gender division of labour. This division of labour can be both a source of inequality in terms of the hours and drudgery of men's and women's relative work routines, and a source of difference in dependence on and hence interest in common pool resources (CPRs). In rural South Asia, not only do women and girls typically have longer workdays than men and boys,[1] they also bear responsibilities which link them to forests and village commons in particular ways. For example, rural women are largely responsible for cooking and cattle care and for gathering fuel and fodder,[2] hence they bear the primary costs of fuelwood and fodder scarcities.[3] Similarly, men are especially affected by scarcities of timber, given that making or repairing agricultural implements or houses fall mainly in their domain.

There is, however, a critical difference between these two concerns—namely the everyday nature of women's subsistence need for firewood and fodder, which puts them under persistent pressure, and the occasional nature of men's subsistence need for timber, which allows them greater flexibility. Village women recognize this difference. As a group of them told me in Gujarat, in 1995, 'men can afford to wait for a while because their main concern is timber, but women need firewood daily.'

Gender differences in *the extent* of dependence on CPRs, however, arise from women's lesser access to private property and income-earning opportunities. Most rural women neither own nor directly control arable land (Agarwal 1994), which can be an important private source of supplementary products such as firewood, or cropwaste for fuel and fodder, or other non-wood forest products (NWFPs). Women also have lesser access than men to employment and other

[1] See e.g. Acharya and Bennett (1982), Akram-Lodhi (1996), Saxena (1995), and Sen (1988).

[2] Apart from numerous small-scale surveys, a large time-use survey of 12,750 households for six Indian states, including Gujarat, specifically establishes this (see GOI 2000a). For rural Nepal, Yamanaka and Ashworth (2002) find that on average girls work twice as long as boys and on heavier tasks.

[3] Fodder may fall in both male and female domains, and women's shortages in collection may be made up by men purchasing fodder, especially where there is a flourishing dairy industry in which men see financial gain.

sources of income (through which they might buy fuel and fodder). They have fewer employment opportunities, lesser occupational mobility, lower levels of training, and lower payments for the same or similar work.[4] Due to the greater task-specificity of their work, they also face much greater seasonal fluctuations in employment and earnings than do men, and have less chance of finding employment in the slack seasons (Agarwal 1984, Ryan and Ghodake 1980). This, and the constraints on women's physical mobility due to domestic responsibilities, security considerations, and (in some communities) female seclusion norms, also increase their dependence on *local* availability. Given women's primary responsibility for fuel and fodder, their restricted access to land and earning opportunities becomes a particular constraint. Women in landless households or in female-headed households (which are often more poverty prone) are placed at an obvious disadvantage. But even in male-headed households with land, where women can claim some advantage from family endowments, there is no guarantee of access to male-controlled income for purchasing, say, firewood, or to family land for growing firewood-yielding species.[5]

Forests and local commons also provide important supplements to daily subsistence diets and cushions during periods of scarcity. Women are again the main collectors of such items. In a survey in Andhra Pradesh (south India), village women identified seventy-nine species of uncultivated leafy greens that they gather for food, in addition to roots, tubers, and fruits; and in Bangladesh's Tangain district, such uncultivated plants are found to provide, on average, 65 per cent of the food weight of poor landless households and 34 per cent of the food weight of better-off landed households (Mazhar et al. 2007). In 1988, during a field trip in Meghalaya (eastern India), just on a short walk through the local woods the woman I was accompanying had gathered 10–12 varieties of herbs and plants which she planned to use for cooking. Daniggelis (1997) documents a similar dependence on wild greens and other food items collected by rural women among high altitude Rai and Shrepa communities in Nepal. During drought and famine, household coping mechanisms reveal a considerable dependence on 'famine foods' gathered mainly by women and children for survival (Agarwal 1990). Forests also serve a number of other functions for women—privacy where villages lack toilets, spaces for respite from the eagle eyes of mothers-in-law, and a place for social interaction and even for a clandestine picnic when they go in groups to gather firewood (Enslin 1990). In general, therefore, gender inequalities in access to private property resources and embedded social norms create gender differences in dependence on CPRs across most wealth and asset groups, even if in varying degree.

These gendered dependencies have other implications. Differences in the nature of forest use can lead, for example, to differences in how women and

[4] See discussions in Agarwal (1986b, 1984) and Bardhan (1977).

[5] All such claims can be subject to negotiation, with women usually operating from a weaker bargaining position. On the issue of bargaining and gender relations, see especially Agarwal (1997c).

men prioritize particular plant species. Women tend to prioritize fruits, fodder, firewood, and non-wood products, and men tend to prioritize species which provide timber (Chen 1993, Brara 1987). Where children graze animals women also prefer shady trees (Brara 1987). A number of participatory rural appraisal (PRA) exercises undertaken by the Agha Khan Rural Support Programme (India) (AKRSP(I)) in rural Gujarat, reveal a further fine tuning of observed gendered choices.[6] In fruit species, for example, women are found to be keen on local fruits that children like, such as tamarind, jamun (a berry), amla, and sitaphal. For fuelwood, I found in my own research that women differentiated between smoky and smoke-free species. Such gender differences in preferences and dependence means that men and women are likely to bear differential costs due to the non-availability of particular items.

All these factors can, in turn, lead to gender differences in the impact of forest decline and degradation.[7] Notably, though, similar effects can arise when *access* to the forest is restricted under community forest management.

1.2 Impact of Forest Decline and Degradation

Stemming from differences in the nature and extent of dependence on forests, women and men can be affected differently by forest decline and degradation, or restrictions on forest access, in terms of at least six critical aspects: time, income, nutrition, health, social-support networks, and knowledge systems. Each of these effects is important in rural South Asia, although their intensity and interlinkages can differ regionally, due to variations in ecology, agricultural technology, land distribution, and social structures.[8] A systematic decomposition of effects by regions is not attempted below, but the illustrative examples are regionally contextualized.

On time

As the main gatherers of fuel, fodder, and water, it is primarily rural women's working day (already averaging 10–12 hours) that tends to get lengthened with the depletion of or reduced access to forests. Firewood, for instance, is the most important source of rural domestic energy in India (providing around 76 per cent

[6] AKRSP(I)'s PRAs in five villages in 1997–98 showed a consistent pattern of women choosing mainly fruit, fodder, and firewood species and men choosing mainly timber species such as teak, kher, and bamboo (personal communication in 2007 by Mahendra Patel, senior AKRSP(I) staff member who had done some PRAs himself).

[7] A decline in forests implies a reduction in forest area as land is shifted to other uses. Degradation implies a worsening of forest condition–e.g. a fall in canopy cover and density of growth or a reduction in biodiversity.

[8] For a detailed regional mapping of some of these variables for South Asia, see Agarwal (1994). For a mapping of additional variables such as poverty incidence, rainfall, and selected gender indicators, see Agarwal (1997b).

of energy used for cooking and heating: NCAER 2001–02: 32). Much of this is gathered and not purchased even by the better-off, but especially not by the poor.[9] Over time, there has been a several-fold increase in firewood collection time in most regions (see Table 2.1). In the early 1990s, in many Gujarat villages (in western India), for instance, even a 4–5 hour search yielded little apart from shrubs, weeds, and tree roots which did not provide adequate cooking fuel. Girls' education can also suffer if they are pulled out of school to help mothers collect firewood (Biswas 2009, Chopra et al. 2007).

Fodder collection, likewise, takes longer with a decline in CPRs. As a woman in the hills of Uttarakhand state (earlier in Uttar Pradesh) in north-west India put it:

> When we were young, we used to go to the forest early in the morning without eating anything. There we would eat plenty of berries and wild fruits... drink the cold sweet (water) of the *Banj* (oak) roots... In a short while we would gather all the fodder and firewood we needed, rest under the shade of some huge tree and then go home. Now, with the going of the trees, everything else has gone too. (Village women cited in Bahuguna 1984: 132)

In that region, in the 1980s, according to a grassroots activist, the growing hardship of young women's lives with ecological degradation led to a spate of suicides among them. Their inability to obtain adequate quantities of water, fodder, and fuel caused tensions with their mothers-in-law (in whose youth forests were plentiful), and soil erosion compounded the difficulty of producing enough grain for subsistence in a region of high male outmigration (Bahuguna 1984).

On income

The extra time spent in gathering fuel, in turn, reduces the time women have for crop production, thus adversely affecting crop incomes, especially in hill communities where due to high male outmigration women are often the primary cultivators. A study from Nepal is indicative (Kumar and Hotchkiss 1988): it found that the substantial increase in firewood collection time due to deforestation significantly cut into women's crop cultivation time, leading to an associated fall in the production of maize, wheat, and mustard which are primarily dependent on female labour in the region. These are all crops grown in the dry season when there is increased competition from fuel and other collection activities.

Similar implications for women's as well as the household's income can arise with a decline in common grazing land and associated fodder shortage. In my 1993 survey of some villages in three Indian states (Rajasthan, Gujarat, and the Kumaon region of Uttarakhand), I found not only an increase in the time spent by women and children in fodder collection, but a growing dependence on market purchase in a hill economy dependent on animal traction for agriculture

[9] In the 1990s, 80 per cent of households using firewood as cooking fuel in rural India and 90 per cent in rural Nepal gathered it largely from the commons (see NCAER 2001–02 for India, and GoN 2004: 41 for Nepal). See also Chapter 9.

Table 2.1. Time taken and distance travelled for firewood collection in different regions

State	Year of data	Firewood collection[a]		Data source
		Time taken	Distance travelled	
Bihar (plains)	c.1972	n.a.	1–2 km/day	Bhaduri and Surin (1980)
	1980	n.a.	8–10 km/day	
Gujarat (plains)				
• Forested	1980	once every 4 days	n.a.	Nagbrahman and Sambrani (1983)
• Depleted		once every 2 days	4–5 km	
• Severely depleted		4–5 hr/day	n.a.	
Karnataka (plains)	n.a.	1 hr/day	5.4 km/trip	Batliwala (1983)
Madhya Pradesh (plains)	1980	1–2 times/ week	5 km	Chand and Bezboruah (1980)
Rajasthan				
Alwar plains	1986	5 hr/day (winter)	4 km	Author's observation in 1988
Ajmer plains (average: all seasons)	1970s	1.9 hr/journey	1.9 km	Survey by author in 1993
	1990s	2.1 hr/journey	2.1 km	
Three districts (13 villages)	2000	2.3 hr/journey	1–3 km	Laxmi et al. (2003)
Uttar Pradesh				
Chamoli (hills)				
• Dwing	1982	5 hr/day[b]	Over 5 km	Swaminathan (1984)
• Pakhi		4 hr/day		
Garhwal (hills)	n.a.	5 hr/day	10 km	Agarwal (1983)
Kumaon (hills)	1982	3 days/week	5–7 km	Folger and Dewan (1983)
Kumaon (hills) (average: all seasons)	1970s	1.6 hrs/journey	1.6 km	Survey by author in 1993
	1990s	3–4 hrs/journey	4.5 km	

Notes: [a] Firewood collected mainly by women and children.
[b] Average computed from information given in the study.
n.a. Information not available.

(Agarwal 1997b). In the Kumaon village, for instance, 84 per cent of the sample households were purchasing at least part of their fodder, compared with only 8 per cent two decades ago. With the decline in grazing lands and hike in fodder prices, landpoor households in all the regions surveyed had also reduced their number of large animals.[10] And where grazing was still possible, while twenty

[10] In my current survey also, many households in both Gujarat and Nepal reported the sale of animals due to fodder shortages (see Chapter 9).

years ago boys and/or men usually took the animals out, now (as in Kumaon) girls often did so, while their brothers attended school, thus widening the gender gap in literacy.

A scarcity of gathered items from forests and village commons can also reduce women's incomes directly. Of course forests can be and often have been direct sources of livelihoods and incomes for *both* women and men, especially among the poor or particular occupational groups. Hence forest degradation or restricted access to existing forest produce can adversely affect the livelihoods of both genders, but the impact would be felt differentially. The collection and sale of seasonal NWFPs, if available in the local forest, are done mainly by women, as is the sale of firewood. In India, the collection of NWFPs provides supplementary seasonal incomes to several million women (GoI 1998), and these items are estimated to account for two-fifths of the forest department's revenue (GoI 1999a). Selling firewood to urban areas was also an important source of employment for women in eastern and central India in the 1970s and 1980s (Bhaduri and Surin 1980), and remains so in some parts, although its extent has again declined with lesser availability and restrictions on collection for sale, after the JFM programme was launched. Similarly, men who are, say, blacksmiths or carpenters and use the forest for fuel or raw material can be affected adversely by degradation or restrictions on access. Here there is no clear marker to suggest which gender might do worse—it would vary by context. But insofar as women have fewer occupational options than men, especially due to their lower mobility, and given that NWFP collection is widespread, we would expect women to be the worse affected.

On nutrition

As the area and productivity of village commons and forests fall, so does the contribution of gathered food in the diets of poor households, with adverse nutritional effects. Negative nutritional effects can also arise because efforts to economize on firewood can induce shifts to less nutritious foods which need less fuel to cook or can be eaten raw; or force people to eat partially cooked food which could be toxic, or to eat leftovers which could rot in a tropical climate, or to miss meals altogether (Howes and Jabbar 1986). Indeed, the fact that malnutrition can be caused as much by shortages of fuel as of food has long been part of the conventional wisdom of rural women in many regions when they observe: 'It's not what's in the pot that worries you, but what's under it.' A trade-off between the time spent in fuel gathering versus cooking can also adversely affect the meal's nutritional quality, if women are compelled to, say, reduce the diversity of items cooked, or to cook food which might need less time to prepare but has less nutritional content.

Although these negative nutritional effects impinge on the whole household, women and female children bear an additional burden because of gender biases in intra-family distribution of food and health care in South Asia.[11] There is also

[11] For a survey of this evidence, see among others Agarwal (1986b).

little likelihood of poor women being able to afford the extra calories for the additional energy expended in fuel collection.

On health

Apart from the indirect health consequences of nutritional inadequacies, rural women are heavily dependent for household energy on the unprocessed biofuels they can themselves gather. Ninety-four per cent of rural domestic energy in India comes from traditional biofuels, such as firewood, cropwaste, and cattle dung (NCAER 2001–02).[12] There is a similarly high dependence in Nepal (GoN 2004). The use of these fuels is one of the most important environmental health hazards facing women and children in developing countries.[13] Indoor smoke from solid fuels (unprocessed biofuels plus coal) is globally responsible for 35.7 per cent of lower respiratory infections, 22.0 per cent of chronic obstructive pulmonary disease (COPD), 2.5 per cent of trachea, bronchus and lung cancer, and a higher incidence of tuberculosis, cataracts, and asthma (WHO 2002: 70).[14] Those at greatest risk from these diseases, however, are women who do most of the cooking, and young children playing near or in their mother's laps (Modi et al. 2005: 28). Women are found to suffer disproportionately more than men from acute respiratory infections in addition to COPD. Women's mortality risk from smoke-related infections is assessed to be 50 per cent higher than for men (Goldemberg et al. 2004: 6) and 60 per cent of the 1.6 million deaths annually due to inhaling fuel smoke from cooking indoors are of women (Modi et al. 2005: 28). Pregnant women risk still births or having low birth weight babies (Misra et al. 2005a).[15] Cumulative exposure worsens the health risk over time (Biswas 2009). Children are also at direct risk. In India, in 2000, an estimated 200,000–300,000 children died due to acute lower respiratory infections linked with biomass fuels (Misra et al. 2005b). In South Asia, young girls inducted to help mothers cook face higher exposure to smoke than boys who are sent out to play.

Although firewood itself is by no means a clean fuel, forest degradation can worsen this situation in several respects. As noted above, some species are smokier than others and as biodiversity declines it becomes more difficult to find less smoky varieties. Shifts to inferior fuel substitutes, such as driftwood or cropwaste, are also becoming common due to firewood shortages (Agarwal

[12] Even better-off rural households are often highly dependent on these fuels: see Natarajan (1995) and Narain et al. (2005) for India; GoN (2004) for Nepal; and Chaudhuri and Pfaff (2003) for Pakistan. Chaudhuri and Pfaff found in their analysis of 2,366 rural households that even the richest quintile used wood and dung in substantial degree.

[13] Most traditional biofuels are unprocessed organic material used in its primary form. The smoke produced during their combustion contains pollutants such as particulates, carbon monoxide, nitrogen and sulphur oxide, formaldehyde, and benzopyrene.

[14] See also CSE (2001) on the enhanced risk of tuberculosis and cancer, and Pokhrel et al. (2005) on cataracts leading to blindness.

[15] Misra et al. (2005a) find that women in India cooking with unprocessed biomass fuels are twice as likely to have experienced two or more stillbirths as those using cleaner fuels.

2001), and this can worsen the health effects, both for women and girls and for infants playing in smoky kitchens. Additional indirect negative health effects can result from firewood shortages due to the extra time and energy women and girls need to spend on collection. As scarcity increases so does the possibility of cuts, falls, and back pain incurred in the process of collecting firewood from thorny sources or increasingly difficult terrains (IRADe-ENERGIA 2009).

On social support networks and public spaces

Large-scale deforestation and the population displacements that can accompany it can disrupt the social support networks with kin and neighbours built especially by women through daily social interaction, marriage alliances, and complex gift exchanges (for details see further below). These networks provide economic and social support, especially for poor women, in diverse ways, such as through reciprocal labour-sharing arrangements during peak agricultural seasons, loans taken during droughts and other crises, and the borrowing of small amounts of food stuffs, fuel, fodder, etc., even in normal times (Agarwal 1990).[16] Also such support strengthens women's bargaining power within families.[17] Once disrupted, these networks, spread across nearby villages, cannot be reconstituted easily.[18] Indeed, large-scale deforestation can erode a whole way of living, interpersonal support, and individual freedoms, especially for women (see also Fernandes and Menon 1987).

On women's indigenous knowledge

The gathering of forest products demands, as well as creates, a wide knowledge of the properties of plants, roots, and trees. Food items, in particular, require an elaborate knowledge of the nutritional and medicinal properties of plants, not only those that are part of daily diets (such as the leafy greens mentioned above) but also those not normally used but critical for tiding families over prolonged

[16] These are apart from the widely documented patron–client types of relationships.

[17] At several points in this chapter and elsewhere, I use the term 'bargaining power'—a concept that has been applied in a number of fields, including in game theory by economists. Here I evoke it as a useful concept without implying the formalization of game-theoretic models. Elsewhere (see Agarwal 1997c), I have developed the bargaining *approach* as it might be applied both to intra-family relations and to situations beyond the household, as well as to qualitative factors such as social norms and perceptions. Notions of explicit and implicit bargaining power and overt and covert forms of bargaining that underlie the complexity of social relations are also discussed therein. See also discussions in Seiz (2000) and Sen (1990). Sen (1990) focuses specifically on intra-household bargaining and gender relations, while Agarwal (1997c) presents a framework that covers four major arenas—the household, the community, the market, and the State—and discusses what factors could affect women's bargaining power in each arena, including the interactive effect of the other arenas.

[18] It is notable that in the early 1990s, during the Narmada Bachao Andolan, a major social movement against the Sardar Sarovar Dam being built across the Narmada river in India, entire villages resisted displacement in some cases, citing the disruption of their neighbourhood networks as one of the reasons (my visit to the displacement site in 1992).

shortages during climatic disasters. Although women are by no means the sole repositories of local knowledge, there is a gender difference and gender specificity to that knowledge, caused by differences in the products that women and men extract from CPRs, their frequency of extraction, the distances from which they extract, and their years of living near forests with diverse products.[19] Methods of extracting daily use products such as tree fodder can in fact make an important difference to whether the biomass declines or regenerates. Among many South Asian communities, women also usually do the seed selection work and have detailed knowledge of traditional crop varieties.[20] This continues to be the case in many communities even today. Women in Andhra Pradesh's Medak district, for instance, grow up to twenty-four crop varieties per year, preserving the seeds with care (personal observation, 2004). The wider range of products women collect in many communities relative to men can also make for gender differences in knowledge of biodiversity.[21] The degradation of forests or lack of access to them can undermine the material basis on which women's (and men's) knowledge of natural resources and processes is founded and the processes of everyday contact by which it is acquired and kept alive, leading to its gradual eclipse.[22]

* * *

The effects described above are not confined to women but tend to impact on women in greater measure than men. Similarly, although the effects are not confined to poor women, since rural women of all classes use forests and commons in some measure, the poor tend to be more adversely affected, given their limited access to private resources and hence greater dependence on what can be gathered free. Moreover, as noted above, similar effects can arise when there are severe restrictions on access to forests under community forestry programmes that make inadequate allowance for the gendered and class nature of forest use.

2. GENDERED INTERESTS AND FOREST CONSERVATION

Tracing the gender and class differences in forest dependence and in the effects of environmental degradation is important, not only for what it reveals in itself, but

[19] See e.g. Berkes et al. (1998), Chen (1993), Daniggelis (1997), Gaul (1994), Jewitt (2002), Gururani (1996), Pandey (1990), and Rusten and Gold (1991). Marriage patterns can also affect this knowledge. Jewitt (2002) found that brides in Jharkhand (India) who came from less forested areas and married into forested ones had to learn about forest products from their mothers-in-law.

[20] Among the Garo tribals of north-east India in the early 1960s, Burling (1963) found that women knew of some 300 indigenously cultivated rice varieties. In Nepal, women were found to do the seed selection work among virtually all communities in the 1970s (Acharya and Bennett 1981), and I understand this has not changed much since.

[21] See e.g. Daniggelis (1997), Howard (2003), and Mazhar et al. (2007).

[22] Jewitt's (2002) finding (noted above) that brides coming from poorly forested areas know rather little about forest products and forest use practices is indicative.

also for understanding the diversity of interests that can prevail on efforts at forest conservation. This diversity is obscured in a notable and influential body of work on gender and the environment that falls under the rubric of 'ecofeminism', as discussed below.

2.1 Are Women More Conservationist than Men?

A considerable literature, much of which emerged in the 1980s and which falls under the broad banner of 'ecofeminism', argues that women are likely to be more conservationist than men, since they are closer to nature than men.[23] There are two variants of the argument. One is that women *are* in fact closer to nature than men, and that this closeness can affirm more nurturing and caring values both between humans and between humans and 'non-human' nature. Some trace this closeness to historical and cultural factors, others mainly to women's biology.[24] The other variant of the argument is that women are *identified* as closer to nature and men as closer to culture. Nature is seen as inferior to culture, hence women are seen as inferior to men. The domination of women and the exploitation of nature are interrelated and seen as having historically emerged together from a common world view that is rooted in a system of ideas and representations, values and beliefs, which places women and the non-human world hierarchically below men.[25] This presumed link between women and nature is argued to give women a special motivation in ending the domination of nature, and by implication their own subordination.[26]

Elsewhere (Agarwal 1992, 1998a), I have critiqued the ecofeminist position in detail on several counts, as have others.[27] Here it suffices to touch on selected aspects relevant to the present discussion. For instance, not only is the idea that women are the main conservationists rather untenable, but much of ecofeminist writing (in both its western and Third World variants) posits women as a unitary category and ignores socio-economic heterogeneity among women. Arguments tracing a universally caring attitude of women toward nature fail to convince in the face of varying behaviour across classes, regions, and contexts. Urban women who use little firewood or fodder, and women from rich peasant households who

[23] For a detailed discussion on this literature, see Agarwal (1992, 1998a).

[24] See e.g. Merchant (1980, 1990) and Shiva (1988) for historical and cultural explanations, and Salleh (1984) for biological explanations.

[25] The emergence of these ideological connections is traced variously to historical shifts in how nature is viewed (Merchant 1980), or to patriarchal constructs (Shiva 1988). Merchant (1980), for instance, traces it to a shift from the world view of nature as a living organism to nature as something to be harnessed for human benefit and advancement.

[26] These arguments are fairly characteristic of ecofeminist formulations (especially but not only the early ones), even given differences among ecofeminists on other counts (for details, see Agarwal 1992, 1998b). Although the debate on gender and the environment has been shifting toward other perspectives, including feminist environmentalism, many of the ecofeminist arguments remain influential and continue to be debated (see e.g. Buckingham 2004, and several articles in Eaton and Lorentzen 2003).

[27] See especially, Biehl (1991), Davion (1994), Jackson (1993), Li (1993), Nanda (1991), Sinha et al. (1997), and Zimmerman (1987).

may obtain much of what they need from family land, depend rather less on communal forests than poor rural women. Poor women, given their substantial dependence on common pool resources, can be faced with a serious conflict between their interests in forest conservation and their survival needs, as indicated poignantly by the words of the near-landless woman from Uttarakhand at the beginning of this chapter, where she poses the difficult choice between saving a green tree and satisfying her children's hunger. In the face of acute shortage, therefore, the very values that women are argued to possess, namely values of nurturing and caring for others, especially children, might lead women not toward conservation but its opposite.

Uttarakhand, in fact, is where Shiva (1988)—the best-known Indian exponent of ecofeminism—draws most of her examples. And although Shiva distinguishes Third World women from the rest, like most western ecofeminists she does not differentiate between women of different classes and castes—differences which are quite apparent in this region. Indeed her generalizations conflate all Third World women into one category. This conflation also sidesteps the potential conflict between women's interest in conservation and their subsistence needs, or between the interests of poor women and well-off women due to differences in the acuteness of those needs. Property rights and institutional arrangements can also impinge on attitudes toward protection. Women might be strongly protective toward their community forest, for instance, while drawing on State-protected forests in the vicinity.[28] Basically, there is little to suggest a biologically rooted connection between women and nature, or even of a culturally specific one which transcends ecological location and the compulsions of survival.

An alternative approach lies in recognizing that people's relationship with nature, their interest in protecting it, and their ability to do so effectively are significantly shaped by their material reality, their everyday dependence on nature for survival, and the social, economic, and political tools at their command for furthering their concerns. Ideological constructions of gender, of nature, and of the relationship between the two would impinge on how people respond to an environmental crisis, but cannot be seen (as in ecofeminist discourse) as the central determinants of their response.

This alternative theoretical perspective, which I have termed *feminist environmentalism* (Agarwal 1992, 1998a), recognizes that *both* women and men would have an interest in forest conservation and regeneration, but their interest would stem from *different* (and at times *conflicting*) concerns, rooted in their respective responsibilities, and the nature and intensity of their dependence on these resources, as outlined above. Men's interests can be traced mainly to their need for small timber for agricultural tools, and logs for house construction or repairs, which are their responsibility. Women's interests are linked more to the availability of fuel, fodder, and seasonal NWFPs, for which they are more directly

[28] I found this to be a common practice during my field visits in the Uttarakhand hills in 1993 and 1998. See also Sinha et al. (1997), and Chapters 6 and 9 of this volume.

responsible. Both would also have an interest in forests insofar as they provide supplementary incomes, but men and women are likely to draw on different forest products for this purpose. The gendered nature of stakes in forests thus cannot be delinked from the gender division of labour.[29]

How would we expect these to play out in approaches to conservation? In far from straightforward ways.

2.2 Shared and Divergent Interests

We would expect both shared and divergent interests in conservation across class and gender lines. Both men and women, for instance, would share an interest in conservation insofar as they draw on local forests for everyday subsistence. There would also be shared interests, in that even given the gender division of labour and responsibilities there is shared consumption within households, so that acute shortages of firewood which might prevent women from cooking a meal, or shortages of timber which might prevent men from repairing a leaky roof, would create a jointness of gender interest.

Interests can diverge across gender lines, however, on at least three counts: the nature of the product that men and women are mainly concerned with; the time horizon within which it needs to be obtained; and the gestation period for the product to grow. Given the noted differences in preferences and priorities regarding species, men and women can differ on what to conserve, what to replant, and what to extract. Similarly, the differences in sporadic versus everyday needs can affect views on how often to extract. But there is a third, typically little considered element. Men's main interest—timber—apart from being needed sporadically, takes more time to mature than women's main interests—firewood, fodder, and NWFPs. In a newly regenerating forest, men will thus have a low time preference. They will want to hold off extraction to allow the timber to mature, and since theirs is not an everyday need they would also be better able to wait longer. By contrast, women, who need firewood and fodder daily, will tend to have a higher time preference than men—they would thus want the product earlier rather then later. The products they use also have a shorter gestation period which can allow early and frequent extraction.

These aspects impinge on the *motivational* dimension of conservation. But the gendered nature of interests in particular species also has practical implications for conservation. Timber extraction, for instance, can involve heavy lopping or felling and this can prove much more destructive of the forest than the extraction of fodder or firewood. Firewood—typically collected in the form of twigs and fallen branches, or breaking dried wood—need cause no harm at all.[30] Hence

[29] This formulation also helps to take account of atypical contexts where men are significant collectors of forest products, including medicinal plants, and tend to be more knowledgeable about their use than women (see e.g. Jewitt 2002, and Corbridge and Jewitt 1997).

[30] In the 1980s, an estimated 75 per cent of firewood used as domestic fuel in India's rural households was so gathered (Agarwal 1986a). See also Lele (1994).

although in the short term men might appear to be more conservationist, in the long term if they extract timber they could prove to be less so. Women, by contrast, insofar as they are keen on early extraction of forest products might appear to be less conservationist, but insofar as their forms of extraction are less (or not at all) destructive, in practice they could prove to be more conservationist, in both the short and the long run.

Effectively, therefore, we have a situation here of cooperative conflict.[31] A shared interest in forest improvement provides scope for women and men to cooperate in forest protection, but differences in the nature and time horizon of men's and women's interests provide scope for gender conflict over when and what to extract. This conflict can remain implicit or spill over explicitly.

The class dimension can play out similarly, in terms of heterogeneity among women. Poor landless women would share with women of landed households an interest in forest regeneration, since women across all classes draw upon forests in considerable degree for daily needs, especially of fuel.[32] But to the extent that landless women are more dependent on the local forest, they would tend to have a higher time preference than landed women and would want more and earlier extraction. There can also be preference differences between the better-off and the poor in the priority they attach to different forest products, or to different uses of the same product.[33] Here an interest in forest improvement that is shared by women of all classes would provide scope for cooperation among them, but class differences in the immediacy and extent of their needs could be cause for conflict between them.

These class–gender dualities can play out in various ways in terms of the commitment to protect and the extent of extraction. It is important to recognize these potential complementarities and conflicts within a long time horizon, to understand women's responses to environmental conservation. As yet they are rather little recognized in the gender and environment literature, especially but not only in the body of work that propounds the ecofeminist perspective. In fact, a number of these weaknesses also creep into the general writing on gender and the environment in South Asia (and even elsewhere). Some of this writing, although quite insightful from the perspective of gender justice and equity, pays little attention to hierarchical heterogeneity among women, and spells out a linear narrative of women as a unified category, with innate tendencies toward nurturing and conserving. Equally there is little attempt to delineate the contexts in which men and women, and women as a heterogeneous group, might cooperate, and those in which they might be in conflict. *Conceptually*, it is important to recognize this potential for conflict in particular contexts, even if, as I will

[31] For elaboration on the idea of cooperative conflict, see Chapter 1 n. 22.

[32] See also n. 12.

[33] For examples, see Sarin and Khanna (1993), Davidson-Hunt (1995), Sharma (1995), and SARTHI (1997–98). Sharma, for instance, finds that a local tree species, dhawra (anogeissus latifolia), in Panchmahals (Gujarat), is valued by poor Naik households for its gum, which they sell, and as firewood by the better-off who have other livelihood sources.

demonstrate in later chapters, *in practice* in most contexts there need be no necessary divergence between conservation needs and subsistence claims.

An additional factor that can impinge on motivation is the potential for attitudinal changes in relation to the environment. Arun Agrawal, in his book *Environmentality*, argues that the very process of monitoring and protecting a resource can be a transforming experience, and can convert diehard non-carers to staunch 'environmental subjects', people who would, for instance, place environmental concerns over economic concerns. Such subjects can be both men and women. In the course of my fieldwork, I too have come across villagers, not dissimilar to Agrawal's Hukum Singh—a young village leader in north-west India who, in a few years, had converted from someone little interested in forests, to a staunch supporter of environmental conservation. But for every such convert there are numerous others in Agrawal's study that remain driven solely by economic interests. The question which remains unanswered in Agrawal's analysis and is at the heart of my framework is this: what choices do people have to supersede survival needs, even if they espouse a 'mentality' for environmental conservation? To what extent did Hukum Singh's transformation, for instance, stem from learning-by-doing (monitoring forests), and to what extent because he was now economically better off, or because his sons and daughters-in-law had taken over the burden of procuring forest items of daily need? Equally, we can ask: is a poor woman's preoccupation with extracting items of daily use from the forest due to her lack of an environmental consciousness—an 'environ-mentality'—or simply because, despite not wanting to cut green branches, what else can she do 'when [her] children's stomachs hurt if there is no firewood to cook them a meal'?

This brings us to another complex and compelling issue—namely the potential gap between having an interest in something and being able to promote that interest. On the one hand, women are likely to have a greater proclivity to cooperate in groups than men, for the reasons given below; on the other hand they are more constrained in their ability to exercise agency. This duality has relevance not only for women's participation in environmental governance, but for all forms and levels of governance.

3. BETWEEN INTERESTS AND ACTION

3.1 Are Women More Cooperative than Men?

At least two types of factors impinge on the question: are women more cooperative than men? One, the nature of social networks, and two, the nature of conflicts and conflict-resolution processes. Networks based on relations of trust and reciprocity are found to facilitate subsequent collective functioning (Baland and Platteau 1996 and White and Runge 1994). The overall density of social ties in a group can also improve its prospects for collective action (Marwell and Oliver 1988), as can a prior history of successful cooperation (Seabright 1997a). Gender differences in the nature and history of cooperative networks and interdependencies could thus impinge on the formation and functioning of environmental groups.

Women and men tend to have different types of networks predicated on social norms that separate and circumscribe male and female domains. As a result, certain types of networks tend to be more within women's domains and others more within men's domains. In South Asia, for example, women are often the main actors in complex gift exchanges and in some communities in forging marriage alliances as well.[34] Also, the main crop-cultivation tasks that rural women perform—such as transplanting, weeding, and harvesting—are all group tasks, whereas many of the tasks performed mainly by men, such as ploughing, irrigation, and threshing, either need fewer persons or have been substantially mechanized (Agarwal 1984). In several parts of South Asia, customary forms of labour exchange still survive among women, but have largely disappeared among men (as I found during my field visits in 1998–99), not least due to the gendered nature of the agrarian transition, whereby men have moved in much greater extent than women to non-farm occupations (Agarwal 1998b). Women's networks can thus provide a foundation for solidarity among them which would be conducive to the successful functioning of their forest protection groups.

Women are also more dependent than men on localized networks and everyday forms of cooperation, given their restricted economic resources and physical mobility. This increases the cost they may incur from non-cooperation, especially but not only in poor households. Moreover, they have a greater need to *sustain* these networks, given their fewer exit options: as anthropologists note, in the absence of substantial assets or financial resources in their control, 'friendships among women are . . . often cemented by small acts of cooperation and mutual aid' (Sharma 1980: 190). This could involve small monetary loans, sharing surplus home produce, helping to cook for guests on ceremonial occasions, and so on. This everyday accumulation of social capital falls especially in women's domain, while market linkages are more typical for men. In addition, women seek to extend kinship and ritual ties to deal with their vulnerability after marriage, since unlike men, most women have to leave their parental homes (and often their birth villages) on marriage (Minturn 1993, Sharma 1980).

These intersecting networks of informal cooperation among women within neighbourhood clusters, work clusters, or at the village level can be important sources of solidarity for organized collective action, as found both in India and elsewhere (see e.g. Hart 1991, on rural Malaysia). Several grassroots activists whom I interviewed in September 1998 in the Uttarakhand hills, for instance, emphasized the importance of traditional labour exchange systems (*palta*). Champa, a grassroots worker from an NGO in the UP hills, put it emphatically:

[34] On gift exchanges, see Elgar (1960), Sharma (1980), and Vatuk (1981). On marriage alliances, see Sharma (1980) and Minturn (1993).

In my 15 years of experience of working with women, I can say confidently that where there is a *palta* system it helps greatly in forming a *sangathan* [group]. In fact a *sangathan* can be built on the back of the *palta* system.

Author: Do men also have *palta*?
Champa: Yes, as in land levelling, building houses, cutting wood, and organizing religious functions. But these activities are more occasional. For women, *palta* is integrated into their daily existence. Also now with male outmigration the system is mostly sustained through women.

Women's interdependence also facilitates group functioning. Given the intersecting nature of rural women's networks and their substantial dependence on them for everyday survival, they would be less tempted to free ride, since doing so would reduce their ability to seek help from fellow women on other counts, and the overall cost of sanctions would be greater for women then for men, given women's fewer outside options. Similar considerations might also make them resolve conflicts faster, and so sustain collective action. In Andhra Pradesh (south India), for instance, when I asked a women's group doing collective farming whether men's and women's groups resolved conflicts differently, I was told:

Men have bigger fights; they get physical. We women may shout but finally we resolve the conflict before getting up from the meeting.

Author: Why is there this difference?
Women's group: Men say: Why should we sit here. If we get up and leave, the problem too will go away. Women reflect more. *They say: even if I am fighting with her now, I have to go together with her for weeding or fetching water, or if I don't have flour in the house, I will have to borrow from her. This is always at the back of our minds.* We also understand each other's problems and mistakes better. (Emphasis mine).

Recent systematic research also indicates that women tend to display more solidarity with other women. A study of forty-six groups with varying gender composition, managing natural resources across diverse cultural contexts in Asia, Africa, and Latin America, found that groups with more women had greater solidarity and better conflict resolution (Westerman et al. 2005). The experimental psychology research discussed in Chapter 1 suggests too that women tend to display solidarity with female partners, and in general tend to be more cooperative and egalitarian and display more altruism and trust than men.

A related issue is whether women are less divisive than men. Lower divisiveness and greater group homogeneity can be conducive to cooperation. Although group homogeneity is not a necessary condition for successful cooperation (and there could be instances where heterogeneity might help),[35] overall socio-economic homogeneity is typically noted to facilitate cooperation.[36] Heterogeneity could take various forms: hierarchical heterogeneity (which I had distinguished from heterogeneity per se in Chapter 1) can be manifest in economic inequality (e.g.

[35] See Baland and Platteau (1996), and Marwell and Oliver (1988).

[36] See e.g. Bardhan (1993), Malhotra et al. (1990), and Baland and Platteau's (1996: 344) summing up of empirical evidence on successful collective action among village communities.

class differences) and social inequality (e.g. caste hierarchies), while heterogeneity based on ethnic or religious differences may or may not be hierarchical. A community can be relatively equal in economic terms while being heterogeneous in other respects (Seabright 1997b), but both forms of difference can be sources of conflict.

There are several reasons to expect less class and social divisiveness among women, even in communities where *households* are so differentiated. One, women's class position is much more vicarious than that of men: a well-placed marriage can raise it, widowhood, desertion, or divorce can lower it. Hence, to the extent that women, even of propertied households, do not own property themselves, they face a significant risk of poverty. In northern South Asia, it is not uncommon to find rural women married into rich households being left destitute on widowhood or divorce (Agarwal 1994). Two, since, even in relatively better-off households, tasks such as firewood collection for home use are usually women's responsibility, shortages affect women across a wide economic spectrum of households, giving them a common stake in action that enhances fuel and fodder availability. Three, women are usually less connected than men to local power structures: this can increase their prospects of cooperation. During my 1998–99 fieldwork I found that several community forestry groups which had dissolved because men were divided by political factions, had subsequently re-emerged as all-women groups, since women were not similarly factionalized. Four, women appear better able to overcome initial conflicts and discords within their groups. The Self-Employed Women's Association (SEWA), for example, working in the highly caste-divided villages of Gujarat, found that within a year of their forming groups poor women overcame divisions predicated on caste politics. Renana Jhabvala, from many years of experience with SEWA, told me in 1998: 'most women were not keen to keep up such divisions, despite pressure from the men of their community.' It is also possible that where women typically marry outside the village (as in north India), women's networks, forged and maintained outside their natal village, are freer from animosities created by family feuds than those of men who continue to live in their birth village after marriage. In other words, the greater permeability of women's networks across class and social lines, and women's typically greater distance from local power nexuses, make for better prospects for group action among women than among men, in heterogeneous communities.

This suggests that all-women forest protection groups might perform differently from mixed-gender groups in terms of long-term sustainability, since they are less likely to be torn by conflict due to hierarchical heterogeneity or political factionalism. At the same time, there are factors pulling in the opposite direction, in terms of social constraints on women's freedom and ability to participate in community groups.

3.2 Freedom to Cooperate

How much 'agency-freedom' do women have to act in their own interest or in the interlinked interests of forest regeneration? Agency-freedom, as Amartya Sen (1985: 203) defines it, is that which 'the person is free to do and achieve in pursuit of whatever goals or values he or she regards as important'. In the gender and environment literature it is not uncommon to assume that given women's stake in environmental protection, they will be effective agents of change. Ecofeminist discourse in fact effectively constructs women as full-fledged agents, and takes little account of a possible gap between women having an interest in environmental protection and their ability to translate that interest into effective action. But is having an interest in changing something enough to initiate the process of change?

In practice, we find that women's involvement in environmental management is unlikely to emerge automatically, since having a stake in the protection of natural resources does not appear to be a sufficient condition for catalysing women's environmental action. Although this would also be true of men to a degree, in that acting collectively rather than individually does not happen automatically in the natural order of things, women, even if sufficiently motivated, face gender-specific constraints (such as restrictive social norms) in initiating collective action or in exercising agency-freedom. Hence although there are cases of women forming patrol groups to protect degraded forests even when men's groups exist, there are also many cases where despite acute shortages of firewood and fodder women take no action (see also Agarwal 1997a). In other words, there can be a disjuncture between women's interests in environmental conservation and their ability to act on those interests.

It can also be the case that women are more able to participate in certain types of environmental activism (e.g. that which is informal or agitational in nature) than in activism that is formal and regular in nature. It is helpful here to distinguish between agitational collective action and 'cooperative' collective action, and between formal and informal groups. Agitational collective action is sporadic, situation specific, and can involve extra-local mobilization for calling attention to a given local situation, or for protesting against the action of some extra-local authority, usually the State. While this too requires a degree of cooperation, it is of a different nature from what I call cooperative collective action which involves regular monitoring and decision-making. The CFIs of the present study belong to the latter category.

Similarly, we can distinguish between formal and informal groups. Formal groups are those which are clearly delineated and have the authority, derived either through the State or the village community, to make and enforce rules. Informal groups lack both clear delineation and such authority.[37] Some argue that informality provides the advantage of flexibility, but when the demarcation of formality and informality is along gender lines, with formality being linked with authority and informality being divested of authority, occupying only an informal space can systematically disadvantage women.

[37] A given group may of course have formal and informal components in its functioning, but my distinction relates not to the group's functioning but to its recognized authority. See also Stewart (1996), who characterizes formal groups as clearly delineated and subject to agreed rules of membership and operation, and informal groups as unclear, sporadic, and varying. In my delineation, however, the presence of formally conferred authority is also of importance.

Most formal CFIs in South Asia are male dominated, with, at best, a marginal female presence. Mixed groups with significant female presence are proportionately few and all-women's groups even fewer. In Nepal all-women groups constituted only 3.8 per cent of all CFIs in 2000 (GoN 2000), and in India (where there is no comprehensive data base but some state-level figures are indicative) they constituted only 0.5 per cent of the 1,006 Joint Forest Management groups surveyed in Madhya Pradesh around 2002, and 0.7 per cent of the 5,000 or so self-initiated groups surveyed in Orissa during 2000–04.[38] The emergence of all-women CFIs often tends to be highly context specific, linked usually to a prior history of women's groups being formed by a local NGO or donor agency (around credit, health, etc.), or the higher availability of NWFPs in an area, or because of a gender-aware local leader, and so on (see Chapter 4 for elaboration). In Nepal, all-women's groups also typically control very small plots of degraded forest land, while male-controlled CFIs receive larger forests and in better condition. In mixed-gender groups, apart from nominal presence, a range of factors, discussed in Chapter 5, can prevent women from attending meetings, or speaking up at them, or being taken seriously when they do speak up. Their limited participation in decision-making, and so in the framing of forest use rules, monitoring, benefit distribution, etc., can have adverse implications for both distributional equity and efficiency (as explored in Part II of this volume). Moreover, formal CFIs are only rarely initiated directly by women themselves.

Typically, women's self-initiated forest activism takes the form of informal protection groups and agitational collective action. Despite their limited presence in male-dominated CFIs, for instance, women often play an active role in protection efforts, keeping an informal lookout or sometimes forming informal forest protection groups when they find that men's groups are ineffective or non-existent.[39] Usually these are patrol groups which help improve protection. In almost all the villages I visited, women recounted cases of apprehending intruders, persuading women whom they caught breaking rules to desist, fighting forest fires alongside men (or even in men's absence), and so on. In many ways, women's patrol groups appear to be extensions of women's everyday forms of cooperation and social networking, and women's virtual absence from men's formal protection groups tends to reflect the power of gender exclusion that characterizes many of men's other networks.

Women also often have a significant presence in agitational collective action. They have been highly visible, for example, in protest demonstrations held by forest protection movements, such as the much-publicized Chipko movement (popularly characterized as the tree-hugging movement) catalysed by villagers in

[38] The Madhya Pradesh information is based on a questionnaire fielded for me by the state's forest department, covering eighteen forest divisions, and the data for Orissa were collected by the networks of the NGO, Regional Center for Development Coooperation (RCDC), covering sixteen districts (RCDC 2005).

[39] Personal observation in Gujarat and the Uttarakhand hills. See also Sharma and Sinha (1993), Viegas and Menon (1993), and Agarwal (1997a).

the hills of Uttarakhand in 1973, to protest against the commercial exploitation of their local forests. Observers also comment on the spontaneous nature of women's agitational protests in mass movements. The fact that women are often visibly present, sometimes even in the forefront of protests organized by environmental groups, however, is no guarantee that this will enhance women's involvement in decision-making. Women rarely find entry into the regular decision-making forums of the organizations spearheading these movements.[40] Rather these movements tend to replicate the history of early peasant struggles in South Asia, such as the Telangana and Tebhaga struggles in India in the 1940s, in which women made substantial contributions in various capacities, but did not hold significant decision-making positions.[41]

Even in the Chipko movement, although women were central to the protests, decision-making power remained largely with men. On occasion, women did take stands in opposition to the men, as in 1980 when in one village they successfully prevented the local oak forest (their major source of firewood) from being axed, for building a potato seed farm that the village men wanted for its potential cash benefits (Sharma et al. 1987). But such opposition remained sporadic, and did not advance women's formal authority within the movement.

In any case, in local resource management, agitational collective action can complement but not substitute for institutions that monitor resource flows and the regeneration of stocks. It is thus important for women to participate in both. At a minimum, such participation requires group membership and is linked with membership eligibility conditions. But effective participation requires that women attend meetings and speak up at them, so that they can have an impact on the decisions made. In other words, there can be *degrees of participation* in collective action (as elaborated further in Chapter 5).

3.3 Between Cooperation and Conflict

The complexity of gender differences in dependence on forests, in social networks and knowledge systems, in specie-preferences and approaches to conservation, and in the freedom to cooperate, noted above, can have implications for many aspects of local forest governance. Traced broadly in Chapter 1 these effects will be examined in more depth in the body of this book, but a few points warrant highlighting.

Notwithstanding socio-economic differences, village communities dependent on forests have many reasons to cooperate in managing this common pool resource, in particular for its immediate and long-term use value, apart from its intrinsic worth. This shared interest can, at the very least, lead a group of men

[40] See e.g. Sharma et al. (1987) for the Chipko movement.

[41] See Lalita et al. (1989) and Custers (1987) on the peasant movements of Telangana and Tebhaga respectively. For other mass movements, see Sen (1990). See also the discussion on these movements in Agarwal (1994).

and women to act collectively in defining boundaries that demarcate those that are included from those excluded from the protected forests, thus creating what is commonly termed a 'social fence' (as opposed to a physical fence). As will be seen in Chapter 7, even villagers with potentially divergent interests are typically unified in their efforts at keeping away 'outsiders' (that is, those from another village, or non-members). This, in itself, increases the quantum of forest products available to the 'insiders' and provides an important incentive to cooperate.

Within the village, however, the gender, class, caste, occupation, or other characteristics of those cooperating can play out in potentially conflictual ways, in relation to how the benefits generated from protection are shared, for instance what forest products are extracted and how they are distributed. Women, who have less holding capacity because they need the resource every day, might be in conflict with men who need the resource now and again. Poor rural women who have no fall-back in terms of private land could be in conflict with women who have family land. Groups occupationally dependent on forests for raw material or fuel may be in conflict with those with other livelihood sources. And people who value forests for their intrinsic worth may be in conflict with those who see the forests mainly in instrumental terms. All the above parties would have an interest in cooperating insofar as cooperative arrangements are more likely than non-cooperation to promote the objectives they have reason to value. But they could be in implicit conflict over whether and how that which becomes available with protection is shared. Indeed, contestation (or bargaining) over available forest products can be an ongoing process, since distribution is not a one-time event—the products change as the seasons pass and as the forest ages and regenerates.

In terms of governance, this contestation is key to the framing of forest use rules. Men's sporadic need of a long-gestation product such as timber and women's daily need for fast-growing products such as firewood, and the associated difference in time preferences, create divergent interests in terms of extraction rules. Consequently groups that have more women in them might frame different rules from those that have few or none. Class differences among women can have a similar although weaker effect, since most women depend on the same forest products, even if in varying degree. What rules emerge, however, would also depend on women's relative bargaining power within the group.

A second major, but less visible, area of potential conflict within the village, which has important implications for governance outcomes, stems from gendered social norms that define whether and to what extent women have access to public decision-making forums. Potentially, for instance, there is much to be gained by including women in CFI governance in terms of improved forest condition. Women's social networks, different from men's, can create gendered channels of communication which can be particularly effective in spreading information among other women about CFI functions, including rules for forest use. Women's informal forest protection groups based on such networks can improve protection. Women's greater ability to transcend social difference and political divisiveness, noted above, could reduce intra-group conflict and make for sustained cooperation. Their knowledge systems could benefit the processes of forest regeneration. And their interest in and promotion of particular species (if different from men's) could enhance biodiversity. There could also be equity gains from women's involvement, both indirectly insofar as improving forest condition would increase the availability of items women use from the forest, and directly by increasing women's access to those products.

In practice, however, patriarchal social norms can prove to be a major barrier to women contributing in any of these ways, and more generally in exercising agency-freedom, to the detriment not only of women themselves but also of the community. This conflict is subtle and tends to be revealed in the many indirect ways in which women seek to promote their interests, such as by complaining about firewood shortages to their husbands, to male EC members, to NGO workers, or even to researchers such as myself. Non-compliance with CFI rules is another instrument of implicit bargaining that women tend to use.[42] In other words, in gendered collective action we need to peer under the surface of women's overt cooperation to see if conflicts lurk beneath. Women's individual and covert forms of bargaining, however, are likely to have limited power, in contrast to, say, overt negotiation by a group of women, be it over access to forests in CFI decision-making bodies or over social norms within the community.[43]

4. CONCLUDING COMMENTS

Extending the issue of women's interests to the context of environmental governance helps us to focus on aspects that are little discussed in the gender and politics literature, wherein the question of women's participation has been raised most consistently. In particular, when dealing with common pool resources, the time dimension becomes especially important both in the regeneration capacity of the resource and in the need for the resource. That the forest products of particular interest to men and women are not only different but vary in their gestation periods and the frequency with which they are needed can be the basis for conflict between women and men, and between women of different socio-economic groups (even while there is scope for cooperation despite those differences in the joint project of forest protection and regeneration). These differences, which are rather little recognized in the women and environment literature (and even less in ecofeminist writings), could prove key to understanding ground-level gendered responses to environmental change. On the ground, cooperative conflicts can play out in the making of forest use rules, in the extent to which the rules are followed, in the vigilance with which the forest is protected, and in the outcomes for forest

[42] See also Scott (1985) on the weapons of resistance used by the weak, and Agarwal (1994) on the many forms of resistance and implicit tools of bargaining that women, in particular, use.

[43] It is easier, for instance, to penalize an individual woman who transgresses seclusion norms than a group of women who do so collectively (Agarwal 1994).

condition and equity. These conceptual threads will weave through the empirical core of this book.

Before we turn to the empirical analysis, however, consider in the next chapter the history of women's exclusion from formal institutions of public decision-making—environmental and other—in South Asia. Chapter 3 also outlines recent efforts in the region at enhancing women's nominal presence in public bodies through a system of quotas and the process of decentralized governance.

3

From Absence to Negotiated Presence

> A woman can take virtually no overt leadership.
>
> (Mandelbaum 1970: 272 on village councils, summarizing numerous ethnographies up to the 1960s)

> Khasi women inherit and hold property, but they have no right to vote in the election of chiefs.
>
> (Bhattacharya 1985: 56)

> And now the Entwives are only a memory for us, and our beards are long and grey.
>
> (Tolkien 1967: 100)

In a wonderful flight of poetic imagination, Tolkien in the *Lord of the Rings: The Two Towers* leads us into a primeval forest in Middle Earth, inhabited by tree-like creatures—the great Ents. When the hobbits, Pippin and Merry, ask for help against the dark forces, Treebeard the oldest of the Ents convenes an Entmoot—the equivalent of a forest council. He explains the purpose of the meeting not only to those who turn up, but also to those who could not come. As he elaborates, 'I have still got to explain things . . . to those that live a long way off . . . and [to] those that I could not get round to before the Moot, and after that we shall have to decide what to do. . . . [I]t is no use denying, we shall be here a long time yet: a couple of days very likely' (Tolkien 1967: 108).

In this impressively democratic and inclusive method of decision-making, however, there is a significant absence. There are no women—none in the Council, none in the forest. The Ent-trees in the Entmoot are all male. Also, in this lush forest we find no women searching for firewood or fodder or medicinal herbs or berries or wild vegetables—all the things that it is in women's domain to collect. Tolkien with a deft flick of storytelling tells us that the Entwives—female Ents—who kept order and peace and cultivated gardens—have long disappeared. In other words, women and their work have been made invisible. Moreover there is no hint that Entwives were ever invited to an Entmoot.

This story perfectly captures the essence of the term 'participatory exclusions' that I had coined in 2000 to describe how formally democratic institutions could effectively exclude particular categories of people. It is a story of male councils of decision-making and of women's invisibility in these bodies that has unfolded over the centuries across many continents. It is also a story that metaphorically highlights the process of women losing customary claims to nature's wealth and its biodiversity as men establish new mechanisms of control and access.

We need a giant leap forward from Ent time and the sharp eye of economic historian Jane Humphries to spot the women among the forests of middle England. She describes how these forests were used in the late eighteenth and nineteenth centuries when they were common wealth—and makes women visible again. Humphries (1990: 40) notes, 'Women were . . . the principal gatherers of fuel: in Cornwall they would cut furze in early summer from thickets up to ten feet high . . . and in Surrey bring home prodigious loads of wood or sacks of fir cones picked up in the woods a mile or more away.' She garners evidence of women 'bent nearly double under loads of firewood, "toiling painfully along, with hats or bonnets pushed awry . . . occasionally [with] tiny urchins, too small to be left at home alone, clinging to their mothers' frocks"'. And she describes how women and children gathered 'all the food that was for free: watercress from running streams, rabbits, pigeons, wild raspberries, wild plum and blackberries, crabapples, hazel nuts, chestnuts, walnuts'. So here we have women drawing on nature's wealth to create family livelihoods, and through the knowledge of nature they acquire and pass on to their grandchildren they also create social wealth. All this Humphries makes visible, but on governance she is silent.

The enclosure movement in Britain restricted even this access, converting common wealth into private wealth. In the process it enhanced women's burdens and their dependence on husbands and fathers, and adversely affected them in many other ways. Today a different type of enclosure of the commons—this one by communities—is doing something similar to women in other regions. We see this duality—women's central stake in and knowledge of forests, and their absence (or limited presence) in forest-related decision-making—in many parts of the globe, but most especially in the forests of India and Nepal.

This chapter traces the history of South Asian women's absence in traditional institutions of governance (including environmental governance), and the process of negotiation through which they have sought to establish a presence in modern institutions of governance (legislatures and community bodies). It highlights the intertwined processes that led to the creation on the one hand of more democratic and decentralized institutions, and on the other hand of spaces for women within these institutions. At the same time, I argue against the conflation of processes that led to decentralized government and those that led to decentralized *environmental* governance, pointing to mostly independent and parallel developments that propelled the latter. Hence although women's entry into local government facilitated their entry into other local institutions, by setting a precedent, it did not guarantee it. Both types of institutions also continue to carry a historic baggage of assumptions about the numbers (or proportion) of women needed for effective functioning, and about any women being able to represent all women's interests. It is important to trace this history to understand the constraints and assumptions that continue to circumscribe women's effective participation in public bodies.

1. A HISTORY OF ABSENCE

1.1 Women in Local Governance

Historians of South Asia appear to have paid rather little attention to women in governance, except for the focus on women's struggle for suffrage and a place in the legislatures from the latter part of the nineteenth century, coinciding with the region's anti-colonial struggles. A history of women's role in (or absence from) public decision-making in other contexts remains to be written. By this I mean a history not of queens and consorts but of women's interactions within customary institutions of village and town decision-making, such as in caste and tribal councils, village general bodies, village courts, and so on. The limited information that I could glean is from ethnographies and colonial accounts—some dating to the nineteenth and early twentieth centuries,[1] others undertaken mostly in the 1950s–1970s—which reconstruct the past through oral histories, or by recounting a long-standing tradition. Most village ethnographies make at least a passing reference to traditional village councils but women receive no mention except in the rare cases when they played some role. Typically the councils appear to have been marked by women's absence, save in the exceptional community which allowed them voice, or the occasional woman who, by virtue of circumstance (e.g. the absence of suitable men) or personality, carried influence beyond the private realm. Structurally, there was little space for women's direct inputs in public forums. The space that exists today has been negotiated through a range of processes, including quotas and reservations, as discussed further below.

Customarily, at the village level, legislative and judicial functions were performed by local councils such as caste panchayats (usually consisting of the prominent and elderly men of the caste), village panchayats (cross-caste), tribal councils, village *samaj* (community) groupings, village courts, councils of elders, and so on (for details see Appendix 3.1).[2] These bodies differed somewhat in their membership and level of operation (caste/tribe, single village, or multi-village), but they had at least two notable features: first, men of age and influence were

[1] In particular, I examined some thirty volumes of *Castes and Tribes* relating to different parts of India: see Bhargava (1949), Crooke ([1896] 1974), Enthoven ([1920] 1975), Iyer ([1912] 1981), Nanjundayya and Iyer ([1928] 1975), Risley ([1891] 1981), Russell and Hiralal ([1916] 1975), Sherring ([1881] 1975), and Thurston and Rangachari ([1909] 1975). In addition, see Roy ([1912] 1970), and Baden-Powell ([1896] 1957).

[2] Apart from references included in Appendix Table 3.1 which relate to the late 19th and early 20th centuries, several South Asian ethnographies, mostly covering the 1950s to the early 1980s, give some information on local councils: For India see Bailey (1957), Chowdhry (2007), Cohn (1965), Dube (1955), Epstein (1962), Furer-Haimendorf (1985), Lewis (1958), Luschinsky (1962), Majumdar (1978), Mandelbaum (1970), Mathur (1964), Minturn and Hitchcock (1966), Newell (1962), and Per-Lee (1981). For Bangladesh, see Arens and Beurden (1977), Hoque (1987), Jahangir (1979), and Jansen (1983). For Pakistan, see Ahmed (1986), Elgar (1960), and Lindholm (1982). For Sri Lanka, see Yalman (1967).

given primacy; and second, women were typically excluded. Most village councils consisted only of elderly, influential males. '[The] reveren'd sit on polished stones, the elders in a ring' (Roy [1912] 1970: 67). In multi-caste/community contexts, either influential males from all caste groups were represented, or only members of the dominant caste who settled disputes for all castes and religious groups (including Muslims) in the village (Cohn 1965, Srinivas 1955, Chowdhry 2007).

Overridingly, however, women—except in rare communities or contexts—were excluded from both caste and tribal councils and within all systems of kinship, be they patrilineal (where inheritance and descent was through the male line), matrilineal (where inheritance and descent was through the female line), or bilateral (where inheritance and descent was through both sons and daughters).

Deviations from this generalized female exclusion were uncommon and were found only among a few communities. And even then women could at best attend and speak up in council meetings; they could not take decisions or enforce them.[3] Among the Bhats (Muslim entertainers) of northwest India, for instance, all adults could attend village council meetings and women sometimes constituted one-third or more of those present (Luschinsky 1962). Similarly the Santal tribals of eastern India allowed women to attend the meetings, but customs differed across villages on how much they could participate, ranging from those where 'even women may join the discussion' (Sachchidananda 1968: 85) in an assembly of adult males, to villages where women could not participate 'unless personally accused, and then only in cases of extremely reprehensible nature, such as witchcraft' (Somers 1977: 13). The matrilineal Garos of Meghalaya (northeast India), discussed further below, also allowed women to attend and speak at council meetings, but they could not enforce the rules. In most other regions and communities, however, women could not even attend meetings, and (especially, but not only, in northwest India) even those who were a party in a dispute were represented by male family members, and the dispute was settled by male authority in accordance with male-defined rules and customs.[4] Typically, therefore, women had little say in the framing, interpretation, or enforcement of such rules or customs.

Women were also rarely allowed headship of the village or of extended families. The village headman was the representative authority in village affairs, whose functions and clout varied between communities (see Appendix 3.1). Some headmen had substantial power (vested in them by the villagers/clans etc.), including the power to apportion village land to new settlers, serve as custodians of village common property and sacred groves, and even preside over village councils. Other headmen played only a ceremonial role.[5] The important common factor was that these headships were confined to males and were usually hereditary.

[3] See, for instance, Luschinsky (1962) on the Bhats; Archer ([1946] 1984), Sachchidananda (1968) and Somers (1977) on the Santals; and Burling (1963, 1997) and Kar (1982) on the Garo.

[4] See, e.g. Chowdhry (2007) for Haryana and Luschinsky (1962) for Uttar Pradesh.

[5] Examples of powerful headmen are found more commonly in south and east India than in northwest India (in line with Baden-Powell's ([1896] 1957) observations for pre-British India), although

There are rare accounts among the Santals of headmen's widows trying to step into their husbands' shoes, and for a while even performing all the headman's duties, but they were not formally given that designation by the community (Archer [1946] 1984: 4, 9–10). Mandelbaum's (1970) review of numerous ethnographies relating especially to the first half of the twentieth century, and his own field research, further confirm that women were not accepted as leaders in this respect.

Notably, this pattern was somewhat different, but not substantially so, among matrilineal and bilateral communities. Although the dominant kinship pattern across South Asia was patrilineal, present-day Meghalaya, Kerala, and the Laccadive Islands in India had a significant presence of matrilineal communities, while in Sri Lanka most communities were either bilateral or matrilineal.[6] Matrilineal communities appear to have provided women with more voice than patrilineal ones. Among the Garos of Meghalaya and the Chittagong Hills (now in Bangladesh), for instance, women were free to openly express opinions in tribal council meetings (Burling 1963, 1997). But jural authority for settling disputes and enforcing penalties still lay with the men.[7] Burling (1997: 59) observed, for instance, that although 'the women always sat clustered nearby when a dispute was being discussed' and 'did not hesitate to express their opinions', 'formally it was the men who debated the issues. They decided what to do, and they carried out the decisions.'

Moreover, the heads of clans, tribes, or extended families were customarily male, even among matrilineal groups. Hence among the Khasis of Meghalaya (north-east India), although inheritance passed through women, and the *syiems* (chiefs) were men from the female line of the family, women were not part of the Council, and could not vote when chiefs were elected (Bhattacharya 1985: 57). Nor could they become *syiems* unless there were no male heirs, and even then they 'did not rule but merely held office to preserve it in the regular line. When a woman was appointed *syiem*, the state was administered by a Durban or Council *in her name*' (Rao 1985: 37, my emphasis). Female *syiems* could play ceremonial roles, even be spiritual heads, such as high priestesses, but did not dispense justice or wield executive powers (Gurdon [1907] 1981, Bhattacharya 1985).[8] Similarly, among the matrilineal Nayars of Kerala (an upper-caste matrilineal community in southern India), although women were the bearers of property and at least till the early twentieth century enjoyed considerable sexual freedom, it was the *karanavan*—the seniormost male (usually the maternal uncle or older brother of the seniormost woman)—who commanded paramount authority. He managed

geography is clearly not a rigid marker since there are also some accounts of authority-wielding headmen in north-west India and parts of Pakistan, who convened and made the final decisions in village councils (see Elgar 1960, Lindholm 1982, and Crooke ([1896] 1974).

[6] See Agarwal (1994), for a regional mapping.

[7] See Burling (1997: 59) and Kar (1982: 58).

[8] In the Khasi 'states' with hereditary chiefs, in theory there was provision for a woman to succeed to office in the absence of specified categories of men. In practice, the chance of this happening was small, given the long list of men who preceded her.

the *taravad* (joint family estate), was legally responsible for its junior members, and represented the family in caste assemblies and interactions with higher authorities in the kingdom.[9] Rare cases of Nayar women becoming *karanavans*, managing the *taravad*, and even enjoying some political power did exist, but only in the absence of suitable males in the female line, or if the *taravad* males were minors (Moore 1983, Balakrishnan 1981, Aiyar 1883). The system did not provide for female *karanavans* in the normal course. Among the royalty, again, there are examples of Nayar queens who directly governed and even acquired reputations for good governance, including one who promoted female education in the late nineteenth century (a point much emphasized by Nobel Laureate Amartya Sen), but in the general population there was clearly a gendered separation of the public and private spheres of decision-making. Among bilateral communities also, such as the majority Sinhalese of Sri Lanka, although women could manage their individual or family property, men monopolized customary institutions with jural power. They were the headmen and village council members (Yalman 1967). Women were typically excluded from such bodies.

Of course, village/caste councils were themselves by no means institutions of democratic functioning. And the inclusion of women appears to have been more likely where the community itself was egalitarian, whatever its kinship or inheritance system. For instance, both the Garos (tribal, matrilineal) and the Santals (tribal, non-matrilineal) who allowed women to be present in council meetings were customarily egalitarian—economically and socially—unlike most communities which disallowed women's presence. Elsewhere, age, property, and caste all played a role in who dominated village decision-making processes. But while many men too did not have a voice in these bodies, unlike women they were not excluded as a gender. Also among all groups (matrilineal, bilateral, patrilineal) men's control of the public decision-making domain gave them critical influence over the modification of legal and social rules when external conditions began to change in significant ways, especially under British colonial rule (Agarwal 1994). To move from a situation of such substantial exclusion to inclusion was not going to prove easy.

1.2 Women in Green Governance

South Asian *environmental* history tells us even less about women in governance than the social history of the region. Most influential writings on the region's environmental history provide us with little information for assessing, even to the extent Jane Humphries does for England, how women used or related to the forests.[10] People are described as ungendered entities, subsumed into general categories such as 'villagers' and 'tribals', even when the context clearly indicates

[9] Gough (1961), Buchanan (1807). See also discussions in Agarwal (1994).

[10] See e.g. S. Guha (1999), Grove (1995), Sivaramakrishnan (1999), Chakravarty-Kaul (1996), Phillip (2003), and Anderson (2000), among others. R. Guha (1989) mentions women's work in cultivation, but he too is silent on their use of forests.

the subject is likely to be a woman. Numerous articles in Grove et al. (1998) on the environmental history of South and South-East Asia follow this pattern.[11] Tucker's (1998) piece on the western Himalayas, for instance, which focuses on non-timber forest products, including fruits, flowers, medicinal roots, and leaves—items which we know from contemporary sources (e.g. Gaul 1994; Gururani 1996) are mainly collected by women in the region—speaks of 'rural *people's*' traditional use of the forests, and the impact of British regulations on the 'villagers'. Saldanha (1998), writing about the ecological history of Thana district in Bombay Presidency, similarly traces the impact of forest regulations in the late nineteenth century on the 'tribals' and 'non-tribals' who, she notes, depended on local forests variously for domestic and agricultural needs, including fruits, roots, berries, small game, fuel, timber, and grazing. She describes the hardships faced by 'the villagers' due to forest restrictions on wood collection and grazing, and how 'the landless' and 'tribals' responded, including by stealing wood for farm implements or headloads of firewood for personal use and sale in the village. Some ungendered subjects (pp. 719–20) admit: 'We bring fuel from the jungle... The forest guards object to our taking wood of any kind from the forests... but we disregard [their] objection and remove the wood. If we did not do so we would starve.' It is more than likely that those speaking here are women, since it is they who mainly collect firewood, and even today women in many regions admit slipping into government-regulated forests behind the guard's back for firewood and fodder (see Chapter 9). But they are not identified as women by the author.

Similarly, Padel's (1998: 910) entire discussion on the forest knowledge of 'tribals' on 'how to grow and gather plants and animals for food' remains ungendered. Anderson (2000: 49), likewise, describes the Irula tribe as follows: 'A young Irula... sees fruits, herbs and the like as gifts from the forest.' Even careful environmental historians, such as Sivaramakrishnan (1999), conflate women into 'villagers' when describing the history of forest activities which are obviously gendered, and it can be inferred that the subjects are women. In discussing the draft Indian Forest Act of 1865, for instance, Sivaramakrishnan (1999: 172, emphasis mine) notes: 'hardship for *villagers* gathering fuelwood, thatch grass, and fodder was anticipated... ' The one exception is his passing citation of an 1880s British account which mentions firewood sale by Paharia women for family subsistence. However, other scholars, as noted, conflate gender in this activity as well. Possibly, such silence on the gender of subjects stems from a similar one in the historical sources used by these authors, but this cannot entirely be the case since some well-known sources such as Elwin ([1939] 2007) do gender their descriptions. In any case, even the lacuna has not been commented on, and this conflation carries into most contemporary writings.[12]

[11] Even the one exception, namely Damodaran (1998), makes only a passing reference to women (as collectors of mahua flowers), although she develops a more gendered perspective in her 2002 piece discussed further below.

[12] See e.g. Agrawal (2001: 21 n. 21), who uses the term 'villagers' even when the respondent can be identified as being a woman. In more recent years, some historical work is beginning to emerge on

For information even on what men and women collected from the forest, we have to turn directly to colonial administrators and chroniclers writing about India's castes and tribes in the late nineteenth and early twentieth centuries. Although they too typically conflate people into ungendered entities, there are exceptions. Russell and Hiralal ([1916] 1975) and Elwin ([1939] 2007), for instance, describe how among the Baigas of central India, women collected fruits and roots as food to tide over seasonal shortages, as well as leaves, flowers (mahua) for liquor, and sal seeds. Men collected roots especially during drought and famine (see also, Prasad 2003). Crooke ([1896] 1974: 286) describes how women were 'believed to possess secrets for charms and medicines' and sold roots and herbs collected from the jungle. We can also gather that women collected famine foods from Damodaran's (2002: 153) gleanings from famine commission reports of the 1890s, including descriptions of Oraon tribal women foraging in gangs for edible plants during times of extreme scarcity. And we get two rare colonial accounts of forest land being gifted to or through women. Crooke ([1896] 1974: 331) finds that among the Korwa tribe in Chota Nagpur, women were assigned a piece of forest of their very own for hunting and for collecting roots and wild fruits; and that 'no one else dares to interfere with her domain, and the right is strictly enforced by the council'. Among the Bhar community, however, the bride's father gifted a small patch of forest for cultivation to the bridegroom, and not to his daughter (Crooke[1896] 1974). These tantalizing descriptions still tell us little, however, about women's role in forest *governance*.

To infer women's place in environmental governance historically, I therefore rely on a tangential approach, using ethnographic/historical information on governance in general. This material indicates that women were users of the commons but had little role in decisions regarding the commons. Typically, the village headman was the representative authority managing the commons. In many regions he decided how wasteland would be allocated and what access would be granted to village forests, grazing lands, and water sources.[13] This authority came specially into play for new settlers. In some areas the headman even represented the community in negotiations with the government.[14] Among the Santal tribals, the headman maintained the sacred groves, arranged tree planting, and looked after grazing grounds and communal wells (Archer ([1946] 1984); and in the colonial period he was charged with preserving trees not only in the commons but also on cultivated land, and had to report any infringements of the rules to the deputy commissioner (Sachchidananda 1968). To a lesser

gender and ecology (e.g. Prasad 2003 and Damodaran 2002), but this is still not on gender and ecological governance.

[13] See, e.g., Somers (1977) and Sachchidananda (1968) for Bihar; Roy ([1912] 1970) for Bengal; Mohapatra (1991: 8–9) for Chotanagpur (then in the undivided Bihar province and now in Jharkhand state); and Yorke (1985) for Andhra Pradesh. In parts of Sri Lanka the landowners elected a separate headman for irrigation (Yalman 1967: 30–1).

[14] See Chakravarty-Kaul (1996: 265) on the Indian Punjab in the late nineteenth and early twentieth centuries.

extent than the headman, but also important in particular regions, were a range of other entities such as feudal lords (as in Rajasthan: Gold and Gujar 2002), clan chiefs (as in north-east India), networks of agnatic kin (brotherhoods, bhaicharis), and families of first settlers, who exercised authority over forests or over the allocation of usufruct rights in common land, and sometimes over selected forest produce, such as certain types of wood and non-wood products.[15]

Other custodians of forests, such as forest guards, employed by the colonial government to enforce forest use rules, were also male. And the van panchayats (forest councils) established in the Uttar Pradesh hills in India by the British in the 1930s, in response to a long period of agitation by local communities against the government's curtailment of their rights to forest use, were similarly male controlled. Although women were not formally excluded from van panchayats, effectively they remained excluded, even into the contemporary period. Of the twenty-eight van panchayats that Agrawal (2001: 21) studied, only one had a woman member.[16] Broadly we could thus venture that unlike in Tolkien's imagined Middle Earth, representative authority rather than democratic consultation typified commons governance in South Asia. And women played little role in this.

Indeed, in contrast to South Asia's regional and cultural diversity in women's access to immovable property and in their mobility and marriage patterns that I mapped in *A Field of One's Own*, there appears to have been substantial regional and cross-community *uniformity* in women's historical exclusion from public decision-making forums. This does not make cultural geography irrelevant in the present discussion, but it does mean that it had limited impact on this count *historically*, although it could still have important implications in efforts to enhance women's public participation today.

Against this background of women's (almost) exclusion from public decision-making bodies, the changes, first in the top echelons of government in the early twentieth century and later at the village level, especially in the 1990s, can only be termed dramatic. These changes are traced below through two trajectories: (1) the spread of the idea that women should be part of public decision-making, initially in the late nineteenth and early twentieth centuries, in the negotiation over and entry of women into the legislatures, and subsequently in the 1980s–1990s for including women in institutions of local governance; and (2) the shifts in thinking and activism which led to the idea of participatory forest management. The results of these developments, however, as I will argue, were mixed—an increase in numbers within new institutions of governance, but constrained in effectiveness by being embedded in social norms and contexts where traditional village councils, and long-standing lines of gendered authority, continue to hold sway.

[15] Here too there could be gendered hierarchies; for instance, in Chotanagpur's Munda villages, descendants from the mother's side of the founding family needed prior permission from the father's side to take wood for domestic and agricultural use (Chaudhuri 1993: 69).

[16] See also TERI (1995). Changes on this front are recent, and occasionally all-woman van panchayats may be found (personal observation during fieldwork, 1998).

2. NEGOTIATING A PRESENCE

Women's struggle to find a place in public decision-making in South Asia can be characterized as successive waves of effort and policy shifts which broadly coincide with, but are not identical to, the periods popularly identified in the international women's movement as the three 'waves of feminism'. The shifts are best demonstrated by examining the Indian experience in some detail, given both the paucity of equivalent material on other parts of South Asia, and the shared historical experience between India and several other countries in the region, such as present-day Pakistan and Bangladesh.

In India, the first wave of policy shifts enabling women's entry into public bodies in the late nineteenth and early twentieth centuries coincided with, indeed was nourished by, the anti-colonial struggle, the opening up of places in government for Indians under colonial rule, and the emergence of national women's organizations lobbying for universal suffrage and legislative positions. This culminated in women getting the right to vote (albeit on restricted terms) and their formal entry into the legislatures. The second wave of policy shift—roughly around the mid-1970s to early 1990s—coincided with and was propelled by the women's movement in South Asia and internationally, and a parallel emphasis in development discourse on participatory development and decentralization. This culminated in the 73rd and 74th Constitutional amendments in 1993. The former reserved one-third seats for rural women in the village, block (or other intermediate level), and district councils, and the latter for urban women in municipalities. The third wave or rather push to change policy from late 1990s onwards—again propelled by the women's movement within the region and by the focus of international agencies on women's low representation in parliaments globally—is still on the surge. In India, this is the (yet unsuccessful) struggle to reserve one-third seats for women in parliament. Alongside are the continuing efforts to make women's presence effective, rather than remaining simply nominal, within institutions of local governance.

It is important to understand these historical processes, since they shaped policies on women's inclusion not only within institutions of government but also more widely, such as within institutions of environmental governance. For instance, the terms of women's entry into local government strongly influenced the guidelines for including women in institutions for managing natural resources such as forests, water, and biodiversity. Indeed, not only is the history of South Asian women's role in green governance intertwined with the history of women in governance more generally, but the social factors which constrain women's effective participation are also largely common across various institutions of local governance. The question of what proportion of women and which socio-economic class of women might prove effective is also of common interest. (To distinguish the decentralized arms of government from other institutions of local governance, such as community forestry institutions, I use the term local *government* for the former and the term *governance* more generically.)

2.1 Waves of Policy Shifts

Women's early struggles to enter state institutions of governance date to the late nineteenth and early twentieth centuries when the British colonial government in India began to allow greater representation of Indians.[17] The early twentieth century, in particular, brought substantial legislative changes which led to the inclusion of Indians in legislatures and executive bodies, and the establishment of a restricted form of parliamentary democracy in which Indians could participate in elections. Enfranchisement was based on property ownership. Elections in the 1920s brought a fair number of Indians into both the provincial legislative councils and the central legislative assembly, where they could debate government policy.[18]

Parallel to this, women were campaigning for universal suffrage as well as positions in the legislatures, alongside a push for social reform legislation. Several women's organizations emerged at this time, such as the Women's India Association (WIA), the National Council of Women in India (NCWI), and the All India Women's Conference (AIWC), established in 1917, 1925, and 1927 respectively (Forbes 1981). These organizations were national in scope but had branches in several provinces, and during the late 1920s and 1930s they expanded both numerically and geographically, with membership reaching the thousands (Everett 1979: 71–4). In addition, numerous women's organizations were formed in the provinces. These brought with them a wider cross-class and cross-regional constituency than embodied in the national women's organizations which were constituted largely of educated, middle-class, urban women (Forbes 2000).

At this time, the colonial government also introduced the idea of separate electorates for certain social groups, on grounds of religion (Muslims), caste,[19] and gender. Separate electorates meant that both voters and candidates would come from the targeted group—e.g. only women would vote for women (as opposed to reservation of a proportion of seats for them where the voters would come from the general population). Women's organizations did not favour separate electorates but the government's proposal did mean that women had emerged as a special constituency. Several factors underlay this recognition. The most important appears to have been the idea that women have different perspectives and interests from men—an idea that was pushed both by women's organizations and the men who supported them. According to Forbes (1979), the ideological argument for women's franchise, which also underscored the argument for their entry into the legislatures, was that women's lives and interests were so different from men's that they needed separate representation. Differences between

[17] Only some broad parameters are mentioned here to mark the context. For more details on the complex constitutional history of that period, see especially Brown (1994), Robb (1976), and Sikri (1960), as well as the discussion in Agarwal (2002).

[18] By 1940 Indians also constituted 50 per cent of the Indian civil service (Brown 1994: 247).

[19] Seats were first reserved for Scheduled Castes and Tribes (SCs/STs) under the Government of India Act of 1935 passed by the British. After Independence, the Constitution of India also recognized SCs/STs for affirmative action measures, but based on a more complete list compiled by the states.

women (based on class, caste, or religion) were minimized under an idealized notion that they were all 'sisters under the sari' (Forbes 1979: 18). Some AIWC members within small local women's groups questioned the ability of elite women to represent the interests of all women (Singer 2007: 38), but these differences did not prevail in the negotiations of women's groups with the government. A related idea was that men were 'handicapped' in dealing with issues such as marriage, divorce, labour, and child welfare which were seen as needing a woman's perspective (Singer 2007: 43). Another important factor was women's participation in large numbers alongside men in the civil disobedience movement and in public demonstrations against the colonial government. This not only made women's contributions visible, it also (according to Singer), created 'a debt' that the Congress party (which led the anti-colonial struggle and formed the government after Independence) continued to recognize well after Independence. Alongside, a strong social reform movement in the late nineteenth and early twentieth centuries spearheaded by some male reformers, and focusing on the social disabilities that women faced, created a climate conducive to enhancing women's voice. Finally, but not the least, women's organizations carried these demands to policy forums and into the streets.

Although the complex history of women's negotiations with the government cannot be traced here, it is notable that their demands had at least two divergent effects. On the one hand it effectively underscored the point that women were a political constituency that could not be ignored. On the other hand, ironically, the very argument that women constituted a special group and would bring a special perspective to the political domain also gave weight to solutions such as separate electorates which were applied to other social groups, such as Muslims, although (as noted) women's groups themselves opposed separate electorates and favoured a place in the general electorate.[20]

By 1929, Indian women had won the right to vote in all provinces (Forbes 2000: 101), although enfranchisement was based either on their husband's tax status or on their being literate.[21] Universal adult suffrage was granted only in 1949 when Independent India adopted its Constitution (Singer 2007). In the 1920s women also gained restricted eligibility to membership (through election or nomination) in some of the Provincial Councils (Everett 1979: 112) and later in the Federal Legislatures (Sikri 1960).

These pre-Independence changes had several implications for later developments. On the positive side, they created a precedence of women participating in and winning seats in the legislature—thus bringing them into decision-making. Women gained direct experience in voting and political campaigning and some voice in legislative debates during a critical period of political transition. On the negative side, women continue to be bracketed with minorities as groups facing

[20] Women's organizations were also influenced by Mahatma Gandhi's strong opposition to separate electorates for Scheduled Castes as versus reservations for them within the general electorate.

[21] For the 1937 elections, some 43 per cent of adult males but only 9 per cent of the adult females were enfranchised (Everett 1979: 137).

social and economic disabilities (although the idea of separate electorates was abandoned after Independence). Also the notion that there are a set of issues to which women can bring a special perspective continues to hold sway in the granting of traditional portfolios to women politicians (such as health, and women and child welfare), with some shifts away from this stereotyping in recent years.

In formal terms, the first wave of policy shifts, at the highest levels of government, brought only a small percentage of women into parliament, but in symbolic and strategic terms it was an important gain. *Structurally*, however, gain in the legislatures was in itself insufficient to enhance women's presence in village-level governance. Given the hold of traditional village councils, which were male dominated and based on age and social hierarchies, what was clearly needed as a first step was institutions of governance built on ideas of *democratic* participation. In other words, decentralized government was in some sense a necessary condition for women's entry into local government, although it was not a sufficient condition. This required a further separate struggle. Indeed, women's entry into local governance, including into green governance, in India, and in South Asia more generally, is closely linked with the idea of decentralization, albeit not automatically resulting from the process of decentralization, to which I now turn.

2.2 Decentralization

At its broadest, decentralization involves the administrative, fiscal, and democratic devolution of power and resources by governments from its top tiers to its bottom tiers, and aims to give communities democratic voice and influence over the issues that affect their daily lives (Manor 1999), even if in practice it may fall well short of these aims. In India, early moves toward decentralized government date to the colonial period, when statutory village councils were set up in the 1920s, following the recommendation of the Royal Commission on Decentralization in 1909 and the Government of India Act of 1919.[22] The move was aimed primarily at improved administration. The idea took firmer root in the immediate post-Independence period of the 1950s when, influenced by the Gandhian vision of local self-sufficiency, India launched the community development programme (Frankel 1978). The Constitution of India also built into its Directive principles of State Policy (article 40) the organizing of gram panchayats (village councils) as units of self-government.

Neither in India nor elsewhere, however, was decentralized governance the dominant paradigm at this time. Rather, Keynesian and Leninist approaches to economics, the attraction of the Soviet model of planning for newly industrializing economies to 'catch up', and the political need to consolidate national

[22] Even earlier, in 1882, Lord Ripon, Viceroy of India, promoted the idea of popularly elected local institutions to oversee specified functions.

identities in the post-colonial period propelled most developing countries toward centralism. In the 1970s, faith in this approach was shaken economically as well as politically, by both global and local factors: stagflation (stagnant growth with high inflation) in western economies, growing inequalities and disappointment with political leaders to deliver prosperity in newly independent countries, and the oil shocks. This cluster of factors (varying by country) led many politicians to seek answers in decentralization (Manor 1999: 36).

There was also intellectual support for decentralization in the standard economic preoccupation with incentives and efficiency. The following argument by Binswanger and Deininger (1997: 1999), although made in the 1990s, was not atypical of emergent thinking in the 1970s: 'Decentralization of political, fiscal, and administrative power may change incentive structures for political participation and the ability of previously powerless groups to participate, thus creating conditions for bargaining which are more conducive to efficiency.' In India, Gandhian social activism provided additional pressure for the revival of Gandhian ideas that had coexisted (albeit uneasily) alongside more centrist visions of development.[23] The idea of decentralization also found fertile ground in the ongoing debates among activists and academics on poverty, economic inequality, urban bias, and the need to empower the economically and socially disadvantaged. Decentralization was seen as a way of correcting 'the multiple failures of the bureaucratic and centralized apparatus of the Indian development state' (Chaudhuri 2007: 160).

An important strand in the decentralization debate was about equity and voice for local communities, closely intertwined with the idea of 'participation'. Indeed participation was a key concept in the arguments favouring administrative decentralization, although it was evoked in other contexts as well. Internationally, for instance, it was a much discussed issue in the context of post-colonial developments in the 1960s.[24] In the 1980s 'participation' in governance as a key element in building a robust democracy added strength to the idea of decentralization, although unlike decentralization which was seen mostly in instrumental terms, participation was seen as having intrinsic worth, in its promise of giving political voice to the local, the poor, and to women. These interlinkages also eased the path to women's inclusion in local government, although they did not ensure such inclusion.

2.3 Women in Local Government

Neither decentralization nor women's gains in parliament were sufficient conditions for women's entry into *local* government. The pre-Independence statutory village councils set up in the 1920s made no space for women (Buch 2000).

23 See e.g. Manor (1999) and Jain (2007), among others.

24 See various issues of the *Ideas and Action Bulletin*, launched in 1959 by the UN Food and Agricultural Organization.

Although some states enacted laws to elect council members, women were eligible neither to stand for election nor to vote. In fact several states specified that only adult males could form the electorate, and some also stipulated that no woman could vote or be elected (Buch 2000). Even the request to form a statutory village panchayat could only be made by resident males.

This male-bias eased somewhat after Independence. In the 1950s, in a series of meetings, the Central Council of Local Government noted that block panchayats should coopt two women interested in working among women and children. They suggested two women rather than one, since 'a solitary woman is unable to express herself freely' (cited in Buch 2000: 35). The 1957 Balvantray Mehta Committee made similar recommendations for village panchayats, as did the 1965 Santhanam Committee Report (GoI 1965: 13) which reiterated that at least two women should be included since 'where there is only one, she feels rather isolated and if there are at least two women members they will be able to contribute more effectively in the deliberations of the panchayat'. Following such recommendations, several states enacted laws in the 1950s and 1960s for coopting one or two women. This set the precedent for 'at least two women' in local institutions of governance, and of linking women's participation in government with their responsibility for women and children's welfare. Most village and town councils, however, were marked by women's absence, save for an occasional token woman, as seen from village ethnographies of the period. The more dramatic changes came in the second wave of policy shifts from the mid-1970s to the early 1990s. These shifts culminated in the reservation of one-third seats for women in India's institutions of local government in the early 1990s (as well as in Pakistan and Bangladesh around the same period), and to a more limited extent in Nepal.

The post-Independence debates for women's inclusion in local government in India followed the trajectories of those around women's entry into legislatures on some counts, and departed from them on other counts. The most important commonality was ideational. There was acceptance of the idea that women's presence in public decision-making was an important indicator of 'women's upliftment' and social reform. Women were also seen as likely to bring to social issues a different perspective from men, and further that certain issues could be dubbed 'women's issues', even though there was no clarity on what these issues might be, beyond, say, linking children's welfare with women's welfare. The second important common feature was the recognition, especially by the Congress party, that a debt was owed to women for their substantial contribution in the freedom movement. Both factors no doubt underlay the Congress party's target in the 1950s of having at least 15 per cent women in the legislatures (Singer 2007). The third carryover feature from pre-Independent debates was the idea of reservation. While separate electorates were rejected in the framing of Independent India's Constitution, the seat reservation for scheduled castes and tribes that was built into the Constitution potentially opened a similar route for women.

At the same time, in the discussions around local government, there were several points of departure from the earlier debates on women in the legislatures.

First, in ideational terms, some early government committees which focused on the political representation of women linked the need for women's participation to that of nation building and especially the building of an effective democracy. The Santhanam Committee Report (GoI 1965), for example, saw women's presence as necessary not just for correcting historic inequities but also for establishing a fully functioning democracy, where women were citizens and their active participation as voters and representatives was an index of a healthy democracy.[25] In line with this perspective, and deviating from the Balwantray Mehta Committee (GoI 1957: 127) that two women should be *coopted* into panchayats, the Santhanam Committee (GoI 1965: 13) recommended direct elections of women in local government and a minimum of two women at every level.[26]

Also at the ideational level, the discourse on participatory and equitable development—with antecedents in the 1960s—impinged on including women in the development process (see also Singer 2007: 91). This paralleled the discussion on decentralization and on giving greater autonomy to local-level institutions, discussed further below. Second, apart from traditional women's organizations, such as the AIWC, which continued to play a role, a proliferation of new pressure groups emerged (especially from the mid-1970s), such as women's organizations linked with new political parties, autonomous (non-party) women's groups, and several thousand NGOs working on developmental issues.[27]

The shifting historical emphasis on women in government was of a piece with shifting national concerns. In the colonial period, gaining control of the top echelons of government was the aim of the anti-colonial movement in which women and minorities negotiated a space. In the post-Independence period the agendas were wider and deeper—intertwined with the aims of development, the strengthening of democratic institutions, and the involvement of all citizens in nation building. The discussions on including women in public decision-making reflected these concerns.

The recommendations of various government committees on decentralization (and especially those mentioned above) were taken up by some states long before the 73rd Constitutional Amendment of 1993 which reserved seats for women in local government. In the late 1980s, several states in southern and western India—regions with more women-friendly cultural norms—mandated 20 to 30 per cent women's representation in village councils. Some additionally mandated that a certain percentage of village council chairpersons would be women.[28] A few

[25] In general also, as Frankel (1978: 104) observes, a panchayat was seen as 'an instrument for redistribution of political power in favour of the peasant and landless classes', and to break the stranglehold of 'narrow notions of caste or faction' in traditional communities.

[26] Subsequently, the Asoka Mehta Committee (GoI 1978) recommended that panchayats be made an integral part of the government decision-making and not simply agencies for implementing government schemes.

[27] Estimates of development NGOs in the late 1990s range from 3,700 (Development Alternatives 1998) to 25,000 (VANI 2000).

[28] See e.g. Singer (2007: 103), Manikyamba (1989), and Kaushik (1993). In some states, the inclusion of even one woman was a notable break with tradition (see e.g. Chaki-Sircar 1984, for Manipur).

northern states also introduced reservations, but only for 'at least two women'. However, earlier perceptions continued that the women elected to the councils would represent the interests of all women, and would promote women's issues under the banner of women and child welfare.

The 73rd Amendment to the Indian Constitution through the Constitution (73rd Amendment) Act, 1992 (notified in 1993), provided the basis of a broad-based representation of women, formalized in a three-tier structure—at the village (gram), intermediate (block/taluka/mandal) and district (zilla) levels—henceforth called the Panchyati Raj Institutions (PRIs). Under the amendment, one-third seats were to be reserved for women as members in each PRI across the country, at all three levels. In addition, seats were reserved for SCs and STs in proportion to their populations, and within these categories too one-third seats were reserved for women as members. The overall reservation of one-third seats for women members in a council was, however, inclusive of any SC/ST woman member. Hence all councils would have at least one-third women members (and some could have more since women could also contest from unreserved seats). Moreover, there was recognition of women as chairpersons, and one-third of all chairpersons' seats in PRIs were reserved for women—these reserved constituencies would rotate every five years. The 74th Amendment (Constitution (74th Amendment) Act 1992) provided similar reservations of one-third seats for women as members in each municipal body, and as chairpersons in one-third of the municipal bodies. The women were to be elected directly, with five-year terms. As a result of the Act, over a million village women (including about 86,000 chairpersons and vice chairpersons) were elected across the country, with statutory powers, albeit with (restricted) budgetary allocations.

These constitutional amendments faced little opposition,[29] although they were passed by a parliament which had very few women legislators. As at the time of Independence, what won was the power of the idea that women's presence was important on various counts. Indeed, the idea of a substantial inclusion of women in panchayats had been promoted by many women's pressure groups at least since the mid-1970s when the Committee on the Status of Women in India (GoI 1974: 304–5) recognized women's low political representation and recommended the setting up of all-women panchayats 'to ensure greater participation of women in the development process' and to look after village-level development programmes for women and children.[30] Subsequently, the *National Perspective Plan for Women* (GoI 1988: 164–6) specifically called for 30 per cent reservations for women in Panchayati Raj Institutions, as well as 30 per cent reservation of the executive heads of all such bodies. It also recommended that 30 per cent of all candidates fielded by all political parties should be women. Women's pressure

[29] See Singer (2007) and Gaiha et al. (2000).

[30] The Committee was divided on reservations: some supported reservations at all levels, from panchayats to parliament, others wanted no reservations at all, and yet others supported reservations in local bodies but not in parliament (GoI 1974: 302–5, 354–7). Notably, the clubbing of women with children, in arguments favouring women's representation, continued.

groups kept the idea alive in the public domain, even though there were segments opposing representation. Many male MPs supported the policy, not merely 'to portray themselves in a positive light' (as Singer 2007: 124 argues), but (as indicated by the parliamentary debates preceding the 73rd Amendment) out of a genuine belief in social reform, a vestige perhaps of the history of male-supported social reform in the pre-Independence period.

The magic figure of one-third, however, does not appear to have been an Indian invention. In fact it was popularized internationally as *the* critical mass needed for women to be effective. Although there is no easy way to trace the path, it appears to have emerged especially from research in Scandinavia, in which Dahlerup's (1988) study was among the early ones to emphasize this percentage. More generally too, world attention was focused on gender inequality through the World Conferences on Women in Mexico in 1975, and in Nairobi a decade later. The writings and activism that accompanied this attention brought the issue of women's exclusion from public decision-making into policy discussions.

Following India's 73rd Constitutional Amendment, each state enacted a Conformity Act with its own provisions within the broad framework of the amendment; a few states also gave village panchayats judicial powers to serve as *nyaya* panchayats for settling disputes (Ray and Basu 1999). The Conformity Acts differed in the kinds of issues prioritized by state governments and had implications for whether gender needs or environmental concerns might be taken up (as discussed in Chapter 10).

In several other parts of South Asia also, although reservations in parliament have had a chequered history, reservations in local governance have moved along a trajectory not dissimilar to India's. Both Pakistan and Bangladesh now have one-third reservation for women at all tiers of local government; and Nepal reserves twenty per cent (although there is a demand for more, following the country's 2008 Constituent Assembly elections). Sri Lanka has no reservations at present, but there is a demand from civil society groups for one-third reservations in local government (see summary in Table 3.1).[31] Also common across South Asia is the focus on numbers rather than an interrogation of what those numbers might achieve for women. Efforts to assess the impact of presence are now ongoing, but *ex post facto.*

In the moves for reservation in local government, four points are of particular note. First, it was assumed (with no firm basis in evidence) that the women elected would be interested in and able to represent all women simply because they were women. Second, even though in India seats were reserved for women in the SC/ST category, this was more an attempt to correct a historical disadvantage than to bring through SC/ST women a different perspective to women's issues than that offered by upper-caste women.[32] In terms of defining interests, women's gender

[31] Personal communication, Kumari Jayawardena, 2007.

[32] In Nepal, after the 2008 Constituent Assembly Elections, the demand by a section of women that dalit women should be recognized as a distinct category for representation in parliament, similarly

Table 3.1. Reservation for women: South Asia

Country	Reservation/quota policy		Figures
	National legislatures	Local governance	Per cent women in lower house of parliament (in 2004)
Bangladesh (Pre-1971)	Shared policy with Pakistan with a few reserved seats		Not available
(Post-1971)	Reserved seats for limited periods: 30 in 1979–82 (lapsed in 2001)	33% in three tiers of local governance: village, union, zilla (Local Government Act No. 20)	2.0
India	None	One-third reservation for women among members in three tiers of Panchayati Raj Institutions: village, intermediate and district, in rural areas. Also one-third of all chairpersons' seats reserved for women (73rd Constitutional Amendment in 1993). One-third reservation for women among members in municipal elections in urban areas Also one-third of all chairpersons' seats reserved for women. (74th Constitutional Amendment).	8.8
Nepal Pre-2008[a]	5% of 60 seats in national assembly; 5% of party tickets in elections	20% reservation for women in two tiers of local government (district and village local bodies) (Local Self-Government Act 1999)	5.8
Pakistan	A few seats since 1956 but 17% (60 out of 342) in national assembly (lower house) since 2002	One-third reservation at all tiers: union council, tehsil and district. Also in town councils for urban areas (The Local Government Ordinance, 2000)	21.6
Sri Lanka	None	None (but demand by civil society for one-third reservation)	4.4

Note: [a] These figures relate to the situation before the April 2008 Constituent Assembly elections. The elections led to 33% women in the Assembly. In local councils also there is now a demand for a higher level of reservation.

Sources: Author (for India); Khawar (2005) and Rai (2005) for other countries. For recent information on Nepal see http://www.iknowpolitics.org/en/node/6191.

identity was privileged over other identities such as those derived from caste, class, religion, or ethnicity. This assumption simplifies the social context within which women (and men) are located and the impact of that context on constraints to their effective participation.[33] In fact, the assumption that all women necessarily have common interests needs interrogation and empirical testing, as does the assumption that women representatives will promote and prioritize women's interests in decision-making. This returns us to an important thread in this book about the potential as well as the limitations of mere presence.

Third, the Panchayati Raj Institutions with one-third women coexist with women-less traditional village councils of caste and tribe. The former draw on modern ideas of equality and democracy; the latter draw on customs which are still deeply patriarchal in many communities. Also the former are typically limited to the exercise of executive authority, and only have judicial authority in a few states, while many traditional panchayats perform both judicial and other functions. The strength of the traditional panchayats varies regionally, and in some areas was already declining in the 1960s (Mandelbaum 1970), while in other areas, as in Haryana state (north-west India), even today caste panchayats remain 'wholly male, patriarchal bodies that use their united collective power for repressive ends rather than egalitarian or democratic ones' and 'wield dictatorial power ... as a parallel legal system ... enforcing gender and caste codes' (Chowdhry 2007: 12 n. 13).[34] The functioning of PRIs cannot be disassociated from this potentially conflictual interface between the modern and the traditional. Indeed, other institutions of local governance, such as those managing community forestry, have to contend with this interface more centrally, in the formal rules for gender inclusion and the way those rules are implemented within community forestry institutions.

Fourth, the discourses preceding the 73rd Constitutional Amendment and the amendment itself have set a precedent for other local institutions. For a start, and most importantly, the norm of having 'at least two women', which dates back to the 1950s, has been adopted in a number of contexts in which government has intervened, including in many institutions for forest governance (as elaborated later). Only occasionally has this been scaled up to one-third women. The 'at least two' or 'at least one-third' is usually treated as a cap rather than a floor. Moreover, even such spillover effects from local government to other local institutions in terms of including women did not occur immediately. Just as decentralization of government was a necessary first step for gender-inclusive government, so decentralizing forest management was a necessary first step for gender-inclusive forest

appears to be driven more by the idea of justice than by a stated possibility that dalit women will bring a special perspective.

33 See also Gaiha et al. (2000) on concerns about the representation of the poor in the panchayats.

34 Although Chowdhry's (2007) focus is on marriage alliances that invite extreme punishments from caste panchayats if villagers transgress local custom, the authority that caste panchayats command also impinges on the overall social climate that works to the detriment of women and their rights as citizens, in all kinds of ways.

governance. Decentralization of government, however, did not imply decentralization of forest governance. This process had a somewhat independent trajectory, as discussed below.

3. DECENTRALIZING FOREST GOVERNANCE

The move to decentralized government created conditions conducive to devolving control over natural resources to communities on grounds of both efficiency and equity, but neither the concept of decentralized government nor that of participation was specific to *environmental* governance.

Nevertheless many writers on community forestry in India and Nepal locate their analysis centrally within the framework of decentralization in local government (see e.g. Hobley 1996, Agrawal 1999a).[35] The close link which Hobley (1996) and many others seek to establish between the move toward decentralized government and decentralized environmental governance appears justified to some extent for Nepal, where the 1982 Decentralization Act empowered village councils in a number of ways, including to form people's committees to use, conserve, and afforest forest land (Hobley 1996, Agrawal 1999a). But in India in the 1980s the decentralization debate was not couched in relation to forests or other common pool resources.[36] Nor were the PRIs empowered to control government forests (even if they could control forests located on panchayat land). Control over government forests lay firmly in the centralized charge of the forest department with its entrenched and hierarchical bureaucracy.

Also in both India and Nepal the move from top-down State-directed forest management to community involvement in forest governance was a result of complex parallel processes, in which three factors were of particular importance: State failures in forest protection; examples of community success in forest conservation and resistance to top-down State control; and the theoretical debate on property rights and conservation.

3.1 State Failures

Over 90 per cent of the forest lands in India and Nepal are government owned which, until the introduction of community forestry on a countrywide scale in

[35] In a somewhat different way, Baumann and Farrington (2003) also conflate decentralized government and decentralized forest management, by failing to distinguish between the potential control PRIs can exercise over forest resources, and the control that village communities were given over degraded forests by the forest department under Joint Forest Management.

[36] Even in Nepal, the student demonstrations that preceded the 1982 Act were for replacing the 1961 partyless panchayat system with multiparty democracy and were not specifically focused on decentralized *forest* management.

the 1990s, were largely government managed through their forest departments.[37] The inefficiencies of centralized control became especially apparent in the early 1970s. In that period, both South Asia and many developing regions awoke to a sense of an environmental crisis, fuelled on the one hand by satellite images of rapid forest degradation which alarmed environmentalists, and on the other hand by the human face of the crisis revealed by shortages of daily items faced by village communities dependent on the commons. In India, for instance, between 1972–75 and 1980–82 the country lost an estimated 1.3 million hectares of forest cover a year. In 1985–87 only 19.5 per cent of the country's geographic area had forest cover and 40 per cent was degraded, with less than 0.4 canopy cover (Agarwal 1992: 130).[38] Village commons, likewise, both degraded over time and declined in area: between 1950 and 1984 their area fell by 26–63 percentage points (varying by state), across seven states (Jodha 1986).

In Nepal a similar alarm at the loss of forest cover followed the findings of the Land Resources Mapping Project in the early 1980s which used a countrywide 1978–79 aerial photographic coverage as its base. This project revealed that only 28 per cent of all forest area could be termed 'well stocked'; the rest had been reduced to open forest or shrub (Gilmour and Fisher 1991). Writings from the Worldwatch Institute in Washington DC also fuelled a crisis view of forest disappearance and domestic energy shortages in developing countries (Eckholm 1975, 1976).

The initial response of governments and international organizations to these ecological and human crises involved launching 'social forestry programmes' in the late 1970s and early 1980s, traversing a range of property rights regimes and systems of management. In India this involved three types of tree-planting schemes:[39] direct planting by the forest department on government land (within forests, or along roads and water bodies); encouraging village communities to plant trees on community land (the 'community forestry' component); and encouraging individual farmers to plant trees on private land (the 'farm forestry' component). As elaborated in Agarwal (1986a), although the farm forestry component had a considerable success in some regions, such as Gujarat, the other components failed in terms of both efficiency (e.g. ensuring the survival of planted trees) and equity (e.g. providing for the daily needs of fuel and fodder of the local poor). Tree survival rates were poor and targets for community forestry fell short by up to 90 per cent in some Indian states (World Bank 1983a, 1983b). The causes of these failures, analysed in Agarwal (1986a), lay especially in the top-down approach to scheme implementation with little involvement of and few incentives for local

[37] Van panchayats, set up in the 1930s, were an exception to this, but they were confined to one state.

[38] Measures of degradation can vary, of which canopy cover is but one (Lele et al. 1998).

[39] This was supplemented by steps to reduce fuelwood use by promoting biogas plants (anaerobic digesters producing methane gas as biofuel) and improved wood-burning stoves, most of which failed to have much impact, due especially to the top-down forms of implementation, with little consultation with women users for adapting the designs to their needs (Agarwal 1986a). See also discussion in Chapter 11.

communities, insecure property rights, and the undermining of existing user rights. The government's takeover of village land for tree planting, and the failure to elicit community support when the schemes were initiated, led to widespread local hostility and resistance.[40] Women typically did not feature in such schemes or, at best, were caretakers in tree nurseries with little say even in the choice of species. The real 'success' story, with plantings far exceeding targets, was that of farm forestry, practised mainly by the richer farmers who sought to reap quick profits from fast-growing commercial varieties, eucalyptus being a great favourite.

In large part, therefore, social forestry proved to be neither social nor forestry. It neither revived forests nor met people's subsistence needs. All this raised serious doubts about the ability of the State to develop what was a communal resource without some significant involvement of the resource-using communities. It is only in rare cases that the social forestry schemes overcame their weaknesses and provided a basis for community cooperation, which later served as useful experience for establishing a more participative community forestry experiment (Joshi 2000).

The typical top-down approach to forest management has a long and chequered history. In India, environmental historians trace that history especially to the second half of the nineteenth century when the colonial government established centralized control over most of the country's forests, following the Indian Forest Act of 1878, which divided forests into four categories: reserved, protected, private, and village. Most forest land fell under the first two categories, wherein local residents were given virtually no use rights in reserved forests, and highly restricted rights to those that had prevailed customarily in protected forests. Centralized control was further cemented by the 1927 Indian Forest Act. This control was used to extract revenue through timber export and large tracts were exploited for building ships and railways, or cleared for agriculture and other uses.[41]

India continued with a centralized approach to forests in the immediate post-Independence period, investing rather little in the sector while extracting substantially from forests to service other sectors (Joshi 2000).[42] In particular, the 1976 National Commission on Agriculture (NSA) Report emphasized production and extraction over people's needs. A number of bills in the early 1980s, such as the 1981 Draft Forest Bill which was later shelved due to widespread opposition from environmental activists (see Fernandes and Kulkarni 1983), were based on the NCA's recommendations. It was not until 1988 that a more community friendly forest policy was framed (GoI 1988). This policy gave centrality to forest management for fulfilling local subsistence needs and conserving the environment, and

[40] Similar failures occurred in other countries: see Hoskins (1979a) for Niger and Senegal; Eckholm (1979) for Ethiopia; and Aguilar (1982) for the Philippines.

[41] For more detailed discussions on these and related processes see Sivaramakrishnan (2000), R. Guha (1989), Joshi (2000), and Agarwal (1986a).

[42] The 1952 Indian Forest policy, for example, placed what were termed national interests over local needs, and limited the rights of local communities to forest produce.

moved away from the earlier emphasis on forest exploitation for commercial and industrial use and revenue maximization. The emphasis now was on protecting the rights of forest dwellers and 'meeting the requirements of fuelwood, fodder, minor forest produce and small timber of the rural and tribal populations' subject to the forest's carrying capacity, based on community (including women's) involvement (GoI 1988). This policy formed the basis for the Government of India's JFM programme for promoting community forestry on government forest land, through the involvement of local village communities and voluntary agencies. A circular issued by the Secretary (Environment and Forests), Government of India, on 1 June 1990, to all states and union territories, set out the contours of this new policy, and the states then passed individual orders with detailed specifications (see SPWD 1993 for the full text of the circular and the initial orders passed by fourteen states).[43] Several factors, discussed below, led to this shift in approach.

3.2 Community Forestry Successes

In contrast to the failures of centralized government-driven forestry, the 1970s saw emerging successes in forest protection by communities. Some were linked with forest movements such as Chipko in north-west India and Appiko in Karnataka (south India); others resulted from efforts by concerned villagers to initiate protection; and yet others were encouraged by forest officials (as in West Bengal, eastern India). The Chipko movement was the best publicized of community responses, with substantial participation by women (as described in Chapter 2). While everyday needs triggered village resistance to the commercial exploitation of local forests, the language in which the resistance was couched was deeply conservationist. The songs and folklore on which the movement drew, linked forests with improved soils, recharged water sources, and clean air:

> Do not axe these oaks and pines—
> nurture them, protect them.
> From these trees the streams get their water
> And the fields their green
> Look how the rhododendron smiles in the forest . . .[44]

Chipko turned existing perceptions upside down—from forest department as protectors and people as destroyers of forests, to the opposite, namely communities as forest protectors and forest officials as responsible for degradation

[43] The most recent move toward strengthening the rights of customary forest users over forests has been the passing of the Scheduled Tribes and Other Traditional Forest Dwellers (Recognition of Forest Rights) Act 2006 (henceforth called the Forest Rights Act 2006). The Act was passed after substantial inputs and lobbying by grassroots groups, and it remains contested, especially in relation to its potential effect on forest conservation, which some argue could be adverse and others the opposite.

[44] Translated from a Gharwali folk song by Ghan Shyam Shailani.

through their promotion of commercial interests.[45] Another folk song sung by Chipko activists evocatively illustrates this: 'What if the fence itself wrecks the field, if the water itself ignites the fire?' The Gandhian underpinnings of the Chipko movement helped highlight the image of communities as conservationists, since it linked subsistence needs to sustainable forest conservation, and commercial extraction to long-term non-sustainability. Mahatma Gandhi's words—'There is enough for everyone's need, but not for anyone's greed'—were also evoked.

Alongside, especially in eastern India (in states such as Orissa and Bihar), forest protection groups initiated variously by village councils, youth clubs, and village elders were being discovered, or were emerging. Some claimed a conservation history of 20 to 100 years, found especially in tribal areas where people were strongly dependent on forests and had some tradition of community resource management. By the late 1980s an estimated 3,000 to 4,000 communities had established control over about 10 per cent of the State's forests (Poffenberger et al. 1996: 34). There were also the van panchayats (some of which had survived and others had been revived by NGOs) which in 1995 were estimated to be 4,805, covering about 0.24 m ha of forest area in eight districts now in Uttarakhand state (Saxena 1995: 63).

In addition, there were examples of communities that had begun to manage degraded forest area in the late 1970s and 1980s with encouragement from local forest officials, such as in West Bengal (the Ararbari and Purulia experiments) and Haryana (the Sukhomajri experiment). The Ararbari and Purulia experiments are among the most cited accounts of early State-initiated participatory approaches to forest management, but many less-noticed, informal, forest protection efforts by communities in West Bengal—as many as 842 by one estimate—also mushroomed concurrently between 1980 and 1988, triggered by demonstration effects between neighbouring villages (Joshi 2000: 8). Most interestingly, 'front-line workers' of the forest department and members of the field-level staff of the West Bengal Subordinate Forest Service Association (WBSFSA) catalysed community forest protection, seeking a policy change to ensure worker safety, an improved work image, and a desire to build good relations with the villagers among whom they worked and lived (Joshi 2000). In fact, Joshi argues that WBSFSA's campaign was more influential than either the Arabari or the Purulia stories in propelling a policy change and the passing of an order in 1989 by the West Bengal government, to establish a co-management arrangement between the government and village communities on degraded government forest land.[46] This order substantially influenced the one passed by the central government in 1990, which formally ushered

[45] There are numerous detailed accounts of the Chipko movement from varying perspectives—see e.g. Jain (1984), Sharma et al. (1987), Shiva (1988), R. Guha (1989), and Agarwal (1986a, 1992), among others.

[46] These local developments in the 1980s are often missed by otherwise insightful accounts of that period by social scientists and environmental historians.

in JFM across the country. Similar experiences of collaboration between the forest department and villages have been documented in some other states.[47]

These examples demonstrated both that villagers could cooperate among themselves and collectively manage a common pool resource and that field-level forest officials could cooperate with the villagers. The accounts of these success stories were spread via the media, in conferences and gatherings, and in books and articles. Also important was direct pressure on the State by NGOs and environmental activists on behalf of forest-dependent communities, for the protection of their traditional rights and livelihoods, and for drawing on the conservation ethic that many argued was intrinsic to tribal communities and so would benefit forest regeneration. A rare government document—the 1982 *Report of the Committee on Forests and Tribals* brought out by the Ministry of Home Affairs—also recognized that local communities could be potential partners and contributors to forest protection.[48]

These experiences of State failure and grassroots success, in turn, influenced the property rights debate which in intellectual terms had long recommended State or private management of forests for efficient conservation. The outcome of this debate in favour of community forestry was an additional element in paving the way to decentralized forest management, not only in South Asia but also more globally.

3.3 The Property Rights Debate

The property rights debate was focused on the question: what kinds of institutional arrangements would best promote environmental conservation—State, private, community, or co-management—each of which involves a different property rights regime?[49] At the heart of this debate were two interlinked issues: people's incentive to conserve and their ability to cooperate. Prevailing economic theory painted a pessimistic picture on both counts.[50] Drawing on three interrelated 'models'—Hardin's (1968) 'tragedy of the commons', the prisoner's dilemma in game theory, and Olson's *The Logic of Collective Action*—it was argued that guided by individual self-interest, people would tend to free ride, each person expecting the others to do the same, leading to over-extraction of natural resources on the one hand and failure to cooperate on the other. In Hardin's classic example of two herders grazing their animals on the commons, for instance, an individual herder would keep adding animals to his herd for immediate benefit rather than

[47] See Pathan et al. (1991) and Poffenberger et al. (1996).

[48] The report (cited in Baland and Platteau 1996: 242) argued: 'A national forest policy should recognize the positive role of the people in maintaining forests and environment in unambiguous terms and not merely in its implications.'

[49] For useful discussions on property rights regimes, see Schlager and Ostrom (1992) and Ostrom and Schlager (1996).

[50] All of them rested, in particular, on the assumption of the self-interested utility-maximizing individual which dominated orthodox economics.

for long-term common interest, leading to overgrazing and the 'tragedy of the commons'.[51]

The 'prisoner's dilemma' model in game theory helped formalize the logic underlying Hardin's description, wherein in a two-person game, each acts in isolation in her/his own interest on the basis of individual rational calculation, on the presumption that the other will too. This leads each of them to a worse outcome than would be attained through cooperation. Olson added to this pessimistic outlook, suggesting that no cooperation would be possible, since people would have no incentive to contribute toward a collective good, if they could not be excluded from its benefits once the good had been produced. They could simply free ride on the efforts of others, and, assuming that everyone in a community thought this way, none would help produce the collective good without 'coercion or some other special device to make individuals act in their common interest' (Olson 1965: 2).

These writings had enormous influence especially among economists, many of whom concluded that it was 'impossible for rational creatures to cooperate' (Campbell, cited in Ostrom 1990: 5).[52] Some suggested that the solution to a potential tragedy of the commons lay in centralized State control over forests, pastures, etc.[53] Others suggested privatization of the commons, arguing that private owners would have more incentive to conserve the resource, since they would reap the rewards.[54] However, as several people pointed out, for State control to result in efficient outcomes, the fulfilment of a number of conditions would be required, such as accurate information of local commons, the ability to monitor and sanction, and no enforcement costs.[55] These conditions are seldom met in practice. In practice, centralized forest management has been plagued with problems of rule enforcement among hostile local populations deprived of traditional use rights, high monitoring costs, inadequate information on local ecology, corruption in the forest bureaucracy and its collusion with contractors and industrial interests, and so on.[56] Not surprisingly, centralized State management of forests across the developing world speaks substantially of State failure and inefficient outcomes.

Similarly, it was noted that private property regimes would be inefficient in practice, except under special conditions.[57] Apart from the practical infeasibility of dividing vast resources among private owners, private monitoring would also

[51] Other scholars extended the example to diverse contexts, such as local forests and fisheries (Ostrom 1990).

[52] In the 1970s by one count there were already 2,000 papers on the prisoner's dilemma game (Ostrom 1990: 5).

[53] See also Heilbroner (1974), Ehrenfeld (1972), Carruthers and Stone (1981), and arguments in Ostrom (1990).

[54] For instance, Lloyd (1833, cited in Baland and Platteau 1996: 14).

[55] See e.g. Ostrom (1990) and Baland and Platteau (1996), among others.

[56] See e.g. Baland and Platteau (1996), Agarwal (1986a), and Ostrom (1990), among others.

[57] See Baland and Platteau's (1996) discussion on the conditions needed for privatization to work: well defined and complete property rights, no enforcement costs, the existence of markets (for

have been prohibitively costly, especially where access was historically determined through a complex mosaic of rights and privileges. Moreover, there is no reason to expect private preferences to favour conservation over profitable exploitation, or individuals to be well informed about ways of conserving complex ecosystems. Forests are also a communal resource with many externalities, a global public good held in trust for future generations in which millions of communities, and not just a few individuals, have a stake.

Acceptance of village communities as managers of local commons required crossing the hurdle of prevailing theory both by questioning narrow assumptions about *homo economicus* driven mainly by self interest, and by taking account of ground experience wherein many communities have historically cooperated for protecting the commons, under a range of common property regimes. A number of developments helped cross these hurdles. Economic theorists began to recognize that cooperation was possible under specific conditions and to move toward less pessimistic predictions.[58] Empirical studies showed that free riding was not a dominant trait in village communities.[59] It was also recognized that in describing the 'tragedy' what Hardin had in mind was a situation of open access rather than regulated common property under community protection.[60] There were parallel debates among practitioners and public intellectuals on community involvement in forest governance. Some focused on critiques of top-down afforestation programmes and the importance of participatory forest management by communities (e.g. Agarwal 1986a, Aguilar 1982, Hoskins 1979b). Others highlighted that village communities, as long-standing users and custodians of forests, offered the best solution for greening the villages (e.g. Agarwal and Narain 1989 for India). Yet others, while in favour of community forest management, also cautioned that village inequalities could undermine cooperation (e.g. Agarwal 1986a and Cernea 1981).

Communal management of common pool resources was argued to have several potential advantages, including village knowledge of local ecological, economic, and social conditions and constraints; the ability to effectively monitor the resource; and a small enough size to make rules through consensus, to change rules if conditions so warranted, and to resolve conflicts at low cost. Incentives

products supplied by the resource), and of markets that are perfect and competitive. In the real world these conditions are difficult to satisfy.

[58] Theoretically, within game theory, for instance, there was a shift from the classic prisoner's dilemma model toward the recognition that cooperation can arise under various conditions, such as repeated games; frequent interactions which enable learning and build trust and reciprocity that can reduce free riding; small group size where everyone knows each other and peer pressure can rein in/penalize free riders; and social and moral norms (Baland and Platteau 1996 provide an excellent summary of and discussion on these developments).

[59] See e.g. Bromley and Chapagain (1984) and Wade (1988). For more recent work on the better conservation outcomes of village managed forests, compared with State managed forests, see Somanathan et al. (2008).

[60] See e.g. Bromley (1986 cited in Gilmour and Fisher 1991: 40), and Baland and Platteau (1996).

could be provided through regulated access to forest products.[61] Globally, the link with community management and conservation was specifically mooted in the *Brundtland Report* (1987: 64–5) which argued that: 'The pursuit of sustainable development requires [*inter alia*] a political system that secures effective citizen participation in decision making', and that 'greater public participation in the decisions that affect the environment ... is best secured by decentralizing the management of resources upon which local communities depend, and giving these communities an effective say over the use of these resources'.

Thus both theoretical and empirical developments, interactively, opened up the intellectual space to convince a larger group—including many economists with influence in policy circles—that communities could successfully govern the commons.[62] Basically the shift involved a recognition that there were contexts in which free riding could be contained and cooperation succeed, especially if groups were small, cohesive, and norms of trust and reciprocity prevailed. Community forestry embodies a notable shift in the idea of forest governance from top-down to participatory, creates a new system of communal property rights as co-management between civil society and government, and sets the basis for a new form of collectivity. In fact, dozens of countries have now entered into such arrangements for forest protection (Agrawal and Gibson 2001).

In India the formalization of decentralized forest management took the form of the JFM programme, initiated through the earlier-mentioned central government circular of 1990, followed by individual orders passed by each state (each varying in its operational details). The basic idea behind the JFM programme was to establish a partnership between the state forest department and village communities, with a sharing of responsibilities and benefits from the regeneration of degraded forest land, subject to a joint agreement.[63] The state-level orders allow the participating villagers usufruct rights to most non-timber forest products and a 25–50 per cent share (varying by state) of the mature timber when finally harvested. This provides incentives to villagers, and the assumption of a shared common interest is expected to enhance prospects of cooperation. NGOs can act as catalysts in group formation. Indeed, some scholars argue that the 'core set of ideas' applied in JFM had widespread appeal in many other parts of the world, and that these ideas could be seen as constituting a 'global paradigm shift toward what is commonly called participatory forest management, but which might more comprehensively be termed socially responsible forestry' (Sundar et al. 2001: 233).

[61] See Ostrom (1990) and Baland and Platteau (1996), among others.

[62] Although some of these academic developments were subsequent to the policy shift toward community forest management in South Asia and in many other regions, they were important for keeping up the momentum and strengthening support for the idea within national governments and international agencies.

[63] National parks and sanctuaries (which came under 'protected areas') were excluded from JFM, as were forests that were not degraded. None of the states, however, specified what qualified as degraded forest, except Karnataka which specified a canopy cover of 0.25 density or less. Madhya Pradesh demarcated 'degraded' from 'well-stocked' forests and allowed villagers to manage the latter as well, but gave them more restricted rights than under the former.

Table 3.2. JFM characteristics: Gujarat and All-India

Characteristics	Gujarat	All-India
JFM committees (number)	1,424	84,632
Forest area under JFM (m.ha)	0.16	17.33
JFM area as a percentage of total forest area	8.37[a]	22.37[a]
Forest area per committee (ha)	113	n.a.
Social characteristics of households under JFM		
• Scheduled castes	5,748 (3.8)	1,582,898 (18.9)
• Scheduled tribes	123,347 (82.7)	2,729,433 (32.5)
• Other groups	20,096 (13.5)	4,072,277 (48.6)
• All households under JFM	149,191 (100.0)	8,384,608 (100.0)
Average number of households per JFM committee	105	99[b]
Average number of tribal households per JFM committee	87	32[b]

Notes: Figures in brackets give the percentage of JFM households from each social category.

[a] Calculated on the basis of the JFM forest area given in Bahuguna (2004) and the GoI (2003) figure of 1.91 million ha of total forest area in Gujarat and 77.47 million ha in all-India.

[b] Calculated on the basis of the JFM forest area given in Bahuguna (2004).

Sources: Bahuguna (2004), GoI (2003).

Today, technically, JFM covers all states. In 2000, when I did my survey, there were (as noted in Chapter 1) an estimated 84,000 such groups, involving about 8.4 million rural families and protecting 17 million ha or 22.4 per cent of India's recorded forest area (Table 3.2).[64] Just over half of the JFM families across India belonged to disadvantaged groups, namely scheduled castes and tribes, while in Gujarat state, where I conducted my 2000–01 survey, 86 per cent belonged to these social groups. Many of the newer CFIs were constituted by the forest department, but many of the older ones were NGO-initiated or self-initiated, formed as informal bodies and later formalized as JFM groups. Some pre-existing groups, however, still continue to function informally.[65]

Parallel to India, Nepal too shifted to community forestry in the 1990s. The Forest Act of 1993, operationalized in 1995 with the formulation of Forest Regulations 1995, allows the District Forest Officer (DFO) to hand over the management of any part of the national forest in the form of a community forest directly to those identified as forest users and constituted into forest user groups. Even good forest land can be so transferred. Under the Act, these groups are

[64] Of these groups, not all would have completed registration formalities.

[65] This is either out of choice, or because of the problem of converting into JFM groups, given that under the 1990 order JFM was established on degraded forest land, while many of the self-initiated groups were protecting denser forests or forests that had revived through their protection efforts. The central government guidelines of 2000, however, recommend extension of JFM eligibility to forests with more than 0.4 crown density. These are defined as 'good forests', but it is left to state governments to decide whether or not to transfer good forests to villagers. The rights and responsibilities of villagers in relation to good forests are also expected to be different from those in relation to degraded forests (see GoI 2000b).

entitled to 'develop, conserve, use and manage the forest, and sell and distribute forest products independently by fixing their prices, according to an operational plan' (GoN 1995: 9). This plan can be amended by the users from time to time after informing the DFO. Communities can thus derive all the benefits from the areas they manage (except exporting timber, which is banned).[66] Around the year 2000 there were about 9,100 community forestry institutions (CFIs) involving 1 million households and covering 0.66 m ha or 11.4 per cent of Nepal's 5.8 m ha of forest land (GoN 2000), mostly located in Nepal's hill districts.[67] In addition there are a number of self-initiated groups and indigenous protection efforts going back a few decades (Gilmour and Fisher 1991).

3.4 The Question of Women's Inclusion

Traditionally women as forest users held the same rights as men to local forest resources, and these rights fluctuated with that of the community to which they belonged. In fact their rights were more extensive than men's, since women typically collected non-timber forest products, while timber cutting, which was more in men's domain, was highly restricted. At the same time, forest guards, village headmen, and forest officials were predominantly males in the centralized systems of forest management.

Decentralization of forest management created conditions conducive to women's entry into forest governance, but did not assure it. Women are rather sparsely located in the noted two-tier governance structures of the new CFIs, namely in the General Body constituted of all members and the Executive Committee of 9–15 members. In India, the eligibility rules for membership in the GB and EC, as prescribed by the initial state-level JFM resolutions, varied by state. In the GB, some states allowed membership to only one person per village household, others to one man and one woman per household, a few to all village residents, and so on. In 1993, of the fourteen states that first initiated JFM, six allowed GB membership to only one person per household (Table 3.3). This was inevitably the male household head. In 2000, eight of the twenty-two JFM states on which there was information used this criteria. In eight others (in some after rule amendments), both spouses, or one man and one woman, could be members. But this still excluded other household adults. In West Bengal, where the woman automatically became a member by virtue of her husband being a member, it was he who was seen as the primary member. Only three JFM states allowed membership to all village adults, including Gujarat where I did my 2000–01 survey. In practice, even here, usually only one person per household formally

[66] The government, however, retains the right to reclaim any forests seen to be mismanaged by the CFIs.

[67] The CFIs are termed Forest User Groups (FUGs) in Nepal. Throughout this book, however, the term CFI is used generically to cover all kinds of community forestry groups, including FUGs, as well as India's JFM groups, van panchayats, self-initiated groups, and so on.

Table 3.3. JFM criteria for general body membership

Membership criteria	1993 (N=14)	1998 (N=21)	2000 (N=22)	2002–03 (N= 25)
One person per household	Bihar, Jammu & Kashmir, Karnataka, Madhya Pradesh, Maharashtra, Tripura[b]	Assam, Arunachal, Pradesh,[a] Bihar, Jammu & Kashmir, Maharashtra, Rajasthan, Sikkim, Tripura[b]	Assam, Arunachal Pradesh[a], Bihar, Jammu & Kashmir, Maharashtra, Manipur, Sikkim, Tripura[b]	Assam, Arunachal Pradesh,[a] Bihar, Manipur, Sikkim, *Uttar Pradesh*[a]
One male and one female per household	Andhra Pradesh, Himachal Pradesh, Orissa, *West Bengal* [c]	Andhra Pradesh, Himachal Pradesh, *Madhya Pradesh,* Orissa, Tamil Nadu, West Bengal,[c] *Karnataka,*[c] Kerala	Andhra Pradesh, Himachal Pradesh, Orissa, *Rajasthan*, Tamil Nadu, West Bengal,[c] Karnataka,[c] Kerala	Andhra Pradesh, Himachal Pradesh,[e] *Jammu & Kashmir,* Kerala, Orissa, *Punjab,* Tamil Nadu, *Tripura,* West Bengal
Any interested village adults	Gujarat	Gujarat, *Haryana*	Gujarat, Haryana, *Madhya Pradesh,*	Chattisgarh, Gujarat, Haryana, Jharkhand, *Karnataka,* Madhya Pradesh, *Maharashtra, Rajasthan*[d]
No clear representation indicated	Punjab, Haryana, Rajasthan	Punjab, Nagaland,[b] Uttar Pradesh	Punjab, Nagaland,[b] Uttar Pradesh	Mizoram, Nagaland[b]

Notes: The italicized states have moved toward more women-inclusive rules compared with the previous year(s).

[a] One adult per family, but at least 30% of total registered members will need to be women.

[b] In Tripura only families with at least one wage earner are eligible. In Nagaland only landowning households are eligible.

[c] In West Bengal, if the husband is a member the wife automatically becomes a member. In its 1990 order only one person per household could be a member; this was modified in 1991 to include women. In Karnataka, if one spouse is a member the other automatically becomes a member.

[d] All willing adults can join, but at least one-third should be women.

[e] At least 50% should be women.

Sources: SPWD (1993, 1998), *Van Sahyog* (2002–03) and some individual state orders.

joined. This was typically the male household head, although the local NGOs were trying to encourage more women to join (with varying degrees of success). The prescribed gender composition of the EC under JFM similarly varied. Most states specified a minimum number of female members and some also required the inclusion of a low-caste or landless member (Table 3.4).

Over time, in many of the states, the membership criteria for both the GB and the EC have moved toward greater inclusion of women, as a result of pressure from national-level bodies, donors, activists, and academics (Tables 3.3 and 3.4). And in 2000 the central government issued new guidelines to state governments

Table 3.4. JFM criteria for women's representation in the EC

No. or % of women[a]	1993 (N=14)	1998 (N=21)	2000 (N=22)	2002–03 (N=25)
Min 1	Punjab	Punjab	Punjab	
Min 2	Gujarat, Himachal Pradesh,[b] Jammu & Kashmir, Karnataka, Maharashtra	Gujarat, Himachal Pradesh,[b] Jammu & Kashmir, Karnataka, *Madhya Pradesh*, Maharashtra, Sikkim	Gujarat, Himachal Pradesh,[b] Jammu & Kashmir, Karnataka, Madhya Pradesh, Maharashtra, Sikkim	Gujarat, Himachal Pradesh,[b] Jammu & Kashmir, Maharashtra, *Uttar Pradesh*,
Min 3	Andhra Pradesh, Orissa	Kerala, Orissa	Kerala, Manipur Orissa, *Rajasthan*	Manipur, Orissa, Rajasthan
Min 2 max 5		Tamil Nadu	Tamil Nadu	
Min 2 max 5	Bihar	Bihar	Bihar	Bihar
Min 30% or 1/3		Andhra Pradesh *Haryana*, Uttar Pradesh	Andhra Pradesh Haryana, *Madhya Pradesh*	Chattisgarh, Haryana, Jharkhand, Karnataka, *Kerala*, Madhya Pradesh, *Punjab*, *Sikkim*, *Tripura*
Around 50%				*Andhra Pradesh*, *Tamil Nadu*
Unspecified	Haryana, Madhya Pradesh, Rajasthan, Tripura, West Bengal	Assam, Arunachal Pradesh, Nagaland, Rajasthan, Tripura, West Bengal	Arunachal Pradesh, Assam, Nagaland, Tripura, Uttar Pradesh, West Bengal	Arunachal Pradesh, Assam, Mizoram, Nagaland, West Bengal

Notes: The italicized states have moved toward more women-inclusive rules compared with the previous year(s). Min = minimum, max = maximum.

[a] Total specified EC members vary: typical number is 9–15 members.

[b] Out of a total of 9–12 EC members, 5 are village representatives, of whom 50% should be women. This works out to a minimum of 2–3 women in the whole EC.

Source: SPWD (1993, 1998), *Van Sahyog* (2002–03) and recent state orders for Madhya Pradesh, Rajasthan, and Sikkim.

that at least one-third of the EC members should be women (GoI 2000b), but at the time of my survey there was little general awareness of these guidelines, or action based on them, and even today there is a notable gap between the guidelines and practice.

In the self-initiated CFIs the situation is worse, since they replicated the customary exclusion of women from village decision-making bodies. In Orissa, for example, during my field visits there in 1998–99, I found that a large number of the CFIs were initiated by all-male youth clubs and included no women at all in

CFI decision-making. Subsequently a 2000–04 survey by RCDC (2005) found that 48 per cent of the 5,000 self-initiated groups studied were all male, and among the mixed groups two-thirds had less than one-third women, indicating that male dominance remains the pattern.

In Nepal, the community forestry programme is different from JFM in some respects (as elaborated in Chapter 4), but particularly on two counts. Nepal allows even good forest land to be transferred to communities and its members can come from several toles (a tole is between a hamlet and a village in size). Households in one tole can be members in more than one CFI if they live close to those forests and can prove customary usage of them, whereas under JFM, typically one village manages one forest. The two-tier governance structure of CFIs in Nepal is, however, like that of JFM groups, with a general body which elects/selects an executive committee of some 9–15 members. Membership in Nepal's CFIs at the time of my 2000–01 survey was defined on a household basis, rather than on an individual basis (see also, Seeley 1996). In male-headed households the man's name alone was thus entered in the membership list, except among all-women CFIs. Including women in ECs was not mandatory either, and although some of the guidelines on CFI formation, issued from time to time, mentioned figures for women's inclusion (one-third in 1991, no figure in 1996, and 50 per cent in 2001), few CFIs followed the guidelines in practice, since it was simply required that women be encouraged to participate in the ECs. The new 2009 guidelines go a step further in suggesting the inclusion of one man and one woman per household in the GB, and the appointment of 50 per cent women on the EC, with a woman as either the chairperson or the secretary (GoN 2009).[68] But these guidelines are again not legally binding, and it remains to be seen how they will be implemented on the ground.

In both countries, community forestry is meant to improve forest condition as well as supplement local needs. Of these the most basic is firewood for domestic fuel which, as noted, is still largely a non-monetized good in rural areas, gathered mostly by women and children. Many non-wood products, including fodder, are also gathered from the forest mainly by women. As the primary subsistence users of forests women are thus potentially the main stakeholders in institutions of forest regeneration, but are not adequately recognized in that capacity. In this context, four points (discussed further in the chapters that follow) are of particular note.

First, in the JFM orders in India or the guidelines in Nepal which specify the composition of the GBs and ECs, the idea that a certain percentage of women should be in the EC is based on a priori assumptions of what might be considered reasonable or fair in terms of gender representation. In India, the most common criterion, to begin with, was the inclusion of *at least two women* in the EC. This is a purely arbitrary number, and its precedent can be traced to the recommendations of the 1950s and 1960s committees for decentralized local government

[68] Translated for me from the Nepali by Bharat Pokharel, Kathmandu, 2009.

which suggested the inclusion of at least two women, recognizing that a lone woman would feel intimidated. More recent specifications, which require the inclusion of one-third women, are also arbitrary and their effectiveness as a critical mass needs to be empirically verified.

Second, women's presence in community forestry has been promoted largely in nominal terms. There has been limited discussion on effective participation and virtually no discussion on two significant questions: what would be the impact of women's presence, if any? Whose interests would the women so included represent, and to whom would they be accountable? The first question needs empirical probing, as attempted in the chapters which follow. On the second question, since the members of the EC are usually nominated and accepted by broad consensus rather than by formal election (unlike in the PRIs), there is no clear constituency to whom they are accountable, except in the general sense of being accountable to the village community. We might assume that women in the EC will represent women's interests and bring women's concerns to the EC's attention, but there is no in-built institutional mechanism to arrive at an understanding of what those issues are. Hence EC members, including women, might raise issues they may personally see as important rather than issues arrived at through prior consultation with others. In the gender and environment literature, an important and recurrent argument for including women in forest governance is that women and men have different and complementary interests in forests, and it is usually assumed that all women have interests in common. The argument has some validity in that virtually all rural women depend on forests for basic needs, but as with the pre-Independence discussions for including women in legislatures, this commonality of interests among women appears to have been overstated, papering over potential conflicts across socio-economic classes (as discussed in Chapter 2). For identifying such conflict in interests and possibly resolving them, we need, at the least, some process of deliberation (as discussed in the concluding Part III of the book).

Third, institutions of forest governance are embedded in communities with varying cultural norms and histories. In particular, they lie within two opposing forces, one which seeks to correct a historic gender disadvantage that women have faced, by seeking their inclusion in institutions of governance, the other that perpetuates that disadvantage, through traditional social norms which confine women or which separate public/private domains along gender lines. These forces, pulling in opposing directions, can play out in CFIs in a range of ways, as will be apparent especially in Chapter 5.

Fourth, there can be a potential conflict between institutions of local government (e.g. the village panchayat) and institutions of forest governance (e.g. the CFIs).[69]

[69] Village councils can take up natural resource management as one of the 'subjects'. Technically, in the case of forests, as noted above, their jurisdiction does not extend to government forest land which CFIs are protecting, but JFM orders in some states require the inclusion of a panchayat member in the CFI's EC.

Where there is a lack of clarity in the respective jurisdictions of the two institutions, or where village councils and CFIs have conflicting agendas (e.g. if village councils are more politically driven and CFIs more economically driven), or where village councils have little experience in forest management, their attempts to intervene in the functions of CFIs could undermine the latter. This concern has been raised by NGOs especially in the case of van panchayats in the Uttarakhand hills,[70] but is likely to be relevant elsewhere as well (see e.g. Sivaramakrishnan 2000). Village councils may also be too large a unit for managing a local forest or giving it priority (Baumann 2000; TERI 2004). Hence decentralized government bodies and decentralized forest governance need not be in sync, and concerted efforts may be needed to realize potential synergy between the two institutions. For women the implications would further depend on what interest women councillors take in forest governance and in gender equity agendas within CFIs (a point I return to in Chapter 11).

4. CONCLUDING COMMENTS

South Asia's history of governance in general and of environmental governance in particular has been marked by the invisibility of women, both in historical accounts and (if we go by ethnographic records) in actual practice. Almost universally, women were excluded from council membership, and in most communities were not encouraged even to attend committee meetings. They were usually represented by male family members even when the disputes involved themselves. This was so as a rule across communities, including matrilineal ones, the rare exceptions being some tribal groups with strongly egalitarian traditions. Moreover, local governance was neither participative in scope nor democratic in conception. Typically, traditional village affairs, including allocation of rights over the commons, were managed variously by hereditary headmen acting on behalf of the villagers, or by caste/tribal/village councils, or by feudal lords. In other words, unlike in Tolkien's imagined Middle Earth there is little evidence of any tradition akin of an Entmoot, let alone of one which provided space and voice to women.

This began to change substantially in the early part of the twentieth century with the emergence of democratic institutions that also included women in limited extent, riding on the wave of anti-colonial struggles and social reform movements. Women not only participated in substantial numbers in the freedom movement, but also raised demands for a right to vote and a place in the legislatures. The recognition of women as a special constituency with distinct

[70] See e.g. TERI's (2004) research on van panchayats and PRIs in Uttarakhand. Concerns have also been expressed by many about the potential adverse effect of trying to introduce JFM type institutions in van panchayat areas (Sarin et al. 2003).

interests, their contribution to the anti-colonial movement, the emergence of national and provincial women's organizations with lobbying power and skills, the backdrop of social reform, and the spirit of inclusiveness in the Independence movement bore fruit, initially in the form of separate electorates for women akin to those for Muslim minorities, and in time in universal adult suffrage granted under Independent India's Constitution.

This first wave of policy shifts toward inducting women into public office in the high echelons of government did not, however, lead to similar inclusion in institutions of local government. Such inclusion required, as a first step, a process of decentralization and a parallel emphasis on participatory development. Such a process took place in the 1950s, leading to the setting up of statutory village councils on democratic principles, and a limited inclusion of women in these councils. This opened up the space for a second wave of policy shifts in the 1980s and 1990s. This time the shifts involved a reservation of one-third seats for women within local government, not only in India but in most parts of South Asia, including to a restricted extent in Nepal. In India, the discussions and recommendations on a minimum number or percentage of women in local administration which took place in relation to women in PRIs had an impact on all institutions of local governance, and even on demands for reservations within parliament. And 'at least two women' or one-third women became the two markers for drawing up guidelines even for institutions of green governance.

Although decentralization of government and moves toward including women in local government set a precedent for including women in forest governance, it did not guarantee it. It was first necessary to decentralize the institutions of forest governance themselves, from State controlled and managed to community controlled and managed. State failure and contrasting community success in local conservation, shifts in theoretical debates on property rights and cooperation, and pressure from civil society and communities, all led to the move to community forest management. Women's inclusion followed, but in limited extent and in nominal terms.

This intertwined legacy of local institutions continues, as do the assumptions that women share common interests across socio-economic divides. The preoccupation with numbers (or percentages) also persists. But, as noted in Chapter 1, we now need to ask: to what extent can simply having more women help in influencing policy decisions and their outcomes? Would the commonality of interests stemming from shared experience and common dependence on community resources be enough for women's inclusion in decision-making to make a difference? These questions beg empirical testing, which is what Chapters 4 to 9 seek to do. They focus on the impact of women's presence (or absence) in the EC, on five aspects:

- Women's effective participation in decision-making as versus simply nominal presence;

- The nature and strictness of forest use rules made by the CFIs—rules in which explicitly or implicitly every member of the village community has an interest;
- The extent and forms of violations, change in violations over time, and penalties given for rule-breaking;
- The efficiency outcomes of institutional functioning in terms of improvement in forest condition; and
- The equity outcomes of institutional functioning in terms of the experience of shortages of firewood and fodder—two of the main resources that households need on a daily basis, and that women especially seek to provide.

Effectively, therefore, I will empirically examine the impact of the EC's gender composition on women's participation and institutional outcomes. I also test whether there is a threshold percentage at which women begin to participate more effectively. Chapter 4, which follows, outlines how the data on which the analysis is based were collected. Based on these data and some additional information, I then present, in broad brushstrokes, a profile of the study areas, as a background to the empirical analysis in Chapters 5 to 9.

APPENDIX 3.1

Local Governance and Gender: Mid-Nineteenth to Early Twentieth Centuries

Appendix 3.1 Local Governance and Gender: Mid-Nineteenth to Early Twentieth Centuries

Region	Community	Period	Representative authority	Authority and duties	Village decision-making body	Author
NORTH-WEST INDIA						
Himachal Pradesh	Caste villages	Long-standing customs	Headman (*lambardar*)			Parry (1979)
North-west India (North-western Provinces and Oudh)	74 castes and tribes	Late 19th century	Headman. Typically hereditary, but in some cases appointed or elected to chair each meeting	Substantial authority in the social sphere, exercised predominantly to settle disputes of marriage, divorce, wife ill-treatment, adultery, etc., and less commonly to settle economic disputes. Consulted on marriage proposals.	Typically tribal or caste council constituted of adult males.	Crooke ([1896] 1974)
Punjab	Caste village	Late 19th, early 20th centuries	Headmen (*lambardars*)	Represented the interests of co-sharers of the commons to the government.		Chakravarty-Kaul (1996)
Rajasthan	5 castes and tribes	Late 19th century	Headman. In one case headman of 51 villages	Substantial.	Collecting dues for the government; other duties unclear.	Sherring ([1881] 1975)
Uttar Pradesh hills	Caste villages, Dom community	Long-standing customs	Headman.	Authority jointly shared with village council members, to settle disputes of all kinds (social, religious as well as relating to judicial matters).	Hill panchayat	R. Guha (1989)

WEST INDIA						
Bombay province	63 castes, tribes or religious groups	Early 20th century	Headman. In one caste he headed 12 village panchayat. Sometimes hereditary, typically selected on basis of wealth and age. Some Muslim communities had no headman	Substantial: especially settled social disputes, and was consulted on social matters.	Caste, tribal, or village council	Enthoven ([1920] 1975)
EAST INDIA						
Bihar	Santals (tribal)	Early 20th century	Headman (*manji*)	Maintained sacred groves, arranged tree planting, looked after village grazing land, abandoned land, communal wells, and other common property.		Archer ([1946] 1984)
Chotanagpur, (now in Jharkhand state, earlier part of Bihar province)	Caste groups (initial settlers)	Late 19th century	Headman (variously called *pradhan/munda/ manjhi*) represented the corporate village	Substantial authority. Represented the village in economic matters. Granted cultivation rights in the commons and rights in forest use.		Mohapatra (1991)
Bihar	Mundas, Oraon, Kharia (tribals)	Long-standing customs	Hereditary headman (*munda*)	Substantial authority. Empowered by the British to preserve trees in the village forest, village commons as well as on cultivated land, and reported to the deputy commissioner any infringement of protected forest rules.	Tribal panchayat constituted of influential, elderly men. Women and young were excluded	Sachchidananda (1968)

(continued)

Appendix 3.1 Continued

Region	Community	Period	Representative authority	Authority and duties	Village decision-making body	Author
Bihar	Santals (tribal)	Long-standing customs	Hereditary headman	Probably similar to that held by headman among Mundas, Oraons, etc., as described above.	Tribal panchayat (democratic) constituted of all village male adults with equal voice; women could join discussion	Sachchidananda (1968)
Bihar	Santals (tribal)	Long-standing customs	Hereditary headship, but had to be endorsed by household heads constituting village council	Authority to apportion common areas, and protect growing and full grown trees. Controlled public access to grazing lands, water resources, and woods.	Tribal council constituted of male adults with equal voice; women even if a party in the dispute were represented by male relatives.	Somers (1977)
Bihar	Korwa (tribal)	Late 19th century			Tribal council, responsible for ensuring that the piece of forest given to a woman on marriage for hunting and collecting roots and fruits, was not interfered with.	Crooke ([1896] 1974)
West Bengal	Bagdis (tribal)	Long-standing customs	Hereditary headman	Presided over Dal (tribal) council. Settled disputes but based decisions on consensus within the council.	Dal was council constituted of senior, influential males of village. Also ad hoc councils.	Dasgupta (1986)
West Bengal	60 castes and tribes	Late 19th century	Headman, typically not hereditary, although some cases of hereditary ones could be found.	Settled social disputes, also inheritance matters. Sometimes headed several villages.	Presided over caste or tribal council, and sometimes over village councils.	Risley ([1891], 1981)

NORTH-EAST INDIA						
Assam	Nagas	Long-standing custom	Headman			Allen et al. ([1905] 1993)
Manipur	Caste village	Early 20th century	Villagers (members of the panchayat)		Panchayat formed only of village men.	Chaki-Sircar (1984)
Meghalaya (earlier in Assam) Rensanngri village; and Chittagong Hills (now in Bangladesh)	Garos (matrilineal tribe)	Long-standing customs	*Nokma* (always male) *Loksars* (always male) elected by *nokmas*	Ceremonial functions, little jural authority. More authority than *nokma*, presided over tribal council.	Tribal council presided over by *loksars*. Women could be present, speak in disputes concerning themselves and had a say in deciding penalty, but not in enforcing it	Burling (1963, 1997)
Meghalaya	Garos (matrilineal tribe)	Long-standing customs			Tribal council. Women could not dispense justice.	Kar (1982)
Meghalaya	Khasis (matrilineal tribe)	Long-standing customs	*Syiem* (clan chiefs, hereditary, adult males in the female line. Women could hold office if no male heirs)	Jural authority over clan. A woman *syiem*, however, was only a nominal/ceremonial head. A *syiem*'s functions were performed by the council in her name.	Clan and village councils.	Rao (1985); Bhattacharya (1985)
Nagaland	Nagas	Long-standing customs	Village headman			Furer-Haimendorf, [1939] 1976

(*continued*)

Appendix 3.1 Continued

Region	Community	Period	Representative authority	Authority and duties	Village decision-making body	Author
CENTRAL INDIA						
Madhya Pradesh (Ramkheri village)	Caste village	Mid-19th century, till 1946	Village headman	Statutory authority up to 1946.	Village committees of 8 representatives (all men) set up in 1946. Later in 1956 a seat reserved for women).	Mayer (1960)
Central Provinces	59 castes and tribes	Early 20th century	Village headman	Settled social disputes. In some communities also settled land disputes.	Caste, tribal, or village panchayats.	Russell and Hiralal ([1916] 1975)
SOUTH INDIA						
Southern India provinces	48 castes and tribes	Early 20th century	Caste headman	Settled intercaste disputes. Sometimes jurisdiction extended to other, less dominant castes.	Caste, tribal, or village panchayats.	Thurston and Rangachari ([1909] 1975)
Andhra Pradesh	Gonds (tribal)	Long-standing customs	Headman		Tribal panchayats to settle disputes	
Andhra Pradesh	Gonds (tribal)	Long-standing customs	Headman	Chaired village council meetings. Could call even a few prominent householders to discuss village matters. Council enforced customary law.	Village council of adult householders chaired by headman. Women had no voice, but were called if party to a dispute or as witnesses.	Furer-Haimendorf and Furer-Haimendorf (1979)
Andhra Pradesh (Adilabad district)	Gonds (tribal)	Long-standing customs	Headman		Allocated to new immigrants which area of forest they could clear and cultivate.	Yorke (1985)

Cochin	13 castes and tribes	Early 20th century	Caste or tribal headman	Presided over caste or tribal assembly. Settled disputes.	Caste or tribal council	Iyer ([1912] 1981)
Karnataka (Mysore, western Ghats)	Caste villages	Early 19th century	Hereditary chief (*munigar*)	Had jural authority to settle disputes and could also let out fields for cultivation.		Buchanan (1807)
Karnataka (Mysore)	45 castes and tribes	Early 20th century	Caste or tribal headman	Settled social disputes, some also settled property and factional disputes.	Caste, tribe, or village panchayats. Sometimes did not head a panchayat.	Nanjundayya and Iyer ([1928] 1975)
Karnataka (Mysore)	Caste village	Mid 19th century	Thakur (upper-caste) landlord; chiefs (hereditary); headman	Landlord was de facto ruler and judge for lower castes; Chiefs and headman could convene the panchayat.	Panchayat constituted of the chiefs.	Marriott (1955).
Kerala	Nayars (matrilineal caste)	16th to early 20th century	*Karanavan* (family head). Usually male. Woman could become *karanavans* in absence of suitable men, but not clear if her role went beyond management of estate.	Performed various functions of head, managed estate, and represented family in village affairs.	Village council. Extended families represented by *karanavans.*	Gough (1961), Balakrishnan (1981)

Part II

The Impact of Presence

4

Fieldsites and Field Profile

> Our village is called Mor—the village of peacocks—because we have a large number of them in the area. One day we had all gathered at a house for a wedding when a peacock rushed into the courtyard. It was being pursued by someone and had no place to hide in the forest. This gave us a clear signal that our forest was so depleted it could not protect our wildlife. We decided right away to call a meeting and discuss how to protect the forest. Gradually everyone came around to the idea that we should form a protection group.
>
> (Mor CFI, Panchmahals, Gujarat, author's survey, 2000–01)

> We began protecting fifteen years ago. Narabhir is the gateway of the upland government forest, which was being used freely for cattle camping, timber extraction, and the collection of medicinal herbs. Located on the boundary of Gorkha and Dhading districts, people from both sides used these forests for fodder, firewood, and timber. The forest was deteriorating and the forest line receding. We realized the situation was grave when getting a headload of firewood or fodder required a walk of two to three hours. So we called a meeting of our thirty-two village households and decided to form an informal protection group in the winter of 1986. Some ten years later we received a formal certificate from the forest department.
>
> (Narabhir CFI, Gorkha, Nepal, author's survey, 2000–01)

Long before community forestry was formally launched in India and Nepal, the adverse effects of forest degradation led some communities to begin informal protection. The subsistence nature of their local economy, their relatively small-sized villages, and a high dependence on village forests for daily needs provided fertile ground for successful cooperation. The history of CFI formation in the sample sites also bears this out. Over time, CFIs have emerged here in diverse ways—some are self-initiated, others catalysed by local NGOs, and yet others by the forest department.

In the state of Gujarat, for instance, where my India-related fieldsites are located, many villages began informal protection around the mid- or late 1980s, that is, some years before Joint Forest Management formally began. Such self-initiated groups can be found in each of the three survey districts (Narmada/Bharuch, Sabarkantha, and Panchmahals) but the early starters are most common in Panchmahals where 38 per cent of the surveyed CFIs began protection before 1990, compared with 6 per cent and 14 per cent in Narmada/Bharuch and Sabarkantha respectively (Table 4.1). Some of Panchmahals' villagers decided to protect their forest when they saw large-scale tree felling for constructing a local dam. Others saw danger signals when the local wildlife lost its habitat, as in Mor village whose compelling story is recounted above. Yet others were energized into action by the severe fodder and firewood shortages they experienced, when even rootstalks were being pulled out by those in acute need. In the two other Gujarat districts, by contrast, local NGOs had a bigger hand in initiating the CFIs. Here most of the self-initiated groups also approached these NGOs for help very soon after starting protection.

In Nepal, about half of the sample CFIs were catalysed by the forest department and half by the villagers, either on their own or with external support, and later formalized by the department (Table 4.2). Three-quarters of the CFIs in Baglung/Parbat and a quarter in Gorkha were initiated with the department's help. However, some self-initiated CFIs also emerged in the Nepal fieldsites through a demonstration effect, as neighbouring hamlets or excluded groups saw successful regeneration of forests in the vicinity and decided to start a protection group of their own. I came across several all-women's groups that had asked the forest department for forest land to protect, such as the one in Kala Kuna (Box 4.1) or that in Gaja Deurali, Baglung, described below:

> We started protecting the forest in 1998. We thought that men are always away from the village and we are the ones who go to the forest, so we should form a group. We formed this FUG [forest user group] in 1999. (Author's survey 2000–01)

A move from informal protection to formal recognition of the CFI, however, is a multi-stage process. In Gujarat, formalization involves two main steps: obtaining an Adhikar Patr (deed of rights) from the forest department and registering the CFI as a society under one of the state's Society Acts. Nepal has a more complex four-stage process, involving a range of interactions between the forest staff and those wanting to set up a forest user group (Pokharel 1998, Hobley 1996). Here the support of a local NGO or forest ranger can prove crucial in helping groups navigate the steps involved.

CFIs formed in various ways constitute the basis for my empirical analysis. In this chapter, I outline the process of fieldsite identification and sample selection, and describe the socio-economic and ecological character of the study districts from which the data were collected. Based on this data I also broadly profile the CFIs and their functioning. This provides a picture of institutional design and important background information for the chapters that follow. Readers eager to move to the empirical analysis, however, could go directly to those chapters and refer back to this one for more detailed information.

Table 4.1. Gujarat: CFI initiation (% CFIs)

CFI characteristics	By district			By EC gender composition		All CFIs (N=65)
	Narmada/ Bharuch (N=16)	Panchmahals (N=21)	Sabarkantha (N=28)	≤2 EC Women CFIs (N=31)	>2 EC Women CFIs (N=34)	
Who initiated the CFI?						
Villagers alone	50.0[a]	52.4	46.4[a]	54.8	44.1	49.2
Villagers with NGO help	50.0	38.1	46.4	41.9	47.1	44.6
Villagers with FD help	0.0	9.5	7.1	3.2	8.8	6.2
Percentage protecting pre-1990	6.2	38.1	14.3	19.4	20.6	20.0
Formalization of CFI						
1990–95	75.0	47.6	46.4	45.2	61.8	53.8
After 1995	25.0	52.4	53.6	54.8	38.2	46.2

Notes: N = number of CFIs

[a] In several of these cases villagers approached the NGO soon after starting protection.

Source: Author's survey, 2000–01.

Table 4.2. Nepal: CFI initiation (% CFIs)

CFI characteristics	By district		By EC gender composition		All CFIs (N=70)
	Gorkha/ Dhading (N=36)	Baglung/ Parbat (N=34)	All women CFIs (N=27)	Other CFIs (N=43)	
Who initiated the CFI?					
Villagers alone	30.6	20.6	40.7	16.3	25.7
Villagers with FD help	25.0	76.5	40.7	55.8	50.0
Villagers with NGO help	41.7	0.0	14.8	25.6	21.4
Others	2.8	2.9	3.7	2.3	2.9

Note: N = number of CFIs.

Source: Author's survey, 2000–01.

Box 4.1. Gujarat and Nepal: illustrative histories of CFI formation

Gujarat

Asundriya village CFI (Panchmahals)

Around 1978 or thereabouts, when the Panam Dam was being constructed, the entire forest was cut down by private contractors. They left nothing but stones. There was no employment for the poor. People would sell firewood in this area to survive while the contractors had sold off the wood earlier in truckloads. We heard that in Kotha village logs were being taken from the forest but had been stopped by the village leaders who put up a resistance with the help of fellow villagers. It led to a scuffle but still they took away the wood. Some people also made charcoal. We met and decided that something would have to be done, and soon. We decided that there will be no cutting of trees either by the villagers or outsiders. We formed an informal committee and appointed a watchman. This was the beginning of our protection. (Narrated by Somabhai, the elder who had catalysed the formation of this CFI.)

Ode village all-women CFI (Sabarkantha)

Initially we were not familiar with the concept of a *mandali* [CFI]. Then a woman from our village after a visit to her birth village told us of the *mandali* they had formed there and how the village had prospered as a result. Some of us were very excited to hear this and wanted to start one but did not know how to go about it. Then the NGO VIKSAT helped us. In the beginning there were only five women but gradually we became ten and then more. We were taken by the NGO to training camps in other villages to learn about various aspects of running a *mandali* and providing leadership. Initially the village men were not supportive, but slowly they came round when they saw we were doing good work for the village. However, there were still some men who were not happy with the idea of women running a *mandali* and put obstacles in our path, but we got unexpected help from the forest department, which announced plans to rejuvenate barren lands and undertake plantations. The department is also supporting us in other ways. Now, as you can see, the forest is thriving and so is our *mandali* (Narrated by the EC women.)

Nepal

Gai Odar CFI (Gorkha)

There was a big area of bushy forest in the Manbu VDC. It was open for grazing, tree cutting, and slash and burn cultivation till the late 1970s. Population growth and the extension of cultivated area led to a decline in forest land. We began to experience a shortage of forest products for daily use. During the 1980s, we could not find even a stick for tethering a goat in the forest. We discussed this at a village meeting and reached a consensus to start protection around 1984–85. The forest was known as 'Paleko ban' (literally meaning protected forest). It regenerated gradually. Situated on the upper side of the village, no one could enter the forest without first entering the village, so we did not employ a guard in the beginning. Later when the forest condition improved somewhat, and our neighbours were attracted to it for firewood and fodder, we found it necessary to keep a forest guard. (Narrated by the EC.)

Majhi Khola CFI (Gorkha)

The Majhi Khola forest was dense and full of wild animals and birds till about 20 years ago. We had a small population then. There were no settlements in Naukilo and Syaule bazaar. The forest was used only by the people from Daraigaun. Gradually as the population increased and a road was constructed, two settlements—Syaule bazaar and Naukilo bazaar—emerged, and forest degradation started. By the 1990s it had become very degraded. All of us living in the surrounding areas experienced the shortage and requested Save the Children US to help us undertake plantations. Save the Children accepted our request and helped us. We put in voluntary labour for pitting, planting, sowing seeds, and other activities. After that, the villagers agreed to protect the plantation. We started a patrol group and one person from each household went daily by rotation. We continued protection for one year and then in 1992 applied for formalizing our protected area as a community forest. The DFO sent a Ranger to prepare the constitution and operation plan that year. Finally, in 1994, we received the CF certificate. (Narrated by the EC.)

Kala Kuna, all-women's CFI (Baglung)

Before turning this forest into a CF, the people from Dharapani and Ghunthikhet looked after it. When the forest was handed over to the community we charged NRs. 100 each from the households of Thotneri and Ghaakhet who wanted to join the forest user group. In the beginning there were only men in the Samiti. Then there was a conflict over leadership. The women also spoke up and said that they would like to take over control. Initially, we had thought we would give women one plot in the forest to protect and keep control of the remaining two plots. But a Ranger said we should not split the forest; we should either give it intact to the women or mange it all ourselves. The women said they could look after the whole forest and asked that they be given all of it. So it was handed over to them and they formed an all-women samiti. (Narrated by the vice-chairwoman's husband.)

1. FIELDSITE SELECTION

The empirical basis of this study is primary data collected in 2000–01 for 135 CFIs, of which 65 are located in Gujarat state in west India and 70 are located in selected districts of Nepal's middle hills.[1] The antecedents to this fieldwork lie in earlier research visits by me to a range of fieldsites in both countries, starting in 1995. In that year, I first visited CFIs in the three Gujarat districts selected for the current survey. In 1998–99, I also travelled extensively across seven states of India (including Gujarat) and two districts of Nepal, undertaking focus group discussions and key informant interviews in 94 villages.

This initial fieldwork was illuminating and revealed many of the concerns mentioned in Chapter 1 that compelled me to do a more systematic follow-up study. In particular, it revealed women's substantial exclusion from the decision-making bodies of CFIs, despite their considerable stake in forest resources and ability to contribute to forest regeneration. At the same time, it raised the question: would having more women in the CFI's main decision-making body—the Executive Committee (EC)—lead to different outcomes, such as

[1] In Nepal, the district is the highest administrative division which is further subdivided into village development committees and municipalities. In India, the highest administrative division is the state, which is further subdivided into districts. Gujarat is however bigger in size (in terms of area and population) than Nepal as a whole.

women's greater participation in meetings, the formulation of different forest use rules, better forests, less firewood and fodder shortage, and so on? These questions became the basis for further intellectual exploration.

Fieldwork for my follow-up survey began in October 2000 and was mostly completed by late 2001. It was undertaken, as noted, in three districts of Gujarat (Narmada/Bharuch, Panchmahals, and Sabarkantha) and three of Nepal (Baglung, Parbat, and Gorkha), with a small spillover of the sample into Dhading district in Nepal.[2] Henceforth, I refer to the survey year as 2000–01, although some supplementary data were also gathered during 2002–03, to fill data gaps in Gujarat and complete one more CFI in Nepal (which had been put on hold due to the imposition of national emergency in late 2001). Even in 2000–01, fieldwork in Nepal was undertaken against the backdrop of an ongoing Maoist insurgency which restricted the number of potential study sites. In Gujarat, similarly, some gap-filling could only be completed after normalcy returned, following communal violence in the state in 2002. The empirical analysis based on this data set is supplemented by insights from my 1998–99 fieldwork.

Both prior to and for the 2000–01 study, my interest was to examine the functioning and impact of CFIs from a gender perspective. My main focus was not, however, on why CFIs are formed in some villages and not in others, nor on what impact the presence as versus the absence of a CFI has on forest condition; rather it was on the impact of women's presence on the outcomes of CFIs that had already been formed. I describe below the process of fieldsite selection for this purpose.

1.1 CFI Governance Structure

The site selection criteria depended, to begin with, on the governance structure of CFIs in the region. Community forest management in Nepal and Gujarat has both similarities and differences. The differences lie not only in the fact that Nepal allows even good forest land to be transferred to communities, while Gujarat villagers can get only degraded land, but also in who constitutes the management group. In India usually a single village manages a given forest and its jurisdiction is based on village administrative boundaries.[3] In Nepal several toles can manage a single forest and villagers from a given tole can be users of more than one forest,[4] with one tole on average containing around twenty households in my

[2] The reasons for selecting Gujarat and these districts in Nepal are given further below.

[3] This is the predominant pattern, although there can be occasional exceptions. During my 1998 field trip to Orissa, for instance, I found a CFI formed with five forest villages jointly protecting one forest.

[4] The Forest Regulations of 1995 clearly state that: 'While handing over a forest area as a community forest, the boundaries of the villages, towns, and districts shall have no effect' (GoN 1995: 12).

study area. The sketches below (not to scale) illustrate the difference between CFIs in India and Nepal. In the sketch of Malekpur village (Gujarat) the forest belongs to and is managed entirely by Malekpur's villagers. In contrast, Barahathan CFI in Nepal is managed by villagers in three toles—Danda, Gaunswara, and Gaune. They have rights to use not only the Barahathan community forest

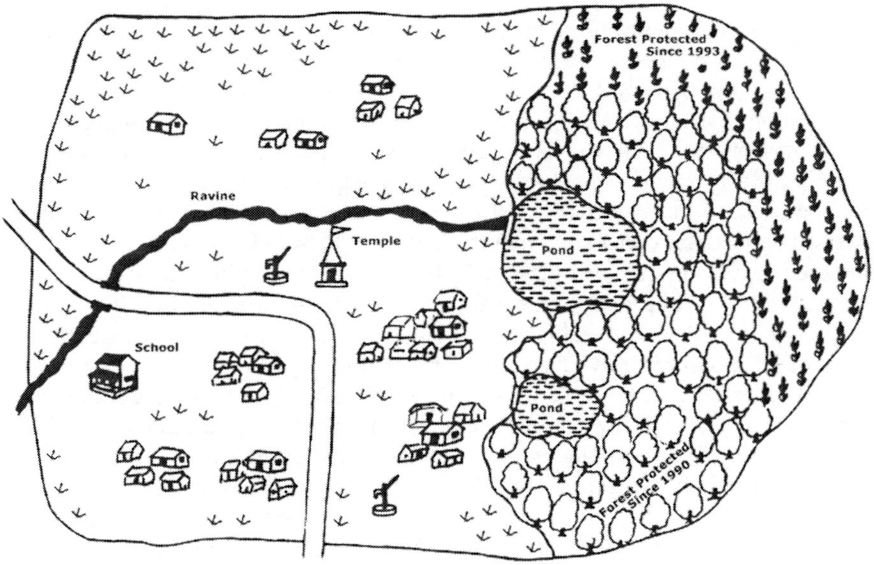

Figure 4.1. Gujarat: villager's sketch of Malekpur village, Sabarkantha

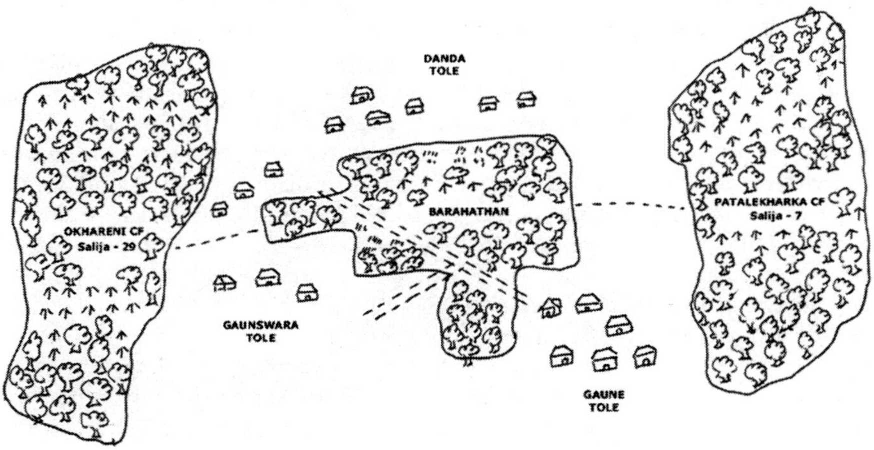

Figure 4.2. Nepal: villager's sketch of Barahathan Community Forest, Parbat

but also the neighbouring Okhareni community forest. Basically, customary usage (which can cut across villages) and proximity to the forest play an important part in Nepal's CFI formation.

Notwithstanding these and related differences, however, CFIs in both Nepal and most states in India (including Gujarat) have a broadly similar governance structure, which is what was relevant for our sample selection. It is (as noted in Chapter 3) a two-tier structure, with a GB in which the village households/forest users can be members and an EC selected or elected from the GB. Identifying GB members, however, is far from straightforward. In some Indian states, for instance, CFIs charge membership fees, others take none. Within a state, some CFIs collect nominal fees from the required minimum percentage of village households, simply to fulfil the basic criteria for registering a CFI, but effective membership (on which benefit distribution is based) depends on their contribution to protection. In Nepal, often no joining fee is charged, and all customary users are effectively considered members of the GB, but distinctions may be made between regular users and occasional users; hence identifying the users can be a complex exercise in practice. In contrast to the fuzziness underlying GB membership, however, EC membership is clear cut, as are its tasks and responsibilities. It is involved in almost all CFI decisions either on its own or in consultation with the GB (as elaborated later). The EC thus provides a firmer and more robust basis for examining the effect of gender composition on CFI functioning, and the EC's gender composition was therefore used for sample selection.

I was interested in a sample which would allow me to compare CFIs that had (a) ECs with two or fewer women and those with more than two women; and (b) all-women ECs with those that had male members. The reason for this categorization is given further below. I also needed CFIs that were active at the time of selection and had been formed at least a year prior to selection, so that their functioning and impact could be studied. It needs mention that whatever the gender composition of the EC, the membership of a CFI itself (namely its general body) is constituted of both men and women in the community.

Prior to sample selection, identifying the region for the survey involved a multi-stage process. I first identified the state in India and the districts in Nepal in which to conduct the survey. Second, I identified the districts and blocks within the chosen state in India and the Village Development Committees (VDCs) within the identified districts in Nepal from which the sample would be selected. Third, based on the gender composition of their ECs, CFIs in the identified blocks/VDCs (as relevant) were divided into two non-overlapping strata for Gujarat: those with ≤ 2 EC women and those with >2 EC women; and three non-overlapping strata for Nepal: all-women, ≤ 2 EC women, and >2 EC women. Sample selection was done at this final stage: CFIs were selected from within each of these strata, using stratified random sampling. It may be noted that choosing the state/district and the CFI universe involved a process of *identification* based on other information. Only at the last stage—for choosing the CFIs—was selection done through statistical methods.

1.2 State/District Identification

To decide where to locate the study, I required, at a minimum, baseline information on the gender composition of the ECs, when the CFIs were formed, and whether they were active. In India, none of the state forest departments, in the normal course, collects data on the social profile of the CFI's governance structure. Nor do research studies provide such data for entire districts or states.[5] Gujarat was an exception—here such data were being collected by three NGOs for the sites where each had an ongoing community forestry programme, predominantly in one district. The NGOs were AKRSP(I), SARTHI, and VIKSAT,[6] working respectively in Narmada/Bharuch (earlier Narmada was part of Bharuch district), Panchmahals, and Sabarkantha. The choice of Gujarat, rather than another Indian state, was thus dictated mainly by the fact that these three district-level NGOs had information on the gender composition of CFIs. This information, updated through my own efforts in some cases, also showed a sufficient variability and covered an adequate number of CFIs for the sample. Gujarat, and within Gujarat these districts (Figures 4.3 and 4.4), thus became an obvious choice for the study. My familiarity with Gujarat's community forestry programme through prior visits, and some understanding of the local language, Gujarati, also made this site attractive.

In Nepal, by contrast, the forest department has a comprehensive and regularly updated cross-country data base on community forestry which gives the gender composition of the ECs. On this basis I could identify the districts for selecting a gender-differentiated sample of CFIs, including all-women CFIs (that is, CFIs with all-women ECs). Given the sparseness of all-women groups, however—they constituted only about 3.8 per cent of the country's CFIs at the time of the survey—I used their presence as the starting criteria for identifying the districts. In addition, the regions had to be safe, given the ongoing Maoist insurgency,[7] and physically accessible to enable close supervision of the research.

Only 10 of Nepal's 75 districts had 12 or more all-women groups. Of these, 5 were inaccessible due to security reasons or remote location. From the remaining five districts, based on various forms of accessibility I identified three—Baglung,

[5] In 2000–01, I tried to field a questionnaire for generating such data through the state forest departments. After a year or more of effort, a few states sent back completed questionnaires for small numbers of CFIs, except Madhya Pradesh which covered 1,006 CFIs across 18 forest divisions, largely due to the interest taken by Mr A. P. Dubey, then the Chief Conservator of Forests. This was too late for the state to be a potential site for my sample survey, but the results are cited in Chapters 2 and 3. An ongoing NGO project to collect such information in Orissa state was also incomplete when my study began, but is now complete (RCDC 2005), and is again cited in Chapters 2 and 3.

[6] The acronyms stand respectively for Agha Khan Rural Support Programme (India), Social Action for Rural and Tribal Inhabitants of India, and Vikram Sarabhai Center for Development Interaction.

[7] The districts (and VDCs within districts) which posed security risks were identified by consulting forest department officials and the security maps available with the International Centre for Integrated Mountain Development (ICIMOD) in Kathmandu.

Figure 4.3. India (Gujarat) and Nepal

Parbat, and Gorkha (see Figure 4.5). The first two are contiguous, with a similar ecological and social profile, and, in both, the same donor, NUKCFP (the Nepal-UK community forestry programme), had an ongoing involvement in forestry projects. But each had only 14 CFIs with all-women ECs, insufficient to take only one district on its own. The two districts were thus clubbed together for sample selection. Gorkha with 42 all-women groups was treated as a separate unit. Subsequently, a VDC from the adjoining Dhading district, but contiguous to Gorkha, was identified to provide substitute cases, when four of the originally selected Gorkha cases became insecure.

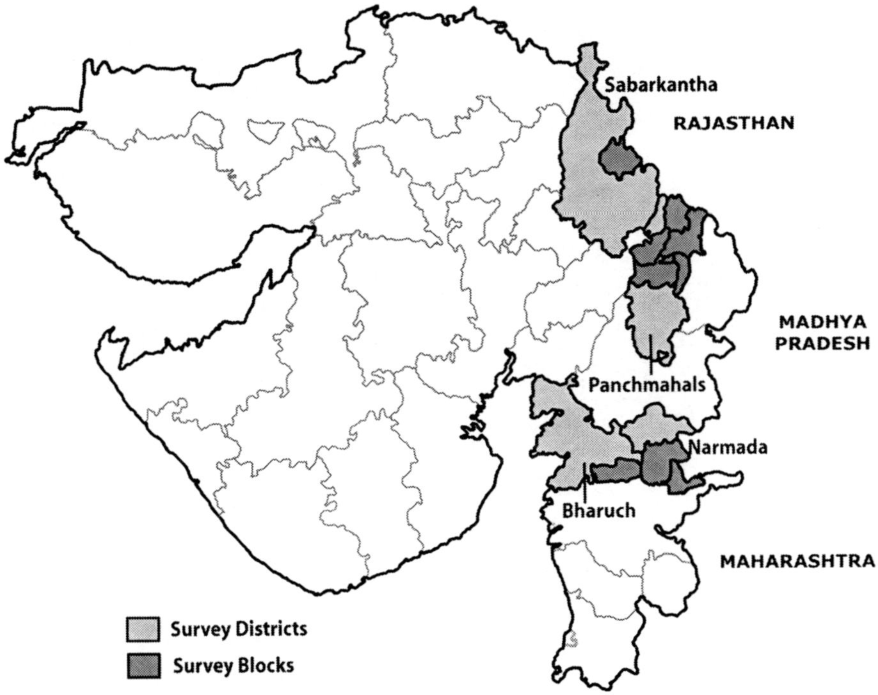

Figure 4.4. Gujarat (fieldsite districts)

1.3 Sample Selection Criteria

The sample selection process is described in detail in Appendix 4.1. Here a few points need highlighting. My main criterion for sample selection was the gender composition of the ECs, stratified, as noted, into mutually exclusive categories. In Gujarat, the two-woman marker stemmed from the fact that including at least two women in the EC was required in Gujarat (as also in several other Indian states). The antecedents for this specification go back to the recommendations of the Balwantray and Santhanam committees on decentralization in India, discussed in Chapter 3. In practice, many CFIs fail to reach this minimum, others interpret at least two women to mean *at most* two women and include only two, and yet others exceed this number. Nevertheless this is a relevant criterion, since including only two women can be seen as a nominal way of following the rule, and including more than two women as a departure from the minimum requirement. Gujarat had very few all-women's ECs, hence the Gujarat sample was based

Figure 4.5. Nepal (fieldsite districts)

only on the two strata division in each district. Each district was sampled separately.[8]

In Nepal, as elaborated in Chapter 3, including women in ECs is not mandatory, although occasional 'guidelines' encourage women's inclusion, sometimes mentioning percentages. The ECs in my sample were in any case all formed in the 1990s when the 2001 guideline suggesting 50 per cent women did not apply. For consistency and to enable comparative analysis with Gujarat, I therefore used the criteria of ≥ 2 and <2 EC women for selecting the mixed CFI's in Nepal's sample as well, in addition to all-women CFIs which were common in some Nepal districts. Also, based on information provided by the local NGO (in Gujarat) or forest official (in Nepal), non-functioning CFIs were omitted, since my purpose was to study active institutional functioning.

Six researchers in Nepal and six in Gujarat who knew the local dialect undertook the fieldwork, travelling in teams of two (typically one male and one female).

[8] Subsequent to my survey, the GEER Foundation, Gujarat, undertook a census of JFM groups and found there were 1,417 groups in 2003 (GEER 2005). Unfortunately their report does not give the gender composition of each group, and instead aggregates total male members and total female members across all the groups by forest division. On this basis we find that only 18.4 per cent of EC members across the state were women. For the forest subdivisions where my research is based, Narmada/Bharuch (Rajpipla division E and W), Panchmahals (Godhra division), and Sabarkantha (Sabarkantha division N and S), the figures were 17.6 per cent, 18.2 per cent, and 20.6 per cent women respectively. If each, typically 11 member, EC had at least two women, the percentage of women would come to 18.2. The actual figures indicate that in Gujarat as a whole there were barely two women per EC and in Narmada/Bharuch there were less than two at the time of the GEER census.

In addition, FECOFUN—the federation of community forest users in Nepal—sent a local male staff member who was familiar with the village location and routes to accompany each Nepal team.[9] He did not, however, participate in the data gathering process, to guard against any bias being introduced. Given the physical remoteness of many villages in Nepal's middle hills, the researchers often stayed over in the village itself. This involved hardship but also helped build rapport with the informants. In Gujarat, similarly, each team of two researchers was introduced to the villagers by the local NGO staff members, who then absented themselves during the research interviews. In both Gujarat and Nepal, each team spent on average three and a half days in the field for every CFI, although in Gujarat I also personally undertook follow-up visits to many sites.

Fieldwork involved two types of challenges: difficult physical terrain in the Nepal sites and security concerns in both Gujarat and Nepal, but especially the latter. The Gujarat fieldsites were fairly accessible by motorable roads, but many of the Nepal fieldsites, located in the middle hills, could only be reached by foot after a half or full day's trek. Also, despite the security filters used in VDC identification, the researchers were still at some risk both from Maoists and from the Nepalese army and police who could mistake them for Maoists, as could the villagers. To minimize potential problems, several precautions were taken, such as translating the questionnaire into Nepalese so that it was obvious this was simply a survey on community forestry. Where possible, the researchers also carried letters of introduction for the CFI chairperson from the District FECOFUN chairperson or the government's district authority. Despite these precautions the research teams faced moments of alarm (see Box 4.2).

Although almost all of the cases were completed before Nepal's security situation deteriorated substantially and emergency rule was imposed in late 2001, three CFIs in the Baglung/Parbat area remained. During the national emergency, public gatherings were disallowed; hence focus group discussions, which were central to my research methodology, could not be conducted. After emergency rule was lifted in December 2002 and the security situation eased partially, one more CFI was completed, and two were dropped altogether since substitutes in secure areas could not be found easily. Also, during fieldwork, the researchers discovered that the gender composition of a few ECs had changed after the forest department had recorded the information on which the sample selection was based. These were all cases of mixed-gender CFIs since, in most part, all-women CFIs tend to remain all-women over extended periods.

Overall, we therefore have a sample of 65 CFIs in Gujarat and 70 in Nepal. Tables 4.3 and 4.4 give the district-wise and gender-wise breakdown. For these CFIs, a mix of detailed quantitative and qualitative information was obtained on the CFI's history; the many facets of its functioning; the characteristics of EC members, the protected forest, and the forest-using population; and the features

[9] FECOFUN is an all-Nepal federation of forest users initiated in late 1995, and has several million members drawn from almost all of Nepal's 75 districts (see also Chapter 10).

Box 4.2. Fieldwork challenges

Narrated by Bidya Bhurtel, project team member

* * *

We faced a unique challenge, arising mainly from the Maoist insurgency, while doing fieldwork in the remote hills of Nepal in 2000–01. At that time the Maoists often intervened to 'uproot' what they saw as feudal attitudes and characteristics, in order to radically change the socio-cultural structure of the countryside. Often those identified as 'people's enemies' were tried in the 'people's court' and meted out punishment. Many ended up with broken limbs or worse. Against this backdrop there was widespread distrust among villagers, and outsiders faced a tough task in winning people's confidence. The further we went from the district centres the more likely we were to be interrogated by the villagers or by the Maoists. Dealing with village suspicion and non-cooperation was particularly challenging. I clearly recall one such situation.

After almost a two-day walk from Baglung Municipality, the headquarters of Baglung district, my co-researcher, Shyamu Thapa, and I reached Kharbang, a trade centre between Baglung and Gulmi districts in the western part of the country. Our local helper, deployed by FECOFUN, was supposed to meet us at Kharbang. In that rugged and remote place where communication facilities are available to very few, accurate planning is impossible. When we arrived, our helper was nowhere to be seen and our target for the day was to reach Saknyar VDC, roughly a two-hour walk from Kharbang. Since it was getting late, we could not afford to wait long and decided to walk to Saknyar on our own.

We set off around 4.30 p.m. Tired to the bone and frustrated, we used our last bits of energy to reach the village located on top of a low hill. We knew the names of the local FUG members whom we had to contact first. We tried to find the FUG chairman's house assuming that he had been informed of our visit and was expecting us. Typical of the hill terrain, the village was spread over a large area. At least a five- to ten-minute walk separated each house, so as soon as we reached the first house, we asked the woman inside where we could find the chairperson. She did not utter a word and went inside, closing the door behind her. We got a similar reception in the next house. Since it was late winter and getting dark by the minute, we could not find a single soul to direct us. Around 7.30 p.m., just as we reached the third house, we met a middle-aged man. Although he pretended not to notice us, we knew he was observing us. We asked him whether he knew where the FUG chairman lived. He pointed to a dark space uphill. We requested him to take us there. He refused and said he had urgent work downhill. We had no option but to try the next house. This was bolted from outside. It was then that we really began to worry and get scared. Still we kept pushing uphill. In about 15 minutes we located a well-lit and better-looking house. On reaching it, we realized that it belonged to a relatively wealthy person. Hearing our voices, a man emerged. He turned out to be a retired army man. Luckily for us, he agreed to let us sleep in his veranda. So without eating anything, except some biscuits and water that we carried, we went to sleep in a corner. They had already eaten their evening meal and showed no interest in entertaining their late evening guests.

Next morning, our host agreed to show us the FUG chairman's house. To our utter surprise, the 'chairman' was the same man who had misdirected us the evening before. We managed to gather some more members of the executive committee, and explained why we were there, and also showed them the permission letters granted to us by the District Development Committee. The rest of our work went smoothly. After a couple of days the chairman opened up and told us that the Maoists had come to his house some days ago and threatened to severely punish him for misusing the community forest. He said one of the Maoists looked just like me, so he had tried to escape from us the first evening since, he said, it was difficult to make out with certainty who we were in the dark.

Table 4.3. Gujarat: EC gender composition

Districts	≤2 EC women CFIs	>2 EC women CFIs	All CFIs
		No. of CFIs	
Narmada/Bharuch	8[a]	8	16[a]
Panchmahals	11	10	21
Sabarkantha	12	16[b]	28[b]
All districts	**31**	**34**	**65**
		% CFIs	
Narmada/Bharuch	50.0	50.0	100.0
Panchmahals	52.4	47.6	100.0
Sabarkantha	42.9	57.1	100.0
All districts	**47.7**	**52.3**	**100.0**

Notes:
[a] Includes 5 cases of all-men CFIs.
[b] Includes 3 cases of all-women CFIs.
Source: Author's survey, 2000–01.

Table 4.4. Nepal: EC gender composition

Districts	All-women CFIs	≤2 EC women CFIs	>2 EC women but not all-women CFIs	All CFIs
		No. of CFIs		
Gorkha/Dhading	16	11[a]	9	36[a]
Baglung/Parbat	11	9[b]	14	34[b]
All districts	**27**	**20**	**23**	**70**
		% CFIs		
Gorkha/Dhading	44.4	30.5	25.0	100.0
Baglung/Parbat	32.4	26.4	41.2	100.0
All districts	**38.6**	**28.5**	**32.9**	**100.0**

Notes:
[a] Includes 4 cases of all-men CFIs.
[b] Includes 1 case of all-men CFIs.
Source: Author's survey, 2000–01.

of the village where the CFI was located for Gujarat, and of one of the CFI toles for Nepal. Nine different questionnaires were fielded at several levels: the CFI, the village/tole, the household, the individual (key informants), and the forest department (Appendix 4.2 describes the type of information obtained at each level). The CFI was my principal focus. Here four questionnaires were fielded, using focus group discussions with members of the executive committee, the village/tole men, the village/tole women, and any outlier/marginalized community in the village/user group. In addition, in both regions, gender-disaggregated information was obtained on attendance at EC meetings from registers kept by the secretaries of many CFIs. The EC was also a useful source of information on aspects of the village/tole and its population, but for land ownership and selected population characteristics a separate questionnaire was fielded through an educated youth from the village/tole.

Individual interviews were also conducted with two former EC members (one man and one woman) from different households, and with one male and one female adult in a sample of member and non-member households. These individual-level interviews are used in the book only for qualitative illustration and for enriching the quantitative analysis. Information on forest condition was obtained from several sources. In Gujarat this included assessments by a forestry expert in the research team and by the villagers, supplemented by assessments of forest cover provided by the GEER Foundation (Gandhinagar) based on satellite imagery. In Nepal, apart from the villagers' assessments, the forest officials also fielded questionnaires, giving information from the department's files on the area and condition of the forest when it was transferred to the community, and the officer's own assessment of forest condition at the time of my survey. This gave me a fairly reliable measure of change in condition over the period of protection. (The Gujarat forest department lacked similar information.)

Since each Gujarat CFI is linked to a specific village in membership and functioning, while in Nepal one CFI can draw members from many toles, and residents in one tole can be members of more than one CFI, Nepal's tole-level information is not representative of its CFI population in the way that Gujarat's village-level information is. Gujarat's village data could thus be used in the quantitative analysis while Nepal's tole data could only supplement the EC information, in addition to providing a qualitative perspective. Also, given this difference, the Gujarat and Nepal samples could not be clubbed together for analysis without losing information available for Gujarat but not for Nepal. They have thus been analysed separately. Below I broadly describe the characteristics of the study districts and fieldsite villages.

2. DISTRICT AND VILLAGE CHARACTERISTICS

2.1 Districts

Gujarat

Gujarat state is located in a semi-arid zone of western India. Administratively divided into 25 districts, it has a geographic area of 19.6 million hectares (m ha). In 2001 it had a population of about 51 million, 63 per cent of which was rural. Economically, it is one of India's more prosperous states with a lower incidence of

Table 4.5. All-India and Gujarat: forest characteristics (1991, 2001)

	1991	2001
All India		
Area under forest cover (m ha)	63.94	67.55
Percentage geographic area under forest land	23.43	23.38
Percentage geographic area under forest cover	19.45	20.55
Gujarat (state level)		
Area under forest cover (m ha)	1.19	1.52
Geographic area (m ha)	19.60	19.60
Percentage state geographic area under forest land	9.89	9.69
Percentage state geographic area under forest cover	6.07	7.73
Forest cover in Gujarat as a percentage of all-India forest cover	1.86	2.24
Percentage Gujarat forest cover under dense forest (>40% crown area)	52.27	57.2
Percentage Gujarat forest cover under open forest (canopy >10–≤40% crown area)	44.39	42.8
Percentage Gujarat forest cover under mangrove forests	3.33	-
Gujarat (district-wise)	1995	2001
Bharuch (Percentage district geographic area under forest cover)	} 13.74	4.37
Narmada (Percentage district geographic area under forest cover)		38.14
Panchmahals (Percentage district geographic area under forest cover)	11.54	13.45
Sabarkantha (Percentage district geographic area under forest cover)	9.15	12.58

Sources: Calculated from *Forest Survey of India Reports* (see GoI 1996, 2001, 2003).

poverty (13.2 per cent) than all-India's (27 per cent);[10] higher male and female literacy rates; and a higher level of industrialization and urbanization. (In contrast, my field-study districts are poor and largely agricultural.) Much of the state has been deforested over the years. In 2000–01, when I undertook my survey, about 10 per cent of Gujarat's geographic area was administratively designated as forest land but only around 8 per cent was actually under tree cover as measured by satellite data, compared to the all-India averages of 23 per cent and 21 per cent of forest land and forest cover respectively (Table 4.5). Gujarat's forest-covered area constituted 2.2 per cent of India's forest cover. Of Gujarat's forests, 57 per cent were dense (>40 per cent crown cover) and the rest were open forest (10–40 per cent crown cover).

Between 1991, when the community forestry programme was formally launched in India, and my survey in 2000–01, Gujarat's forest cover increased by 0.33 million hectares (m ha), as did its dense forest. In the same period, the state's forest-covered area as a percentage of India's forested area also increased from 1.86 to 2.24. Given

[10] The poverty figures are the official figures based on the 1999–2000, 55th round of the National Sample Survey (NSS). Although more recent figures from the 61st round, 2004–05, of the National Sample Survey are also available, the earlier ones are more relevant given the time of the survey, and in keeping with the other indicators taken from the 2001 census.

that the all-India forest cover increased alongside, Gujarat did proportionately better than many other states. It would be reasonable to attribute a fair part of this improvement to the success of communities protecting the state's forests. Indeed, community forestry appears to have contributed to an overall improvement in forest condition not just in Gujarat, but in many other states.[11]

Within Gujarat, the fieldsite districts are located fairly close to one another in the south-eastern part of the state (Figure 4.4). Unlike the state as a whole, the main survey districts are predominantly rural, with populations dependent mainly on low-productivity, rainfed agriculture. Their agricultural holdings are small (and getting smaller), unequally distributed, and largely unirrigated. All three districts come within the Eastern Zone where the incidence of rural poverty is 25.4 per cent, almost twice that for Gujarat state.[12] Literacy levels are also lower than for all-Gujarat.

The forests in these districts, as in the state more generally, are dry deciduous, although both Narmada and Panchmahals have pockets of moist deciduous forest in their ravines and depressions. Teak—a hardwood—is the dominant species (Champion and Seth 1968). Narmada has the largest proportion (38 per cent) of its geographic area under forest, again dominated by teak (Table 4.5), but the district average cloaks large intra-district disparities since several forest sanctuaries raise the average forest density, even while the village forests are highly degraded. Sabarkantha and Panchmahals, in contrast, have only 12–13 per cent of their geographic areas under forest and much of it is 'open forest' with rather little tree cover. But again there is intra-district variation. Much of Sabarkantha's forest (81 per cent) is concentrated in five blocks, including Bhiloda block where my study is located.

Topographically, the survey sites are typically dotted with low-lying hills with forest land interspersed by cultivable plains. However, except where protected by communities, the hills are largely denuded of vegetation, leaving the soil shallow and exposing the rocks beneath. Grassroots workers report that in the early 1980s parts of Gujarat were so acutely degraded that even sweeping the hillside with a broom yielded little more than a few twigs and leaves. The tree-covered hills where communities are now protecting the forests thus stand in stark contrast to those that have been stripped bare. Here, high rainfall concentrated over a brief period has also led to a heavy loss of topsoil over time.

The three NGOs whose sites form the basis of my sample have much in common. They are all located in environmentally degraded areas which they seek to restore, especially through forest regeneration. All of them began work on community forestry in the early 1980s, focusing on poor, disadvantaged populations; and all aim to build village institutions that are participatory, inclusive, and can make the disadvantaged more self-reliant and independent of the NGO over

[11] Of course the benefit derived by local communities from an improvement in forest cover depends also on how much useful biomass is produced and how accessible it is institutionally (see also Lele et al. 1998).

[12] These are the official poverty figures (headcount ratios) which are computed by zones rather than districts for Gujarat, using the 1999–2000, 55th NSS round (calculated by Abhijit Sen, member Planning Commission, personal communication, 25 April 2007).

time. There is one notable difference, however, between AKRSP(I) and the other two NGOs in the village institution responsible for community forestry. AKRSP(I) promotes what it calls Gram Vikas Mandals (GVMs or village development societies) which are responsible not only for community forestry work but also other development projects such as watershed development, irrigation, and employment generation.[13] Although all the sixteen AKRSP(I) fieldsites had community forestry as their dominant focus, only a few had forestry as the *sole* focus. SARTHI (in Panchmahals) and VIKSAT (in Sabarkantha), however, were concentrating on community forestry at the time of my study. Here CFIs were responsible only for forest management, and there were separate village institutions for other development work. This makes for some differences in the functioning of the CFIs in the three districts. Panchmahals, where SARTHI is based, also contains many more self-initiated forest protection groups, constituted by a village elder or group of elders, than found in the other district sites. SARTHI later helped strengthen and formalize these initiatives. Most of the CFIs in my study are registered as cooperative societies.[14]

All three NGOs are today broadly gender aware and seek to enhance women's participation in the village institutions they promote. This was not always the case. In the mid-1990s when I first visited there, gender sensitization was in the early stages. But from around that time, when donor agencies and independent observers pointed to women's near absence in the CFIs, the NGOs began to make special efforts to promote women's participation in various ways, such as by forming women's credit or health groups, providing leadership training, organizing cultural events to bring women out of their homes, and taking villagers on 'exposure visits' to other CFIs in their own region or in other NGO sites to broaden people's approach.[15] AKRSP(I) also began to conduct gender-sensitizing workshops for the staff, and soon thereafter it began promoting Mahila Vikas Mandals (MVMs or women's development societies) parallel to its GVMs, to help women gain self-confidence and experience in group functioning. The mid-1990s constituted something of a turning point for SARTHI as well, when it began to encourage women's membership in its general body, especially following the inputs of a gender consultant, Madhu Sarin.[16] Similarly, around that time, VIKSAT made more concerted efforts to involve women, especially through leadership training. On the ground, however, till 2000–01, all three NGOs had only mixed success in inducting women into community forestry. In AKRSP(I)'s

[13] Post-2000, AKRSP(I) also experimented with other institutional forms, but these proved unsatisfactory and the NGO then returned to the earlier GVM structure (personal communication, NGO staff in Bharuch, April 2007).

[14] Within this category, VIKSAT's and many of AKRSP(I)' s CFIs are registered as Tree Growers' Cooperative Societies (TGCs), the by-laws of which were formulated by VIKSAT (personal communication, VIKSAT staff).

[15] Raju (1997), Rathore (1996), SARTHI (1997–98), and my conversations with the NGO staff members.

[16] It organized women's savings and health groups to increase their self confidence, as well as exposure visits to other CFIs: see e.g. Rathore (1996) and SARTHI (1997–98).

field area, for instance, even in 2000, CFIs with all-male ECs were not uncommon, and barring a few of VIKSAT's CFIs, women had not been office bearers in any of the sample sites.

In recent years, the three NGOs have began to promote women's self-help groups (SHGs) especially to increase women's experience in group functioning, but by and large SHGs have remained separate from the CFIs, except where the field staff has made concerted efforts to link the two institutions. Efforts were also made from the mid-to-late 1990s to 'scale up' local institutions by forming CFI federations. These lateral and vertical linkages between local institutions have enormous potential for strengthening women's voice in CFIs, as discussed in Chapter 10.

Nepal

The Nepal fieldsites are quite different from Gujarat's, topographically, ecologically, and socially. Nepal is largely a mountainous country with a population of 23.2 million (in 2001) and a geographic area of 14.7 m ha. It is thus smaller than Gujarat state both in area and population size (which is a little over half of Gujarat's).

Three main topographical belts run along the country's width, broadly parallel to each other, defining three distinct ecological zones. The topmost division—the Himalayan belt—has high mountains and the fringes of the Tibetan Plateau. The middle part—the middle hills—contains the lower mountains and hills; and the southern-most belt—the Terai—consists of plains in the Himalayan foothills (see also Ojha 2005). These three belts respectively cover 7, 44, and 49 per cent of the country's population, 86 per cent of which is rural, and an estimated 37 per cent of the rural families are 'ethnic'.[17] The middle hills, where my research is located, is socially heterogeneous, with a substantial presence of ethnic groups, such as the Newars, Tamangs, Magars, Gurungs, and Thakalis who follow a mix of Buddhist and Hindu religious traditions; upper-caste Hindus, especially Brahmins and Chhetris; and lower-caste Hindus and dalits identified by their caste occupations, such as porters, blacksmiths, and cobblers. The broad geographic and caste demarcations define a range of gender norms. Among the ethnic groups women are, in general, physically mobile, economically active, and not subject to seclusion practices. Upper-caste Hindus tend to be more gender conservative, but those located in the middle hills are less so compared with those in the Terai plains, and social restrictions on Hindu women have also been declining overall (Bennett and Gujurel 2006). Landlessness is also low in the area: 6–13 per cent of households in the study districts are landless (GoN 2001).

Some 40 per cent of Nepal's geographic area, and 50 per cent of its middle hills, is forested (Table 4.6). Unlike in India, there is no regularly updated, reliable, district-wise data base on forests, despite the substantial national and international donor attention paid to Nepal's forests. Hence information was gleaned from various

[17] While the dividing line between ethnic and other groups is not clear cut, it is a commonly used division in Nepal, and will be used here as a broad marker.

Table 4.6. Nepal: forest characteristics

Characteristic	Source of information	Nepal	Gorkha	Dhading	Baglung	Parbat
Total geographic Area (in m ha)	Nepal Census (GoN 2001)	14.72	0.36	0.19	0.18	0.05
Total forest area: forest + shrub (m ha)	GoN (1999) for all Nepal and NDII (2006) for districts	5.83	0.17	0.11	0.13	0.02
Percentage geographic area in Nepal under forest	GoN (1999) and NDII (2006)	39.6	47.5	56.0	71.0	40.8
Percentage geographic area in middle hills under forest	NDII (2006)	49.6	—	—	—	—
Percentage total households in forest user groups	ICIMOD and CBS (2003:84)	n.a.	63.6	68.1	62.3	84.8

Notes: There is no comprehensive data base that would provide consistent information on Nepal's forests, district-wise. The above information was gleaned from several different sources.
n.a: not available. m ha = million hectares. 1 m ha = 10,000 sq. km.

Sources: GoN (1999, 2001), NDII (2006), ICIMOD and CBS (2003).

sources which shows that Nepal is substantially more forested than India, with forests in better condition. This is also true for the study districts where 41 per cent (in Parbat) to 71 per cent (in Baglung) of the geographic area is estimated to be under forest. These percentages tell us little, however, about the extent of forest *cover* (on which there is no comprehensive data), but field reports indicate that in Nepal, as in India, degradation was moving apace in the 1980s, a key factor leading to the launch of the community forestry programme in 1993 (Hobley 1996).

2.2 Village/Location

The sixty-five Gujarat villages and seventy Nepal CFI sites of my sample broadly reflect the ecological conditions in the district. In the case of Nepal they also reflect the overall social and economic conditions. The Gujarat sample villages, however, are much more economically and socially backward than indicated by the district averages. The people are mainly tribals, living on the edge of subsistence, dependent largely on low-productivity rainfed agriculture, supplemented by cattle tending and dairying, making bamboo products for sale, and migrating seasonally for wage work. It is a drought-prone region, where rainfall failure can lead to serious animal loss and aggravate distress migration. On the one hand, people's dependence on the local forest provides a strong incentive for collective action to conserve the resource; on the other hand it can lead to a high time preference to satisfy immediate needs, which can undermine cooperation. The proclivity to migrate can also make it more difficult to sustain cooperation. However, mostly men migrate, except in situations of drought and high landlessness when the entire family may do so. The pattern of male migration makes it even more important to involve women members in CFI management.

On average, the Gujarat survey villages are medium sized, with a population of about a thousand, spread over 6 hamlets and 183 households per village (Table 4.7). To much greater extent than the districts in which they are located, the sample villages are dominated by scheduled tribe households—85 per cent on average per village. This concentration stems partly from the overlap between tribals and forests (not just in Gujarat but in India as a whole: Poffenberger et al. 1996), and partly from the decision of the three NGOs to work among the more disadvantaged who tend to be the tribals. Unlike the Narmada/Bharuch sites, both Panchmahals and Sabarkantha also have a notable minority of other backward castes (OBCs). OBCs tend to follow restrictive social norms for women similar to those followed by upper-caste Hindus, although even the tribals have, to some extent, been influenced by such norms and by conservative socio-religious movements. In the manner of upper-caste Hindu women, therefore, many tribal women also partially veil their faces, covering their heads and eyes in public meetings in the study sites.

The economic profile of the villages varies across the three district samples (Table 4.7). The Narmada/Bharuch sites have the largest percentage of landless households—21 per cent compared with only 2–3 per cent in the other field-sites—as well as a higher percentage of households with migrant males, many of which are likely to be de facto female headed. Inequality among those owning land is high—the average Gini coefficient is 0.32 for the full sample—but district-wise inequality is highest in the Narmada/Bharuch villages and lowest in Panchmahals. Modernization in terms of health and education facilities in the village, and by the aggregate infrastructure index I have computed, is, however, lower in the Narmada/Bharuch sites than in the other two districts. Electricity is available in most of the sample villages but not every house is connected. Most of the surveyed villages are located within two kilometres of a motorable road but at variable distances from the nearest town. Good connectivity to roads or good overall infrastructure, however, need not improve forest condition, since it can also make it easier to steal and sell timber or reduce the overall commitment to protect. Some 68 per cent of the villages have a mahila mandal.[18] These women's associations, as noted, are typically like self-help groups. Some are confined to

[18] The history of mahila mandals in India goes back to the 1950s when the government launched its community development programme, but many became inactive over time. They were revived in the 1970s for facilitating women's involvement in the rural economy (Jain and Reddy 1979). In parts of India, such as Himachal Pradesh and the Uttarakhand hills, they have also been quite active in forest protection (Davidson-Hunt 1997, and personal observation). Unlike many government-promoted mahila mandals, those promoted by NGOs also tend to be more gender aware and active, although their class composition can affect the nature of their interventions (on this, see Chapter 6).

Table 4.7. Gujarat: survey villages, characteristics

Village characteristics	By district			By gender composition		All CFIs (N=65)
	Narmada/ Bharuch (N=16)	Panchmahals (N=21)	Sabarkantha (N=28)	≤2 EC women CFIs (N=31)	>2 EC women CFIs (N=34)	
Average village population	831	1109	981	1192	797	985
Average no. of village hhs	168	184	191	226	144	183
Average no. of village hamlets	3	8	6	6	6	6
Village caste composition (%)						
Scheduled caste	0.3	2.7	1.1	2.2	0.4	1.5
Scheduled tribe	98.2	76.8	83.9	83.6	86.5	84.8
Other backward castes	0.2	20.5	11.5	11.8	12.1	11.9
Upper caste	1.3	0.0	3.5	2.4	1.0	1.8
Percentage villages with mahila mandals	87.5	57.1	64.3	61.3	73.5	67.7
Percentage village households with migrant males[a]	34.1	4.1	4.9	11.1	11.8	11.4
Percentage village households without adult male heads	6.9	4.0	4.5	5.1	4.5	4.9
Average land owned in village (ha.)	1.2	0.9	0.8	1.0	0.9	0.9
Percentage landless households in village	21.2	1.7	3.1	6.8	6.6	6.7
Gini coefficient for village landowning households (mean)	0.36	0.29	0.32	0.32	0.32	0.32
CFI years of functioning (yrs of formal protection)	6.5	4.8	5.8	5.8	5.6	5.7
Percentage villages by level of educational institution						
Primary (up to class 5)	62.5	38.1	42.9	35.5	55.9	46.2
Secondary (up to class 8)	37.5	38.1	50.0	48.4	38.2	43.1
Higher sec. (up to class 12)	0.0	23.8	3.6	12.9	5.9	9.2
College	0.0	0.0	3.6	3.2	0.0	1.5
Percentage villages with primary health centres or sub-centres	6.25	33.3	42.9	29.0	32.4	30.8
Percentage electrified villages	93.8	100.0	96.4	96.8	97.1	96.9
Village infrastructure index[b]	2.4	3.3	3.5	3.3	3.1	3.2
Village to town (km)	12.4	14.8	7.3	10.2	11.7	11.0
Village to motorable road (km)	4.0	0.8	1.6	2.3	1.6	1.9

Notes: N= number of CFIs.

[a] There was no information for one CFI in Panchmahals.

[b] Aggregate of electrification, health, and education facilities: see definitions in appendix tables at the end of the book.

Source: Author's survey, 2000–01.

saving and credit, others also focus on women's health and related concerns, and many local NGOs encourage their formation to make women self-confident and experienced in public interaction.

Village characteristics differ rather little by the EC's gender composition in contrast to the noted district-wise differences. There is not much difference, for example, between CFIs with >2 women relative to those with ≤ 2 women in the population's caste composition, incidence of migration, land inequality or landlessness, or overall infrastructural index. The main differences lie on other counts: villages where the CFI has more than two EC women have somewhat smaller populations, and are more likely to have women's associations and primary health centres.

In the Nepal sites where forest users can come from several toles, each CFI draws members from five toles on average. Brahmins are the dominant caste (42 per cent) and ethnic communities (33 per cent) come second (Table 4.8). In other words, unlike the Gujarat sample where tribal groups dominate, in Nepal upper-caste presence is fairly substantial. As in Gujarat, however, most of the CFI members are located in toles which have amma samuhs (women's associations), or a women's savings group, many of which were formed before the CFIs started. Amma samuhs are not simply savings and credit societies. They perform varied functions, and sometimes even generate funds for community work, such as

Table 4.8. Nepal: survey location characteristics

Location characteristics	By district		By EC gender composition		All CFIs (N=65)
	Gorkha/ Dhading (N=36)	Baglung/ Parbat (N=34)	All-women CFIs (N=27)	Other CFIs (N=43)	
Average no. of toles in CFI[a]	5	5	4	6	5
Average no. of households in each tole[a]	17	21	19	19	19
Average no. of households in CFI	87	112	87	107	99
Dominant caste[b] (% CFIs)					
Brahmin	37.1	47.1	38.5	44.2	42.0
Ethnic	40.0	26.5	38.5	30.2	33.3
Mixed and other	22.9	26.4	23.1	25.6	24.7
Percentage CFIs with women's association (amma samuh)	58.3	61.8	77.8	48.8	60.0
Percentage member households with migrant males	16.3	16.6	13.6	18.0	16.5

Notes: N is the number of CFIs.

[a] The figures have been rounded.

[b] Based on EC's response to the question: what is the dominant caste among your members?

Source: Author's survey, 2000–01.

building a bus stop or temple. Men's savings groups are less common. Consider now the broad characteristics of the EC.

3. EC CHARACTERISTICS

3.1 Gender Composition

In Gujarat, although JFM requires CFIs to have at least two women in the typically eleven-member EC, many lack even two, while some go beyond. Overall about half the CFIs in my sample have ≤ 2 EC women and about half have >2, as a result of the initial selection (Table 4.9). Only a quarter of the ECs (excluding the all-women ones), however, are constituted of one-third or more women members, the proportion that many have argued is needed for women to be effective in public decision-making. Having only two women does not provide this percentage in a standard eleven-member EC in Gujarat. Also none of the mixed-gender CFIs has more than 55 per cent EC women.

Although Nepal, as noted, has no mandate for including women, in practice all-women CFIs are common in the study area. At the same time, most mixed-gender CFIs fail to include one-third EC women. My sample has 39 per cent all-women CFIs, but among other CFIs (that is other than all-women ones), only 37 per cent have one-third or more women EC members (calculated from Table 4.10), and none has over 64 per cent.

Why do some ECs have a large percentage of women and not others? To effectively answer this question, we would need a random selection of CFI's from an unstratified universe, and then an analysis of the factors affecting EC gender composition

Table 4.9. Gujarat: EC gender composition, disaggregated (% CFIs)

EC characteristics	Narmada/ Bharuch (N=16)	Panchmahals (N=21)	Sabarkantha (N=28)	All CFIs (N=65)
Gender composition				
≤2 EC women	50.0	52.4	42.9	47.7
>2 EC women	50.0	47.6	57.1	52.3
Percent women in EC				
0	31.2	0.0	0.0	7.7
>0–<15	0.0	0.0	7.1	3.1
≥15–<25	31.2	52.4	35.7	40.0
≥25–<33	6.3	23.8	25.0	20.0
≥33–<100	31.2	23.8	21.4	24.6
100	0.0	0.0	10.7	4.6

Note: N= number of CFIs.

Source: Author's survey, 2000–01.

(treated as a dependent variable). My research was not designed to address this question since my interest was in examining the effect of a given gender composition, in whatever way the latter may have come about. Nevertheless I probed the question of the EC's gender composition within my sample, to see if there were any systematic factors underlying the composition which might also affect, say, forest use rules or forest regeneration, and which could thus affect the interpretation of my econometric results in the chapters that follow.

I probed this by examining the history of CFI formation through case studies, revisiting the Gujarat sites in 2007 for discussions with the local NGO staff and EC members in some of the villages, and discussions with my Nepal research team and local NGOs there. The explanations that emerge point to non-systematic factors and a high degree of context specificity, often varying from CFI to CFI. These explanations can broadly be categorized into five: (i) a history of women's prior group activity (unrelated to forestry); (ii) a shift in NGO thinking and gender-sensitizing programmes held by them for their staff; (iii) ad hoc interventions by NGO staff members; (iv) special features of the forest and village location, and motivated village leaders; and (v) prevailing social influences.[19] Broadly, CFIs which have more than two women in the EC appear to be linked with one or more of these factors, as outlined below:

Table 4.10. Nepal: EC gender composition, disaggregated (% CFIs)

EC characteristics	Gorkha/ Dhading (N=36)	Baglung/ Parbat (N=34)	All CFIs (N=70)
EC Gender composition			
0 women	11.1	2.9	7.1
>0–≤2 women	19.4	23.5	21.4
>2–<100 women	25.0	41.2	32.9
100 women	44.4	32.4	38.6
Percentage women in EC			
0	11.1	2.9	7.1
>0–<15	8.3	11.8	10.0
≥15–<25	8.3	8.8	8.6
≥25–<33	11.1	14.7	12.9
≥33–<100	16.7	29.4	22.9
100	44.4	32.4	38.6

Note: N= number of CFIs.
Source: Author's survey, 2000–01.

[19] These explanations are gleaned from: (a) the case studies of CFIs; (b) discussions during a field revisit in April 2007 with Gujarat NGO staff members in AKRSP(I), SARTHI, and VIKSAT who were involved in the initiation of CFIs in the 1990s; (c) discussions with village EC members during the revisit to some of the Gujarat fieldsites in April 2007; and (d) discussions with my Nepal research team and NGOs that had worked in the fieldsites earlier.

History of women's group activity

First, it is well recognized that collective action in the past can lead to similar action subsequently (Seabright 1997a; Baland and Platteau 1996). In my fieldsites, many CFIs with >2 EC women appear to have had a stronger history in this regard than other CFIs. In Narmada/Bharuch, for instance, in several CFIs with >2 EC women, AKRSP(I) started MVMs (women's development groups) *alongside* the GVMs, which encouraged women to also be active in the GVMs. This simultaneity was missing in many of the CFIs with $\leq$ 2 EC women where the MVM was started *after* the GVM was already in place, which proved less effective since male GVM members were then less open to including women. Similarly, in Panchmahals, in several of the villages with >2 EC women in the early 1990s, Save the Children (an international organization) promoted smokeless stove programmes for women and encouraged women's involvement in primary school education through parent–teacher groups. In several of Sabarkantha's CFIs with >2 EC women, likewise, a local NGO (not VIKSAT) formed women's groups for development activities in the 1990s. VIKSAT was also more involved in CFI formation in villages which ended with >2 EC women than in those with $\leq$2 EC women. In the former, their staff were often present in gram sabhas (all-village meetings) during which the initial EC was selected, and on grounds of social inclusiveness they encouraged the participation of women.

In Nepal, similarly, two organizations with programmes for women had a substantial presence in the 1990s, especially in Gorkha. Save the Children US undertook (among other things) gender-sensitizing training for community workers, and in 1995 produced a guide for trainers on gender analysis (Parker et al. 1995). CARE, another international NGO, was similarly active, again specially in Gorkha, where it 'inherited' many of the women's groups formed by Save the Children and encouraged its own, under its women and development programme (CARE 2000). Several Gorkha CFIs mentioned both organizations during my field survey. Although neither was active in community forestry when my survey was conducted, their prior work with women would explain the emergence of more all-women CFIs in this district. Similarly, in Baglung/Parbat, the presence of the Nepal UK forestry project, with its positive gender approach, encouraged CFIs to include more women in their ECs.

Nepal also has a high presence of amma samuhs in communities with all-women groups. These women's associations, many of which were formed before the CFIs emerged, are active locally, and about half the CFIs mentioned that their presence had enhanced women's participation. Without precise information on when each amma samuh was formed we cannot establish causation, but the correlation coefficient between the presence of an amma samuh and the percentage of women in the EC is 0.39 and significant at the 1 per cent level. These influences in the Nepal sites are, of course, general in nature which would apply across the region, and cannot explain why specific CFIs included more women than others, *within the same region.* To throw light on this, we need more context-specific information than is available for Nepal.

Shift in NGO thinking

Second, the mid-1990s was a watermark in terms of gender-sensitive interventions in Gujarat, but in different ways in different districts. In Narmada/Bharuch, around 1994–95, I personally witnessed considerable discussion within the NGO about the need to enhance women's participation in GVMs. Subsequently, gender-sensitizing workshops were also held for the staff. It is notable that 75 per cent of AKRSP(I)'s CFIs with >2 EC were formalized after 1995. The correlation coefficient between the percentage of women in the EC and the timing of CFI formation (i.e. before or after 1995) for the Narmada/Bharuch subsample is 0.60 and statistically significant at 5 per cent.

However, a similar type of intervention by a gender consultant in the Panchmahals fieldsites, in the mid-1990s, had a different impact. It helped increase women's presence in the GB rather than the EC. As a senior SARTHI staff member said: 'we were paying more attention to overall GB membership and not to the EC composition when the group (CFI) was formally registered. Once an EC is formalized, it is more difficult to change its composition. But, in any case, we were not giving this priority.'[20] Instead, the SARTHI staff and some of the villagers pointed to a fascinating variety of context-specific factors for explaining variations in EC gender composition, including the role of individual staff members, and the forest's shape and location, as detailed further below.

In Nepal, a less direct external influence appears to have been the formation of FECOFUN in 1995. The federation's constitution mandated that 50 per cent of its office bearers should be women. This sent an important message that women should be part of CFI decision-making. HIMAWANTI—a cross-country network (headquartered in Nepal) linking women's grassroots groups working on natural resource management—was also formed around the same time.

Ad hoc interventions by NGO staff

Third, some NGO staff members played a catalysing role. The Panchmahals story clearly highlights this. Gender-sensitive Kishore bhai, for instance, simply told the villagers that the criterion of 'at least' two women did not mean a maximum of two women but a minimum of two women, so anyone who wished to join could do so. This, he said, led many more women to come forward, and/or led ECs to induct more women. He had worked with five of the ten CFIs with >2 EC women, and with none of the CFIs with ≤2 EC women. Several other Panchmahals CFIs with high female presence also have interesting individual stories: in one case, a field worker trained by SARTHI took a delegation of women from his village on an 'exposure' visit to VIKSAT's sites, and paid special attention to the

[20] It is notable that the GB's composition does not automatically affect the EC's composition, except insofar as those inducted into the EC need to be members of the GB. Most JFM orders, including that for Gujarat, lay down separate criteria on how the EC should be constituted (see Chapter 3).

EC's gender composition when the CFI was registered. In another village, SARTHI itself organized an exposure visit for women.

Location and motivated village leaders

Fourth, some of the villages had special geographic features. In three of Panchmahals villages with >2 EC women, the EC members said that the inclusion of three or four women was dictated by the logic of protection. The CFI chairman of Falwa village, for instance, told me that they decided to include four women on their EC since their forest stretched longitudinally along the village, as did the village hamlets. Four women, each living in a hamlet near the forest, could keep a lookout for women intruders: 'Just one or two women would not have helped. Who would then have watched the remaining forest?'[21] EC members in Panchmua and Charada villages gave somewhat similar explanations. Their forests are divided into several segments, and this feature lent itself better to hamlet-wise protection, and hence to women in several hamlets keeping a lookout for intruders.[22] Of course not all CFIs with segmented forests have >2 EC women, since much also depends on the attitude of the village leaders. But overall, CFIs with segmented forests are found more likely to have ECs with >2 women than other CFIs.

Cross-fertilizing influences among neighbouring villages also had an impact. In Sabarkantha, three of the villages with >2 EC women (Patiakua, Rampur, and Ambabar) are neighbours, and share a village council. According to VIKSAT staff, in Patiakua, dairy activity which involves women and the potential for fodder from the forest whetted women's interest in the CFI. In Rampuri, Urmila Ben, who later became her CFI's president, had seen her father serve as an EC member in her birth village and so took an active interest in JFM in her marital village. Ambabar village women were influenced by both Patiakua and Rampuri.

Similarly, in two of Sabarkantha's villages, VIKSAT staff attributed the high presence of women in the EC to substantial availability of non-wood forest products which are collected and sold mainly by women. Men here also wanted to involve women in protection work, in order to keep out women from neighbouring villages who might be attracted to their forest for these very products.

Social influences

Fifth, locally specific conservative influences discourage women's involvement in some CFIs. Two of the Panchmahals villages, for instance, are located near Rajasthan state which has strong female seclusion norms. In these villages the socio-religious Bhagat movement—with its emphasis (among other things) on female modesty—is also strong (see also Mann 1993). Two of Sabarkantha's

[21] Personal communication from the elderly male EC president who had initiated the CFI.

[22] See further below on how forest segments have been identified and counted.

villages, similarly, are dominated by conservative male leaders. The absence of these influences increased the likelihood of more women joining the EC.

On the demand side, NGO staff and village leaders in Gujarat gave three main reasons for wanting to induct more than the required two women in the EC: one, women could help protect the forest better because they could dissuade other women from breaking forest use rules; two, women as the main users of the forests needed to have a say in CFI decisions; and three, since women constituted half the village population it was only fair that they should be involved in village institutions. The leaders also explained that they tended to favour women who were literate, had demonstrated leadership qualities (e.g. if they had served in some other institution, such as the village council), and had time to devote to the institution. In practice, however, these favoured criteria were not always fulfilled by the women who actually served on the ECs.

* * *

The above discussion highlights that the factors explaining the EC's gender composition are *diverse and highly context specific, rather than systematic.* Some factors are historical, some locational, some are linked with dynamic NGO staff or village leaders, some stem from the forest's location and settlement pattern, or the availability of forest products of particular interest to women, or the absence of disabling gender norms. It is also notable that those seeking to include more women are typically driven by an interest in gender justice and women's empowerment, rather than by the idea that women might make different kinds of decisions from men. None mentioned, for instance, that women and men might favour different forest use rules. Occasionally gendered social norms came into play, as where the village leaders justified including women so that the forest would be better watched. But these considerations impinged on the formation of ECs *prior to* the formulation of forest use rules or to any visible impact on forest condition—in other words, there is no reason to expect reverse causality here. Nor is there any indication that the context-specific factors that underlie the EC's gender composition have a systematic relationship with decisions on forest use rules or forest condition outcomes.

CFIs, once formed, tend not to change much in their EC composition. Typically, there is no formal election of the EC. Rather, selection is done by a broad consensus through a show of hands as a person's name is proposed in a GB meeting. Usually the same people are reselected every few years, unless migration, death, a mishandling of funds as office bearers, or an inability to devote time to CFI work requires their replacement. In fact, in Gujarat, at the time of the survey, 79 per cent of both male and female EC members had either served on the EC at least once before, or belonged to a CFI where the EC had not changed since inception.

In Nepal also, the EC is selected rather than formally elected. I personally observed the process in some cases and found that selection was done in an open fashion, with someone proposing the name, and if the candidate agreed she or he would be selected through a show of hands. Here again it was quite common for a person to have served on the EC for several consecutive periods: 68 per cent and 73 per cent of the current male and female EC members respectively had either been on the EC before or belonged to a CFI where the EC had remained unchanged.

3.2 Other EC Features

Gender apart, other socio-economic characteristics of the EC such as its caste composition, age, literacy level, and land ownership can also affect governance. As already noted, the ECs in the survey sites are dominated by scheduled tribes (Table 4.11). EC members (both men and women) are typically in their early forties, almost all are married, and 72 per cent are literate, although there is considerable regional variation in literacy, especially female literacy. Overall literacy is highest in the Sabarkantha ECs (about 80 per cent) and lowest in Panchmahals (about 61 per cent), where female literacy is also very low (21 per cent) relative both to male literacy in this district and to female literacy in the other two districts.

Regionally, ECs also differ substantially in their inclusion of the landless. In the Narmada/Bharuch sites, although village landlessness is substantial, only 10 per cent of EC members are landless, indicating considerable under-representation. The opposite is true for Panchmahals—here village landlessness is very low, but 14 per cent of all EC members and 52 per cent of women EC members are from landless households. The presence of landless women in the EC, as we will see in Chapter 6, makes a notable difference to the strictness of forest use rules that the CFI formulates. But even among landowning EC members, the mean land owned across the sample is only 1.2 ha, and (as at the village level, so for the EC) the Gini coefficient of inequality is moderately high—0.33.

In Nepal, the EC's caste composition is much more diverse than in the Gujarat sample (Table 4.12). For a start, about half the EC members, on average, are Brahmins, while ethnic communities constitute another 40 per cent. The notable Brahmin presence, however, does not, in itself, imply 'elite capture'—a term used in the literature to highlight the disproportionate influence exercised over village institutions by the economically or socially powerful. In CFIs for which I have information on the caste composition of the toles from which forest users come (the data was not comprehensive), a comparison of tole caste composition and EC caste composition indicates that Brahmins dominate ECs where the general body of CFI members is also predominantly Brahmin. The same holds for the ethnic population. In other words, these groups appear to be represented on the EC broadly in proportion to their presence in the forest user population. Steenhof et al.'s (2007) study in three other Nepal districts also bears this out.[23] Moreover,

[23] They also compared the proportion of particular caste/ethnic groups in the population with their proportions in the ECs of forestry groups, and found that the proportions were fairly close. Women's representation, however, was disproportionately low.

Table 4.11. Gujarat: other EC characteristics

EC characteristics	By district			By EC gender composition		All CFIs (N=64)[a]
	Narmada /Bharuch (N=16)	Panchmahals (N=20)[a]	Sabarkantha (N=28)	≤2 EC women CFIs (N=31)	>2 EC women CFIs (N=33)[a]	
Average no. of members in EC						
All EC members	11	11	11	11	11	11
Male EC members	9	8	7	9	7	8
Female EC members	2	3	4[b]	2	4[b]	3[b]
Caste composition (%)						
Scheduled caste	0.0	0.0	4.2	3.8	0.0	1.8
Scheduled tribe	100.0	76.2	89.5	82.7	92.6	87.8
Other backward caste	0.0	23.8	6.2	13.5	7.4	10.4
Percentage illiterate EC members						
All members	26.9	39.2	20.7	21.5	34.4	28.2
Male members	18.1	26.3	12.4	17.1	20.6	18.6
Female members	63.6	78.6	37.4	47.9	56.4	54.3
Average age of EC members						
All EC members	39.7	44.8	44.9	43.6	43.6	43.6
Male EC members	40.5	45.6	46.8	44.1	45.5	44.7
Female EC members	36.2	42.4	41.1	40.4	40.7	40.6
Average land owned by EC (ha)	1.6	1.0	1.1	1.3	1.1	1.2
Percentage EC members from landless households						
All EC members	9.9	14.1	1.3	9.1	6.1	7.5
Male EC members	10.1	1.8	1.5	4.8	2.7	3.9
Female EC members	9.1	51.8	1.0	34.0	11.4	17.4
Gini coefficient of land owned by EC	0.39	0.35	0.30	0.34	0.33	0.33

Notes: N= number of CFIs.
[a] In one CFI no information could be gathered on EC members' characteristics other than their sex.
[b] The average includes members of the 3 all-women ECs.
Source: Author's survey, 2000–01.

only a quarter of the ECs are entirely single caste, although in 57 per cent a single caste constitutes 80 per cent or more members (table not reproduced here).

The average age of the Nepal EC members (as in Gujarat) is around 42, almost all are married, and 67 per cent are literate (Table 4.12). There is a large gender gap in literacy—82 per cent of the men and only 55 per cent of the women EC members are literate. But these figures are notably higher than the district literacy

Table 4.12. Nepal: other EC characteristics

	By district		By EC gender composition		All CFIs (N=70)
	Gorkha/ Dhading (N=36)	Baglung/ Parbat (N=34)	All-women CFIs (N=27)	Other CFIs (N=43)	
Average no. of members in EC					
All EC members	11	12	12	11	12
Male EC members	4	6	—	8	5
Female EC members	7[a]	6[a]	12	3	7[a]
Caste composition of EC (%)					
Brahmin	44.6	55.6	48.4	51.1	50.1
Dalit	7.6	9.5	10.1	7.6	8.5
Ethnic	47.1	32.3	41.6	38.7	39.8
Muslim	0.5	0.0	0.0	0.4	0.2
Others	0.2	2.5	0.0	2.2	1.4
Percentage illiterate EC members					
All EC members	32.9	33.5	43.8	26.1	33.2
Male EC members	11.4	22.8	—	17.8	17.8
Female EC members	45.6	43.6	43.8	46.7	44.7
Average age of EC members (yrs)					
All EC members	39.6	43.7	38.6	43.5	41.6
Male EC members	42.8	47.4	—	45.4	45.4
Female EC members	37.6	40.2	38.6	39.0	38.8
Average land owned by EC (ha.)	1.0	0.6	0.8	0.8	0.8
Percentage EC members from landless households					
All EC members	0.8	2.1	0.6	1.9	1.4
Male EC members	0.0	2.6	—	1.5	1.5
Female EC members	1.2	1.6	0.6	3.0	1.4
Gini-coefficient of EC land ownership[b]	0.28	0.32	0.31	0.29	0.30

Notes: N is the number of CFIs.

[a] The average includes all-women ECs; hence the high figures for female EC members.

[b] Due to incomplete data this could not be calculated for 3 CFIs. Here N = 67.

Source: Author's survey, 2000–01.

rates for both men and women, suggesting that the communities place a value on literacy in selecting EC members of both sexes. Virtually all EC members own some land, but the low representation of the landless in the Nepal ECs reflects low landlessness in the population as a whole. Let us now examine what kinds of forests the CFIs are managing.

4. FOREST CHARACTERISTICS

The Gujarat and Nepal sites differ not only ecologically but also in the size and quality of the forests they received for protection. In Gujarat, the average size of forest protected by CFIs—165 ha—is fairly large, although some have as little as 15 ha and others up to 500 ha, and one has 1,537 ha (Table 4.13). Where the forests are very large, as in several Sabarkantha and Panchmahals sites, the villagers receive only a part of it formally in their deed of rights. Effectively, however, most villagers maintain that they protect all the forest in their village, since there is no physical fencing to separate the protected part from the rest of the government forest, and a guard or patrol group's presence deters people from entering even the area that has not been formally given to the CFI to protect. These can be counted as positive externalities.

All the Gujarat CFIs report that when they started protection the forest land was degraded or very degraded. In fact, as already noted, according to the JFM rules in 2000, only degraded land could qualify for JFM. Most Gujarat villages are protecting at least some natural forest,[24] although, especially in Narmada/Bharuch, a fair amount of plantation and gap-filling, or what is termed 'enrichment planting', has also been done (Table 4.14).[25] Some villages have single segment contiguous forests, others have non-contiguous, multiple segments: about half the Gujarat CFIs have one segment, a quarter have two, and the rest have three to six. In some, the natural topography—a stream, gully, or hill—serves as a divider; in others segments emerge when forest land is encroached upon for cultivation or for building homesteads. An assessment of the number of segments is based on sketches made for each village in Gujarat by a local person, after the survey was completed.[26] In Figures 4.6 and 4.7, for instance, Bhatela village has one segment and Patedi village has six. Forest segments have also been used as an explanatory variable in the empirical analysis. Methodologically, this variable, gleaned from maps, has not, to my knowledge, been used before by anyone as an explanatory factor.

All three districts had some plant species in common, such as teak, bamboo, and khair. But Panchmahals and Sabarkantha had much greater diversity than Narmada/Bharuch, and Sabarkantha had several seasonal species of non-wood forest products, such as timru or mahua, which the villagers traditionally collected and sold (see Appendix 4.3). Many of these forest products which were earlier

[24] 'Natural forest', as used here, does not imply a forest in some pristine state. Human interventions go back centuries, and especially during the colonial period silviculture practices greatly altered the ecology. I use the term mainly to distinguish areas where no identifiable planting or gap-filling was done, from areas where it was.

[25] 'Enrichment planting' is done for increasing plant density (i.e. the number of plants per hectare) in an already growing forest stand (Watson et al. 2000). In highly degraded forests, the entire area may take the form of a plantation.

[26] Such sketches could not be made for the Nepal sites, since the state of emergency and insecurity in the country, and the physical remoteness of many sites, ruled out revisits for this purpose.

Table 4.13. Gujarat: forest area protected by type (ha)

Region and gender composition	Total area protected		Gap filled and Plantation area	
	Mean	Range (min–max)	Mean	Range (min–max)
		By District		
Narmada/Bharuch (N=16)	57.9	20–120	46.9	20–120
Panchmahals (N=21)	224.6	15.3–546	5.1	0–25
Sabarkantha (N=28)	181.4 [131.2][a]	15–1536.8 [15–365.2][a]	5.5 [5.7][a]	0–50 [0–50][a]
		By EC gender composition		
≤2 EC women (N=31)	173.3	15–546	17.7	0–120
>2 EC women (N=34)	157.3 [115.5][a]	20–1536.8 [20–470.7][a]	13.6 [14.0][a]	0–60 [0–60][a]
All CFIs (N=65)	164.9 [143.5][a]	15–1536.8 [15–546][a]	15.6 [15.8][a]	0–120 [0–120][a]

Notes: N= No. of CFIs.

[a] Mean values and range without outlier Wageshwari village with its forest of 1536.8 ha.

Source: Author's survey, 2000–01.

Table 4.14. Gujarat: forest characteristics (% CFIs)

Forest area and condition	By district			By EC gender composition		All CFIs (N=65)[a]
	Narmada/ Bharuch (N=16)	Panchmahals (N=21)[a]	Sabarkantha (N=28)	≤2 EC women CFIs (N=31)	>2 EC women CFIs (N=34)[a]	
Natural forest only	0.0	66.7	75.0	61.3	47.1	53.9
Plantation only	18.8	0.0	0.0	3.2	5.9	4.6
Both natural forest and plantation	81.3	33.3	25.0	35.5	47.0	41.5
Forest condition (natural and plantation) when protection began[b]						
Very degraded	50.0	20.0	75.0	51.6	51.5	51.6
Degraded	50.0	80.0	25.0	48.4	48.5	48.4

Notes: N = number of CFIs.

[a] Forest condition data for one CFI was unreliable; here the N values are 20, 33, and 64 for Panchmahals, >2 women CFIs and all-CFIs respectively.

[b] Villagers' assessment.

Source: Author's survey, 2000–01.

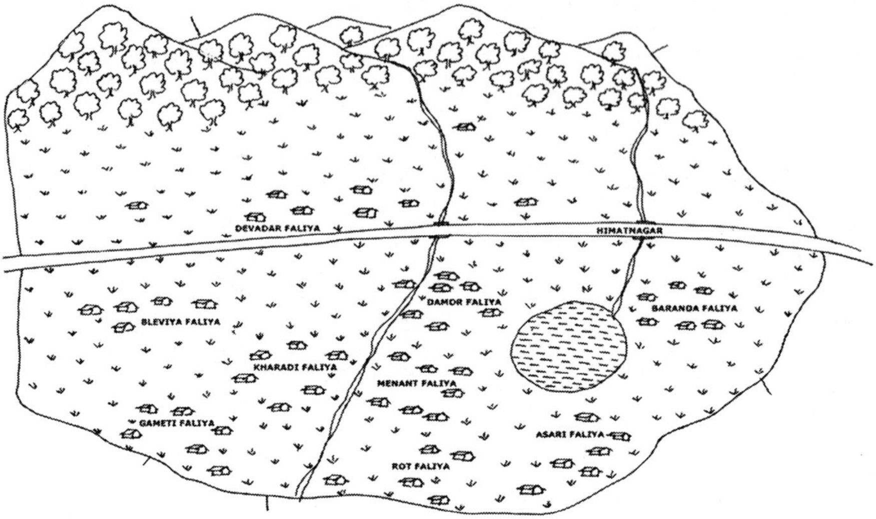

Figure 4.6. Gujarat: villager's sketch of Bhatela village, Sabarkantha

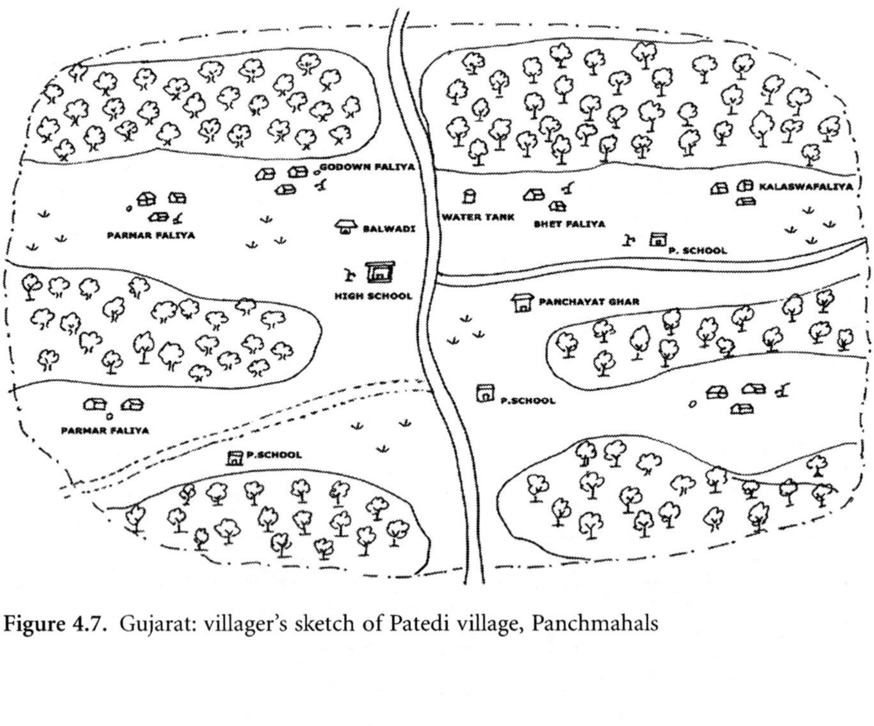

Figure 4.7. Gujarat: villager's sketch of Patedi village, Panchmahals

available in profusion, are now scarce. Also Panchmahals and Sabarkantha have a local firewood species called kada which has little commercial or timber value but substantial fuel value.[27] Ganda babul (prosipus juliflora) is another species used mainly for firewood. CFIs, especially in Panchmahals, therefore allow women to cut these species, when (and if) the forest is opened for such collection.

In the Nepal sites, community forests are much smaller in size—about 34 ha on average—than in Gujarat, the smallest being close to 4 ha and the largest 160 ha (Table 4.15). None has the very large forests found in some Gujarat villages. Indeed, as noted, different parts of one contiguous forest are sometimes protected by different CFIs in Nepal. The forests they protect are usually in one segment. About half of Nepal's CFIs protect only natural forest with no additional plantation, and just over a third protect areas which also have some plantation (Table 4.16). But less than a tenth have plantations alone—all such cases are located in Baglung/Parbat. Receiving a plantation forest can be both advantageous and disadvantageous. On the negative side, it can mean that the forest area was so highly degraded that it needed planting to acquire tree cover. Plantations also require more effort to protect in the early stages, and tend to be less biodiverse than natural forests. These negative features apply especially where the CFI is protecting only plantation area. On the positive side, planting for gap-filling can help rejuvenate a natural forest and revive its bare patches. In general, Nepal's CFIs received better quality forests than Gujarat's CFIs. Only 16 per cent of Nepal's CFIs reported that their forest was very degraded at the time of handover (relative to 52 per cent of Gujarat's) and about 26 per cent also reported they received good or very good forests. By the Nepal forest department's assessment, again, 24 per cent of the forests handed over had thick or medium canopy and 44 per cent were medium or old in age.

Within this overall picture, there are striking gender differences. Nepal's all-women CFIs received on average half the forest area and in much more degraded condition than that received by other CFIs (Table 4.15 and 4.16).[28] A larger percentage of all-women CFIs compared with other CFIs also tend to have only natural forest, and a much smaller percentage have both natural forest and plantation. Insofar as a combination of both is advantageous, in this respect also all-women CFIs are worse off than other CFIs in the forest they receive for protection. This disadvantage is compounded by the predominantly young forests received by all-women groups, none of whom received old forests, while 14 per cent of the other CFIs did. Receiving a small, degraded, and young forest reduces a CFI's freedom to extract forest products and could affect the incentive to protect, as discussed in Chapter 6. Despite this initial disadvantage, however,

[27] Kada is probably Holarrhena antidysenterica, although it could also be Wrightia Tinctoria. Both species are found in the area and used only for firewood (see also the *Gazetteers of the Bombay Presidency*: GoM [1883] 2006).

[28] The forest area per household among the all-women groups also works out to approximately half that for the other groups (0.25 ha versus. 0.48 ha).

Table 4.15. Nepal: forest area protected by type (ha)

District/gender composition	Total forest protected (ha.)		Total area per household (ha.)		Natural forest area (ha.)		Plantation area (ha.)	
	Mean	Range (min–max)	Mean	Range (min–max)	Mean	Range (min–max)	Mean	Range (min–max)
				By district				
Gorkha/ Dhading (N=36)	33.1	3.9–160	0.4	0.07–2.2	31.4	3.6-160	1.7	0–16.8
Baglung/ Parbat (N=34)	34.1	4.9–105.2	0.3	0.07–1.5	24.2	0–90	10.0	0–50
				By EC gender composition				
All-women CFIs (N=27)	20.9	3.9–75.2	0.2	0.07–0.7	16.9	0–75.2	4.0	0–41
Other CFIs (N=43)	41.6	4.9–160	0.5	0.08–2.2	34.8	0–160	6.8	0–50
All CFIs (N=70)	33.6	3.93–160	0.4	0.07–2.2	27.9	0–160	5.7	0–50

Note: N = number of CFIs.

Source: Author's survey, 2000–01.

groups with all-women ECs tend to perform better than other groups in terms of improvement in forest condition, as we find in Chapter 8.

Species diversity is another indicator of forest condition. Overall in the Nepal sites, fodder and fruit species are less common than firewood and timber species. Regionally, Baglung/Parbat CFIs appear to have more biodiversity—some of the plant varieties reported here receive no mention in the Gorkha/Dhading sites (see Appendix 4.3). Among their main species, three-quarters of the CFIs have some firewood species, and about half have some timber species. The prevalence of species that can be used for firewood is especially high in Baglung/Parbat (Table 4.17). However most of these species are also useful as timber and therefore strictly guarded. None mentioned a firewood species like Panchmahals' kada, which has little use as timber. Once these forests have been transferred to the CFIs, whether and to what extent their condition improves depends on how well the institution functions.

5. SOME ASPECTS OF CFI FUNCTIONING

The process of local forest management involves a wide range of functions, collective coordination, negotiations within the village and with the forest department, and various types of decision-making. Some decisions are undertaken at the time of CFI formation, such as defining membership and identifying

Table 4.16. Nepal: forest characteristics (% CFIs)

Type of forest, condition, and age	Percentage CFIs with given forest characteristics				
	By district		By EC gender composition		All CFIs
	Gorkha/ Dhading	Baglung/ Parbat	All-women CFIs	Other CFIs	
	N=36	**N=34**	**N=27**	**N=43**	**N=70**
Natural forest only	75.0	32.4	63.0	48.8	54.3
Plantation only	0.0	17.7	7.4	9.3	8.6
Both natural forest and plantation	25.0	50.0	29.6	41.9	37.1
Forest condition (natural and plantation) when CFI was formed: (villagers' assessment)					
Very degraded	16.7	14.7	22.2	11.6	15.7
Degraded	61.1	55.9	51.8	62.8	58.6
Good	22.2	23.5	25.9	20.9	22.9
Very good	0.0	5.9	0.0	4.6	2.9
Forest age when CFI formed					
Young (≤20 years)	50.0	61.8	63.0	51.1	55.7
Medium (>20 to ≤50 years)	38.9	32.3	37.0	34.9	35.7
Old (>50 years)	11.1	5.9	0.0	14.0	8.6
Forest canopy when CFI formed[a] (forest department assessment)	**N=32**	**N=28**	**N=21**	**N=39**	**N=60**
Thin canopy	37.5	42.9	57.1	30.8	40.0
Patchy canopy	46.9	25.0	33.3	38.5	36.7
Medium canopy	3.1	3.6	4.8	2.6	3.3
Thick canopy	12.5	28.6	4.8	28.2	20.2

Notes: N = number of CFIs.
[a] For forest canopy the N values are given separately because of missing values for this variable.
Source: Author's survey, 2000–01.

members, framing a constitution (in Nepal), demarcating the forest boundary, and preparing a micro-plan. Other decisions are made on an ongoing basis. Some key elements of CFI functioning are described below for providing a background, but particular aspects are further refined, as relevant, in the chapters which follow.

5.1 Defining Membership

Who is a member of the CFI? The notion of CFI membership while simple in principle is complex in practice. Members constitute the general body, and membership not only creates collective responsibility for institutional management and

Table 4.17. Nepal: forest species by potential use (% CFIs)[a]

Species by potential use[b]	By district		By EC gender composition		All CFIs (N=64)
	Gorkha/ Dhading (N=36)	Baglung/ Parbat (N=28)	All-women CFIs (N=25)	Other CFIs (N=39)	
Firewood	67.9	83.3	72.8	75.8	74.6
Fodder	28.5	25.7	21.7	30.9	27.3
Timber	53.9	48.2	48.9	53.1	51.4
Fruit/medicinal plants	17.7	11.0	18.9	12.2	14.8

Notes: N= number of CFIs with information.

[a] Percentage of main species which provide the noted product (main species range between 5 and 10).

[b] Derived from Appendix 4.3

Source: Author's survey, 2000–01.

gives villagers a say in decision-making, but it also constitutes the basis for benefit sharing, which, for many, is perhaps the most important initial reason for joining. In principle, all village households (in Gujarat) and all customary users (in Nepal) can be members. In practice several criteria can define membership.

To begin with, the universe of potential members is somewhat different in Gujarat and Nepal. In Gujarat, as noted earlier, there is a one-to-one relationship between a village and the forest it controls; hence only households in that village have responsibility for and can benefit from the protected area. In Nepal, by contrast, those using and managing the CFI can come from several villages/toles. This difference has both negative and positive features. On the positive side, the Gujarat structure creates clear lines of responsibility and property rights, and is administratively simpler to handle. But the downside is that it takes no account of prior customary user rights which may extend to more than one village. This can lead to inter-village conflicts between those who now have control over the forest and those whose customary access has been denied. These problems are mostly avoided in Nepal, since all traditional users living in the vicinity of the forest can become members of the CFI.[29] Often people are thus members of more than one CFI: in 76 per cent of the CFIs in my Nepal sample people reported being members of at least one other CFI and in some cases of more than one (Tables

[29] There could of course still be social exclusion for other reasons, such as internal caste conflict, but that has to do with social divisions and not institutional design. Similarly, CFIs sometimes distinguish between so-called primary users (those who customarily used the forest regularly) and secondary users (those who used the forest occasionally for a specific purpose or product), and give more rights to the former: see Hobley et al. (1996: 13). I understand, however, that this is more likely a practice among larger CFIs and not built into the formal regulations (personal communication, Bharat Pokharel, 2009).

Table 4.18. Nepal: membership and fee

CFI characteristics	By district		By EC gender composition		All CFIs (N=70)
	Gorkha/ Dhading (N=36)	Baglung/ Parbat (N=34)	All-women CFIs (N=27)	Other CFIs (N=43)	
Membership in other CFIs (%)					
Not member of another CFI	25.0	23.5	7.4	34.9	24.3
Member of one other CFI	58.3	64.7	66.7	58.1	61.4
Member of more than one CFI	16.7	11.8	25.9	7.0	14.2
CFIs with no membership fee when CFI started (%)	69.4	76.5	63.0	79.1	72.9
Average membership fee for late joiners (among CFIs charging a fee) (IRs.)	525.2	1120.8	604.1	941.4[a]	804.4

Notes: IRs. = Indian Rupees. NRs. = Nepali Rupees. The conversion rate is fixed at 1 IRs. = 1.6 NRs
N is number of CFIs.
[a] Some charge as much as IRs. 5600.
Source: Author's survey, 2000–01.

4.18). This can allow them some benefits, even if their own forest is highly degraded.

These differences apart, both Gujarat and Nepal share further on-ground complexity in how membership gets defined, especially for identifying legitimate beneficiaries. Gujarat CFIs charge IRs. 11 per person from the founding members, while most Nepal CFIs either charge no initial fee, or a nominal amount. In any case, the initial fee is simply a starting point. As forest condition improves and new people want to join, many CFIs in both Gujarat and Nepal charge a higher fee. This represents an implicit valuation for the work put in by the founding members, the benefits of which will be reaped by the late joiners. About 50 per cent of the Nepal CFIs say they charge a late joiners fee, which is somewhat arbitrarily fixed and can be as high as IRs. 5,600 in some cases.

A further complication arises when additional persons from member households want to join the CFI but are reluctant to pay a high fee if the household gets only one share of any forest product distributed. To encourage women to join where their husbands are already members proves especially difficult if there is a high fee for late joiners. When I visited some of the Sabarkantha sites in 1998, for instance, despite VIKSAT's encouragement few women were willing to join as second members, unless they were promised an additional share of the benefit. This the village committees were unwilling to do.

For benefit sharing, a second criterion for membership also becomes important. Many CFIs link benefits to contribution toward protection, such as by contributing toward the guard's pay or by patrolling. Those who depend on wage labour for a livelihood or migrate for work, are faced with financial and time constraints which disadvantage them on this criterion. Also, this criterion uses the household rather than the individual as the basis of membership, since people contribute to a guard's pay or to patrolling on a household basis (with family members substituting for one another in a patrol), whereas membership fees are paid on an individual basis. This difference between the two criteria can also make it difficult to move from household shares to individual shares.

5.2 Decision-Making

Setting the criteria for membership is only one among a wide range of decisions in which a CFI is involved. Others include site selection, preparing micro-plans/operational plans, deciding on protection methods, framing forest use rules, specifying and implementing penalties for rule-breaking, organizing forest pruning and cleaning operations, raising nurseries for tree planting, supervising extraction and distribution of forest products, setting prices for forest products sold, resolving conflicts within the village and between villages, organizing visits to other CFI sites as a learning process, managing the community fund, and so on.

These decisions are made variously by the EC, the GB, and the forest department, with the EC playing the primary role on most counts. Although technically the EC acts on behalf of the GB, effectively it enjoys considerable authority and autonomy. It is involved in almost all of the CFI's decisions, whether made on its own and then ratified by the GB, or made in consultation with the GB. On some counts, discussion in the GB can be essential, such as organizing patrol groups or hiring a guard, the extraction of forest products and their distribution or sale, and tree selection and planting—activities in which the involvement of all the members is necessary. But on other counts the EC may not seek the GB's involvement, nor may such involvement be practical. In Nepal, for instance, since members are physically scattered across toles, well-attended GB meetings are often difficult to organize. This dependence on the EC for most aspects of the CFI's functioning is also perhaps inevitable since the GB is usually expected to meet only once a year and the EC once a month. More frequent meetings can be called, if needed, but typically only some CFIs meet even with this regularity or keep a full record of the proceedings. Records for EC meetings are better kept than for GB meetings. Sometimes interested CFI members may turn up at an EC meeting even if they are not on the committee, swelling its numbers, although this is not usually the case. The NGOs which are significant actors in the Gujarat sites play a role more as facilitators than as formal decision-makers and may be present in some meetings and not in others.

The forest department's role is again limited in terms of the everyday functioning of the CFI, but is central on selected counts. In Gujarat, broadly the department helps the CFI prepare its plans for forest development, mediates in cases of serious rule violation that the CFI reports to it, and has a hand in the choice of species in enrichment planting. On timber cutting, however, its role is central. The CFIs cannot normally cut timber even for cleaning and pruning the forest without the department's prior permission. On this count, therefore, EC/GB discretion is limited, sometimes leading to conflicts between the CFIs and forest officials when the latter deny them permission to harvest. Occasionally CFIs may give timber on request (typically a written request) to someone in acute need, or following a natural disaster.

In Nepal the department's role is especially important at the time of handover when it helps frame the CFI's constitution and its operational plan. The constitution spells out the responsibility and authority of the forest user group, lists the EC members and office bearers, outlines the process of penalizing for rule violations, and elaborates on a range of other points. The operation plan, among other things, specifies the forest boundaries, the silviculture practices to be followed (termed forest promotion activities and involving periodic thinning/pruning/cleaning operations in the forest, as well as tree planting), the forest products that will be collected, sold, or distributed, the method of protection, and the penalty provisions for various types of rule violations. A number of activities that could harm the forest are also prohibited by the operational plan, such as clearing the forest area for cultivation, building huts in the forest, and so on.[30] The constitution and operation plan have to be approved formally by the DFO. Both can be revised if needed, after discussion in and approval by the general body, and the DFO needs to be informed of such changes. The forest department also has a say in the fixing of prices for the sale of forest products to outsiders and, as in Gujarat, is a key figure in any decision to clean and prune the forest or harvest timber. In both Gujarat and Nepal, the community forest can be taken back by the department in case of serious deviations from the work plan, or if the group's activities are found to be harming the forest.

Within these broad parameters, when you actually observe CFIs on the ground, as in my survey, it is clear that in practice they exercise a fair degree of functional autonomy on particular counts, such as in organizing protection, distributing non-timber products, and overall management, as outlined below.[31]

5.3 Protection Methods

The forests are protected by a mix of methods which change over time and sometimes by season. In Gujarat, when the CFIs were initiated, they depended mostly on patrolling or informal lookout. On average, only 18 per cent of the Gujarat CFIs employed a guard, typically paid in cash or in both cash and kind. In

[30] This description of the constitution and operation plan is based on Nepal's Forest Act 1993 and Forest Regulation 1995 (GoN 1995).

[31] These observations relate to the sample and regions studied. The extent of autonomy a CFI enjoys or the degree of control the FD exercises can (and does), however, vary regionally, especially across states in India.

Table 4.19. Gujarat: protection method (% CFIs)

CFI characteristics	By district			By EC gender composition		All CFIs (N=65)
	Narmada/ Bharuch (N=16)	Panchmahals (N=21)	Sabarkantha (N=28)	≤2 EC women CFIs (N=31)	>2 EC women CFIs (N=34)	
Protection method when CFI formed[a]						
Informal lookout	12.5	52.4	3.6	29.0	14.7	21.5
Patrol group	68.8	33.3	75.0	54.8	64.7	60.0
Guard	12.5	14.3	17.9	12.9	17.6	15.4
Guard + patrol group	6.2	0.0	3.6	3.2	2.9	3.1
Protection method, in 2000–01[a]						
Informal lookout	43.8	57.1	7.1	32.3	32.4	32.3
Patrol group	31.2	14.3	42.9	25.8	35.3	30.8
Guard	25.0	28.6	25.0	29.0	23.5	26.2
Guard and patrol group	0.0	0.0	17.9	6.4	8.8	7.7
Almost no protection	0.0	0.0	7.1	6.4	0.0	3.1

Notes: N is the number of CFIs.
[a] This was the primary protection method. Informal lookout supplements patrol groups and guards as well.
Source: Author's survey, 2000–01.

some CFIs guards protected the forest on their own and in others their efforts were supplemented by a patrol group. Alongside, informal vigilance was common everywhere (Table 4.19).

At the time of my survey, however, patrolling had declined in all the fieldsites and dependence on solely informal protection or on guards had increased—by then 34 per cent of the CFIs kept a guard. Several factors contributed to the change. To begin with, patrolling needs voluntary labour and is difficult to maintain on a regular basis for extended periods, since people tend to slacken over time. As the institution matures, in many CFIs villagers see less need for regular patrolling because their neighbouring villages know that they are protecting the forest, and many neighbours are now also protecting their own forests, so each is wary of the other and has a stake in ensuring that the rules are followed. Both these factors (one on the supply side, the other on the demand side) have contributed to a decline in patrolling and a move to informal lookout. The villagers' responses below are illustrative:

> Initially five men would patrol. We would decide which five would go and inform them the night before. When people heard we were patrolling they stopped coming to steal. Earlier usually men came to steal timber, mostly from the Naik [low caste, usually poor] community . . . After 3–4 years, it became increasingly difficult to get people to patrol. In the other village people get grain to patrol but not in this one. So people have less incentive. Now we have informal protection. (EC members, Ramdev Na Muada village, Panchmahals, Gujarat, author's survey 2000–01)

> Initially we took turns to protect. One person would go for patrolling from every household. Every household would give 5–10 kg of grain as payment for this. After a year we decided to have a fixed group of five persons. This went on for two years. Finally we decided to keep two watchmen. (EC members, Mor Undara village, Panchmahals, Gujarat, author's survey, 2000–01)

> We have dealt with all our problems fairly and people of the neighbouring villages are quite aware how serious we are about our forest so they think twice before they come into our forest now. (EC members, Rukhal village, Bharuch, Gujarat, author's survey, 2000–01)

> When protection first started, we followed the rotation method. A man or woman from each household had to take a turn. We cannot employ a watchman since we have no money in our community fund. We have a small forest and we can see it from a single place even through informal vigilance. (All-women EC, Bhadaurepani Mahila CFI, Baglung, Nepal, author's survey, 2000–01)

However, as the forest regenerates and product availability increases, more formal protection is often needed both overall and in certain seasons. Prior to the monsoon, for instance, everyone wants to store firewood, and just after the monsoon, people sneak in if there is a good crop of fodder. Extra firewood is also needed during wedding seasons. During these periods, therefore, many CFIs are more vigilant. EC members from Rukhal village (Bharuch) reported: 'Men and women come to steal according to the season. Just after the monsoon the women come during the day to steal fodder and the men come at night to steal timber.' 'The main difficulty arises in the monsoon when there is too much agricultural work. Our neighbouring villages try to take advantage of this and we have to be very alert.' Some also employ a guard in such seasons, and depend on limited patrolling or informal lookout in other months.

There is another interesting variation on protection methods in Panchmahals where the NGO, SARTHI, distinguishes between unified protection, hamlet-wise protection, and household-wise protection. The first is typical where the forest is constituted of one or two large segments. The second is common where the forest is divided into several segments of reasonable size—here protection is often done by clusters of hamlets located closest to those segments. Household-wise protection is uncommon, tends to overlap with other forms of protection, and is usually found where the forest is fragmented and there is no large hamlet near a forest patch. Here households closest to the patch are made responsible. This can lead to rather inequitable results however, since families living near such patches exert territorial rights over them and follow their own ad hoc extraction systems. Despite this, the forest usually does improve, largely because the users are fewer and the households keep a strict vigil against intruders.

Women seldom become guards or go for formal patrolling, although they sometimes substitute for male family members. Only ten of my study CFIs included women in their patrol groups, usually as replacements for absentee males. During my 1995 field visit to Gujarat, I had similarly found that women were rarely part of formal protection. But they play a critical role in informal protection, which is also recognized by many village men. Indeed, as we had noted, this was one of the important reasons given by some male village leaders for inducting women into their ECs. Sometimes women form their own informal 'lookout' groups, and enthusiastically recount stories about apprehending intruders (see also Agarwal 1997a). Women's absence from the formal groups, however, reduces the efficiency of protection in a cultural context where men cannot physically catch female intruders, given the risk of being accused of molestation. Although this is recognized by both men and women, cultural norms can win over efficiency considerations. At the same time, even by their informal efforts, women, on joining the EC, can improve protection and hence forest condition in a variety of ways (see Chapter 8).

In Nepal, to greater extent than in Gujarat, the CFIs kept guards when they first started protection, either as sole protectors or to supplement a patrol group or informal lookout. But, as in Gujarat, patrolling declined over time, or continued selectively by season, intensifying during festival and wedding seasons when villagers expected more theft. Unlike in Gujarat, however, in Nepal dependence on guards has also declined over time. At the time of my survey, only a third of the CFIs kept a guard (usually paid in cash), while a fifth still did patrolling, and the rest kept only an informal lookout (Table 4.20). Like Gujarati women,

Table 4.20. Nepal: protection method (% CFIs)

CFI characteristics	By district		By EC gender composition		All CFIs (N=70)
	Gorkha/ Dhading (N=36)	Baglung/ Parbat (N=34)	All-women CFIs (N=27)	Other CFIs (N=43)	
Protection method when CFI formed[a]					
Informal lookout	16.7	23.5	29.6	14.0	20.0
Patrol group	38.9	14.7	25.9	27.9	27.2
Guard	38.8	52.9	37.0	51.1	45.7
Guard + patrol group + other	5.6	8.8	7.4	7.0	7.1
Protection method in 2000–01[a]					
Informal lookout	44.4	47.1	51.9	41.9	45.7
Patrol group	25.0	20.6	25.9	20.9	22.8
Guard	25.0	32.3	22.2	32.5	28.6
Guard + patrol group + other	5.6	0.0	0.0	4.7	2.9

Notes: N is the number of CFIs.
[a] This was the primary protection method. Informal lookout continues alongwith patrol groups and guards.
Source: Author's survey, 2000–01.

Nepalese women also rarely become guards, but are more involved in patrolling than in Gujarat. This is partly because Nepal's all-women CFIs sometimes have all-women patrols, and partly because women are subject to less restrictive social norms among hill communities.

5.4 Forest Use Rules and Penalties

In addition to protection, a crucial CFI function is the formulation of rules for forest use. These rules determine whether and which products are extracted from the forest, and by what method, and so determine the benefits derived and the incentives for protection.

In Gujarat, before formal protection began, the forests were used mostly for subsistence, except for seasonally available NWFPs, such as timbru leaves, which were customarily collected for sale (Table 4.21). After protection began, more formal rules were instituted. These were made largely by the villagers themselves with only a small percentage seeking help from the local NGO or the forest department (Table 4.22), although such agencies could have had an indirect influence, through general discussions with the villagers around conservation or equity issues.

When initiating protection, almost all the CFIs tend to restrict the entry of people and animals and disallow cutting of any kind of wood—drywood, greenwood, or small timber. In fact, the ban on cutting timber species without permission goes back many decades, but was not always enforced effectively. After protection begins, technically some CFIs continue to allow the collection of fallen twigs and NWFPs, but there is often little to collect. Also, where

Table 4.21. Gujarat: forest use before CFI formed (% CFIs)

Forest use/ products extracted	Home use	Sale	Both	Item not available in forest	Forest not used for item	No. of CFIs with information
Firewood	88.5	0.0	11.5	0.0	0.0	61
Fodder	93.3	0.0	0.0	6.7	0.0	60
Grazing	96.7	0.0	0.0	1.7	1.7	60
Small timber	70.5	0.0	1.6	13.1	14.8	61
Leaf litter	80.3	1.6	3.3	8.2	6.6	61
Timru leaves	21.3	47.5	11.5	11.5	8.2	61
NWFPs	32.8	32.8	6.6	13.1	14.8	61
Cremation wood	69.0	0.0	1.7	13.8	15.5	58

Notes: Percentages are based on number of CFIs with information.
NWFPs = non-wood forest products.

Source: Author's survey, 2000–01.

Table 4.22. Gujarat: forest use rule-makers (% CFIs)

Who made the forest use rules?	By district			By EC gender composition		All CFIs (N=62)[a]
	Narmada/ Bharuch (N=15)	Panchmahals (N=20)	Sabarkantha (N=27)	≤2 EC Women CFIs (N=29)	>2 EC Women CFIs (N=33)	
Villagers alone	66.7	80.0	88.9	79.3	81.8	80.6
Villagers with FD help	6.7	10.0	7.4	3.4	12.1	8.1
Villagers with NGO help	26.7	10.0	3.7	17.2	6.1	11.3

Notes: N = number of CFIs.

[a] Information was available only for 62 out of 65 cases. Percentages have been computed based on the cases for which there is information.

Source: Author's survey, 2000–01.

vigilance is strict, villagers treat this as an effective ban on collecting any product.

Both ecological conditions and the ability of CFI members to bargain with the EC impinge on the rules made, and the rules outlined in Table 4.23 and Figure 4.8 are the net result of these and other factors explored in Chapter 6. From the table we note that rules can range from a complete ban on collection to open always,[32] with varying degrees of restrictions in between. However, the full range of rules does not apply to all products. Tree cutting for any purpose is never fully open, and seldom allowed on a regular basis even under supervision, while the seasonal collection of many non-wood products is allowed freely in most cases.

When the tree canopy is thin, grass fodder can be substantial and in a cattle-based economy many CFIs open the forest seasonally for fodder extraction, sometimes through procedures for systematic collection and distribution (e.g. in equal bundles given to each participating household or via plot allocations), at other times allowing free collection, but restricting entry to one person per household. These varied arrangements are detailed in Chapter 6. When the tree canopy thickens and there is insufficient fodder for extracting and distributing on a systematic basis, and there are few new shoots that can be damaged, some CFIs allow grazing. NWFPs, where found, can also usually be collected freely, and are sold by poor women to supplement family income. And a fair proportion of CFIs—either unrestrictedly or on forest opening days—allow the collection of twigs, fallen branches, and drywood by hand. In Panchmahals, in particular, rules in many CFIs have moved from a strict ban during the early years of protection,

[32] 'Open always' does not mean 'open access'. It means open only for the community protecting the forest, but not for residents of other villages. Open access would imply open for anyone, including outsiders.

Table 4.23. Gujarat: forest use rules after CFI formation (% CFIs)

Forest use/ products extracted	Rules					No. of CFIs with information
	Open always[a]	Open occasion-Ally	Partial ban[b]	Given on request[c]	Full ban	
Fallen twigs	58.5	23.1	0.0	0.0	18.5	65
Drywood (cutting)	26.2	29.2	3.1	0.0	41.5	65
Greenwood	14.8	29.6	0.0	0.0	55.6	54
Grass fodder	49.2	40.0	0.0	3.1	7.7	65
Grazing	40.0	1.5	26.2	7.7	24.6	65
Timber species for firewood	0.0	0.0	0.0	1.5	98.5	65
Timber for agricultural implements	5.0	5.0	0.0	27.5	62.5	40
Timber for house building or repair	0.0	1.5	1.5	9.2	87.7	65
Leaf litter	82.1	10.7	0.0	0.0	7.1	56
NWFPs	78.3	15.0	1.7	1.7	3.3	60
Cremation wood	0.0	0.0	1.7	5.1	93.2	59

Notes: Percentages are based on number of CFIs with information.
NWFPs = non-wood forest products.
[a] 'Open always' means open for the village community, but closed to others. It does not mean 'open access'.
[b] Partial ban normally implies that collection is banned in some parts of the forest (usually where there is a plantation, gap-filled parts, or young shoots).
[c] Given on request for special need or natural disaster.
Source: Author's survey, 2000–01.

to 'chutti' (opening occasionally), or more access for drywood cutting without an axe, after the CFIs were formalized. This leniency was also possible due to the noted availability of firewood species such as kada and ganda babul. Cutting timber species for firewood is still banned, however. And, unlike for fodder, virtually no Gujarat CFIs practice systematic extraction of firewood under supervision and formal distribution even on forest opening days, except when there is pruning and cleaning at intervals of a few years. Overall, therefore, notwithstanding the somewhat greater leniency exercised by some CFIs, the limited extraction of firewood has brought little relief from persisting shortages in most villages (as detailed in Chapter 9).

In Nepal, similarly, before community protection started, the forests were used mainly for personal use and rather little for sale. This overall picture did not change much after protection started (Table 4.24). Formal rules were set in place: this was often in consultation with the forest department, especially in the case of all-women CFIs (Table 4.25). But given that the forests were on average in better condition than in Gujarat, the CFIs could, if they wished, allow more extraction than possible in the Gujarat villages. In practice, however, except for twigs collection, toward which the Nepal CFIs show more leniency than Gujarat, for

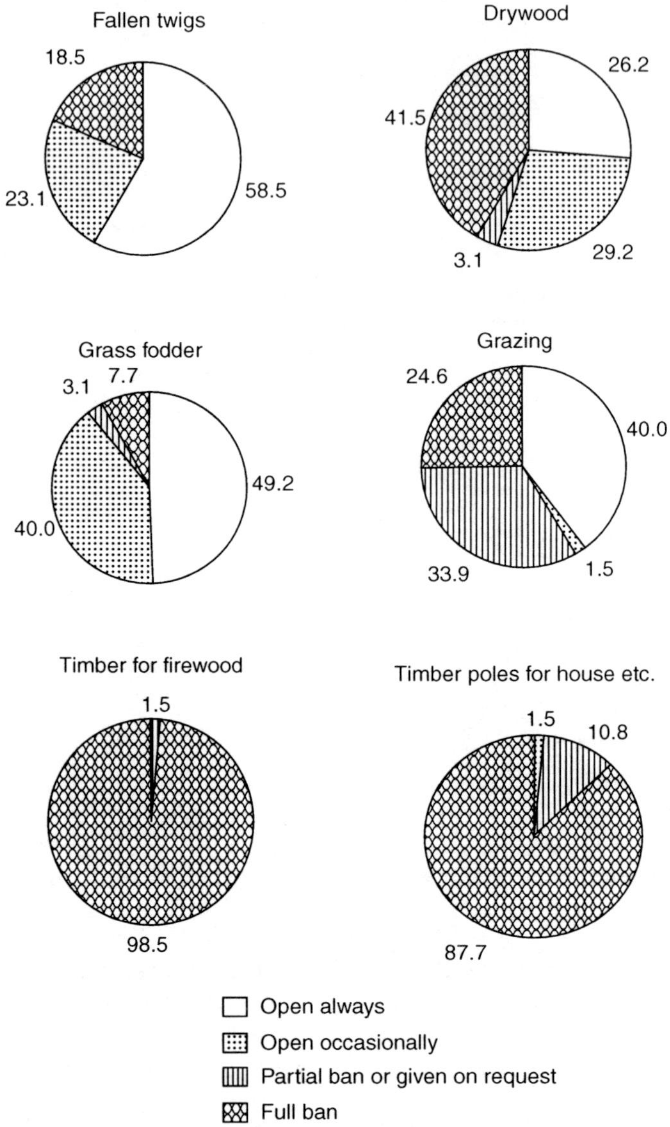

Figure 4.8. Gujarat: forest use rules after CFI formation, product-wise

Table 4.24. Nepal: forest use prior to and after CFI formation (% CFIs)

Forest use/products extracted	At the time of informal protection (N=62)				After CFI formed (N=68)			
	Home use	Sale	Both	Not used	Home use	Sale	Both	Not used
Firewood	77.4	0.0	3.2	19.4	77.9	0.0	0.0	22.1
Fodder	85.5	0.0	0.0	14.5	83.8	0.0	0.0	16.2
Grazing	71.0	0.0	0.0	29.0	54.4	0.0	0.0	45.6
Timber[a]	64.5	1.6	3.2	30.7	58.8	0.0	0.0	41.2
Leaf-litter	64.5	0.0	0.0	35.5	58.8	0.0	0.0	41.2
NWFPs	40.3	1.6	1.6	56.5	38.2	1.5	0.0	60.3
Cremation wood	32.3	0.0	0.0	67.7	29.4	0.0	0.0	70.6
Other[b]	6.5	0.0	0.0	93.6	8.8	0.0	0.0	91.2

Notes: N is the no. of CFIs. NWFP = non-wood forest products.
[a] Includes 'small timber', that is, wood with a girth of <3 feet.
[b] This includes items such as grass for thatching, white clay, etc.
Source: Author's survey, 2000–01.

Table 4.25. Nepal: forest use rule-makers (% CFIs)

Who made forest use rules?	By district		By EC gender composition		All CFIs (N=70)
	Gorkha/ Dading (N=36)	Baglung/ Parbat (N=34)	All-women CFIs (N=27)	Other CFIs (N=43)	
Villagers alone	27.8	14.7	11.1	27.9	21.4
Villagers with FD help	44.4	85.3	77.8	55.8	64.3
Villagers with NGO's help	27.8	0.0	11.1	16.3	14.3

Note: N is the number of CFIs.
Source: Author's survey, 2000–01.

all other products we see much greater strictness (Table 4.26 and Figure 4.9). Cutting drywood, for instance, is only allowed when the forest is opened occasionally, perhaps once or twice in the year or on special request (Table 4.26). Similarly, even for twigs, less than half the CFIs allow collection on a regular basis, while the remaining do so only on special opening days, and 13 per cent ban even this, either fully or partially. Hence in Nepal, as in Gujarat, women in most CFIs complain about firewood and fodder shortages. Timber cutting is allowed, but subject to the provisions built into the operational plan and in consultation with the forest department. CFIs also give out timber on occasion, under special circumstances, if requested.

The counterpoint of rule-making is formulating penalties for rule-breaking. Prescribed penalties are more formally spelt out in the Nepal sites than in Gujarat,

Table 4.26. Nepal: forest use rules after CFI formation (% CFIs)

Forest use/ products extracted	Rules					No of CFIs with information
	Open always	Open occ.	Partial ban[a]	Given on request[b]	Full ban	
Fallen twigs	45.7	41.4	4.3	0.0	8.6	70
Drywood (cutting)	1.4	90.0	1.4	1.4	5.7	70
Tree fodder	0.0	31.4	7.1	1.4	60.0	70
Grass fodder	41.4	51.4	2.9	0.0	4.3	70
Grazing	27.1	5.7	14.2	0.0	52.9	70
Timber[c]	0.0	0.0	0.0	62.9	37.1	70
Leaf litter	40.0	37.1	2.9	0.0	20.0	70
NWFPs	48.8	7.0	9.3	0.0	34.9	43
Cremation wood	20.5	7.7	5.1	12.8	53.8	39
Other[d]	20.0	20.0	0.0	0.0	60.0	5

Notes: Percentages are based on number of CFIs with information.

[a] Partial ban normally implies that collection is banned in some parts of the forest (usually where there is a plantation, gap-filled parts, or young shoots).

[b] This means it is normally banned, but can be given in case of special need or a natural disaster.

[c] Includes 'small timber'.

[d] Includes white clay, charcoal, etc.

Source: Author's survey, 2000–01.

and vary by product. In Gujarat, broadly, cutting drywood and greenwood for fuel can invite reprimand or fines, sometimes along with confiscating the implement (usually an axe) and the stolen product. For grazing most impose no penalty, while one-third impose fines, with or without confiscating the animals. However, for timber cutting fines dominate, imposed alone or with a range of additional measures, and serious logging can lead to a formal complaint to the authorities (Table 4.27).

In Nepal, the prescribed penalties are dominated by fines for most products (be it for drywood, timber, or fodder: Table 4.28); and the prescribed fines for non-members are often twice those for member households. While the Gujarat sites had no formal penalty for collecting NWFPs, in Nepal fines are also mandated for such products in many CFIs. At the same time, notwithstanding the domination of fines, informal penalties are not uncommon in practice, even in Nepal. Public reprimand, in particular, is not usually prescribed, but it is often used at the EC's discretion. Reporting to the forest department or to the police is rare since the villagers often say they feel out of their depth in dealing with public agencies, and unlike in India the institutional arrangement is not one of co-management with the forest department. There are also differences (explored in Chapter 7) between actual violations by product and persons, and perceptions about who breaks the rules and for what product.

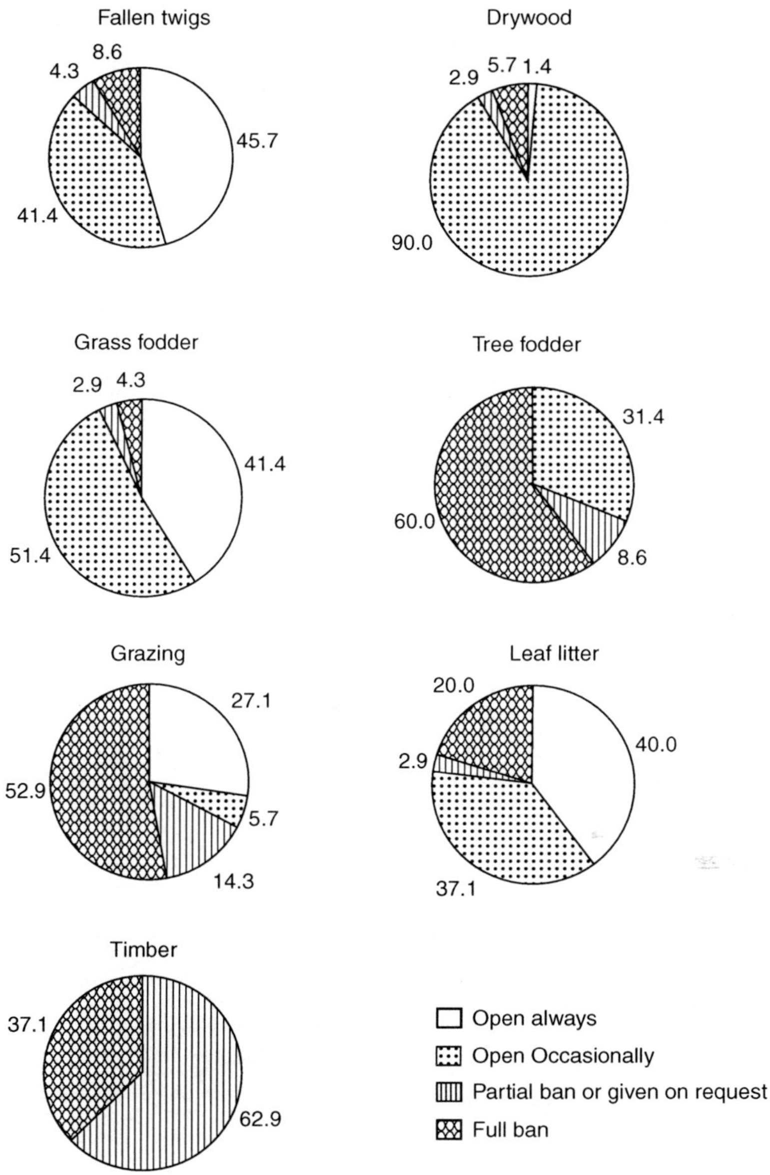

Figure 4.9. Nepal: forest use rules after CFI formation, product-wise

Table 4.27. Gujarat: penalty provisions[a](% CFIs)

Form of violation	Penalty specified						No of CFIs with information[b]
	No Penalty	Public reprimand	Warning	Fine	Product and implement taken	Report to forest dept.	
Drywood cutting	31.4	14.3	34.3	11.4	8.6	0.0	35
Greenwood cutting	0.0	12.8	35.9	33.3	17.9	0.0	39
Grazing	40.0	4.0	24.0	32.0	0.0	0.0	25
Timber cutting	0.0	7.1	21.4	42.9	21.4	7.1	42
NWFP collection	100.0	0.0	0.0	0.0	0.0	0.0	64

Notes: Percentages are based on number of CFIs with information.

[a] These are broad-based specifications and unlike for Nepal (below) are seldom formalized in writing.

[b] The remaining CFIs either have no rules for that item or the information is missing.

Source: Author's survey, 2000–01.

Table 4.28. Nepal: penalty provisions (% CFIs)

Form of violation	Penalty specified				No. of CFIs with information[a]
	Public reprimand	Fine	Implement taken	Other	
Drywood cutting	0.0	96.8	1.6	1.6	63
Greenwood cutting	1.5	97.0	0.0	1.5	67
Fodder cutting	0.0	100.0	0.0	0.0	38
Grazing	6.8	86.4	2.3	4.6	44
Timber cutting	0.0	93.8	3.1	3.1	65
NWFP collection	16.7	58.3	16.7	8.3	12
Other[b]	0.0	90.0	2.5	7.5	40

Notes: Percentages are based on number of CFIs with information.

[a] In the remaining CFIs either the actual penalty for a given item is not specified in the operational plan and it leaves it to the EC to decide, or the information is missing.

[b] Other violations can include wild life hunting, encroachments, stealing boulders, being absent from meetings or patrol duty, destroying plants, careless clearing of undergrowth, collecting soil from the forest, or stealing multiple products.

Source: Author's survey, 2000–01. Data provided by the EC was cross-checked with the CFI's operational plan where available.

5.5 Community Fund

Fees, fines, the sale of forest products, and forest-related income-generating activities all help build a community fund: 69 per cent of the Gujarat CFIs and 100 per cent of the Nepal CFIs have such a fund, holding a medium amount of around IRs. 12,000 in Gujarat and IRs. 5,000 in Nepal. In Gujarat, on average, groups with >2 EC women have half the funds of groups with ≤ 2 EC women and in Nepal, all-women's groups have a third of the funds that other groups control. In both regions, the money is used mostly for giving loans to community members for various purposes, followed by expenditure on forest management, such as paying for the guard and community development activities. Expenditure on religious and social activities is also important in Nepal. Notably, the funds are not used for the particular problems women face, such as persistent firewood shortages. Basically, domestic fuel is seen as a private concern and not as a community responsibility. And women's presence on the EC is not enough to shift this perception in a way that would lead CFIs to allocate some of the funds for alleviating these shortages.

5.6 Conflicts

Collective action around the range of CFI activities described above can also lead to conflicts. Some conflicts are implicit, such as those embedded in class and gender relations, while others can be explicit, such as rule violations by villagers or outsiders, within-village disagreements over the sharing of forest products, encroachments on forest land for cultivation, free riding in labour contribution during forest cleaning and cutback operations, a misspending of community funds by CFI office bearers, and inter-village disputes over the forest boundary. Typically in Gujarat I found that villagers (especially men) were often hesitant to report *intra*-village conflicts to an outside researcher such as myself, out of loyalty toward fellow villagers, but *inter*-village conflicts were described readily. Women, however, were usually more open and trusting even about intra-village conflicts. I give below a flavour of the conflicts.

Conflicts over the distribution of forest products were more commonly reported in Nepal, than in Gujarat. Consider these examples:

> It happened about four years back. We were involved in a forest clearing operation. The forest was divided into five plots. The members who had participated in plot no 3 quarrelled during firewood distribution, because some of them had hidden a few bundles. The issue reached the EC. Those who had hidden the firewood were identified and the firewood seized. Some members wanted to terminate their CFI membership, but we decided on a lesser punishment and simply refused to give the offenders any firewood that year. (Balju Kang CFI, Gorkha, Nepal, author's survey, 2000–01)

> Initially we used to call the members for a forest clearing operation and would allow those who came, including hired labourers, to take the harvested wood. But some members were unhappy with this system and said that the firewood should be distributed equally among the member households. So we will change the system and distribute firewood only to members for a small fee. (Bhangeri Mahila CFI, Gorkha, Nepal, author's survey 2000–01)

A related conflict was over labour contributions:

> We had a small conflict about labour contributions to harvest thatch grass. Some member households did not provide labour. Those who did wanted to exclude the shirkers from

using the fund generated from the grass. We are still discussing the matter. (Kalika Dhoden CFI, Dhading, Nepal, author's survey, 2000–01)

Similarly, in both Gujarat and Nepal, but especially in the latter, conflicts over misuse of funds are not uncommon. Two cases are illustrative. The first case concerns the non-transfer of funds from one EC to another.

The previous EC has not handed over the community fund of over NRs. 8,000 to the new EC. Basically the chairman of the previous EC did not want to leave his post, but the villagers did not like him and terminated his position in an emergency meeting. He was angry and refused to hand over the fund. We are trying to resolve this. (Balju Kang CFI, Gorkha, Nepal, author's survey, 2000–01)

The second case relates to a conflict over fund use between an all-women and an all-male CFI:

It happened between Gairi Khola all-women's group which had a community fund in a joint account with an all-male CFI. The conflict between women and men members developed because the all-male EC overdrew the money and spent it on constructing a community building without the consent of the all-women EC. The conflict has yet to be resolved. (Gairi Khola CFI, Gorkha, Nepal, author's survey, 2000–01)

Overall, boundary disputes are not common, and where they do occur they tend to be more in the Nepal sites than in Gujarat, possibly because in the latter community forests are administratively allocated to particular villages. Sometimes such disputes are settled through discussion with representatives from the disputing villages or CFIs, but often boundary disputes remain unsettled for long periods. A case each from Gujarat and Nepal is illustrative:

At present we have conflict with Bhudrasan village over our forest area limit which we are sure we will win. We have a map that says that the forest range we are protecting belongs to our village. They are very adamant about their claims, but we have government documents in our favour. These people are pressing us to bow down but we will not do so. The conflict remains unresolved. VIKSAT and the forest department are helping us to resolve it. (Patiakua village, Sabarkantha, Gujarat, author's survey 2000–01)

The Tangrang VDC people are claiming a patch of our forest as their forest. Last year, they harvested the patch without informing us. Later, when we discovered this, we told them that it is our forest. We hope to solve the problem with the help of the District Forest Officer. (Dullav CFI, Gorkha, Nepal, author's survey, 2000–01)

Women play rather little role in conflict resolution in Gujarat but they are active in Nepal, speaking up and offering solutions, especially where there are several of them on the EC (Gai Odar CFI, Gorkha, Nepal, author's survey, 2000–01).

Yes, there are four women in the samiti now. And they also play a vital role in resolving conflicts. Once, the EC decided to sell ground grass because it was not sufficient to distribute among the 41 member households. The women opposed the decision, however, and the EC had to distribute the grass among the members.

5.7 Villagers and Forest Department

On many counts, but especially in settling major conflicts such as over forest boundaries, getting permission for forest cleaning operations, and harvesting the timber, the community's relationship with the forest department can prove key. Conversations with villagers in both Nepal and Gujarat indicated that relations with the forest department had improved notably since community forestry began. Moreover, in answer to a specific question posed to the Nepal ECs on whether their relationship with the department had improved, worsened, or remained the same, 80 per cent affirmed an improvement, and only a few expressed mixed feelings.[33] A sample of responses illustrates this:

> Our relationship is better than before. Earlier, we were very afraid of Rangers. When they came we were always worried that they had come to impose fines on us. Now they come to our house, talk in a friendly way and give very good suggestions about the forest. (Baglung CFI, Nepal, author's survey, 2000–01)

> It is a mixed relationship—sometimes better than before, at other times worse. For example, when the DFO invites us for training, or for a workshop or an exposure visit, we feel we have good relationship. But when the Ranger stops us from distributing timber without consulting the DFO, even to those who really need it, while letting contractors collect valuable herbal medicines and timber, we feel cheated. (Gorkha CFI, Nepal, author's survey, 2000–01)

> When the forest was under the government's control we were always afraid of being caught and fined by Rangers. Nowadays they are helping us and are friendlier. (Baglung CFI, Nepal, author's survey, 2000–01)

Moreover, 95 per cent of the Gujarat CFI members and 88 per cent of the Nepal CFI members said that the forest they were protecting was like their own, and most of the rest said that they and the forest department co-owned it. All this portends well for institutional sustainability and forest conservation.

6. CONCLUDING COMMENTS

In this chapter I have given a profile of the study regions, the sample selection process, the factors (non-systematic) underlying the EC's gender composition, the CFI governance structure, and how the CFIs function in the study sites. This provides a background to the empirical analysis that follows. Additionally, protection and monitoring, formulating appropriate rules for forest use and methods of benefit distribution, and the setting in place of graduated penalties for rule violation and mechanisms for conflict resolution, are all significant elements of the conditions identified by Ostrom (1990: 90) and others for building

[33] Similar data were not collected for Gujarat. To avoid any potential tension with the forest department, I have not given the names of the Nepal CFIs in these quotations.

long-enduring institutions for governing the commons.[34] Ostrom (1990) also emphasizes participative methods of making and implementing rules, and of prescribing penalties and resolving conflicts with the full involvement of the forest users. Empirically, however, this literature, with its focus on household-level analysis, does not grapple with the potential negative impact of *women's* non-participation in institutional functioning on the sustainability of CPR governance and its outcomes.

In the chapters that follow I empirically examine the impact of women's proportionate presence in the EC on five aspects: their effective participation in CFI decision-making, the nature of rules framed by the CFI, rule violations and penalties, the condition of the forest, and the incidence of firewood and fodder shortages. An understanding of these aspects is essential not only in the interests of environmental and institutional sustainability, but also because the outcomes can affect basic survival. As we were told, in village after village, in rather similar ways: 'We want our forest to improve because then our lives will also improve.'

[34] See, among others, Wade (1988), McKean (1986), Lam (1998) and the review in Baland and Platteau (1996).

APPENDIX 4.1

Details of Sample Selection

Details of the sample selection for both Nepal and Gujarat are given below. Nepal is discussed first since it had special features which propelled the sampling procedure. For uniformity, the same methodology was used for Gujarat.

1. NEPAL

The sample selection was done through a four-stage process. (i) Identification of appropriate districts (Nepal has no states, only districts); (ii) identification of safe and accessible VDCs within the districts; (iii) stratification of CFIs by a threefold EC gender composition, in the identified VDCs; and (iv) selection of the CFIs, using random sampling within each strata. The process is summarized in Table A4.1

District identification was subject to certain constraints. First, the districts had to have a reasonable number of CFIs in three mutually exclusive categories of EC gender composition: all-women ECs, ≤ 2 women ECs, and >2 women (but not all-women) ECs. The incidence of all-women CFIs—which are relatively rare—was used as the initial identification criterion. Second, districts and VDCs had to be safe and physically accessible (some districts were inaccessible due to the Maoist insurgency, or difficult physical terrain, or remoteness of location). Third, CFIs had to be active and should have been formed at least a year before selection, so that their impact on forest condition and institutional functioning could be studied.

CFIs were identified initially from three districts—Baglung, Parbat, and Gorkha, with Baglung and Parbat being clubbed together to provide an adequate CFI population in each category. The CFIs that were safe and accessible and had been active for at least a year constituted the universe. This came to 367 CFIs in Baglung/Parbat and 226 in Gorkha. After stratifying them into the three gender composition categories, a simple random sample (without replacement) of 12 CFIs was taken from each category for Baglung/Parbat jointly and for Gorkha on its own. Later, the changing security scenario and high Maoist presence in the upper hills of Gorkha rendered four initially selected CFIs inaccessible, and these were substituted by those of the same gender composition set, but located in Dhading district, in a VDC adjacent to Gorkha's lower boundary and with a similar topography. In Baglung/Parbat two cases had to be dropped altogether for want of appropriate substitutes. The total sample for Nepal came to 70. The sampling fractions came to 16 per cent and 9 per cent of the CFI populations of Gorkha/Dhading and Baglung/Parbat respectively, and 12 per cent overall.

In the above sample selection, I deviated from the standard method of making the sample size for each stratum proportional to its occurrence in the population, and used instead equal allocation of 12 CFIs from each stratum, implying disproportionate sampling. A disproportionate sample is often used when a stratum constitutes a very small

Table A4.1. Nepal: region identification and sample selection

Stages of identification	Total	Identified/selected	Reason
Districts	75 districts	3 districts identified	Out of Nepal's 75 districts only 10 had $\geq$12 all-women CFIs. Of these 5 were unsafe or physically remote. Of the remaining 5, 3 districts were identified: Baglung, Parbat and Gorkha. Baglung and Parbat were contiguous, had similar ecology and an international donor working on forestry in both. But each had only 14 all-women CFIs so they were clubbed for CFI selection. Gorkha had 42 all-women CFIs, so it was taken separately.
VDCs (in accessible districts)			Within identified districts some VDCs were inaccessible due to Maoist insurgency. These were not included in the population sampled.
CFIs in accessible VDCs	367 CFIs in Baglung / Parbat were clubbed	The total CFIs were divided into 3 strata by gender composition. From each stratum 12 CFIs were drawn, using simple random sampling without replacement (SRSWOR).	36 CFIs were initially selected. Later, two could not be completed because of the declaration of national emergency in Nepal. The final sample for Baglung/Parbat consisted of 34 CFIs.
	226 CFIs in Gorkha	Same as above: The total CFIs were divided into 3 strata by gender composition. From each stratum 12 CFIs were drawn, using SRSWOR.	36 CFIs were initially selected for Gorkha, but 4 had to be replaced due to security problems. For this purpose, a VDC in adjacent Dhading district was taken, and in it 4 replacement CFIs with the same gender composition as those dropped from Gorkha were chosen. The final sample for Gorkha/Dhading consisted of 36 CFIs.
	Total sample: 70 CFIs (See also Tables 4.4 and 4.10 in main text).		

percentage of the universe and proportionate sampling cannot produce sufficient numbers in that group for detailed statistical analysis,[35] as was the case for the all-women CFIs in Nepal. Time and cost constraints impinged on limiting the number to 12 CFIs in each stratum.

2. GUJARAT

The Gujarat sample selection involved a three-stage process: (i) Identification of appropriate districts; (ii) identification of active CFIs and dividing them into two strata by EC gender composition; and (iii) selecting the CFIs using stratified random sampling within each strata. The process is summarized in Table A4.2 below.

The districts identified needed to have information on the gender composition of ECs, and (as in the case of Nepal) the CFIs had to be active at the time of selection, and to have been formed at least a year prior to selection. The CFIs were divided into two mutually exclusive categories (strata) of ECs: $\leq$2 women and >2 women, since Gujarat has hardly any CFIs with all-women ECs. Within each stratum, given time and cost constraints, the planned sample, as in the case of Nepal, was restricted to 12 CFIs per stratum in each of the

Table A4.2. Gujarat: region identification and sample selection

Stages of identification	Total	Identified/selected	Comment and final sample size
Districts	3 districts	3 districts	These had baseline data through NGOs working on community forestry in the state.
CFIs in Narmada/ Bharuch	16 CFIs	All 16 CFIs	Final sample for Narmada/Bharuch consisted of 16 CFIs.
CFIs in Panchmahals	43 CFIs	The total CFIs were divided into 2 strata, by gender composition. From each stratum 12 CFIs were drawn, using SRSWOR.	24 CFIs were initially selected, but two CFIs were found to be inactive, and two had a common EC. Final sample consisted of 21 CFIs.
CFIs in Sabarkantha	45 CFIs	The total CFIs were divided into 2 strata and 14 CFIs were drawn from each, using SRSWOR.	Final sample consisted of 28 CFIs.
		Total sample: 65 CFIs (see also Tables 4.3 and 4.9 in main text)	

[35] See e.g. Cargan (2007: 241) and Pedhazur and Schmelkin (1991: 333). Disproportionate sampling is also used in World Health Surveys (see www.who.int/entity/healthinfo/survey/whssampling-guidelines.pdf). See also Walker et al. (1990: ch. 2) on fixed sample size allocations where there is under-representation of certain categories of the population, as was done in the ICRISAT village data collection in India—a data set that has been used widely by economists in many countries.

three districts. This meant identifying 24 CFIs in each study district, making for a total of 72. In practice the sample turned out to be somewhat smaller, as explained below.

Of Gujarat's three study districts, the NGO AKRSP(I) in Narmada/Bharuch was found to have an active community forestry programme in only 16 sites at the time of the survey. I selected all of them for the study. In Panchmahals and Sabarkantha there were 43 and 45 NGO-associated active CFIs. In each district, the CFIs were divided into two mutually exclusive stratums of $\leq$2 EC women and >2 EC women. In Panchmahals, from each stratum, 12 CFIs each were randomly selected, making a total of 24. Later, two CFIs were found to be inactive due to internal conflicts, and two contiguous forestry sites had a combined governance structure and so were consolidated into one. This gave a total sample of 21 CFIs for Panchmahals. In Sabarkantha, to make up (at least in part) for the smaller Narmada/Bharuch sample, 14 (rather than 12) CFIs were selected through random sampling from each of the two strata. Of these, at the time of the actual survey, two were found to have shifted from $\leq$2 women to >2 women, giving the district-wise sample sizes of 16, 21, and 28, and a total sample of 65. The sampling fractions came to 100 per cent, 49 per cent, and 62 per cent for Narmada/Bharuch, Panchmahals, and Sabarkantha respectively, and 62 per cent overall. In the sampling, for uniformity with Nepal, I used the same methodology of equal allocations within each stratum for Gujarat as well.

APPENDIX 4.2
Details of Data Collected

Sources, methods used, and data description

1. ***Source***: Executive Committee (EC) questionnaire (for both Gujarat and Nepal)
   Method used: Group interview/discussion with Executive Committee members
   Data collected

   - Characteristics of each member: name of EC member, sex, age, marital status, education, land owned, caste, whether or not he/she is an office bearer. These characteristics were obtained for the EC operating at the time of the survey, and in the year the CFI was formalized, plus for whatever years in between that information was available.
   - Characteristics of the general body: number of members (by sex if available) and caste groupings.
   - History of CFI formation, why, when, and who initiated it; when was protection started; how was the CFI formalized, etc.
   - Forest protected: total area, plantation area, condition now (extent degraded, canopy cover, age, main species), and change in condition since the CFI was formed.
   - Participation in EC meetings, separately for male and female EC members: attendance and speaking up in meetings; reason for non-attendance or not speaking up; difficulties faced in attending; potential advantages of having more women in the EC including impact on attendance and speaking up; whether and how information on EC decisions was shared with villagers; impact of being an EC member on her/his social status, etc.
   - CFI functioning: activities undertaken; main decision-makers for given activities (EC, GB, both, other); protection method at the time of CFI formation, changes therein and reason for change; women's participation in protection.
   - Forest use: products taken from forest before protection began and at the time of CFI formation, and changes therein.
   - Rule-making: details of forest use rules by main forest products at the time of CFI formalization; whether forest opened for extraction (frequency of opening, and items extracted, etc.); who made the rules? Changes in rules since the CFI was formed and why.
   - Product distribution: distribution method used for items extracted, in particular for firewood, fodder, and timber.
   - Penalties specified for rule violation; details of actual violations, and penalties given in practice.
   - Women EC members: main cooking fuel used; sources of firewood used; whether shortages faced for firewood and fodder; difficulties due to shortages and coping strategies.
   - Fee charged for CFI membership.
   - Community fund: sources, amounts, and uses.
   - Gender differences in preferences of forest species.
   - Forest/CFI related conflicts: details of conflicts, how resolved, and women's role in resolving them.
   - Views on sustainability of CFI and on forest conservation, relationship with forest department, etc.

2. ***Source:*** EC questionnaire (for both Gujarat and Nepal).
   Method used: Information obtained from written records kept by the secretary of the EC.
   Data collected: Details of EC and GB meetings held: date, attendance by gender, issues discussed.

3. ***Source***: EC questionnaire (for Gujarat and Nepal).
   Method used: Group interviews with the EC members.
   Data collected (for Gujarat only): Details about village: Distance of village from nearest town and motorable road; village infrastructure: health centre, educational institution, electrification, number and location of hamlets, presence of women's associations in the village.
   Data collected (for Nepal only): Total members in CFI, membership in another CFI, presence of women's associations in the CFI toles.
4. ***Source***: Two village-level questionnaires, one for male villagers, the other for female villagers (for Gujarat only).
   Method used: Focus group discussion with male and female villagers in separate groups.
   Data collected: Assessment of forest condition when protection began; participation in choosing the species planted; main cooking fuels used; sources of firewood; firewood shortages faced before CFI formed and at the time of the survey, difficulties experienced, and coping strategies. Similarly whether fodder and timber shortages were experienced, difficulties faced, and coping strategies. How many are members of CFI? Difficulties faced in attending and speaking up in EC and GB meetings; benefits of women's membership in EC or GB; participation in protection; awareness of protection methods, forest use rules, penalties for rule violation, benefit sharing methods, community fund, etc. Details of rule violation (who violates, catches intruders, actual cases of violation) and details of penalties prescribed and given; CFI conflicts and how resolved. Membership in a women's association or savings group, perception of costs and benefits of CFI, and additional qualitative follow-up questions.
5. ***Source***: Villagers of specially disadvantaged community if any (for Gujarat only).
   Method used: Focus group discussion with members of the disadvantaged community.
   Data collected: Membership in CFI, participation in GB meetings, main sources of cooking fuel used, firewood and fodder shortages experienced, and coping strategies before and after CFI formed, benefits received from CFI, problems faced due to forest closure, rule violations, participation in other village activities.
6. ***Source***: Two tole-level questionnaires fielded in one major tole, one with male members, one with female members (for Nepal only).
   Method used: Focus group discussions with male and female tole members (in separate groups) in the tole selected.
   Data collected: History of CFI formation; socio-economic details about tole members (caste composition, migrant households, main occupations, land ownership pattern); infrastructure in tole (education and health facilities, electrification); sources of main forest products used before and after CFI formed; preferred tree species and participation in choosing species for planting; details of cooking fuel used and sources before and after CFI formed; whether facing firewood, fodder, or small timber shortages, difficulties due to any shortages and coping strategies; participation in GB meetings; forest protection methods used; gender differences in knowledge of forest; awareness of forest use rules and penalties, of forest products distributed and methods of distribution, and of penalties prescribed; details of actual rule violations and penalties given; CFI related conflicts and how resolved; perceived costs and benefits of CFI; any additional follow-up qualitative questions by context.
7. ***Source***: Village-level questionnaire (for Gujarat only).
   Method used: Census for each household by educated villager.
   Data collected: Land owned, caste group, whether the household has a migrant male.
8. ***Source***: Village-level maps (for Gujarat only).
   Method used: Map (not to scale) drawn by a person employed through the local NGO and its accuracy verified by the NGO and elderly villagers.
   Data collected: Maps showing location of forest segments, hamlets, road, gullies, etc.

(*continued*)

9. ***Source***: Key informant questionnaire (Gujarat and Nepal).
   Method used: Individual-level interviews in each CFI with one former male and one former female EC member of different households.
   Data collected: Position held in EC; demographic and socio-economic details of informant; attendance and speaking up in EC meetings as a member and problems faced; participation in CFI activities; use of forest by product and purpose; cooking fuel used, problems faced due to firewood shortages and coping strategies; awareness of forest use rules and penalties prescribed; knowledge of actual rules broken, by whom and for what; impact of being an EC member on household and community relationships; membership in other groups; views on whether the CFI and the forest will be sustainable; any additional follow-up qualitative questions by context.
10. ***Source***: Household-level survey for members and non-members (Gujarat and Nepal).
    Method used: Individual-level interviews with household head and spouse in 150 households in Gujarat and 108 in Nepal (in each case divided into member and non-member households).
    Data collected: Similar to key informant survey.
11. ***Source***: Forest department questionnaire (for Nepal only).
    Method used: Filled by a forest officer, based on written records, except for the officer's assessment of forest condition at the time of the survey.
    Data collected: Information on when CFI formalized; number of toles from which members come; details of CFI members, such as their number and caste composition; forest handed over in terms of area, age, main species, canopy cover, overall condition, plantation area; details of micro-plan and constitution.
12. ***Source***: Village-level forest survey by researcher (for Gujarat only).
    Method used: A visit by one member of the research team with a degree in forestry to each forest in the Gujarat sample to assess the state of the forest. Different parts of the forest were visited, notes taken, and an overall assessment rank given, based on the information collected.
    Data collected: Information on forest condition by visual assessment of the height and girth of trees, density of forest cover, signs of regeneration, signs of cutting and other damage, evidence of regeneration, and so on.

Note: During focus group discussions, the researchers took detailed notes and also taped some parts, if the villagers had no objection. The questionnaires were filled later, based on the notes and tapes. This allowed the discussion to flow uninterrupted and also allowed the researchers to ask clarificatory or context-specific follow-up questions not included in the questionnaire. With two researchers per team, one could conduct the discussion and the other could take notes, interchangeably.

APPENDIX 4.3

Main Plant Species in Sample Sites

GUJARAT

Narmada/Bharuch	**Panchamahals**	**Sabarkantha**
	Aawal (Cassia aurintifolia)	
Bamboo (Dendrocalamus strictus)	Bamboo	Bamboo Dhavad (Anogeissus Latifolia), Dhove
Khair (Acacia catechu), Khakra (Butea monosperma)	Kada (Holarrhena antidysenterica or Wrightia Tinctoria), Khair, Khakra	Kada, Khair
	Mahua (Madhuca indica)	Mahua Nilgiri (Eucalyptus globulus Labill.)
Sesum (Dalbergia latifolia)	Sadad (Terminalia tomentosa)	
Teak (Tectona grandis)	Teak, Timru (Diospryos melanoxylon)	Teak, Timru Umbio

NEPAL

Gorkha/Dhading	**Baglung/Parbat**
Amala (Emblica officinalis), Angeri (Lyonia Ovalifolia) Badkaulo, Bardhairo, Bakaino (Melia azedarach), Bhalayo (Semecarpus anacardium) Bhanj (Q. lanata), Barro (Terminalia bellirica), Bilaune (Maesa chisia); Buddhangero	Amala, Ainselu (Rubus sp.), Angeri Bhanj, Barro, Bhalayo, Buddhangero
Chilaune (Schima Walichii); Chiuri (Bassia butyracea)	Champ (Hemiltonia suaveolens); Chilaune, Chiuri, Chutro (Berberis aristata Dc); Chaplaya, Chautari Dabdabe (Garuga pinnata), Dar (Boehmeria regulusa), Dudhilo (Prunus cerasoides); Dhairo (Woodfordia fruticsa), Dhalne, Dhursal (Colebrookea oppositifola L), Dhuyekath
Gurans (Rhododendron)	Gurans
Harro (Terminalia chebula)	Harro
Jhingane (Eurya acuminata); Jamun (Syzygium cumini)	Jhingane
Kafal (Myrica esculenta), Kalikath (Symplocos pyrifolia) (Myrsine capitellata); Kangyo (Grevillea Robusta); Khasru (Quercus semecarpifolia); Katus (Castanopsis indica); Khayer (Acacia catechu); Kyamuna (Careya Arborea), Khallu	Kalikath, Katus, Khasru, Koirala (Bauhenic variegata), Khallu
Lankuri (Fraxinus floribunda)	Lankuri, Laligurans (Rhododendron arboretum)
Mahua (Madhuca indica)	Mahua Nigalo (Arundinaria falcate) Okhar (walnut, Juglans regia)
Padake (Albizia lucidior), Padkeulo; Putalikath (Cosmos sulphureus)	Painyu (Prunus cerasoides); Phirphere
Saaj (Terminalia Alata); Sal (Shoria Robusta); Salla (Pinus roxburghii); Sisso (Dalbergia latifolia)	Saaj, Sal, Salla, Sisso
Thakal (Argemone Mexicana)	Timur (Zanthoxylum armatum)

Note: The biological names of species are given in brackets, where identifiable.
Source: Author's survey, 2000–01.

5

From Exclusion to Empowered Engagement

> If we were to attend meetings, the men will say, oh you haven't cooked my meal on time. What happened to my tea? . . . Why haven't you fed the cattle? Men make a big fuss about every small thing; so we are afraid when it comes to going out of the house for something that's not considered work.
>
> (EC women, Panchmua CFI, Panchmahals, Gujarat, author's survey, 2000–01)

> Women protect women—with more women, things would be better. The numbers here are too small to make a big difference.
>
> (Woman legislator in the USA, Thomas 1994: 102)

> Men and women should be equally represented in the samiti [EC]. Then it would make it easier for us to speak, to participate in decision-making and to get decisions implemented in favour of women. The population of male and female is almost equal in our village.
>
> (EC women, Jana Chetna CFI, Baglung, Nepal, author's survey, 2000–01)

The women of Nepal's Jana Chetna CFI, in one clear statement (above), provide some of the key reasons for enhancing women's presence in public decision-making. They argue the case not only on grounds of equity and justice but also for the potential impact on decisions made and implemented. Most importantly, they highlight how increasing women's proportionate strength would enhance their ability to participate actively in the decision-making process itself, rather than remaining simply nominal members of the decision-making body. Yet empirically we know rather little about this critical intermediate step, namely the link between women's proportional strength in a forum and their active participation in it.

Indeed there is a curious divide between two notable bodies of work on women's participation. On the one hand we have the gender and green governance literature which focuses largely on women's participation in local institutions in developing countries, and the factors (especially cultural) underlying women's limited presence and voice.[1] Notwithstanding their insights, the focus of these studies on women's relative exclusion misses the potential impact of

[1] For an illustrative listing of the studies, see Chapter 1 n. 58 in this volume.

women's greater inclusion on their participation. On the other hand, we have the gender and politics literature which concentrates largely on the impact of increasing women's strength in legislatures on the type of legislative change they tend to bring about. This misses the in-between process, namely how their greater numbers might empower women to participate more effectively. Understanding this process appears to be important even in western contexts, as the few studies that have examined it demonstrate. Flammang (1985), for instance, in her study of women county supervisors in California found that women were more likely to speak out and pursue their goals when more women were present,[2] while Dahlerup (1988) noted that the timings of meetings began to be adjusted to women's convenience, and discussions became less aggressive in tone, when women constituted one-third of the Scandinavian legislators. In the context of local green governance, however, understanding the process of women's participation is of particular importance, since women's effective involvement (such as by attending meetings and speaking up at them) is a necessary initial step for them to influence institutional outcomes. And we need to identify not only the constraints but also the conditions under which, despite the constraints, women can assert their presence.

One of the factors which many argue would make women more effective in public forums is their proportionate strength in the forum—the greater their presence the more their effectiveness. A closely related discussion is that on critical mass—a threshold presence which is argued to help women move from being nominal to effective participants. There is no consensus, however, on what constitutes a threshold level. As elaborated in Chapter 1, Kanter (1977a, 1977b) does not provide a specific figure, but argues that 15 per cent would constitute merely a 'token' presence while 40–50 per cent could prove more effective. Many other writers—mostly focused on western legislators—also place the percentage variously between 15 and 50. In the context of US legislators, for instance, some mention 15 per cent (Saint-Germain 1989), others 25 per cent (Carroll and Taylor 1989), and yet others 50 per cent (Thomas 1994). Thomas stresses that even 25–30 per cent is not enough for women legislators to influence overall policies and a figure closer to parity might be needed. Similarly, Lovenduski (1997: 718) argues for 20 per cent from her research on the British House of Commons, while Bratton and Ray (2002) and Dahlerup (1988)—the former empirically the latter discursively—emphasize 30 per cent for women in Nordic countries. Although

[2] See also Thomas' (1994) discussion on US women legislations, as well as her detailed interpretation of Flammang's study. On the latter, Thomas (1994: 89) points out that having female majorities among supervisors in Santa Clara county (California) in the early 1980s had two effects: One, 'the presence of supportive colleagues (other women) encouraged female representatives to speak out and participate in the process rather than exhibit the reticence to which they might otherwise have resorted'. Two, the women on the board felt freer to pursue issues which they might not have pursued in other circumstances, out of fear that their choices would be considered deviant or that they would be poorly supported.

empirical verification of effective proportions is, to date, rather limited,[3] among policy-makers and practitioners globally it is the figure of one-third that has become widely accepted as *the* critical mass.

This debate on gender proportions in the gender and politics literature can be extended creatively to the question of women's participation in local forest governance in ways that has not been done so far. Long-standing assumptions and propositions about women's participation in local institutions also need more rigorous empirical testing.[4] In this chapter I examine the factors that disable and enable women's effective participation in the decision-making process, using both qualitative evidence and quantitative analysis. In doing so, I also seek to throw light on the contested issue of critical mass, although, as will be seen, empirically identifying a critical mass effect is far from easy.

I begin with a typology of participation and then describe women's involvement in CFI functioning and outline the obstacles that can constrain that involvement. It is striking how many of these obstacles are common across contexts. I then empirically analyse what underlies the extent of women's participation in CFI decision-making as measured by women attending meetings, speaking up in them, and holding office. In particular, does having more women on the EC enhance their attendance and voice? And is there a proportionate presence which is especially effective? Also what role do other factors play in helping women overcome social constraints, such as support from external agents, personal attributes (education level, age, leadership qualities, and so on), or compelling circumstances.

1. PARTICIPATORY EXCLUSIONS

1.1 A Typology

Participation in decision-making is a complex concept. Definitions of participation differ, as do views on whom it is expected to involve, what it is expected to

[3] Exceptions include Studlar and McAllister (2002) and Bratton and Ray (2002). For many scholars, data constraints limit empirical testing (see e.g. Thomas 1994; and discussions in Schwindt-Bayer and Mishler 2005, and Goetz 2008).

[4] Most existing studies on gender and natural resource management, when providing statistics (and not all do), rarely go beyond cross-tabulations. The few scholars who have sought to statistically test the effect of gender (variously defined) on natural resource management by controlling for other factors have focused on the impact on project performance, and not on the process of women's participation itself. Prokopy (2004), although in the context of water management, does measure women's attendance at committee meetings, but not whether women's numbers affect that attendance. She tests the effect of women's participation on the effectiveness of rural water supply projects and finds none.

achieve, and how it is to be brought about.[5] At its narrowest, participation in a group is defined in terms of nominal membership (e.g. Chopra et al. 1990, Molinas 1998), and at its broadest in terms of a dynamic interactive process in which the disadvantaged have voice and influence in decision-making (e.g. Narayan 1996, White 1996). In terms of objectives, at its narrowest participation is judged almost entirely by its potential efficiency effects and at its broadest by its ability to enhance equity, efficiency, empowerment, and environmental sustainability (Uphoff 1991). In other words, participation can have a range of levels.

Community forestry institutions provide a rich basis for examining all these facets of participation and the extent to which they are fulfilled. Although meant to operate on democratic principles and to involve and benefit all sections of the community, effectively such institutions can exclude significant sections, especially women.[6] These 'participatory exclusions' can, in turn, have a negative effect on both equity and efficiency outcomes. Methods of exclusion, however, can range from the obvious, such as exclusion from formal membership of a group, to the subtle, such as exclusion based on social norms which silence voice. A person's ability to be effective in a public forum requires *both* presence and voice, and the former does not guarantee the latter.

In the typology given in Table 5.1, achieving effective participation would involve a shift from the lower to the higher levels, with levels being defined by how active its members are. This is unlike some earlier typologies, where, for instance, self-initiated activity is seen as the highest level of participation. In fact

Table 5.1. Typology of participation[a]

Form/level of participation	Characteristic features
Nominal participation	Membership in the group.
Passive participation	Being informed of decisions *ex post facto*; or attending meetings and listening in on decision-making, without speaking up.
Consultative participation	Being asked an opinion in specific matters without guarantee of influencing decisions.
Activity-specific participation	Being asked to (or volunteering to) undertake specific tasks.
Active participation	Expressing opinions, whether or not solicited, or taking initiatives of other sorts.
Interactive (empowering) participation	Having voice and influence in the group's decisions; holding positions as office bearers

Note: [a] This is a modified version of the typology presented in Agarwal (2001).

[5] See, among others, Bagadion and Korten (1991), Cernea (1991), Chopra et al. (1990), Cohen and Uphoff (1977), Isham et al. (1995), Michener (1998), Molinas (1998), Narayan (1996), Paul (1987), Pretty (1995), Uphoff (1991), and White (1996).

[6] Similar issues can arise in participatory research on natural resource management where participant selection from among the community can itself be gender inequitable, and the level of collaboration with local NGOs can range from contractual to collegial (see Johnson et al.'s 2004 review of fifty-nine such projects in developing countries).

not all self-initiation need signify participatory success of the programme. A set of disadvantaged persons may, for instance, opt out of the main group where they have no voice, and set up their own group. But this exit option cannot compensate for their lack of voice within the main group, if the latter controls most of the resource.

What is the nature of women's participation in South Asia's CFIs? CFI functioning entails taking a wide range of decisions about rules and procedures and the responsibility for their implementation. The two tiers of a CFI's governance structure—the GB and EC—are jointly responsible for most of the decisions, through a process of deliberation. We noted in Chapter 4 that the EC is involved in virtually all the CFI decisions, some on its own, some in conjunction with the GB and the forest department. Even when the GB is said to decide issues on its own, the EC is a part of that GB and remains a core decision-making unit with considerable power. For women's concerns to be *effectively* represented the presence of women EC members is thus important. But equally, to be effective within the EC, women EC members need to attend meetings, speak up at them, hold office, and so on. In terms of my typology, they need to move from being absent or nominal members to being interactive (empowered) participants.

1.2 Facets of Women's Participation

Where are women currently placed in terms of effective participation in the CFIs? To answer this question, I first provide an overview, based mainly on my 1998–99 fieldwork in India and Nepal and case studies by others on these two regions, supplemented by my 2000–01 survey. This gives a broad regional picture that goes beyond the survey areas and highlights the widespread nature of gender exclusions and constraints. I then present the more in-depth quantitative analysis of how differing levels of gender inclusion may matter, based on my 2000–01 survey.

Nominal participation

With some exceptions, such as all-women groups, typically female participation in most CFIs is low. In India, in nominal terms, till the late 1990s, women generally constituted less than 10–15 per cent of the general bodies in most JFM groups.[7] Even in states such as Gujarat which had liberal membership specifications that allowed all adults to join the GB, the percentage of women in the GB was usually small; and even where NGOs were active the figure seldom reached parity with men. In recent years, with changes in JFM orders in some states, women's numbers could be expected to improve in the GB, but not uniformly across all states.

[7] Roy et al. (*c.*1992), Guhathakurta and Bhatia (1992), and Narain (1994); also my field visits 1998–99.

More importantly, women are sparsely represented in the ECs (again barring some exceptions). In 20 JFM groups studied in West Bengal, 60 per cent had no women in the EC, and only 8 per cent of the 180 EC members were women (Sarin 1998). Although, as detailed in Chapter 3, the JFM resolutions of most states require that the EC include some women, and the provisions have become increasingly women-inclusive over time, in practice there remains a wide gap in implementation. Also the women when included are often nominated not by other women as their representatives but by influential village men. Landless families, similarly, although present in most GBs are barely represented in the EC. In my 2000–01 sample as well, the landless are found to be poorly represented, with the notable exception of some CFIs in Panchmahals (Gujarat), where the local NGO made a particular effort to encourage their inclusion.

Occasionally this familiar pattern changes and we find ECs with several women and even all-women.[8] But they remain the exception. As noted in Chapter 2, around 2002 there were only 0.5 per cent all-women groups among the thousand or so JFM groups surveyed for me by the Madhya Pradesh forest department; and such groups constituted only 0.7 per cent of the 5,000 or so self-initiated groups surveyed by RCDC (2005) in Orissa (almost half of these groups were of all-men). Indeed, self-initiated groups and van panchayats have tended to be even more women exclusionary than the JFM groups.[9] A study of 50 van panchayats in the 1990s found that only 9 had any women (TERI 1995; see also Agrawal 2001).[10] Mixed-gender groups with a high female presence (say with 30 to 50 per cent women in the EC) are similarly uncommon, and are found only in selected pockets of India.[11]

In Nepal, similarly, in overall terms (not specific to this study's sample), women's presence in the general bodies of most CFIs remains sparse, although there is likely to have been some improvement since the early years of community forestry when there were hardly any women members. Dahal (1994: 78), for instance, had found that only 3.5 per cent of the CFI members in the cases he had studied in eastern Nepal were women. Other studies had noted that often those who joined were poorly informed of the group's activities; some were even

[8] See e.g. Correa (1997), Adhikari et al. (1991), Mansingh (1991), Regmi (1989), Singh and Burra (1993), and Raju (1997), and Chapter 4, this volume.

[9] For the self-initiated groups see Kant et al. (1991), Singh and Kumar (1993), and RCDC (2005), and for van panchayats, see Sharma and Sinha (1993), TERI (1995), and Agrawal (2001). My field visits in 1998–99 covering both kinds of groups also indicates this. It is possible that van panchayats are more women inclusive now, influenced by developments in other local institutions, but there are no figures to indicate to what extent.

[10] It is possible that van panchayats may now include more women (influenced by increasing numbers of women in the elected village councils) but there are no recent figures to confirm this.

[11] See e.g. Narain (1994) and Viegas and Menon (1993). My field visits in 1998–99 also indicate this, as does the 2003 census of Gujarat's CFIs (see Chapter 4 n. 8), although NGO intervention can make a difference.

unaware that they were members.[12] EC membership in Nepal is more women-inclusive than in Gujarat, but only to a degree. For example, taking the universe from which I chose my survey sample, only 55 per cent of the 367 CFIs in Baglung/Parbat and 40 per cent of the 226 CFIs in Gorkha had more than two women, which meant that a large proportion still had only two or fewer women. Moreover, as noted in chapter 4, in the country as a whole at that time, only 3.8 per cent of the CFIs had all-women ECs controlling as little as 1.1 per cent of CFI forest land (GoN 2000). In my data, I therefore specifically included all-women groups through disproportionate sampling.

ECs with a high female presence can arise from a complexity of factors. Those in my survey appear to have arisen as a result variously of historical, demographic, or locational specificities, interventions by NGOs or international donors, the presence of a gender-sensitive village leader, and so on (as elaborated in Chapter 4). In rare cases women had themselves initiated CFIs, either in areas where there were none,[13] or where, frustrated by their lack of voice in an existing male-dominant group, they decided to set up their own group on available forest land.[14] Although such initiatives are encouraging, CFIs formed by women as an exit option are an unsatisfactory solution to their exclusion from the male forums which still control most of the forest.

Passive participation

Without being members, women usually hear little of what transpires at GB or EC meetings; that is, they are not even passive participants. Women across the different regions characteristically complain that men do not inform them (see also Box 5.1):

> Typically men don't tell their wives what happens in meetings. Even if there is a dispute about something, they don't tell us; nor do they volunteer information about other matters. (Women to author, Khairpada village, Narmada, Gujarat, 1999)

> The men seldom inform us of discussions in meetings. When we ask them they say: 'why do you want to know?' If we were members we would be better informed. (Women to author, Jamai village, Madhya Pradesh, 1999)

Even among women who are GB or EC members, many remain absent from meetings, or attend irregularly. If they do attend many fail to speak up, and if they speak they report that their opinions usually carry little weight. Consider some characteristic responses:

> What is the point of going to meetings? We would only sit silently. (Women to author, Panasa village, Orissa, 1998)

[12] See e.g. Moffatt (1998), and periodic Reports of the Nepal-UK Community forestry programme, Kathmandu.

[13] See e.g. Adhikari et al. (1991), Singh (1993), Agarwal (1997a), and Chapter 4.

[14] Field observations in Orissa in 1998–99 and in Nepal during my survey in 2000–01 (see also Chapter 4).

Men don't listen, except perhaps one or two. Men feel they should be the spokespersons. (Woman to author, Garbe Kuna CFI, Kaski district, Nepal, 1998)

I attend van panchayat meetings, but I only sign, I don't say much. Or I say I agree. (Woman van panchayat member to author, Sallarautela village in the Uttarakhand hills, 1998)

Hence even those who are members often remain passive participants, far from the active or interactive level in my typology.

Consultative participation

Male CFI members and forest officials seldom consult or involve women when framing forest use rules or preparing micro-plans for forest development. Some women hear about the plans through their husbands, others not at all (Guhathakurta and Bhatia 1992, and my 2000–01 survey). Since women, as the main fuel and fodder collectors, often know more than men about the attributes of fuel and fodder trees (Chapter 2), a failure to consult them means that their existing knowledge of diverse species does not enrich forest regeneration programmes. At the same time, women have less chance of acquiring new knowledge, such as about new silviculture practices, since they are rarely part of the CFI teams that receive such training (Agarwal 2001). This is ironic, since involving women would help not only to draw upon their knowledge of ecological practices, but also to incorporate their tree preferences within plantation programmes, ensure that locally desired species are planted, and enhance their commitment to protecting them. Here social norms that exclude women become barriers to what would be in the best interests of forest conservation.

Activity-specific participation

Despite their limited presence in formal decision-making, however, women do get drawn into specific activities, especially protection. In formal terms, protection is typically done through a male guard or an all-male patrol group constituted by member households. Because of social norms and safety issues, female guards are rare (I found them only in Nepal), and only a small percentage of patrols have both sexes or women alone. Mixed patrols are more common in central and western India, and all-women patrols are more likely to be found in the hills of India and Nepal where women's outdoor work participation is high and where men migrate to towns in many households (Agarwal 2001, Buchy and Rai 2008).

Notwithstanding their limited formal role in many regions, women everywhere keep an informal lookout. Sometimes, building on their social networks and everyday forms of cooperation, they even form patrol groups parallel to men's because they feel men's patrolling is inadequate. Women are better able than men to dissuade other women from breaking the forest use rules, to catch female intruders, contribute to fighting forest fires, and so on. None of this, however, adds up to interactive participation.

Active and interactive participation

Limited nominal presence also reduces the prospects of women's interactive participation. The occasional cases of CFIs with a high or all-women presence, however, enable us to see (further below in this chapter) whether women are more active in such groups. In addition, there are examples of individual women with innate leadership qualities who speak up and swing decisions, and even become office bearers. Occasionally too, as noted above, a group of women initiates a CFI and runs it with success. But we cannot rest on these exceptions. If forestry institutions are to be fully participative and inclusive, it is important that women have an active presence not by exception but as a rule. What constrains women's effective participation?

2. CONSTRAINTS ON WOMEN'S EFFECTIVE PARTICIPATION

The obstacles to women's participation are complex and varied and I do not seek to quantify them here. Rather, culled from qualitative evidence I present below a broad view of the kinds of factors that tend to come into play, although all of them would not apply to all regions or contexts. Broadly, the barriers can be categorized as follows:

- Membership criteria defining who can join the GB and EC
- Social norms that define women's appropriate roles and behaviour
- Social perceptions regarding women's abilities
- Entrenched territorial claims of men
- The culture of public discourse
- Personal endowments and attributes (e.g. women's educational levels, property status, age, etc.)
- Household endowments and attributes (e.g. where women fall within structural hierarchies, such as of class and caste).

Membership criteria

The first hurdle can be the criteria for membership in the GB or EC of a CFI. In India, we have already seen that these criteria vary by state (Chapter 3). States which allow membership to only one person per household are the most exclusionary for women, since that one person is usually the male household head. States which allow one man and one woman per household to join are more inclusive, but still exclude other female adults living in the same households. The most inclusive are states that allow all adults to join—such states are few. In the EC again, while some states require that one-third of the members be women, others, such as Gujarat (until recently), merely specify that there should be *at least* two women (typically interpreted as a *maximum* of two). In Nepal, one set of criteria apply to the whole country, but membership is again on a household basis in the GB; and for the EC, although (as noted in Chapter 3) guidelines advise women's inclusion this is not mandatory and is not always followed.

In recent years, the formal membership criteria have moved toward greater inclusion of women and the poor in both India and Nepal. More Indian states, for example, now allow all villagers to join the GB. More also specify that one-third of the EC be women; and two states (Andhra Pradesh and Tamil Nadu) specify 50 per cent women (see Chapter 3). Several states mention the inclusion of the lower castes and the landless as well. But there are still states which have not moved forward on any of these counts, and retain the same criteria that they had formulated when issuing their first JFM orders almost two decades ago. Implementation of the changed membership criteria also remains weak, not least due to gaps in awareness about the changes even within forest departments, but especially at the village level.[15] Among many self-initiated groups (which lack formal membership rules), women are denied entry into the CFIs to even greater extent, due to long-standing conventions that traditionally excluded women from public decision-making forums.

Social norms

Where membership is not an obstacle, social norms can still circumscribe women in various ways. The gender division of labour is the most important and the most universal constraint. Rural women's responsibility for childcare, housework, and the collection of firewood and water, in addition to their share of agricultural work and cattle care, makes for high work burdens and time constraints. Men are reluctant to share not just domestic tasks but often even cattle care. This seriously restricts women's ability to attend lengthy meetings held at inconvenient times:

> There are problems in attending meetings since we need to cook and serve the evening meal. The meeting is long. We also have to feed the cattle. (Woman to author, Barde CFI in Karnataka, 1998)
>
> Women have a lot of problems. They can cut grass quickly, but who will give grass to the buffaloes if we come to a meeting? Women's work is a constraint. (Arti Shrestha, grassroots organizer, to author, Kaski district, Nepal, 1998)
>
> We want women to come to our meetings, but who will take care of the children? (Man to author, Bansur CFI in Karnataka, 1998)

[15] I found substantial awareness gaps during my fieldwork in 1998–99 in several states, and again in recent conversations during 2008–09 with forest department officials in some states. Inadequate dissemination of information about changes in guidelines has a long history. A study of nineteen West Bengal CFIs in the 1990s, for instance, found that even four years after the membership criterion was amended to allow women's inclusion in the GB along with their husbands, barely two-fifths of the members knew of the change (Raju 1997).

In the van panchayat villages that Mansingh (1991) studied, women's attendance thinned over time since, as most women said, they did not have time to 'sit around for [the] four hours that it took to have a meeting in the middle of the day'.

In my 2000–01 survey, the one factor which almost every group of women mentioned, when asked what would help them attend meetings, was someone sharing housework and childcare (see Boxes 5.1 and 5.2). In all-women groups, women often bring along small children to meetings. But in mixed-gender meetings men frown upon children's presence as distracting.

Box 5.1. Gujarat: EC women's perceptions about attending meetings

EC women's illustrative answers to the question: what would help you attend EC meetings regularly?

* * *

Kanjai CFI, Narmada

W1: If our work at home is shared by other family members, we would have more time for *mandali* meetings.
W2: We have to be informed on time about the meetings. Then we can go regularly.
W3: Our home routine is fixed. If there is a change in that we can attend regularly.

Chorimala CFI, Sabarkantha

Having more women in the EC will help. Also they need to tell us in advance and even consult us about the *mandali*'s activities.

Patedi CFI, Panchmahals

W1: If the meetings are held at a time when we are free from domestic work, that would help. The problem is that women are overburdened with housework in our village.
W2: If we neglect housework then our husbands will shout at us. In any case, we would have to do the work even if we attend meetings. So our work only piles up. If the men tell us that it is ok to let housework be, that will be encouraging.

Boriya CFI, Panchmahals

If we are informed in time, that would help. If there are more women that also would be good. If we had less housework we would have a lot more time for meetings.

Sabuti CFI, Narmada

W1: If we are informed regularly about the meetings we will attend more regularly.
W2: Usually we make it a point to attend meetings.

Charada CFI, Panchmahals

If women had more time and were informed in advance about the meeting, we would go. Often we are not informed about the meeting.

Siladari CFI, Sabarkantha

I attend most of the meetings. I am absent only if there is some urgent work.

Nansalai CFI, Panchmahals

W1: If they ask us when to have the meetings then we can tell them a convenient time.
W2: If the housework is reduced then we will have time to attend meetings.

(*continued*)

Box 5.1. (Continued)

Kunda CFI, Panchmahals

There is a lot of work in the house. Our husbands will not let us attend meetings if we neglect our work.

Navi vasahat CFI, Panchmahals

For us to attend the EC meetings more often the *mandali* has to become more regular. Also, if more people are involved, if the forest department gives us more benefits, then EC meetings will be attended regularly.

Panchmua CFI, Panchmahals

W1: A woman's work is never finished, so time is a problem.
W2: To run the house, both men and women have to work. So women will just have to find time to attend meetings if they are really interested.

Ramdev Na Muada CFI, Panchmahals

If more women were allowed to speak, if we had the opportunity to speak, we would attend.

Makroda CFI, Sabarkantha

We just have to organize our schedules a little better.

Note: The responses are based on focus group discussions with EC women. Although many women were present, usually only a few served as spokespersons.
Source: Author's survey, 2000–01.

Box 5.2. Nepal: EC women's perceptions about attending meetings

EC women's illustrative answers to the question: What would help you attend EC meetings regularly?

* * *

Chitradevi CFI, Gorkha

W1: Men should allow us to attend meetings. They must help us in household chores.
W2: My mother-in-law always gets angry with me when I attend meetings.

Dadhibari CFI, Baglung

I would attend meetings regularly if the meeting were not held early in the morning when I have to cook.

Ekin Dhara CFI, Baglung

W1: I am alone at home. My husband and son work outside the village. I have a *sasu* (mother-in-law) who is 84 years old. I have to look after her, in addition to all the housework and agricultural work. I like to come to meetings but I have too many problems at home to come regularly.
W2: I don't have that problem and I attend meetings regularly.

Gaderi Dhaireni CFI, Baglung

I would attend meetings more often if there were someone in my house to prepare meals, milk the buffaloes, clean the *goth* of dung, etc.

Ludi CFI, Gorkha

Without family support we can't attend meetings regularly. Lack of awareness is another problem. Village women need to understand the importance of a CFI.

Kanno Bhanchuwa CFI, Baglung

W1: In the beginning, men used to say—you are a woman, sit far way.
W2: It would be easier if there were more women.

Narabhir CFI, Gorkha

W1–W2: We can attend the meetings regularly if someone assists us in housework.

Siddha CFI, Gorkha

W1–W2: In our view, male members of the family should help us. If men took care of the children and cooked the food we would attend the meetings regularly. Also meetings should be held in the afternoon. That is the appropriate time for women; we cannot manage time in the morning.

Tarang Khola Judipakha CFI, Gorkha

W1: If our society and my family recognized me as a social worker, they would object less to my attending meetings.
W2: If society recognized men and women as equals, both would be free to attend meetings.
W3: I also think that men and women should have equal status in society so a woman can easily go to public places.

Bajani Pakho CFI, Baglung

Only women with grown-up children can attend regularly.

Bhadkhore CFI, Baglung

I do come to the meetings regularly. I will keep doing so unless I am ill.

Chamere CFI, Baglung

W1: If my husband did not shout at me and if he encouraged me I would participate in meetings and other activities.
W2: I would participate more if my children were grown up and my in-laws did not always question me when I went to the meeting (she is a young daughter-in-law who is also literate).

Majh Katera CFI, Baglung

The main thing is how interested someone is. If you are interested you attend the meeting.

Urleni CFI, Baglung

When we have to attend a meeting we cut fodder for our animals the day before and feed the animals before leaving the house for the meeting.

Jana Chetna CFI, Baglung

W1: It is in our self-interest to attend EC meetings.
W2: It would be easier for me to attend if meetings were held near my place.

Note: The responses are based on focus group discussions with EC women. Although many women were present, usually only a few served as spokespersons.
Source: Author's survey, 2000–01.

Social norms also tend to segregate village public space along gender lines. Spaces where men congregate (such as tea stalls and the marketplace) are spaces that women of 'good character' are expected to avoid or not loiter in (Agarwal

1994). Restrictions are fewer for older women, but never entirely absent. These notions carry over to formal village meetings. A fear of reputation loss or family reprimand makes many women uncomfortable with attending CFI meetings, unless the men explicitly invite them:

They don't call us, so we don't go. (Women to author, Roopkheda CFI in Madhya Pradesh, 1999)

The meetings are considered for men only. Women are never called. The men attend and their opinions or consent are taken as representative of the whole family—it's understood. (Woman in a van panchayat, Uttarakhand hills, cited in Britt 1993: 148)

Rural women and men can't sit together. But we convey our decisions to them. (Man to author, Chattipur CFI, Orissa, 1998)

Although some forms of gendering village space are no longer feasible, given the mandatory entry of women into elected village councils as a result of seat reservations, the ideology of segregated spaces persists in attitudes and expectations. In addition, gendered behavioural norms, whether internalized by women or imposed by threat of gossip, reprimand, or violence, restrict women in male-dominated CFIs in myriad ways, placing strictures on their visibility, mobility, and voice. Female seclusion norms are the most restricting. Although traditionally uncommon amongst hill, tribal, or ethnic communities where my current research is based, such norms (e.g. veiling) are now being adopted by many even within these communities (as in Gujarat) in imitation of upper-caste Hindu practices associated with high social status. More pervasive, however, is the social emphasis on self-effacement, shyness, and soft speech that many women imbibe even when they do not veil.

Gendered behavioural norms also create subtle hierarchies, such as by requiring women to sit on the floor while men, especially older ones, sit on cots or chairs. Even where everyone sits on a level, typically women (including EC members) sit on one side or at the back of the meeting space. This makes them less visible and effective in raising a point, while issues raised by male members who sit in front receive priority. Moreover, when senior family males are present, women hesitate in attending meetings, or speaking up at them, or opposing the men publicly. The hierarchy that marks 'respectful' family behaviour thus carries over into community spaces (see also Raju 1997 and Hobley 1990).

Women cannot speak in front of elderly male relatives, and they have to observe *purdah*. (EC women, Bhamri CFI, Panchmahals, Gujarat, author's survey, 2000–01)

Even if women attend meetings, they cannot voice their opinions; they cannot speak against the opinions of their seniors. When the men have finished speaking that is the end of the meeting. (Satibama, Nepal, cited in Hobley 1990: 309)

We wonder when we speak whether we have said the right thing. We are afraid that men might complain that what we say is irrelevant. (Women in Namunadas Mahabir CFI, Parbat, Nepal, author's survey, 2000–01)

The collective action literature has typically emphasized the enabling positive side of social norms, but from women's viewpoint these examples reflect the disabling 'dark side' of gendered social norms.

Social perceptions

There is, not uncommonly, a divergence between what a person actually contributes or is able to do, and perceptions about her contributions and abilities. Incorrect perceptions about women's abilities are reflected in men's reluctance or ambiguity toward including women. Men often view women's involvement in CFIs as serving no useful purpose and tend to downplay their potential contribution. During my field discussions with mixed groups, for instance, when men answered my questions women would listen attentively and keep the children quiet. But when I spoke with the women, the men would smile, implying: Why ask her, what does she know? On my persisting, they would begin chatting among themselves, or interrupt the women and answer questions on their behalf, or just get up and leave.

Equally indicative of men's perceptions are some of their direct responses:

> Calling all the women to the meeting just hampers the work of the agenda . . . It is true that women are the real users of the forest but our women have not yet participated in the meetings. They don't know much, they don't give solid opinions. I am a man, I attend the meeting. If I am prepared to make the female members of my family act according to what I say, why should they attend the meeting? (Male respondent in Nepal, cited in Hobley 1990: 310)

> Women can't make any helpful suggestions. (Village male to author, Arjunpur village, Orissa, 1998)

> Women are illiterate. If they come to meetings, we men might as well stay at home. (EC chairman to author, Ghusra CFI, Dang district, Nepal, 1998)

In some cases I asked the men who justified women's exclusion on the ground that women were illiterate, whether they themselves were literate. It turned out that many were not!

Illiteracy can be debilitating for both sexes, but the association of illiteracy mainly with women in people's minds (clearly a perception bias), and women's internalization of 'illiteracy as a disability' (Buch 1999: 182), compounds their disadvantage. More generally, women's capabilities and contributions in CFIs tend to be discounted not only by village men but also often by male forest officials. This was especially the case in the early years of JFM. In West Bengal, for instance, women complained to Narain (1994) that male officials discouraged them from coming to the forest office, and rebuked them if they came in the evening. Roy et al. (1993: 15–16) similarly note that 'the forest officers put very little value on what [women] say and always crosscheck with the men to verify the truth of [women's] words'. Since the forest service staff is also largely male (Narain 1994), lines of authority and gender overlap here, although in recent years the gender sensitization of forest officials has diluted their gender bias and cases of officials advocating women's inclusion have been growing. Some village men readily admit that they included two women on the EC because of the forest department's intervention, rather than because they thought women might make a valuable contribution: 'There is no advantage in having women in the EC. We have been told by the forest officials that we must have two women in the committee, that is why we have included them' (male EC member to author, Pathari CFI, Karnataka, 1998). The men were clearly responding to stereotypical notions of women's capabilities and roles. Stereotypes, as Krieger (1995: 1199) argues, 'influence how incoming information is interpreted, the causes to which events are attributed, and how events are encoded into, retained in, and retrieved from memory. In other words, stereotypes cause discrimination by biasing how we process information about other people.'

Within this general picture, there are exceptions where the men say they want to involve women in decision-making. These exceptions stem from two types of motivation. One, rather uncommonly, men recognize (and say so explicitly) that women's contribution would be valuable. Two, and more commonly, men want to include women for negative instrumental reasons. There is a popular male perception, for instance, that women as everyday users of the forest are the ones who most frequently violate forest use rules, hence their presence in meetings could help reduce violations: '[Since] women are the ones who cut the wood, if they came to meetings they would understand the need to protect the forests.' Women are also seen as best able to dissuade other women from stealing forest products. In my 2000–01 survey I found (as recorded in the minutes) that often in GB meetings which had high female attendance, women had been called merely to inform them that they should take firewood from only certain species of trees and desist from touching others, when the forest was opened. There was rarely a recognition that women could contribute to rule-making or to the ecological knowledge pool.

Entrenched claims and control over community forums

Opposition to including women is also stronger where men's claims are already entrenched, for instance, where CFIs begin with only male members, or where men feel they have a prior claim to the forest. I found this to be the case in a variety of contexts, but two examples are illustrative. In a Karnataka village, men reacted to my suggestion that they should include women as follows: 'Women have DWACRA,[16] they have savings groups, why don't you leave community forestry to us men?' And in a village in Orissa state (India), a group of young men formed a forest protection committee and barred women from entering the forest. Women responded by demanding their own patch of forest to protect because (they said): 'If we have our own forest, we would not need to ask the men each time for a bit of wood.' 'They are not willing to give us even a patch to protect. Why would they be willing to give us a whole tree if we asked?'

Men can also promote their own interests better than women through their prior control over community structures and village public forums. An example

[16] DWACRA: Development of Women and Children in Rural Areas. This is an anti-poverty programme of the Indian government under which, among other things, women's groups are given subsidized loans for income-generating activities.

from Uttarakhand is illustrative. Here women from one van panchayat told me that when they closed off a patch of open grazing land to protect, the men objected and insisted on getting the grazing reopened. They could do so because of their greater say within community forums. Poor low-caste men too are disadvantaged in this respect, relative to the upper-caste rich.

Culture of public discourse

The aggressive culture of public interaction in male-dominated forums is another reason women give for not going to meetings, saying they feel threatened by men's behaviour:

> When we open our mouths, men shout us down. (Village women in Harimari village, West Bengal, cited in Raju 1997)
>
> If men drink and say something to us, we don't like it. They fight with us, so we don't go to the meetings. (Village women to author in Khabji village, Gujarat village, 1999)
>
> Men drink a great deal here . . . and start abusing us . . . If one woman is abused, ten men stand up and agree with the abuser saying, yes, she deserves this. (Village women to author in Deolikhal village, Uttarakhand hills, 1998)

The men I interviewed often agreed with women's observations that men often drank and fought in meetings. Some said so outright: 'There are often fights in the meeting, so women will not come' (village men to author, Hanasur village, Karnataka, India,1998).[17]

Endowments and attributes: personal and household's

The fact that rural women typically lack personal property such as land and are seldom well connected politically reduces the weight of their opinions; and their limited experience of interaction in public forums undermines their effectiveness. Some of these disadvantages can be overcome if the women are older, married, have leadership qualities, and the self-confidence to speak up. In some regions, the active women members are usually widows or older married women living in their parental homes (Narain 1994, Britt 1997), women whose social position, as Britt observes, 'enables them to travel more freely, speak more loudly, and assume the posture of local leaders'. Such women tend to have greater autonomy and usually carry a lower burden of domestic work than young married women.

Finally, the economic and social position of the woman's household is likely to matter in hierarchically heterogeneous communities, for instance where the village is multi-caste and dominated by the upper-castes (class and caste are illustrative; other features, such as ethnicity, could similarly impinge on the social

[17] In fact, women, in quite diverse cultural contexts, including the USA and UK, mention their discomfort with aggressive language in male-dominated forums and find the use of rumours, abuse, threats, and a constant questioning of their integrity to be commonplace forms of intimidation (Barry 1990, Cockburn 1987).

dynamics). The impact of such hierarchy, however, need not be linear. On the one hand being low-caste and poor can reduce a person's bargaining power within a predominantly upper-caste community, and lower-caste men can be similarly affected as lower-caste women. On the other hand, lower-caste poor women compared with upper-caste women are less subject to social norms that restrict their mobility and stifle speech. Hence when issues of survival are involved we might expect them to be more willing to speak up publicly in ways that neither their husbands nor upper-caste women might—a point reinforced by my survey.

* * *

Many of the above constraints that women face in CFIs are shared by women in other local institutions and across regions. Studies of village councils, water users' associations, and local development groups, for instance, also find that women are restricted by conservative social norms and perceptions, and the double burden of domestic work.[18] In Buch's (1999) study of 843 women village councillors in three Indian states, the councillors cited time conflicts with domestic work, livelihood burdens, and institutional demands as the main factors restricting their ability to attend meetings.[19] Illiteracy (50 per cent of the women councillors were illiterate) and lack of cooperation by male officials and community members also undermined their authority. Buch found that male community members commonly mentioned women's illiteracy as a reason for dissatisfaction with their work, even if women were doing well in practice. This constraint is compounded where women themselves accept illiteracy as a disability and lose self-confidence (see also Behar and Kumar 2002). In fact, several studies of village councils note that the gender gap in literacy negatively affects both community perceptions and women's actual effectiveness.[20] It is perhaps not surprising that elected women councillors face constraints similar to those faced by women EC members in CFIs, since both operate in the same local milieu. It is discouraging, however, that women's entry into panchayats has not empowered women in other forums—at least not yet.

There is also a striking similarity across regions within South Asia, in the way village women talk about the difficulties they face in public participation. This is

[18] See, among others, Prokopy (2004), Weinberger (2000), Buch (1999), Shamim and Kumari (2002), Ray (1992), Behar and Kumar (2002), and several case studies in Baviskar and Matthew (2009).

[19] Indeed, even within political institutions, women repeatedly mention time constraints due to lack of family support for housework as an important factor underlying their low participation, in cultural contexts as diverse as Chile, Turkey, the USA, and the UK. See Franceschet (2001) for Chile; Arat (1983) for Turkey; Fuller (2000) and Andersen (1975) for the USA; and Barry (1990) for the UK. In some studies, women mentioned that husbands' attitudes and domestic work were bigger hurdles than class differences between women, since they developed cross-class solidarities with other women in the course of their activism (Corcoran-Nantes 1988 and Soulliere 1996).

[20] See e.g. Shamim and Kumari (2002) for Bangladesh and India; Ray (1992) for Haryana, India; and Behar and Kumar (2002) for Madhya Pradesh, India. The latter even record a case of a woman chairperson in a village council who was duped by a hostile male councillor into signing a no-confidence motion against herself!

apparent in the quotations given above, in which women from quite diverse parts of India and Nepal describe the same kinds of barriers. We would have expected constraints to be substantially less in south India where there are fewer restrictions on women's mobility and public interaction, than in west or north-west India (as mapped in Agarwal 1994). We found, however, that women in the southern states of Karnataka and Andhra Pradesh spoke about male exclusionary practices in the CFIs in very similar ways to women in regions with more social restrictions, such as Gujarat in the west, or Uttarakhand in the north-west, or Madhya Pradesh in middle-India.

What appears to be playing out here is South Asia's historical legacy of women's near universal exclusion from public decision-making, across regions and communities (as outlined in Chapter 3). *On this count*, therefore, cultural and geographic variation in gendered norms and perceptions does not appear to make much difference.[21] Moreover, regional differences in women's social situation are relatively narrow in the context of CFIs, since a large proportion of them are still located amongst tribal communities in India and hill communities in Nepal. As more CFIs are formed in hierarchically heterogeneous contexts, however, regional/cultural differences in women's participation could become more apparent. Such differences could also affect CFI responsiveness to NGO attempts at promoting women's participation—we would expect regions and communities with historically less gender bias to be more responsive.

3. EFFECTIVE PARTICIPATION: EMPIRICAL DESCRIPTION

Notwithstanding the constraints noted above, are there factors that might still enable women to be effective in public participation and decision-making? In particular, would a substantial female presence, in and of itself, make a difference? Here I explore this question empirically.

My sample contains a sufficient variation in the EC's gender composition for us to test the overall impact of higher female presence on their effective participation, as well as test for critical mass (threshold) effects. I have used only CFIs with mixed-gender ECs, since our interest is in the effect of women's proportional strength *relative to men* and the associated gender dynamics on women's participation. In other words, I have excluded all-women and all-men ECs. In Gujarat 88 per cent (57 out of 65) and in Nepal 54 per cent (38 out of 70) of the total

[21] Norris and Inglehart (2001: 137) note, on the basis of their global study, that even in countries such as 'Australia, the United States, and Spain . . . favourable attitudes toward women's leadership are not sufficient by themselves to produce breakthroughs, since some social structures and institutions continue to act as barriers'. See also Paxton and Kunovich (2003), who empirically examine the effect of culture and ideology on women's political representation globally, using the World Values Survey data, and find it to be an important predictor.

sample consisted of mixed-gender ECs. In the Gujarat sample the typical EC has 11 members, and about 45 per cent of the mixed-gender ECs have 1–2 women and another 45 per cent have 3–4 women. Only one has 6 women (the highest number). In Nepal again, the typical EC has 11–13 members. About 40 per cent of the mixed-gender ECs have 1–2 women, another 29 per cent have 3–4 women, while none has more than 7 women.

This sample distribution, however, is not representative of the universe, since the sample was purposively selected. As detailed in Chapter 4, broadly probing what factors underlay why some ECs had few women and others many, I found a mix of context-specific, non-systematic factors (historical, locational, NGO-influenced, leadership-related, institutional, and demographic), which varied from village to village. For instance, some CFIs with more women on the EC were located in regions with a prior history of women's group activity (although unrelated to forestry); other CFIs had forests with substantial potential for producing seasonal products that women collect; yet others had a gender-sensitive NGO staff member who had encouraged women's inclusion, and so on. Here our interest is in examining whether, and in what ways, women's strength on the EC impinges on their effective participation, whatever were the ad hoc factors that led to their initial presence. I examine three dimensions of effectiveness: attendance at EC meetings, speaking up at the meetings, and holding office.

3.1 Attendance at Meetings

Information on meeting attendance is based on the recorded minutes of meetings held. Fifty-seven per cent of the 57 mixed-gender CFIs in Gujarat, and 100 per cent of the 38 mixed-gender CFIs in Nepal, had records on attendance by gender. This gave me a sample of 303 and 335 meetings (in 32 and 38 CFIs) for the two regions respectively—large enough to proceed with the analysis, despite the lack of coverage of all the meetings held. For both Gujarat and Nepal the analysis covers meetings for all the years the CFI has functioned.

It is commonly argued in South Asia that there is little point in nominating or electing women to village public bodies, since their husbands will end up effectively representing them. In my sample, only two women in Gujarat and six in Nepal said that they had on occasion been represented by their husbands in EC meetings. These cases are not part of the analysis, since the records of meetings gave the names of those attending, and it was ascertained that the persons mentioned actually attended the meeting.

How frequently do the women EC members attend EC meetings? Are they more likely to attend if there are a larger percentage of women in the EC? On attendance, two aspects are of particular importance. First, for gender representation there should be at least some female presence in every meeting, namely there should be as few meetings as possible with no women. The indicator used for this is the percentage of meetings in each CFI that had no women. Second, we would like to capture any critical mass effect. Our argument here is that a lone woman on the EC is less likely to attend than one who has company. We might expect this on the grounds that village women would be better placed to overcome restrictive social norms if there are other women to keep them company, to motivate each other to attend, and to make their presence in the traditionally male space more socially acceptable within the community and family. This effect, however, may be greater where ECs have very few women, and may decline beyond a point as women feel less compelled to attend if several others are attending anyway.

Capturing a threshold effect is not straightforward since simply increasing women's numbers on the EC will increase the mathematical probability of at least one woman attending a meeting. In other words, even if each woman's likelihood of attending is independent of every other woman's likelihood of attending, simply increasing the overall numbers will lead to more women attending. What we need to test is whether the likelihood of each woman attending is *dependent* on the percentage of women in the group. To test this I calculated the average proportion of EC women attending a meeting, or what I term the female attendance rate per CFI, as below.

Female attendance rate for CFI A $= \frac{1}{n}\sum_{i=1}^{n}\frac{w_i}{w}$ where w_i is the number of EC women attending the ith meeting (i=1, 2 . . . n); w is the number of EC women in CFI A; and n is the number of meetings held in CFI A. As an illustration, if CFI A has 3 women in the EC and holds 4 meetings, each attended by 2, 3, 1, and 0 EC women, the female attendance rate in this CFI is $(2/3 + 3/3 + 1/3 + 0) \div 4 = 0.5$. If there is a threshold effect, we would expect this attendance rate to rise as the proportion of women on the EC increases, but not in a linear way.

If the attendance rate does not rise, or rises rather little until some critical proportion of EC women is reached and then rises significantly, then we can conclude that there is a threshold effect around that proportion. It could taper off subsequently. In the next section I test this through regression analysis by examining whether the female attendance rate is significantly related to particular percentages of women on the EC. Below I simply describe women's attendance as measured by these two indicators.

In Gujarat, 26 per cent of the EC meetings had no women attending, while in 16 per cent of the meetings one-third or more of those attending were women (Table 5.2).[22] Hence a large percentage of meetings had no female presence and only a small percentage had the popularly emphasized one-third. Women's attendance improved with more women in the EC. For instance, in ECs with $\leq$2 women only 59 per cent of the meetings had some women attending, while in ECs with $>$2 women there were women in about 87 per cent of the meetings.

[22] On women's poor attendance at meetings despite a nominal presence, see also Quddus et al. (2001), who studied local government in Bangladesh. For India, Buch (1999) found that out of the 843 village women councillors she interviewed, only 66 per cent of those serving as members, but 82 per cent of the chairwomen, reported attending meetings regularly.

Table 5.2. Gujarat and Nepal: percentage EC meetings with women attending (mixed-gender CFIs)

Percentage attendees who are women	Gujarat			Nepal		
	≤2 EC women (136)	>2 EC women (167)	All CFIs (303)	≤2 EC women (139)	>2 EC women (196)	All CFIs (335)
			% EC meetings			
0	41.2	13.2	25.7	36.0	6.1	18.5
>0–<15	25.7	16.2	20.5	38.1	17.3	26.0
≥15–<25	16.9	21.6	19.5	15.1	14.3	14.6
≥25–<33	8.1	27.5	18.8	9.4	17.9	14.3
≥33	8.1	21.6	15.5	1.4	44.4	26.6

Note: Figures in brackets give the number of meetings.
Source: Author's survey, 2000–01.

Table 5.3. Gujarat and Nepal: female attendance rate (mixed-gender CFIs: means)

	Gujarat (32)	Nepal (38)
CFIs with given number of women in the EC		
≤2 women	0.43	0.45
>2 women	0.54	0.58
CFIs with given % of women in the EC		
<25% women	0.39	0.43
≥25–<33% women	0.74	0.56
≥33% women	0.42	0.59
All CFIs	**0.50**	**0.53**

Note: Figures in brackets give the number of CFIs.
Source: Author's survey, 2000–01.

In contrast, there were no EC meetings where men were entirely absent. In Nepal, women's overall attendance was better than in Gujarat—there was at least one woman in about 82 per cent of the meetings. But like Gujarat, women's attendance improved as their presence in the EC increased. For instance, women were present in 94 per cent of the meetings where the EC had >2 women members, but were present in only 64 per cent of the meetings where the EC had ≤2 women.

In both Gujarat and Nepal, the female attendance rate was also notably higher among ECs with more than two women relative to those with two women or less; and much higher for ECs with 25 to 33 per cent women relative to those with less than 25 per cent women. After reaching this level, however, it declined substantially in Gujarat and levelled off in Nepal (Table 5.3). In other words, the highest female attendance rate occurred when there were 3–4 women in a typical EC of 11–13 members.

3.2 Speaking Up

Attending meetings is only one step toward women's effective participation, albeit an important one. The second measure of participation is whether women who attend meetings speak up at them. Information on speaking up is based on responses by EC women and men to the question 'how many of you spoke up in the last three EC meetings you attended?', and grading their answers into 'none, some, and most'. If half or less of the women EC members said they had spoken up they were categorized under 'some' and if over half had done so they were categorized under 'most'. Women EC members were also asked additional questions about problems encountered in attending or speaking up at meetings. In the focus group discussions with village women, similarly, additional questions were posed on aspects such as firewood shortages and awareness about CFI decisions.

Speaking up is a more complicated variable than attending meetings, since women's silence can have several different connotations. For example, even if women feel empowered to speak up, not all of them will speak. If they agree with the point being made, they may remain silent or simply nod. As one EC member in a Gorkha CFI clearly put it: 'I would have spoken if there had been anything that I did not agree with.' At the same time, even when they have something to say, village women, unless they have self-confidence, tend not to speak in male-dominated committees. Here the presence of other women may be necessary for even one woman to speak. Given the nature of this variable, it is not possible to identify a potential threshold effect, but we can examine whether the chances of at least one woman speaking up are greater if there are more women in the EC, using the same gender composition intervals as used for women's attendance.

In Gujarat, in 36 per cent of the ECs, women reported being completely silent in meetings, while men reported that at least some of them had spoken up in all the meetings (Table 5.4). In fact, even in ECs with more than two women, in over a third of them the women had remained silent. The substantial gender gap does suggest that diffidence rather than silent acquiescence is at play. As we will see from the regressions, a considerable presence is needed for Gujarat women to speak up. When asked whether their speaking up had changed any EC decisions, 17 per cent said it had, but again the percentage was twice as high among ECs with more than two women than in ECs with less than two women (namely 21 per cent relative to 10 per cent).

In Nepal, women tend to be somewhat less socially constrained—in about 75 per cent of the CFIs at least some of the women reported speaking up at EC meetings (Table 5.4). Also in about one-third of the CFIs the women EC members felt they had had an impact on decisions at some point in time or other—this was again far greater than in Gujarat. In both regions, however, women said that it would be easier for them to speak up if there were more women in the EC (see also Boxes 5.3 and 5.4). Men, in contrast, tended to voice their views irrespective

Table 5.4. Gujarat and Nepal: speaking up in EC meetings (mixed-gender CFIs: % of CFIs)

How many spoke up in last 3 EC meetings attended?	Gujarat			Nepal		
	≤2 EC Women	>2 EC Women	All CFIs	≤2 EC Women	>2 EC Women	All CFIs
	Female EC members			Female EC members		
	(N=16)	(N=20)	(N=36)	(N=14)	(N=23)	(N=37)
None	37.5	35.0	36.1	42.9	13.0	24.3
Some	50.0	35.0	41.7	57.1	34.8	43.2
Most	12.5	30.0	22.2	0.0	52.2	32.4
	Male EC members			Male EC members		
	(N=23)	(N=27)	(N=50)	(N=15)	(N=21)	(N=36)
None	0.0	0.0	0.0	0.0	0.0	0.0
Some	34.8	29.6	32.0	26.7	23.8	25.0
Most	65.2	70.4	68.0	73.3	76.2	75.0

Note: N = number of CFIs with information.

Source: Author's survey, 2000–01.

Box 5.3. Gujarat: EC women's perceptions about speaking up at meetings

EC women's illustrative answers to the question: would having more women on the EC help you speak up?

* * *

Sabuti CFI, Narmada

We think that there should be at least five women in the EC—that would help us be more vocal.

Golanpur CFI, Panchmahals

The presence of more women will give us support and confidence. It makes a difference when there are other women in meetings.

Falwa CFI, Panchmahals

Yes there should be more women. That will help the *mandali* as a whole.

Dehloch CFI, Panchmahals

W1: If there are more women in the EC, that helps. More women attending meetings always encourages other women to speak. Women should have separate meetings first if they cannot speak in front of the men.

W2: The presence of more women in meetings will help. Women's meetings should be held separately from other meetings. That way, women can be given a space where they can talk amongst themselves. Women have to be given the freedom to speak and that will happen in an all-women meeting.

W3: It helps women share their concerns in public if there are more women in meetings. If there are very few women they get tongue-tied and can't speak out about their concerns, so there should be more women.

W4: Yes, we think that more women in the EC will also understand our point of view more clearly.

Sakwa CFI, Bharuch

To speak up, one needs self-confidence and so if there were more women it would help, but only to a certain extent.

Boriya CFI, Panchmahals

If we have meetings separately then women will speak. If women attend in large numbers then it is better for other women too.

Machod CFI, Panchmahals

W1: Yes, it makes a difference, but not all women speak, so it depends.
W2: It is difficult to say, because if men don't want to let us speak, they will not.

Kalyanpur CFI, Sabarkantha

Men don't allow us to talk. We need more women so that we can get each other's support.

Sattalav CFI, Panchmahals

There are five women in the EC. That is a good number.

Jetpur CFI, Sabarkantha

There should be 50% women in the EC.

Makroda CFI, Sabarkantha

External help as such cannot help us. We have to have that inner confidence when the moment comes. And if we feel that we have to speak up, or we realize we will lose if we don't, then we will speak.

Malekpur CFI, Sabarkantha

Yes it will help if there are 4–5 women.

Note: The responses are based on focus group discussions with EC women. Usually only a few served as spokespersons.
Source: Author's survey, 2000–01.

Box 5.4. Nepal: EC women's perceptions about speaking up at meetings

EC women's illustrative answers to the question: would having more women on the EC help you speak up?

* * *

Bhalu Khola CFI, Gorkha

Yes we would speak up more if there were more women around to encourage us.

Majhi Khola CFI, Gorkha

Of course, yes. Otherwise we hesitate to speak in front of males and the respected members of the community.

Tarang Khola Judipakha CFI, Gorkha

Yes, of course it would be better. In fact, we should have 50% women and 50% men.

Gai Odar CFI, Gorkha

W1: The attitude of the family members should be positive.
W2: Training and awareness programmes are essential in our area. This will help us speak in the meetings and understand our rights and responsibilities as citizens.

(*continued*)

Box 5.4. (Continued)

Bajini Pakho CFI, Baglung

W1: If there are more women in the EC we can support each other. We can share our problems and raise our voice in front of men.
W2: If we have more women in EC, men will certainly listen to us.

Thanmale CFI, Gorkha

W1: We can speak up only in women's meetings, so it is better to have more women members in the EC. Villagers are familiar to us, but we can't speak in front of them. We also feel shy in front of strangers.
W2: We should have 50% men and 50% women in our EC.

Kanno Bhanchuwa CFI, Baglung

Men would not listen to women two years ago, now they respect us. If there were more women in the EC it would be easy for us to talk.

Ludi CFI, Gorkha

It depends. If we can't speak up due to lack of awareness then there is no sense in bringing more women into the EC.

Bhadkhore CFI, Baglung

W1: Yes, more women will help those who hesitate to speak up.
W2: We need both men and women in the Samiti.

Bhagwati Chisapani CFI, Baglung

If we are in majority we would speak in the meeting.

Gaderi Dhaireni CFI, Baglung

Yes, if there were more women in the EC, it would be easier for us to explain things to village women.

Jana Sewa CFI, Baglung

I would not feel shy to speak if there were more women.

Majh Katera CFI, Baglung

W1: Of course, it would help. It is women who can understand other women's problems clearly.
W2: If there are more women, we can talk more easily.

Saure Pakho CFI, Baglung

W1: Yes, it will be easier for us if there are more women in the *samiti*. In front of women, we feel less hesitant to open up about our problems.
W2: We cannot share our concerns or explain what we want to men in the EC because we are uneducated. With women we can talk about our concerns more easily.

Note: The responses are based on focus group discussions with EC women. Usually only a few served as spokespersons.
Source: Author's survey, 2000–01.

of the EC's gender composition. In other words, while substantial male presence restricted women's voice, substantial female presence did not restrict men.[23]

3.3 Office Bearing

A third aspect of participation is holding official positions within the EC, such as those of president, vice president, secretary/joint secretary or treasurer/co-treasurer. How frequently do EC women hold such positions? Rarely in Gujarat but commonly in Nepal—only 5 per cent (3 of 57) of Gujarat's mixed-gender CFIs relative to 42 per cent of Nepal's had female office bearers at the time of the survey. The Gujarat figures indicate that simply having more women on the EC is not a sufficient condition for women to break this glass ceiling. All three CFIs where women held office in Gujarat—two as presidents and one as vice president—were located in Sabarkantha, where the local NGO, VIKSAT, had imparted women leadership training. In Nepal, however, where cultural norms are less restrictive, women hold office more commonly, although still much less than men. At the time of my survey, about half of the male EC members and 13 per cent of the female EC members were holding office on average. But women were typically vice presidents, joint secretaries, and co-treasurers and rarely presidents, secretaries, or treasurers.[24] In other words, they usually occupied supportive rather than leadership positions. Nevertheless the contrast between Gujarat and Nepal warrants some comment.

There can be several reasons for the higher participation of women in Nepal relative to Gujarat by all the indicators. First, in Nepal's middle hills, women are less socially restricted across all communities than in the Gujarat sample. In the latter, despite a dominance of tribal communities (among whom women are usually less constrained than among Hindu caste groups), women face restrictions due to a visible adoption of upper-caste norms. In village meetings, for instance, even tribal women commonly cover their heads and veil parts of their faces with their saris when they sit in public meetings, even though veiling was never traditionally practised among tribal groups in these parts. Also in Nepal, as noted earlier, FECOFUN—the federation of forest user groups—built into its constitution that half of its office bearers would be women. The influence of this could have percolated to village-level forest user groups as well. Most of the women office bearers were literate, in particular the secretaries who keep the minutes of meetings, but the position of co-treasurer was also often filled by illiterate women, probably because the effective work is done by the male treasurer with accounting skills.

[23] The experimental games literature indicates similar gender patterns. Sell (1997), for instance, using US undergraduates as subjects, found that women cooperated more in all-women groups, since they felt more empowered there than as minorities in a mixed-gender group, while men cooperated more in predominantly female groups, in which they expected to carry more influence than in all-male groups.

[24] Keeping women out of the more powerful positions within decision-making, even while including them overall, is also noted in other contexts. Heath et al. (2005), for instance, find that among Latin American legislators, women are kept out of the more powerful standing committees, notwithstanding the increase in female presence in the legislatures.

Below I statistically examine through regression analysis, whether women's proportional strength on the EC affects their effective participation, after controlling for a number of other factors which could also impinge on this.

4. FACTORS AFFECTING PARTICIPATION: REGRESSION ANALYSIS

4.1 Measurement and Hypotheses

Women's effective participation (the dependent variable) covers three dimensions: attending EC meetings, speaking up at EC meetings, and holding office. For Gujarat, given the very few office bearers, the analysis was confined to indicators of attendance and speaking up, namely, the percentage meetings with no women for all the years that the CFI had functioned, the average female attendance rate, and the extent to which women spoke up at meetings. For Nepal, in addition to

Table 5.5. Participation: list of explanatory variables

Explanatory variables included in the regressions	
Gujarat	Nepal
EC characteristics	**EC characteristics**
Gender composition of the EC	Gender composition of the EC
Percentage EC women from landless household	Average age of EC members
Average land owned by all EC members	80% single caste: $\geq$80% EC members are from one caste
Percentage illiterate female EC members	Percentage illiterate female EC members
	Gender gap in illiteracy
	Number of EC members
CFI characteristics	**CFI characteristics**
Who initiated the CFI?	Who made forest use rules?
CFI formation period (before and after 1995)	CFI formation period (before and after 1996)
Forest protection method	
Village characteristics	**Location characteristics**[a]
Gini coefficient for land owned by villagers	Number of toles to which CFI members belong
Percentage village households with migrant males	Percentage member households with migrant males
District where CFI is located	District where the CFI is located
Special interest characteristics	**Special interest characteristics**
Firewood shortages faced by majority of village households	Firewood shortages faced by majority of member households
	Individual characteristics of EC members
	Literacy, age, land owned, marital status, caste, prior experience of serving on the EC

Note: [a] As noted in Chapter 4, for Gujarat we have village-level characteristics since each CFI is linked with a specific village, but in Nepal there is no clear set of 'village characteristics', since a CFI can cater to people from several toles. Hence, for Nepal, I have used 'location characteristics' instead.

these three indicators, there are three for office bearing—whether or not an EC member becomes an office bearer (separately tested for men and women), the percentage of current female EC members who are office bearers, and the gender gap in office bearing, measured as the difference in the percentage of current male and current female EC members who are office bearers.

Four types of factors could impinge on the prospects of women's participation on all these counts: EC characteristics (including gender composition), CFI characteristics, village/location characteristics, and special interest characteristics. All these are group variables. In addition, for office bearing, we also have individual EC member characteristics. Table 5.5 contains the full list of explanatory variables used in the final equations. We are especially interested in the impact of the EC's gender composition. We would expect, for instance, that the greater the proportion of women in the EC the more likely that women will attend meetings, speak up at them, and hold office. At the least we can expect simply a numbers effect. In addition there can be a critical mass effect. I hope to capture any threshold effect through the female attendance rate, by testing how it responds to changes in the percentage of women in the EC. It is unlikely that a single threshold point holds in all contexts. I have therefore divided the proportion of women in the EC into three intervals: CFIs with <25 per cent EC women; CFIs with ≥25–<33 per cent EC women; and CFIs with ≥33 per cent EC women. These intervals were selected since, as noted earlier, a quarter or one-third (and especially the latter) are usually treated as markers representing the relevant critical mass. These divisions also worked well for the sample distribution. In Gujarat, 95 per cent of the ECs fall in the 15–50 per cent range and there are no mixed-gender ECs with over 55 per cent women. In Nepal 71 per cent of the ECs fall in the 15–50 per cent range and there are no mixed-gender ECs with over 64 per cent women.

Although our interest is particularly in the impact of the EC's gender composition, some related gender variables could also affect women's participation, such as whether the EC women are literate, their economic status (e.g. whether they come from landless or landowning households), or the prevalence of problems of special concern to women, such as firewood shortages. Illiteracy could be an obstacle especially to women speaking up and holding office, the former because it reduces women's self-confidence and negatively affects men's attitudes toward women, and the latter because holding office can involve tasks which need literacy. Similarly age can matter: older women face fewer social restrictions on their mobility and on speaking in public and could be better placed to hold office. The woman's economic status could, however, go either way. The landless would tend to be motivated more than the landed to attend meetings and speak up at them because they have more at stake, but they might be less able to attend meetings due to time constraints stemming from job search and wage work demands. The results will show which of these opposing pulls prevails. The EC's caste composition could also affect women's participation—greater social homogeneity would encourage women to attend meetings and speak up at them, greater heterogeneity is likely to have the opposite effect. In the Gujarat sites tribal communities dominate (88 per cent of EC members are tribals) and there is rather little caste variation, but in the Nepal sites ECs do have caste differentiation and here the effect of social heterogeneity could be examined.

Another factor that can motivate women to participate is shortages of essential items like firewood. (A CFI was taken as a site of firewood shortages if discussions with women EC members and village women indicated that the majority of households were facing a shortage.) For many women, forest closure has increased firewood scarcity (see Chapter 9). EC women may thus attend meetings and speak up at them in order to draw men's attention to the problem. Village women also tend to exert pressure on women EC members to take up this matter within the EC. For speaking up, the method of protection can similarly matter, especially if guards are employed, since guards tend to be stricter than village patrols, and women often have arguments with guards over firewood theft. These conflicts come up for discussion in EC meetings, and require women to respond.[25]

At the CFI level, we would expect women to have a higher effective participation where external agents such as NGOs or the forest department have been involved in its functioning (e.g. in the CFI's initiation or its rule-making), since they would tend to infuse less conservative attitudes than those traditionally prevalent in the community. Participation could also depend on when the CFI was formed. In Gujarat, for instance, as elaborated in Chapter 4, around the mid-1990s when donor agencies and independent observers pointed to women's low involvement in the CFIs, the NGOs began to make special efforts to enhance women's participation in various ways. I therefore used 1995 as a marker to see if participation was greater among CFIs formed after that year. In Nepal, 1996 is used as a marker for office bearing, since that was the year when FECOFUN ratified its women-inclusive constitution.

In addition, locational/geographic characteristics could affect participation in complex ways. The district where the CFI is located, for instance, embodies various forms of institutional and social influences: in Gujarat the NGO in each district has a somewhat distinct approach to institutional functioning; and in Nepal, Baglung/Parbat have an important donor presence in community forestry, while Gorkha/Dhading have had rather limited interventions on this count. Similarly, in Gujarat's Panchmahals and Sabarkantha districts, the effect of the Bhagat socio-religious movement is stronger than in Narmada/Bharuch, broadly leading to more conservative gender norms in the former districts. Other location factors, not specific to a district, are economic and demographic, such as job-related migration and inequalities in village land ownership. Higher

[25] The effect of the protection method could only be tested for Gujarat. In Nepal, the inclusion of the protection method as an explanatory variable in the speaking up equations caused problems of 'hidden collinearity'. This can occur, for instance, in logistic analysis when several explanatory variables are dummies, leading to missing standard errors for one or more of the estimated coefficients. The solution is usually to drop the variable due to which this occurs.

male outmigration can increase the time constraints on the women left behind and so adversely affect their ability to attend EC meetings. Village landlessness can have the same effect, but migration is a more direct measure. Inequalities in village landownership—a measure of economic heterogeneity in the village—can also exert pressure on women by creating a conflictual dynamics. In Nepal, locational variables are limited to CFI districts, the number of toles from which the CFI members are drawn, and the percentage of CFI member households with migrant males. There are no village-level variables, however, given the absence (noted in Chapter 4) of a one-to-one relationship between the village and the CFI in Nepal. Also while conceptually we would expect the above variables to affect women's effective participation, in practice some are not usable for both regions. For instance, there is rather little caste variability in the Gujarat ECs and little landlessness in the Nepal ECs (only 1.4 per cent were landless on average).

For office bearing (examined only for Nepal), there is information on each EC member's education, caste, age, marital status, prior history of having been on the EC earlier, and land owned by the person's family. I am therefore able to test the impact both of these individual characteristics and various CFI characteristics, in particular its gender composition, on the likelihood of a person holding office. To this end, I have specified two equations—one for women and one for men. In both, the dependent variable is dichotomous and takes a value of 1 if a woman (or man) EC member is an office bearer and 0 otherwise. The data relates to those who were EC members at the time of the survey and either held office then or had done so in the past. The explanatory variables include both individual and CFI characteristics (with standard errors adjusted for clustering within CFIs).[26] For women office bearers, I also examine whether the likelihood of each woman becoming an office bearer rises notably after we reach a particular proportion of women on the EC (namely if there is a threshold effect), using a graph for tracing the change in probabilities. In addition, I specify two more equations in which I confine myself to group variables to test whether having more women on the EC increases the overall proportion of EC women members who became office bearers, and affects the gender gap in the proportion of male and female members who become office bearers.

Across all the equations, our primary interest is in the impact of the gender variable, which is consistently included in each equation. All the equations also contain those non-gender variables which are conceptually important to test, but the models differ somewhat in relation to additional explanatory factors. Some gender composition variables are continuous and others binary. The continuous gender variable is simply defined as the percentage of women in the EC. In addition, several gender dummies are used. The estimation procedures also vary across the equations. For attending meetings, since the dependent variables are continuous the estimation procedure used is ordinary least squares (OLS) with robust standard errors, that is the standard errors are corrected for hetero-

[26] For elaboration on the issue of clustering within samples, see especially Deaton (1997: ch. 2).

skedasticity. For speaking up, since the dependent variable is binary, logistic analysis is used. In office bearing, I use two different methods. For examining the likelihood of an individual EC member becoming an office bearer (using both the individual characteristics of EC members and the group characteristics of CFIs as explanatory variables), I apply logistic analysis; and for the equations relating to the percentage of women EC members who are office bearers and the gender gap in office bearing I use OLS with robust standard errors.

Finally, to reiterate, the analysis is based only on CFIs with mixed-gender composition, that is, all-men's groups and all-women's groups have been excluded, since our interest is in factors that affect women's effective participation vis-à-vis men.

4.2 Regression Results

The regression results are summarized in Tables 5.6 to 5.11. The definitions of variables used and descriptive statistics are given in appendix tables (AE.1–AE.6) at the end of the book.

Attending meetings

The EC's gender composition, as hypothesized, has a significant positive effect on women attending meetings; that is, the more women there are in the EC the lower the percentage of meetings with no women. In both Gujarat and Nepal, the percentage of EC meetings with no women attending is significantly less if ECs have ≥25–<33 per cent women (or ≥33 per cent women) than if they have <25 per cent women. In both regions, there is a 36-point difference in the percentage of meetings with no women between ECs with ≥25–<33 per cent women and those with <25 per cent women (Table 5.6, Equation 1; Table 5.7, Equation 1). Beyond one-third EC women, however, the gain is limited and tapers off. These results do not translate into a critical mass effect since they do not tell us much about the effect of gender composition on the likelihood of each woman attending a meeting. They do, however, provide a strong case for having more women on the EC, given our interest in ensuring at least some female presence at each meeting.

Moreover, the female attendance rate (the average attendance rate for EC women per meeting) does help identify a potential threshold effect. For Gujarat we find that the attendance rate among ECs with ≥25–<33 per cent women is significantly higher by 0.35 relative to ECs with <25 per cent women, and significantly higher by 0.28 relative to ECs with ≥33 per cent women. In other words, ECs with women within the proportions of ≥25–<33 per cent have a significantly higher female attendance rate than ECs outside these proportions. Beyond 33 per cent there is a dropping off. Either this is because some women assume others will attend anyway, as the number of women increases from 3 to 4–5 in a typical 11-member EC (but there is no qualitative evidence to suggest

Table 5.6. Gujarat: factors affecting women's attendance in EC meetings (mixed-gender CFIs)

	Dependent variables	
	Percentage meetings with no EC women	Female attendance rate[a]
Equation no.	1	2
Statistical method	OLS (r)	OLS (r)
No. of observations	32	32
R^2	0.64	0.62
Explanatory variables	**Coef.**	**Coef.**
GenComp4: dummy (≥25–<33% EC women = 1)[b]	−35.96*** (0.004)	0.35*** (0.001)
GenComp5: dummy (≥33% EC women=1)[b]	−20.00† (0.102)	0.07 (0.512)
Average land owned by all EC members (ha)	−21.88** (0.015)	0.24*** (0.000)
% EC women from landless households	−0.12 (0.413)	0.003* (0.052)
Who initiated the CFI: dummy (villagers =1)	31.73*** (0.003)	−0.21** (0.017)
CFI formation period: dummy (post-1995=1)	−19.73* (0.076)	0.09 (0.370)
Gini coefficient for land owned by villagers	150.82** (0.025)	−1.09** (0.033)
% village households with migrant males	0.46 (0.109)	−0.004* (0.052)
Constant	7.66	0.55

Notes: [a] Average proportion of EC women per meeting.
[b] Reference category GenComp3: Dummy (<25% EC women=1).
OLS (r) = OLS regressions with robust standard errors.
Numbers in parenthesis are *p*-values. Significance: *** at 1%, ** at 5%, * at 10%, † at close to 10%.
The difference between the coefficients of GenComp4 and GenComp5 (the gender composition intervals ≥25–<33% and ≥33%) is not significant even at 10% in Eqn. 1, but it is significant in Eqn. 2 at 5%.

this), or the effect is not showing up after 33 per cent, given the rather few CFIs with more than 33 per cent EC women with gender information on attendance. Nepal's results, however, give a clear threshold effect. The attendance rate is higher by 0.23 among ECs with ≥25–<33 per cent women compared to ECs with <25 per cent women. Beyond 33 per cent although the rate is still significantly greater than with <25 per cent women it is not significantly different from ECs with ≥25–<33 per cent women. In other words the rate tapers off after 33 per cent. Interestingly, in both Gujarat and Nepal, the critical mass figures—25–33 per cent—are in line with those that are popularly afloat, underlining the importance of having at least one-quarter to one-third women in decision-making bodies.

The comfort of numbers in increasing attendance is also emphasized by women themselves. During focus group discussions women often mentioned that having more women in the EC would help them both attend EC meetings and speak up at them. Some sample responses are given below (see also Boxes 5.3 and 5.4):

If more women attend, if the tradition in the village changes then we can go to EC meetings regularly. (EC women, Mor CFI, Panchmahals, Gujarat, author's survey, 2000–01)

Yes, if there were more women in the Mandali [CFI] it would be good. That would encourage women to attend meetings and speak up. (EC women, Gayasavar CFI, Narmada, Gujarat, author's survey, 2000–01)

It will help to have more women. It is also important that women attend meetings, because if women do not attend men will take all the decisions. (Village women, Panchmua CFI, Panchmahals, Gujarat, author's survey, 2000–01)

Factors other than the EC's gender composition, such as land ownership (or its lack) among EC members, the EC's average age, gender-friendly external agents, and CFI location, impinge on meeting attendance and attendance rates as well. For instance, women are found more likely to attend meetings both where there is a higher percentage of landless women in the EC *and* where there is an overall higher average area owned by EC members (Table 5.6, Equation 2).[27] Landless women tend to attend because of the acute problems they face with forest closure (such as firewood shortages) and *despite* their time constraints from wage work, or the absence of male members due to outmigration.[28] Women from households with more land tend to attend because they are somewhat less time constrained than landless women, and although they may be less forest dependent their interest in firewood and fodder availability is still strong.[29] In other words, for somewhat differing reasons, women from both ends of the spectrum of land ownership tend to attend meetings.

In Nepal, as noted, there is very little representation of the landless in the EC for this variable to have an impact. Nevertheless, the Nepal results demonstrate in a different way that women's special interests can compel them to turn up for meetings: for instance, they are more likely to attend where there are firewood shortages (by both attendance indicators: Table 5.7, Equations 1, 2). By attending meetings EC women get a chance to raise this issue of critical importance to themselves and to their constituencies. Indeed, that a higher percentage of landless women in the EC or the experience of firewood shortages is significant (the former in Gujarat, the latter in Nepal) indicates that high dependence on the

[27] There is a high correlation (0.81) between average land owned by all EC households and average land owned by female EC households in Gujarat. I used the former as a proxy since the latter was also highly correlated with the percentage of landless women in the EC.

[28] Behera (2006) similarly found high attendance of poor women at village council meetings in Andhra Pradesh.

[29] See also Chapter 2 in this volume and Narain et al. (2005) for cross-class dependence on the commons for firewood. In the case of fodder, landed households with their typically larger stocks of livestock would, in fact, tend to have more interest than the landless, even if they can draw on private resources for a part of their needs.

Table 5.7. Nepal: factors affecting women's attendance in EC meetings (mixed-gender CFIs)

	Dependent variables	
	Percentage meetings with no EC women	Female attendance rate[a]
Equation no.	1	2
Statistical method	OLS (r)	OLS (r)
No. of observations	34	34
R^2	0.67	0.38
Explanatory variables	**Coef.**	**Coef.**
GenComp4: dummy (≥25–<33% EC women = 1)[b]	–36.93*** (0.000)	0.23* (0.062)
GenComp5: dummy (≥33% EC women=1)[b]	–36.53*** (0.000)	0.20* (0.055)
Average age of EC members	−0.97* (0.079)	0.014* (0.083)
Who made forest use rules: dummy (without FD help =1)	11.91** (0.049)	–0.11 (0.166)
% CFI member households with migrant males	−0.04 (0.788)	−0.004 (0.182)
Firewood shortage: dummy (if shortage = 1)	−11.28 * (0.063)	0.19* (0.055)
Constant	86.97	−0.20

Notes: [a] Average proportion of EC women per meeting.
[b] Reference category GenComp3: dummy (<25% EC women).
OLS(r) = OLS Regressions with robust standard errors.
Numbers in parenthesis are *p*-values. Significance: *** at 1%, ** at 5%, * at 10%.
The difference between the coefficients of GenComp4 and GenComp5 (the gender composition intervals ≥25–<33% and ≥33%) is not significant at 10% in either equation.

forest is an important factor encouraging women to attend meetings, despite restrictive social norms and time constraints. Firewood shortage, as we will see below, is also significant in explaining whether women will speak up at meetings in Gujarat, although it was not found significant in explaining attendance in Gujarat (these latter results are not presented here).

The age of the EC members makes a difference as well—ECs with a higher average age are found more likely to attend in Nepal. Older people tend to have more time for meetings, and older women in particular are usually relieved of some of their household tasks by daughters-in-law. A woman EC member expressed this graphically:

> My workload has decreased at home because I have a daughter-in-law now and my daughter has also grown up. But since the Mandali [CFI] started I am very busy attending meetings, attending workshops and going to training programmes! (Woman EC member, Vajapur CFI, Sabarkantha, Gujarat, author's survey 2000–01)

Gender-progressive external agents also have an impact.[30] In both Gujarat and Nepal, women are found more likely to attend meetings where the forest department (FD) or an NGO have catalysed the CFI or helped in the framing of its forest use rules. One or the other variable is significant in most of the equations. Especially in Gujarat, as a result of pressure from women's organizations and gender specialists in recent years, civil society organizations as well as government officials have begun to place emphasis on women's presence in public decision-making, influenced too by gender quotas in village councils. Hence they often tend to be more gender-progressive than traditional village leaders, most of whom still remain embedded in a culture of conservative social norms and gender role expectations, notwithstanding an occasional exception. A related significant factor in Gujarat is the date of CFI formation. Women are found more likely to attend meetings among CFIs formed after 1995 (Table 5.6, Equation 1) when local NGOs took measures to increase the gender sensitivity of their staff and villagers.[31]

Locational economic factors matter in both regions. In Gujarat, the higher the economic inequality in village land ownership, the poorer is women's attendance by both attendance indicators. Also the higher the percentage of village households (or member households in the case of Nepal) which have migrant male members, the more likely are women to be absent from meetings (the coefficient is significant in Gujarat, but not in Nepal). Although we lack information on whether any EC women themselves came from migrant households, in general high outmigration increases the work burden of the women left behind, leaving them less time to attend to community work. Overall, village economic inequality, as reflected in various indices (among which the results show a consistency), tends to reduce women's participation in meetings, but this negative effect can be overcome partly by inducting landless women directly into the EC—women who, as noted, have a particular stake in attending meetings.

Much of this is as hypothesized. However, some factors which can influence women's attendance are difficult to capture statistically, in particular the timing of meetings and women's responsibility for childcare, housework, and cattle care. The burden of domestic work is consistently mentioned by women as a critical constraint (see also Boxes 5.1 and 5.2).[32]

> We want to attend meetings, but it is difficult when you have the responsibility of the house, the field, the children, the cattle. We can manage a limited number of things in a day. (EC woman in Kanjai CFI, Narmada, Gujarat, author's survey, 2000–01)

[30] I term those individuals and organizations 'gender progressive' which work toward reducing or eliminating the inequities (economic, social, political) that women face in relation to men, in laws, practices, policies, etc. Gender-progressive laws or policies would have a similar connotation.

[31] I did not include this variable for Nepal since there was no such date-specific input here; the formation of FECOFUN is relevant mainly for office bearing where the date of formation *is* used as an explanatory variable.

[32] Meetings held at awkward times can even restrict women parliamentarians (see e.g. Franceschet 2001 for Chile, and Arat 1983 for Turkey).

For me, either my husband should be at home or someone should help with my housework. Otherwise, I cannot attend the meetings regularly. (EC woman, Bhalu CFI, Gorkha, Nepal, author's survey, 2000–01)

The timing of EC meetings is context specific and amenable to change if the CFI so decides, but the gender division of labour tends to be rather inflexible.

Speaking up at meetings

Men don't stop us from speaking, but they do all the talking. (EC women, Moscut CFI, Narmada, Gujarat, author's survey, 2000–01)

Men do not listen to us. Sometimes they insult us. Sometimes they ask us to keep quiet. Therefore, if there is a majority of women, we will feel more confident in speaking up. (EC women, Gahate Armana CFI, Baglung, Nepal, author's survey, 2000–01)

Speaking up, as discussed above, is a much more complex behavioural issue than simply attending meetings. In principle, each EC woman may be expected to attend a meeting, but not each woman who attends may be expected to speak. Speaking up, even if there are no social constraints, can depend on the dynamics of the meeting—for instance, whether a woman speaks can depend on whether or not the point she wants to make has already been made by someone else, or warrants repetition. Nevertheless there is an aspect of speaking up which can depend on the presence of other women, namely in helping village women overcome their shyness and diffidence. Hence we would expect at least some women to express their views, if there are more women around to support them. Even the mere presence of other women can help make the public space less male dominated and provide women with the silent strength of numbers. In the equations, I base my interpretations on the significance of the marginal effect, even if the coefficient of the variable is not significant.

In both Gujarat and Nepal, the EC's gender composition is found to be important in determining whether at least some women express themselves in meetings (Tables 5.8 and 5.9). The greater the percentage of women on the EC the more likely that some or most women will speak up. In Gujarat, for example, the marginal effect for gender composition indicates that the probability of women speaking up is 5 per cent higher for every 1 point increase in the percentage of women on the EC (Table 5.8, Equation 1). Further, the probability of at least some women speaking up is 48 per cent greater among ECs with ≥33 per cent women compared to ECs with <25 per cent women and also significantly greater relative to ECs with ≥25–<33 per cent women (Table 5.8, Equation 2). For Nepal, similarly, the probability of at least some woman speaking up is 27 per cent higher in ECs with ≥33 per cent women compared to those with <25 per cent women (Table 5.9, Equation 2). These do not translate into threshold effects since we are not measuring the likelihood of each woman speaking up. Indeed, as noted, it is unlikely that every woman will speak at a meeting even when able to. What the results do illustrate, however, is that with more women on the EC at least some will tend to speak up. In this sense, it is similar to the 'no woman attending'

Table 5.8. Gujarat: factors affecting women speaking up in EC meetings (mixed-gender CFIs)

	Dependent variable: Do women speak up in EC meetings: dummy[a]			
Equation no.	1		2	
Statistical method	Logit		Logit	
No. of observations	34		35	
Pseudo R^2	0.54		0.38	
Explanatory variables	**Coef.**	**ME**	**Coef.**	**ME**
GenComp2: % EC women	0.35** (0.016)	0.05** (0.013)		
GenComp4: dummy (≥25– < 33% EC women = 1)[b]			–0.99 (0.398)	–0.21 (0.430)
GenComp5: dummy (≥33% EC women=1)[b]			4.03 (0.172)	0.48*** (0.007)
% EC women from landless households	0.06** (0.020)	0.01** (0.033)	0.05 (0.151)	0.01* (0.094)
% illiterate EC women	0.006 (0.785)	0.001 (0.786)	0.01 (0.522)	0.002 (0.527)
Protection method: dummy (guard=1; patrol or informal lookout=0)	5.27** (0.030)	0.59*** (0.001)	2.75** (0.037)	0.42** (0.010)
District2: dummy (Panchmahals=1)	−5.31** (0.037)	−0.77*** (0.001)	−5.04 (0.128)	−0.81*** (0.002)
District3: dummy (Sabarkantha=1)	−5.08* (0.076)	−0.82*** (0.001)	−1.94 (0.303)	−0.40 (0.288)
Firewood shortage: dummy (if most have shortages = 1)	3.45* (0.086)	0.67** (0.022)		
Constant	−10.42		0.19	

Notes: [a] If some or most women spoke up in any one of the last 3 EC meetings = 1; if none spoke up = 0.
[b] Reference category is GenComp3: dummy (<25% EC women).
The marginal effect (ME) is for a discrete change from 0 to 1 for dummy variables, and for a one unit change for continuous variables.
Numbers in parenthesis are p-values. Significance: *** at 1%, ** at 5%, * at 10%
In Eqn. 2, the difference between the coefficients of GenComp4 and GenComp5 (the gender composition intervals ≥25–<33% and ≥33%) is significant at the 10% level.
Difference in models
In Eqn. 1, gender composition is a continuous variable. In Eqn. 2 gender composition is constituted into interval dummies; also firewood shortage was not included in Eqn. 2 due to 'hidden collinearity' (see n. 25 in the text on what 'hidden collinearity' implies).

variable, in that greater numbers can ensure that at least some women will attend a meeting.

EC women themselves consistently say—in 78 per cent of the CFIs in Gujarat and 85 per cent in Nepal—that the presence of other women helps them greatly in voicing their views, because of the encouragement, support, and self-confidence this provides. The following responses are typical (see also Boxes 5.3 and 5.4):

It helps to have more women because then women will not be dominated or feel shy. After all, if there is only one woman and ten men, how will she speak? Women need each other to

Table 5.9. Nepal: factors affecting women speaking up in EC meetings (mixed-gender CFIs)

	Dependent variable: Do women speak up in EC meetings: dummy[a]			
Equation no.	1		2	
Statistical method	Logit		Logit	
No. of observations	34		34	
Pseudo R^2	0.34		0.34	
Explanatory variables	**Coef.**	**ME**	**Coef.**	**ME**
GenComp2: % EC women	0.08* (0.077)	0.01** (0.046)		
GenComp4: dummy (≥25–<33% EC women = 1)[b]			1.91 (0.256)	0.14 (0.168)
GenComp5: dummy (≥33 % EC women=1)[b]			2.79* (0.067)	0.27** (0.043)
% illiterate EC women	0.004 (0.755)	0.000 (0.752)	0.008 (0.571)	0.001 (0.559)
80% single caste: dummy (≥80% EC members from single caste = 1)	1.38 (0.181)	0.16 (0.259)	1.70 (0.114)	0.02 (0.173)
Who made forest use rules: dummy (without FD help =1)	1.57 (0.262)	0.15 (0.274)	1.58 (0.260)	0.14 (0.278)
District: dummy (Baglung/Parbat=1)	2.33† (0.105)	0.29 (0.143)	2.16† 0.101)	0.25 (0.139)
Firewood shortage: dummy (if shortage = 1)	1.50 (0.180)	0.18 (0.210)	1.98 (0.201)	0.24 (0.238)
Constant	−4.57		−4.15	

Notes: [a] If some or most women spoke up in any one of the last 3 EC meetings =1; if none spoke up = 0
[b] Reference category is GenComp3: dummy (<25% EC women).
The marginal effect (ME) is for a discrete change from 0 to 1 for dummy variables, and for a one unit change for continuous variables.
Numbers in parenthesis are *p*-values. Significance: ** at 5%, * at 10%, † at close to 10%.
In Eqn. 2, the difference between gender composition intervals ≥25–<33% and ≥33% (GenComp4 and GenComp5) is significant at 10%.
Difference in models
In Eqn. 1, gender composition is a continuous variable. In Eqn. 2 gender composition is constituted into interval dummies.

be able to speak up. (Village woman, Panchmua CFI, Panchmahals, Gujarat, author's survey, 2000–01)[33]

Another notable factor observable from the Gujarat results is the effect of special interests in inducing women to speak up: there is a 67 per cent greater probability of women speaking up at meetings where the village has reported

[33] We had noted earlier that even in a very different cultural context, namely the United States, increasing women's proportionate strength is found to enhance women's ability to express their views (Flammang 1985, Thomas 1994).

firewood shortages than where there are none (Table 5.8, Equation 1). Firewood shortages affect both poor and well-off women in an everyday sense, providing them an incentive to attend meetings. In addition, women are found more likely to speak up in ECs with more landless women (the marginal effect is significant though small). That landless women tend to attend and speak up at meetings is interesting but not surprising, given their noted high dependence on the local forest, and the difficulties they face from forest closure. They need to speak up to promote their interests, such as by pushing for more lenient forest use rules that allow some extraction of firewood where none is currently allowed, or that allow more extraction than is currently allowed. Overall it is notable that including more landless in the EC increases the likelihood not only of women attending meetings but also of their speaking up at them.[34]

An additional piece of this story lies in the finding, also from Gujarat, that where the CFI is protected by a guard rather than by a patrol group or other method, women tend to speak up more—there is a 59 per cent higher probability of women speaking up in CFIs with a guard than if there is none (Table 5.8, Equation 1). There appear to be at least two reasons for this. First, women, especially poor women, tend to get caught by the guards for stealing firewood and often enter into altercations with them.[35] Guards, as noted, are usually stricter than patrols, hold more formal authority, and tend not to let intruders get away (see also Chapter 7). EC meetings are an important forum for resolving such conflicts, and EC women are more compelled to speak up or be called upon to speak where such conflicts involve village women. Second, households contribute toward the upkeep of guards by paying in cash or kind, and women are likely to give their views or be asked their views where CFIs keep guards, since ensuring regular payments requires consensus among EC members, including women. In fact, sometimes CFIs even call a special General Body meeting of the whole village to ensure that payments are made, especially before the forest is opened seasonally, since where protection is by guards only those who have contributed to the guard's pay are usually allowed to gather forest produce (as elaborated in Chapter 4).

A few other factors warrant mention. In both Gujarat and Nepal, the district where the CFI is located matters—women tend to speak up more in CFIs located in some districts (Narmada/Bharuch in Gujarat and Baglung/Parbat in Nepal) than in others. Contrary to expectation, however, illiteracy among female EC members has virtually no effect on the likelihood of them speaking up in either Gujarat or Nepal.

[34] The necessity of finding wage work can also lead women from poor households to challenge restrictive social norms and speak up (see Agarwal 1994). In general, in South Asia, female work participation outside the home tends to be higher among the poor, and female wage labour in agriculture is predominantly from landless and landpoor households (Agarwal 1984).

[35] On women's altercations with guards in Gujarat's CFIs, see also Sharma (1995), Sarin (1995b), and Narain and SARTHI (1998).

Office bearing

The third dimension of women's effective participation is holding office. For Nepal, where one or more women held office in 42 per cent of the mixed-gender CFIs, I could explore which types of women were more likely to do so, and whether women were more likely to hold office in ECs with more female members. I examined these diverse dimensions in the two ways mentioned earlier, one using the individual characteristics of EC members along with the CFI's group characteristics in the same regression and also tracing the threshold effect through a graph, and the other using only CFI characteristics and gender composition intervals.[36]

We find that a woman EC member is significantly more likely to hold office the larger the proportion of women in the EC (Table 5.10, Equation 1). In addition, Figure 5.1, which gives the probability of an EC woman holding office as a function of the percentage of women on an EC, reveals a threshold effect. It shows that increasing women's proportions on the EC has very little effect on the probability of a woman holding office until we reach around 25 per cent EC women, after which we see an increasingly larger impact till we just cross 50 per cent EC women. Subsequently, the size of the effect, while still positive, begins to decrease. Or, to put it differently, the slope of the curve (i.e. the change in the likelihood of a woman holding office) rises notably at around 25 per cent EC women and continues till around gender parity, and then begins to decline. The threshold can thus be argued to lie around 25 per cent, which is when the probability increases noticeably from an almost flat curve before. We might think of this as a minimum necessary to make a difference, but clearly increasing women's proportions beyond 25 per cent and going toward parity would be desirable to further improve a woman's chances of holding office. For men, by contrast (as Figure 5.1 shows), the EC's gender composition makes little difference to their probability of holding office.

In addition, the regression results (Table 5.10, Equation 1) show that a woman EC member is more likely to hold office if she is literate (the probability is 14 per cent higher for literate women members than illiterate ones), and is currently single, that is unmarried, widowed, or separated (the probability of being an office bearer is 31 per cent higher for a single woman than for a currently married one). She is less likely to hold office where traditional leaders have more influence in EC functioning (as reflected in the rule-makers' dummy), and the more members the EC has—a larger EC increases the competition for each position. That single women are more likely to become office bearers may be attributable to their having more time for CFI work and greater individual autonomy than women with spouses. Indeed, several village leaders in both Gujarat and Nepal told me that literacy and having time to serve on the committee were among the attributes villagers looked for when nominating people (and especially women)

[36] The gender composition interval dummies could not be included in the logistic equations involving individual characteristics, due to problems of hidden collinearity.

Table 5.10. Nepal: factors affecting likelihood of EC member holding office (mixed-gender CFIs)

	Dependent variable: current EC member who is or has been an office bearer dummy[a]			
	Female EC office bearers		Male EC office bearers	
Equation no.	1		2	
Statistical method	Logit		Logit	
No. of observations	134		299	
Pseudo R^2	0.29		0.10	
Explanatory variables	**Coef.**	**ME**	**Coef.**	**ME**
GenComp2: % EC women	0.13*** (0.000)	0.015*** (0.000)	0.002 (0.746)	0.001 (0.746)
EC member's literacy (literate =1)	1.24** (0.031)	0.14** (0.034)	1.56*** (0.000)	0.35*** (0.000)
Land owned by EC member's household (ha)	–0.07 (0.853)	–0.01 (0.852)	0.50*** (0.009)	0.12*** (0.009)
EC member's age	0.02 (0.514)	0.002 (0.506)	0.003 (0.755)	0.001 (0.755)
EC member's marital status (currently married =1)	−1.81** (0.018)	−0.31* (0.062)		
EC member's caste (upper-caste Hindu =1)	–0.04 (0.898)	–0.005 (0.900)	–0.19 (0.373)	–0.05 (0.373)
If EC member has been on EC before	–0.55 (0.180)	–0.06 (0.161)	0.56** (0.047)	0.14** (0.044)
Who made forest use rules: dummy (without FD help =1)	–0.81* (0.069)	–0.09* (0.066)	0.18 (0.350)	0.04 (0.349)
Number of EC members	–0.16*** (0.006)	–0.02** (0.018)	–0.14*** (0.006)	–0.03*** (0.006)
No. of toles in CFI	0.06 (0.458)	0.007 (0.484)	–0.04 (0.259)	–0.01 (0.259)
CFI formation period: dummy (post-1996=1)	0.74 (0.152)	0.09 (0.160)	0.03 (0.904)	0.01 (0.904)
Constant	–4.88		–0.268	

Notes: [a] If current EC member is or has been an office bearer =1; if she/he has never been an office bearer = 0.
The marginal effect (ME) is for a discrete change from 0 to 1 for dummy variables, and for a one unit change for continuous variables.
Numbers in parenthesis are *p*-values. Significance: *** at 1%, ** at 5%, * at 10%.
In both equations individual-level characteristics are combined with group-level variables, with the standard errors corrected for clustering within a CFI.
In Eqn. 2, marital status was not included since all the men except four were currently married.

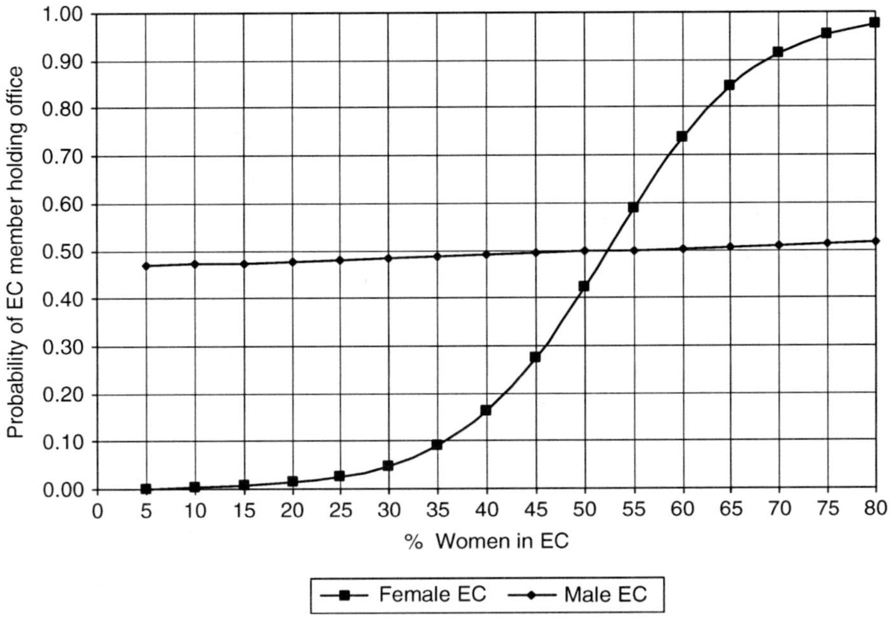

Figure 5.1. Nepal: probability of an EC member holding office (mixed-gender CFIs)

Note: The figure is based on Table 5.10, Eqn. 1 and Eqn. 2. Predicted probabilities of an EC member holding office were obtained for specified values of the percentage of women in the EC, holding all other explanatory variables at their mean values.

to the EC. The date when the EC was formed (namely before or after FECOFUN's constitution was formalized) does not make a significant difference. It is possible that the impact is too diffused to be captured directly, even if the influence has percolated down through external agents such as forest officials and donors. That external agents can make a difference is indicated by the rules dummy—women are more likely to be office bearers where forest officials are more involved in rules formulation than where the villagers do so mainly on their own. For a male EC member the likelihood of holding office is greater the more land he (or his household) owns, if he is literate, and if he has had prior EC experience (Table 5.10, Equation 2). As with women, a large EC reduces each male EC member's chance of becoming an office bearer, but unlike for women the gender composition of the EC has no significant effect.

The second set of results, based only on group characteristics, show that the percentage of EC women becoming office bearers is indeed higher if they belong to ECs with ≥33 per cent women in comparison to those with <25 per cent women as well as those with ≥25–<33 per cent women (Table 5.11, Equation 1). There is a 28-point difference between ECs with <25 per cent women and those with ≥33 per cent women in the percentage of EC women holding office. In

Table 5.11. Nepal: factors affecting percentage of EC women holding office (mixed-gender CFIs)

	Dependent variables	
	% women EC members who are office bearers	Gender gap in office bearing[a]
Equation no.	1	2
Statistical method	OLS (r)	OLS (r)
No. of observations	38	38
R^2	0.47	0.49
Explanatory variables	**Coef.**	**Coef.**
GenComp4: dummy (≥25–<33% EC women = 1)[b]	9.79* (0.078)	–8.25 (0.424)
GenComp5: dummy (≥33% EC women=1)[b]	27.94*** (0.000)	–38.51*** (0.000)
% illiterate EC women	–0.08 (0.169)	
Gender gap in illiteracy[c]		0.18* (0.061)
Who made forest use rules? dummy (without FD help=1)	–2.67 (0.574)	14.09* (0.061)
No. of toles in CFI	2.09* (0.065)	–3.89** (0.035)
CFI formation period: dummy (Post 1996=1)	1.62 (0.669)	–4.73 (0.449)
Constant	–8.40	67.61

Notes: [a] Gender gap in office bearing: % male office bearers minus % female office bearers at the time of survey.
[b] Reference category GenComp3: dummy (<25% EC women=1).
[c] Gender gap in illiteracy: % illiterate female EC members minus % illiterate male EC members.
OLS (r) = OLS regressions with robust standard errors.
Numbers in parenthesis are *p*-values. Significance: *** at 1%, ** at 5%, * at 10%.
The difference between the coefficients of GenComp4 and GenComp5 (the gender composition intervals ≥25–<33% and ≥33%) is significant at 5% in both equations.

addition, ECs with one-third or more women are linked with a significantly lower gender gap in office bearing, although this gap is greater where illiteracy among female EC members is higher than men's (Table 5.11, Equation 2).

Of course being an office bearer does not automatically give the woman influence over decisions, but since appointing women to office is not mandatory in Nepal it is unlikely that most of them are merely figureheads, although some may be. A few whom I personally interviewed were articulate and active and some gave concrete examples of the decisions they had influenced. Studies of India's village councils are also indicative and present a mixed picture, with some council chairpersons (pradhans) being figureheads and others being active. Women office bearers can, however, affect outcomes. For instance, in a study of two Indian states women pradhans were found to prioritize different public goods from male pradhans (Chattopadhyay and Duflo 2004), and although the performance of first-time women pradhans tended to be underrated by the villagers due to a negative perception bias about women, the bias declined with second-time women pradhans, suggesting that greater exposure to women leaders can make a difference (Beaman et al. 2008, Duflo and Topalova 2004).

Further discussion

Direct observation by me and my field staff of the dynamics of seventeen EC meetings in as many sample villages, during a follow-up exercise in Gujarat, reinforced many of the above conclusions, and provided further insights. Three features of these meetings were striking. First it was indeed the case that where there are several women in the EC, at least some turn up for meetings, and where many turn up they tend to be more vocal. If there are only two or fewer women they feel intimidated. However, albeit unusually, an older articulate woman who has leadership qualities can speak up and persuade the men even in ECs with low female presence; in such cases other women might simply nod without saying anything themselves. Second, a dominant male president can silence women even if they are one-third of the EC; indeed he can silence the men too, as I found in one Gujarat village where seating arrangements at the meetings replicated the typical pattern of men sitting on chairs or benches and women sitting on the floor on one side, with the president holding forth and dominating the decision-making process. Third, just as a dominant male president can silence women so a sympathetic one can empower them. At an EC meeting in one Panchmahals village, two of the four women EC members made several interesting observations, but for these to sway the final decision the male president had to reinforce women's opinions. The issue under discussion was the location of a water trough for cattle that would cater to two hamlets. When no consensus seemed in sight, one of the women suggested that it be located in the middle of the two hamlets and near a well, so that both hamlets could use it and filling it would also be easier. Some men objected, saying: 'We can't accept what you are suggesting simply because you are saying so,' but the president pointed out that it was the most reasonable solution, to which everyone then agreed.[37]

Although such gender-sensitive male presidents are rare, over time, as women's presence in CFI decision-making becomes more commonplace, negative male attitudes and social norms are also likely to change, as observed for women pradhans. Here again women's greater numbers in ECs can help. Also, prior group activity by village women, even if unrelated to forestry, could enhance women's presence, attendance, and speaking up in ECs, due to the experience women gain through such activity.

[37] The meeting was attended and recorded on my behalf by Kishore Bhai and Rugha Bhai, who are former and current SARTHI staff members respectively.

5. CONCLUDING COMMENTS

Women's proportional strength in the EC is found to be consistently important in enhancing women's participation in governance, not just nominally but effectively. For a start, the more women there are on the EC the greater the likelihood of them attending EC meetings, speaking up, and being office bearers. Having more women ensures that there is at least some female presence in most meetings. The attendance rate also improves and there is evidence of a critical mass effect. Woman's attendance rate is significantly higher in CFIs where a quarter to a third of the EC consists of women compared with ECs with less than a quarter women. The likelihood of at least some women speaking up, however, becomes significantly greater at a somewhat higher level of women's presence, namely among ECs with a third or more women members. And although increasing women's proportional strength on the EC does not increase their chances of becoming office bearers where social norms are strict (as found in Gujarat), it does enhance their chances of holding office where those norms are more pliable (as found in Nepal). Here again we find a threshold effect—the EC needs to have at least a quarter women for it to be probable that a woman will hold office. Going beyond a quarter, however, improves her chances further.

Discussions on the impact of women's presence in public forums have focused almost entirely on the decisions women take, rather than on the process of decision-making. My results show that women's proportional strength is important even for the process. Moreover, in terms of *effective* proportions, one-third has become widely accepted, largely without empirical verification. I find a critical mass effect that lies within a somewhat wider range—such as between a quarter to a third for women's attendance—but it is still fairly close to the popularly emphasized percentage. This provides empirical support for the popular view and strengthens the policy argument for promoting at least these proportions of women in public decision-making bodies.

On office bearing, additional measures would be needed to break the glass ceiling effect, where it exists. Here mandating a certain percentage of women office bearers, accompanied by leadership training, may be necessary. In Gujarat, for instance, in the three CFIs where women had held office and become presidents or vice presidents, they had received leadership training. Such training can enhance women's capabilities and also signal to the community that women too can be, and deserve to be, effective leaders. In Nepal this message was conveyed through demonstration by the women-inclusive nature of FECOFUN's constitution. Such a message, however, simply lays the ground for inducting women into office, it does not guarantee it. Social norms also play a role: in Nepal's middle hills the less restrictive environment that women face, even among the upper castes, clearly helps in increasing their public participation, although even here measures to build women's self-confidence and experience can prove important, as recent donor attempts demonstrate (LFP 2007). A woman's personal attributes, such as her education and the time she can devote to CFI work, can also affect her chances of becoming an office bearer.

It is notable that where women have a personal stake in the outcomes of meetings (e.g. if they are experiencing firewood shortages or persistent conflicts with guards) they are more likely to attend meetings and/or speak up at them. It would be interesting to test this in other institutional contexts as well. Women's class position also matters but not in the expected way. The finding that ECs with a higher percentage of landless women have greater female attendance and voice indicates that being poor and female does not necessarily confine a person to the bottom of the pyramid. Landless women are less constrained by social norms and status considerations, face altercations with guards in greater measure, and have more stake in forest access, compelling them to attend meetings and speak up. Apropos the discussion in Chapter 1 about the heterogeneity of women's interests, this also highlights the importance of distinguishing between women, and including more disadvantaged women in community institutions of governance.

Some scholars have argued that conditions of socio-economic inequality can seriously constrain the disadvantaged from participating in public forums (e.g. Fraser 1990). My results suggest, however, that prior equality is not essential for women to assert themselves. In fact, women from disadvantaged households, especially if present in sufficient numbers, can be more outspoken in public forums than women from well-off households, since they have less to lose by way of social status, and much to gain if the decisions go in their favour.

Women's participation is thus mediated by a number of factors, including the individual attributes and skills of those composing the EC. This cannot always be captured statistically but it does suggest that while women's greater presence on the EC can play a critical role in increasing this participation, there are also aspects beyond mere numbers that would help make that presence effective.

Overall, the results indicate that the EC's gender composition is a fairly good proxy for women's effective participation. And by examining the effect of gender composition on rule-making, rule violations, forest quality, and the experience of firewood and fodder shortages in the chapters that follow, we can plausibly assume that we are capturing the effect of women's participation on these dimensions.

6

Rules and Rule-Makers

> Rules are prescriptions that define what actions . . . are *required, prohibited,* or *permitted,* and the sanctions authorized if the rules are not followed.
>
> (Ostrom et al. 1997: 38)

> The male members of the forest committee have difficulties implementing the rules. Women could discuss these problems with the men. Perhaps more 'mid-way' rules would be, in the long run, more effective . . . more viable.
>
> (Nepalese village women, cited in Britt 1993: 148)

Rules that define what is 'required, prohibited, or permitted' are widely recognized as central to the functioning of institutions governing common pool resources (CPRs).[1] Indeed, Ostrom (1990) identifies the formulation of rules that are congruent with local conditions and the collective mechanisms of rule-making as among the key 'design principles' for building sustainable institutions for CPR governance.[2] But are the rules likely to differ depending on who frames them? In particular, are men and women likely to frame different rules of forest use due to, say, differences in responsibilities and priorities? Village women often suggest (as above) that involving them in rule-making would affect not only the pattern of rules but also whether they are complied with. If so, the gender composition of the rule-making body could impinge critically on institutional functioning and its outcomes.

Research relating to other types of institutions, such as legislatures and village councils (some descriptive, some empirical, and some, less commonly, involving careful statistical analysis), although diverse in its context, presents a near consensus that women compared with men tend to have distinct priorities or preferences in public policies; and the few studies that have tested this find the differences to be statistically significant.[3] For environmental governance, however, there is surprisingly little work on whether women's presence in institutions managing natural resources, such as forests, is likely to make a difference to the

[1] On the importance of CPR rules see, among others, Ostrom (1990), various articles in Ostrom et al. (1997), Baland and Platteau (1996), McKean (1986), Wade (1988), Agrawal (1997), Arnold and Campbell (1986), Bardhan (2006), and references therein.

[2] By a 'design principle' Ostrom (1990: 90) means 'an essential element or condition that helps to account for the success of these institutions in sustaining the CPRs and gaining the compliance of generation after generation of appropriators to the rules in use'.

[3] For elaboration and references, see Chapter 1.

decisions made, in particular the rules formulated for forest use and product extraction. Existing discussion is limited and largely inferential, with virtually no theorizing on why we might expect gender differences in rule-making, or statistical testing of the actual impact of women's participation in rule formulation.

In this chapter, I seek to bridge this conceptual and empirical gap and also carry forward the discussion in Chapters 1 and 2 on the complex character of women's interests. I examine whether the gender composition of the EC makes a difference to forest use rules, especially their extent of strictness. Do groups with more women in their ECs, for instance, make less or more strict rules? Does the inclusion of poor landless women make a particular difference? Do all-women groups make rules of different strictness from, say, mixed-gender groups? Before we address these questions, however, consider why the nature of rules matters.

1. WHY RULES MATTER

The most important set of rules made by CFIs are those relating to forest use, involving the extraction and distribution of forest products (also termed by some as 'allocation rules': Agrawal 1997). Penalties for violating these rules could be seen as a secondary set of 'rules', but effectively penalties are a means of ensuring rule compliance, and not all CFIs specify detailed penalties (see Chapter 7).[4] Forest use rules determine what forest products are allowed to be extracted and distributed, in what quantity and frequency, by what means, when, and by whom. The rules matter for their potential impact on institutional sustainability, as well as on the equity of benefit sharing and on forest conservation.

Consider firewood extraction. Potentially the rules can range from a complete ban on collection to varying degrees of permissible extraction. For instance, the collection of fallen twigs may be allowed, but breaking or cutting drywood from the trees may be banned; or extracting drywood may be allowed if done by hand, but not with an axe. Some CFIs may permit such extraction throughout the year, others only for a few days annually; and anyone may be permitted to enter the forest in this period or only one or two persons from member households.[5] Other forest products may similarly be subject to varying restrictions, leading to numerous permutations of overall rules.

On such rules would depend the benefits derived by the local population from forest protection. This impinges, first, on the incentive and commitment to protect the forest, since protection involves bearing costs and people expect

[4] Monitoring rule compliance, occasional tree planting, clearing undergrowth, and so on, are essentially 'activities' that CFIs undertake, rather than rules.

[5] Ostrom et al. (1997: 42) term the rules of extraction 'scope rules' and eligibility conditions on who can extract as 'boundary' rules. In the present discussion, however, no additional purpose is served in using that nomenclature, and I include both scope and boundary rules under the term 'forest use rules'.

appropriate benefits. These costs could either be direct, such as contributing to patrolling time or paying for a guard, or indirect, such as forgoing resource use by complying with the prescribed rules.[6]

Second, rules can have differential consequences by class and gender. Strict rules (a complete ban on extraction, for instance) affect the poorest households and women in general more adversely, given their substantial dependence on forests for subsistence. Women may end up spending more time and energy in firewood collection, economizing on fuel use, or using inferior and more health-damaging fuels as substitutes (Agarwal 2001 and Chapter 2). Poor, landless women would be the most adversely affected. In other words, the equity and welfare outcomes of CFI formation could depend on forest use rules, and the costs of strictness would be shared unequally across gender and class lines.

Third, rules can affect forest condition but in somewhat complicated ways. Strict rules, if implemented effectively, can benefit regeneration, but overly strict rules (e.g. virtually no forest use or extraction) could prove to be counterproductive socially and ecologically. Socially, for instance, very strict rules are difficult to enforce and could increase violations and conflicts, with potentially damaging effects on forest condition. South Asia's colonial history is replete with examples of forest fires caused by resentful villagers whose customary collection rights were curtailed.[7] Ecologically, uncleared undergrowth can increase the risk of fires, and tree growth may be poorer without periodic pruning. Moderate rules, by contrast, may prove beneficial for conservation by encouraging village cooperation, as well as by permitting forms of extraction that can enhance biomass regeneration. Forest use rules thus need to be neither so lenient as to degrade the resource further (by over-extraction), nor so strict as to undermine people's incentive to protect and the ecological benefits of selected extraction. The appropriate level of strictness would be that which is adapted to ground conditions.

The *process* by which the rules are made—bottom-up or top-down—can also affect their impact. Even those who suffer adverse consequences may accept strict rules, if they are involved in rule-making, that is if the rules are made in a participative way rather than imposed from above. Women, for instance, may be more accepting of strict rules even at the cost of an increase in their burden of firewood and fodder procurement, if they are consulted, represented, or allowed to directly participate in rule-making. Among water users' groups, for example, Bardhan (2006) found a positive association between rule compliance and participation in rule formulation. In other words, the very involvement in rule-making of those most affected by the rules and who are expected to follow them could prove important for institutional sustainability. The EC's gender composition can help capture the impact of women's presence both on the rules made and (implicitly) on the process by which they are made.

6 Of course in some contexts people can transcend material incentives and come to view conservation as having intrinsic worth: see e.g. Agrawal (2005) and Buchy and Rai (2008).

7 See e.g. Bhattacharya (1992), Sivaramakrishnan (1999), and R. Guha (1989).

What kinds of rules might be in women's interest to formulate? Given their everyday dependence on local forests for firewood and fodder, lenient rules which allow substantial extraction would appear to be in their interest. However, immediate and long-term interests can vary. Short-term interests may lie in immediate extraction, but long-term interest would lie in deferred and sustainable extraction (in other words, in framing stricter rules that allow resource regeneration). If the forest is highly degraded, immediate extraction may not even be an option. But as a forest improves, the CFI would need to decide when to start extracting and how much to extract. Here negotiation between different parties, especially between villagers and EC members, and amongst the EC members, can play a part; and the EC's gender composition and the intersection of gender and class can prove important. The poorer a woman, for instance, the less her capacity to defer current consumption and the more likely is she to be interested in lenient rules. These aspects are empirically examined further below. But let us first consider the kinds of rules found in the study sites.

2. DIVERSITY OF FOREST USE RULES

2.1 Overview

In 1998–99, when I was travelling across India and Nepal interviewing villagers about their community forest programme, I was struck both by the commonalities in the forest use rules across the country and by their remarkable diversity. The commonalities related on the one hand to the almost universal ban on timber felling, except under highly restrictive conditions, and, on the other hand, to the relative leniency toward certain types of seasonally available non-wood forest produce, such as timru leaves and mahua flowers. The diversity lay especially in the varied methods of extracting different types of fodder (e.g. cutting grass, plucking tree fodder, or allowing grazing) and, to a limited extent, firewood. Rules for these products differed not only between states and ecological zones, but at times even from village to village. I found such variations across the seven states that I visited in 1998–99, and again across the districts in my 2000–01 survey in Gujarat and Nepal.

Framing such diverse forest use rules involves various types of decisions, such as whether to extract, what to extract, how much to extract, and how to distribute what is extracted. Embedded herein are not only specifications for regulated forest use but also a concern for conservation (e.g. whether to allow grass cutting unrestrictedly or by plot rotation). Affecting these decisions, as noted, is a complex interplay of ecological conditions and negotiations/interactions between different parties with varying interests (such as EC members, other villagers, and external actors). Ecologically, for instance, the regeneration of a highly degraded forest may require banning the entry of all humans and animals and forbidding any kind of wood cutting. However, with low or non-existent tree cover and a ban on grazing, a good harvest of grass can be reaped, especially post-monsoon. Similarly, woody biomass revives if the rootstock is intact, but haphazardly. Some shoots need pruning a few years into protection, and the cut wood can be distributed. Also trees generate a flow of twigs and fallen branches. Seasonal non-wood forest products may revive as well. As the forest ages, however, there is less risk of trampling on young shoots. Grazing can then be allowed, although goats could still cause damage, because, as the villagers remark, 'the goats eat everything'. One Gujarat villager further explained to me: 'In the beginning there was a rule that animals should not be allowed to graze in the protected area. This was decided because there was a danger that they will eat the saplings. Now the rules have changed as the plants have grown and they are under no danger.'

Potentially, therefore, with protection, a degraded resource can yield benefits to the community in the form of grass fodder and drywood (the former seasonally, the latter more continually) and, depending on local biodiversity, many other products as well. In addition, it can yield timber when mature. In contrast, if the forest already has good tree cover when the community receives it, there may be less grass and more of other products. Whether or not these potential benefits are reaped, however, depends on the rules. Here there is scope for different segments of the population and other interested parties to negotiate and exercise influence.

The emergent rules—reflecting both ecological conditions and negotiation/influence—can show considerable diversity by product, CFI, and region. Tables 6.1 and 6.2 and appendix Tables A6.1 and A6.2 illustrate this variation. These rules were formulated and practised at the time when CFIs began formal protection (although some villages in Gujarat had begun informal protection prior to this).[8] Broadly, I found five levels of strictness in rules, although not all applied to each product: complete ban on collection; partial ban (e.g. a ban on collection in certain seasons, or on grazing by certain types of animals, such as goats); given on special request, in case of personal exigency or natural disaster; occasional opening for a specified period with specified conditions for collection; and open always (meaning open for the protecting village but not for other villages). Cases with partial ban and those that give a product on special request have been clubbed in the tables.

In Gujarat, the most lenient rules—'open always'—are for seasonal NWFPs and fallen twigs, and the strictest rules apply to timber cutting which is banned in all the CFIs, although a few entertain requests (sometimes required in writing) for a special need. In fact, in some of the Panchmahals villages in Gujarat, even written requests are first vetted by a *nishpaksh samiti* (impartial committee) appointed by the EC, which investigates whether the request is based on a genuine need. The villagers themselves devised this innovative method of cross-checking. Fodder cutting and grazing are subject to rules of moderate strictness. Also, as noted in Chapter 4, in parts of Gujarat such as Panchmahals, CFIs

[8] In Nepal, information provided by the EC could be cross-checked in many cases with written records dating to the time of CFI formulation. Gujarat lacked such records but follow-up questions about rule changes provided some cross-checking of the original rules (see also Chapter 4).

Table 6.1. Gujarat: forest use rules after CFI formation by gender composition (% CFIs)

Products extracted, strictness rules and weights (in brackets)	Open always (1)	Open occasionally (2.5)	Partial ban or given on request[a] (2.75)	Full ban (3)
		≤2 EC women CFIs (N = 31)		
Fallen twigs	64.5	29.0	0.0	6.4
Drywood (cutting)	29.0	29.0	3.2	38.7
Grass fodder	48.4	35.5	3.2	12.9
Grazing	32.2	0.0	45.2	22.6
Timber species for firewood	0.0	0.0	0.0	100.0
Timber poles for house building, etc.	0.0	3.2	9.7	87.1
		>2 EC women CFIs (N =34)		
Fallen twigs	52.9	17.6	0.0	29.4
Drywood (cutting)	23.5	29.4	2.9	44.1
Grass fodder	50.0	44.1	2.9	2.9
Grazing	47.1	2.9	23.5	26.5
Timber species for firewood	0.0	0.0	2.9	97.1
Timber poles for house building, etc.	0.0	0.0	11.8	88.2
		All CFIs (N=65)		
Fallen twigs	58.5	23.1	0.0	18.5
Drywood (cutting)	26.2	29.2	3.1	41.5
Grass fodder	49.2	40.0	3.1	7.7
Grazing	40.0	1.5	33.8	24.6
Timber species for firewood	0.0	0.0	1.5	98.5
Timber poles for house building, etc.	0.0	1.5	10.8	87.7

Notes: See Chapter 4 for a more detailed breakdown of rules by products, including for NWFPs.
N= Number of CFIs.
[a] Partial ban normally implies that collection or grazing is banned in some parts of the forest (usually where there is a plantation, or gap-filled parts, or young shoots). In case of a special need or natural disaster, a product may also be given out to households on request.
Source: Author's survey, 2000–01.

distinguish between timber species and species used mainly as firewood, like kada and ganda babul, which have little commercial value but substantial fuel value. These can be cut by women on forest opening days.

Almost all the Gujarat forests in my sample were heavily degraded when informal protection started and most villagers began by banning all collection, although the ban on cutting timber without permission has a long history. Technically some CFIs continued to allow the collection of fallen twigs and NWFPs, but often there was little available of either. Also, where vigilance was strict, villagers presumed this meant an effective ban on all products. In some areas, such bans substantially increased women's firewood collection time and distance travelled (Sarin 1998, Agarwal 2001). When neighbours started protecting, these options too were foreclosed, and most women switched in part to

Table 6.2. Nepal: forest use rules after CFI formation by gender composition (% CFIs)

Products extracted, strictness rules, and weights (in brackets)	Open Always (1)	Open occasionally (2.5)	Partial ban or given on request[a] (2.75)	Full ban (3)
		All-women CFIs (N=27)		
Fallen twigs	44.4	44.4	0.0	11.1
Drywood (cutting)	0.0	96.3[b]	0.0	3.7
Tree fodder	0.0	33.3	3.7	63.0
Grass fodder	40.7	55.6	3.7	0.0
Grazing	22.2	3.7	14.8	59.3
Timber	0.0	0.0	51.8	48.2
Leaf litter	44.4	33.3	0.0	22.2
		Other CFIs (N=43)		
Fallen twigs	46.5	39.5	7.0	7.0
Drywood (cutting)	2.3	86.0[b]	4.7	7.0
Tree fodder	0.0	30.2	11.6	58.1
Grass fodder	41.9	48.8	2.3	7.0
Grazing	30.2	7.0	14.0	48.8
Timber	0.0	0.0	69.8	30.2
Leaf litter	37.2	39.5	4.6	18.6
		All CFIs (N=70)		
Fallen twigs	45.7	41.4	4.3	8.6
Drywood cutting (cutting)	1.4	90.0[b]	2.8	5.7
Tree fodder	0.0	31.4	8.5	60.0
Grass fodder	41.4	51.4	2.9	4.3
Grazing	27.1	5.7	14.3	52.9
Timber	0.0	0.0	62.9	37.1
Leaf litter	40.0	37.1	2.9	20.0

Notes: See Chapter 4 for a more detailed breakdown of rules by products. N = Number of CFIs.

[a] Partial ban normally implies that collection or grazing is banned in some parts of the forest (usually where there is a plantation, or gap-filled parts, or young shoots). In case of a special need or natural disaster, a product may also be given out to households on request.

[b] In most of these CFIs this drywood is extracted as part of pruning/thinning operations, which some perform annually and others less frequently.

Source: Author's survey, 2000–01.

inferior fuels—cropwaste, twigs, even straw. Women's complaints about strict closure were frequent and bitter.

Protection, however, allowed fodder and wood to regenerate. In an economy where cattle play an important role, many CFIs instituted formal methods for fodder harvesting in both Narmada/Bharuch and Sabarkantha, but not in Panchmahals where grass was sparse, and the land was covered largely with bushes. In terms of trees, the hardy teak that characterizes the area readily revived where rootstock was intact. The initial pruning provided cut wood which was distributed among the villagers, but since cutting was done at intervals of several years, it did rather little to alleviate chronic fuel shortages. Over time, some CFIs, in response to women's complaints, began opening the forest once or twice annually for a few days at a time, typically around the two main Hindu festivals—Holi in the spring and Diwali in the early winter—when people have additional needs and migrants return. But many other villages continued with their bans despite biomass availability and women's pleas. In Narmada/Bharuch, for instance, all the CFIs continue to ban greenwood cutting and 88 per cent ban even drywood collection.

In Nepal, since the forests transferred to communities were on average in better condition and more biodiverse than in Gujarat, the CFIs could, if they wanted, allow more extraction. In practice, the rules they made are stricter on many counts (Table 6.2). Drywood is cut periodically but infrequently. Similarly, less than half the CFIs allow twigs collection on an open basis, and in Nepal, as in Gujarat, women in most CFIs complain of firewood shortages. Timber (typically 'small timber' of <3 feet girth), however, is more often given out on request in Nepal (63 per cent of the sample CFIs allow this) than in Gujarat.

An illustrative feel for the fascinating variety of fodder and firewood rules for extraction and distribution, among those that extract these products, is given in appendix Tables A6.3 and A6.4 (based both on my 2000–01 survey and my 1998–99 fieldwork).[9] A brief look at these rules is important not only because they demonstrate local innovativeness in rule-making, but also because they can have significant equity effects. Broadly, three types of principles/norms are implicit in the distribution methods formulated by the CFIs: market determined, contribution, and need. Each principle implies a different equity outcome. 'Contribution' (in terms of membership fee, protection efforts, labour inputs, etc.) is the dominant criterion underlying distribution rules in most CFIs. The contributors get equal access to the forest, or equal amounts of fodder or firewood. Auctions are undertaken in a few cases, and distribution by need is rare. Contribution as a distributive principle is egalitarian but not equitable in that it disadvantages the poor and women, who are less in a position to contribute to formal protection efforts financially or in terms of patrolling time. A move from the principle of contribution to that of need would require a shift in societal values where the better-off are willing to relinquish some of their claims in favour of those who need the products more. At present, rather few are so willing.

2.2 Fodder Extraction and Distribution

In both Gujarat and Nepal, fodder rules are the most fine tuned. They vary not just in whether fodder can be extracted, but also how it is to be extracted and distributed. I found tree fodder being extracted only in the Nepal fieldsites. Grass fodder, by contrast, is extracted periodically in many sites, and especially in Narmada/Bharuch and Baglung/Parbat most CFIs have formal procedures for cutting and distributing fodder.

Almost all CFIs that permit fodder extraction open the forest seasonally, once or twice a year for a week to ten days, allowing entry to one or two persons per

[9] These do not include cases where fodder collection is banned altogether or always open for the community.

member household. A few admit non-members, but for a higher fee.[10] Distribution methods, however, vary greatly—some CFIs show a considerable concern for equality, others a gross disregard for it. CFI 1 (Gujarat) in appendix Table A6.3, for instance, has been following an egalitarian system for nine years. On its annual opening, two persons can go in to cut the grass and tie it in bundles. Ten per cent of the bundles go to the EC; the rest are distributed equally among the participating households.[11] CFI 16 from another part of India, namely Uttarakhand state, also provides an example of an egalitarian system, but different from CFI 1 in its specifics. On the morning of the forest opening day, one member per household (usually a woman) lines up and answers a roll call. When the person taking the roll call signals 'go', the women run, as in a race, rushing to the greenest patch they have identified the day before. Sometimes they sprain their ankles in this rush. Despite this, most women in the village feel they have an equal and fair chance to get good fodder, although they would like a less competitive and stressful access system.

At the other end of the spectrum are CFIs that disregard equity altogether, treating fodder like a market good and auctioning it. Although auctions reduce monitoring costs, they can lead to elite capture of the product. In CFI 22 in Nepal, for instance, the grass area is annually divided into three plots, each of which is auctioned to the highest bidder. The remaining households have to buy fodder from the successful bidders at a price the latter set. In some other CFIs, a few rich bidders get all the grass and the auction money goes into a community fund (e.g. CFI 18). Women usually have little say in the use of funds, which are used for giving loans to members, or for community development, paying the forest guard, and so on, and not for relieving fuel and fodder shortages. This also means that many of those who have been protecting the forest may get nothing or may have to buy grass at high prices. During my 1998–99 fieldwork, I heard the bitterest complaints about forest use rules from women where grass was auctioned.[12] Below I give some samples from my 1998 discussion with women in Ghusra village, Dang district, Nepal:

> The community forest belongs to the men. We own nothing. Even the grass is auctioned off. Whoever pays more gets it.

> The money obtained from grass and firewood is kept by them in their fund. We have not seen one penny of it. We buy grass, which is auctioned by bundles.

[10] Membership itself, as noted in Chapter 4, is not a straightforward concept and can depend on various criteria: payment of an initial membership fee, contributing toward protection, being identified formally as forest users (in Nepal), and so on.

[11] Distribution of fodder by making equal bundles and allocating the bundles by various methods (including through a lottery system) is also found in other regions. McKean (1986), for instance, describes similar procedures in her study of community forest management in Tokugawa Japan.

[12] I understand that auctioning is now rarely practised in the middle hills.

In fact, successful bidders can also cause damage by careless and excessive extraction, as found by Agrawal (1997) in Kumaon (India), where too such auctions were deeply resented.

Between the two extremes—equal bundles and auctions—are a complex array of distribution systems, with varying equity effects. In Nepal, for example, CFI 21 ensures non-partisan distribution by randomly assigning a plot (with a fixed price according to the amount and quality of grass) to each household. And CFI 23 is a rare case where poor households are charged less, and households with their own pastures do not get a plot. The lack of even a patch of private grassland and restrictions on grazing can create another problem—keeping the cattle tied and stallfed. Occasionally, women resort to humour to highlight a daily anxiety. One woman in Devistan CFI (Nepal) put it jocularly: 'I tried to keep my ox tied but could not. It seems it is going to be a Prime Minister. It is always going around to people's houses in the village, as if to ask for votes!'

2.3 Firewood Extraction and Distribution

Unlike fodder, the extraction and distribution of firewood (as drywood and greenwood), is seldom based on a regularized system and the contrast between fodder and firewood is striking. In Gujarat, virtually none of the CFIs has formal procedures for cutting and distributing firewood (Table 6.3). People can simply collect available drywood when the forest is opened. The only exception is where cleaning/pruning/thinning (locally termed 'cutback') is done—a skilled job undertaken for enhancing tree growth by lopping off uneven shoots and branches, and clearing the undergrowth. The cut wood is usually tied into bundles and distributed equally among the participating households. But this cutback is done only once every few years. The contrast with fodder is starkest in Narmada/Bharuch, where most CFIs have banned drywood cutting but many carefully supervise fodder extraction (see appendix Table A6.4, and also Chapter 9).

In Nepal, although most CFIs do extract firewood periodically through formal procedures, this is again as part of the standard silviculture practice of pruning and clearing, undertaken either every winter or every two to five years. Many CFIs simply divide the cut wood equally among those contributing labour, but some have evolved more complex systems (Table A6.4). In CFI 10 (Nepal), for instance, the forest is divided into five blocks, each of which is further subdivided into seven plots. Each plot is supervised by a team of participating members who weed, cut, and prune. All participating households get equal amounts of firewood, but the teams that have done the best work are rewarded with more, and large families can ask for some extra. Although the method of distributing the cut wood can vary, the periodic pruning/clearing procedure is mandatory under the 'operational plan' prepared by the CFI, in consultation with the forest department, when the forest is transferred to the community. The procedure is meant to improve the forest and is not put into place specifically for the benefit of participating households, although women may benefit by default from the cut

Table 6.3. Periodic extraction rules for fodder and firewood

Region	Tree fodder	Grass fodder	Firewood (drywood and greenwood cutting)
GUJARAT			
Narmada/ Bharuch	Not extracted	Around 69% of the CFIs allow periodic cutting, and most have formal procedures for extraction and distribution.	Extraction is banned by most CFIs. None has formal procedures for extraction and distribution.
Panchmahals	Not extracted	Only 19% of CFIs allow periodic cutting, but none has formal procedures for extraction and distribution.	About 52% of CFIs allow periodic collection, but none has formal procedures for extraction and distribution.
Sabarkantha	Not extracted	About 39% of CFIs allow periodic cutting, but only some have formal procedures for extraction and distribution	About 29% allow periodic collection, but very few have formal procedures for extraction and distribution.
NEPAL			
Gorkha/ Dhading	Most CFIs ban collection. The 11% that allow periodic extraction and distribution have formal procedures.	Only 17% have periodic grass extraction, and another 6% give out on request. A few specify formal procedures for extraction and distribution.	About 83% organize periodic extraction and distribution, mostly under formal procedures, but as part of mandatory forest pruning/clearing operations. Some do so annually and others less frequently. Only some also open the forest for informal collection.
Baglung/ Parbat	About 53% of the CFIs formally organize periodic extraction and distribution.	Most of the CFIs—88%—formally organize periodic extraction and distribution.	About 97% organize formal extraction and distribution, but as part of mandatory forest pruning/clearing operations. Some do so annually and others less frequently. Only some also open the forest for informal collection.

wood that is distributed. In addition, a few CFIs open the forest periodically to allow members to collect twigs and branches without supervised distribution.

Why does firewood get less attention from the community than fodder? Several factors (discussed further in Chapter 9) appear to impinge on the relative importance given to fodder—the role of animals in the local economy, the financial cost of procuring fodder if not obtained from the forest, and gender bias. In Nepal draught animals are needed for hill cultivation, and in several Gujarat sites there is a flourishing milk economy.[13] Hence men share with women a significant interest in fodder while firewood is predominantly in women's domain. Also families that cannot collect fodder freely have to buy some, or sell off their animals. Many households report a fall in their animal stocks and an increase in fodder purchase, since protection began. Formal extraction and distribution of forest products require careful supervision. Typically men supervise. Given the potential costs associated with fodder shortages, male CFI members clearly think it worthwhile to put in the time and effort for fodder extraction, but are less willing to put in the same work for extracting firewood, which is seldom purchased, and the costs of shortages (extended collection and cooking time, adverse health effects) are non-monetary, less visible, and borne mainly by women and children.

All products are thus subject to some regulation, but CFIs differ in complex ways in the strictness of their rules. How might the group's gender composition impinge on these diverse rules, in particular their extent of strictness?

3. FACTORS AFFECTING STRICTNESS OF RULES

3.1 Measuring Strictness of Rules

Given the complexity and range of forest use rules, we need some kind of aggregation to compare rules across CFIs. For this purpose, I have computed an aggregated strictness index. Some additional analysis was done product-wise. The index is specified as follows:

$$S = w_1 P_1 + w_2 P_2 + \ldots\ldots\ldots\ldots\ldots w_n P_n = \sum_{i=1}^{n} w_i P_i$$

where S is the strictness index, $P_1, P_2, \ldots\ldots P_n$ are the n forest products/uses, and $w_1, w_2, \ldots\ldots w_n$ are the weights based on the degree of strictness of rules for that product/use.

All the forest products are weighted equally, since there was no obvious justification for weighting them differentially.[14] However, for each product, the degree of strictness is weighted differentially, as below:

- Full ban = 3
- Partial ban, and 'given on request' (on personal need or natural disaster) = 2.75 since these are closer to a full ban than to 'open occasionally'

[13] In interviews with 145 Gujarat households and 108 Nepal households in my fieldsites, 78 per cent of the former and 91 per cent of the latter reported owning large animals.

[14] For instance, fodder extraction in Nepal can take the form of plucking tree fodder, cutting grass fodder, or grazing. All three serve as cattle feed and access can depend on availability and other factors. There is no obvious reason for giving different weights for different types of fodder.

- 'Open occasionally' = 2.5 since this is closer to a full ban than 'open always' but less close than a 'partial ban'; and
- 'Open always' = 1

The value of *w* ranges between 1 and 3.[15] The number of forest uses included in the index is six for Gujarat and seven for Nepal. For Gujarat, the index includes rules for fallen twigs, drywood, timber species for firewood, grass fodder, grazing, and timber poles for house building, etc. For Nepal, the index includes rules for fallen twigs, drywood, tree fodder, grass fodder, grazing, timber for various uses, and leaf litter. The strictness index lies between 6 and 18 for Gujarat, and 7 and 21 for Nepal. The percentage of CFIs with given strictness scores for different items is given in Tables 6.1 and 6.2. The variations we observe are largely related to firewood and fodder rules. Occasionally other items, not listed in the tables, are also extracted, such as wood for cremation, or non-wood products such as flowers, wild vegetables, and berries, but information on these items was lacking for many sites, or not relevant (the forest had none). Hence these products are not included in the index.

3.2 Hypotheses

What factors are likely to affect the strictness of the rules formulated? Table 6.4 lists the factors that I examine empirically. Of course not all factors that might affect the rules can be captured quantitatively or directly. Perceptions about who is most likely to violate the rules is a case in point. There is a general (and often incorrect) perception, for example, that women are more likely to break rules than men: 44 per cent of CFIs in Nepal perceived women alone to be the main violators, although only 13 per cent of identified violations were by women alone (see Chapter 7). Male EC members are thus less willing to open the forest for extracting dry firewood on the argument that women will also take greenwood. Women recognize this bias:

> When we ask for permission to take dry twigs men say: what is the guarantee that you won't cut green branches? You might cut more. The men don't listen to us. (Village women to author in Sabarkantha, Gujarat, 1995)

Similar perceptions can colour how the landless are viewed. Perception bias cannot be quantified readily, but its potential effects, as subsumed in other variables, are discussed below under monitoring constraints.

[15] Any system of weightage would have an element of ad hocism. Here the logic is that between the two extremes—total ban and open always—lie rules which allow some extraction, but the extent (e.g. opening up the forest for a few days annually or via special permission for a specific need) deviates only in small degree from a full ban. The given weights reflect this relative closeness to a full ban, such as 2.50 and 2.75, which are close to the weight of 3 for a full ban and distant from the weight of 1 for open always. However, using slightly different weights, for instance by reducing those for open occasionally by 0.25 points, does not change the results in terms of the statistical significance of most of the explanatory variables.

Table 6.4. Rule-making: list of explanatory variables

Explanatory variables included in the regressions[a]	
Gujarat	Nepal
EC characteristics	**EC characteristics**
Gender composition of the EC	Gender composition of the EC
Average age of all EC members	Average age of all EC members
Percentage EC women from landless households	Percentage Brahmins in EC
Percentage all EC members from landless households	Average land owned by EC members
Gini coefficient for land owned by EC	Gini coefficient for land owned by EC
	CFI characteristics
	Member of another CFI
	Who made forest use rules?
Forest characteristics	**Forest characteristics**
Forest area protected (ha)	Forest area protected (ha)
Forest segments	Interactive term of forest area and gender composition
Gapfilled plus plantation area (ha)	Forest age
	Forest canopy
Village characteristics	**Location characteristics**
Presence of a women's association in the village	Presence of a women's association in the community
Total households in the village	Number of toles
Percentage landless households in village	District in which CFI is located

Note: [a] The table lists the variables finally used in the analysis. However a number of additional variables were also tested but found to be consistently insignificant in explaining the variation in the dependent variable. These were not included in the final equations, given sample size constraints.

My empirical analysis focuses in particular on the characteristics of the EC, the CFI, the population, and the resource (forest) base. These are all likely to matter by impinging on people's time preferences, monitoring costs, and resource constraints; and each of these can have gender and class dimensions. External agents can also influence rule formulation. Consider why we might expect these factors to make a difference.

Time preference

Unlike many other kinds of rules, those relating to environmental resources deal with the choices we make today for benefits that will accrue in the future, either to us or to our children. Hence rules will reflect time preferences, predicated on the ability or willingness to defer current consumption.[16] The greater this ability and

[16] There is a substantial economics literature on time preferences, but see especially a much-cited paper by Becker and Mulligan (1997).

willingness, the lower the time preference. Gender, age, economic status, and caste status—individually and/or interactively—can all affect this.

First, we would expect women's time preference to be much higher than men's, given notable gender differences in the use of and dependence on local forests and commons, as spelt out in Chapter 2. In particular, women's primary responsibility for firewood and fodder, their substantial dependence on common pool resources for procuring these items, and the everyday nature of their dependence, all make it more difficult for women to defer current use for future benefits. When forests are closed it is women who bear the immediate burden of finding alternative sources for items of daily use. In contrast, men's much more sporadic use of the forest for timber to make agricultural implements or for house building and repairs, and their greater ability to make up for shortfalls through purchase, would make for a lower time preference. However, insofar as women, relative to men, tend to think more about children's needs than personal needs—and there is substantial evidence that they do[17]—they might be more willing to endure the current costs of conserving forests. Hence, although in general we would expect women's presence in the EC to be associated with less strict rules insofar as self-interest prevails, they might make more strict rules if concern for their children's future prevails and the forests need time to recover. The one caveat to this would again be landless women who lack other means of fulfilling even their children's immediate needs.

Second, we would expect the elderly to have lower time preferences than the young, since the former would be more concerned about leaving behind a good forest as a legacy for their children.[18] Also older people, especially older women living in extended families, tend to have grown up children and daughters-in-law to carry the burden of finding alternative sites for fuel and fodder if the forest is closed.[19] In contrast, younger people who face the immediate costs of fuel or fodder shortages would be more inclined toward lenient rules. Hence the greater the EC's average age the stricter would we expect the rules to be.

Third, economic class, especially women's, would influence time preferences. Women from landless households are likely to have a higher time preference than those who have family land as a supplementary source of fuel, fodder, leaf litter,

[17] For instance, women are found to spend the income under their control primarily on family needs, especially children's needs (Mencher 1989, Noponen 1991). And the mother's assets are found to make a substantially greater difference to child survival, nutrition, health, and education than the father's assets (Thomas 1990, Duraisamy and Malathy 1991). Some also argue that women tend to think more in terms of family welfare than personal welfare (Sen 1990; Beneria and Roldan 1987).

[18] Some people, assuming a purely self-interested individual, might well argue to the contrary, namely that the elderly will have higher time preferences since they have less time to live. But such an assumption would mean ignoring cultural norms or social arrangements (such as interdependent living in joint families in South Asia) that promote other-regarding preferences, or the global evidence on altruistic inter-generational transfers of wealth which require that you consume less today to pass on something to your children (see also Stark 1995, Falk and Stark 2001).

[19] See also Gururani (1996) who describes such shifts in burdens from older to younger women, especially daughters-in-law, in the Uttarakhand hills (India).

etc. The more land the EC members own, the fewer difficulties they would face from strict closure.[20] We would thus expect ECs with a higher percentage of landless members, and especially of female landless members, to veer toward more lenient rules, and ECs with higher average land ownership to veer toward stricter rules. The effect of inequality in EC landownership (Gini coefficient) could go either way, depending on whether the interests of the landpoor or the landed prevail. In my sample, however, the range of inequality is low since no EC member owned over 4.2 ha in Gujarat or over 2 ha in Nepal (where almost all EC members owned some land).

Fourth, time preferences might differ by caste. The Upper-castes tend to be better off and also place more social restrictions on women's mobility. They thus depend less on local forests for items of daily use than the lower castes, and so would tend to suffer less hardship from restrictions on forest use.[21] ECs with more Brahmins, for instance, would therefore tend to veer toward stricter rules. Nepal has a fair degree of caste variation, but in the Gujarat sample tribal communities dominate.

Monitoring costs

Monitoring costs—actual or perceived—are another major factor impinging on rules. Both strict forest closure and periodic extraction involve supervision, but in different extent. Forest closure requires continuous monitoring over an extended period (by patrolling, keeping a guard, informal lookout, or some combination of these). Opening up the forest for controlled extraction requires short-term but complicated supervision to ensure that only the eligible enter and take only what is authorized. Given the monitoring costs of periodic opening, we might expect the CFI rule-makers to be somewhat reluctant to make rules that allow extraction.

The costs of both types of monitoring costs—daily protection and periodic extraction—would be affected by village and forest characteristics, such as population size, forest area protected, and the number of forest segments. The more numerous the village households, for instance, the more difficult it would be to oversee periodic extraction, thus creating tendencies toward stricter rules. Villages that have a large landless population might also go for greater strictness, expecting the forest-dependent landless to break rules if the forest is opened. This could arise as much from *perceptions* about the likelihood of rule violation, as from evidence that the landless break rules more often. Such perception bias can

[20] Of course landowners also need fodder for maintaining bullocks for cultivation, and more leaf litter for manure—items which they could potentially obtain from the commons. However, the substantial weight of the empirical evidence, at least for India, suggests that in overall terms the landed draw much less from the commons than the landless (Jodha 1986), possibly because the labour cost of such collection is greater compared with obtaining these items from one's own field. There can of course be deviations from the overall pattern for specific items, such as firewood, for which dependence on the commons is noted to be high across all classes (Narain et al. 2005, Natarajan 1995).

[21] See e.g. GoN (2001) for Nepal and also discussion of the regression results in this chapter.

be substantial, as will be discussed in Chapter 7. Actual and perceived difficulties of monitoring would also be linked to forest size, but the effects could move in either direction. Rules could be stricter in large forests insofar as extractions are more difficult to monitor in larger areas, or they could be less strict since more can be extracted without harming regeneration.[22] Both aspects would play out simultaneously. Forest segments (non-contiguous parts) could also affect monitoring costs. A segmented forest is difficult to supervise in a centralized way. In Panchmahals (Gujarat), for instance, villages with more segments tend to protect hamlet-wise, through communities located near a forest patch keeping an informal lookout. These communities need incentives to protect, such as being allowed to extract. This would make for less strict rules. This was tested for Gujarat but not for Nepal, both due to data gaps in Nepal and because most of Nepal's CFIs protect one segment carved out of the larger forest, rather than a historically inherited forest encroached upon and fragmented over time, as in Gujarat.

Gender can also impinge on monitoring in various ways. For instance, all-women's groups (as in Nepal) compared with other groups are likely to be more constrained in supervising extractions and may therefore opt for stricter rules.

Resource constraints

Forest characteristics—its size, condition, age, and segments—can also constrain forest use. Forest size per se would have a mixed effect, as noted above. A large forest reduces the resource constraint so that potentially more biomass can be extracted sustainably through less strict rules, but size increases the monitoring constraint which could lead to stricter rules. The age of the forest can matter, in that younger forests are more vulnerable to being damaged by people and animals, and would need stronger restrictions on entry. This could change as the forest ages. Improvement in canopy cover could likewise affect the availability of different forest items (e.g. a decrease in grass fodder but an increase in tree fodder) and so affect rules.[23] Similarly, the larger the gap-filled or new plantation area, the stricter are the rules likely to be, to protect young growth. In principle this strictness could decline over time, but in practice rules, once made, can prove to be 'sticky' and difficult to alter.

A gender dimension is indirectly linked to forest size and condition. We noted in Chapter 4 that in Nepal, all-women groups are systematically allocated smaller,

[22] Total forest size and total village households thus matter, each independently, apart from interactively. I therefore chose to keep both variables rather than a standardized forest per household measure. There is also a high correlation between total forest size and forest per household (0.88 in Gujarat), and substituting the latter for the former did not change the regression results in terms of which variables were significant.

[23] Of course product availability and regeneration processes are also affected by other factors, such as the type of plant species found or promoted in the region. And canopy can improve with forest age, but it can also vary by tree specie and season. Such factors should be kept in mind, although they could not be fine-tuned for the regression analysis.

younger, and more degraded forests than other groups. This leaves them less freedom to extract forest products and would propel them toward stricter rules. The interactive effect of gender and forest size has been examined through an interaction term (namely, the forest area protected multiplied by the relevant gender variable).

Resource constraints can of course be eased somewhat if the community can draw on alternative sources for fuel and fodder, such as their own land or other forests in the vicinity. In Nepal, for instance, people can belong to more than one CFI, and so access other protected forests. This option can allow a community to better protect its own by making stricter rules, especially where its own forest is small and degraded. Of course if every CFI responded in this way there would be strict rules all round. However, we would normally expect villagers to join another CFI only if they thought there was a reasonable chance of accessing its products. And there are many independent factors affecting rules which could lead some CFIs to be more open than others.

External influences

Finally, NGOs, donors, the forest department, and a women's association could all influence the rules as 'external agents', either directly if CFIs seek their help for framing rules, or indirectly through their influence on EC members. The effect of the forest department versus villagers and donors (in Nepal), and of the women's associations (in both Nepal and Gujarat) are measured directly through dummy variables. A women's association could support the EC women but it can also oppose them, especially if the class composition of the association is different from that of the EC. Typically women's associations in Gujarat are constituted of somewhat better-off women than those in Nepal. In some Gujarat districts, such as Narmada/Bharuch, however, almost all the villages have a women's association so these cannot explain rule differences here. Moreover, in Gujarat as a whole, 81 per cent of CFIs reported that villagers alone made the rules (Chapter 4), so external involvement in rule-making is not used as an explanatory variable in the Gujarat analysis, although there is indirect NGO influence in these sites. Some indirect effects of external agents such as NGOs and donors are also captured by the district dummies.

* * *

To test the above hypotheses, regressions were run jointly for all districts and also separately for each one, since some of the explanatory variables have district-specific characteristics, such as a large percentage of landless women on the EC, or a high incidence of gap-filled or plantation area, or forests of large size, the effects of which can get obscured in the aggregate analysis. In addition, product-wise analysis was undertaken for each important forest product for which the rules varied sufficiently to make comparisons relevant. For some variables, the direction of effects can differ between products. Some effects may therefore show up in the product-wise analysis which might get cancelled out in the aggregate index.

The product-wise indicators have been formulated as dichotomous variables. For all products, other than tree fodder (in Nepal), the focus of comparison is 'open always' versus 'open occasionally' clubbed with 'partial ban' and 'full ban', since there are rather few cases of complete ban for some of the products. For tree fodder, however, since there is no case of 'open always', the comparison is between 'full ban' and 'partial ban' plus 'open occasionally'. I use ordinary least square (OLS) regressions with standard errors corrected for heteroskedasticity for the aggregate strictness index, which is a continuous variable (albeit within a limited range), and logistic regressions for the product-wise analysis.

It needs mention that I do not expect potential problems of omitted variable bias or reverse causality in relation to the EC's gender composition, which is the explanatory variable we are most interested in. As discussed at some length in Chapter 4, a specific probing revealed that the factors which underlie variations in the EC's gender composition are largely non-systematic and context-specific, often varying by village. The forest use rules are also highly variable and product-specific. Hence, there is little reason to expect that some omitted variable would systematically affect both EC gender composition and rules in a given direction. Reverse causality, again, is unlikely since rules are made *after* the EC is formed. In other words ECs are constituted in time 't' and in turn formulate forest use rules in time 't+k'. Subsequent changes in the EC's gender composition are moderate (20 per cent in Gujarat and 16 per cent in Nepal), and in these cases the rules' strictness category has shifted in only three CFIs in Gujarat and four in Nepal. Moreover, I found no evidence of a change in the EC's gender composition as a conscious response to the potential effects of women's presence on rule formulation. Thus while gender composition can have a bearing on the rules made, the reverse appears unlikely.

4. REGRESSION RESULTS

The regression results are summarized in Tables 6.5 to 6.6 and appendix Tables A6.5 and A6.6. The variable definitions and descriptive statistics are given in appendix tables (AE.1–AE.6) at the end of the book. The notes at the bottom of each table explain the reasons for omitting some of the variables in particular equations.

4.1 Gender Variables

The gender results (which are robust across different specifications) have some expected and some surprising features. As expected, the impact of the EC's gender composition is significant in most equations for both Gujarat and Nepal. For Gujarat, gender is significant for each district-wise run, although not in the all-district equation (Table 6.5). For Nepal, gender is significant for all districts taken together and for Gorkha/Dhading, although insignificant for Baglung/Parbat (Table 6.6).

Table 6.5. Gujarat: factors affecting strictness of rules all districts and district-wise

Dependent variable	Strictness index			
Region	All districts	Narmada/ Bharuch	Panchmahals	Sabarkantha
Equation no.	1	2	3	4
Statistical method	OLS (r)	OLS (r)	OLS (r)	OLS (r)
No. of observations	59	16	20	28
R^2	0.24	0.69	0.92	0.48
Explanatory variables	**Coef.**	**Coef.**	**Coef.**	**Coef.**
GenComp1: dummy (>2 EC women = 1)	0.70 (0.346)	5.57** (0.029)	−4.11*** (0.006)	1.73* (0.075)
Women's association: dummy (Assoc. exists=1)	1.33* (0.099)		2.73*** (0.003)	−0.18 (0.853)
% EC women from landless households	0.03 (0.121)		−0.07* (0.058)	
% all EC members from landless households	−0.06 (0.305)	0.09 (0.223)	0.21** (0.042)	
Average age of all EC members[a]	−0.01 (0.899)			
Gini coefficient for land owned by the EC	−1.97 (0.612)	−15.68* (0.064)	1.42 (0.698)	−6.47 (0.155)
Forest area protected (ha)	0.00 (0.804)	0.04 (0.126)	0.004 (0.210)	0.003** (0.048)
No. of forest segments	−0.57† (0.105)	0.20 (0.800)	−0.24 (0.363)	−2.28*** (0.007)
Gap-filled plus plantation area (ha)	-0.001 (0.955)	0.001 (0.984)	0.15* (0.067)	−0.11*** (0.000)
Total households in village	0.01** (0.041)	0.02** (0.035)	0.01*** (0.004)	0.01** (0.017)
% landless households in village	0.07* (0.085)	−0.04 (0.510)	0.10 (0.304)	0.20*** (0.000)
Constant	12.98	10.98	11.60	15.69

Notes: [a] Average age of the EC was also found to be insignificant in the district-wise runs and so was not included in the final equations, given sample size constraints.
OLS (r) = OLS regressions with robust standard errors.
Numbers in parenthesis are *p*-values. Significance: *** at 1%, ** at 5%, * at 10%, † at close to 10%.

Notes on the models
Narmada/Bharuch: Eqn. 2: Women's association was not included as an explanatory variable due to low variability: 14 out of the 16 villages had such an association. Similarly % EC women from landless households was not included since only two CFIs had landless women EC members.
Sabarkantha: Eqn. 4: The % EC women from landless households was not included since only one CFI has landless women EC members, and overall also very few CFIs had any landless EC members.

Table 6.6. Nepal: factors affecting strictness of rules all districts and district-wise

Dependent variable	Strictness index				
Region	All Districts			Gorkha/ Dhading	Baglung/ Parbat
Equation no.	1	2	3	4	5
Statistical method	OLS (r)	OLS (r)	OLS (r)	OLS (r)	OLS (r)
No. of observations	67	67	67	35	32
R^2	0.52	0.53	0.47	0.54	0.38
Explanatory variables	**Coef.**	**Coef.**	**Coef.**	**Coef.**	**Coef.**
GenComp: dummy (all-women EC = 1)	2.49** (0.012)			3.44** (0.044)	0.71 (0.555)
GenComp2: % EC women		0.04** (0.019)	0.02* (0.059)		
Women's association: dummy (assoc. exists=1)	0.11 (0.851)	–0.17 (0.814)	–0.40 (0.576)	–0.86 (0.392)	0.79 (0.353)
Average age of all EC members	0.18*** (0.005)	0.19*** (0.001)	0.23*** (0.000)	0.24** (0.019)	0.04 (0.644)
Average land owned by EC members (ha)	1.08 (0.140)	1.15** (0.049)	1.01* (0.092)	2.60** (0.033)	–0.18 (0.728)
Gini coefficient for land owned by EC	6.51** (0.045)	5.41** (0.037)		10.54 (0.107)	0.80 (0.784)
% Brahmins in EC	0.02** (0.017)	0.02** (0.019)	0.02** (0.045)	0.03* (0.056)	0.01 (0.410)
Member of another CFI: dummy (if member =1)	0.89 (0.235)	0.79 (0.270)	1.30** (0.042)	0.80 (0.476)	–0.11 (0.929)
Who made forest use rules (no help from FD = 1)	0.62 (0.365)	0.66 (0.321)	0.48 (0.512)	1.01 (0.305)	–1.20 (0.155)
Forest area protected (ha)	0.01 (0.334)	0.03* (0.073)	0.01 (0.484)	0.02 (0.123)	0.01 (0.183)
Interactive term 1: forest area with GenComp	–0.06** (0.036)			–0.04 (0.457)	–0.07* (0.096)
Interactive term 2: forest area with GenComp2		–0.001* (0.090)			
Forest age: dummy (medium or old=1)	–0.26 (0.651)	–0.20 (0.746)		–0.93 (0.214)	–0.76 (0.458)
No. of toles	–0.05 (0.649)	–0.06 (0.501)	–0.04 (0.683)	–0.16 (0.480)	0.07 (0.524)
District: dummy (Baglung/ Parbat=1)	2.44*** (0.001)	2.52*** (0.001)	2.36*** (0.002)		
Constant	2.48	1.23	1.95	–2.35	15.10

Notes: OLS (r) = OLS regressions with robust standard errors.
Numbers in parenthesis are *p*-values. Significance: *** at 1%, ** at 5%, * at 10%.

Differences between the models
All districts: Eqn. 1 uses the gender dummy; Eqn. 2 includes gender as a continuous variable to reveal the effect of forest area protected; Eqn. 3 omits the interactive term and the forest age dummy to reveal the effect of membership in another CFI

Additional runs: Eqn. 1 was also run by using two dichotomous gender variables: all-women dummy and >2 EC women dummy, with ≤2 EC women as the reference category. CFIs with all-women ECs made stricter rules than those with ≤2 EC women but were not statistically different from CFIs with >2 EC women. It is notable that both all-women groups and >2 women groups received smaller forests than ≤2 women groups.

It is the direction of the relationship, however, that is unexpected. With the exception of one district, CFIs with more EC women consistently make stricter rules, whether we compare groups with >2 EC women and those with ≤2 EC women for Gujarat, or we compare all-women groups and other groups for Nepal. The exception is Panchmahals in Gujarat. Here CFIs with >2 EC women are significantly less strict by the strictness index than CFIs with ≤2 EC women.

The product-wise results follow a similar pattern on this count. In Gujarat, for instance, although gender is only significant for drywood cutting, ECs with more than two women make stricter rules (Appendix Table A6.5).[24] In Nepal, similarly, all-women ECs relative to other ECs tend to make stricter rules for grass collection and grazing (Appendix Table A6.6). In addition, since Panchmahals was an exception in the aggregate index, I examined product-wise rules for this district separately. Here gender was only significant for grazing, but again the direction of the relationship, as with the aggregate index, was toward lenient rules—ECs with >2 women relative to ≤2 women had less strict rules, veering toward open always as versus ban or open occasionally (table not reproduced here).

In other words, of the five sub-regions—Gorkha/Dhading, Baglung/Parbat, Narmada/Bharuch, Sabarkantha, and Panchmahals—women's greater presence is associated with more strict rules in three, a neutral effect in one, and less strict rules in the last, after controlling for other factors.

Why are rules typically stricter in CFIs with more EC women? And why are such CFIs in Panchmahals an exception? The answers appear to lie in a combination of factors. First, in all the sites, except Panchmahals, the vast majority of EC women belong to landed households, and most ECs have no landless members. Women here are thus better placed to fulfil their firewood needs (at least in part) from their own land, and so are better able to accept stricter rules than women from landless households. In Panchmahals, on average, 52 per cent of the female EC members are landless, compared with only 9 per cent in Narmada/Bharuch, 1 per cent in Sabarkantha, and 1.4 per cent in Nepal as a whole.[25] Also 60 per cent of Panchmahals's ECs relative to only 12 per cent of those in Narmada/Bharuch, 4 per cent in Sabarkantha, and 10 per cent in the Nepal fieldsites have any landless women (Table 6.7).

The overall representation of the landless in the Panchmahals ECs is also disproportionately higher than their presence in the village population. This is not the case in the other districts. For instance, on average, only about 2 per cent of Panchmahals' village households are landless compared with 14 per cent of Panchmahals' EC members (Table 6.7). In Narmada/Bharuch, by contrast, although 21 per cent of village households on average are landless only 10 per cent of EC members are landless. In Nepal, landlessness among the EC is very

[24] I also examined grazing for all districts together, but none of the variables was significant.

[25] Landlessness here reflects an EC member's household property status, and not the individual property status.

low—1.4 per cent of all EC members are landless in the sample, and only 11 per cent of all ECs have any landless EC members. The high proportion of landless women among the women EC members in Panchmahals, compared with the other Gujarat fieldsites as well as with Nepal, coupled with the disproportionately high percentage of landless per se in the Panchmahals ECs (again mainly due to the presence of landless women) relative to their percentage in the village population, would also explain why women's greater presence is associated with less strict rules in Panchmahals.

Women from landless households will understandably veer toward less strict rules because of their greater forest dependence. Also, as we found in Chapter 5, landless women, if present in sufficient proportions, are usually found to be less inhibited in speaking up for their concerns than landed women, especially where basic survival issues (such as firewood shortages) are involved. We can thus infer that the presence of landless women in the EC has played a role in moving the rules toward greater leniency. This is further established by the Panchmahals results (Table 6.5, Equation 3). We find that over and above having more women in the EC the higher the percentage of landless women among them the less strict are the rules, while simply having more landless in the EC (that is, including landless men) makes for stricter rules. Poor men, unlike poor women, are more likely to go along with other men, since firewood is seen as a female concern and poor men who speak up on their wives' behalf can be labelled as 'henpecked'.[26]

Of course women of all households gain if the CFIs allow more firewood and fodder extraction, since the rules apply to all and even the landed own only small plots. But the benefits are especially important for the landless. Women from landed households are less compelled than those from landless households to make a case for lenient rules and battle this out with male EC members.[27] This does suggest that, in particular contexts, what can make a difference is not simply more female presence in decision-making, but a representation of women who have a particularly strong stake in the outcome, such as poor women.

A second explanation, relevant specifically for Nepal, lies in the earlier-noted resource constraint that CFIs with more EC women face. In particular, the smaller-sized, more degraded forests that all-women groups received leaves them less free to make rules that allow periodic extraction. A gender interest in making less strict rules is thus mediated by their resource constraint. The

[26] During my 1998–99 fieldwork I commonly observed that poor men, especially if low caste, would not take up their wives' cause in meetings, even if in personal conversations they admitted that their family was facing acute firewood shortage.

[27] There is no obvious way of knowing whether all the women have consented to stricter rules, or whether some or even most have merely kept silent because of social constraints and their internalization of social norms that restrict their agency, as argued by some feminist scholars (see e.g. Fierlback 1997). As noted in Chapter 1, however, constraints that operate individually need not operate in equal measure for a group, and, as found in Chapter 5, a higher presence of women can reduce social restrictions and person reticence.

Table 6.7. Gujarat and Nepal: average land owned and landlessness among EC members

Districts	% landless households in village[a]	% landless EC Members[a]			% CFIs with over–representation of landless in EC[b]	% ECs with female landless members	% ECs with any landless members
		Men	Women	All			
GUJARAT							
Narmada/ Bharuch (N=16)	21.2	10.1	9.1	9.9	18.8	12.5	43.8
Panchmahals (N=20)	1.7	1.8	51.8	14.1	60.0	60.0	60.0
Sabarkantha (N=28)	3.1	1.5	1.0	1.3	10.7	3.6	14.3
All districts (N=64)	**6.7**	**3.9**	**17.4**	**7.5**	**28.1**	**23.4**	**35.9**
NEPAL							
Gorkha/ Dhading (N=36)	n.a.	0.0	1.2	0.8	n.a.	8.3	8.3
Baglung/ Parbat (N=34)	n.a.	2.6	1.6	2.1	n.a.	11.8	14.7
All districts (N=70)	**n.a.**	**1.5**	**1.4**	**1.4**	**n.a.**	**10.0**	**11.4**

Notes: N= number of CFIs.

[a] Computed for each district as a whole. The figures are, however, very close to the means of village-wise percentages. Not all villages have landless households.

[b] Over-representation is computed here for each CFI by subtracting the percentage of landless households in the EC from the percentage of landless households in the village. The remaining CFIs either have under-representation or have no landless in the village.

n.a. = not applicable, since the village is not the forest protecting unit in Nepal.

interactive term between gender and forest area also indicates this (Table 6.6, Equations 1, 2). While both gender and forest size are positively related to strictness, the coefficient of the interactive term, although rather small, is significant and negative. This suggests that if women had more and better forests at their command they would veer toward less strict rules. Also, again especially for all-women groups, the monitoring constraint can be high, since it is sometimes more difficult for women alone to take time off and organize the kind of careful supervision that is needed for fodder or fuelwood extraction, or to obtain male cooperation for this purpose. In other words, as hypothesized, gender affects rule formulation in a complex way, mediated especially by the economic situation of the EC women (as found in Gujarat), as well as the greater resource and monitoring constraints that all-women groups tend to face (as found in Nepal).

The effect of women's associations (mahila mandals) also appears to play out along class lines. In Gujarat, the associations tend to be constituted more of women from landed households. This is probably why CFIs with mahila mandals tend to make stricter rules (Table 6.5, Equations 1, 3; appendix Table A6.5, Equation 2).[28] Indeed, in Panchmahals, villages with mahila mandals make stricter rules even while the ECs with more women veer toward leniency. In Nepal, the women's associations (amma samuhs) are more class-mixed and have a neutral effect in all equations.

4.2 Other (Non-Gender) Explanatory Variables

Apart from the EC's gender (and class) composition and women's associations, some other variables are also striking. First, as hypothesized, age and caste are significant in Nepal. The average age of the EC members is consistently and positively linked with stricter rules in Nepal (although not in Gujarat), in almost all the equations (aggregate level as well as product-wise). Older EC members, as noted, bear less of the burden of strict forest closure since they tend to have grown-up children, especially daughters-in-law, to help, and also frequently say they want to leave behind a good forest for their children and grandchildren. Indeed the one consistent refrain in interviews with villagers in almost every CFI was that they hoped their children had learnt to love the forest and would continue protecting it, 'as their parents and grandparents have done'. Also in their environmental histories they recount that many older villagers had led the protection efforts after seeing the effects of degradation at first hand,[29] and they continue to persuade the young to carry this effort forward: 'The old people keep saying that we should protect the forest. Now people are starting to understand that' (forest users in Chitradevi CFI, Gorkha, Nepal, 2000).

Similarly, caste can matter: the Nepal results consistently indicate that ECs with more upper-caste (Brahmin) members have stricter rules. Brahmins tend to use the local forests less than other groups, either because they are more land endowed or due to stricter social norms for women, or both. Nepal's Hill Brahmins, for example, are much less dependent on firewood for cooking than other hill communities: in the 2001 census 61 per cent of them reported firewood as their main fuel, compared with around 80 per cent of the ethnic communities such as the Tamangs and Magars, and around 90 per cent of the dalits (GoN 2001). Economic inequality, measured by the Gini coefficient of land owned by

[28] See also Davidson-Hunt (1995) who found that mahila mandals in her two study villages in Himachal Pradesh (India) were dominated by upper-caste women. When the mahila mandals took up forest protection they formulated strict forest use rules, leading to tensions with lower-caste women who depended on the forests for their livelihoods and subsistence needs.

[29] See Chapter 4 and also Agrawal (2005) and Buchy and Rai (2008) on how villagers can become conservationists over time.

EC members, is also linked with stricter rules in Nepal, both overall and for twigs collection, as well as stricter rules in Gujarat for drywood collection. The only exception is the district-level result for Narmada/Bharuch where the EC's Gini coefficient is linked with less strict rules.

Second, again as hypothesized, the variables associated with monitoring difficulties (actual or perceived) significantly affect the strictness of rules in several equations, especially for Gujarat. Rules tend to be stricter the more the village households, the greater the percentage of landless villagers, and the larger the forest area. Supervising periodic forest opening, as noted earlier, is seen to be more difficult with large populations and landlessness, since villagers assume that the needier will steal unauthorized forest products, if allowed to enter the forest for selected extraction.[30] The link between strictness and the size of the village population is consistent across Gujarat and for all the district-wise runs. However, the positive association between forest size and strictness (in some of the Gujarat and Nepal runs) is the net result of two opposing forces: the higher cost of supervised extraction with larger forests pulling toward greater strictness, and more resource availability pulling toward lesser strictness. The monitoring constraint wins out here. Another kind of monitoring problem is linked with forest segments. We find in Gujarat, as hypothesized, less strict rules in segmented forests. Such forests are difficult to guard through a centralized system and, as noted earlier, communities allow nearby hamlets to extract firewood and other products as an incentive to protect their patch.

Third, forest characteristics matter, although selectively. In Panchmahals, the larger the newly planted area the stricter the rules, since entry can negatively affect new shoots. The opposite is the case in Sabarkantha where plantations are more mature. Forest canopy and age similarly have an impact. In Nepal, rules for tree fodder are less strict where the forest canopy is dense. This makes sense given that thicker canopies can yield more tree fodder without damaging the tree.[31] For grazing, similarly, CFIs with older forests tend to be less restrictive presumably because there are fewer young saplings that animals can trample or eat. Forest size, as already discussed, can have divergent effects on monitoring and resource availability. But the resource availability problem (without any monitoring fallout) can be alleviated to some extent where communities have legitimate access to another local forest, as possible in Nepal. Here we find some limited indication that CFIs whose users are also members in another CFI tend to make stricter rules (see Nepal's results: Table 6.6, Equation 3; appendix Table A6.6, Equation 2). As women of the Jana Jagaran CFI, an all-women's group in Baglung, Nepal, explained:

[30] Based on their early fieldwork in Nepal, Arnold and Campbell (1986) similarly noted that if communities felt they could not easily control an open harvest, they preferred to stop collection altogether.

[31] The thickness of the tree canopy was used as an explanatory variable only for tree fodder for which it is directly relevant.

We bring most of the firewood from the other side—the Mauyeni community forest. We can fetch dry fallen branches all the time. It is a large forest of mahua trees. So we can protect our own better.[32] (Author's survey, 2000–01)

During my 1998–99 fieldwork, I found that this approach was also fairly common in many regions in India. In the Uttarakhand hills, for instance, van panchayat villages often drew upon government reserve forests for firewood and medicinal herbs, leaving their own community forests intact.[33] Sometimes women would walk up to 12 kilometres to access a reserve forest. The Gujarat villagers have no legal access to another forest, so they underreport usage if there is a government forest in the vicinity which they use clandestinely.

Fourth, inter-district differences (the district dummies) were consistently insignificant in the Gujarat analysis (models not presented in the tables), but significant in Nepal in several equations. The gender-related differences between districts, however, are much better captured by the district-level equations, discussed above. Finally, external agents other than women's associations have an insignificant impact on rule-making, although some indirect effects are likely to be subsumed in the district dummies.

4.3 Further Discussion

We have examined the factors affecting the rules as formulated around the time formal protection began. Do the rules change over time? In principle, rules need to be reviewed periodically and adjusted to changes in forest condition and the size of the forest-dependent population, or altered if the rules initially formulated are found too strict or too lax or too inequitable. Most CFIs, however, continue with the initial rules. About 30 per cent in Gujarat and 16 per cent in Nepal mention introducing occasional changes, but typically this is in the distribution methods, and only sometimes in strictness of rules. An interesting example is that of Rampuri village in Gujarat where the woman president of the EC—one of the rare Gujarat CFIs with a woman office bearer—suggested that the EC consult the village women about the grass extraction rules. Earlier when grass was extracted, those supervising the operation received a percentage of grass bundles. However, the women suggested that the villagers should be allowed to keep the fodder and pay the supervisors in cash, otherwise the villagers had to make up the balance by buying fodder from the market at a higher price. This suggestion was accepted and now the supervisors receive cash payments—something which has also benefited the men who now spend less on grass purchase (see also CFI 8, appendix Table A6.3). In Nepal, similarly,

[32] Indeed, many all-women CFIs join another CFI with this expectation, although the promise of access that membership in another CFI provides, may not always be fulfilled in practice.

[33] Gururani (1996) also documents this for Uttarakhand and Davidson-Hunt (1995) for Himachal Pradesh.

some CFIs have shifted from auctioning grass to equal distribution, in response to villagers' complaints.

At times, the changes in rules also impinge on strictness and not simply on the method of distribution—occasionally the rules become stricter but usually they move toward leniency. In Gujarat, most of the changes involve allowing fodder cutting and grazing where these were banned before, while rule changes allowing more firewood extraction are largely confined to Panchmahals, probably due to the influence of landless EC women there and the EC's response to village women's bitter complaints about firewood shortages. In Nepal also, the limited shift toward leniency is largely for fodder and grazing. Notably, though, of the mixed-gender CFIs which changed the rules, 56 per cent in Gujarat and 75 per cent in Nepal are those with more than two EC women. This suggests that women's greater presence on the EC *does* give them more influence in CFI decision-making, although the rule changes appear to be largely ad hoc and reactive, rather than based on an assessment of the ecological potential for extraction, or on a discussion with people about their needs.

5. CONCLUDING COMMENTS

Within the overall regulation regime of CFIs, forest use rules are marked by considerable diversity and their extent of strictness varies by product, and further by the characteristics of the forest, the population served, and the composition of the decision-making bodies. The gender composition results are both expected and unexpected. As hypothesized, the group's gender composition does make a significant difference to the rules formulated, but the direction of the difference is unexpected. Given the pressures on village women, especially for firewood and fodder collection, I expected them to favour extraction today rather than years later, and so push for lenient rules. I found, however, that CFIs with more women made stricter rules, except in Panchmahals (Gujarat) where such CFIs made less strict rules. The high presence of landless women among the Panchmahals ECs which made less strict rules and their low presence elsewhere is clearly one factor underlying this difference. Another is the limited freedom that Nepal's all-women groups have for making lenient rules, given the smaller and poorer forests they received. Age is also a mediator. Older EC members, including older women, tend to make stricter rules, probably because of lower time preferences and lower personal costs from strict closure. In other words, the difference women's proportionate strength makes to forest use rules is tempered by their class, age, the nature of the product, and the resource constraint that women-dominant ECs face.

How might we expect the structure of rules associated with women's greater presence (stricter in some regions, less so in others) to play out in terms of equity, institutional sustainability, and conservation? To begin with, less strict rules would imply more equitable outcomes, since they allow greater extraction of products such as firewood which would benefit women (particularly the poor) in an immediate sense. CFIs with a high representation of landless women on the EC which veer toward less strict rules are thus likely to be more equitable than CFIs with a low presence of landless EC women.

We would also expect institutional sustainability to be higher among CFIs with a high proportion of EC women, especially the landless, since by involving those most dependent on the forest the CFIs are more likely to make socially acceptable rules and ensure greater commitment to rule compliance and protection. Overall this would thus help better fulfil the principles identified in institutional analysis as important for building enduring CPR institutions.

The effect on conservation is somewhat more difficult to predict, but overall it is likely to be positive insofar as the rules are adapted to social and ecological conditions. In the Gujarat sites, where highly forest-dependent tribal communities dominate and landlessness is non-trivial in several parts, and where the protected forests are relatively large and non-timber firewood species are common, the less strict rules made by CFIs with a notable presence of landless EC women appear appropriate socially as well as ecologically. In contrast, the rules made in women's absence can be overly conservative in ecological terms, while being socially inadequate. This inference is also supported by data on biomass regeneration and extraction collected by a set of scholars and practitioners in two Panchmahals villages. These villages, which had only two women in their ECs, were found to be extracting less than 10 per cent of the firewood they could extract sustainably, sustainable extraction being defined as 50 per cent of the annual biomass generated (Ravindranath et al. 2000; also see Chapter 9 for details). Here women's complaints about firewood shortages were also acute. We can therefore surmise that involving more landless women in rule-making, and making rules more lenient in those Gujarat villages where they are currently very strict, could improve conservation by enhancing the social acceptance of rules, while maintaining ecological sustainability.

In Nepal, however, the stricter rules framed by all-women groups appear to be ecologically appropriate, given their smaller and poorer forests, and could also prove to be fairly acceptable socially, since the region has a low incidence of landlessness. Moreover, that the women voluntarily make stricter rules, despite any personal hardship (and even when, as with all-women ECs, they largely control rule-making), indicates that their governance practices are informed by a notable concern for conservation. Hence here also the induction of more women into ECs is likely to benefit the forests. Chapter 8 will further examine these propositions.

Finally, the results in this chapter support a point made in Chapter 1, namely, that community decisions on local resource use involve the rule-framers in choices that can affect them personally. This personal stake can bring to the surface potential conflicts of interest—self-interest versus other people's interests, or immediate interest versus long-term interest. And such interests can have gendered dimensions. Community-level decision-making also helps highlight the importance of *process*, and of participatory rule-making and rule adaptation in response to changes in ecological conditions and social dissatisfaction. But rather than rely on ad hoc systems of feedback (e.g. women's complaints), institutional mechanisms need to be set up for receiving feedback from the users, especially the more disadvantaged, such as poor women.

APPENDIX TABLES

Table A6.1. Gujarat: rules for forest use, district-wise (% CFIs)

Products extracted, strictness rules, and weights given	Open always (1)	Open occasionally (2. 5)	Partial ban or given on request (2.75)	Full ban (3)
		Narmada/Bharuch (N=16)		
Fallen twigs	68.8	6.2	0.0	25.0
Drywood (cutting)	12.5	0.0	0.0	87.5
Grass fodder	31.2	68.8	0.0	0.0
Grazing	25.0	6.2	43.8	25.0
Timber species for firewood	0.0	0.0	0.0	100.0
Timber poles for house building, etc.	0.0	0.0	0.0	100.0
		Panchmahals (N=21)		
Fallen twigs	61.9	38.1	0.0	0.0
Drywood (cutting)	38.1	52.4	4.8	4.8
Grass fodder	57.1	19.0	4.8	19.0
Grazing	42.9	0.0	42.9	14.3
Timber species for firewood	0.0	0.0	0.0	100.0
Timber poles for house building, etc.	0.0	4.8	23.8	71.4
		Sabarkantha (N=28)		
Fallen twigs	50.0	21.4	0.0	28.6
Drywood (cutting)	25.0	28.6	3.6	42.9
Grass fodder	53.6	39.3	3.6	3.6
Grazing	46.4	0.0	21.4	32.1
Timber species for firewood	0.0	0.0	3.6	96.4
Timber poles for house building, etc.	0.0	0.0	7.1	92.9
		All districts (N=65)		
Fallen twigs	58.5	23.1	0.0	18.5
Drywood (cutting)	26.2	29.2	3.1	41.5
Grass fodder	49.2	40.0	3.1	7.7
Grazing	40.0	1.5	33.8	24.6
Timber species for firewood	0.0	0.0	1.5	98.5
Timber poles for house building, etc.	0.0	1.5	10.8	87.7

Note: See also notes in the text of Table 6.1.

Table A6.2. Nepal: rules for forest use, district-wise (% CFIs)

Products extracted, strictness rules, and weights given	Open always (1)	Open occasionally (2.5)	Partial ban or given on request (2.75)	Full ban (3)
		Gorkha/Dhadhing (N=36)		
Fallen twigs	63.9	22.2	5.6	8.3
Drywood (cutting)	2.8	83.3[b]	5.6	8.3
Tree fodder	0.0	11.1	13.9	75.0
Grass fodder	75.0	16.7	5.6	2.8
Grazing	47.2	8.3	13.9	30.6
Timber	0.0	0.0	72.2	27.8
Leaf litter	58.3	16.7	2.8	22.2
		Baglung/Parbat (N=34)		
Fallen twigs	26.5	61.8	2.9	8.8
Drywood (cutting)	0.0	97.1	0.0	2.9
Tree fodder	0.0	52.9	3.0	44.1
Grass fodder	5.9	88.2	0.0	5.9
Grazing	5.9	2.9	14.7	76.5
Timber	0.0	0.0	52.9	47.1
Leaf litter	20.6	58.8	2.9	17.6
		All Districts (N=70)		
Fallen twigs	45.7	41.4	4.3	8.6
Drywood (cutting)	1.4	90.0	2.8	5.7
Tree fodder	0.0	31.4	8.5	60.0
Grass fodder	41.4	51.4	2.9	4.3
Grazing	27.1	5.7	14.3	52.9
Timber	0.0	0.0	62.9	37.1
Leaf litter	40.0	37.1	2.9	20.0

Note: See also notes in the text of Table 6.2.

Table A6.3. Grass fodder collection rules—examples from India and Nepal, 1998–99 and 2000–01

State/country/CFI	Days open	No of persons	Method
Gujarat, India (based on my 2000–01 survey)			
CFI 1 (Narmada)	A few days per year	2/hh. Members only. Usually women go	The cut grass is tied into bundles, 10% of which are given to the EC and the rest are distributed equally among the participating households. For distribution, the bundles are placed in equal piles and each pile is given a number. Each member picks a number at random and takes the relevant pile. They have followed this rule for nine years.
CFI 2 (Narmada)	8–10 days per year	2/hh. Both members and non-members can go. Usually women go	Of the grass that the members cut, 25% goes to the CFI and the rest is equally divided among the participating member households. Of the grass that the non-members cut 50% goes to the CFI. Those wanting more can buy back grass from the CFI. The non-members are charged more than members.
CFI 3 (Narmada)	A few days per year	1/hh. Only members can enter	The forest area is divided into two parts. One part is open for cattle grazing and the other is protected. On the latter, members can cut grass and tie it into bundles, the size of which is pre-decided by the EC. The bundles are then divided equally among the participant households.
CFI 4 (Sabarkantha)	2–3 days per year (around October–November) until all the grass is cut	1/hh. Only members can enter	All the grass cut is collected in a common place and all the participating households get equal shares. If a household is present for only one day, then that household's share is calculated according to one day's labour contribution.
CFI 5 (Sabarkantha)	One week	No bar on numbers, but only members can enter	Members cut grass and make bundles. A percentage of the bundles are given to the CFI and the rest are distributed among the members. The CFI grass is sold and the proceeds are used to pay the guard's salary.
CFI 6 (Sabarkantha)	5–6 days in November or December	1/hh. Only members can enter	Each member receives a token. The grass is cut in line under supervision, a patch at a time. From what they cut, the members can take as much grass as they want.
CFI 7 (Sabarkantha)	One week after monsoon each year	1/hh	Participating households can take as much grass as they want. There is no formal method of distribution.

(*continued*)

Table A6.3. (Continued)

State/country/CFI	Days open	No of persons	Method
CFI 8 (Sabarkantha)	4–5 days per year	1/hh for cutting, but they can ask other family members to help carry the grass home	Their system has been changing over the years since protection began. (a) First year: the forest was opened for 4–5 days and any number of persons per household could collect and take as much as they wanted. Some 50–60 persons came. (b) Second year: Each member household was given a token. A roll call was held on the forest opening day; 10–12 persons supervised the operation. Everyone had to stop cutting by noon and make bundles. Each household that came to cut grass donated one bundle to a pile and took the rest. The bundles in the pile were divided equally among the supervisors. The tokens were returned to the supervisors at the end of the day. These rules were made by the male EC members. But the village women were unhappy about contributing fodder to the supervisors. Then a woman was elected as EC president—one of the few women to hold office. At her suggestion the village women were asked what rule changes they wanted and the rules were changed accordingly. (c) Third year: the rules suggested by the women were followed. The token system was kept in place but the method of paying the supervisors was not pre-decided. When three days worth of grass was left, all 226 women who came to cut were asked how they would like to pay. They calculated the value of the grass, and how much they could pay in cash. They decided to pay the supervisors in cash. Otherwise these households had to buy grass for their own use at a higher rate.
CFI 9 (Sabarkantha)	10 days per year after discussion in meeting	1/hh for cutting.	Each participant is given a token. The forest is divided into four plots and ten people supervise each plot. Sometimes women also serve as supervisors. Each

			participating household is assigned to one of the 4 groups, and each group is sent to cut one plot. About 300 out of 400 village households participate.
Madhya Pradesh, India (based on my 1998–99 fieldwork)			
CFI 10[a]	8 days per year	2/hh	Each household cuts grass separately which takes it home in a cart. IRs.100 is charged per cart load.
CFI 11[a]		1/hh	All households cut and collect separately. Each household can take one cartload free
CFI 12[a]	10–15 days per year	1/hh. Both members and nonmembers can cut. Plenty of fodder	Each protecting household gets a patch of grass. They can cut the grass themselves or hire others to do so. They have to pay for the patch in cash at a rate decided by the CFI
Uttarakhand, India (**based on my 1998–99 fieldwork**)			
CFI 13[a]	Once a year	No specification	Each household is charged IRs. 15 for the right to cut grass. They plan to raise this to IRs. 20. Sometimes a few families cut all the grass and donate the money to the mahila mandal.
CFI 14[a]	Once each monsoon season	1 woman/hh	Households receive the right to cut on payment. The charges can vary. Earlier each household paid IRs. 50 for the whole season. This was later reduced to IRs. 25 per household. The money obtained goes into the CFI fund. The CFI collects IRs. 500 or more per year.
CFI 15[a]	Once a year	1/hh	Households get a pass allowing them to cut. They have to pay IRs. 2 per bundle. The money collected is used to pay the guard IRs. 100 a month.
CFI 16[a]	Once a year	1/hh	A register is kept of all the member households. On the forest opening day one woman can come per household and a roll call is taken. The women line up, and when the roll caller says 'go' the women race to get to a good patch of green. Some fall and hurt themselves in the process.

(*continued*)

Table A6.3. (Continued)

State/country/CFI	Days open	No of persons	Method
Nepal **(cases based on my 1998–99 fieldwork. The rest are based on my 2000–01 survey)**			
CFI 17[a] (Kaski)	Once a year	not specified	Each member household pays NRs. 40 for the right to collect grass. They are able to collect 10–15 baskets. The market value is NRs. 25 per basket. The money collected by the EC is used to cover part of the guard's salary.
CFI 18[a] (Kaski)	Once a year	not specified	The grassy area is divided into plots. The users decide how many plots to make but 6 plots is usual. Each plot is given an initial value and then auctioned. Each person puts a bid on a piece of paper with her/his name. Each household can bid for more than one plot. The highest bidder gets the plot. The rich with few animals often bid high to show off while poorer households with more animals cannot get enough grass. Sometimes, 4–5 households bid for all the grass and the rest got nothing. The money collected from the auction goes into a community fund. It is a very unequal system of distribution. Women are unhappy with auctioning.
CFI 19[a] (Dang)	7 days per year	1/hh	Member households pay NRs. 10 for the right to collect and only dry grass can be cut for bedding, while cutting green grass is forbidden
CFI 20[a] (Dang)	n.i.	not specified	The grassy area is divided into blocks and a reserve price is fixed for each block. The blocks are then auctioned. The successful bidder usually divides the block into plots and sells villagers the right to collect grass from these plots.
CFI 21 (Baglung)	Once a year	not specified	The grass is on hilly slopes. Each slope is assigned one of three alphabets (A, B, C) according to the quality of grass it can yield. Each hill is divided into as many plots as there are households. Each plot is assigned a price and a number. Each household gets a randomly assigned number. Those unhappy with their assigned plot can exchange it with another household. Those who want two plots can get a second one from another household by paying its price.
CFI 22 (Baglung)	Once a year after the monsoon	not specified	A GB meeting is called and the names of those who want grass are noted down. The grassy area is divided into three plots and each plot was auctioned to a

			single bidder. The remaining households have to buy what they need from the bidders. This reduces the EC's supervision cost, since protecting the grass is then the responsibility of the successful bidders, but the distribution is very unequal.
CFI 23 (Baglung)	Once a year	not specified	The forest is divided into 30–5 plots which villagers can buy, each at a price fixed by the EC. The poor are charged a lower price than the rest. Those who have their own pasture land are not allowed to buy plots.
CFI 24 (Baglung)	Once a year	not specified	Those who need grass have to submit an application to the EC. The EC scrutinizes the applications. The landless get priority. The forest is divided into plots and each member household needing grass can get a plot. Only a limited number of households can get plots at one time. But rather few need fodder from this forest, since many can go to an adjacent government forest or use their own fields.
CFI 25 (Baglung)	Two weeks once a year	1/hh can enter	Each household can take one bundle of fodder per day free of cost from the natural forest. In the plantation, the area is divided into plots and those who need grass can get cutting rights at the price fixed by the EC.
CFI 26 (Baglung)	Once a year	not specified	The grass is auctioned to the highest bidder and those wanting grass can buy it from the successful bidder.
CFI 27 (Baglung)	Twice a year for 15 days each	1/hh for one day	The member who is allowed entry can take as much as she can carry out at one go. (This condition puts a limit on how much a person takes.)

Notes: hh = household. n.i.= no information. [a] These cases are based on my 1998–99 fieldwork. The rest are based on my 2000–01 survey.

Table A6.4. Firewood collection rules—examples from India and Nepal, 2000–01

State/country/CFI	Days open	No of persons	Method
Gujarat, India (based on my 2000–01 survey)			
CFI 1 (Narmada)	A few days only	Not specified. All member households can participate	This is a formal cutback and forest clearing operation. All firewood is cut and made into bundles. Each bundle is given a number. Each member family can pick a number and get its share by a lottery method. About 5% of the firewood goes to the EC.
CFI 2 (Narmada), all-male	A few days	Not specified. All member households can participate	This is a formal cutback and forest clearing operation. The cut firewood is collected and made into bundles of different sizes. Member households that have participated in the cutting and other CFI activities get larger-sized bundles than those who have been less active.
Nepal (based on my 2000–01 survey)			
CFI 3 (Gorkha)	Once a year in January/February	All member households can participate	This is an annual forest clearing operation. The harvested wood is tied into bundles with a rope of 'five hands' length. This is given to those providing the labour. A packed lunch is also provided as an incentive.
CFI 4 (Gorkha)	Once a year in winter for 7–15 days	All member households can participate	This is an annual forest clearing operation. Those who want to participate have to pay an entrance fee of NRs. 20 per member household. Teams of users are formed with 7 persons per team. The wood is collected and distributed equally on the last day.
CFI 5 (Gorkha)	Once every few years for a few days	All member households can participate	This is forest clearing work. The participants can take as much wood as they have harvested and no fee is charged.
CFI 6 (Gorkha)	Once a year	All member households can participate	Informal collection is allowed. No knife can be taken into the forest. Drywood and fallen twigs and branches can be collected by hand. A fallen tree can also be taken if someone can carry it without cutting it in the forest.
CFI 7 (Gorkha)	Once a year in winter	All member households can participate	This is an annual forest clearing operation. Earlier the harvested firewood was distributed equally. Then the EC switched to selling the firewood. This led to complaints of firewood shortages, so they reverted to the practice of equal distribution among the participants.

CFI 8 (Gorkha)	Once in seven years	All member households can participate.	This is a forest clearing operation. Participating households have to pay a fee of NRs. 10. The firewood is distributed according to the household's labour contribution.
CFI 9 (Gorkha)	Once a year in winter	All member households can participate.	This is an annual forest clearing operation. Earlier all the wood was divided into bundles using a five hand length of rope. NRs. 25 was charged for each such bundle. The villagers complained about the method so they began dividing the forest into plots among the member households. Each individual can clear the plot and take the firewood at NRs. 15 per bundle.
CFI 10 (Baglung)	Once a year in winter	All member households can participate. Usually one person per household goes. If no one can go, the household pays Rs. 70 for the labour cost	This is a forest clearing operation. The forest is divided into 5 blocks. Each block is subdivided into seven plots each. The users are constituted into seven teams and a team leader and vice-leader are selected for each team. Users are randomly assigned to teams. All the teams have to weed, cut and prune. The firewood generated is made into piles. Each household is given an equal amount of firewood, but the teams that do the best work are rewarded with extra. Also large sized households can ask for extra firewood. If households experience shortages during the year, they can request the EC to open up the forest for seven days around the time of a major winter festival. One person per household can enter for a fixed period after paying an entry fee of NRs. 50. Only fallen drywood can be taken.
CFI 11 (Baglung)	Opened when there is need for cutting and pruning the trees	1 person per member household is called to work	This is a forest clearing operation. On the first day, a few able bodied men climb the trees to prune them and cut the branches. The next day another set of men cut the branches and make piles of firewood. The women help in gathering the cut pieces in one place. Stacks of firewood are measured by a given length of rope. Each stack is two arms rope length and width and five arms in height. The stacks are divided equally among the member households. NRs. 5 is charged per stack. Any leftover twigs and branches can be taken without charge.

Note: The village numbers are simply sequential and do not relate to the same villages as in the previous table.

Table A6.5. Gujarat: factors affecting strictness of rules, product-wise (all districts)

Dependent variable	Twigs collection rules 1: dummy[a]		Drywood cutting rules: dummy[a]		Grass fodder cutting rules: dummy[a]	
Equation no.	1		2		3	
Statistical method	Logit		Logit		Logit	
No. of observations	59		59		55	
Pseudo R^2	0.20		0.34		0.16	
Explanatory variables	**Coef.**	**ME**	**Coef.**	**ME**	**Coef.**	**ME**
GenComp1: dummy (>2 EC women = 1)	0.90 (0.183)	0.22 (0.167)	1.98* (0.060)	0.23** (0.050)	0.56 (0.417)	0.14 (0.410)
Women's association: dummy (assoc. exists=1)	0.95 (0.206)	0.23 (0.178)	3.06** (0.011)	0.45** (0.011)	0.71 (0.354)	0.17 (0.337)
% EC women from landless households	0.00 (0.967)	0.00 (0.967)	0.02 (0.354)	0.00 (0.334)	0.02 (0.221)	0.01 (0.222)
% all EC members from landless households	–0.01 (0.932)	–0.00 (0.932)	–0.12 (0.147)	–0.01 (0.144)	–0.06 (0.345)	–0.02 (0.345)
Gini coefficient for land owned by the EC	–3.29 (0.376)	–0.81 (0.375)	8.77* (0.099)	0.90 (0.112)	–2.74 (0.475)	–0.68 (0.474)
Forest area protected (ha)	0.01* (0.093)	0.002* (0.097)	0.01** (0.048)	0.001** (0.032)	–0.00 (0.839)	–0.00 (0.839)
No. of forest segments	–0.47 (0.182)	–0.12 (0.180)	–0.62* (0.086)	–0.06* (0.092)	–0.47 (0.176)	–0.12 (0.176)
Gap-filled plus plantation area (ha)	0.00 (0.880)	0.00 (0.880)	–0.04 (0.227)	–0.00 (0.223)	0.00 (0.900)	0.00 (0.900)
Total households in village	0.01* (0.090)	0.001* (0.092)	0.01† (0.101)	0.001** (0.050)	0.01* (0.057)	0.001* (0.058)
% landless households in village	0.02 (0.642)	0.00 (0.641)	0.14** (0.029)	0.01** (0.030)	0.07 (0.122)	0.02 (0.122)
Constant	–1.53		–6.67		–0.65	

Notes: [a] Dummy for twigs collection/drywood cutting/grass fodder cutting rules: If full ban or partial ban/given on request or open occasionally = 1; open always = 0.

The marginal effect (ME) is for a discrete change from 0 to 1 for dummy variables, and for a one unit change for continuous variables.

Numbers in parenthesis are *p*-values. Significance: ** at 5%, * at 10%, † at close to 10%

Table A6.6. Nepal: factors affecting strictness of rules, product-wise (all districts)

Dependent variable	Twigs collection rules: dummy[a]		Grass fodder cutting rules: dummy[a]		Tree fodder cutting rules: dummy[b]		Grazing rules: dummy[a]	
Equation no.	1		2		3		4	
Statistical method	Logit		Logit		Logit		Logit	
No. of observations	67		67		67		67	
Pseudo R^2	0.27		0.56		0.27		0.39	
Explanatory variables	**Coef.**	**ME**	**Coef.**	**ME**	**Coef**	**ME**	**Coef**	**ME**
GenComp: dummy (All-women EC=1)	0.91	0.22	1.90	0.38*	0.14	0.03	2.35*	0.21**
	(0.268)	(0.248)	(0.109)	(0.070)	(0.874)	(0.873)	(0.055)	(0.036)
Women's association: dummy (Assoc. exists=1)	0.83	0.20	−0.86	−0.18	−0.94	−0.21	0.05	0.00
	(0.272)	(0.260)	(0.426)	(0.391)	(0.251)	(0.221)	(0.955)	(0.955)
Average age of all EC Members	0.18**	0.04**	0.27**	0.06**	0.07	0.02	0.21**	0.02**
	(0.018)	(0.018)	(0.028)	(0.043)	(0.320)	(0.319)	(0.045)	(0.047)
Average land owned by EC members (ha)	0.90	0.22	2.18	0.48	−0.67	−0.16	2.45*	0.24*
	(0.302)	(0.303)	(0.157)	(0.173)	(0.452)	(0.451)	(0.064)	(0.051)
Gini coefficient for land owned by EC	8.25**	2.05**	10.17*	2.25	3.14	0.73	0.35	0.03
	(0.041)	(0.041)	(0.097)	(0.110)	(0.410)	(0.409)	(0.948)	(0.948)
% Brahmins in EC	0.02**	0.005**	0.00	0.00	−0.001	−0.00	0.02*	0.00†
	(0.048)	(0.049)	(0.745)	(0.747)	(0.919)	(0.919)	(0.096)	(0.103)
Member of another CFI: dummy (if member =1)	0.98	0.24	2.55	0.56*	0.43	0.10	0.08	0.01
	(0.302)	(0.277)	(0.137)	(0.062)	(0.627)	(0.633)	(0.937)	(0.938)

(continued)

Table A6.6. (Continued)

Dependent variable	Twigs collection rules: dummy[a]		Grass fodder cutting rules: dummy[a]		Tree fodder cutting rules: dummy[b]		Grazing rules: dummy[a]	
Who made forest use rules (no help from FD = 1)	0.45 (0.581)	0.11 (0.575)	2.50* (0.075)	0.45** (0.035)	0.23 (0.798)	0.05 (0.796)	0.02 (0.980)	0.00 (0.980)
Forest area protected (ha)	0.02 (0.160)	0.00 (0.160)	−0.01) (0.669)	−0.00 (0.672)	0.01 (0.549)	0.00 (0.551)	0.02 (0.287)	0.00 (0.255)
Forest canopy: dummy (Dense=1, Thin=0)					−2.02† (0.105)	−0.34*** (0.007)		
Forest age: dummy (Medium or old=1)	0.23 (0.740)	−0.06 (0.739)	0.04 (0.963)	0.01 (0.963)			−2.27** (0.049)	−0.26** (0.035)
No. of toles	−0.06 (0.677)	−0.02 (0.677)	0.18 (0.456)	0.04 (0.450)	−0.35** (0.026)	−0.08** (0.028)	−0.18 (0.372)	−0.02 (0.398)
District: dummy (Baglung/Parbat=1)	1.17 (0.144)	0.28 (0.122)	6.13*** (0.001)	0.88*** (0.000)	−2.48** (0.011)	−0.53*** (0.002)	3.68*** (0.009)	0.41*** (0.002)
Constant	−14.11		−21.99		1.72		−11.14	

Notes: [a] Dummy for twigs collection/grass cutting/grazing rules: full ban or partial ban/given on request or open occasionally = 1; open always = 0.
[b] Dummy for tree fodder cutting rules: full ban = 1; partial ban/given on request or open occasionally = 0.
The marginal effect (ME) is for a discrete change from 0 to 1 for dummy variables, and for a one unit change for continuous variables.
Numbers in parenthesis are *p*-values. Significance: *** at 1%, ** at 5%, * at 10%, † at close to 10%.
For tree fodder cutting rules (Eqn. 3) I substituted the forest canopy dummy for the forest age dummy, since the former is what matters for tree fodder availability and its effect can be captured directly.

7

Violations and Penalties

> The women do not cut green trees for timber. Sometimes they might pick up one or two twigs for the evening's meal. That does not make much difference to the forest.
>
> (Male EC members, Ekin Dhara CFI, Baglung, author's survey, 2000–01)

> When we were men in the *samiti* it was women who did 75 per cent of the stealing from the forest. Now we have given them [women] the responsibility, so violations have decreased.
>
> (Husband of EC member, Kala Kuna all-women CFI, Baglung, author's survey, 2000–01)

> The villagers are saying that the penalty for grazing animals is very high. Sometimes animals wander into the forest unintentionally. They are demanding that there should be no penalty in such cases.
>
> (Male EC members, Chamere CFI, Baglung, author's survey, 2000–01)

Violations and penalties tell us many different stories about institutional functioning, social relations, and perceived effects on forest condition. Violations can signal how well the institution is functioning and how well people are cooperating. They could indicate, for instance, whether village residents have accepted the rules of forest use; and whether neighbouring villages have recognized the social fencing created by the communities protecting the forest. They also indicate which forest use rules are locally appropriate. Violations can be out of subsistence need or out of greed. High levels of violation could imply non-acceptance of forest use rules (non-cooperation) or simply over-dependence on the forests for essential everyday requirements. In the latter case, the answer may lie not in strict rules and their enforcement but in finding alternative means and sources of satisfying basic needs. Similarly, intra-village or inter-village conflicts can arise from rule violations, and effective methods of conflict resolution could prove critical for the institution to endure over time.

The nature and extent of violations can also affect the condition of the forest, but not in a straightforward way. It would depend, for instance, on which forest products are stolen and by what method. Products such as firewood take the form of flows, and if women violate a ban on firewood collection by picking up twigs and fallen branches it may do no harm to the forest. Products such as timber, however, are in the nature of stocks, the theft of which could degrade the forest over time. Moreover, as elaborated in Chapter 6, *perceptions* about potential violators can affect the strictness of forest use rules and so indirectly impinge on equity outcomes. Similarly, the penalties specified (graded by the seriousness of the violation), the process by which they are enforced, and how disputes get settled, are argued to be key elements in building sustainable CPR institutions (see Ostrom 1990, Agrawal 1997, among others). Penalties can serve as deterrents as well as signifiers of how serious a view a community takes of different types of rule-breaking.

The EC plays a central role in enforcing penalties, with varying degrees of inputs from the GB and the forest department. Does women's presence on the EC reduce their proclivity to break rules, as is one of the oft-stated expectations of village men? Are there gender differences in the nature of violations? Do ECs with more women use different methods of dealing with rule violators than men? Attempts at simple quantification, however, would miss the complexities involved in measuring and interpreting rule-breaking, since so much remains unreported or hidden in the interstices of social relations, especially of class and gender relations.

To begin with, communities tend not to readily reveal the full extent of rule violations to an outside investigator, although some may be more willing than others to share what they know. Also, people may not remember all the violations where not all violations are recorded or subject to formal penalties. Second, there can be gaps between perceptions about violations and actual violations because of stereotyping by gender, class, ethnicity, etc. Data on violations collected by simply asking people who the violators are can be biased due to such stereotyping. Third, hidden factors can underlie the incidence of violations. A low incidence of rule-breaking, for instance, need not imply voluntary acceptance of the rules, since some community members may have been coerced into following the rules. Hence whether or not a set of rules is followed reveals as much about the appropriateness and acceptance of the rules by the community as about their enforcement. Also motivations for rule-breaking can range from extreme need, such as poor women cutting greenwood because they have no other fuel source, to greed, such as people cutting timber for profit. Fourth, there could be selective enforcement of penalties, depending on the nature of violation or the identity of the violator: enforcement may be harsher against those with less clout in the community, such as the poor and the lower castes, or it could be less harsh against these very people on compassionate grounds. Similarly, friends, relatives, or valued acquaintances may be treated more leniently than others.

Some of these issues are general and would apply to the wider dilemma of 'crime and punishment' in society. When people break rules, for instance, it could imply that the rules are too strict and we should re-evaluate and change them, or it could mean that we need better enforcement of existing rules. Other issues arise from the local context. The enforcers can have a conflict of interest, for example, if the violator is someone they know. These are not abstract questions. They centrally affect how we interpret the information on rule-breaking and what we do about rule-making and enforcement. Yet they are rather little discussed in the existing literature on environmental governance.

In this chapter I will first elaborate on some of the measurement and conceptual difficulties, and then examine through the lens of gender the extent and nature of rule violations and changes in them over time, the gap between observed and perceived violations, and formal penalty rules versus the penalties actually imposed.

1. DILEMMAS OF MEASUREMENT

1.1 Underreporting

Communities seldom want to openly admit of rule violations in a village meeting in front of outsiders, especially violations by their own members. There is often a sense of embarrassment in admitting to rule-breaking since it could reflect negatively on the character of the villagers and on their ability to protect. I found interesting gender differences in this regard, however, during my 1998–99 fieldwork in India. Women were much more willing to talk about rule-breaking than men. In some of the group meetings with both men and women present, when I asked about violations and the women started answering, some of the male leaders would signal silently with their eyes that the women should not answer the question. In one or two cases the women openly disagreed: 'There is no harm in telling the truth. She is like our sister and also a teacher, so we must give her the correct picture.' If the women fell silent due to men's quiet pressure in public, and I spoke to them in private, they would readily recount cases of violation.[1] In my 2000–01 survey on which this chapter is largely based, we collected data from both men and women and both on incidents of rule-breaking and village perceptions of violations. In Gujarat where written records on rule-breaking were rare, these actual cases provided the hard evidence. In Nepal, many CFIs did keep written records of violations and penalties in their EC meeting registers. Here cases recounted by the villagers provided supplementary information.

1.2 Perceptions and Memory Recall

Answers about the frequency of violations, for what product, and by whom, are subject to perception bias and memory recall problems (in the absence of written records). Perception bias can arise because people see certain categories of persons as more likely to be violators than others. Since women often complain about firewood shortages and strictness of rules, the EC men (and sometimes even EC women) assume that women are the main violators (as elaborated

[1] Several studies using experimental games also find that women tend to display higher levels of trust than men (see e.g. Innocenti and Pazienza 2006, and Dreber and Johannesson 2008).

further below). Stereotyping by gender and caste can also lead to a perception bias.[2] Moreover, for minor offences, especially those relating to drywood collection or grazing, people are sometimes let off easily by the guard or patrol group and these do not become part of collective memory. Hence violations, especially minor ones, tend to be underreported.

1.3 Non-Voluntary Cooperation

Frequent violations signal that the rules are too strict and need amending, or that they were arrived at without a consensus (since even strict rules may be accepted if made through a participatory process). But even when rule-breaking is low it need not imply that the rules are appropriate or accepted by the community. In particular, women or other disadvantaged categories of people may be coerced into complying. Historically, in South Asia (as in many other regions, including medieval England), forests were often preserved by the power that the feudal lord exercised over the economic and social life of the village (Gold and Gujar 1997, Baland and Platteau 1996). Similarly, using their power, husbands or community members have been known to threaten women with reputation loss or even with violence if they break the rules of collective functioning. In India, women in some communities report that they follow the rules because their husbands have threatened to beat them if they did not (Sarin 1995a; author's interviews in Gujarat, 2000–01). More commonly, women fear reprimand. As some men in a Gujarat village said: 'women have to be controlled because they are liable to cut wood' (my field survey 2001). Some village bodies also shame husbands if their wives break the rules (my fieldwork, 1998–99). In these circumstances, women may appear to cooperate (follow the rules) out of coercion rather than consent, even when the costs from cooperation outweigh the benefits: these would be termed cases of non-voluntary cooperation (see also, Agarwal 2006).

1.4 Selective Enforcement

Although CFIs specify formal penalties for various types of violations, enforcement may be selective for a range of reasons: the minor nature of the transgression, instrumental factors, or social bias. Where the transgression is small (e.g. an animal has strayed into the forest or someone has sneaked in for procuring some drywood), the patrol group or guard may simply let off the culprit with a

[2] Such stereotyping is common in many contexts and countries. In the USA, for instance, due to racial stereotyping, white police officers are more likely to see blacks than whites as potentially guilty of a crime. There is a vast literature on racial bias in the American criminal justice system, but see especially Stuntz (2006) and Schott (2001). Race apart, certain categories of people may also be stereotyped: gypsies, for instance, are often labelled as thieves in Europe.

warning. For illustration consider my interview with a watchman (viz. the guard employed by the villagers) from Mor Undura village (Gujarat) in 2001:

Q: If village women enter the forest do you penalize them or leave them with a warning?
A: Sometimes I do let them go with a warning when they come to take firewood. The forest is almost completely closed so they have nowhere to go. I confiscate the wood and let them go.
Q: How frequently does this happen?
A: Two or three times a week.
Q: Are these mainly young women?
A: No, women of all age groups come.
Q: What do you do with the wood you confiscate?
A: I let it lie in the forest.
Q: Do you sometimes let them take the wood?
A: No. I don't. They plead with me, saying they are 'poor things', but I don't let them play on my sympathy. There is no 'poor thing' in my vocabulary. Not for a single branch, not for a single stem!
He starts to laugh!

Even in Nepal where most offences are recorded in the EC minutes, small transgressions are sometimes given the miss. As the EC of Mauribhir CFI, Baglung, reported in 2000: 'Stealing small amounts of forest products such as firewood and fodder is not considered a big issue. The members themselves decide the penalty and it is not written into the minute books.'[3]

The EC or the patrol group may also decide not to penalize violators from a neighbouring village for instrumental reasons. For instance, where the passage to the main road is through that village, or they have other reasons for not disrupting cordial relations with their neighbours, they might use persuasion or a discussion with the elders of that village, rather than impose formal penalties.[4] In 2001, for instance, EC members from three Gujarat villages gave us the following accounts:

Whenever we caught someone [from another village], we would explain to them that we were protecting our forest and ask them to stop coming to steal. We did not bring them into the village since that would have caused conflict with another community. Sometimes one person came, sometimes two or three. This happened two to three times. They even brought axes. (Ramdev Na Muada village, Panchmahals)

People from the nearby village come to steal our wood. We try to make them understand, even warn them, but they don't stop. We cannot take strict action since during the rains we have to pass through this village to go to Shyamalaji. If we fight with them they can refuse us passage and they are taking advantage of our dilemma. (Nanasameera village, Sabarkantha)

[3] Agrawal (2005), in the context of Kumaon (India), similarly notes that written records underestimate violations, especially of illegal grazing and grass cutting.

[4] See also Agrawal (2005) on the fine line villagers in Kumaon had to walk in terms of sanctioning violations without eroding community relationships.

We have never really fined anyone as yet, although I am sure there is some fine listed in the books. The reason for not fining is that we all live close to one another and fining them would spoil our relationship. If they understand and don't repeat their mistake, then it is ok by us.

Once we saw a couple of women from our neighbouring village stealing grass and we yelled at them. They got scared and left. I don't think they have ever come back for more grass. (Vajapur village, Sabarkantha)

In contrast, certain categories of persons may be penalized more than others in a selective enforcement of rules. In Arun Agrawal's (2001) study of a van panchayat village, for instance, women constituted 70–80 per cent of the reported offenders between 1951 and 1991. Most were poor and low caste. Agrawal suggests that this was not only due to their greater dependence on the forest but also because the forest council was dominated by high-caste men who applied the rules more strictly to poor, low-caste women. In my study areas, caste dominance was not important but class did play a role. On several occasions, I heard poor women in Nepal complain about a selective application of rules. In one case they did so in a formal EC meeting at which I was present. The women, all from poor households, who were being fined, complained that when the watchman's female relatives broke the rules, they were never penalized (see Box 7.1). However, this selectivity is more likely when the violation is of a small order. It is more difficult to be selective for major items, such as timber, and I found that even the rich and upper-caste could not easily escape penalties for timber theft.

Many subjective dimensions thus impinge on the reporting of rule violations and the enforcement of penalties. Nevertheless, it is important to draw on written records and the verbal recounting of cases, where possible. Typically people tend to better recall or record incidents that lead to formal penalties than incidents where violators were let off with only a warning. Although this may lead us to underestimate overall violations and overestimate the more serious ones, it gives a good indication of which violations the villagers count as serious offences. Also, as I found, separate interviews with women informants can prove helpful when recording cases, since women tend to be more willing to talk about them.

2. RULE VIOLATIONS

Who breaks the forest use rules—men or women, those from within the village or from outside, and for what products? Are violations less likely if there are more women in the EC? Are there gender differences in the nature of violations, say in the products stolen?

There are several reasons why we might expect such gender differences. First, we would expect violations by women to be fewer where the EC has more women.

Box 7.1. Nepal: bargaining over penalties at an EC meeting

Author's visit to a community forest in Dang district, in December 1998

* * *

When we arrived, an EC meeting was in progress in the school hall. Three women had been caught stealing firewood from the community forest four days ago. The EC was discussing how much fine to impose on them. Ten men and 7 women are present. The EC men wanted to impose a fine of NRs. 40 but the culprits were arguing that the wood was not worth that much and were suggesting a lower fine of NRs. 25.

M1 (male): We must stick by the rules.
F1 (female): We will pay the fine and take the wood. We know nothing more.
M2: The punishment is not for you, but for what you did. Everyone has an equal right to the forest and must participate in improving it. You must pay NRs. 40 each.
F1: Make it NRs. 25 not 40 or 30.

The male secretary then read out the rules from a register and pronounced the penalty.

'NRs 30 is the fine; NRs 30 is the value of the wood; You can keep the wood and together pay a total of NRs 60. If you had paid the fine straightaway, without argument, we might have charged less, but now you also have to pay for wasting the EC's time.'

F2: I am poor, I have no brother.[a] I am alone and have to do all the work by myself. The *chowkidar* [guard] does not protect well. *Samiti* members should go have a look—many others also steal from there. They are not caught or fined.
F1: Someone from the *chowkidar*'s household also stole grass and wood on Saturday. Why was she not fined?

This comment led to an argument. A woman EC member said: 'no one went to steal from the *Chowkidar*'s house.'

F2: 'Yes someone did. It was Saturday and we were all together.'

As a parting shot she says to the secretary: 'Either you should fine the women of the *chowkidar*'s household or you should return our money.'

Women from the *chowkidar*'s household were present and sitting on one side. They said: 'We did not go to steal. Where is the proof? We did not go with implements, we picked up the wood by hand. If there is a small fine for that, we could pay it. I only fetch twigs and drywood.'

Finally the three women who had been caught had to pay up. F1 also paid for F3—an elderly woman who had remained silent throughout. F2 paid for herself, but was clearly unhappy. Each was given a receipt.

Later I asked the secretary who the three women were. He said: 'They are all poor. F1 is low caste. She has a house and a buffalo but no land. F2 is unmarried. She has a brother but lives with her mother. She is not as poor as she was making out to be. F3 is old and landless. She does not even have homestead land. Her husband and son are working in India.' I then asked the secretary: 'Is it true that the *chowkidar*'s family women steal?' He said: 'Possibly, but we need proof. The woman must complain in writing.'

Note: [a] Brothers are expected to support sisters in times of need. This comment is meant to signify that she has no one to support her. In reality she did have a brother but he was not very helpful.

As elaborated in Chapter 6, women's presence in the EC would enhance awareness about the rules among village women, since women EC members are more accessible to female than to male EC members. EC women are also better placed than EC men to persuade village women to follow the rules, and their vigilance can help better intercept female intruders. Culturally too it is easier for women than for men to physically catch women intruders. Second, given the gender division of labour we would expect gender differences in the products taken—women in general are more likely to be involved in firewood and fodder violations and men in timber violations. Third, there can be gender differences in the implementation of penalties. Women may have a different approach to dealing with violations from men. What does the evidence tell us? Consider first the actual incidents of violation, and then perceptions about violations.

2.1 Actual Violations Reported

There are striking similarities between Gujarat and Nepal in the products for which rules are broken and by whom. On many other counts, also, there are notable parallels between the regions.

Incidence of violation

In Gujarat, 68 per cent of the CFIs reported actual incidents of violation. We get a mean of 2.6 incidents per CFI over the five and a half years on average that CFIs have been functioning, or 0.5 violations per CFI year.[5] Narmada/Bharuch villages reported much higher average violations per CFI than the other two districts. CFIs with more than 2 EC women compared to those with 2 women or less reported slightly lower mean violations per CFI (2.5 and 2.6 respectively), as well as lower mean violations per CFI year, but neither set of differences was statistically significant.

Nepal's CFIs keep better written records than Gujarat's, although if we add up the documented and recounted cases the percentage of Nepal CFIs with information on actual violations—70 per cent—is not very different from that for Gujarat. On average, in Nepal, there were five to six reported violations per CFI over the protection period, with rather little difference across districts. A somewhat smaller percentage of all-women CFIs relative to other CFIs reported any violations (67 per cent and 72 per cent respectively). All-women CFIs also reported lower mean violations per CFI (4.2 vs. 6.1) and per CFI year (0.9 vs. 1.4).

[5] The years of CFI functioning vary between 2 and 10, although 15 per cent of the villages (mostly in Panchmahals) said they had begun informal protection earlier.

The regression analysis further helps us assess whether the EC's gender composition affects the number of violations per CFI year, after controlling for other factors which might impinge on violations as well. Some of these other factors are common to Gujarat and Nepal, such as the period and method of protection (by a guard or other means) and the district in which the CFI is located. Other factors are region-specific, such as the average land owned by village households, the percentage of landless households in the village, the distance of the village from the road (for Gujarat), and the number of toles (for Nepal). The standard errors have been corrected for heteroskedasticity, and the definitions and descriptive statistics are given in the appendix tables (AE.1–AE.6) at the end of the book.

Gender is significant for Nepal but not for Gujarat (Tables 7.1 and 7.2). In Nepal violations per CFI year are lower among groups with all-women ECs relative to other groups. Also, in both Gujarat and Nepal, violations per CFI year decrease as the number of years of institutional functioning increase (that is the older the CFI), suggesting an acceptance of institutional protection over time.

Table 7.1. Gujarat: factors affecting reported violations

Dependent variable	Total no. of violations per year of CFI functioning
Statistical method	OLS (r)
No. of observations	44
R^2	0.36
Explanatory variables	**Coef.**
GenCompl: dummy (>2 EC women=1)	−0.003 (0.977)
CFI years of functioning[a]	−0.12*** (0.003)
Protection method: dummy (Guard=1)	0.19 (0.252)
Average land owned by village households (ha)	−0.20 (0.478)
% landless households in village	−0.002 (0.694)
Distance of village from road (km)	0.004 (0.913)
District2: dummy (Panchmahals=1)	−0.28* (0.083)
District3: Dummy (Sabarkantha =1)	−0.15 (0.373)
Constant	1.54

Notes: [a] This also indicates years of formal protection.
OLS (r): Ordinary least square regressions with robust standard errors.
Numbers in parenthesis are *p*-values. Significance: *** at 1%, * at 10%.

Table 7.2. Nepal: factors affecting reported violations

Dependent variables	Total no. of violations per year of CFI functioning
Statistical method	OLS (r)
No. of observations	49
R^2	0.22
Explanatory variables	**Coef.**
GenComp: dummy (all-women EC =1)	−0.73* (0.096)
CFI years of functioning	−0.18* (0.053)
Protection method: dummy (if guard used =1)	0.59 (0.174)
No. of toles	−0.18** (0.036)
District: dummy (Baglung/Parbat=1)	0.15 (0.710)
Constant	2.98

Notes: OLS (r): Ordinary least square regressions with robust standard errors. Numbers in parenthesis are *p*-values. Significance: ** at 5%; * at 10%.

Landlessness in the village (in Gujarat), however, does not significantly affect violations, contrary to popular perceptions that the landless are the ones most likely to break the rules. Violations per CFI year are also lower in Panchmahals relative to the Narmada/Bharuch and Sabarkantha fieldsites.

Nature of violations and violators

People break rules most frequently for timber in both regions, and for firewood and fodder or grazing to lesser extent. In Gujarat, almost half the reported cases are of timber cutting; firewood comes next (28 per cent), then grazing (14 per cent). There is rather little reported rule-breaking for other products (Table 7.3). Timber, in fact, accounts for most of the reported violations in Narmada/Bharuch and Panchmahals and a fair percentage in Sabarkantha.[6] Firewood, by contrast, accounts for a rather small percentage of violations in Narmada/Bharuch, but is important in the other two districts. While CFIs of different gender compositions vary little in terms of firewood violations, timber accounts for a much higher percentage of violations in ECs with fewer women (Table 7.3).

In Nepal, however, for all CFIs taken together, although the highest percentage of reported violations is again for timber, firewood and fodder are very close behind (Table 7.4). District-wise, timber theft overshadows all other thefts in

[6] The district-wise tables are not reproduced here for either Gujarat or Nepal.

Table 7.3. Gujarat: actual violations reported vs. perceptions by EC gender composition (% violations)

	Actual violations reported (based on number of violations)			Perception of violations (based on number of CFIs)		
	≤2 EC women (N=51)	>2 EC women (N=58)	All CFIs (N=109)	≤2 EC women (N=27)	>2 EC women (N=33)	All CFIs (N=60)
	% violations by product/type			% CFIs reporting main item stolen		
Firewood	25.5	29.3	27.5	51.8	72.7	63.3
Fodder	2.0	1.7	1.8	3.7	3.0	3.3
Timber [a]	52.9	41.4	46.8	37.0	21.2	28.3
Grazing	15.7	12.1	13.8	7.4	3.0	5.0
Forest fire	0.0	3.4	1.8	n.i.	n.i.	n.i.
Other	3.9	12.1	8.3	n.i.	n.i.	n.i.
	% violations by gender of violator			% CFIs reporting main violators by gender		
Men	51.0	51.7	51.4	29.6	39.4	35.0
Women	19.6	22.4	21.1	11.1	24.2	18.3
Both	15.7	6.9	11.0	59.3	36.4	46.7
Gender not given	13.7	19.0	16.5	0.0	0.0	0.0
	% incidents by insider/outsider status of violator			% CFIs reporting main violators by insider/outsider status		
Insiders	58.8	37.9	47.7	18.5	18.2	18.3
Outsiders	41.2	62.1	52.3	51.8	48.5	50.0
Both	0.0	0.0	0.0	29.6	33.3	31.7

Notes: [a] Includes 'small timber', that is, wood with <3 feet girth
n.i. = no information or no mention of any kind of violation.
Source: Author's survey, 2000–01.

Gorkha/Dhading while in Baglung/Parbat, firewood, fodder, and grazing each account for a fifth of all violations. Also, while the stealing of forest products constitutes the most important form of violations, a fifth of rule-breaking takes other forms, such as encroachments into the forest area, carelessly or deliberately causing forest fires, destroying saplings while clearing undergrowth, or not turning up for patrol duty.

The rule-breakers are typically men alone in both regions (Tables 7.3 and 7.4 and appendix Tables A7.1 and A7.2). In Gujarat, about half the reported violations are by men alone, a fifth by women alone, and the rest by both sexes or with gender not reported. Men are the main violators both in CFIs with ≤2 EC women and those with >2 EC women. These gender differences are most marked in Narmada/Bharuch, where 75 per cent of the reported violations are by men alone, while in the other two districts the gender differences are much smaller (appendix Table A7.1). Given the predominance of timber violations in

Table 7.4. Nepal: actual violations reported vs. perceptions by EC gender composition (% violations)

	Actual violations reported (based on number of violations)			Perception of violations (based on number of CFIs)		
	All-women CFIs	Other CFIs	All CFIs	All-women CFIs	Other CFIs	All CFIs
	% violations by product/type[a]			% CFIs reporting main item stolen		
	(N=75)	(N=178)	(N=253)	(N=22)	(N=41)	(N=63)
Firewood	20.0	18.0	18.6	9.1	4.9	6.3
Fodder	24.0	14.6	17.4	27.3	7.3	14.3
Timber	25.3	19.7	21.3	4.6	12.2	9.5
Grazing	4.0	16.9	13.0	13.6	4.9	7.9
Forest fire	1.3	5.6	4.3	n.i.	n.i.	n.i.
Leaf litter	2.7	6.7	5.5	n.i.	n.i.	n.i.
Other[b]	22.7	18.5	19.8	45.4	70.7	61.9
	% violations by gender of violator			% CFIs reporting main violators by gender		
	(N=74)	(N=189)	(N=263)	(N=22)	(N=40)	(N=62)
Men	64.9	72.0	70.0	9.1	27.5	21.0
Women	18.9	11.1	13.3	59.1	35.0	43.6
Both	14.9	5.8	8.4	31.8	37.5	35.5
Gender not given	1.4	11.1	8.4	0.0	0.0	0.0
	% violations by insider/outsider status of violator			% CFIs reporting main violators by insider/outsider status		
	(N=74)	(N=189)	(N=263)	(N=22)	(N=41)	(N=63)
Insider (CFI member)	78.4	77.8	77.9	68.2	46.3	54.0
Outsider	21.6	22.2	22.1	18.2	31.7	27.0
Both	0.0	0.0	0.0	13.6	22.0	19.1

Notes:
[a] For 10 cases there was no information on the nature of violation, although there was information on who the violator was.
[b] 'Others' are violations unrelated to forest products, such as encroachments into the forest area, careless cutting of valuable plants when clearing bushes and undergrowth, being absent at the time of tree planting, not turning up for patrol duty or for meetings, abusing EC members or the guard, and so on.
N is the total no. of incidence of violations. n.i. No information: these were not mentioned by the villagers.
Source: Author's survey, 2000–01.

Narmada/Bharuch, it is not surprising that men are the main violators there, while in the other two districts, where rules are also broken for firewood and grazing, both sexes are reported to be responsible. This is in keeping with the generalized pattern of relatively distinct gender domains—timber falls mainly in men's domain and firewood mainly in women's. Everywhere, both insiders (villagers) and outsiders (from other villages) break the rules, but male rule-breakers are typically from within the village while female culprits usually come from neighbouring villages.

In Nepal, again, men alone account for 70 per cent of the total violations reported, and women alone for a substantially smaller proportion, which is in keeping with the lower incidence of violations for firewood compared with timber. Three-quarters of all violators came from within the user community, unlike in Gujarat where violators were mostly from outside. This suggests that the rules are not being accepted by many of the CFI members in the Nepal sites and the institution needs more consensus building or rule amendment. At the same time, around five notable violations on average over the protection period, and just over one violation per year of CFI protection, are not substantial, even given the non-recording of minor violations.

Women's violations are fewer than and different from men's for several reasons. Women are not involved in timber cutting, which is seen as a major offence and is banned in almost all the CFIs, except where men bring women along to reduce the possibility of being penalized, if caught. Women break rules mainly for firewood and fodder (or grazing) and these are seen as less serious offences. Also for security reasons women seldom venture into the forest on their own after dark which is when the more serious timber cutting takes place. This again reduces the potential for such rule-breaking by women.

Typically men steal timber by sneaking into the forest at night to cut branches which they then hide somewhere, hoping to return at a convenient time to retrieve them. If a patrol group or guard spots illegal cutting, they search for the wood and sometimes find the hidden logs in the forest. If necessary, the patrol group also checks people's homes in its village and confronts the culprit if it finds wood of the cut species, the source of which the house owner cannot explain. Usually the culprit confesses.

The people of Khabji village (Gujarat) recounted a typical case of timber stealing. The EC members while patrolling found that wood had been cut from the plantation area. They searched the village and found wood of the same species in the house of a former EC member who admitted to breaking the rules. He was fined IRs. 51 and the money was deposited in the CFI community fund.

Imposing and collecting a fine is easier when the culprit is a fellow villager. Offenders from another village can threaten violence, although most stop short of actually carrying out the threat. Sometimes men ask women to accompany them, since it is more difficult for the male guard or male patrol group to physically catch women for fear that they may be accused of molesting the women. The following case recounted by the EC of a village in Panchmahals, Gujarat, is illustrative.

> Around 1991, two or three men and two or three women came from the Naik phalia of a nearby village,[7] to cut dav trees for timber. They cut 25 to 30 poles. Our watchman caught them red handed. The culprits responded defiantly: 'This is not your forest, it is the government's forest. We used to cut here earlier and will continue to do so.' They chased the watchman with an axe. The women also threatened the watchman saying, 'we will

[7] Naiks are a low-caste group and typically poor.

register a case of rape against you. We will say you took our ornaments.' Then they departed, leaving the timber behind. The watchman reported this to his village CFI. A group of CFI members retrieved the cut wood from the forest. Some villagers wanted to take legal action but others felt this would lead to trouble for the village, and decided against such action. However, the intruders never returned.

Whoever catches people cutting timber is vulnerable to physical attack. Consider a case from another village in Panchmahals, as recounted by a male EC member in 2001:

It happened about a month and a half ago. It was evening, after 5.00 p.m. From my house I saw that some persons were cutting wood. I sought the help of 5 persons who were working in the village temple and took them along to catch the culprits. Two men and four women had come to cut teak. We caught them and brought them back to the village, along with the cut wood. One woman ran away and informed her own villagers. Then her village people came with implements (one rod of iron and one wooden pole with a long handle) to beat me, as I was returning home. These were villagers from Junakhera. We were able to take away their implements and catch the two who had come to beat me. Our relatives also came to help. The whole group was made to apologize in writing and promise never to return.

(Comment by my research team: 'We saw the paper. Eight people had signed it on 14 October 2001. But the paper carried no apology. It said that they had brought the implements in self-defence!')

This case is fairly typical of timber violations. Sometimes, however, even firewood cutting can lead to serious altercations between forest guards and poor women who desperately need firewood, as happened in Manchod village, Panchmahals, Gujarat:

Initially we were three watchmen. Each had a different beat. Then the new watchman joined. One day he stopped four Naik women from cutting wood. The women surrounded him and beat him up. He also hit back and one woman was injured. Then the women returned to their hamlet, and the watchman told us what happened. The women registered a court case against the watchman but later the case was dismissed. (Author's interview with the watchmen, 2001)

How should we read these examples? On the one hand they suggest quite serious conflicts over resources, both within villages and across villages. On the other hand, it is interesting that most of these stories end with the violators from neighbouring villages accepting the social boundaries, suggesting that with time the institution gains legitimacy within the region. The one factor which can disrupt this acceptance is the growth and regeneration of valuable timber species (as discussed further below).

Do these patterns differ with the gender composition of the EC? Not hugely, but there are some points of interest. In Gujarat, although the overall incidence of rule-breaking does not vary much among CFIs, in cases where ECs have more women a much smaller percentage of the violations are for timber so that rule-breaking is potentially less destructive of the forest. Also a much lower proportion of violations in such CFIs are by insiders, suggesting that the rules are broadly followed by the villagers, and their primary challenge is to curb rule-breaking by male outsiders. In Nepal, on the positive side, overall violations are significantly fewer per CFI among all-women groups compared with other groups. And the products stolen are spread evenly between timber, fodder, and firewood. On the negative side, however, all-women's groups tend to have a larger percentage of timber and fodder violations, albeit a much smaller percentage of grazing violations and forest fires, relative to other groups. The implications of this for forest condition are mixed—negative on timber violations but positive on preventing forest fires. The distribution between insiders and outsiders, aggregated across the sexes, does not differ between all-women CFIs and other CFIs. But given the overall high proportion of violations by insiders, the challenge here is to prevent rule-breaking from the CFI's own members, especially men, and suggests that there is still some way to go for arriving at rules that people are willing to comply with, and at mechanisms for more effective prevention.

2.2 Perceptions of Violations

Perceptions about who violates the rules and for what product, however, differ notably from the information gleaned from reported incidents, namely those narrated by the respondents and/or found in the written records. The comparison is broadly indicative and revealing, although admittedly the unit of measurement for actual violations is the number of incidents recorded, while perceptions are based on the responses of the EC members to questions such as: 'Are violations mostly by women, men or both? Are they mostly from within the village/user group or by outsiders? What are the main products people steal?' Focus group discussions indicated that the perception of the villagers did not differ much from that of the EC.

In Gujarat, the dominant perception is that the main violators are both men and women. In actual cases reported, it is mainly men alone who break the rules (Table 7.3). The dominant perception is also that it is mainly outsiders who break the rules, followed by both outsiders and insiders. Actual violators are in almost equal measure insiders as well. In fact, there is a notable underestimation in the EC's (and villagers') stated perception of violations by insiders alone. Also timber violations are perceived to be much lower and firewood violations to be much higher than indicated by the actual cases reported. Male-dominated groups (with ≤ 2 women) tend to particularly underestimate (in their perceptions) the extent of violations by men alone, and by insiders alone.

In Nepal, as in Gujarat, there is a notable gap between perceptions about violations and actual violations (Table 7.4). Typically in people's perception it is women alone who mainly break forest use rules but the analysis of actual cases shows that only 13 per cent of the violations are by women alone and 70 per cent by men alone. Interestingly, on this count, CFIs with all-women ECs and other CFIs both show a wide gap between perceptions and actual cases reported, and hold women responsible for rule-breaking in large extent (Table 7.4). For instance, only 9 per cent of the all-women's groups see men alone as the main violators, while in actual cases 65 per cent of the violations in all-women CFIs were by men alone. Similarly, the overall perception in 54 per cent of all CFIs is that violations are by insiders alone, while observed cases indicate that a much higher percentage (78 per cent) of the violations is solely by insiders. Here perceptions among the all-women's groups are somewhat closer to the observed violations than the perceptions of other groups which substantially underestimate insider involvement. Also, as in Gujarat, perceived timber theft is substantially underestimated. Overall, therefore, perceived violations by women are overestimated and by men alone, insiders alone, and for timber are underestimated.

* * *

The commonality between the Gujarat and Nepal results is notable. In both regions, about 68–70 per cent of the CFIs report actual cases of violations. In both, the actual violators are predominantly men alone. In both regions, the perceptions substantially underestimate violations by men alone and overestimate violations by women alone. Of course, some part of this gap between perceptions and observed violations could be because minor offences by women (such as entering the forest for collecting twigs when that is banned) affect perceptions but fail to register as actual cases. But the considerable gap between perceptions and observation does suggest that people are underestimating violations by village men and overly blaming village women or clubbing them with the men. In conversation, male villagers often refer to women as the main culprits.[8]

Perception bias is of interest in and of itself. But it can also have other fallouts. The perception that women are the main violators, for instance, often translates into stricter rules that seek to keep women out of the forest—male EC members are reluctant to open the forest at all or for longer periods. And such bias can deflect attention from violations by male insiders.

The EC's gender composition also appears to make a difference in the incidence of observed violations, at least in Nepal. As the regressions showed, all-women CFIs report a significantly lower incidence of overall violations compared with other groups. However, there is not much difference in Nepal between all-women groups and other groups in terms of who violates or for which product. In both types of groups, male insiders stealing timber dominate. In Gujarat, although groups with more than two EC women do not differ from other groups in the overall incidence of cases, their lower percentage of timber violations is a positive feature implying lesser chance of the forest being damaged.

[8] See also Agrawal (2005: 1) who cites a representative male villager in Kumaon (Uttaranchal, India): 'Women are the worst [offenders]. With a small hatchet, they can chop so many branches, you will not believe [it].'

2.3 Changes as the CFI Ages

As an institution matures and gets established, we would expect violations to decline for several reasons. For a start, people in neighbouring villages/communities would come to recognize the social boundaries and be less likely to steal from the protected forest, as illustrated by some of the examples given above. Within the village, similarly, systematic enforcement of penalties can deter rule-breaking. Over time, however, the dynamics can also change by product, as commercially valuable products regenerate. In Gujarat, for instance, teak is a valuable commercial species which regenerates quite fast with protection. This can tempt both insiders and outsiders to steal timber.

The evidence highlights this mixed effect. On the one hand, the vast majority—80 to 85 per cent—of the CFIs in Gujarat and Nepal perceive a decline in violations, although the proportion that report such improvement is much greater among CFIs with more EC women. The regressions discussed earlier also showed that violations per CFI year declined in both Gujarat and Nepal, the longer the CFI had been around. On the other hand, there are significant differences in the proportion of rules broken by product and by gender as the years of formal protection increase. This is seen from a series of regressions that I ran for Gujarat, with the percentage of violations by men alone, by women alone, for timber, and for firewood as the dependent variables. Violations by men alone and women alone are not mirror images since there are also violations attributable to both men and women. The explanatory variables include the EC's gender composition, the years for which the CFI has been functioning, the protection method, the percentage of landless households in the village, the number of village hamlets, district dummies, and the distance of the village from the road.[9] In the case of firewood violations, additional explanatory variables include dummies for firewood shortages and whether another local forest (typically a government forest) is being used for firewood collection.

The results presented in Table 7.5 are revealing. The percentage of violations by men and for timber are positively related to the CFI's age, while violations by women and for firewood are negatively related. This supports the idea that the growth of valuable teak over the years becomes an attraction for men who are the ones who cut the timber. On the other hand, women who meanwhile switch to other fuels such as cropwaste to a fair extent appear to accept the rules against firewood cutting. Violations by women and for firewood thus tend to decline as the CFI ages. In addition, villages located near forests which women can use for firewood collection, as an alternative to their own community forest, have a significantly lower percentage of firewood-related violations (Table 7.5, Equation 5). District-wise the percentage violations by men and for timber are higher in Narmada/Bharuch compared with the other districts, while the

[9] Distance from the road or from the town could both be potential explanatory variables. The former was used since it is access to the road which we might expect to matter more for, say, transporting stolen timber out, rather than the town per se. Both were tested, however, and neither was found significant, possibly because timber theft in these Gujarat villages is more for local use than for sale.

Table 7.5. Gujarat: factors affecting violations by gender and products (all districts)

Dependent variables	% violations by men per CFI	% violations for timber per CFI	% violations by women per CFI	% violations for firewood per CFI[a]	
Equation no.	1	2	3	4	5
Statistical method	OLS (r)	OLS (r)	OLS (r)	OLS (r)	OLS (r)
No. of observations	44	44	44	42	37
R^2	0.20	0.15	0.38	0.33	0.37
Explanatory variables	**Coef.**	**Coef.**	**Coef.**	**Coef.**	**Coef.**
GenComp1: dummy (>2 EC women=1)	10.20 (0.425)	4.24 (0.753)	5.94 (0.529)	−2.18 (0.869)	−1.47 (0.912)
CFI years of functioning	5.66* (0.092)	5.32* (0.086)	−3.09* (0.083)	−5.85** (0.024)	−5.62* (0.095)
Protection method: dummy (guard=1)	−10.52 (0.423)	−5.90 (0.650)	−10.03 (0.275)	−1.97 (0.861)	−7.34 (0.597)
% landless households in village	0.07 (0.920)	0.23 (0.714)	−0.36 (0.213)	0.58 (0.331)	0.73 (0.220)
No. of hamlets in village	3.52 (0.195)	1.38 (0.625)	2.18 (0.217)	−0.45 (0.844)	4.24* (0.098)
Distance of village from road (km)	−2.32 (0.633)	−5.81 (0.225)	3.25 (0.261)	3.37 (0.471)	−0.34 (0.934)
District2: dummy (Panchmahals=1)	−38.15* (0.064)	−17.62 (0.428)	26.99** (0.032)	48.55** (0.013)	
District3: dummy (Sabarkantha =1)	−35.48* (0.095)	−26.51 (0.190)	7.03 (0.466)	33.09* (0.077)	
Use of another local forest for firewood: dummy (If used=1)					−34.57** (0.018)
Firewood shortage: dummy (If most have shortage=1)				−1.24 (0.927)	−10.71 (0.483)
Constant	33.10	38.02	10.45	25.69	49.12

Notes: [a] Firewood shortages are included only in equations 4 and 5 which concern firewood violations.
OLS (r): Ordinary least square regressions with robust standard errors.
Numbers in parenthesis are *p*-values. Significance: ** at 5 %, * at 10%.

Difference between models
Eqn. 5 includes use of another forest for firewood and excludes the district dummies to demonstrate the effect of the former on firewood violations. Access to another forest is highly correlated with a district dummy.

opposite is the case for the percentage violations by women and for firewood. Finally, the number of hamlets is linked with higher percentages of firewood violations. None of the other variables was significant in any of the equations.

In Nepal, similar regressions were run, but none of the explanatory variables was significant. This is perhaps not surprising in relation to violations for timber and by men since many of Nepal's community forests had some valuable timber from the start, leaving less likelihood of observing *change* over time.

3. PENALTIES SPECIFIED AND ENFORCED

Most CFIs have formal penalties for rule-breaking which differ product-wise, but there is flexibility and EC discretion in implementation, and here again gender plays a role.

3.1 Penalties Specified

How are rule-breakers dealt with? In general, penalties are more fully specified and implemented in the Nepal sites than in Gujarat. This has to do with the history of forest protection and the degree of formalization of the institution in the two countries. In many of the Gujarat sites, forest protection was initiated by the villagers and they tend to deal with violations in a somewhat ad hoc way rather than through a clearly specified set of penalties. In Nepal, by contrast, penalty provisions are built into the operational plan drawn up by the CFI with the forest department when the forest is officially handed over to the community, although the plan can be modified from time to time with the approval of the general body and the District Forest Officer (see also Chapter 4).

In Gujarat, formal penalties range from public reprimand to filing a police case, and vary by product (see Chapter 4 for details). Collecting fallen twigs or non-wood produce, for instance, entails no penalty. Some CFIs lack penalty provisions even for drywood cutting and grazing, or have less severe penalties for them than for greenwood and timber cutting. These latter are considered serious offences which all CFIs penalize, typically through a fine, but if timber logging is involved they may even file a case with the forest department or the police.

In Nepal also fines dominate, and more than in Gujarat. This is the main penalty specified in over 95 per cent of Nepal's CFIs, irrespective of the product and the CFI's gender composition. But the fines are quite finely tuned. They increase progressively for repeat offences, vary by the value of the species cut, and are usually higher if the offence is by a non-CFI member. Public reprimand is rarely specified, except for cases where someone might enter the forest with an axe or a sickle, or if cattle stray in inadvertently. Seasonally available non-wood products such as fruits, wild vegetables, flowers, berries, tubers, and herbs can be collected freely in most CFIs, as long as people don't carry an implement into the forest. Implements are frowned upon because they can also be used to cut greenwood, and can harm the forest in ways that collection by hand tends not to.

3.2 Penalties Given

A large proportion of the violators are caught through a process of 'informal lookout', whereby a person going about her or his daily tasks sees and catches (or reports) an intruder. Sometimes EC members themselves catch intruders, again through informal vigilance, as do village women. In fact, vigilant villagers can prove to be central since they constitute 'the eye' at all times, but guards are also important and effective (Table 7.6). In Gujarat, about one-fifth of the violations were detected by guards and another one-fifth by patrol groups. As an incentive, some CFIs give a part of the fine money (up to 50 per cent in some cases), or of the cut wood confiscated, to the person who catches the intruder. In Nepal, guards are generally more common than patrol groups, and are therefore more likely to catch intruders than those patrolling. In fact, who catches the intruders is

Table 7.6. Gujarat and Nepal: implementing penalty rules by EC gender composition (% violations reported)

Implementing penalty rules	Gujarat			Nepal		
	≤2 EC women	>2 EC women	All CFIs	All-women CFIs	Other CFIs	All CFIs
Who caught the violators?	N=48	N=50	N=98	N=67	N=185	N=252
Villagers informally	39.6	48.0	43.9	37.3	38.9	38.5
Patrol group	25.0	14.0	19.4	4.5	2.7	3.2
Guard	18.8	24.0	21.4	17.9	29.2	26.2
EC	14.6	12.0	13.3	37.3	29.2	31.4
Others	2.1	2.0	2.0	3.0	0.0	0.8
Who decided the penalty given?	N=33	N=42	N=75	N=74	N=187	N=261
EC	76.5	54.8	64.5	66.2	83.4	78.5
GB	2.9	2.4	2.6	23.0	11.8	14.9
EC+GB	5.9	9.5	7.9	9.5	4.8	6.1
FD	2.9	16.7	10.5	0.0	0.0	0.0
Other[a]	11.8	16.7	14.5	1.4	0.0	0.4
Penalties given	N=36	N=48	N=84	N=74	N=187	N=261
Warning	13.9	14.6	14.3	1.4	0	0.4
Reprimand	2.8	2.1	2.4	4.0	19.2	14.9
Fine[b]	61.1	35.4	46.4	86.5	73.8	77.4
Products and/or implements taken	5.6	27.1	17.8	1.4	1.6	1.5
Forest department/ police	8.3	18.8	14.3	0.0	1.1	0.8
Removal from CFI	0.0	0.0	0.0	0.0	0.5	0.4
Several forms of penalty	0.0	0.0	0.0	5.4	3.2	3.8
Other[c]	8.3	2.1	4.8	1.4	0.5	0.8

Notes: N is the no. of violations. The figures vary depending on the number of cases for which there is relevant information.

[a] Cases where the watchman, patrol group, or villagers who caught the intruder have on their own decided on the penalty—typically they let the culprit off with a warning, but sometimes they also confiscate the stolen product.

[b] Along with the fine, usually the products stolen are also confiscated.

[c] In Gujarat, these are cases where the person was beaten up or there was no information on the penalty imposed. In Nepal these are cases where the person was asked to undertake some task without charge.

Source: Author's survey, 2000–01.

broadly in keeping with the method of protection. Appendix Tables A7.3 and A7.4 give a flavour of some sample cases describing the nature of violations, who violated, who caught the intruder, and the penalty given.

Insofar as the violations lead to formal punishments (and not all do), penalties are decided mainly by the EC, especially among male-dominated ECs (Table 7.6). In Gujarat, for instance, the EC alone decided penalties in 76 per cent of the cases with $\leq$2 EC women, compared with 55 per cent of the CFIs with $>$2 EC women. In Nepal, similarly, penalties were decided by the EC in only 66 per cent of the all-women groups, compared with 83 per cent of other groups. Groups with more women on their ECs, more often than other groups, consult the general body (in Nepal) and the forest department (in Gujarat). Nepal's all-women CFIs possibly consult the GB more because they feel less confident in meting out penalties for serious offences involving men without such consultation.

The punishments meted out are a mix of strictness and leniency. Typically fines are imposed. In Gujarat, often the product stolen is also confiscated, and sometimes so are the implements used. Fines and a warning may also jointly do the trick, as in Charada village in Panchmahals, Gujarat (author's survey, 2000–01):

> Last year, about seven men and five women came from Pataria village to cut firewood. They came with sickles, ropes, and axes. We caught them and took their implements away. Later they came back for their implements and asked us why we had confiscated them. We held a meeting in their village and explained that we have a CFI and do not allow outsiders to cut wood in our forest. They were fined IRs. 50. They have not returned since. We used the money for tea and snacks in our meeting.

In Nepal, fines were imposed for three-quarters of the reported violations, and public reprimand for most of the rest, even though in the formal rules, as noted, reprimand is not a recognized form of punishment for most products. Warnings and reprimand are more common for drywood cutting or grazing infringements. In general, actual penalties are somewhat more lenient than those formally specified (Table 7.6). In imposing penalties, the villagers take into account not only the product stolen but also the circumstances. The predominance of fines is probably related to the fact that timber stealing is the main offence.

The case below, from Badgaun Chaur CFI (Parbat, Nepal), illustrates how both the nature of the violation and the context can impinge on the penalty given. Here the EC exercised both strictness and circumstance-specific leniency. Two male EC members recounted the incident to the survey team in 2000, as below:

> In the past, we had caught many *bhotes* [caste of hill merchants], usually men, who used to transport different materials from the Kushma bazaar to the surrounding hills by mules. They used to graze their mules in this forest, and were occasionally caught and penalized by the District Forest Office. The main road that goes to the bazaar lies in the middle of the forest. After the forest was handed over to the community to form a CFI, our watchman caught some of the *bhotes* in the first few years and reported them to the EC. They were fined between NRs. 100 to NRs. 1000. After a while they stopped coming.

But grazing violations were not limited to the *bhotes*. Some CFI members also used to graze their animals in the forest. We caught some of them and initially forgave them. They were from Baglung. One was from our village. He was dissatisfied with the demarcation of the forest. He had actually protected a part of the forest by himself before handover. But later when the government forest was turned into a community forest, the area protected by him became part of this community forest. That is why he started destroying the forest deliberately. We did not know this initially, so we reported him to the authorities who sent him to prison. But a week later when we learnt the truth, we had him released, after discussing the case in our GB meeting. Now, the problem is solved. He has also become a member in the CFI and is very cooperative.

A second illustrative example is of villagers from a neighbouring area who inadvertently entered the Simle community forest in Gorkha, which was being protected by an all-women group. Taking account of the circumstances, the women settled the matter pragmatically, but amicably.

Once, our neighbouring community forest group had arranged a forest clearing operation for harvesting the firewood. The participants unknowingly entered our forest and harvested the firewood in about one ropani land. When we heard this, we went to the forest and stopped their work. The latter called their EC members, who arrived immediately. They realized that their members had crossed into our forest inadvertently. They admitted their fault and we excused them, but we did not give them the harvested firewood. We sold it to our members later.

Although it is difficult to say how systematic this was, my impression is that all-women groups more often than mixed-gender groups tend to use persuasion rather than confrontation to settle disputes. Some say so explicitly:

At the beginning some non-members of Baniya and Bhanjyang villages came to collect forest products but they gradually stopped coming when we convinced them not to. We had a policy of convincing people rather than punishing them. So far, therefore, we have not punished anyone. (Discussion with EC members in Sipligane's all-women EC in Gorkha, which had been protecting for three years by 2000)

Women also more often than men tend to use warnings and persuasion for firewood cutting. Consider a snippet of my interview with two male EC members in Boriya CFI, Panchmahals, Gujarat (author's survey, 2000–01):

Author: Have women caught other women stealing through informal lookout?

M1: Three years ago, Jumuna ben [a woman villager] caught *gujjar* women from Godhar village who had brought their *dharias* [sickles] to cut firewood. She told them, 'we have a protection group in our village,' and took away their cut wood and sickles. Later she let them go with the cut wood but warned them not to ever return.

M2: There was another case where some five to six poor Naik women came from our own village a year ago. But Mani ben stopped them. She was cooking and heard the sound of *dharia* so she went to investigate and saw the Naik women. She told them off and prevented them from cutting further. She added: 'you cannot cut firewood here; if you do everyone will blame me since this forest is near my house.'

Similarly, in Panchmua CFI, Panchmahals, Gujarat, a woman EC member recounts (author's survey, 2000–01):

> A year ago, I stopped two women cutting firewood. They were from our own village. I told them not to cut. They left the firewood and went away. They were poor and were cutting the wood for home use, so I let them go.

Male-dominated committees are often less sympathetic or understanding, and earlier we had noted cases where the poor and lower caste were more vulnerable to being penalized that those with good social connections.

Serious cases of timber cutting, however, are dealt with severely, whoever is the culprit, and here both male and female EC members take a strong stand. Even the rich and upper-caste cannot usually get away. Consider some illustrative examples. The first one relates to a forest fire caused by a well-off, upper-caste male member who was being supported by the CFI chairman. Not only was the culprit penalized, but his supporter had to renounce his office as well. The second case concerns an EC member who had to pay the fine despite his protests.

> Nobody had seen who had caused the forest fire. All the members gathered in a local temple and one by one proclaimed their innocence: 'I did not cause the fire in the forest.' A Brahmin male, Chudamani, was silent, so the group realized he was the culprit. They decided to fine him Rs. 10,000. Chudamani did not deny his crime but said the penalty was too high and started bargaining. The EC chairperson (a relative of Chudamani) favoured Chudamani and argued that the fine was too high. Finally, the fine was set at NRs 4,000. Later, however, for supporting a culprit and showing partiality the chairman had to resign from the EC and the group selected a new chairman. For a long time Chudamani did not pay the penalty. Finally, the EC forwarded the case to the Gorkha district branch of FECOFUN which persuaded him to pay the full penalty. (Recounted by EC members of Tanrang Khola Judipakha CFI, Gorkha, Nepal, author's survey, 2000–01)

> A patrol team found that some wood had been cut in the forest and they had a hunch that someone from our village was responsible. They did a thorough check of all the houses and found the wood in the house of an EC member. The member claimed that he had been framed but the patrol team was adamant about his guilt and finally he had to pay a fine of IRs. 101. (Bhangoria CFI, Narmada, Gujarat, author's survey, 2000–01)

Villagers are usually reluctant to go to the forest department or the police unless the case is serious. And some have later regretted doing so, since the forest department kept the confiscated wood. The case described below from Siladari CFI, Sabarkantha, Gujarat (author's survey, 2000–01), is illustrative:

> Three or four days ago a man from our village was caught cutting teak. We confiscated the wood and deposited it with the EC chairman. The culprit was asked to pay a fine and told he could take the wood for a fee. But the man sneaked into the Chairman's house when the latter was away and stole the teak back. We then called the forest department which imposed a penalty of IRs. 1,500/- and also took away the wood. We should have enforced the penalty ourselves. This way we lost both the money and the wood. Next time we will think twice before involving the forest department.

In contrast, in Nepal where the forest department is not available to play such a mediating role, since the CFIs are not set up under a 'joint' management arrangement, members sometimes rue being on their own when they face serious external intrusions, and say they find it difficult to deal with official agencies or file formal complaints.

4. CONCLUDING COMMENTS

The incidence and pattern of violations reveals important aspects of governance, such as the acceptability of forest closure rules by the villagers and their neighbours, the effectiveness of enforcement, gender- and product-related differences in responses, and the mediation of penalties by social relations. There is intrinsic worth in mapping these patterns for what they reveal about CFI functioning. In particular, they alert the community about any need for course correction in the interests of institutional sustainability. This is quite apart from the potential impact of violations on forest condition.

We also find a complex web of stories hidden in rule violations and the enforcement of penalties. Although most CFIs report some violations, the average number of serious cases is not high and declines with time as the CFI matures. A disaggregation by product, however, shows that violations decline for some products and not for others. In particular, the proportion of timber violations tends to rise while that of firewood tends to fall. Further, and linked to this, the proportion of violations by women declines and that by men increases.

Indeed, gender plays out in notable ways, both in the incidence of violations and their pattern. In Nepal, for example, all-women CFIs have significantly fewer overall violations compared with other groups. In both regions, women break rules mainly for firewood and fodder and men mainly for timber. Although women are sometimes complicit in timber thefts, this is typically in support of male family members who ask the women to accompany them. Moreover, in Gujarat, the noted decrease in the proportion of violations by women and for firewood, and the increase in the proportion of violations by men and for timber, as the CFI ages, points to gender differences in adapting to the rules and the lure of growing timber stocks.

Interestingly, in both Gujarat and Nepal there is a notable gap between perceptions and actual cases of reported violation. Actual violators tend to be mainly village men cutting timber, but in popular perception women are the ones most likely to sneak into the forest for firewood, given half a chance. This perception bias feeds into men's justification for strictly curtailing forest entry, thus reducing women's access to firewood and other forest products, with adverse gender and class equity effects. Notably too, especially in Gujarat, the gap between perceptions and actual violations is much greater among male-dominated groups which tend to substantially underestimate the extent to which insider men alone might be breaking the rules.

Penalties for timber cutting, however, tend to be strict both in specification and enforcement, while those for firewood and fodder theft are usually less so. It is likely that this difference reflects the expected impact on the ecosystem. Not all forms of violations need degrade the forest or undermine its ability to regenerate. Most ecosystems can tolerate a certain degree of intervention without harm. What matters is the form and frequency of violation. Timber cutting, especially the clear felling of trees, or the frequent lopping of green branches for any purpose, could cause a lot of damage, but taking drywood for fuel need not. Hence women's rule-breaking would usually prove less potentially harmful than men's. In fact, paradoxically, in CFIs which strictly ban forest entry, violations involving grazing or the collection of dry twigs or leaf litter could even prove beneficial by removing biomass that could otherwise catch fire in the dry season.

APPENDIX TABLES

Table A7.1. Gujarat: actual violations by district (% violations)

Item, gender, and insider/outsider	Narmada/ Bharuch (N=36)	Panchmahals (N=38)	Sabarkantha (N=35)	All Districts (N=109)
		% violations by product/type		
Firewood	2.8	44.7	34.3	27.5
Fodder	0.0	0.0	5.7	1.8
Timber	61.1	50.0	28.6	46.8
Grazing	16.7	2.6	22.9	13.8
Forest fire	0.0	0.0	5.7	1.8
Other	19.4	2.6	2.9	8.3
		% violations of gender		
Men	75.0	44.7	34.3	51.4
Women	0.0	39.5	22.9	21.1
Both	5.6	13.2	14.3	11.0
Gender not given	19.4	2.6	28.5	16.5
		% violations by insider/outsider status of violator		
Insiders	55.6	42.1	45.7	47.7
Outsiders	44.4	57.9	54.3	52.3
Both	0.0	0.0	0.0	0.0

Source: Author's survey, 2000–01.

Table A7.2. Nepal: actual violations by district (% violations)

Product, gender, and insider/outsider	Actual violations		
	Gorkha/ Dhading	Baglung/ Parbat	All Districts
	% violations by product/type		
	(N=139)	(N=114)	(N=253)
Firewood	15.8	21.9	18.6
Fodder	13.7	21.9	17.4
Timber	33.8	6.1	21.3
Grazing	7.2	20.2	13.0
Forest fire	6.5	1.8	4.3
Leaf litter	5.8	5.3	5.5
Firewood and fodder	0.0	0.0	0.0
Firewood, fodder, and timber	0.0	0.0	0.0
Others[a]	17.3	22.8	19.8
	% violations by gender of violator		
	(N=138)	(N=125)	(N=263)[b]
Men	61.6	79.2	70.0
Women	16.7	9.6	13.3
Both	8.0	8.8	8.4
Gender not given	13.8	2.4	8.4
	% violations by insider/outsider status of violator		
	(N=138)	(N=125)	(N=263)
Insider (villagers)	63.8	93.6	77.9
Outsider	36.2	6.4	22.1
Both	0.0	0.0	0.0

Notes: N is the total no. of violations.

[a] 'Others' include violations unrelated to forest products, such as encroachments into the forest area, careless cutting of valuable plants when clearing bushes and undergrowth, being absent at the time of tree planting, not turning up for patrol duty or for meetings, abusing EC members or the guard, and so on.

[b] For 10 cases although there was no information on the nature of violation, there was information on who violated.

Source: Author's survey, 2000–01.

Table A7.3. Gujarat: illustrative examples of violations and penalties

Date and nature of violation	Who violated	Who caught the culprit	Penalty given: by whom and what
Narmada: Bedoda village			
April 1998: Cutting of a Kher tree from the protected forest.	Four persons came from Bedoda village. Three ran away and one was caught.	Four villagers heard the sound of a tree being cut while working on their farms.	Villagers brought the culprit to the village and tied him up for the whole night, but he escaped in the morning.
November 1997: Nine logs of teak were found cut from the protected area. After searching everywhere in the village 5 more logs were found.	Three people came at night from a nearby village.	Villagers caught them.	EC decided the penalty and kept all the logs.
Narmada: Khanjal Village			
November 1995: 128 plants were damaged by cattle while grazing in the protected plantation.	Four or five people came from Sabuti village.	EC members	The EC imposed a fine of IRs. 10 per plant. The total came to IRs. 1280 but the offenders refused to pay up.
April 2000: 20 logs of teak were cut and hidden near the river.	Not known	Patrol group found the wood but could not catch the culprit.	None given.
October 2000: Grazing animals while the patrol team had gone back for lunch.	Two or three people came from Sabuti village.	Patrol group	The EC imposed a fine of IRs. 25.
Narmada: Khabji Village			
August 2000: Some trees had been cut from the protected area.	Male insider (former EC member)	Patrol group saw that some trees had been cut. They searched the village and found the same species in a male member's house. When confronted, he confessed to cutting the wood.	The EC imposed a fine of IRs. 51 which it deposited in the community fund.

July 1998: grazing animals in the protected plantation	4 male insiders	Patrol group during the day	The EC fined them IRs. 5 each, which it added to the community fund.
Panchmahals: Asundriya village			
1995: Pastoralists of the Bhedwal shepherd community from Kutch pitched tents and grazed their sheep in the protected forest	Several families of the Bhedwal tribe brought their sheep and pitched a tent in the village. They told the watchman that the forest department (FD) had given them permission to do so. The watchman said: 'You can't stay even if you have permission.' There was a scuffle. The watchman's son had an arrow and chain. The Bhedwal took away the arrow but the son hit out with the chain. The villagers were informed and 70 of them came to drive away the Bhedwal. The Bhedwal women pleaded that they be allowed to stay for 2–3 nights, then they would leave. They were allowed to stay.	Watchman	The villagers asked the Bhedwal to pay IRs. 500 for permission to stay. The Bhedwal claimed they had already paid the beatguard.[a] When confronted, he denied taking the money. The villagers believed the Bhedwal and reprimanded the beatguard and also took up the matter with the FD, saying, 'if you do not resolve this there will be conflict and our people will get killed. You ask us to protect the forest and then give outsiders rights here. Who will be responsible?' When the Bhedwal left they had to pay IRs 15 for the broken arrow.
March 2000: Cutting 5 poles of teak from the protected forest	The villagers suspected that some people were coming from Godhar to cut timber. To catch them, 10 villagers (including the secretary and president of the CFI) along with the beatguard and the forester went to the forest around midnight. They saw 10 men from Godhar cutting teak. The beatguard blew his whistle and caught the culprits.	Villagers, EC members, beatguard and forest department officials.	The culprits were beaten up by the villagers and sternly warned never to return, otherwise they would face legal action. The cut wood was used for the Holi fire. The trees from which the poles were cut have since coppiced.

(*continued*)

Table A7.3. (Continued)

Date and nature of violation	Who violated	Who caught the culprit	Penalty given: by whom and what
Sabarkantha: Nava Bhateli village			
November 1999: Firewood stealing	Twelve village women were caught in the afternoon with headloads of fuelwood.	Patrol group	Since the offenders were very poor they were let off with a warning.
March 2000: 20–25 teak poles and 2 Neem trees were cut.	Six or seven outsiders, but they escaped into the darkness before the patrol group reached there at midnight.	They were not caught	The EC kept the wood and registered a complaint with the forest department. When the latter took no action, the villagers complained to a higher authority. As a result the beatguard was suspended.[a]
March 2001: headloads of fuelwood	A number of women came in the evening from nearby Jaysingpura village.	Patrol group	The offenders were kept in the forest till evening, although the women kept complaining that their children were waiting and the cattle had to be milked.

Note: [a] A beatguard is the guard employed by the forest department, while the watchman is the guard employed by the villagers.

Source: Author's survey, 2000–01.

Table A7.4. Nepal: illustrative examples of violations and penalties

Date and nature of violation	Who violated	Who caught the culprit	Penalty given: by whom and what
Gorkha: Amalghari Sera CFI, mixed-gender			
7–12–1998: cutting timber poles	One man and a woman, both CFI members	EC members	EC seized the timber.
26–1–1999: cutting a green log for firewood	Male CFI member	EC members	EC seized the timber.
18–12–1999: cutting a tree	Outsider males	Watchman	The EC and members decided to seize the timber and fine NRs. 500.
Gorkha: Janajagriti Mahila CFI, all-women			
17–9–1997: firewood collection	Male CFI member	EC member	The EC decided on public reprimand.
11–11–1997: logging timber	Male outsider with sons	CFI members	The EC and CFI members imposed a fine of NRs. 500.
12–4–1999: tree fodder and timber poles	Two male outsiders	CFI members	The EC fined them NRs 300 each.
6–11–1999: firewood and fodder	One man and three women (all CFI members)	CFI members	The EC imposed a fine of NRs. 50 each.
2–9–2000: timber and tree fodder	Two men and one woman (all CFI members)	CFI members	The EC and CFI members imposed a fine of NRs. 5,000 for timber and NRs. 100 for two bundles of leaf fodder.
Parbat: Kala Kuna CFI, all-women			
6–10–1996: cutting branches when the forest was opened only for cutting fodder	Male CFI member	CFI woman leader	The EC fined him NRs. 50.
5–1–1997: cutting *mauwa* tree for timber	Five male CFI members	Patrol group	The EC fined them NRs. 50 each.
31–8–1999: cutting fodder	Male CFI member	Patrol group	The EC fined him NRs. 75.
4–1–2001: cutting *nigalo*	Four male CFI members	Patrol group	Yet to be decided in a GB meeting.
Baglung: Labdipakha CFI, mixed-gender			
15–3–2000: cutting a *chiuri* tree	Male CFI member	EC vice chairman	EC fined him NRs. 100.
17–5–2000: grazing oxen	10 male CFI members	CFI member	EC fined them NRs. 20 each.
17–5–2000: cutting grass	4 men and 2 women (all CFI members)	CFI member	EC issued a warning.
17–5–2000: cutting green branches	Male CFI member	CFI member	EC fined him NRs. 50.
17–5–2000: cutting another villager's tree	Male CFI member	CFI member	EC fined him NRs. 100.

(*continued*)

Table A7.4. (Continued)

Date and nature of violation	Who violated	Who caught the culprit	Penalty given: by whom and what
Baglung: Namunadas Mahabir CFI, mixed-gender			
12–2–1999: digging stones	3 outsiders	CFI members	EC fined NRs. 300 per person.
28–12–2000: cutting drywood for firewood	Male CFI members	EC member	EC confiscated their implements and later fined them NRs. 24 each.
1–2–2001: taking a log for making a beehive	Ward chair's brother	EC member	EC fined him NRs. 80 (the ward chair paid NRs. 40 for him).
25–4–2001: cutting 28 timber poles	Male CFI member	EC member	EC and GB fined him NRs. 200.

Source: Author's survey, 2000–01. Information obtained from EC minutes and account books, supplemented by discussion with the EC.

8

Conservation and Regeneration

> At night men can go for patrolling. But men alone cannot protect the forest effectively. Just as we need both sexes to run the house so we need both sexes to protect the forest.
>
> (Women to author, Mehru CFI, Sabarkantha, Gujarat, 1998)

> A good forest will bring more rain and help us control soil erosion. Our children will get fruits and berries to eat.
>
> (Woman EC member, Rukhal CFI, Bharuch, Gujarat, author's survey, 2000–01)

> The forests were being degraded very quickly and we were losing all our wildlife as well. Now by bringing back the forest we hope we can bring back the wildlife too.
>
> (Male EC member, Mor CFI, Sabarkantha, Gujarat, author's survey, 2000–01)

In 1995, I was taken by the local NGO worker, Vijay, to see a community forest in a Gujarat village. For a while, Vijay and I sat under the shade of a large banyan tree chatting with the village women who were preparing a tree nursery. I asked the questions, Vijay translated them into Gujarati, and the women answered, briefly and formally. After a while Vijay left to complete an errand. The atmosphere changed. The women came closer, began to talk more animatedly, touching my hand often. Although I missed the details it was clear that they did not think the men were protecting the forest well. They had therefore formed their own informal patrol group. Pulling me to my feet they walked me through the forest, along their patrol route. Every now and again they would stop to point out the illegal cuttings which the men's formal patrol had missed, noting: 'Men don't check carefully for illegal cuttings. Women keep a more careful lookout.'

During that visit, and on subsequent visits in 1998–99 and 2000–01 to other parts of India and to Nepal, it was women who often took me to the forest site, sometimes along with the men, at other times on their own. They did so whether or not they were on the Executive Committee, and sometimes even when they had bitter complaints about the men turning a deaf ear to the firewood shortages they were facing since protection began. They would point out with pride how well the trees were growing or relate a story about a theft they had thwarted.

This duality—the pride in a regenerating forest alongside their resentment at the difficulties they are facing in procuring firewood and fodder, the knowledge that they could contribute in important ways to forest management, laced with their feeling of marginalization within the decision-making process—marks the deeply conflicted nature of women's relationship with forest protection. They recognize the need to make sacrifices by limiting extractions so that their children can inherit a better forest, with 'fruits and berries to eat', but they also recognize that men alone cannot do this well, and resent not being consulted to work out a system of rules that could be more 'midway', more flexible, less hard on their daily lives. As a result, they sometimes cooperate voluntarily by following the rules, sometimes 'non-voluntarily' because of pressure from spouses or peers, and sometimes they break the rules.

Indeed, as elaborated in Chapter 7, violations are not uncommon. Some villagers break rules out of necessity, such as poor women who have no other source of firewood and fodder; others do so for profit, such as the men who steal timber for selling. But most ecosystems are resilient to some extraction and spoilage[1]—resilience being the capacity of an ecosystem to withstand shocks and surprises and to rebuild itself if damaged. Between total destruction and zero intervention are intermediate levels of extraction which allow forest ecosystems to regenerate.[2] Of course, once they get severely degraded, as many of these community forests have been, they cannot be restored to the way they were some decades ago. Some species are hardier than others and the new growth could be dominated by the hardier varieties, while some species may disappear altogether.

Under the community forestry initiatives in India and Nepal, attempts to regenerate degraded forests are therefore unlikely to bring back the lush biodiversity of years gone by, that some community elders remember from childhood—'dense and full of wild animals and birds'. But they can bring back at least some of the species, in a sustainable way. How well are they doing so? In particular, what impact can women's involvement in the decision-making of CFIs have on forest condition?

As elaborated in Chapter 1, studies on the impact of women's participation in public policy-making bodies (from legislatures to village councils) have focused almost entirely on the nature of policies formulated and not on their implementation and impact. At the same time, the gender and green governance literature (mostly relating to forests), has concentrated predominantly on women's limited presence and voice in the governing institutions and on gender equity effects, neglecting questions of efficiency, in particular the impact that women's greater presence could have on forest condition. An occasional study does suggest that women's involvement could enhance forest biodiversity or improve forest regeneration, but there is little statistical testing of propositions, barring a few exceptions.[3] This chapter focuses on this neglected aspect. Specifically, I examine the

[1] See also Agrawal's (2005: 150) observations on this in the context of the Uttarakhand hills (India).

[2] See also discussion in www.asiaforestnetwork.org/pub/pub06.htm.

[3] Exceptions include Agarwal (2006), in which I present a few early results based on my current survey; Agrawal and Chhatre (2006) who examine the impact of several variables (including gender) on forest condition in Himachal Pradesh; and Agrawal et al. (2006) who focus on the impact of

effect of the EC's gender composition on forest condition and changes therein, using a range of indicators to measure forest condition.

1. FOREST PROFILES: FIELDSITES

The Gujarat and Nepal CFIs differ both ecologically and in the size and quality of their forests. The Gujarat sample, as described in Chapter 4, falls in a semi-arid climatic zone characterized by dry deciduous forests, many located on hilly terrain. All the CFIs described their condition as degraded or very degraded when they began protection and some barely had even rootstock intact (Table 8.1). In Panchmahals, with many community-initiated CFIs, the protected sites were mostly left to regenerate naturally. In the other two districts, gap-filling ('enrichment') tree planting was undertaken on degraded patches to increase plant density. On average, the protected forests are substantially smaller in Narmada/Bharuch (58 ha) relative to Sabarkantha (181 ha) and Panchmahals (225 ha). Gender-wise CFIs with >2 EC women, compared with ≤2 women, also have somewhat smaller forests.

The Nepal sample is located in a sub-tropical zone characterized mainly by deciduous forests. The average size of the sample forests—34 ha—is much smaller than Gujarat's, but the forests when transferred to communities were in better overall condition and had more biodiversity. This was both because Nepal's forests are generally less depleted and because its community forestry policy (as noted) allows the handing over of even good forest land to communities, while Gujarat's JFM programme (until very recently) only allowed the transfer of degraded forests. The Nepal forest department's records show that three-quarters of the sample CFIs received forests that had thin or patchy canopies at the time of transfer, while a quarter had medium or thick canopies (Table 8.2). Overall

women's participation on forest condition in Madhya Pradesh. There are, however, problems of definition and interpretation with Agrawal and Chhatre's gender variables, which are defined in terms of 'gender conflict' and 'gender relations', but neither is related to forest governance (I appreciate Arun Agrawal sharing the definitions). Gender conflict is based on villagers' response to the question 'what is the nature of gender conflict in the village?' and villages that report any conflict (even unlinked with the forest) are classified as having conflict. It is unclear why conflicts unrelated to forests should affect forest condition. This may well explain the authors' finding that more conflict is linked with better forest condition, contrary to what we might expect. 'Gender relations' is measured by asking whether women have held several or a few or no positions of authority in village institutions. Again these institutions are not necessarily linked to forests, nor is it clear what 'few' or 'several' might denote. From their results it is thus difficult to infer how gender might affect forest condition. Similarly in Agrawal et al. (2006), women's participation in meetings and patrolling is positively related to forest regeneration, but both participation and regeneration are based on yes/no responses by the committee head, which are rather weak measures, given the complexity of measuring both participation (see Chapter 5) and change in forest condition (this chapter). Data lacunae (e.g. the gender composition of committees is not given) and data discrepancies (e.g. more women are reported as attending committee meetings than are on the committee) raise further questions about the reliability of their results.

Table 8.1. Gujarat: forest area and forest condition when protection began

Forest characteristics	By district			By gender		All CFIs
	Narmada/ Bharuch	Panchmahals	Sabarkantha	≤2 EC women	>2 EC women	
	(N=16)	(N=21)[a]	(N=28)	(N=31)	(N=34)[a]	(N=65)[a]
Forest area protected (mean ha)	57.9	224.6	181.4	173.3	157.3	164.9
Forest condition when protection began (villagers' assessment) (% CFIs)						
• Very degraded	50.0	20.0	75.0	51.6	51.5	51.6
• Degraded	50.0	80.0	25.0	48.4	48.5	48.4

Notes: N= number of CFIs.

[a] Forest condition data for one CFI was unreliable; hence the N values are respectively 20, 33 and 64 for the Panchmahals CFIs, >2 women CFIs and all-CFIs.

Source: Author's 2000–01 survey.

Table 8.2. Nepal: forest area and forest condition when CFI was formed

Forest characteristics	By district		By gender		All CFIs
	Gorkha/ Dhading	Baglung Parbat	All women CFIs	Other CFIs	
	N= 36	**N=34**	**N=27**	**N=43**	**N=70**
Forest area protected (mean ha)	33.1	34.1	20.9	41.6	33.6
Forest condition when CFI formed (villagers' assessment) (% CFIs)[a]					
• Very degraded	16.7	14.7	22.2	11.6	15.7
• Degraded	61.1	55.9	51.8	62.8	58.6
• Good	22.2	23.5	25.9	20.9	22.8
• Very good	0.0	5.9	0.0	4.6	2.9
Forest canopy when CFI formed (forest department assessment) (% CFIs)	**N=32**	**N=28**	**N=21**	**N=39**	**N=60**
• Thin canopy	37.5	42.9	57.1	30.8	40.0
• Patchy canopy	46.9	25.0	33.3	38.5	36.7
• Medium canopy	3.1	3.6	4.8	2.6	3.3
• Thick canopy	12.5	28.6	4.8	28.2	20.0

Notes: N= Number of CFIs. For forest canopy the N values are given separately since information on this variable was not available for some CFIs.

[a] Some villages began informal protection a few years prior to CFI formalization.

Source: Author's 2000–01 survey.

a much larger percentage of the Baglung/Parbat sites relative to Gorkha/ Dhading received forests with medium to thick forest canopies. Most CFIs in both sets of districts received natural forest, but some received forests on which supplementary tree planting had been done, and a few received only plantations.

In addition, there is the striking difference (also noted in Chapter 4) in the size, condition, and age of forests received by Nepal's all-women groups relative to other groups (Table 8.2). All-women's groups received on average half the forest area (21 ha) of the other groups;[4] and the land was much more degraded both by the forest department's assessment and the villagers' own assessment (Table 8.2). According to the former, 90 per cent of the all-women groups received forests with thin or patchy canopy relative to 69 per cent of the other groups.[5] Over a quarter of the other groups received forests with thick canopies compared with only 5 per cent of the all-women groups. Moreover, a substantially larger percentage of all-women groups compared with the other groups reported receiving a young forest (under twenty years of age), with fewer species of firewood, fodder, and timber. Local forest officials justify giving all-women CFIs smaller and poorer plots on the plea that women alone would be unable to protect the forest effectively; and their management capability first needed to be assessed by giving them small plots. The account of an all-women's group managing the Janajagriti community forest in Gorkha, which received only 7.06 ha, is illustrative:

> When the Thuloban CFI was made we were also inspired to have our own community forest. We first formed a group in 1994 on the advice of a female ranger and prepared the necessary papers. But when we submitted the documents to the DFO [District Forest Officer], he was sceptical and said, 'How can you women protect the forest? You don't know the rules or how to manage, and nobody will accept your decisions.' We said, 'please give us the forest, we will try our best and demonstrate to you within a year that we can do it. We are ready to accept any kind of penalty if we fail.' The community men and the local ranger supported us, which is why we were able to speak so boldly to the DFO. Finally he relented and gave us a small area to protect. (Author's survey, 2000–01)

The actual performance of all-women groups (empirically measured below) in terms of improving forest condition belies this official scepticism. Indeed, as we will see, the enthusiasm and commitment that many such groups bring to their work more than makes up for their lesser experience in institutional management.

[4] If we take the 'other' CFIs on their own, and compare the $\leq$2 EC women groups with the >2 EC women groups, the latter have a smaller total forest area to protect, but are not notably disadvantaged on other counts.

[5] The all-Nepal picture is similar: Buchy and Rai (2008) found from 2004 data that 50 per cent of the all-women CFIs, relative to 25 per cent of mixed-gender CFIs, across Nepal, received forests in poor condition.

2. HYPOTHESES

A broad range of factors could affect the condition of the protected forest, some gender and EC related, others related to the characteristics of the CFI, forest, population, and location.

2.1 Gender- and EC-Related Characteristics

Why would we expect a group's gender composition to affect conservation outcomes? The most important reason is the likelihood of substantially improving the quality of protection if there are more women on the EC. In addition, women's presence would bring to forest management their knowledge of plant species and forest use practices; help incorporate their understanding of what should be extracted and when; and take account of their preferences when enrichment planting is undertaken.

Protection, for instance, has both a preventive and a proactive component. In preventive terms, women when inducted into the EC are more likely to follow the rules which they have had a hand in formulating, and are better placed than men to persuade other village women to comply. They can also bring village women's requests for greater access to forest products to the attention of male EC members. Such persuasion and interaction is important, given the disproportionately high cost of forest closure that women bear in terms of time expended in finding alternative sites for firewood and fodder, and the negative health effects of shifting to inferior fuels such as cropwaste. Women's involvement in making and enforcing rules could also help spread awareness of the rules among village women, who tend to get left out of men's communication channels and persistently complain that even their husbands do not usually inform them about what takes place in village meetings (see also Chapter 5). Women EC members are better placed to reach them and more likely to be listened to, a point that even the men recognize:

> By being on the EC, women's status has increased in the village. They can also explain the rules to others who now listen. (Male EC members to author in Asundriya CFI, Panchmahals, Gujarat, 1998)

The proactive component of protection arises from women's participation in the actual process of protection. Inclusion in the EC is likely to enhance women's motivation and ability to participate actively in protection themselves, as well as motivate other village women to do so, by forming a patrol or keeping an informal lookout as they work in the fields. Women often describe with pride their success in preventing theft, including serious smuggling:

We stopped the smuggling of wood that was being taken by train. The Divisional Forest Officer also supported us. (Village women to author, Jamai CFI, Madhya Pradesh, India, 1999)[6]

In the current survey, 37 per cent of Gujarat's CFIs and 72 per cent of Nepal's CFIs that had patrols reported that women also participated in patrolling, typically by substituting for an absent male family member (some CFIs impose a fine on absentees), but occasionally by joining a mixed-gender patrol on a regular basis. As members of the EC, women can mitigate other women's tendencies to break the rules as well. The following comment by a women's patrol, although from a different region of India, is illustrative:

If an individual woman says to an outside intruder—don't cut—the woman gets a bad name. But if women collectively say 'don't cut', then it is more effective. When we did that, the intruders stopped coming. (Women's protection group to author, Chanauti-Dehra village, Uttarakhand hills, India, 1998)

These and other informal ways in which EC women can make a difference to rule compliance and forest protection cannot all be quantified directly but would be subsumed within the gender composition variable. Simply focusing on women's participation in formal patrolling would substantially underestimate this contribution. The presence of women's associations in the forest protecting community could further strengthen the hands of women EC members who could draw upon these associations to improve protection. Several studies in India have noted the contribution of these associations to forest protection by organizing patrols, sometimes even at night, especially in hill communities.[7]

Another important contribution (although again difficult to quantify) that women inducted into the EC can make to forest improvement is through their knowledge of how and when certain forest products should be extracted when the forest is opened periodically, or which species to promote in planting efforts. As elaborated in Chapter 2, in many regions (albeit not universally) knowledge of forest ecology is gendered: women are often found to be better informed about firewood and fodder species and non-timber forest products, and men about timber species. Their knowledge about the products that they typically collect and which require particular skills in collection can also prove significant in forest conservation efforts, such as how tree fodder should be plucked (excessive plucking can reduce growth) and at what stage of its development—some fodder leaves are best when young, others are poisonous when young (Carter 1992)—or how ground grass should be cut, or medicinal herbs and wild vegetables procured.[8] My conversation with a group of tribal women in Panch Mouza CFI, Orissa (India), in 1998, illustrates women's everyday knowledge of extraction:

[6] Indeed, several studies on India have commented on the women's particular role in stopping timber theft (see e.g. Venkateshwaran 1992 for Orissa, and Raju 1997 for Uttarakhand).

[7] See Davidson-Hunt (1995) for Himachal Pradesh, and Raju (1997) for Uttarakhand.

[8] See also http://www.fao.org/docrep/005/y2328e/y2328e07.htm on the importance of using the correct techniques for procuring fodder and pruning fodder trees for sustainable growth.

Author: What do you gather from the protected forest?
W1: We gather four types of tubers for 3 months, during June–August, some dry fuelwood, and several medicinal herbs.
Author: How do you extract the tubers?
W2: We have ways of digging tubers which are sustainable and do not destroy the original plants. We leave the stub in the ground to allow regrowth. Some people pull out even the roots which destroys the plant altogether. We know more [than most] about forest food. If we had authority, we would ensure that everyone dug tubers in the proper way.

Tubers are simply one among many types of non-timber forest products that contribute to a forest's biodiversity and its usefulness to village communities, even though they may not get counted in more tree-focused measures of forest condition. Other aspects of women's everyday knowledge can prove valuable even for tree growth, such as the skills in tree fodder extraction noted above. Moreover, for forest development and enrichment planting it is useful to know the attributes of different firewood species (some are smokier than others), and different tree fodder species (some help milch cattle produce more milk than others), and to allow for gender differences in tree preferences. Women are also found to make notable contributions when involved in forest management. In Himachal Pradesh, Davidson-Hunt (1995) observed, for instance, that women managing the forest had barred the cutting of green conifer branches for firewood but allowed the collection of fallen needles for animal bedding. Although the ban on lopping was hard on poorer women who needed the firewood, it was helpful for conservation. In some of my Gujarat fieldsites women made valuable suggestions on the harvesting and planting of firewood species, discussed further below. All these aspects provide yet another reason why we might expect women's greater presence on the EC (as a proxy for their overall involvement) to improve forest condition.

The age of women EC members could matter as well. Older women, and older people in general, are likely to carry more authority in prevailing on villagers to follow the rules of forest closure. Age also adds to experience and to social networks which the EC can draw upon in case of conflicts with neighbours over intrusions. Moreover, many older people I met on my field visits in 1998–99, and during the current survey, expressed conservationist ideas and the desire to leave behind a better forest for their children and grandchildren.[9] Overall, therefore we would expect older EC members to be more committed to rule compliance themselves, and to be able to persuade others to do the same. A snippet of my conversation with an elderly woman EC member in Almora district (the Uttarakhand hills, India) in 1998 is also illustrative:

Author: why do you protect the jungle given that you are now old and may not reap the benefits of protection?

[9] On people imbibing conservation values over time, see also Agrawal (2005), Buchy and Rai (2008), and Jewitt (2002)—this last on elderly women's efforts to save the forest for their grandchildren.

Elderly woman EC member: For my grandchildren. The jungle will keep growing. Every home now has a small [tree] nursery, so we all join and ensure that all the households participate.

Gender and age apart, other social characteristics of the EC, in particular its caste composition, can impinge on forest condition. The Gujarat sample, dominated by tribal communities, is relatively homogeneous in this regard, but the Nepal sites contain a fair proportion of both ethnic groups and caste-Hindu groups. Brahmins, the uppermost caste, in particular, tend to carry traditional authority and command respect from those lower down the social hierarchy—their presence on the EC could thus benefit protection. Higher literacy levels among EC members could similarly be linked to a better ability to manage the institution and to command greater respect from their own and neighbouring communities, thus making for better protection. In other words, not only the fact of protection but *perceptions* about those managing the CFIs and their relationships within and outside the village can impinge on the effectiveness of governance.

2.2 Additional Relevant Factors

In addition to the above variables, six types of factors could be expected to affect forest condition: the method of protection, the period of protection, the characteristics of the resource, attributes of the forest dependent community, infrastructure development, and technical inputs.

First the overall method of protection could matter. Rule compliance is likely to be better in CFIs employing guards, since guards carry more formal authority than patrol groups or individual villagers, and also reflect the community's commitment to ensuring good protection where the community pays for them. Protection can improve further if the guard's efforts are supplemented by village patrolling and informal vigilance. Although, in Gujarat, CFIs with different gender compositions differ rather little in their protection methods, in Nepal all-women groups depend more on informal protection than on guards, partly due to financial constraints and partly because their smaller plots are easier to protect informally than the much larger forests of the other groups. Second, the period of protection could matter—the longer the community has protected the forest the better we would expect forest condition to be.

Third, the size, initial quality, and contiguity of the protected forest could affect how well it regenerates. A large forest faces less population pressure but is also more difficult to guard effectively. The net effect on realized forest improvement could go either way. The state of the forest when protection starts could, likewise, impinge on its resilience. Groups that receive a more degraded area begin with an initial disadvantage. Where even the rootstock had been destroyed, as had happened in some parts of the Gujarat sites, the forest would have less resilience. Although the impact of this initial condition could not be tested for

Gujarat, since all the CFIs said their land was degraded to begin with, it could be examined for Nepal based on the forest department's data. In addition, the districts serve as proxies for differences in overall ecological conditions under which regeneration takes place. Contiguity of the forest area measured by the number of forest segments can also make a difference—non-contiguous plots are more difficult to protect formally and could negatively affect regeneration. This was tested only for Gujarat, since Nepal had rather little forest segmentation.

Fourth, forest condition is likely to be affected by the demographic and economic attributes of the forest-dependent population, although not always in obvious ways. The larger the number of population settlements (hamlets for Gujarat, toles for Nepal) to which a forest caters, the more difficult it can be to protect, since more settlements imply greater population dispersion (and sometimes also size), as well as more social heterogeneity—hamlets/toles are often formed around caste/ethnic groups. Such heterogeneity can be the basis of community conflict and undermine institutional cooperation. Both these dimensions would negatively affect conservation outcomes. Similarly high landlessness and/or male outmigration in the community is likely to pull toward poorer forest condition.[10] Landless and migrant households (which too are often landless) are more likely to break rules, given their greater forest dependence.[11] They would also be less able to contribute to protection either financially (toward the guard's pay) or in patrolling time—the latter due to the increased work burden on members left behind in migrant families, and the lack of flexible time available to landless families dependent on wage work.

Fifth, village development, measured through an infrastructure index (arrived at by aggregating village electrification, and education and health facilities), can impinge on the state of the forest in complex ways. On the one hand the availability of alternative energy sources, such as electricity (and also LPG in more developed villages), could help conservation by reducing dependence on the forest for fuelwood; on the other hand the index is a proxy for modernization which could be linked with less conservationist attitudes. The two aspects could thus have divergent effects on forest condition.

Sixth, there are technical aspects to forest management which can affect forest improvement prospects: for instance, clearing forest undergrowth and weeding allows new shoots to breathe and reduces the risk of fire. Also young trees need careful pruning to allow the best shoots to grow. Biomass growth can thus be affected critically by the expertise with which such periodic cutback/clearing operations are performed. Although villagers who have used the forest for long years gain skills through learning-by-doing, this expertise can be enhanced

[10] Given a notable overlap between migration and landlessness, only one or other variable was included in the Gujarat regressions.

[11] The issue of dependence is a complex one—greater dependence gives a local population a stake in forest protection but can also lead to over-exploitation of the resource.

further by technical inputs from forest officials. We would thus expect CFIs with greater forest department inputs to have better forest regeneration.[12] Indirectly forest department involvement would also indicate to villagers that the EC has the backing of state authority and might induce better rule compliance. On the negative side the top-down character of forest department inputs can lower village motivation and sense of autonomy. The net effect would depend on these opposing tendencies. The forest department's involvement in CFI rule formulation is used as a proxy for the department's overall inputs in the Nepal sites. In the Gujarat analysis this variable was not included, given the rather little involvement of the department in rule-making or institutional functioning in my sample.

3. INDICATORS OF FOREST CONDITION

Any empirical assessment of forest condition and changes thereof faces the challenge of defining relevant indicators and finding the data to measure them. Forest condition can be assessed in many ways, such as the density of canopy cover, regeneration, the variety of species, the height and girth of trees, or some mix of these. Aggregating these aspects is not easy. It is also difficult to arrive at an overall average assessment for a large forest, since some parts may be dense, other parts degraded or patchy. Given these complexities, no single measure would give a full picture. I have therefore defined several indicators to measure different aspects of forest condition.

Four sources of information help define the indicators: the researcher's assessment (limited to Gujarat) based on visits by the same expert researcher to all the forest sites; the community's assessment of their protected forest at the time they began protection *and* at the time of the survey (for both Gujarat and Nepal); satellite data-based assessments (for Gujarat); and the forest department's recorded assessment of the protected forest at the time of handover and changes therein (for Nepal). These indicators, described below, would be of methodological interest for other regions and contexts as well.

3.1 Gujarat

I have used four types of indicators for Gujarat. The first three are based on my field survey, and the last on satellite data.

[12] I have in mind specific aspects of technical support from the forest department to help regenerate existing species. This does not contradict the broader historical criticism of the silviculture practices promoted by the colonial administrators under the nomenclature of 'scientific forestry' which, among other things, privileged particular timber species (see e.g. R. Guha 1989).

Researcher's index

For computing this, one of my research assistants with a degree in forestry visited all 65 forest sites in the sample, and I accompanied him to a fair number of these fieldsites. We graded each site on a scale of 1 to 5, at intervals of 0.25, with the value 1 representing the worst condition and 5 representing the best. We arrived at the grade based on a visual assessment of the height and girth of the trees, forest density, signs of regeneration, signs of cutting or other damage, and so on. Different parts of the forest were visited, notes taken, and then an overall grade given. Admittedly this was subjective in nature, but since the same person visited all the sites, any personal bias would tend to be uniform, and our purpose was to arrive at a relative ranking rather than assigning absolute values. This index is treated as a continuous dependent variable in the regression analysis.

Forest canopy (villagers' assessment)

During the field survey, the EC was asked whether the canopy of the protected forest was thick, medium, patchy, or thin. Based on this information a binary variable was constructed: CFIs reporting forests with thick or medium canopy were given a value of 1 and those with thin/patchy canopy were given a value of 0. About 59 per cent of CFIs reported medium or thick canopy.

Change in forest condition since protection began (villagers' assessment)

In the survey, EC members were asked to describe their forest condition at two points in time—when they began formal protection and at the time of the survey—by choosing one of the following options: very degraded, degraded, good, and very good. Comparing information for the two periods, I assessed whether there was a worsening, no change, some improvement, or substantial improvement. CFIs that moved one category down from where they were when protection began were listed as worsening; those moving up one category (e.g. from degraded to good, or good to very good) had 'some improvement in category'; and those that moved up more than one category (e.g. from very degraded to good or degraded to very good) had 'substantial improvement in category'. Except for one case of worsening with unreliable data (and omitted from the analysis), all others reported either no improvement, or some or substantial improvement. In the regressions, 'no improvement in category' is compared with 'some or substantial improvement in category', using logistic analysis.

This assessment of change is based on a comparison of the broad categories into which the villagers placed the forest when protection began and at the time of the survey, and not on their assessment of whether the forest was 'improving' in condition. In fact all the CFIs said their forest was improving, but not all felt it had shifted category from say 'degraded' to 'good'. In other words, forest condition can improve within a given category even if it does not qualify for a category shift.[13]

Geer indices

The remaining two indices for Gujarat are based on satellite data for 1999–2000 (close to my survey period) provided by the GEER Foundation in Gandhinagar, Gujarat. These indices—*Geer degraded forest* (percentage of forest area classified as degraded) and *Geer dense forest* (percentage of forest area classified as dense)—are conceptually similar, hence only Geer degraded forest is used in the regressions. The GEER Foundation's technical team synchronized the village forest area with satellite imagery to establish the percentage of forest area that was degraded or dense. The imagery covers total forest area in the village, which, in some villages, exceeds the protected area. In these cases there could be some underestimation of actual forest improvement with protection.

* * *

Some of the above indicators are assessments of forest condition at the time of the survey in 2000–01 and some explicitly measure changes over time. Normally, differences between CFIs in the current state of their forest cannot all be attributed to the governance institution, since each would have started with a somewhat different initial forest condition. However, in the Gujarat sample, since all the CFIs reported they had either degraded or very degraded forest when protection began, it can be assumed that cross-sectional differences in the current state of the forest broadly reflect differences in the efficiency of governance. In this sense, all the Gujarat measures can be seen as measures of change. I am not depending, however, only on the current forest condition indices. There is also one indicator (based on the villagers' assessment) which explicitly measures change. Moreover, there is consistency between indices; the signs of the correlation coefficients between different indicators are in the expected direction; and in some cases the correlation coefficient is notably high (e.g. it is 0.71 between the researcher's index and the villagers' assessment of canopy cover).

Table 8.3 gives the forest condition profile for Gujarat, by district and gender composition. Most of the indices (taking all districts together) show a considerable variation across CFIs, but almost all the forests show improvement, even though there is still substantial scope for betterment. By the GEER Foundation's satellite-based assessment, although a third of the forest area on average was still degraded in 1999, almost a third was also dense. By the villagers' assessment, 41 per cent of the sites had thin or patchy canopies but the rest had medium to thick

[13] Also, as Lele (1994) emphasizes, villagers' assessments of a good or degraded forest could be affected by the products it provides, and different segments of the population may value different products. My survey, however, did not capture such differences, perhaps because the initial degradation was so high that any regeneration was equally welcomed across the community. Capturing such differences may also need specific probing.

Table 8.3. Gujarat forest condition indicators

Forest condition indicators	By district			By gender		All CFIs
	Narmada/ Bharuch	Panchmahals	Sabarkantha	$\leq$2 EC women	>2 EC women	
	N=16	**N=19**	**N=28**	**N=30**	**N=33**	**N=63**
1. Researcher's Index (mean)	3.6	3.4	3.4	3.2	3.7	3.5
2. Density of forest canopy at time of survey (villagers' assessment) (% CFIs)						
• Thin or patchy canopy	25.0	52.6	42.9	40.0	42.4	41.3
• Thick or medium canopy	75.0	47.4	57.1	60.0	57.6	58.7
3a. Geer index: % degraded forest in village, 1999 (mean)	41.3	29.6	29.6	34.5	30.8	32.6
3b. Geer index: % dense forest in village, 1999 (mean)	18.1	38.8	32.1	31.3	29.9	30.6
4. Improvement in forest condition since protection began (computed from villagers' assessments) (% CFIs)	**N=16**	**N=20**	**N=28**	**N=31**	**N=33**	**N=64**
• No category improvement	18.8	35.0	3.6	22.6	12.1	17.2
• Some category improvement	37.5	50.0	50.0	38.7	54.6	46.9
• Substantial category improvement	43.8	15.0	46.4	38.7	33.3	35.9

Notes: N= Number of CFIs. For indicators 1 to 3, information was not available/unreliable for 2 CFIs. For indicator 4, the information was unreliable for 1 CFI.

Source: Author's survey, 2000–01.

canopies at the time of the survey. Also, in the vast majority of the CFIs—83 per cent—there was some or substantial category improvement in forest condition from the pre-protection situation. A slightly higher percentage of the CFIs with >2 EC women compared to those with $\leq$2 EC women showed a category improvement.

In addition, for 27 of my sample villages in Panchmahals and Sabarkanta the GEER Foundation provided supplementary satellite information for 1991. JFM was launched in 1990, and many of the groups began formal protection around that time or shortly thereafter. We can thus make a limited comparison of change between 1991 and 1999–2000 in the percentage of degraded forest area and dense forest area in these villages, although the data are insufficient for regression analysis. Among these 27 fieldsites, 85 per cent showed an increase in dense forest area (shifting from degraded or open forest to dense). Only two CFIs showed a worsening, with some of the dense areas becoming open forest. Similarly, 78 per cent of the CFIs reported a reduction in percentage area degraded, typically moving from degraded to dense. In other words, on the basis of the indices and this additional information on change, we can say that the vast majority of the

CFIs are doing quite well in terms of forest regeneration and improvement in canopy cover.

3.2 Nepal

For Nepal I use two indicators for forest condition, one based on my field survey, the other on the forest department's records. Both measure change. In Nepal, it was necessary to use direct change measures for assessing the impact of institutional governance, since here, unlike in Gujarat, some CFIs received degraded forests and others received forests in fairly good condition.

The first indicator is the villagers' assessment in 2000–01 of forest regeneration since protection began. The EC members categorized regeneration as poor, good, and very good. The second indicator is change in canopy cover, based on the forest department's assessment at the time of handover (and found in the written records) and a forest officer's assessment at the time of my survey. On both occasions, the forest was described in terms of whether the canopy cover was thin, patchy, medium, or thick. Forests that had moved since handover from an upper to a lower category (e.g. from thick to patchy) were seen as 'worsening'. Those remaining either thin, patchy, or medium at both times were identified as remaining the 'same', and those moving upwards (say from thin to patchy or patchy to medium or thick) were categorized as 'better'. Those that were thick both at the time of handover and in 2000–01—namely which maintained their good condition—were clubbed with 'better', since even sustaining a good forest is a beneficial outcome of community management in a context where there is a real threat of illegal lopping. As there were only two cases of worsening they were clubbed with 'same'. Change by this second indicator therefore involves comparing 'same or worsening' canopy cover with 'better or maintaining thick canopy'.

By both indicators most CFIs registered an improvement in forest condition (Table 8.4). Eighty-five per cent of the CFIs reported good or very good forest regeneration and about half also reported an increase in species (table not reproduced here). Even by the forest department's (somewhat more conservative) assessment, 50 per cent of the CFIs improved their canopy cover and another 17 per cent maintained their thick canopies.[14]

[14] Forest canopy density is often seen as a sign of a healthy forest by foresters (e.g. in India the official assessment of forest health is typically based on whether or not the canopy exceeds 40 per cent: GoI 2003), and forest canopy density is also what is captured by satellite imagery. There could of course be a trade-off between forest canopy cover which blocks sunlight and the regeneration of certain forest products, but the trade-off is less in some contexts than others. For instance, Nepal's hilly slopes allow sunlight to filter through, reducing potential conflict on this count (personal communication, Bharat Pokharel, Nepal Swiss Community Forestry Project, 2008).

Table 8.4. Nepal: forest condition indicators (% CFIs)

Forest condition indicators	By district		By gender		All CFIs
	Gorkha/ Dhading	Baglung/ Parbat	All-women CFIs	Other CFIs	
All forest regeneration in 2000–01 (villagers assessment)	**N=36**	**N=34**	**N=27**	**N=43**	**N=70**
• Poor regeneration	19.4	8.8	18.5	11.6	14.3
• Good regeneration	55.6	70.6	51.8	69.8	62.9
• Very good regeneration	25.0	20.6	29.6	18.6	22.8
Change in forest canopy (forest department assessment)[a]	**N=30**	**N=28**	**N=21**	**N=37**	**N=58**
• No change from thin or patchy[b]	33.3	32.1	33.3	32.4	32.8
• No change from thick forest	6.7	28.6	4.8	24.3	17.2
• Improvement from thin upwards	60.0	39.3	61.9	43.3	50.0

Notes: N = number of CFIs. Change in forest canopy—information was not complete to compute this in 12 CFIs.
[a] The original canopy cover could be thin, patchy, medium, or thick.
[b] Contains 2 cases of worsening.
Source: Author's survey, 2000–01.

District-wise, the Gorkha/Dhading sites on average showed poorer regeneration than Baglung/Parbat but a much larger percentage of them also reported very good regeneration. Gender-wise, although Nepal's all-women CFIs began with poorer forests than the other groups, the picture today is mixed. By the villagers' assessment, although a somewhat larger percentage of the all-women groups relative to other groups reported 'poor' regeneration, a substantially larger percentage of them also reported 'very good' forest regeneration. Moreover, by the forest department's assessment of change in forest canopy, a substantially larger percentage of all-women groups than other groups had improved canopy cover, while about the same percentage of both types of groups showed no change from thin or patchy cover. In the regression analysis (further below) we examine whether all-women groups outperform other groups, despite their initial disadvantage, after controlling for other factors.

4. REGRESSION ANALYSIS

In the regression analysis, I use four indicators of forest condition/change for Gujarat and two for Nepal as dependent variables. The explanatory variables conceptually fall into four categories: Gender and other EC characteristics, CFI characteristics, resource characteristics, and location/village characteristics (see Table 8.5). All the models consistently test for the impact of the EC's gender composition, which is our primary interest. Most models also have several other

Table 8.5. Forest condition: list of explanatory variables

Explanatory variables included in the regressions[a]

Gujarat	Nepal
Gender and other EC characteristics	**Gender and other EC characteristics**
Gender composition of the EC	Gender composition of the EC
Average age of women EC members	Average age of all EC members
Average age of all EC members	Percentage illiterate EC members
	Percentage Brahmins in EC
CFI characteristics	**CFI characteristics**
Protection method	Who made forest use rules in the CFI
Forest characteristics	**Forest characteristics**
Forest area protected (ha)	Forest area protected (ha)
Number of forest segments	Forest canopy at time of handover
Village characteristics	**Locational characteristics**
Presence of a women's association in the village	Presence of a women's association in the community
Number of hamlets in village	Number of toles
Percentage landless households in village	District in which CFI is located
Percentage village households with migrant males	
Infrastructure index for the village	
District where the CFI is located	

Note: [a] The gender composition variables and most other variables were included in all the equations; but a few variables had to be dropped from some equations due to problems of hidden collinearity in the logistic analysis (as indicated in the regression tables). In Nepal, the protection method could not be included in either equation as a result. Also a few variables were consistently insignificant, and given sample size constraints these were not included in the final equations: in Gujarat this includes years of CFI functioning in all the equations (all district and Panchmahals), the infrastructure index in the all-district equations, and women's association in the Panchmahals equations. In Nepal, this includes years of CFI functioning in all the equations.

explanatory variables in common, but in a few equations some variables are not included due to sample size constraints or hidden collinearity (in logistic analysis).[15]

Apart from the all-district analysis, separate analysis is presented for Panchmahals (Gujarat) because the district has some distinct features that get obscured in the aggregate equations, such as the community-initiated nature of many of its CFIs compared with the more NGO-initiated groups in the other Gujarat districts, and the disproportionately high percentage of landless women in many of Panchmahals' ECs compared with other Gujarat districts as well as Nepal. The inclusion of landless women, as noted in Chapter 6, is an important factor underlying less strict rules of extraction in more women-inclusive CFIs in Panchmahals. The Panchmahals case would thus also help us examine whether leniency in rules can impact negatively on conservation.

[15] See n. 25 in Chapter 5 for an explanation of hidden collinearity.

The estimation procedures used are ordinary least square regressions with robust standard errors for continuous dependent variables, binomial logistic regressions for binary dependent variables, and a multinomial logistic regression in the one case where the dependent variable takes three discrete values.

4.1 Potential Econometric Concerns

Survey analysis, as also discussed for rule formulation (Chapter 6), can raise some econometric concerns, in particular omitted variable bias and reverse causality. In the present analysis, however, I do not expect problems on either count in relation to the EC's gender composition, which is the explanatory variable we are most interested in. For instance, a potential argument could be that the EC's gender composition and improved forest condition are both a result of an omitted factor, such as culture: communities with a positive gender attitude might also be more conservation minded. Culture could thus explain both high female presence on the EC and improvement in forest condition. This is unlikely to hold in my study area, however. For example, one popular cultural marker (even stereotype) of gender friendliness and environmental friendliness is caste or ethnicity. Tribal communities are popularly assumed to be less patriarchal and more conservationist. But, even to the extent that these stereotypes apply (and often they do not), community social norms do not vary much across my samples. In the Gujarat sites, most villages are dominated by tribal communities and there is no systematic difference on this count by CFI gender composition. In Nepal, there is greater caste/community heterogeneity, but all the sample CFIs are located in the middle hills where differences in social norms governing upper-caste Hindu women and ethnic women tend to be less sharp than in the plains, and social restrictions on Hindu women have also been declining overall.[16] Similarly, there is no evidence in the study sites of systematic differences between communities in attitudes to forest conservation. In any case, in Nepal I have taken the EC's caste/ethnic composition into account as an explanatory variable. Another potential factor which could be argued to affect both gender composition and forest condition is NGO presence. But an NGO would uniformly affect all CFIs in its area of operation, and differences between NGOs are subsumed in the district dummies.

Hence, although it cannot be fully guaranteed that no variable is omitted, no obvious variable comes to mind that may have been omitted which could simultaneously affect both EC gender composition and forest condition in this region. Also, as discussed at length in Chapter 4, the factors that appear to be associated with the EC's gender composition are diverse and context-specific

[16] Although, traditionally, Hindu women faced more social restrictions than ethnic women in Nepal, this was less the case for Hindu women in the hills even in the late 1970s (Acharya and Bennett 1982); and in recent years social restrictions on Hindu women in general have declined substantially (Bennett and Gujurel 2006).

(often varying from CFI to CFI), and none appears to be linked to observed forest condition.

Similarly, I do not expect a reverse causality bias in my analysis, especially because of time sequencing. EC formation precedes the impact on forest condition. Once formed, most ECs tend to remain largely unchanged for several years, with an occasional member being replaced if she/he wants to discontinue or is suspected of corruption. The causality would thus run from EC formation in time 't' to forest condition in time 't+k'. In other words, while the EC's gender composition could have a bearing on changes in forest condition, the reverse does not appear to be very likely. In Nepal the noted link between EC composition and forest condition again has a time sequence. Although all-women groups tend to get poorer forests, such groups are not formed because there is degraded forest available. Rather all-women groups *once formed* tend to be given more degraded forests.[17]

4.2 Regression results

Tables 8.6 to 8.9 give the regression results, and the appendix tables (AE.1–AE.6) at the end of the book give the definitions and mean values of the variables.

Effect of gender and EC characteristics

In both Gujarat and Nepal, we find that gender matters in a number of ways. The most important gender variable is the EC's gender composition. Several indicators show that in CFIs where ECs had more women, the forests were in better overall condition at the time of the survey, and showed greater improvement in condition over the protection period. The positive gender effect is especially strong in the all-district results for Nepal, and for Panchmahals district in Gujarat. Gujarat's all-district results are less strong, but still significant for two indicators and suggestive for a third.

Beginning with the Gujarat all-district runs, we find that ECs with >2 women relative to those with ≤2 women rank significantly higher in overall forest condition by the researcher's index (Table 8.6: Equation 1). Also the higher the percentage of women on the EC, the lower the percentage of degraded forest area by the Geer index (Table 8.6, Equation 4). Given that all the forests were degraded when protection began, we can take the overall better forest condition, and the

[17] Other potential reasons to expect reverse causality also do not apply in my sample. It can be argued, for instance, that high forest degradation can cause men to migrate out, leaving women to serve on the EC. In other words, more women on the EC could result from poor forest condition. For several reasons this is not the case in my fieldsites. First, the percentage of households with migrant males in the village (for Gujarat) or among the members (for Nepal) does not vary much by a group's gender composition: in Gujarat the percentages are 11 and 12 respectively for CFIs with ≤2 EC women and those with >2 EC women; and in Nepal, the percentages are 14 and 18 respectively for all-women CFIs and other CFIs. Second, male outmigration would, in fact, increase women's household responsibilities, and so reduce rather than increase the likelihood of their joining the EC.

Table 8.6. Gujarat: factors affecting forest condition (all districts)

Dependent variables	Researcher's index	Forest canopy: dummy[a] (villagers' assessment)		Geer: % degraded forest		Forest condition change[b] (villagers' assessment)	
Equation no.	1	2		3	4	5	
Statistical method	OLS (r)	Logit		OLS (r)	OLS (r)	Logit	
No. of observations	57	57		57	60	57	
R^2 or pseudo R^2 as relevant	0.59	0.31		0.20	0.29	0.61	
Explanatory variables	**Coef.**	**Coef.**	**ME**	**Coef.**	**Coef.**	**Coef.**	**ME**
GenComp1: dummy (>2 EC women = 1)	0.32*	−0.06	−0.01	−1.12		2.44 †	0.02
	(0.065)	(0.940)	(0.940)	(0.810)		(0.104)	(0.547)
GenComp2: % EC women					−0.13*		
					(0.090)		
Women's association: dummy (assoc. exists=1)		1.27*	0.30*	4.34	5.76	1.55	0.01
		(0.092)	(0.079)	(0.336)	(0.178)	(0.280)	(0.570)
Average age of women EC members	0.03**	0.03	0.01	−0.70*		0.41**	0.00
	(0.028)	(0.547)	(0.548)	(0.055)		(0.037)	(0.535)
Average age of all EC members					−0.95***		
					(0.009)		
Protection method: dummy (guard=1)	0.61***	1.70*	0.35**	−3.38	−3.96	−1.15	−0.01
	(0.002)	(0.060)	(0.022)	(0.470)	(0.361)	(0.606)	(0.712)
Forest area protected (ha)	0.00**	0.00	0.00	−0.01	−0.01	0.01	0.00
	(0.040)	(0.346)	(0.339)	(0.464)	(0.373)	(0.129)	(0.556)
No. of forest segments	−0.16*	−0.29	−0.07	−0.05	−0.69	−2.27*	−0.01
	(0.082)	(0.438)	(0.436)	(0.981)	(0.733)	(0.078)	(0.545)
No. of hamlets in village	−0.14***	−0.34**	−0.08**	0.76	0.19	−0.35	−0.00
	(0.002)	(0.030)	(0.029)	(0.484)	(0.854)	(0.345)	(0.589)
% village households with migrant males	−0.02**	−0.09**	−0.02**	0.05	0.15	−0.13*	−0.00
	(0.016)	(0.037)	(0.039)	(0.825)	(0.265)	(0.074)	(0.528)
District2: dummy (Panchmahals=1)	−0.44	−3.16	−0.66**	−6.21		−4.85	−0.13
	(0.226)	(0.108)	(0.016)	(0.498)		(0.150)	(0.578)
District3: dummy (Sabarkantha =1)	−1.03***	−3.42*	−0.67***	−4.20		−1.43	−0.01
	(0.004)	(0.080)	(0.009)	(0.644)		(0.536)	(0.662)
Constant	3.74	3.55		58.64	74.35	−5.44	

Notes: [a] Forest canopy: Thick or medium density = 1; thin or patchy =0. [b] Forest condition change: some or substantial improvement in category = 1; no improvement in category = 0. OLS (r) = regression with robust standard errors. The marginal effect (ME) is for a discrete change from 0 to 1 for dummy variables, and for a one unit change for continuous variables. Numbers in parenthesis are *p*-values. Significance: *** at 1%, ** at 5%, * at 10%, † at close to 10%.

lower percentage of degraded area at the time of the survey, as signs of improvement. In this sense, as noted earlier, all of Gujarat's indicators are indicators of change, either implicitly or explicitly. The direct change indicator—based on the villagers' assessment—also shows that ECs with >2 women are more likely to show a category improvement in forest condition than those with ≤2 women, but this result is only indicative, since the marginal effect is not significant.

Panchmahals's gender results, however, are consistently strong and striking (Table 8.7). CFIs with more EC women tend to have better forests and show a greater improvement in forest condition by every single indicator: CFIs with >2 EC women compared to those with ≤2 women perform better by the researcher's index; tend to have a thicker forest canopy and a lower percentage

Table 8.7. Gujarat: factors affecting forest condition (Panchmahals)

Dependent variables	Researcher's index	Forest canopy: dummy[a] (villagers' assessment)		Geer: % degraded forest	Forest condition change: dummy[b] (villagers' assessment)	
Equation no.	1	2		3	4	
Statistical method	OLS (r)	Logit		OLS (r)	Logit	
No. of observations	18	18		19	19	
R^2 or pseudo R^2 as relevant	0.84	0.30		0.68	0.55	
Explanatory variables	**Coef.**	**Coef.**	**ME**	**Coef.**	**Coef.**	**ME**
GenComp1: dummy (>2 EC women = 1)	0.98*** (0.001)	3.86* (0.067)	0.75*** (0.001)	−12.60* (0.078)	3.56* (0.094)	0.57** (0.031)
Average age of women EC members	0.01 (0.479)	−0.02 (0.870)	−0.01 (0.870)	−1.20*** (0.003)	0.12 (0.441)	0.02 (0.445)
Protection method: dummy (guard=1)	0.94** (0.013)	1.41 (0.488)	0.34 (0.444)	0.81 (0.908)		
Forest area protected (ha)	0.00 (0.284)	0.01 (0.326)	0.00 (0.315)	0.07*** (0.002)	0.01* (0.099)	0.00 (0.137)
No. of forest segments	−0.03 (0.742)	0.08 (0.884)	0.02 (0.884)	−0.73 (0.720)	−1.29 (0.173)	−0.25 (0.189)
% landless households in village	−0.05 (0.107)	−0.18 (0.400)	−0.04 (0.400)	0.42 (0.664)	−0.62** (0.047)	−0.12* (0.055)
Infrastructure index	−0.07 (0.558)	0.32 (0.771)	0.08 (0.772)	−9.62** (0.024)		
Constant	2.57	−3.71		101.68	−3.39	

Notes: [a] Forest canopy: Thick or medium density = 1, Thin or patchy =0.
[b] Forest condition change: Some or substantial improvement in category = 1; no improvement in category = 0.
OLS (r) = regression with robust standard errors.
The marginal effect (ME) is for a discrete change from 0 to 1 for dummy variables, and for a one unit change for continuous variables.
Numbers in parenthesis are *p*-values. Significance: *** at 1%,** at 5%,* at 10%

of degraded forest area; and are found more likely to show an improvement in forest condition since protection began (Table 8.7). The probability of an improvement in forest condition category is 57 per cent higher in CFIs with >2 EC women than in those with ≤2 women (Table 8.7, Equation 4). Similarly the probability of the forest canopy being medium or thick as versus thin or patchy is 75 per cent higher in CFIs with >2 EC women compared to those with ≤2 EC women (Table 8.7, Equation 2).

The Nepal results are again consistently strong on the gender effects: both indicators explicitly measure change and by both indicators the forests of all-women CFIs relative to other groups show significantly greater improvement. For instance, there is a 29 per cent greater probability of forest regeneration being very good with CFIs that have all-women ECs than other CFIs (Table 8.8). Similarly, there is a 51 per cent higher probability of an improvement in forest canopy with CFIs that have all-women ECs relative to other CFIs (Table 8.9). The positive effect of women's participation on forest canopy is especially notable, since this is a measure derived from the forest department's assessment of canopy cover recorded at two points in time, and not from the villagers' own assessment of change recorded at the time of the survey. There is consistency, however, in the overall direction of change between the assessment of villagers and that of the forest department.

In both Gujarat and Nepal, the presence of more women on the EC tends to improve forest condition for several reasons, which I had discussed when framing the hypotheses and elaborate here. The most important effect is through better protection. Village women tend to participate in patrolling much more if they are on the EC. This makes for more effective patrolling than when men alone patrol.[18] Women are also found more likely to be in patrols where ECs have more women, and some all-women CFIs in Nepal even have formal women-only patrols. More commonly, however, all-women patrols are informal, consisting of a few women doing a daytime round. The account below of women EC members of the Janajagriti all-women CFI in Gorkha district, Nepal, is illustrative:

> We do not have a formal patrol group. It is an informal one. By this we mean we look after the forest when we go to our fields to work. The samiti (EC) has alerted all the users that they are responsible for looking after the forest when they walk through it or by it. Once we caught a non-member in the forest. We seized his knife and basket and sent him back. We donated the basket and knife to the samiti. (Author's survey, 2000–01)

In addition, women in patrols can nab female intruders more easily than men who risk being charged with molestation if they try to physically catch hold of women culprits.[19] For the same reason, male intruders might also be deterred by women in patrols. As a male patrol group observed: 'Women should get involved in protection because if women stop men from cutting wood, and there is a conflict,

[18] The NGO, SARTHI, also observed that protection improved noticeably in some of its villages after involving women and listening to their suggestions (SARTHI 1997–98).

[19] Some examples are given in Chapter 7. During my fieldwork in India in 1998–99, I came across many more instances where such charges had been made against all-male patrol groups (see Agarwal 2001).

Table 8.8. Nepal: factors affecting forest regeneration (all districts)

Dependent variable	Forest regeneration[a] (villager assessment)			
Statistical method	MLogit			
No. of observations	70			
Pseudo R^2	0.21			
Explanatory variables	**Coef.**	**ME**	**Coef.**	**ME**
Categories compared	1 (Poor) Compared with 2 (Good)	Outcome (1)	3 (Very good) Compared with 2 (Good)	Outcome (3)
GenComp: dummy (All-women EC=1)	1.48 (0.195)	0.04 (0.498)	1.58* (0.083)	0.29* (0.095)
Women's association: dummy (Assoc. exists=1)	−1.92* (0.064)	−0.08 (0.278)	−0.20 (0.784)	−0.01 (0.909)
Average age of all EC members	−0.03 (0.805)	−0.001 (0.723)	0.06 (0.437)	0.01 (0.416)
% Brahmins in EC	0.02 (0.194)	0.001 (0.308)	0.01 (0.417)	0.001 (0.465)
Who made forest use rules:[b] dummy (without FD help=1)	2.73** (0.021)	0.11 (0.287)	1.36 (0.122)	0.22 (0.202)
Forest area protected (ha)	−0.08* (0.053)	−0.003* (0.071)	0.01 (0.442)	0.002 (0.271)
No of toles	0.01 (0.955)	0.002 (0.816)	−0.15 (0.334)	−0.03 (0.320)
District: dummy (Baglung/ Parbat=1)	−0.16 (0.894)	−0.005 (0.902)	−0.06 (0.936)	−0.01 (0.943)
Constant	−0.30		−4.34	

Notes: [a] Forest regeneration: Poor=1; Good=2; Very good=3. As assessed by villagers at time of survey.
The marginal effect (ME) is for a discrete change from 0 to 1 for dummy variables, and for a one unit change for continuous variables. Numbers in parenthesis are *p*-values. Significance:** at 5%,* at 10%.
[b] For this variable, the ME for outcome (2), which is not presented here, was negatively significant at 10%.
In the equation, the Hausman's test indicates that the assumption of 'independence of irrelevant alternatives' (IIA) holds.
FD= Forest department.

Notes on models

For GenComp, I also calculated predicated probabilities at value 1 and value 0 and the difference. The predicted probability for forest condition being very good came to 0.44 with GenComp =1, and 0.15 with GenComp = 0, giving a difference of 0.29, which is the same as the marginal effect.

men can easily be accused of molesting the women patrol members. Men fear this possibility' (Nansalai CFI, Panchmahals, Gujarat, author's survey, 2000–01).

Rule compliance also improves with women on the EC. For a start, once they join the EC women themselves tend to comply more with the rules, as some EC women in Ramrekha CFI, Baglung, Nepal, put it frankly:

W1: We feel the forest is ours. When I was only a CFI member, I used to steal grass from the forest, but after taking responsibility as an EC member I have stopped stealing and feel that the forest should be protected.
W2: We labour hard for this forest. I feel it is like my own baby.

Table 8.9. Nepal: factors affecting forest canopy change (all districts)

Dependent variable	Change in forest canopy: dummy[a] (forest department assessment)	
Statistical method	Logit	
No. of observations	58	
Pseudo R^2	0.38	
Explanatory variables	**Coef.**	**ME**
GenComp: dummy (All-women EC =1)	4.18** (0.010)	0.51*** (0.000)
Women's association: dummy (Assoc. exists=1)	−1.43 (0.142)	−0.21 (0.130)
Average age of all EC members	0.40*** (0.006)	0.06*** (0.001)
% illiterate EC members	−0.03* (0.067)	−0.01** (0.050)
% Brahmins in EC	0.03** (0.045)	0.004** (0.034)
Who made forest use rules: dummy (without FD help=1)	−0.43 (0.660)	−0.07 (0.668)
Forest area protected (ha)	0.02 (0.352)	0.003 (0.353)
Forest canopy at time of handover: dummy (Thick or medium=1)	2.97** (0.027)	0.29*** (0.004)
No. of toles	−0.17 (0.302)	−0.03 (0.306)
District: dummy (Baglung/Parbat=1)	−2.34** (0.047)	−0.38** (0.035)
Constant	−15.30	

Notes: [a] Change in forest canopy: Canopy improvement or thick canopy maintained=1; no change in canopy (remains thin, patchy or medium) or worsening canopy =0. As assessed by the Forest Department at two points in time.
The marginal effect (ME) is for a discrete change from 0 to 1 for dummy variables, and for a one unit change for continuous variables.
Numbers in parenthesis are *p*-values. Significance: ***at 1%, **at 5%, *at 10%

In addition, EC women are better able to spread information about rules among other women, persuade them to follow the rules, and may even motivate them to be vigilant and report intruders. As women EC members of Gayasavar CFI in Narmada (Gujarat) told me, 'women can explain forest rules to other women better than men can'. Observations by some women EC members on their contributions to protection are also illustrative:

One year, EC women did not go for protection, only the men went. But women sneaked in for cutting firewood. So men said to me, you should stop women from cutting since the women don't listen to us when we request them not to cut. So I called a meeting of the women. We decided that ten women would go together every day for patrolling. (Woman EC member and leader to author, Vejpur CFI, Narmada, Gujarat, 1999)

Having women in the CFI helps in protection. Often village women would cut firewood from the protected forest in times of need. We held a meeting and they stopped cutting. We were even able to persuade women from the neighbouring village to stop cutting our forest. (Woman EC president to author, Rampuri CFI, Sabakantha, Gujarat CFI, 1999)

Especially but not only among all-women CFIs, I found that village women often expressed a strong sense of ownership of the protected forest, and kept an informal vigil when going about their daily work, looking out not only for intruders but also forest fires.[20] Sometimes it was their alertness alone which contained the spread of a fire. We had also found in the last chapter that all-women groups compared to other Nepal groups had significantly fewer violations per year of CFI functioning; and in Gujarat violations by women and for firewood declined while violations by men and for timber increased, as the years of protection increased. Moreover, women's collection of firewood, fodder, and non-timber items is less likely to be harmful to conservation compared to men's lopping or clear-felling of trees for timber (see also Lele 1994).

A second notable benefit that women in the EC bring to forest regeneration is through their knowledge of plants and correct extraction practices, their inputs on how to manage and regenerate particular species, and their enhanced cooperation if better account is taken of their preferences when tree plantation is undertaken. Although these aspects are difficult to quantify directly they are of considerable importance, as the qualitative evidence presented earlier in this chapter indicates and to which we can add further examples. For instance, one of the factors underlying the striking Panchmahals results is women's contribution to improved forest management practices, noted by Sarin (1995b) and the SARTHI field staff. Sarin found that where the Panchmahals women participated more in decision-making, they provided visibly valuable inputs. They pointed out, for example, that the over-extraction of kada for firewood from highly degraded patches was preventing its regeneration. They suggested that instead women should be allowed to harvest two other firewood species that were coppicing well and the kada trees be left alone to regenerate. Women also argued successfully for enrichment planting in blank forest patches rather than simply waiting for natural regeneration, as the men were doing. This gap filling, they noted, would require relatively little effort, since the pits where the rootstock had been dug out could be used to plant the saplings. Although this example relates to Panchmahals, there would undoubtedly be similar cases in other areas which await documentation.

A third advantage that groups with more women, compared with groups with few or no women, are found to have in other studies (although not directly tested by me) is better collaboration, solidarity, and conflict resolution. Westerman et al.'s (2005) study, discussed in Chapter 2, empirically establishes this through an analysis of forty-six groups with varying gender composition (all-men, mixed, and all-women) managing natural resources across twenty developing countries.

[20] Davidson-Hunt (1995: 147) also observed this sense of ownership of the forests they protect among women in Himachal Pradesh.

They also find that the capacity for self-sustaining collective action increases with women's presence. Similarly, the experimental games literature discussed in Chapters 1 and 2 points to greater cooperation and solidarity in women majority groups. Enhanced cooperation, again, can greatly benefit institutional functioning and conservation outcomes.

A fourth set of factors that underlie the positive gender effects are those that the Panchmahals results help highlight, but which would have wider relevance. For instance, the more inclusive nature of Panchmahals' ECs, which have a substantially larger presence of landless women than other districts, is likely to have contributed to its strong gender results, in addition to women's management inputs noted above. Inducting landless women into the EC and involving them in the conservation project can enhance rule compliance among landless families, who otherwise tend to remain marginalized and, not infrequently, hostile to forest closure. In addition, that women's greater presence in the EC is linked with improved forest condition in Panchmahals, even though, as noted earlier, such groups make less strict rules, demonstrates that lenient rules, which allow some procurement of firewood and fodder, need do the forest no harm. In fact, as elaborated further below, some extraction can even be beneficial, by helping to clear undergrowth and providing people with more incentive to cooperate, resulting in a positive net effect on forest condition.

Gender effects in the regression results are manifest too through village women's associations and the age of female EC members. An active women's association is significantly linked with thick (as versus thin) forest canopy in Gujarat (Table 8.6: Equation 2), and with good forest regeneration (as versus poor regeneration) in Nepal (Table 8.8). The statistical results, however, are not a full measure of this variable's importance which is revealed more in women's qualitative responses. In several Gujarat villages, EC women told us that women's associations helped them spread the message of forest conservation and encouraged village women to watch out for intruders.

Age has both a gender dimension and a general dimension and, as hypothesized, is found significant in both Gujarat and Nepal for most forest condition indicators. CFIs that have ECs with older women members and older members in general show greater improvement in forest condition. In Gujarat, age is positively associated with better current forest (researcher's index), a smaller percentage of degraded forest area (Geer index), and an improvement in forest condition (Table 8.6, Equations 1, 3 to 5). In Nepal, ECs with older members (including women) are found more likely to show an improvement in forest canopy (Table 8.9). Older EC members (as noted earlier) embody greater experience in CFI functioning, carry more authority and respect within the village, and are more likely to be listened to, making it easier for them to enforce rules and resolve conflicts. Also, as elaborated in Chapter 6, the elderly often tend to be more committed to protection, to have lower time preferences, and are more likely to express explicitly conservationist values. Many older people (men and women), especially in Gujarat, said they had initiated forest protection because they had personally seen the decline of once-lush forests. Indeed, in a few cases in Panchmahals, elderly headmen—the agyavans—belonging to families of hereditary headmen who carried traditional authority, had initiated protection (see also Sharma 1995). The elderly also bear fewer costs in enforcing the rules, since they usually have younger family members to search for firewood and fodder—a support of particular importance to women EC members. And older women are more able to attend EC meetings, and face fewer social restrictions in talking to both male and female villagers and persuading them to adhere to the rules.

The EC's caste and literacy make a difference as well (although only in some equations). Improvement in forest canopy in Nepal is greater in ECs which have a higher percentage of Brahmins and a lower incidence of illiteracy among their members (Table 8.9).

Other relevant factors

A number of factors linked with CFI functioning and the characteristics of the forest, the population, and the location also affect forest condition. Some of these factors are significant in Gujarat, others in Nepal. First, in Gujarat, protection by a guard is associated with significantly better overall forest condition (higher researcher's index, denser canopy: see Tables 8.6 and 8.7).[21] Guards matter not only in what they themselves can do (being paid by the community, they bear more responsibility and carry more authority than village patrols), but also because their presence reflects the community's interest in good protection and rule enforcement.[22] Villagers themselves recognize this:

> When we began protection, the forests also began to grow. With that thefts increased. It was difficult for us to control this. So we decided to keep two or three watchmen. People used to feel that they had a right over the forest, and who were we to stop them? Now everybody knows that we are serious about protection, that is why the thefts have decreased, almost stopped. (EC members, Mor CFI, Panchmahals, Gujarat, author's survey, 2000–01)

> There was a lot of stealing of grass and firewood. Then we kept a guard. Also since we are all women in the EC the incidence of stealing is now very low. If we see someone stealing we try and catch the culprit. We give 50 per cent of the fine collected to the person who catches the intruder. (Women EC members, Ramrekha CFI, Nepal, author's survey, 2000–01)

Even when the community cannot afford a guard throughout the year, they employ one during marriage seasons or festival times when the forest is particularly at risk, since the demand for firewood and timber poles rises. The period of protection, however, is found to have an insignificant effect in all the equations

[21] In the Nepal equations, the forest protection method was not included because of hidden collinearity.

[22] There is a difference between a forest department beatguard who may be imposed top-down on the villagers and likely to face hostility from them (as was the case under the social forestry programmes undertaken by South Asian governments in the 1980s: Agarwal 1986a), and a guard appointed and paid for by the villagers themselves. In some Gujarat CFIs, as noted, it was elderly former watchmen who started informal protection.

for both Gujarat and Nepal and the variable is not included in the final equations presented here.

Second, forest condition is significantly affected by the attributes of the population served by the CFI, which in turn impinges on its ability to protect. Both the all-district equations and the Panchmahals equations for Gujarat bring this out in different ways. In the all-district results, the larger the incidence of migrant households in the village, the poorer is the condition of the forest (Table 8.6, Equations 1, 2 and 5). Migration, as we had noted, reduces a household's ability to contribute to protection and other forest management work. Landlessness, except insofar as it overlaps with migration, has no additional effect.[23] In Panchmahals, however, landlessness on its own does have a negative impact on forest improvement (Table 8.7, Equation 4). Landlessness makes for higher forest dependence (which could increase the proclivity to break rules), and a lesser ability to contribute to protection, time-wise or financially.

Third, as hypothesized, resource characteristics and the constraints they pose affect forest condition and its likelihood of improvement—the fewer the constraints the better the conservation. Larger forests show a greater improvement in forest condition in some equations for both Gujarat and Nepal, but the coefficients are very small so that the effect is limited (Tables 8.6 and 8.8). Panchmahals deviates from this pattern for one equation where large forest size is linked with a larger percentage of degraded area (Geer index). This could imply that monitoring difficulties outweigh the advantage of size; but more likely what underlies this result is the fact that in several Panchmahals villages with large forests some of the degraded forest area in the Geer index falls outside the protection boundary (since, as noted, the satellite data does not distinguish between protected and unprotected village forest land).

Relatedly, the Gujarat results bear out that the more the settlements (hamlets) dependent on the forest the poorer the forest condition and the less the chances of improvement, both due to associated population pressure and because more hamlets mean greater social heterogeneity and possible conflicts of interest. In Nepal, however, the effect of the number of toles is not significant. Possibly pressure on any one protected site is somewhat eased since villagers can join more than one CFI, even if such membership when measured directly was not a significant predictor of forest improvement. Other aspects of initial resource disadvantage that are found to adversely affect forest condition include the number of forest segments (in Gujarat). Non-continuous forest areas are difficult to effectively watch either by a patrol or a guard—in fact CFIs with highly segmented forests do not even bother to keep guards. The district dummies capture the overall impact of locational variation in ecology and population characteristics. In Gujarat, CFIs located in Narmada/Bharuch do better by several indicators than those located in the other two districts, and in Nepal, similarly,

[23] This variable, when tried in the all-district runs, was consistently insignificant (not presented in the tables).

CFIs in Gorkha/Dhading do better in terms of canopy increase than CFIs in Baglung/Parbat.

What about resilience? Does the extent of degradation when protection started matter in the forest's ability to regenerate naturally? The Nepal results support this. We find that forests that started with an initial advantage (e.g. had medium to thick canopy) had a 29 per cent greater probability of showing an improvement in canopy or maintaining a thick canopy, compared with forests which were thin or patchy at the time of handover (Table 8.9). It is therefore especially creditable that all-women groups, most of which started with thin and patchy forests, have done so well in improving their forest condition.

Fourth, the impact of the infrastructure index (a proxy for modernization and lower forest dependence) is weak and significant in only one equation (see Table 8.7, Equation 3, for Panchmahals).[24] A higher index is linked with a lower percentage of degraded forest. Fifth, there is a positive, albeit weak indication that forest department involvement adds to forest improvement: those of Nepal's CFIs in which the forest department provided inputs in framing forest use rules (the proxy for the department's overall involvement) are found more likely to have good regeneration (Table 8.8). The forest department, as noted, can help improve forest condition by the technical inputs it can provide, especially in the CFI's cleaning, pruning, and enrichment operations.

Finally, strict forest use rules (that is, little or no extraction) per se may or may not improve forest condition. On the one hand, it is possible that some of the improvement in forest condition associated with women's greater presence on the EC is attributable to the stricter rules that CFIs with more women make in most of the study districts, with the exception of Panchmahals (Chapter 6).[25] On the other hand, the results for Panchmahals, where CFIs with more women show better forest regeneration, despite making relatively lenient rules, indicate that allowing some extraction need cause no harm. Indeed, very strict rules, such as a total ban on entry, could prove counterproductive, both because the rules can prove to be socially non-viable and increase the tendency of those in acute need to break them, and because ecologically the benefits of regulated extraction on regeneration may not accrue and the forest may also be left more vulnerable to fire. Allowing cattle grazing or leaf litter collection, for instance, helps remove potentially incendiary undergrowth which would otherwise accumulate and could get ignited by a careless cigarette or by someone resentful of the rules.[26] In the course of my fieldwork, several such cases were brought to my attention.

[24] The index was found to be consistently insignificant in the all-district regressions for Gujarat and was not included in the final equations, given sample size constraints.

[25] A similar argument could apply to Brahmins and the elderly on the EC: we found in Chapter 6 that CFIs with a higher percentage of Brahmins and of older EC members tended to make stricter rules.

[26] See Chakravartty (2009) for recent incidents in Gujarat and Agarwal's (1986c) investigative account of a forest fire in the Keoldaro National Park in India. In the latter, a ban on cattle grazing had caused the grass to grow tall, which a careless (or deliberately thrown) cigarette had set ablaze. For historical evidence on similar incidents, see Bhattacharya (1992) and Sivaramakrishnan (1999).

I also directly tested the effect of strictness on forest condition by using the strictness index in the equations presented here, but found it to be consistently insignificant in explaining the condition of the forest and improvements therein. This does not of course imply that open access will benefit conservation. Rather, within the overall regime of protection and regulation, context-specific leniency could prove ecologically beneficial, or at least not detrimental, while leading to more equitable gender and class outcomes in terms of women's (and especially poor women's) access to firewood and other non-timber products.

5. CONCLUDING COMMENTS

We now have another chapter of the story on the difference women's participation can make to governance, by probing a dimension that has been seriously neglected both in the green governance literature and in the gender and politics literature. We examined whether women's greater participation in the governance structure of an institution protecting a common pool resource, such as a forest, leads to better conservation and regeneration. We find that this is indeed the case by a variety of indicators covering different dimensions of forest ecology. As argued here, there can be many reasons for the positive gender effect. Involving women in the EC's decisions enlarges the pool of citizens committed to forest protection and conservation. Even if the rules made are strict and add to women's hardships, if they have been party to the decision they will be more willing to follow the rules themselves, as well as convince other women (and men) to do so. Including women in the EC also improves the spread of information about forest closure rules and the need for conservation among a wider cross-section of people. It increases the number of those keeping watch for transgressors from both within and outside the community of members. And it creates conditions for taking better account of women's knowledge of plants and conservation practices and their preferences for particular species. It can also help instil a conservation ethic in children, thus enhancing 'environ-mentality' among them, motivating them to contribute to sustainable conservation practices. Measures that help enhance women's participation in the governance institutions would thus be beneficial not only because their participation is important in and of itself as a constituent element of successful functioning, but also in an instrumental sense of better fulfilling the conservation objectives of such institutions. A related enabling factor is the presence of a women's association in the community. Although captured only limitedly in the statistical analysis, women's associations (especially if inclusive of poor women) can help improve forest protection, and enhance village women's self-confidence, collective strength, and public presence.

Another dimension, not captured in the statistical analysis but which I believe could prove important, is having more landless women and generally more landless members represented on the EC. Landless EC members can better persuade village landless households to follow the rules set by the CFI. Landless *women* on the EC could have a particularly positive effect since they are the most forest dependent and their reaching other landless village women could make a marked difference to protection. In other words, unlike the effect of *village* landlessness, which we found was detrimental to forest conservation, the effect of landless women on the EC could prove beneficial.

Our finding that the older the female EC members and the older the EC overall, the more effective it is, also points to the positive effect of inducting older women and men into governance. Employing a guard to supplement patrolling by villagers would prove beneficial as well. In addition, the forest department's technical support (including training in pruning and clearing operations) could enhance the effectiveness of the community's conservation efforts, although gender barriers in access to training would need to be overcome. At present, as several women EC members in India and senior women grassroots activists in Nepal told me, such training is usually confined to a few male office bearers. Finally, it appears important to give the community a larger-sized forest in a contiguous patch and in a condition that still allows regeneration, rather than giving it a forest area that is so small or so segmented as to provide little resource support, or so degraded as to have lost its resilience.

9

Shortages Amidst Growing Plenty

We deal with the [firewood] shortages. What problems can men have? They get readymade food to eat. It is women who have to worry about how to cook the meal.

(Women to author, Asundriya CFI, Panchmahals, Gujarat, 1998)

Community forestry aims at improving both conservation and subsistence. The surveyed communities are doing well on the former, but what about the latter? In the early 1980s, faced with degrading forests, women in many parts of India and Nepal were spending several hours a day in gathering firewood. The fortunate ones who lived near good forests needed to go only every few days, but for others, as deforestation grew so did collection time. In Gujarat, for instance, for gathering firewood for home use, women had to go once every four days in the forested plains, every two days in depleted areas, and every day for four to five hours in severely depleted regions (Chapter 2, Table 2.1). When community forestry was initiated, leading to forest closures, collection time and distances travelled increased several-fold. In the villages that Sarin (1995a) visited in the early 1990s in the Indian states of Gujarat and West Bengal, she found that after forest closure walking to neighbouring sites for a headload of firewood added several hours and kilometres to women's journeys. The women I interviewed in Gujarat in 1995 also emphasized that they were now fenced in all directions, as neighbours had begun protecting as well (see Box 9.1). I had expected a change in this scenario by the time I conducted my 2000–01 survey. I found instead that the shortages had persisted, even increased for many, despite growing biomass plenty.

In this chapter I examine this paradox of shortages amidst plenty, and explore the impact of women's presence on the EC in alleviating them. I also address the questions: would greater firewood extraction negatively affect the sustainable regeneration of forests? If not, why isn't more extracted? And why is fodder treated differently from firewood?

Access to benefits from the community forest are of central importance both for institutional functioning and for fair outcomes. We have already found that women's inclusion in the EC improves forest condition and hence the efficiency of outcomes. But equitable benefit sharing is just as important. Does women's presence on the EC also enhance women's prospects of getting more benefits? Firewood remains the most important product for which women have

Box 9.1. Gujarat: forest closure and firewood shortages

Excerpts from author's interviews with village women, Sabarkantha 25 March 1995

* * *

Q: On what issues do women and men differ in Forest Protection Committee meetings?
A: Women face the problem of firewood. Because women protect the forest they should get some benefit from it. Men can afford to wait for a while because their main concern is timber. But women need firewood daily. When we ask for permission to take dry twigs men say: what is the guarantee that you won't cut green branches? You might cut more. The men don't listen to us. We can get some fallen twigs and leaves for only ten days. The forest is closed for the rest of the year.

Q: What do you do then?
A: At the moment it is closed, so we use crop stalks, cattle dung, kerosene. Some have biogas.

Q: What did you do before the closure?
A: We used to go to the Rajasthan border [the adjacent state] for firewood. The route was through our own forest. On the return journey we would pick up drywood from our forest.

Q: Do you go to Rajasthan now?
A: No we can't now, because the route through our forest is blocked. From our forest, we are only allowed to get drywood for ten days in the winter. That's all. We collect enough for two to three months. But in the monsoon we don't know what we will do. Last year they gave us special permission to collect for ten additional days. This year we are hoping for permission again.

Q: Will you get permission?
A: At the last *parishad* meeting they told us they won't give us permission.

Q: If you don't get permission what will you do?
A: We can only call a women's meeting and talk to the men and put forward our problem. We will say: we have to cook, we have no wood. So what now?

customarily depended on the forests. The impact on firewood shortages can thus be seen as the central gender equity effect of forest governance. Although other forest products that are gathered, in particular fodder, are not unimportant, firewood demonstrates gender interests and conflicts better than any other item. It also contrasts with fodder which falls less exclusively in women's domain. I therefore focus here on firewood to see whether women's greater presence on the EC makes a difference, supplemented by analysis for fodder in Appendix 9.1.

An estimated 65–75 per cent of rural households in India and over 90 per cent in Nepal depend on firewood for a part or most of their domestic energy.[1] In the

[1] For India, see especially, NCAER (2001–02) and GoI (1999b). For Nepal see GoN (2004: 41) which reports the 2001 census results. The figures for India differ somewhat by source and the period

early 1990s firewood alone contributed 62 per cent of domestic energy in India and the rest came mostly from other unprocessed biofuels such as cropwaste and cattle dung. These biofuels, along with firewood, accounted for 92 per cent of rural India's domestic energy (Table 9.1). This dependence has not changed substantially since. Indeed the pattern is a familiar one across developing countries where 2.4 billion households still use conventional biofuels for cooking and heating. This includes 90 per cent of rural households in large parts of Sub-Saharan Africa and 70–80 per cent in China (Modi et al. 2005). And much of this firewood is gathered from the commons and private sources: about 80 per cent of India's and 90 per cent of Nepal's rural households that are using firewood gather what they use (see also Chapter 2). This percentage rises to 94 in Nepal's hills (GoN 2004: 41). In other words, firewood for domestic use remains a largely non-monetized good, dependent essentially on the labour of women and girl children for procurement. Among landless households almost all the firewood is collected from community resources, but even among the landowners a notable part is obtained from the commons, and the rest from their own resources. Local availability is therefore of critical importance in determining firewood adequacy. It affects the time and energy expended in collection and the health costs of inferior fuel substitutes.

Moreover, even firewood is not the ideal fuel. As elaborated in Chapter 2, due to fuel smoke ingested during cooking in poorly ventilated kitchens women face a

Table 9.1. All India: sources of rural domestic energy

Energy source	Coal replacement		
	1992–93		2000–01
	(million tonnes)	%	%
Firewood	94.77	61.6	76.8
Cattle dung	26.15	17.0	10.0
Crop residues	20.53	13.4	7.6
Unprocessed biofuels: Subtotal		***92.0***	***94.4***
Coal/soft coke	0.58	0.4	0.5
Kerosene	6.83	4.4	4.3
Others	4.97	3.2	0.7
TOTAL	**153.84**	**100.0**	**100.0**

Source: Natarajan (1995: 43) for 1992–93 and NCAER (2001–02: 32) for 2000–01.

covered by the data. NCAER gives a figure of 74 per cent households using wood for cooking and heating in 2000–01, based on a study of rural stove users and covering around 11,800 households across the country. By the National Sample Survey (GoI 1999b: 34) figures, 62 per cent of rural households were using firewood across India, and 73 per cent in Gujarat in 1998. Natarajan (1995) from an earlier NCAER study gives a figure of 84 per cent rural households for the early 1990s.

disproportionately higher risk than men of acute respiratory ailments, chronic obstructive pulmonary disease, tuberculosis, cancer, cataracts, asthma, and even premature death. Acute respiratory infection from indoor air pollution is also a major cause of child morbidity and mortality. Indeed, all unprocessed biofuels have serious health implications for women cooking over open fires in enclosed spaces, and for children sharing those spaces. And many of these effects are grossly underestimated by families since they lack adequate information (Pitt et al.'s 2005 study for Bangladesh is indicative). Substitute fuels such as cropwaste and dung can be much worse offenders and compound the risks. Moreover, the wood used as fuel itself varies in its attributes, especially smokiness, and the less smoky varieties which have value as timber are typically no longer accessible to women in community protected forests. In fact, firewood of any kind is usually in short supply. Despite an increase in biomass through community forest management, the problem has persisted, indeed paradoxically it has worsened for many households. These observations at the country level are reinforced when we examine in more depth what is happening in the study's fieldsites.

1. FIREWOOD SHORTAGES: INDICATORS AND EXTENT

1.1 Indicators

The vast majority of my sample villages report extensive firewood shortages. Potentially, such shortages can be due either to inadequate availability or inadequate access to what is available. Households located in arid or semi-arid regions, such as Gujarat, for instance, are generally prone to biomass shortages. But equally, shortages can arise if people have inadequate access to available biomass, either because they have no personal resources on which to draw, such as trees on their own land, or because they face restrictions in the use of community resources.

It is not easy to measure shortages directly in a survey. I have used three proxy indicators. The first one is based on whether women EC members and village women in general report shortages. The former were asked whether village women were experiencing firewood shortages at the time when protection began and at the time of the survey in 2000–01. Their responses were supplemented by focus group discussions with village women who were individually asked whether they faced firewood shortages when protection began and in 2000–01. Their answers were aggregated to assess whether none, some, or most of them were facing shortages earlier and currently. Those villages or communities where the majority of the respondents reported scarcity were identified as having a firewood shortage problem. Of course, even where the group discussions did not reflect village-wide scarcity, there could have been landless or near-landless communities that were experiencing problems. However, there was no simple way of measuring shortages across all socio-economic categories in a sample of

CFIs covering so many villages and hamlets/toles. I therefore took as broadly representative the assessment based on discussions with the EC members and the village women who constituted the focus groups.

The second indicator of firewood shortages is the type of fuel used and reported shifts from firewood to inferior fuels such as cropwaste, dung, even weeds. Dependence on inferior fuels is, I believe, a fairly reliable indicator of implicit shortages. Cropwaste or dung are seldom women's preferred fuels and although most households use these fuels in small amounts in certain seasons they tend to be used in substantial extent when there is a firewood shortage. These fuels need more time to ignite and tending to keep alight, thus adding to cooking time and restricting multi-tasking while cooking. The additional smoke also compounds the negative health effects. Women in Sabuti village, Narmada, Gujarat (author's survey, 2000–01), explained this graphically:

W1: We have been managing crop waste. That is the only alternative. It is a poor alternative because cropwaste burns up very fast and you have to keep on feeding the stove with it.
W2: As a result [of firewood shortages], the time and labour spent cooking has doubled. With cropwaste we can't just leave the stove unattended and do other work, in the way we can with good firewood.
W3: With dung the problem is smoke. There is a lot of smoke and our eyes begin to smart and water, and the children are always coughing.

The third indicator of shortages is women's reports that they economize on firewood in various ways, bearing a range of costs. Women's complaints are a supplementary pointer, although not statistically measurable. We find widespread shortages in the study areas on all three counts, in both Gujarat and Nepal.

1.2 Gujarat: Firewood Situation

For most communities, CFI formation has not reduced the overall incidence of shortages despite forest improvement and greater biomass availability: 74 per cent of CFIs in Gujarat reported shortages at the time of the survey in 2000–01 and almost as large a percentage said they had faced shortages when the CFI was formed (Table 9.2). Some two-thirds of the villages which had shortages earlier continued to experience them when the survey was done. And although about 9 per cent of the CFIs reported an improvement (they had shortages earlier but none in 2000–01), 7 per cent reported a worsening (they faced no shortages earlier but faced them in 2000–01). Gender-wise, however, a much smaller percentage of CFIs with >2 EC women compared with CFIs with $\leq$2 EC women reported shortages at the time of the survey.

Persistent firewood scarcity is especially apparent in Panchmahals and Sabarkantha. The Narmada/Bharuch sites are somewhat better off due to the presence of nearby government forests which the villagers draw upon clandestinely. The Sabarkantha villages have rather few alternative sites to go to and the Panchmahals sites have almost none. The village open lands are severely degraded as well.

Table 9.2. Gujarat: firewood shortages when protection began and in 2000–01 (% CFIs)

District and gender Composition	No shortages earlier or in 2000–01	Shortages earlier but not in 2000–01 (improving)	Shortages earlier, and in 2000–01 (persisting)	No shortages earlier, shortages in 2000–01 (worsening)	Number of CFIs with information
		By district			
Narmada/Bharuch	23.1	23.1	46.2	7.7	(13)
Panchmahals	5.3	10.5	73.7	10.5	(19)
Sabarkantha	21.7	0.0	73.9	4.4	(23)
		By EC gender composition			
≤2 EC women	3.7	14.8	70.4	11.1	(27)
>2 EC women	28.6	3.6	64.3	3.6	(28)
All CFIs	**16.4**	**9.1**	**67.2**	**7.3**	**(55)**
Shortages earlier (76.3%)					
Shortages in 2000–01 (74.5%)					

Note: The percentages have been computed only for cases with information available for both periods.

Source: Author's survey 2000–01.

That firewood shortages are widespread is also borne out by the type of cooking fuel used and the shift to inferior fuels, such as crop waste and dung. Of the seventeen Gujarat villages with CFIs, located in four districts, that I had visited during my 1998–99 fieldwork (including some villages which are part of my 2000–01 study), sixteen reported firewood shortages. All of these were substituting cropwaste, dung, or other fuels to bridge the gap. In some, women admitted stealing from the community forest, and as we know from our discussion on violations, stealing is probably more common than people admit in an open group meeting. Some villages reported a five-fold increase in distances travelled for a headload of firewood. A few households even reported changing their cropping patterns in favour of crops such as tur and castor to obtain more agricultural waste for fuel.

My 2000–01 survey data throws further light on shifts in cooking fuel over time. All the villages reported using firewood as well as cropwaste or dung both prior to and after protection. In other words, there has been rather little improvement in the aggregate situation. The figures do not capture the *extent* to which substitute fuels are used. Qualitative evidence from group discussions, however, indicates clearly that the dependence on cropwaste and dung has increased among most households after forest protection started.[2] Moreover, 57 per cent of the survey villages report that they are now using kerosene to

[2] In years of low rainfall even cropwaste can be in short supply.

supplement their needs whereas only 33 per cent did so earlier (see Table 9.3 for the survey period). These Gujarat households normally use kerosene for lighting and for making the morning tea rather than for cooking the main meal.[3] None uses LPG, but a few households have access to clean biofuels such as biogas. This is mainly methane gas, generated through the fermentation of biomass under controlled conditions, which is then piped to the kitchen for cooking, from the tanks where the biomass ferments. The residue in the form of slurry is a rich source of manure. Biogas is used mainly in the Narmada/Bharuch sites where the local NGO took the initiative. In the other sites, although some villagers had biogas plants, there were virtually no functioning units. A discussion with a group of women in Bapda village, Narmada/Bharuch (author's survey, 2000–01), gives some insights into how they view alternative fuels.

W1: We collect firewood everyday in winter and store for later use. Now we have also started using cropwaste.
W2: For certain chores like boiling water or for cooking food that requires simmering we use dung.
W3: For making tea or something quick we use kerosene. But we use it sparingly as it is very expensive and not always available.
W4: We prefer wood to everything else, but we have learnt to adjust to alternatives.
W5: Some of the families in the village have biogas but the plants are not working properly. When they work they are a good alternative for us.
W6: The cost of maintenance and upkeep of biogas is high and in a short period all of them have stopped working.

These perceptions are reinforced by village women's ranking of the fuels they use. For computing this, an effort was made to elicit information from each woman who was present in the focus group discussion. All the women who listed a particular fuel were aggregated. The fuel mentioned by the largest number of women got the first rank, and so on. For the time before protection began, firewood was ranked first in all the villages save one in Sabarkantha, where cropwaste dominated. In 2000–01, several years after protection began, although in the bulk of villages women still ranked firewood first, in 16 per cent cropwaste or dung came on top (Table 9.3). Even for firewood, some of the tree species that women were allowed to collect for fuel generated as much smoke as inferior fuels, while the less-smoky so-called timber species, which women much preferred, were banned. Almost everywhere, however, men typically underplayed the firewood scarcity by asserting either that there was none, or that women were managing just fine with cropwaste. Here are some sample responses by male respondents to the question: do you think women are facing a firewood shortage?

[3] Typically, women don't want to light the fire in the morning, since keeping it alight till the afternoon meal is cooked wastes fuel. Also, lighting the fire only for morning tea and then dousing and relighting it several hours later would involve a lot of extra effort.

Table 9.3. Gujarat and Nepal: Cooking fuels used in 2000–01 (% CFIs)

Cooking fuels 2000–01	Gujarat		Nepal	
	Fuel used by most households	First rank of fuel used by most	Fuel used by most households	First rank of fuel used by most households
Firewood	96.6	87.9	100.0	96.8
Cropwaste	96.6	12.1	67.7	1.6
Dung	93.1	3.4	3.2	0.0
Kerosene	56.9		27.4	0.0
Biogas	15.5		22.6	0.0
Fodder residue			27.4	0.0
LPG			16.1	1.6

Notes: The sum of percentages can exceed 100 since in some villages more than one source gets first rank, implying each is of equal importance.
LPG = Liquified Petroleum Gas.
Source: Author's survey, 2000–01.

Responses in Makroda village, Sabarkantha district

M1: The women have to manage with cropwaste and dung.
M2: Those who are smart enough to grow their own trees can use those.

Responses in Koylamandvi village, Bharuch district

M1: The women have started substituting cropwaste and dung for their fuel requirements.
M2: Families have switched very effectively to these products. Some of them don't even miss wood anymore.

It was usually only in very poor households, where shortages were acute, that men too admitted to the problem.

The sources of firewood (what little they can get), however, have become more restricted. Overall, the majority of Gujarat households depend on the protected forest and their own fields, while about a third collect from the nearby government forests or unprotected forests in neighbouring villages (Table 9.4). Nearly a quarter of the villages report some households purchasing firewood, but they do so almost entirely from within the village or from nearby villages where poorer, low-caste or tribal women collect and sell directly to some of the better-off, typically upper-caste families. Sabarkantha has on average 3.8 per cent upper-caste households compared with 1.7 per cent in the Narmada/Bharuch sample and none in Panchmahals.[4] Upper-caste women, especially in affluent Rajput and Patel households, are the most domestically confined and likely to purchase firewood for at least part of their needs.

Firewood gathering sources, however, vary a good deal by district. In Narmada/Bharuch a large percentage of villages (87 per cent) depend on

[4] Although this did not show up in the survey responses, in Panchmahals too there is some limited intra-village purchase of firewood (Narain 1994, and Bhanji 1996).

Table 9.4. Gujarat: firewood sources used before protection began and in 2000–01 (% CFIs)

Districts and gender	Sources of firewood used					
	Community protected forest	Community protected plantation	Other forest	Village open land	Own fields	Purchase
	Sources of firewood by district before protection started					
Narmada/Bharuch (N=16)	18.8	6.2	87.5[a]	37.5	37.5	0.0
Panchmahals (N=20)	100.0	0.0	5.0	0.0	15.0	0.0
Sabarkantha (N=22)	81.8	0.0	54.5[b]	22.7	90.9	36.4
All Districts (*N*=58)	***70.7***	***1.7***	***46.6***	***19.0***	***50.0***	***13.8***
	Sources of firewood by district in 2000–01					
Narmada/Bharuch (N=16)	6.2	31.2	81.2[a]	6.2	56.2	0.0
Panchmahals (N=20)	100.0	0.0	0.0	0.0	10.0	0.0
Sabarkantha (N=22)	54.5	0.0	18.2[b]	13.6	95.4	59.1
	Sources of firewood by gender composition in 2000–01					
≤2 EC women (N=29)	62.1	10.3	31.0	6.9	58.6	17.2
>2 EC women (N=29)	51.7	6.9	27.6	6.9	51.7	27.6
All CFIs (*N*=58)	***56.9***	***8.6***	***29.3***	***6.9***	***55.2***	***22.4***
	First ranked source for firewood in 2000-01 by district					
All CFIs (*N*=58)	***48.3***	***1.7***	***17.2***	***1.7***	***25.9***	***6.9***

Notes: The sum of percentages can exceed 100 since villagers can use more than one source.
The method used for the ranking is described in the text. N=number of CFIs.
[a] Government forest; [b] another CFI's forest.

Source: Author's survey 2000–01. Based on focus group discussion with village women.

neighbourhood forests (especially those controlled by the government), followed by their own fields, and relatively few use the community forest (Table 9.4). Indeed these other forests are the most important source (first rank) in almost half of the Narmada/Bharuch villages, and although this involves a long walk and stretches women's collection time, it provides an important supplementary fall-back.[5] In contrast, the Panchmahals villages depend almost entirely on their community forests and 90 per cent of them rank this source first, while Sabarkantha villagers depend on a range of sources—their own fields, the community forest, firewood purchase, other nearby forests, as well as open village land. Before protection began, both the Panchmahals and Sabarkantha villages depended heavily on what is now protected forest (100 per cent and 82 per cent of the villages in the two districts respectively reported this: Table 9.4), while the Narmada/Bharuch villages even earlier depended mostly on other government forests since their own were highly degraded and yielded rather little. Several reasons underlie Panchmahals' persisting and substantial

[5] The table with a district-wise breakdown of source ranks is not reproduced here.

dependence on the community forest for firewood: the absence of nearby government-controlled forests, the closure of many neighbourhood village forests which are also now being protected by communities, and the availability of a range of plant species, such as kada and ganda babul, which have rather little use other than as fuel. Panchmahals' high dependence on community forests for firewood does not mean, however, that they get enough for their needs. Quite the contrary.

These figures of course give us only a broad idea of village firewood sources. They tell us little about *intra*-village differences in the use of particular sources, or the importance of a source for a particular class of household. Although difficult to capture quantitatively, such intra-village variation can be important, since women from the landless and landpoor households, with no crops or trees of their own and few cattle, lack even the option of using cropwaste or dung as fuel.[6] Indeed, closures have forced many poorer families to reduce their animal stocks (due to fodder shortages, as discussed in Appendix 9.1), which also reduces their supply of cattle dung for fuel.

How do women cope? The costs women incur provide a third indicator of shortages. The difficulty women mentioned most frequently during focus group discussions was the extra time they spent in gathering firewood and in cooking. Cooking time increases for several reasons. Economizing on firewood requires putting out the fire after each meal and relighting it later. Cropwaste, the main substitute fuel, burns less steadily than good firewood and has to be reignited every time the fire dies out. Both these processes are time consuming. Women also dislike cropwaste or dung because of the smoke generated. They have, however, learnt to cope due to lack of other options:

> Neither cropwaste nor dung is a good alternative to firewood. Both cause smoke. Also cropwaste is not good for cooking, it burns up very fast. You can hardly cook on it, but when there is no firewood, you have to use it. What else can you do? (Woman key informant, Gadh village, Panchmahals, author's survey, 2000–01)

> I used to walk a lot just to get a headload of firewood. That is how we managed. Cropwaste and dung were alternatives, but I don't like using them, so I walked long distances to get firewood. It is difficult to walk so long in the heat, and I have had severe back problems for which I am taking medicines. (Woman key informant, Boria village, Panchmahals, author's survey, 2000–01)

Some also cope by sneaking into the closed forest and risk being caught. And sometimes ECs pull up husbands in public to have them stop their wives from breaking the rules. Over a third of the Gujarat villagers reported stealing firewood from their own or neighbouring community forests and even this is under-reporting. In fact, in villages with acute shortages, altercations with neighbouring villages and with guards are common. In addition to the examples given in

[6] See also Jodha (1986) on the significantly higher dependence on the commons for firewood and fodder among landpoor rural households in India, compared with the landed.

Chapter 7, my discussion in 2001 with a group of five women in Singalgadh village in Panchmahals, Gujarat, is illustrative:

W1: We face more shortage now. Earlier [before protection started] we could get much more firewood, although even then it was not enough and we had to supplement it with maize, cotton sticks, and dung.
W2: We now sometimes try and sneak into the neighbouring village which is also protecting its forest. Last week we went to Khordara village but the villagers chased us away with sticks.
W3: We had an axe and rope so they asked us where we were going. We admitted that we were going to their forest to cut firewood.
W4: There were 3–4 men who confronted us, saying: 'You can't cut firewood from our forest, please go back to your own village.' So we came away.
W5: All of us have problems of firewood and water. When men return in the evening they immediately demand their dinner, but without firewood how can we cook?

Complaints are frequent, sometimes bitter, especially (but not only) in acute situations:

How will we cook if we don't get wood from the forest? What do they expect us to do? (Women in a group discussion, Panchmua village, Panchmahals, Gujarat, author's survey, 2000–01)

The women asked the men: should we burn our hands instead of firewood to light the stove? (Male NGO worker citing women in Panchmahals district, Gujarat, India, 1999)

My interview with a group of women in Panchmua village, Panchmahals, given in Box 9.2 also succinctly illustrates the range of difficulties women face with firewood shortages.

1.3 Nepal: Firewood Situation

In the Nepal sites also, most communities report persistent and often increasing firewood shortages (Table 9.5).[7] About half the CFIs reported they had faced shortages at the time of CFI formation, but two-thirds said they were facing shortages at the time of my survey in 2000–01: 38 per cent reported persisting shortages and 25 per cent said the situation was worse—they had faced no shortages earlier but did so now. Only 13 per cent reported an improvement—they had faced shortages earlier but had none in 2000–01. Baglung/Parbat have a higher percentage of CFIs with persistent shortages compared with

[7] The information for Nepal is based primarily on discussions with the EC, since, as noted in Chapter 4, many geographically scattered toles use a given forest, and no consolidated discussion was possible with people from all the toles. The EC, however, does have representatives from several user toles, and can be seen as providing a broad (if imperfect) representation of the communities.

Box 9.2. Gujarat: women discuss firewood shortages

Author's discussion with a group of women (Panchmua village, Panchamahals, Gujarat, 2000–01)

* * *

Q: Do you face firewood shortages?
W1: Yes, we use dung, tur, maize sticks alongwith firewood and manage somehow.
W2: Yes we have difficulty but we try to manage.

Q: Why is using dung or tur a problem?
W2: Tur and dung both produce a lot of smoke.
W1: They give low heat. Firewood heat is strong and steady. Firewood also catches fire easily.

Q: What do you use firewood for?
W1: For cooking. We use a mix of fuels. For tea we mainly use tur.

Q: What proportions of each do you use?
W1: We use tur and maize sticks the most, then dung, then firewood.
W1: We also use ganda babul from the roadside, especially for heating water. Because of its thorns it is difficult to collect. We heat water outside the home.
W2: I use a mix of fuel—tur, maize, roadside babul, and a bit of wood.

Q: When is firewood available most easily?
W1: In winter. After Diwali the forest is opened up for cutback for one month. We can take as much as we want.

Q to W3: How much did you get this year?
W3: About 15 bundles.

Q: How long will that last?
W3: Right now we are using tur, etc. In the monsoon we will use firewood for one month or so.
W4: I don't go to the forest for firewood. My daughter-in-law goes. She could get only 5 bundles.

Q: How will you survive in the monsoon?
W3: I will get some wood from our own fields and from shrubs near the stream.

Q: Since when have you faced this shortage?
W1: Since 4–5 years after the *mandali* was made. Before that people could freely cut firewood.
W2: Seven years or so ago we went quite far to collect firewood. We used our own forest. It took one hour to go and 1½ hours to return. I would get firewood. I also used some tur. The situation is no different now.

Q: Were you able to get more firewood before the *mandali* was formed or can you get more now?
W1: Earlier we were afraid of the forest department and now we are afraid of the *mandali*. Earlier we could cut at greater leisure. Now we have to cut and run because the *mandali* people keep a careful lookout.
W2: Five years ago it was easier.
W3: Earlier it took 2½ hours. Now it takes 4 hours. Earlier when we went to get firewood we could cut anything we saw. Now we have to search for firewood species.

Q: What is the solution to this shortage? What about biogas?
W1: Yes, we have heard of it. Some nearby villages have it and it works. With help to set it up, we could give it a try.

Gorkha/Dhading, but a lower percentage of worsening. Gender-wise, however, although a lower percentage of all-women groups relative to other groups mentioned persistent shortages, they also had a notably higher percentage of CFIs reporting that people were worse off now than before protection started. This is likely due to the smaller and more degraded forests that such groups received, which reduces their freedom to extract firewood periodically. And although technically they may be members of a neighbouring CFI, in practice not all such neighbours allow firewood collection.

Shifts to inferior fuels are also revealing. Although firewood remains the primary cooking fuel in Nepal (all the households use some) and 97 per cent of the villages ranked it as first among their fuel sources, two-thirds of the CFIs also listed cropwaste as an important source and a fair percentage (27 per cent) use fodder residue—an extremely inferior fuel (Table 9.3). Dung, which is a valuable source of manure in the hill economy, is little used as fuel here, but kerosene and biogas are used by a fifth to a quarter of the households as supplementary fuels—namely in much greater extent than in Gujarat. Firewood is gathered mainly from the community forest, supplemented by the villagers' own fields (Table 9.6). In lesser extent they draw upon nearby government-controlled forests or the forests of other CFIs of which they are members. All-women CFIs are much more dependent on neighbourhood forests than mixed-gender groups. Some, especially in Baglung/Parbat, also purchase firewood.

The costs that Nepalese women incur from firewood shortages and the coping mechanisms they use are similar to those used by Gujarati women, but there are also differences. Smoke from cropwaste is the most frequently mentioned problem (60 per cent of the women facing shortages mentioned this), followed by more time spent in cooking. To cope, women economize in various ways, such as not heating bath water in winter or heating it only for husbands, undercooking food, forgoing winter fires for space heating (even in sub-zero temperatures), giving the cattle unheated feed, and so on. Some of these burdens are acute and specific to the colder climate of Nepal's middle hills compared with the much warmer Gujarat plains. But like their Gujarati counterparts, Nepalese women do not suffer these consequences in silence—they complain:

> We face many problems. We can't afford to buy kerosene. We burn less firewood. Now we don't give our animals cooked feed and so we get less milk. We can't warm the house in winter. I use cropwaste but it produces a lot of ash and the food, the clothes, the house—everything gets dirty. Pine wood releases sticky smoke that makes it very difficult to clean utensils with ash. (Woman EC members, Dadhibari CFI, Baglung district, Nepal, author's survey, 2000–01)

Table 9.5. Nepal: firewood shortages when protection began and in 2000–01 (% CFIs)

Changes in firewood shortages	No shortages earlier or in 2000–01	Shortages earlier but not in 2000–01 (improving)	Shortages earlier, and in 2000–01 (persisting)	No shortages earlier, shortages in 2000–01 (worsening)	Number of CFIs with information
			By district		
Gorkha/Dhading	30.0	13.3	30.0	26.7	(30)
Baglung/Parbat	19.4	12.9	45.2	22.6	(31)
			By EC gender composition		
All women CFIs	23.1	7.7	34.6	34.6	(26)
Other CFIs	25.7	17.1	40.0	17.1	(35)
All CFIs	**24.6**	**13.1**	**37.7**	**24.6**	**(61)**
Shortages earlier (50.8%)					
Shortages in 2000–01 (62.3%)					

Notes: The percentages are calculated based only on cases with information for both periods.
Source: Author's survey, 2000–01.

Table 9.6. Nepal: firewood sources used in 2000–01 (% CFIs)

	Community protected forest	Government-controlled forest	Another CFI	Own trees	Purchase	Village common land	Drift wood
			By district				
Gorkha/Dhading (N=30)	83.3	40.0	30.0	66.7	3.3	3.3	3.3
Baglung/Parbat (N=31)	93.5	32.3	22.6	83.9	25.8	0.0	9.7
			By EC gender composition				
All women CFIs (N=27)	77.8	44.4	48.2	77.8	14.8	3.7	7.4
Other CFIs (N=34)	97.1	29.4	8.8	73.5	14.7	0.0	5.9
All CFIs (N=61)	**88.5**	**36.1**	**26.2**	**75.4**	**14.8**	**1.6**	**6.6**
			% CFIs giving first rank to given sources				
All CFIs (N=61)	**54.1**	**9.8**	**8.2**	**27.9**	**1.6**	**0.0**	**0.0**

Notes: N = number of CFIs.
The rows do not always add up to 100 since in some cases more than one source was mentioned.
Source: Author's survey, 2000–01.

We have been managing with difficulty. We have to use roots, twigs, and *ghaseuta* (fodder remains). Earlier, we used to burn these remains in the fields but now we use them as fuel. (Women EC members, Aaitabare CFI, Gorkha district, author's survey, 2000–01)

W1: We are facing a lot of problems. We use cropwaste, stumps, shrubs, weeds, etc.
W2: The smoke and flying ash from these fuels irritates our eyes. Our clothes get dirty, as does the whole house. (Women EC members, Ludi CFI, Gorkha district, author's survey, 2000–01)

W1: Of course it is not easy to cook with *danth* (maize stalks) and *ghaseuta*. It is smoky and we have to watch the hearth all the time till we have finished cooking.
W2: Yes she is right. We have to keep our other work pending till the food is cooked. (Women EC members, Bajini Pakho CFI, Baglung district, author's survey, 2000–01)

Many times my family has eaten cold food because there is no firewood to heat it. (Woman EC member, Mahibal CFI, Gorkha district, author's survey, 2000–01)

Woman EC member: There are poor people, like the dalits, who especially need firewood. They collect driftwood from the river. Some have kerosene stoves but they also need more firewood.
Elderly male EC member: They also use cow dung. But the problem is not that serious. (Kaligandaki Chhamarke CFI, Parbat, author's survey, 2000–01)

* * *

Whichever way we look at it, therefore, the vast majority of villages in Gujarat and Nepal are facing serious firewood shortages. Barely 10–15 per cent of the CFIs say they are better off because firewood availability has increased since protection began. Does women's greater presence in the EC make a difference? We examine this below.

2. FACTORS AFFECTING FIREWOOD SHORTAGES: REGRESSION ANALYSIS

2.1 Hypotheses

We would expect the incidence and extent of firewood shortages to depend on a range of factors such as the EC's gender composition, the overall availability of the resource (e.g. forest size), access to the forest (e.g. rules for firewood extraction, the number of forest segments, etc.), and access to alternative sources (such as other forests or personal resources). Our interest first and foremost is in whether women's presence in the EC reduces the likelihood of shortages.

The gender effect is likely to be complex since it can play out both directly as well as through other factors (see Table 9.7 for a list of explanatory variables). For a start, it would play out through the rules for firewood extraction. In Chapter 6 we saw that gender composition affects the strictness of rules, but not in a straightforward way. In fact even for a single product there can be varied and complicated arrangements for extraction and distribution, each of which can

Table 9.7. Shortages: list of explanatory variables (for both firewood and fodder)

Explanatory variables included in the regressions[a]	
Gujarat	**Nepal**
EC characteristics	**EC characteristics**
Gender composition of the EC	Gender composition of the EC
CFI characteristics	**CFI characteristics**
Twigs collection rules	Twigs collection rules
Grazing rules	Tree fodder cutting rules
	Member of another CFI
Forest characteristics	**Forest characteristics**
Forest area protected (ha)	Forest area protected (ha)
Forest segments	Forest canopy
Village characteristics	**Location characteristics**
Number of hamlets in the village	Number of toles
Percent landless households in village	
Used another local forest for firewood	
Used another local forest for fodder	
Distance of village from town (km)	

Note: [a] The table lists the variables finally used in the analysis for the regressions relating to firewood (main text) and fodder (appendix). However a number of additional variables were also tested but found to be consistently insignificant in explaining the variation in the dependent variable, and were not included in the final equations given sample size constraints.

make an important difference, such as whether or not the forest is opened for firewood extraction, whether it is opened once a year or more frequently, the number of days for which it is opened, whether people can collect all they want or specified amounts, and whether they can only pick up twigs or also cut drywood from the tree. The full range of these complexities emerges in focus group discussions with villagers and conversations with key informants. Neither the rules variable (discussed further below) nor the gender variable can be fine-tuned to capture such variations comprehensively, but the broad impact of gender and rules, independently and interactively, can be assessed.

Typically, in mixed-gender CFIs women try to persuade the men to open the forest periodically for firewood extraction if it is not opened at all, and to get it opened for a longer period where such opening is already allowed, as illustrated below:

Women want the forest opened for more days than is done at present. Now they only open it for one or two days a year for cutback. That gives us enough firewood only to fulfil one month's needs. (Women's group in Panchmua village to author, Panchmahals, Gujarat, 1999)

Initially they did not open the forest at all. Now they open it for one or two days each year, but for large families this does not help tide over even the monsoon months. Initially women's firewood collection time increased greatly with closure. We used cropwaste, cow dung, and went to the nearby forest for firewood, but now even that forest is closed. All this is enough only for four or five months. Then we use our own land for firewood and kerosene for lighting, but we have no biogas. (Women in Asundriya village to author, Panchmahals district, Gujarat, 1999)

A larger percentage of women on the EC could help reduce shortages in several ways. They could prove more effective in getting the forest opened for firewood collection and for more days. They could persuade the EC to allow the extraction of more species for firewood and to plant firewood species in the gaps within the forest (as some of the women in Panchmahals were able to do: Chapter 8). They may even be able to prevail on fellow EC members to invest in firewood plantations or biogas plants. Most of these dimensions cannot be captured directly and are subsumed in the gender variable.

In all-women ECs, women themselves have control over decisions on firewood extraction, but their ability to do so is subject to the gender-specific constraints we had noted in Chapter 6, namely the smaller and poorer forests that such groups typically receive and the monitoring problems they tend to face, which veer them toward stricter rules. All these can impinge on the effect of gender on firewood shortages. The gender variable is measured through the percentage of women in the EC for Gujarat and through a comparison of all-women groups with other groups for Nepal. In addition, since rules on forest use can play a critical role in the experience of shortages I have also sought to directly measure, at least broadly, the impact of firewood access rules.

Second, resource availability and pressures upon it, as indicated by the forest's size, the number of hamlets dependent on it, and its distance from the town, can matter. We would expect shortages to be less likely the larger the forest area protected, the fewer the dependent hamlets, and the further the village is from a town. The last factor could make a difference by deterring poor village households from clandestinely cutting and selling firewood in the market. Although some may still sell within the village or in a neighbouring one, such sales would increase the overall local supply of firewood and so decrease shortages, even if the extraction was in violation of the rules.

Third, a resource can be available in principle but if access to it is blocked (through strict rules of extraction), shortages can still emerge. Firewood extraction rules are of several kinds (Chapter 6). Some relate to fallen twigs, others to cutting or breaking off drywood, yet others to cutting greenwood, and so on. CFIs which either open their forests occasionally or are open always for such collection (such as for fallen twigs) are less likely to face shortages than CFIs where extraction is completely banned throughout the year. Statistically we can capture only the broad dimension of rules and depend on qualitative evidence for fine tuning. In both regions, twig collection rules have been used in the regressions, specified as dummies. In Gujarat the comparison is between CFIs which have a complete ban on such collection and those which allow such collection occasionally or always.[8] In Nepal the comparison is between CFIs which restrict the

[8] In the Gujarat regressions, I also tried disaggregating the twigs rules dummy to separate out the effects of a full ban, open occasionally and open always, but found no significant difference between open occasionally and open always. In Table 9.8 I therefore clubbed open occasionally and open always. This is a different specification from the twigs dummy used in Table A6.5.

collection of twigs (by a full ban or a partial ban or occasional opening) and those that do not.[9] As discussed above, for the gender effects, even among CFIs that open the forest occasionally there is variation in the frequency and period of opening which can affect shortages.

Forest segments provide a somewhat different indicator of access. A segmented forest is more accessible since settlements are usually interspersed between the segments. Segments are also linked with less strict forest use rules (Chapter 6). At the same time segmentation is associated with poorer forest condition (Chapter 8). The implications of forest segmentation for firewood availability will depend on the net effect of these opposing pulls.

Fourth, we would expect villagers with access to other forests to be less likely to experience firewood shortages. For Nepal, since membership of other CFIs is formally possible this serves as the explanatory variable, although whether this makes a difference will depend on whether these other CFIs have firewood available and distribute it. In Gujarat, such access is not authorized, but village women did report whether they clandestinely used government forests for firewood, and the explanatory variable was constructed on the basis of this information. Another aspect of access is ownership of one's own land. We would expect shortages to be greater the higher the percentage of landless households in the village.

The impact of these factors on the community's experience of firewood shortages at the time of the survey is examined through logistic analysis. The dependent variable—firewood shortages—is defined as a dummy: shortage = 1, no shortage = 0, based, as described above, on the situation reported for the majority of villagers/users. Due to sample size limitations, the regression analysis does not cover changes over time which were discussed above through cross-tabulations.

2.2 Regression Results: Firewood

On gender, we get mixed results—significant for Gujarat, insignificant for Nepal. In Gujarat the EC's gender composition is significant in explaining firewood shortages but only when there are one-third or more women on the EC (Table 9.8). There is a 48 per cent less likelihood of villagers reporting shortages where ECs have $\geq$33 per cent women than if they have less. In the Nepal sample gender composition is not significant—all-women groups and other groups do not differ on this count (Table 9.9) probably because there is rather little difference in their overall firewood extraction rules. Controlling for other factors, the regressions in both regions clearly show that shortages are much less likely where the rules are

[9] There were very few cases of full ban, while open occasionally was usually for cutback and pruning undertaken infrequently and so close to a full ban. The two categories were therefore clubbed.

Table 9.8. Gujarat: factors affecting firewood shortages

Dependent variable	Firewood shortage: Dummy[a]			
Equation no.	1		2	
Statistical method	Logit		Logit	
No. of observations	54		54	
Pseudo R^2	0.38		0.48	
Explanatory variables	**Coef.**	**ME**	**Coef.**	**ME**
GenComp2: % women on the EC	−0.04 (0.342)	−0.005 (0.352)		
GenComp4: dummy (≥33% EC women=1)			−3.36** (0.032)	−0.48** (0.032)
Twigs collection rules 2: dummy[b]	1.24 (0.390)	0.11 (0.264)	3.16 (0.151)	0.13* (0.056)
Forest area (ha)	−0.004 (0.323)	−0.000 (0.347)	−0.004 (0.233)	−0.000 (0.324)
Forest segments	−0.88** (0.023)	−0.10** (0.020)	−1.15** (0.025)	−0.08** (0.048)
No. of hamlets in village	0.43* (0.057)	0.05* (0.084)	0.50* (0.053)	0.04† (0.102)
Used another local forest for firewood: dummy (if used=1)	−2.83** (0.025)	−0.48** (0.033)	−3.75** (0.018)	−0.54** (0.023)
% landless hhs in village	0.02 (0.702)	0.002 (0.705)	0.02 (0.622)	0.002 (0.640)
Distance of village from town (km)	−0.10* (0.082)	−0.01* (0.080)	−0.10* (0.096)	−0.01 (0.173)
Constant	4.19		4.66	

Notes:

[a] Firewood shortages: If most have firewood shortages = 1; if few or none have firewood shortages = 0.

[b] If full ban =1; If partial ban or open occasionally or open always = 0.

The marginal effect (ME) is for a discrete change from 0 to 1 for dummy variables, and for a one unit change for continuous variables.

Numbers in parenthesis are *p*-values. Significance: ** at 5 %, * at 10%, † at close to 10%.

less strict. In Gujarat, we find a 13 per cent lower probability of shortages in villages where the forest is always or occasionally opened for the gathering of fallen twigs than where such collection is totally banned (Table 9.8, Equation 2). In Nepal again, there is a 23 per cent lower likelihood of firewood shortages in villages which are open always for twigs than those where there is total ban or occasional distribution (Table 9.9, Equations 1 and 2).

Statistically, the rules, as measured, indicate whether or not the CFI allows extraction, but the period for which the forest is opened is not captured. To women what matters is both whether the forest is opened and the period for which it is opened, and a good deal of negotiation takes place on both counts. The more nuanced aspects of rules that stem from the number of forest opening days or relating to different categories of firewood (drywood, greenwood, timber

Table 9.9. Nepal: factors affecting firewood shortages

Dependent variable	Firewood shortage: dummy[a]			
Equation no.	1		2	
Statistical method	Logit		Logit	
No. of observations	62		62	
Pseudo R^2	0.14		0.08	
Explanatory variables	**Coef.**	**ME**	**Coef.**	**ME**
GenComp: dummy (all-women EC =1)	−0.27 (0.678)	−0.06 (0.679)	0.13 (0.825)	0.03 (0.825)
Twigs collection rules: dummy[b]	0.99* (0.095)	0.23* (0.087)	1.01* (0.078)	0.23* (0.071)
Member of another CFI: dummy (if member = 1)	1.15 (0.109)	0.27 (0.117)		
Forest area protected (ha)	−0.01 (0.177)	−0.003 (0.176)	−0.02* (0.094)	−0.004* (0.096)
Number of toles	−0.14 (0.254)	−0.03 (0.253)		
Constant	0.45		0.51	

Notes: [a] Firewood shortages: If most have a firewood shortage = 1; if few or none have a shortage = 0.
[b] If full ban or partial ban or open occasionally=1; if open always = 0.
The marginal effect (ME) is for a discrete change from 0 to 1 for dummy variables, and for a one unit change for continuous variables.
Numbers in parenthesis are *p*-values. Significance: * at 10%.

Difference between models
In equation 2 some variables were omitted to reveal the effect of forest area.

versus non-timber species) are not captured here—but the qualitative evidence indicates that these matter a great deal as well.

For illustration, consider the following examples of mixed-gender groups, one where women were able to negotiate the opening of the forest when it was completely closed before, and the other where they could negotiate an increase in the number of open days:

> After our complaints women and men had a joint meeting and decided to open the forest for a few days for firewood collection, since everyone has to cook. (Women to author, Narmada district, Gujarat, 1999)

> The seven-day opening was inadequate. So women users complained. Now they open the forest for eleven days. (Women to author, Laxmi Deurali CFI, Kaski, Nepal, 1998)

Having more women in a mixed-gender EC gives women more negotiating power both on their own behalf (as interested parties) and on behalf of other village women. This is captured in the Gujarat results where one-third women make a significantly greater difference than a lower female presence. But the Nepal results—where we are comparing all-women ECs with other ECs—also indicate that women's presence alone may not be enough to reduce shortages where there is the systematic gender-linked resource constraint, as a result of which such groups may place more strictures on firewood extraction than other groups (Chapter 6).

The results show in other ways as well that access matters a great deal *provided that it is effective and not just nominal.* In Gujarat, villages that effectively use a nearby government managed forest, albeit clandestinely, have a 54 per cent lower probability of facing shortages than other villages (Table 9.8, Equation 2). This access is linked with location. Narmada/Bharuch or Sabarkantha villages, but especially the former, which have access to other (mainly government-managed) forests, have a lower incidence of shortages despite their stricter rules than Panchmahals villages: in the regression (not presented here) when district dummies were included and the dummy for the use of another forest was excluded, Panchmahals showed a significantly greater likelihood of shortages than either of the other districts. In Nepal, however, membership in another CFI does not, in itself, reduce shortages (Table 9.9, Equation 1).

This contrast between Nepal and Gujarat warrants comment. Although most all-women groups are members of another CFI in Nepal, typically this does not translate into effective access to firewood. Two-thirds of the CFIs which had members in another CFI reported that they did not actually use the other CFI in practice. And in Table 9.6 we note that only 8 per cent of all CFIs ranked another CFI as their primary source of fuel. In contrast, in Gujarat, despite the lack of formal access to government forests, the poorer vigilance in such forests relative to community-protected ones enables villagers to use them, and over half the Narmada/Bharuch CFIs ranked them as their primary fuel source. Somewhat ironically, therefore, the Gujarat villages, which have a government forest to steal from, are likely to be better off than Nepal's groups which enjoy formal membership of another community forest, but most lack effective use of it. Shifting the burden of shortages from community-managed forests to government-managed ones does not, however, portend well for the condition of the region's forests overall.

Another (indirect) indicator of access—forest segments (measurable only for Gujarat)—is also significant: the more the segments the less the likelihood of shortage, because women are better able to procure more in their immediate vicinity. Also, as noted in Chapter 4, often where the forest protected is in several segments, protection is more decentralized hamlet-wise. This gives the villagers greater freedom to extract from the segment they are protecting. How sustainable such extraction is remains to be seen, since segmented forests regenerate less well than consolidated ones (Chapter 8).

Access to forests appears to be more important overall than the characteristics of the forest. For instance, in Nepal, although CFIs with a larger forest area are found less likely to face shortages, the marginal effect is small. In Gujarat, forest area is not significant, nor is village-level landlessness, although two other variables impinging on resource availability are significant: villages with more hamlets are more likely to have shortages and those located far from a town are less likely. Distance from a town indirectly reduces shortages, since it reduces the opportunities for selling firewood to outsiders and keeps any such sales within the village.[10]

2.3 A Glance at Fodder Shortages

Although the focus of this chapter is on firewood shortages, a brief comparison with the results for fodder (elaborated in the appendix to this chapter) is of interest. We had noted in Chapter 6 that fodder is treated differently from firewood in the relatively less attention paid to the latter in terms of supervised extraction. We had also noted that firewood is much more exclusively women's responsibility while men also have an economic interest in fodder. We would therefore expect some differences in the impact of a group's gender composition on fodder shortages relative to firewood shortages. Is that the case?

Fodder shortages, like firewood shortages, are widespread. Ninety-five per cent of the Gujarat villages and 67 per cent of the Nepal ones report fodder inadequacies (appendix Table A9.1). They obtain what they can from the protected forest or their own fields, but also cope with shortfalls in various ways: purchasing it if they can afford to, spending more time collecting it, economizing by feeding animals less, and, especially in Nepal, reducing the number of animals (appendix Table A9.2).[11] The regression results, are again interesting. First, in Gujarat, as with firewood the higher the proportion of women on the EC the less the likelihood of fodder shortages, but unlike for firewood it does not need one-third women on the EC to make a difference (appendix Table A9.4). This is probably because men are also concerned about fodder availability. Second, again as with firewood in Gujarat, access is more important than the forest characteristics. Villages with less strict grazing rules, and those that have another forest nearby from where they collect fodder or clandestinely graze their cattle, are found less likely to have shortages, while forest size has an insignificant effect. Third, in Nepal, neither gender composition nor access rules are significant explanatory variables (appendix Table A9.5). Here resource characteristics matter more—larger forests with denser canopies are found less likely to have shortages. Canopy thickness increases tree fodder availability, in particular. Overall therefore, although the firewood and fodder results differ, the differences are subtle rather than substantial.

[10] As noted earlier, although most households consume what they collect, some women from better-off or upper-caste households, who themselves do not go out to gather, tend to buy firewood from tribal women locally.

[11] The issue of fodder shortages is complicated since it can also depend on the number of animals. For instance, shortages can rise with an increase in the animal stock. But the household coping strategies—such as a reduction in animals and efforts to economize on feed—suggest that the shortages are being driven largely by external factors.

3. FIREWOOD EXTRACTION AND SUSTAINABILITY

3.1 Extraction in the Fieldsites

Let us now return to the firewood story. We have seen that firewood shortages can be significantly affected by access to the protected forest, but we lack information on the exact volume of firewood extracted. What we do know is whether CFIs allow any firewood collection and in what context, and how they distribute it. We know, for example, that 58 per cent of the CFIs in the Gujarat sites and 46 per cent in the Nepal sites allow people to pick up fallen twigs (see Chapter 6), but this does not tell us whether there is much available to pick up.

An additional and firmer indicator of actual extraction is whether CFIs formally open up the forest periodically and distribute firewood. Only 29 per cent of the Gujarat CFIs (19 out of 65) extract any firewood through periodic opening on a regular basis. This opening is typically done once a year, usually for a couple of days, and although most have no bar on the amount collected, households cannot gather more than a small percentage of their needs in this period. A few CFIs have done cutback operations, but only once or twice during their several years of protection. Notably also, none of the Narmada/Bharuch fieldsites extracts periodically; and although many of the Panchmahals and Sabarkantha fieldsites have begun doing so, it is mainly a result of women's constant complaints and local NGO intervention. Even here many CFIs have restrictions on whether women can carry an axe to cut dry branches or only gather by hand; and some also restrict the kind of wood that can be taken, by confining extractions to so-called non-timber species which are not the species that women most prefer.

In Nepal, where formal extraction in terms of periodic cleaning/pruning/thinning is built into the operation plan, firewood distribution is more common—90 per cent of the CFIs say they undertake it. However, their regularity varies: although many do so every winter, a fair number also do so only once every alternative year or once every few years. Thus often there is a gap between the operational plan which requires annual extraction, and actual practice. Also, according to field reports (as elaborated further below), sometimes people fail to turn up for the pruning work despite firewood shortages, possibly because the work involved can be heavy and is typically done by men, and a fee is also charged for the firewood (almost all the Baglung/Parbat CFIs charge a fee).

3.2 Can More Be Extracted Sustainably?

Can more firewood be extracted sustainably from the protected forests? Although a clear answer is not possible from my survey, there is persuasive evidence to this effect from a set of coordinated studies undertaken by a network of ecologists, social scientists, and NGOs in a number of Indian villages, including two which are also part of my 2000–01 survey (Ravindranath et al. 2000). They found that much more can be extracted without harming forest regeneration than is being done.[12] The results of these studies, summarized in Table 9.10 and Figure 9.1, indicate how much annual woody biomass is regenerated in the protected forests, how much is extracted as firewood, and the annual need for firewood in twelve villages (all with CFIs) from three Indian states.[13] The studies assume, as a conservative rule of thumb, that half the annual biomass regenerated per year can be extracted sustainably. The estimates of biomass generated are themselves on the conservative side, since they exclude vegetation with a girth of less than 10 cm, some of which can be used as fuel.

In six out of the twelve villages, less than 15 per cent of the estimated need for firewood is being satisfied from the forest, and in none is more than 55 per cent being satisfied in this way. These shortages could be very substantially reduced by extracting more. In ten of the twelve villages, extractions are far below even the conservative extractable limit and of the two villages which show over-extraction, in one—Kharikamathani—extraction is still below the total biomass produced per year.[14] In three villages, extraction is less than 10 per cent of what is possible. If these villages were to extract up to the extractable limit, some, such as Baluji Na Muada, could more than satisfy their firewood requirements, while others, such as Asundriya and Allali, could satisfy a fair percentage (65 per cent and 35 per cent respectively) of their needs. At present Allali extracts nothing at all. Hence while firewood shortages might still persist, they would be less acute if there was extraction within sustainable limits. Currently these three villages satisfy less than 10 per cent of their needs through the community forest.

These results show that the extent of firewood shortages that the women are facing in these villages is not because of inadequate availability of woody biomass in the protected forest but from restricted access to what is available. The very low levels of extraction are due to strict closure regimes, enforced without women's acquiescence. In fact even in nominal terms, at the time of that study, very few of the villages in Table 9.10 had even one woman on its EC.[15] But the question remains: why don't men allow greater extraction, given that firewood is a household need and not just women's need?

3.3 Why Isn't More Extracted?

There could be several potential explanations for under-extraction. The villagers may lack information about how much can be extracted sustainably. There may

[12] In fact, as elaborated in Chapter 8, some forms of extraction, if done well, can actually enhance regeneration and growth, such as careful tree pruning operations in the early period of tree growth.

[13] The studies covered more villages, but those which lacked complete information or had data discrepancies are not included in Table 9.10.

[14] This could well be the case too in the second over-extracting village, Halaker, given that biomass of < 10 cm girth was not counted in the growing stock.

[15] Baluji Na Muada and Asundriya, which are also part of my Gujarat sample, had two EC women each; almost all the others had one or none.

Table 9.10. Firewood: sustainably extractable, actual extraction, and need

Village/state	Forest area (ha) protected	Protection Yrs	Form (in 1996)	Basal area (ha)	Growing stock (t/ha)	Mean annual increment (t/ha/yr)	Sustainably extractable (t/yr)	Actual extraction (t/yr)	Firewood need for village (t/yr)	Extraction as % of extractable	Extraction as % of need	Extractable as % of need
Gujarat												
Asundriya	176[a]	8	SC	14.4	144.5	4.10	361	35	554	9.7	6.3	65.2
Baluji Na Muada,	122	11	SC	44.9	343.4	9.75	595	46	511	7.7	9.0	116.0
Garda	100	6	MC	1.2	58.5	1.66	83	38	264	45.8	14.4	31.4
Kunbar	188	4	MC	2.0	63.7	1.81	170	61	603	35.9	10.1	28.2
Rampur	120	4	MC	3.0	70.2	1.99	119	94	185	79.0	50.8	64.3
Karnataka												
Alalli	73	20	SC	13.8	140.6	3.99	146	0	416	0.0	0.0	35.0
Halakar	20	72	LC	10.5	119.1	3.38	34	107	521	169.8	20.5	12.1
Hunasar	120	100	SC	33.1	266.5	7.57	454	262	496	57.7	52.8	91.5
Kugwe	194	100	LC	24.5	210.4	5.98	580	209	697	36.0	30.0	83.2
West Bengal												
Bhagawatichowk,	53	11	SC	10.5	119.1	3.38	90	54	176	60.0	30.7	51.1
Kapasgaria	25	5	SC	11.3	124.3	3.53	44	8	139	18.2	5.8	31.6
Kharikamathani,	57	3	LC	4.0	76.7	2.18	62	87	161	140.3	54.0	38.5

Notes: Growing stock = 50.66 + (Basal area × 6.52). Woody biomass with a girth of < 10 cm was not included. t/ha = tons per hectare.
Mean annual increment (MAI) = 2.84% of the growing stock.
Sustainably extractable = (MAI × forest area)/2.
For the 4 Karnataka villages, the case study assumes firewood need to be 1.67 kg/capita/day. I have assumed the same for calculating firewood needs for Garda, Kunbar and Rampur, since information on need was not given in the case study.
SC = Strict closure: firewood cutting banned except for a few days per year. In some cases, collection of fallen twigs is, however, allowed all year round.
LC = Lenient closure: firewood extraction in the form of twigs and dry branches allowed throughout the year.
MC = Mixed closure: a combination of LC and cutback/cleaning operations undertaken for a few days each year or every few years.
[a] Ravindranath et al. (2000) give a figure of 182 ha, but the forest department records show that 175.94 ha is the area registered formally as under protection.

Source: Compiled/calculated by author from information given in Ravindranath et al. (2000).

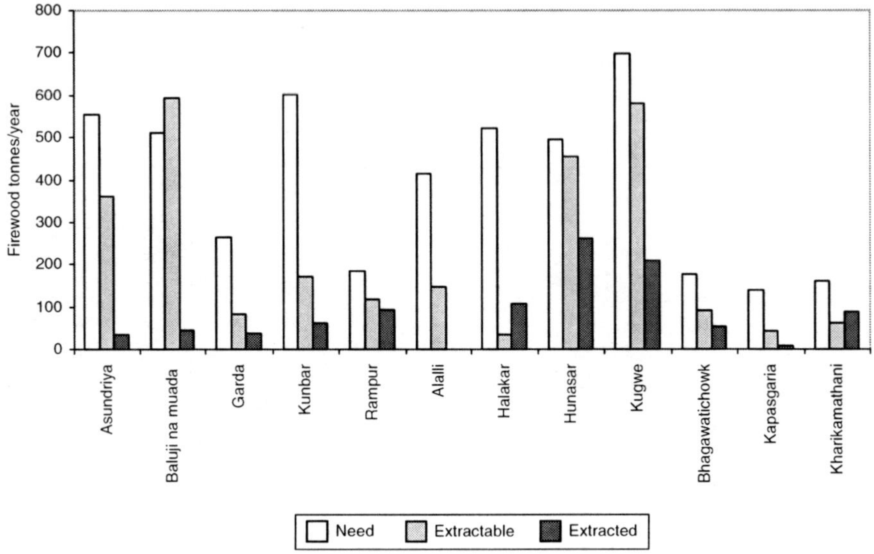

Figure 9.1. Firewood needed, sustainably extractable, and actually extracted in selected Indian villages

be difficulty in getting forest department permission for cutting wood. Supervising extraction could involve a lot of effort. The cost of shortages may be invisible to or be ignored by the male EC members since they are borne largely by women and children in terms of extended labour time and health ill-effects. Where extraction is linked with forest cutback and tree pruning, for which men's labour is needed, men may be unwilling to put in the effort from which mainly women gain. The same can hold for paying fees for any firewood distributed. Or several of these explanations could apply. Consider them in the context of my survey.

First, on inadequate information, although it is true that communities may not have an *exact* idea of how much is extractable, they would have a fair idea. Communities usually have good local knowledge about plants and species; and the fact that they often ban even the collection of dried branches and twigs does not suggest that the real barrier is a lack of knowledge about extractability. Second, while permission is needed for cutting greenwood, this is not the case for drywood. In fact, there are CFIs in both Gujarat and Nepal that do extract drywood, and the Gujarat forest department officials confirmed to me that drywood does not require such permission, while in Nepal such extraction can be built into the operational plan. The third factor—high supervision costs—has relevance, however. Opening the forest for a few days and ensuring that none cuts green branches requires vigilance, but its extent depends on the rules of extraction. Allowing collection without a bar needs less work than forest cutback/pruning and organizing the distribution of cut wood. This is not the whole story, however. A part also relates to whether the costs and benefits of extraction are financial or non-financial and whether they are borne mostly by men or women. Here a comparison of firewood and fodder is revealing.

Men have an interest in fodder, given the returns from cattle rearing for agriculture and milk production, and the monetized nature of fodder. It is notable, for instance, that none of the Narmada/Bharuch CFIs said they extracted firewood formally but 69 per cent mentioned extracting fodder through careful supervision on a regular basis, sometimes once a year, sometimes twice (Table 9.11). And all distributed it through equal bundles which require additional effort. Underlying this interest in the Narmada/Bharuch sites is a thriving dairy economy which makes cattle rearing profitable and fodder valuable, coupled with the considerable availability of grass there in the early years of protection (in much greater extent than in the other sites[16]). Similarly, in Nepal, although cattle are centrally needed for agriculture, the Baglung/Parbat sites located near roads do better on dairy farming than Gorkha's typically remoter villages located on steeper terrain. The average number of milch cattle per farm holding is also higher in Baglung/Parbat than in Gorkha/Dhading (GoN 2001–02). This is probably one of the reasons why only 22 per cent of the Gorkha/Dhading sites compared with 88 per cent of the Baglung/Parbat sites have a system of regular fodder extraction, done typically by selling off grass plots to villagers or charging fees from member households for unrestricted collection. Many are willing to pay these charges since otherwise they would have to purchase fodder from the market: 54 per cent of the Nepal CFIs (and 89 per cent of the Gujarat CFIs) report some fodder purchase. The money for fodder comes mostly from the pockets of men who substantially control the household cash. This makes fodder shortages an issue of immediate concern to men in a way that firewood shortages are not. All this creates a greater incentive for extracting fodder from the protected area than a typically non-purchased item such as firewood.

At the same time, almost all of Nepal's CFIs mention that they do distribute firewood. This distribution is, however, different from that of fodder. The firewood distributed formally in Nepal is an incidental by-product of the silviculture operations mandated in the operational plan as a 'forest promotion activity', under the 1995 regulations guiding the Forest Act of 1993 vis-à-vis community forestry (GoN 1995). Fodder extraction, however, is voluntary in nature and it is up to the CFI to make provision as it considers appropriate. Also in practice, about a third of my Nepal sites do not carry out the forest pruning/thinning operations every year. Some of the CFIs reported too that men don't turn up for these operations or that households don't collect the firewood for which a fee is usually charged. Some illustrative cases are given below:

[16] In Panchmahals, there was rather little fodder grass available (personal communication, Dhansingh Bhai Rathore, SARTHI, Panchmahals).

Table 9.11. Gujarat and Nepal: firewood and grass fodder distribution

	Firewood distribution		Fodder distribution	
	% CFIs opening forest for firewood	Method of distribution (% CFIs)	% CFIs opening forest for fodder	Method of distribution (% CFIs)
GUJARAT	*Drywood*	*Of drywood*		
Narmada/Bharuch (16)	0.0	Not distributed	68.8	Equal bundles 100.00
Panchmahals (21)	52.4	No formal distribution	19.0	No formal distribution
Sabarkantha (28)	28.6	A few distribute formally but infrequently	39.2	A few distribute formally but infrequently
All districts (65)	**29.2**		**40.0**	
NEPAL	*Cutback, etc. but in varying frequency*[a]	*Of cut wood and drywood*		
Gorkha/Dhading (36)	83.3	No bar 13.3 Equal bundles 53.3 Other methods[b] 33.3	22.2	No bar 37.5 Equal bundles 25.0 Other methods[d] 37.5
Baglung/Parbat (34)	97.1	No bar 9.1 Equal bundles 87.9 Other methods[b] 3.0	88.2	No bar 23.3 Plots[c] 40.0 Auction 10.0 Other methods[d] 26.7
All districts (70)	**90.0**	No bar 11.1 Equal bundles 71.4 Other methods[b] 17.5	**54.3**	No bar 26.3 Equal bundles 5.3 Plots[c] 39.5 Other methods[d] 29.0

Notes: Figures in brackets are the number of CFIs.
[a] A nominal fee is charged per bundle even for those contributing labour in the forest cleaning operation.
[b] Other methods include fixing a fee per bundle and allowing purchase of a specified maximum number of bundles.
[c] Distribution by plots is typically by selling them.
[d] Includes a range of methods, such as giving bundles on payment; distribution only to the poor and needy; and grass plots assigned through a lottery system.

Source: Author's survey, 2000–01.

They have to pay money if they want firewood from this CFI. That is why only a small number of people come to collect firewood. (Women EC members, Devisthan all-women CFI, Parbat, Nepal, author's survey 2000–01)

The samiti arranges forest clearing operations and distributes harvested firewood to the participants equally, charging Rs. 2 per bundle. Last year the members did not bother to come so we sold the harvested firewood to the non-members. In fact we sold about 40 bundles of firewood on Rs. 1,000. This year, we are going to ask the villagers whether they are interested in collecting the firewood or not. (Male EC member in all-male Seto Pahar Majhuwa CFI, Gorkha, Nepal, author's survey, 2000–01)

That despite persistent shortages some of the households do not purchase firewood even at a nominal price, while they are willing to pay for fodder, suggests that gender relations are a mediating factor. Both the non-financial cost of firewood extraction (pruning/cleaning etc.) and the financial cost of paying for the cut wood (as noted) are typically borne by men, while women are the main direct gainers of any firewood obtained. Firewood is also seen as a consumption good while fodder as an input into cattle which have economic returns is viewed as an investment.

The above factors, in varying degree, would underlie the much greater attention paid to fodder extraction than to firewood. Women's low representation on the EC adds to this inattention. Whereas men do not hesitate in discussing fodder shortages in a public forum such as an EC or GB meeting, men talking about firewood shortages are seen as bringing a private matter and 'women's problems' into the public domain. Hence, even in households facing acute firewood shortages men usually hesitate to raise this issue from fear of being ridiculed or of not being taken seriously (see also Chapter 6). Women are able to bring their concerns without social embarrassment into the public forum more readily than their husbands. Their greater presence on the EC can thus help.

4. CONCLUDING COMMENTS

A spotlight on firewood shortages helps highlight a gender inequality paradox—persisting shortages of an essential item of daily use, amidst regenerating forests and growing biomass plenty. In the early years of community forestry, the strictness of closure rules led women to walk longer distances in search of fuel. When the neighbouring villages too began to protect, even this option was foreclosed. Many households spent more time searching, switched partly to inferior biofuels, and economized on firewood use, and some were compelled to enter the protected tracts and risk being penalized or insulted by a patrol group or guard. Hence the initial cost of strict closure was borne disproportionately by women.

We would have expected this to change over time. But even after years of protection shortages have not only persisted, they had become more acute in some cases. Yet this is not uniformly so. Villages where the ECs have a larger percentage of women are found less likely to face shortages in Gujarat. Women's voices therefore do count in getting the community to extract more from the protected area. At the same time, all-women groups in Nepal, notwithstanding their substantial control over the decision to extract, are constrained by the poverty of the resource they receive. Also, in many CFIs, men are not always willing to put in the labour for extraction. Hence, the larger context of gender inequalities within which women operate, restricts, in complex ways, the benefits they can draw from the forests under their command.

Moreover, enhancing women's representation may alleviate women's cooking fuel problem, but cannot solve it. What is needed is not just alleviating firewood shortages, but eliminating clean energy poverty. Even village women's complaints stem from observable difficulties in obtaining adequate firewood, time constraints, or the unpleasantness of smoke, and not from less observable long-term health ill-effects associated with firewood or other unprocessed biofuels. Improved stoves with chimneys and better ventilated kitchens which allow smoke to escape can mitigate some of the health ill-effects of unprocessed biofuels. However, the dissemination of such stoves has been largely unsuccessful in India, due to a complexity of factors discussed in Chapter 11 (see also Agarwal 1986a).

Stoves apart, the question of cleaner fuels, other than firewood, still needs to be addressed. Some alternative sources of energy, such as solar, are too expensive for most households, but biogas is very much within the affordable range. The biogas structures now available require only limited amounts of biomass that could be generated by, say, two head of cattle, compared with earlier models which needed four head of cattle.[17] The support of an external agent such as an NGO or a donor agency could help, up to a point. For example, households in several of the Narmada/Bharuch fieldsites in Gujarat and the Baglung/Parbat fieldsites in Nepal have biogas connections, since in the former the local NGO and in the latter the donor agency, NUKCEP, have actively promoted biogas plants. Locally, the community funds generated from CFI membership fees and the sale of forest products could, in principle, be used for community investment in this cheap and clean fuel.

That typically such options are not even discussed at the community level in CFI meetings has much to do with the failure to recognize the firewood problem as a community problem. To bring about this recognition, simply enhancing women's presence in the EC may not be enough. We would also need to look beyond CFIs to strengthen women's hands within CFIs, such as by establishing links with other local women's organizations or, as I term it, creating 'a web of strategic alliances'. This would increase women's bargaining power with local institutions (as discussed in Chapter 10). Village councils in most Indian states, for instance, have funds for promoting alternative rural energy sources. These funds could be tapped if the community so wanted and insisted on it. But (as elaborated in Chapter 11) for domestic energy poverty to be *effectively* eliminated, the involvement of government beyond the local appears crucial. For this, the voices of women in the villages where the fuel crisis is faced need to be heard in the higher echelons of government where energy policies are framed.

[17] Personal observation of small biogas plants promoted by the NGO Chirag in the Uttarakhand hills, 1998–99.

APPENDIX 9.1

Fodder Shortages: An Analysis

> We manage by feeding our cattle the barest minimal fodder they require to survive.
>
> Once the stock of fodder is over we will have no other option but to purchase some from the market.
>
> (Villagers in Makroda village, Sabarkantha, Gujarat, author's survey, 2000–01)

> We have to feed our cattle cropwaste like bajra and jowar, and if that is not enough then we have to buy fodder from people who have extra to spare.
>
> (Villagers in Vadva village, Narmada, Gujarat, author's survey, 2000–01)

In the main chapter we examined the paradox of persisting firewood shortages despite regenerating forests. This appendix supplements and contrasts with the analysis for firewood, by examining the impact of the EC's gender composition on shortages of fodder—the second major product for which villagers in India and Nepal depend substantially on the local commons.

The survey villages in both regions, for instance, practise subsistence agriculture on very small farms and use animal traction in large part for ploughing. It is thus common for landed households to keep one or two bullocks. The Nepal sites, in particular, located in the middle hills, do terraced farming on which land preparation is done almost entirely by animal power (rather then by tractors which are used in plains agriculture). Moreover, in some of the Gujarat villages, especially those located in Narmada/Bharuch, and in parts of Nepal (especially in Baglung/Parbat), dairy farming and hence milch cattle are popular. In somewhat lesser degree than for firewood, but still to a significant extent, women are mainly responsible for cattle care and gathering fodder, although they may get help from children. Especially in Nepal, where cattle are fed both grass and tree fodder, it is typically young women who climb the trees for fodder leaves. Fodder shortages, however, create somewhat less of a burden for women than firewood shortages since, as noted, men are also involved in farming and dairying activities (which can bring in income), and are willing to purchase fodder to make up for shortages. Sometimes households even employ a cowherd collectively to graze their cattle. Community responses to fodder shortages can therefore differ from responses to firewood shortages.

1. EXTENT, COPING, SOURCES, AND DISTRIBUTION

In Gujarat, fodder shortages were assessed through discussion with the EC members as well as focus group discussions with villagers. As in the case of firewood, villages with fodder shortages are those where the EC members reported that most of the households were facing scarcity, supplemented by group responses from village women themselves on whether most, none, or only a few of them were facing shortages.[18] In Nepal, likewise, the assessment is based on the EC members reporting whether or not most of the CFI members were facing shortages. Again, as with firewood, it is possible that the experience of those not attending the discussions (which might include the poorest and the migrant households) is not fully reflected here. However, in the absence of a ready method for measuring shortages across all socio-economic categories in a village, what was reported in the village discussion is taken as a broad indicator.

In both regions, the vast proportion of the CFIs reported persistent fodder shortages and a large percentage said they were worse off than before forest protection began. In Gujarat, for example, 95 per cent of the villages reported fodder shortages (Table A9.1). Only 5 per cent said they had no shortages earlier or at the time of the survey, while 48 per cent mentioned persisting shortages and 47 per cent reported a worsening. Some part of this worsening could be due to lower output because of low rainfall in parts of the region in the previous year, but qualitative evidence and the econometric results show that the shortages are also linked to strictness of forest closure rules. The villagers deal with these shortages in various ways: 89 per cent said they purchase additional fodder, many of them getting into debt in the process (Table A9.2). They also economize by feeding animals less (32 per cent) and even reducing the number of animals they own. Usually these are goats—even CFIs that allow grazing in the forest tend to ban goats. A typical response on this count: 'In the summer months, the bigger animals can be let into the forest to graze, except goats because goats eat everything, even saplings' (villagers in Bambri village, Panchmahals, 2001). The better-off have replaced some of their goats with higher-value milch cattle, but the poor have typically ended up with a net loss since they are unable to maintain large animals, and not many can keep even goats because of the ban on grazing in the forest.

In Nepal, relative to Gujarat, fewer CFIs—67 per cent—reported shortages in 2000–01: 43 per cent said that their shortages were persisting from the time before protection began, while 24 per cent reported a worsening, that is, these CFIs had no scarcity before protection but were facing it in 2000–01 (Table A9.1). Overall, therefore, there is a fodder shortage situation, in most survey sites. To cope, the main response in Nepal has been to reduce their animal stock (70 per cent of the CFIs mentioned this), followed by purchase of grass fodder or straw (among 54 per cent CFIs), more time spent on fodder collection, and feeding the animal less. Indeed, 80 per cent of CFIs said that at least some of their member households had reduced their animal stocks and one-third reported that most households had done so. As in Gujarat, the animals sold off are disproportionately goats. In rare cases, a community may make special arrangements for goat grazing as a goodwill gesture toward poor households.

Animal sales and overall fodder scarcity also lead to other kinds of costs. Some mentioned that now their children go without milk and they themselves drink tea without milk. The responses of women in Gaderi-Dhaireni CFI, Baglung, Nepal (author's survey 2000–01), are illustrative:

W1: We are getting less animal dung for preparing manure.
W2: We don't have enough milk for our children since we cannot keep more than a single buffalo.
W3: We sometimes have to go to far away places to buy fodder, leaving our children and animals hungry for a long while.

[18] The men were also asked this during focus groups discussions with them, but at this broad level there was little difference between theirs and the women's responses.

Table A9.1. Gujarat and Nepal: fodder shortages when protection began and in 2000–01

Fieldsites	No shortages earlier or in 2000–01	Shortages earlier and in 2000–01	No shortages earlier, shortages in 2000–01	CFIs for which information on change is available
GUJARAT				
		By district (% CFIs)		
Narmada/Bharuch	6.2	31.2	62.5	(16)
Panchmahals	0.0	80.0	20.0	(20)
Sabarkantha	9.1	31.8	59.1	(22)
		By EC gender composition (% CFIs)		
≥2 women in EC	3.4	55.2	41.3	(29)
>2 women in EC	6.9	41.3	51.7	(29)
All CFIs	**5.2**	**48.3**	**46.6**	**(58)**
NEPAL				
		By district (% CFIs)		
Gorkha/Dhading	33.3	40.0	26.6	(30)
Baglung/Parbat	32.1	46.4	21.4	(28)
		By EC gender composition (% CFIs)		
All women CFIs	32.0	40.0	28.0	(25)
Other CFIs	33.3	45.4	21.1	(33)
All CFIs	**32.8**	**43.1**	**24.1**	**(58)**

Note: The percentages are calculated based only on cases with information for both periods.
Source: Author's survey, 2000–01.

Table A9.2. Gujarat and Nepal: coping with fodder shortage, 2000–01

Coping strategy	Gujarat (N=58)	Nepal (N= 58)
	% CFIs facing shortages and coping as below	
Feed less	31.5	35.1
Purchase fodder	88.9[a]	54.1[b]
More time spent on collecting fodder	5.6	43.2
Reduced animals	18.5	70.3
Used cropwaste as fodder	14.8	

Notes: [a] Several CFIs mention that some of their members had to go into debt for buying fodder.
[b] Several CFIs mention buying straw and cropwaste for use as animal feed. N= number of CFIs.
Source: Author's survey, 2000–01.

Where do the villagers now get whatever fodder they collect locally? We have this information only for Gujarat. Here CFIs mainly use their own fields, and to lesser degree the protected forest and nearby (largely government-managed) forests (Table A9.3). There are, however, district-wise differences: only Narmada/Bharuch use protected plantations or village common land, since most of the villages in the other two fieldsites do not have much of either. Also, as was the case with firewood, a much smaller percentage of Narmada/Bharuch fieldsites report using the protected forest and a much larger percentage

Table A9.3. Gujarat: fodder sources used before protection and in 2000–01(% CFIs)

Sources of forest	Protected forest	Protected plantation	Other forest	Village open land	Own fields
			Before protection began		
Narmada/Bharuch (N=16)	18.8	6.2	75.0	68.8	87.5
Panchmahals (N=20)	60.0	0.0	0.0	0.0	90.0
Sabarkantha (N=22)	59.1	0.0	50.0	9.1	100.0
All districts (N=58)	**48.3**	**1.7**	**39.7**	**22.4**	**93.1**
			In 2000–01		
Narmada/Bharuch (N=16)	31.2	37.5	68.8	56.2	93.8
Panchmahals (N=20)	70.0	0.0	0.0	0.0	90.0
Sabarkantha (N=22)	31.8	0.0	13.6	0.0	86.4
All districts (N=58)	**44.8**	**10.3**	**24.1**	**15.5**	**89.7**
			First ranked source in 2000–01		
All districts (N=58)	**27.6**	**3.4**	**15.5**	**0.0**	**39.7**

Note: The sum of percentages is not always 100 since some villages use more than one source. N= number of CFIs.
Source: Author's survey, 2000–01.

report using 'other forests' (mainly government-managed forests), compared with the other district fieldsites. Sabarkantha villages depended in fair degree on other forests before protection and only 14 per cent did so in 2000–01. This is probably because earlier Sabarkantha villages used the forests of neighbouring villages, but this option was foreclosed when the latter also started protecting. Similar information on fodder gathering was not collected for Nepal, but from the fodder-related rules described in Chapter 6 we know that 41 per cent of the CFIs allow unrestricted grass fodder collection, about a third allow open grazing, and a large percentage also distribute fodder on a systematic basis. In other words, the community forest (including the plantation area) continues to be an important source of fodder.

Grass extraction from the community forest takes place especially in the initial period of protection, because grass grows well on degraded forest land if no animals and humans enter. Some CFIs distribute this fodder either freely or under supervision but others continue with the ban, either because they fear that young shoots will get trampled or because they do not want to incur the burden of supervising extraction, or simply because they believe in strict conservation practices. Once the canopy cover thickens, there is less fodder in the ground, and at that time allowing some grazing is more common than formal fodder extraction.

Many CFIs, especially in Narmada/Bharuch in Gujarat and Baglung/Parbat in Nepal, have also been opening the forest periodically for distributing fodder formally (see Table 9.11 in the main text). In Narmada/Bharuch, distribution is done by making equal bundles. In Baglung/Parbat, the most common method is to divide the grass area into plots which are sold off to the villagers for a fee. The sale of plots leads to substantial inequalities in fodder access since only those with the ability to pay can get the fodder. Despite periodic distribution, however, the noted shortages persist in most villages and most households. But are shortages less among groups with more women in the EC? I seek to answer this question below.

2. REGRESSION ANALYSIS

The dependent variable is dichotomous: shortage now = 1, no shortage now = 0. The explanatory variables cover characteristics of the EC, especially its gender composition, and of the CFI, the forest, and the village.

We would expect that the larger the percentage of women in the EC the less likely that it would report shortages. This could play out both directly and through the rules for forest use. At the same time, the gender effects for fodder are likely to be less important than for firewood for the reasons already noted, namely that although women bear substantial responsibility for cattle care and fodder collection, men also have a direct interest in ensuring that the animals remain healthy and survive. Shortages are also likely to be more acute the greater the resource constraints, for instance, the smaller the forest area protected or the more the hamlets or toles dependent on it. Forest segmentation, however, could have two opposing effects: more segments give easier access to nearby hamlets and

Table A9.4. Gujarat: factors affecting fodder shortages

Dependent variable	Fodder shortage: dummy[a]			
Equation no	1		2	
Statistical method	Logit		Logit	
No. of observations	58		58	
Pseudo R^2	0.28		0.19	
Explanatory variables	**Coef.**	**ME**	**Coef.**	**ME**
GenComp2 (% women on the EC)	−0.05* (0.081)	−0.01* (0.089)	−0.05* (0.060)	−0.01* (0.062)
Grazing rules: dummy[b]	−1.80** (0.046)	−0.28** (0.014)	−1.57* (0.055)	−0.28** (0.018)
Forest area protected (ha)	−0.002 (0.138)	−0.00 (0.123)	−0.002 (0.261)	−0.00 (0.252)
No. of forest segments	0.79† (0.104)	0.14* (0.067)	0.53 (0.186)	0.11 (0.168)
No. of hamlets in village	0.41** (0.029)	0.07** (0.015)		
Use of another local forest for fodder: dummy (if used =1)	−0.84 (0.310)	−0.16 (0.352)	−1.38* (0.069)	−0.30* (0.078)
Distance of village from town (km)	0.04 (0.526)	0.01 (0.525)	0.04 (0.458)	0.01 (0.454)
Constant	−0.17		2.40	

Notes: [a] Fodder shortage: if most have fodder shortage =1; if few or none have shortage = 0. There were only three cases of no shortages.

[b] Grazing rules: if full ban or partial ban or open occasionally = 1; if open always = 0.

The marginal effect (ME) is for a discrete change from 0 to 1 for dummy variables, and for a one unit change for continuous variables.

Numbers in parenthesis are *p*-values. Significance: ** at 5%, * at 10%, † at close to 10%.

Differences in models

Equation 2 does not include hamlets to demonstrate the effect of access to fodder from another forest.

could thus reduce shortages, but segmentation is linked to poorer forest condition which could increase shortages. Also, the stricter the rules for fodder collection the more is the likelihood of reported shortages. However, the presence of another forest in the vicinity to which the villagers have formal or informal access would have the opposite effect, namely reduce the likelihood of shortages. In Nepal, membership of another CFI again serves as an indicator of such access. In Gujarat, we have information (as with firewood) on the actual use of another forest for fodder. Although fodder collection or grazing is not formally allowed in government forests, people use them anyway.

Our results bear out most of the hypotheses. The EC's gender composition does indeed affect fodder shortages, but as with firewood the results are mixed. In Gujarat, the larger the percentage of women on the EC the less the likelihood of shortages (Table A9.4), but in Nepal the gender composition effect is not significant (Table A9.5).

Improved access to fodder—through less strict grazing rules and the use of another forest—reduces the likelihood of shortages substantially in Gujarat. The probability of fodder shortages is 28 per cent lower with lenient grazing rules compared with strict rules, and 30 per cent lower with access to another forest than with no such access. For Nepal, fodder extraction rules have no significant effect. Also, as with firewood, Nepalese villagers do not gain much from membership of another CFI, either because fodder extraction is banned there as well, or because they have been denied the customary access they had enjoyed. The negative experience of Ludi CFI in Gorkha is illustrative: 'When the Mirkot villagers formed a community forest excluding us, our problem of fodder shortage began.

Table A9.5. Nepal: factors affecting fodder shortages

Dependent variable	Fodder shortage: dummy[a]	
Statistical method	Logit	
No. of observations	60	
Pseudo R^2	0.11	
Explanatory variables	**Coef.**	**ME**
GenComp: dummy (all-women EC=1)	−0.72 (0.277)	−0.16 (0.272)
Tree fodder cutting rules: dummy[b]	0.72 (0.228)	0.16 (0.231)
Member of another CFI dummy: (if member =1)	0.13 (0.864)	0.028 (0.865)
Forest area protected (ha)	−0.02* (0.094)	−0.004* (0.095)
Forest canopy at time of survey: dummy (dense=1; thin=0)	−1.40 (0.225)	−0.24* (0.090)
Constant	2.24	

Notes: For shortages, no distinction was made by people between grass and tree fodder in their responses.
[a] Fodder shortage: if most have fodder shortage = 1; if few or none have shortage = 0.
[b] If full ban =1; if partial ban/given on request or open occasionally = 0
The marginal effect (ME) is for a discrete change from 0 to 1 for dummy variables, and for a one unit change for continuous variables.
Numbers in parenthesis are *p*-values. Significance: * at 10%

Otherwise, since the Ludi and Bhangeri forests were already degraded we had used the Mirkot forest. We were the traditional users of the Mirkot forest.'

Forest condition—dense canopy—however, is linked with a 24 per cent less likelihood of fodder shortages than a forest with thin canopy, and forest size is also negatively related to shortages in Nepal although the effect is statistically small. Both these capture the effect of resource constraints. In Gujarat the more the number of hamlets dependent on the forest and the larger the number of forest segments, the more likely are fodder shortages. This suggests that here also resource constraints matter, although less than access.

3. CONCLUDING COMMENTS

Increase in biomass availability with improvement in forest condition has not alleviated fodder shortages. Shortages not only persist, they have become more acute for a fair percentage who report that they now have shortages when they had none earlier. As a result, people depend more on purchased fodder to feed their animals, and even sell off small animals such as goats, with adverse effects especially on the livelihoods of the poor. Only some of the Gujarat CFIs distribute fodder formally, and although the Nepal CFIs commonly do so, their methods of distribution are inegalitarian, since payments in some form or other are expected in two-thirds of the CFIs. A higher representation of women in the EC does reduce the likelihood of shortages in Gujarat, but it has no significant effect in Nepal.

Part III

Beyond Presence

10

Connecting with Civil Society

Weaving a Web of Strategic Alliances

> Pools of silver shimmer
> from one leaf to another, from one path trodden
> to another . . .
>
> (Coral Bracho, 'Thread in a Spider's Web', 1998)
>
> . . . until the mosses
> take root in the thunder, until from the pulse
> of hand and hand the roots descend.
>
> (Pablo Neruda, 'Pact (Sonata)', [1947] 1975)[1]

If we took a satellite view of the South Asian landscape we would see millions of scattered settlements and forest segments, some dense with trees, others with barely a tree standing. If, however, we lay on our backs on a forest floor and looked up, we might see 'pools of silver shimmer'—a spider weaving its gossamer threads across spreading branches, bridging them. These two images—one looking down from space, the other looking up at space, one of atomization, the other of connection—provide the central metaphors for this concluding section of the book. The first metaphor is of individual village communities seeking to create social fences to protect their forests, and within these communities, women, segregated and marginalized by social norms, struggling to find a voice. The second is of a web of alliances, woven strategically, that could connect communities across villages, and women across communities, and so transform both the ecological and the social landscape.

In the preceding chapters, we have seen that there are compelling arguments for enhancing women's presence in local institutions for governing the commons, both intrinsically (on grounds of equality and justice) and instrumentally—for their beneficial effect on conservation and improved welfare through women's enhanced command over public resources. At the same time, there are serious constraints to women being able to achieve this transformative potential, in particular inadequate numbers and voice, group heterogeneity, and being

[1] Both Bracho and Neruda's verses are translations from the Spanish (see Bracho 1998 and Neruda [1947] 1975).

confined to the local. In the two chapters which constitute this concluding Part III—*Beyond Presence*—I argue that to overcome these constraints we will need institutional innovations, in particular a web of strategic alliances forged horizontally and vertically between diverse grassroots collectivities on the one hand and between civil society and government on the other. Although we still have miles to go for making the kinds of connections that the image of a spider's web evokes or that Pablo Neruda's verse elicits, we can discern modest beginnings of innovative structures on which such associations could be built. I elaborate on these possibilities and also examine how the reach of local institutions and networks could be extended beyond the local, and how higher echelons of government could be made more accessible and responsive to the poor and to women.

Indeed, the concern with strengthening their horizontal and vertical reach is common to many institutions of local governance, be they formed around forests or around other environmental public goods, and it raises questions such as: how can the disadvantaged gain access to public decision-making forums and influence them in their own interest? How can local issues that are critically important to the lives and livelihoods of poor women be brought to the attention of policy-makers and help shape national policy? How do we make the upper echelons of the bureaucracy and parliament accountable to the poor? Can local institutions transform into a green movement for change? More generally, how do we shape gender-egalitarian ideas while advancing gender-egalitarian presence?

Conceptually, I touched on some of these questions in the introductory chapter. Empirically, my results establish that at the community level, including women in sufficient proportions can make a significant difference to institutional functioning and its outcomes. But the results also highlight how, on particular counts, simply increasing women's participation in CFIs is not enough: for instance, despite their participation, shortages of cooking fuel—an item as basic as food in the everyday lives of rural households—persist. How is it that such a basic need has received such inadequate attention from policy-makers and even NGOs and grassroots women's groups? What mechanisms can be devised to establish a two-pronged process of communication: one for strengthening women's voice within civil society organizations, and the other for conveying that voice to all levels of government—from village councils to the bureaucracy and further to the legislature?

In this chapter I address the first lap of this process, namely that of enhancing women's numbers, voice, and influence within the forestry groups, especially through strategic alliances with civil society institutions of similar ilk. In the next chapter I examine the difficulties of engaging with government at different levels, as well as the potential for doing so, and highlight the need for a more transformative politics, both in the realm of ideas and in the realm of practice, to promote more gender-egalitarian and green-responsive goals.

Before examining those processes, however, let me summarize below the main empirical findings of my study and the lessons they hold on the difference women can make to green governance, as well as the relevance of these results for gender and governance more generally.

1. THE IMPACT OF PRESENCE: SOME LESSONS

1.1 Recapitulation

Historically the process of women's inclusion in governance has been slow but notable. In South Asia, until the early part of the twentieth century, public affairs at the local level were managed almost entirely by men. The early twentieth century brought significant changes. In particular, the decentralization of government and later of forest governance provided a basis for women's inclusion in local-level decision-making, although substantial shifts occurred only in the late 1980s and 1990s, with one-third reservation of seats for women in India's village councils and urban municipalities, and more limited reservation in Nepal. In India, the recommendations of various committees that 'at least two women' or 'one-third women' be included preceded the establishment of these gender quotas, and influenced not only the mandates in institutions of government but also the administrative directives for institutions that fell mainly within the purview of civil society, such as CFIs.

There was considerable variation, however, in the formal JFM directives for women's inclusion passed by different Indian states (Chapter 4), and in how the directives got translated into practice by communities. Nepal simply had broad guidelines on women's inclusion in forest management and even these were often non-specific and changing with time. As a result, on the ground, in both Gujarat and Nepal, we observe CFIs which range in their EC gender composition from no women to only women, with most veering toward a mixed group containing one or two women and occasionally more. This variation provided a rich basis for capturing in my study, through a stratified random sample, the impact of varying gender composition on various dimensions of institutional functioning. In Gujarat the CFIs selected across three districts—Narmada/Bharuch, Panchmahals, and Sabarkantha—were predominantly mixed-gender groups. In Nepal, the survey districts—Gorkha/Dhading and Baglung/Parbat—also had a fair proportion of all-women groups, that is groups with all-women ECs, although with both men and women in the general body.

Based on this primary data, my empirical analysis—the core of this book—establishes that women's greater presence in local environmental governance makes a significant difference on many fronts (summarized in Appendix 10.1). It enhances women's effective participation in decision-making; influences the nature of decisions made, especially the rules of forest use and their implementation; curbs rule violations; increases the likelihood of an improvement in forest condition; and reduces the likelihood of women facing firewood and fodder shortages. There is also a critical mass effect in relation to women's participation.

In fact, women's effective participation in decision-making is (and needs to be) our entry point in the field of gender and governance. Examining mixed-gender CFIs we find that increasing women's presence in the executive committee—the CFI's principle decision-making body—does help women move beyond nominal membership to effective engagement. In the company of other women, they are able to transcend conservative social norms and personal diffidence to attend meetings, speak up at them, and hold office. To begin with, simply having more women on the EC of mixed-gender CFIs increases the likelihood of there being at least some female presence at meetings. If there is only one woman on the EC, and if she is absent, there would be no female representation at all. There is also a statistically verifiable critical mass effect, especially for Nepal and indicative for Gujarat: women's attendance rate at meetings is significantly higher on ECs that have between a quarter to a third women, than on ECs which have less than a quarter women. Having a critical mass of women tends to empower each woman in the group to attend meetings. Essentially, in traditional contexts, women are in a better position to go to public meetings if other women are also going. Similarly, the supportive presence of larger numbers of women increases the chances of at least some women speaking up.

The inclusion of *landless* women in the EC makes a particular difference. If present in sufficient numbers, landless women are significantly more likely to attend EC meetings and voice their concerns, since they are less constrained by social norms and more compelled by circumstance (e.g. acute firewood shortages) to raise a voice. Given the potential heterogeneity of women's interests, this alerts us to the importance of also including in institutions of governance women who are economically and socially disadvantaged, and not simply any women, for the interests of the disadvantaged to gain more visibility.

There is a view within the feminist debate that economic and social inequalities can obstruct women's participation in public discussion. We might well expect this a priori, but my analysis (and the experiences of many grassroots women's organizations in South Asian villages, as well as recent research on village councils) suggests that equality is not a necessary precondition for women to express their views.[2] In fact, poor women, especially if present in strength, or with prior exposure to women's empowerment programmes, are found more likely to speak up fearlessly on issues in which they have a high personal stake. As a result, they can often be more effective in public discussions than well-off women. That personal stake matters is further substantiated by my finding that women are more likely to attend meetings and/or speak up at them if they face firewood shortages, or if they need to resolve conflicts with forest guards who catch them stealing firewood.

The impact of women's proportions on women holding office is rather more complex. On the one hand higher proportions are insufficient for ensuring that

[2] I have attended many such meetings (both relating to community forestry and other subjects) where economically and socially disadvantaged women were often the most outspoken, if a fair number of them were present. They were also more willing to speak up in front of government officials on issues that affected them and their families. Behar and Kumar (2002) similarly found, in their study for Madhya Pradesh (India), that village councillors from scheduled caste/scheduled tribe backgrounds tended to be less socially constrained in public speaking. See also Prasad and Haranath (2004).

women will hold office—in Gujarat, for instance, almost no CFIs have women office bearers, no matter what the EC's gender composition. On the other hand, where that initial glass ceiling has been cracked, as in Nepal, the likelihood of women holding office increases significantly among ECs with more women. There is a threshold effect around 25 per cent women which is the minimum percentage needed to make a difference, but the likelihood increases further as we move toward gender parity. A person's individual characteristics also matter. Women who are literate and currently single (widowed, separated, etc.) are more likely to become office bearers, as are men who are literate and landowners. Notably, though, while the EC's gender composition significantly affects the chances of a woman holding office, it has no effect on men holding office.

Regional differences in cultural norms also affect women's participation, although not dramatically. On the one hand, women in both Gujarat and Nepal and across much of South Asia share a history of exclusion from public forums and continue to be constrained by the gender division of labour, social norms and perceptions, and related factors. On the other hand, there are interesting differences between India and Nepal in the likelihood of women attending meetings or becoming office bearers. Nepal tends to have fewer meetings with no women attending than Gujarat, and often has women holding office. This difference stems at least partly from the less restrictive social norms among all communities (including upper-caste Hindus) in Nepal's middle hills, and partly from the impact of external influence, such as the example set by Nepal's forest federation, FECOFUN, through its constitutional mandate that 50 per cent of its office bearers should be women.

Moreover, cultural geography impinges on how substantial a presence women need to have to make an effective difference. In the Gujarat CFIs, although most women belong to tribal populations, the ideology of female seclusion has been growing due to emulation of upper-caste practices and the influence of conservative religious movements. In Nepal's middle hills, by contrast, social restrictions on women's mobility and public presence have been declining even among the upper castes, and remain low among the ethnic groups that are widespread in the area. Hence although women's effectiveness is clearly enhanced by the presence of more women, enabling social norms can compensate for smaller numbers, to some extent.

ECs with higher proportions of women not only enhance women's effective participation in CFIs, such groups also frame significantly different rules for forest use. The difference women make, however, is not always in the expected direction. In general (with the exception of one district), ECs with more women in Gujarat, and all-women ECs relative to other ECs in Nepal, tend to make stricter rules of forest use, that is, they extract less from the forest. We would have expected the opposite, namely groups with more women making more lenient rules, since women need forest products such as firewood and fodder daily and cannot easily defer consumption: with no fuel there would be no food on the table. It would thus be in women's immediate self-interest to push for less restrictive rules which allow more extraction. Women's degree of freedom in framing lenient rules, however, is especially limited by two factors: first, in Nepal, all-women groups face substantial resource constraints—they tend to get on average half the forest area and much more degraded plots to protect than groups with men on the EC. Second, qualitative evidence suggests that groups with only women or predominantly women tend to face a greater monitoring constraint than male-dominated groups in organizing the careful supervision needed for regulated, periodic extraction. In other words, resource and monitoring constraints can restrict women's ability to act according to their immediate interests. But women's responses also suggest that they frame rules responsibly by taking into account the needs of conservation. All-women groups in Nepal, for example, could make less strict rules for short-term gains even at the cost of long-term regeneration. They eschew that temptation, despite internal pressures from the women of their constituency, or their own needs. The following comment by the village women of the all-women EC in Chamere CFI, Gorkha, Nepal, is illustrative:

> There is plenty of dry firewood lying in the forest, so we asked the samiti if it could open the forest during the festival season, but the samiti members did not want to do so because they felt that the regenerated plants would be destroyed by the crowd.

That almost all the EC members in Nepal's CFIs come from landowning families clearly enables them to go toward strictness at less personal cost, since they have a fall-back option of drawing on some form of biofuel (firewood, cropwaste, or dung) from their own land. Landless women lack this choice. And their presence on the EC underlies the results for the one exceptional district—Panchmahals, Gujarat—where CFIs which had high female presence made less strict rules. Unlike other districts, in Panchmahals the women in ECs with substantial female presence were largely landless, and were able to argue for more lenient rules. It is notable, though, that even ECs with more landless women do not veer toward open access; rather they allow restricted procurement, especially of firewood, and for more days in the year.

On the one hand, therefore, not simply their presence but women's class matters in what kind of difference women make. On the other hand, women of all classes balance self-interest with community interest, and immediate needs with long-term forest conservation goals, when placed in decision-making positions.

Similarly, caste and age matter—ECs with a higher percentage of upper-caste members and older members (including older women) make stricter rules. Older people often emphasize the importance of forest conservation for leaving a legacy for their grandchildren. They can also enforce strict rules at less personal cost because their family members can shoulder the extra burden of finding fuel, fodder, etc. The impact of women's presence, and the difference they can make to forest use rules, is thus mediated by their economic and social position and age. Emerging research suggests that some of these characteristics also impact on the positions women take, or the decisions they make, in other contexts. Race, for instance, is found to matter in US legislatures (Bratton and Haynie 1999) and caste in India's village councils (Chattopadhyay and Duflo 2004). At the same time, as I argued in Chapter 1, community-level rule-making has dimensions less likely to be found at higher levels of governance. In particular, community decisions on local resource use affect the rule-framers personally, bringing to the surface potential conflicts of interest—self-interest versus other people's interests, or immediate interest versus long-term interest.

The other side of rule-making—rule violations—is again affected by women's participation. In Nepal's CFIs, for example, ECs with more women have a lower incidence of rule violations, and in Gujarat violations by women and for firewood decline while violations by men and for timber rise, as the years of protection increase. This shift over time is a second generation effect. As timber matures it increases the profitability and hence the probability of theft. It is men who are mainly involved in timber stealing. Women, however, tend to substitute inferior fuel for firewood and thus appear to adapt better than men to strict rules over time. Moreover, procuring firewood—especially if collected as twigs or drywood—is not ecologically destructive in the way that timber harvesting can be.

Another piece of the win-win story with women's greater involvement in green governance—and for conservationists perhaps the most important piece—relates to improvements in forest condition. This is measured through a range of indicators to capture the complexity of effects, but particularly by changes in canopy cover and regeneration, based on assessments by my research team, the villagers, and the forest department, as well as on satellite sources. I found that CFIs with more than two women in the EC compared with two women or less in Gujarat, and all-women CFIs relative to other CFIs in Nepal, were linked with significantly greater improvement in forest condition. Several indicators in the aggregated Gujarat analysis and all indicators in the Panchmahals district-level analysis established this, as did all the indicators in the aggregated Nepal analysis. In Nepal, the performance of all-women groups is especially notable given that they began with poorer and smaller forests than other groups.

There are many reasons why groups with more EC women tend to do well in improving forest condition. Women on the EC help disseminate information about protection rules more widely within the community, since women can reach other women more easily than men. They also bring into the protection enterprise a larger pool of people committed to resource conservation, and women's vigilance, in particular, improves protection since they can better apprehend female intruders than men. Women's presence on the EC also provides more opportunities for village women to contribute their knowledge of plants and species and of ecologically sound extraction practices, as well as convey their preferences when plans for forest development are drawn up. More generally, even if the rules that the EC eventually makes are hard on women, if they are part of the rule-making process they are more likely to themselves comply, as well as persuade others to do so. All this substantially improves protection and community cooperation and so benefits forest condition.

As with rule-making, age also matters in conservation. ECs with older women and older members in general show greater improvement in forest condition. This is probably because they have more experience of forestry as well as of governance, and command greater authority and respect within the village and in the neighbourhood, which increases the likelihood of villagers adhering to the rules made. The interests of efficiency (improved conservation) may therefore be better served by inducting older women and men into governance, although equity goals may do less well, since an older EC makes stricter rules (namely allows less extraction of forest products). It needs emphasis, though, that very strict rules are not necessarily better for conservation. The relationship between strictness of rules and forest conservation is a complex one: overly strict rules can lead resentful villagers to indulge in destructive behaviour, whereas some leniency, which allows sustainable extraction, can prove beneficial both ecologically, by clearing space for new shoots and removing biomass that could catch fire, and socially by increasing the incentive to cooperate.

Other policy pointers stem from the positive effects on forest condition of employing a guard to complement village patrolling, and of receiving technical support from the forest department (including training in pruning and clearing operations). There is, however, need to reduce gender bias in access to such training. It also helps if the community receives a forest of reasonable size, in a single plot, and in a condition that still allows regeneration, rather than a forest that is so small or degraded that it is difficult to revive and can provide rather few initial benefits (a disadvantage faced especially by many all-women CFIs in Nepal). It is to the considerable credit of forest protecting communities that whatever the initial state of the plots they received almost all the protected forests have improved after transfer. And in 85–90 per cent of the CFIs, the villagers were optimistic that the forest and the CFI as an institution would sustain and that their children would follow in their footsteps (see also Box 10.1). The following response of EC members in a Gorkha CFI is typical of this spirit: 'Yes, our children will also protect the forest. The forest is essential for us agriculturists. Our children have learnt from us and in fact are more knowledgeable than us.'

Where the institutions have done rather less well, however, is in addressing women's needs. Indeed, it is paradoxical that despite regenerating forests and growing biomass availability, firewood shortages persist and, in some cases, have even intensified since protection began. This has negative equity and welfare consequences in terms of the time and energy women expend in firewood collection and the health ill-effects that they and their children suffer from the use of smokier fuels as substitutes. In general, in many of the male-dominated committees, there tends to be less extraction of firewood than would be possible to undertake sustainably. The presence of more women in the EC can help to an extent—in Gujarat, CFIs with a larger percentage of female EC members are found less likely to report firewood shortages. They are also found less likely to have fodder shortages. Women's voice, therefore, does count in getting the community to extract more from the protected area. But the persistence of

Box 10.1. Sustainability

When asked if the forest and the CFI would sustain over time, almost all the villagers were optimistic, and expected their children to carry the tradition forward. Indeed, a distinct note of 'environmentality' could be detected in their responses. Some examples of the views expressed are given below.

* * *

Khabji village, Narmada, Gujarat

M1: Yes our forest will survive because it is important to us and we understand the benefits of preserving it not only for ourselves but also for our future generations.
W1: The forest fulfils all our requirements, so we have to ensure that it improves.

Bhadkhore, Baglung, Nepal

M1: Yes, it will survive. We have worked so hard to make this forest as you now see it. It is already so much better than it was in the past.
M2: We will make this forest even better since it helps fulfil our needs, allows us to save money in our community fund, and also provides forest products for those in need from outside this CFI.

Gaderi-Dhaireni, Baglung, Nepal

W: I think people will continue as a group.
M1: The CFI will survive if people receive something from the forest. In the last three years people have benefited and the majority are satisfied. That is why I think the group will survive.
M2: The group will survive for a long time to come. There has been natural growth of species like *teeju* (timber) and *chilaune* and we are also planting new saplings. Grazing has stopped and people work together to clear the shrubs and cut the grass. At most about 2% of the community may be dissatisfied, but the rest are happy with this CFI.

Kheidipada village, Bharuch, Gujarat

M1: We are dedicated to protecting our forest.
M2: In doing so we have spoiled out relationship with some of our best friends. We are looking at the larger picture here. If the forest survives our children will have a better future.
M3: We are saving the forest to save our lives.

* * *

Bhalu CFI, Gorkha, Nepal

W1–W2: The new generation is guided by their parents and by society. Now, we are protecting the forest and they are learning from us, so we think they in turn will protect the forest in the future.
M1–M2: We agree with the women.

Phoksing CFI, Parbat, Nepal

W: We have no alternative sources of firewood for cooking and our children will also have to save it for their children.

(*continued*)

Box 10.1. (Continued)

Urleni CFI, Baglung, Nepal

M: Land in this area is becoming more and more expensive. Soon we will have only buildings and little private forest. Then, only the community forestry will be left for us and our children.

Mahadev Bhogteni, Gorkha, Nepal

W: Yes, our children will also protect the forest. They will do it out of love for this forest just as their parents and grandparents have done.

Source: Author's Survey, 2000–01.

cooking energy poverty also points to the limits of what mere presence in a CFI can achieve.

Moreover, even the noted positive effects of women's participation can depend on the *extent* of their presence. I found substantial support for the idea that women will be more effective if they constitute more than a token minority and on some aspects of participation if they constitute a critical mass. The threshold is found to lie between a quarter to one-third women in the EC for attending meetings and around 25 per cent for women to become office bearers, although for office bearing the results hold only for Nepal, and about 25 per cent is the minimum, since women's chances of holding office continue to rise till there is gender parity. One-third, as noted earlier, has become the popularly accepted cut-off point in arguments for women's presence, on the assumption that this is necessary for women's effectiveness in parliament or other public bodies such as village councils. My results show that a wider range of gender composition is linked to effectiveness, but one-third is still a fairly close approximation. Of course on grounds of gender equality a case can clearly be made for going beyond one-third to gender parity. And this would also improve the prospects of women overcoming the glass ceiling effect in office bearing. In fact, recently some Indian states have legislated for 50 per cent gender quotas in the Panchayat Raj Institutions, and there is also a move to legislate this for all states.[3]

Overall, therefore, women's greater presence in the decision-making body makes a significant and positive difference to the two primary objectives of community forestry—better conservation/regeneration of the resource and satisfying a larger measure of local needs, even though it cannot fully satisfy those needs. The aims of both efficiency (more biomass regeneration and improved forest condition) and distributional equity (e.g. lesser firewood and fodder shortages) are likely to be better realized with more women on the EC, and

[3] The states are Himachal Pradesh, Rajasthan, Madhya Pradesh, and Uttarakhand (*Indian Express* 2008a, 2008b).

equity would be especially better served with the participation of more economically disadvantaged women on the EC.

In addition, although not measurable empirically in all its facets, a range of gender-empowering effects follow when women are present in sufficient proportions, and begin to participate in CFI activities. Speaking up at meetings, influencing decisions, participating in patrolling, holding office, and in some cases even initiating CFI formation by directly asking forest officials for a plot to protect, are all facets of empowerment. The gains that women themselves mention most frequently are enhanced self-confidence and an increase in their ability to attend meetings, to speak up in public forums in front of strangers, to interact with visitors, and to have the opportunity of attending training workshops, meeting new people and making new friends—in short, becoming, as they term it, 'more knowledgeable', and being seen by others as 'responsible persons'. In Nepal, some lower-caste women also mentioned the social advantages of becoming EC members, such as gaining respect in the community. One of them said: 'As a dalit woman no one cared about me until the CFI was formed. Since I was elected to the EC, however, community leaders and women members of the forest group have been consulting me about community forestry' (Gorkha CFI, author's survey, 2000–01).

There are other more complex and subtle signs of women's empowerment as well. No matter the hardship they were facing with strict rules of protection, for instance, women would often show me their community forest with pride. I wondered at this at the time, but realize on reflection that for many women who own neither fields nor homesteads and have few other private possessions, claiming 'ownership' of a public good (till recently controlled by the forest department) is an important form of empowerment. Similarly, the informal patrol groups that women sometimes form, or even the individual vigilance they often exercise, give them a rare opportunity to exert authority, for instance in telling neighbouring villagers to keep away if they venture into their forest. Women experience this too as a form of empowerment.

Women's presence on the EC and greater involvement in CFI activities overall, also helps the CFIs attain many of the characteristics deemed by several scholars as conducive to building successful and enduring institutions for managing common pool resources, but which have not been evaluated from a gender perspective. These include characteristics such as involving resource users in framing and modifying the rules; keeping the rules simple and fair; holding those monitoring the resource condition accountable to the users, such as holding the CFI's executive committee and patrol group accountable to the general body; specifying graded penalties in keeping with the seriousness of the rule violation; involving resource users and/or officials in applying such penalties; and instituting effective mechanisms for discussing problems and resolving conflicts.[4]

[4] See especially Ostrom (1990: 90), McKean (1986), Wade (1988) and the discussion in Baland and Platteau (1996). Here I have paraphrased the list of characteristics, in keeping with the context, rather than stated them literally. These characteristics are broadly in line with Ostrom's (1990: 90) 'design principles' (also discussed in Chapter 6 of this volume).

CFIs which have few or no women in decision-making would be found wanting in relation to all of these characteristics. Women affected by the rules, for instance, would have no hand in formulating them; the rules framed could be unfair to women and resented by them; men who patrol the forest formally would not be accountable to women forest users; women who protect the forest informally would not be accountable to the formal protection committees; women as users or monitors would be excluded from decisions on penalties given; and women would not be party to conflict resolution. In contrast, all these conditions are better fulfilled in women-inclusive CFIs, with women's greater participation in rule formulation, protection, conflict resolution, and forest development. We would thus expect improved performance on all these counts in such CFIs.

1.2 General Lessons for Governance

What lessons and insights do these results offer for gender and governance more generally, and what pointers do they provide for research beyond green governance?

First, the results highlight the importance of tracing the implications of a group's gender composition much before we come to the stage of policy formulation, namely in women's ability to participate effectively in the very process of decision-making. The potential impact of women's numbers on such participation, barely touched upon in relation to women in legislatures, except by rare scholars such as Thomas (1994) and Flammang (1985), and rather little tested empirically, warrants much more attention at all levels and contexts of governance. Equally we need more exploration of the potential constraints that women face in attending and speaking up at meetings. For instance, does the presence of other women motivate women legislators to be present in larger numbers during discussions and express themselves more boldly, as we found in local-level governance? How universal is this across cultures and contexts?

Second the study extends the debate on critical mass. Can we indeed project certain proportions of women's presence—for instance, one-third—as having global relevance? Many scholars strongly support the idea of critical mass a priori, but some also reject it. In fact this is an empirical and not just a conceptual question. My analysis points to the complexity of measuring critical mass effects and the need to go beyond simply the numbers effect. At the same time it affirms, through statistical testing, that popularly floated guesstimates of one-quarter or one-third women are fairly on the mark, at least in relation to women participating in meetings and holding office. These results hold after controlling for a range of other factors. It is of course possible that somewhat different proportions may obtain in other contexts. There is thus substantial scope and need for much more empirical testing of propositions relating to gender and governance in diverse contexts, than has been done so far (see also Dodson 2006).

Third, for policy formulation, the finding that including landless women in decision-making can enhance the effectiveness of women's participation, as well as the nature of decisions made, points to the importance of paying attention to the class and social position of the women who constitute a decision-making body. It also highlights the need to examine in contexts other than green governance the impact of social disadvantage, such as women's class, caste, or race, on the decisions women make. On this count, we cannot extrapolate directly from my results, because class, race, etc. may matter more or matter differently for decisions made at the community level, relative to the national level. It would matter less if, for example, legislators promote laws or policies which do not benefit them personally; and it would matter differently insofar as such legislation or policy gives them political leverage with their constituencies which is not usually the case for women in CFIs.

Fourth, the results demonstrate that the impact of numbers extends much beyond policy formulation to policy implementation and outcomes. Those studying local government could do a similar exercise by examining not simply whether female and male village councillors differ in the particular schemes or public goods they prioritize (on which there is a growing body of work), but whether women are also able to ensure that the schemes are completed in less time and at lower cost. At higher levels of governance it is much more difficult to make these connections by studying only one institution. It can prove difficult, for instance, to trace the impact on communities of a piece of legislation enacted by women parliamentarians, simply by studying parliamentarians, because of the potential disconnect between those framing policies and those implementing them. But we could still address this issue by posing a somewhat different question, such as: are woman legislators more likely than male legislators to maintain a channel of communication with communities, say through links with civil society, to monitor the ground impact of the policies they formulate? These issues are addressed further below, but consider first how we can enhance women's presence, voice and influence.

2. ENHANCING WOMEN'S NUMBERS, VOICE, AND INFLUENCE

Given the importance of women's numbers in a decision-making forum (even while admitting that there are limits to what numbers alone can achieve), and given that a high percentage of women on the EC is not the norm and only some CFIs achieve it, we need to find ways of increasing women's presence in all CFIs. At the same time, for women to be able to promote their interests more effectively there is need to go beyond numbers.[5] I believe at least three additional elements are important: first, increasing women's self-confidence and ability to speak in public forums; second, forging a collective voice as opposed to simply intervening individually; and third, establishing institutional mechanisms wherein women can strategize and carve out collective goals. In addition, to have an impact beyond the village, local bodies would need to have vertical reach to higher levels of decision-making. All these goals, including that of increasing women's numbers, are interlinked and could be furthered by forging strategic alliances with other elements of civil society, as discussed here. We begin with the issue of enhancing women's local-level presence and participation in CFIs.

A number of factors outlined in Chapter 5 can constrain women's effective participation, such as the criteria for defining membership, conservative social norms and perceptions about women's roles and abilities, women's late entry into the institution after men have already established control, the culture of male discourse (e.g. its aggressiveness), the class and social background of the women, and their personal diffidence and lack of self-confidence. How can women overcome some of these constraints and enhance their numbers and voice in CFIs?

2.1 Working within CFIs

Since women's effective participation in decision-making depends, for a start, on their proportions in the main decision-making body, the first step would be to ensure an increase in women's numbers. In terms of formal directives, both Gujarat and Nepal have already moved toward greater inclusion of women in community forestry, as we had noted in Chapter 3. In India, for example, in 2000, the central government's directive to all states was that half of the GB and one-third of the EC members under JFM should be women (GoI 2000c, WINROCK 2006). In Nepal, the 2009 community forestry guidelines suggest the inclusion of one man and one woman per household as GB members, and the appointment of 50 per cent women on the EC. These are encouraging steps forward, although India too like Nepal could move toward gender parity on the EC, and both countries need to take steps to include women from landless households. At the time of my survey only two Indian states, Karnataka and Madhya Pradesh, required CFIs to include one or two landless *persons* (not necessarily women) on the EC (SPWD 1998) and by 2002 six states required this (*Van Sahyog* 2002–03). India's experience also shows that changing the initial rules of entry is not difficult. Support from external agent such as NGOs, donors, and key individuals, and the gender sensitivity brought about by the country-wide women's movement, has given village women implicit bargaining power on this count.[6]

[5] See also Goetz's (2003) distinction between access, presence, and influence.

[6] Personal observation. See also WINROCK (2006) which traces the process by which interventions by NGOs, academics, and others helped to shift JFM policy in women-inclusive directions, although

Moving from directives to practice, however, is neither easy nor automatic. In India many individual states have yet to incorporate the post-2000 directives into their JFM orders. An even bigger hurdle is convincing the communities to implement women-inclusive rules. In Gujarat, as we found, even the minimalist rule of including at least two women in the EC was not being implemented by all CFIs, at the time of my survey. External agent support can help in motivating villagers to some extent, such as by taking them on visits to more women-inclusive CFIs, or sensitizing them on how to interpret the rules in a women-friendly way. As noted in Chapter 4, when an NGO staff member in Gujarat said, 'there should be at least two women' (the stipulated minimum), the villagers interpreted this as implying a maximum of two women, so only two were included, but when he said: 'anyone who wants to can become a member', larger numbers of women joined the EC. External agent bargaining power, however, works best when women's participation is sought from the beginning. Once men's 'territorial interests' get entrenched, women's entry can prove difficult, even if the formal rules are favourable.

Similarly, NGOs and forest department staff can facilitate women's attendance in meetings. Some Indian NGOs working on community forestry have, for instance, promoted the practice of women forming the front rows of a gathering so that they can be better heard and do not need to cover their faces from elderly relatives sitting behind them (SARTHI 1997–98). Other NGOs have used their clout with the community on women's behalf, by stipulating that there be at least 30 per cent women in Governing Body meetings to form a quorum (Viegas and Menon 1993); and some states have now formally stipulated a minimum percentage of women for a quorum, although typically only for the GB and not the EC (*Van Sahyog* 2002–03). Similarly, forest department personnel have, on occasion, played an enabling role by insisting that the meeting would not start until the village men invited the women, brushing aside men's excuses that women were busy with housework. The women, on being so invited, often turned up in strength (Sarin 1998). The recruitment of more women into the forest department as officers and village forest workers would also help. At present, female staff are few and far between (Sarin 1996). Moreover, attending meetings is just one step forward. To have an impact, women also need to express their views and be heard. On this count too, some gender-sensitive NGO personnel have sought to privilege women's voice in mixed-gender meetings, by soliciting and giving weight to their opinions in discussions dominated by village men. I observed this in Gujarat, and Sarin (1996) in Haryana state.

All such efforts by external agents, however, can at best complement and not substitute for strengthening women's own ability to be active in meetings. To increase women's numbers in public forums we need additional institutional mechanisms. For enhancing women's voice, such steps are even more imperative.

the paper pays rather little attention to the impact of research and advocacy by persons outside the donor-driven network.

To some extent, a sufficient number of women EC members can, in itself, enhance women's ability to overcome obstructive social norms and speak up at meetings. This is clearly brought out both by my empirical analysis and the qualitative evidence cited in Chapter 5 of women affirming that they felt empowered by the presence of other women. This feeling of empowerment could strengthen over time as women learn to cooperate with one another and develop a sense of solidarity. Moreover, the needs of survival compel poor women to attend and participate in meetings. But again, in cultural contexts such as South Asia's, where most rural women lack self-confidence and experience in public interaction, we need additional mechanisms to strengthen women's ability to stand up for themselves.

How can women gain confidence and voice in public forums and the capability to deal with the women-unfriendly environments that they often encounter in such forums? There is a growing consensus among NGOs, donors, and elements of the State that the formation of separate women's groups enhances both. Maya Devi Khanal (a Nepalese grassroots activist with long experience in group organizing, including in community forestry)[7] put it emphatically:

> In mixed groups when women speak men make fun of them, so women need to learn to deal with this . . . When women join a [separate] group they gradually lose their fear of making fools of themselves when speaking up . . . Women need their own small groups. This is what I know from my 22 years of experience working with the government and NGOs.

This insight, however, can only point to an intermediary process of building women's preparedness for public participation. Forming all-women CFIs *as a norm* is not the answer, especially since mixed-gender CFIs control the bulk of the community forest resources, carry more clout in the village, and can bring indirect benefits to women members in terms of learning and resource access.[8] All-women CFIs, therefore, can supplement but not substitute for efforts to enhance women's presence in mixed groups.

For an effective and notable impact on women's numbers and voice, and especially poor women's numbers and voice in CFIs, we need a more innovative institutional leap. A substantial potential lies in building strategic linkages between CFIs and local collectivities of women. In particular, I have in mind village self-help groups (SHGs) in India and similar types of groups in Nepal. For illustration I focus especially on India's SHGs on which there is considerable information.

[7] Maya Devi was also the first president of HIMAWANTI, the women's network of grassroots groups managing natural resources in Nepal and in some neighbouring countries.

[8] Koolwal's (2004) study, although not focused on CFIs, is indicative. Comparing all-women groups and mixed-gender groups in an income-generating programme in Madhya Pradesh (India), she found that women in mixed groups achieved higher personal savings relative to household wealth, and participated more and with greater confidence in household decisions.

2.2 Horizontal Linkages with SHGs

There are over 2.2 million SHGs in India, of which 85–90 per cent or more are constituted only of women.[9] An SHG usually consists of 10–12 economically or socially homogeneous self-selected women who pool their savings and rotate lending within the group. One village can have several SHGs. Groups with a proven record of working together for about six months can apply for a bank loan as a proportion of their group savings deposit.[10] Loans, if taken, go to the whole group which then decides their use. Loans tend to be taken for individual or family micro-enterprises rather than group ventures (NCAER 2008). Until the early 2000s, two-thirds of the SHGs were being promoted by NGOs, although now they are also being catalysed by state governments and banks. Many SHGs, especially those catalysed by NGOs, have graduated beyond loan disbursements to social advocacy. Indeed, for many NGOs, forming SHGs around savings-and-credit is simply an entry point for working toward women's empowerment. In this and several other respects SHGs differ from micro-credit groups.[11] The latter are formed basically around credit,[12] often involve women with no proven record of working together, typically dispense loans on an individual basis, and usually do not venture into social advocacy.

Several features of women's SHGs make them particularly attractive as possibilities for strengthening women's presence and voice in community forestry groups. Since SHGs are typically constituted of self-selected women from economically or socially homogeneous backgrounds, the prospects of cohesiveness and cooperation within the group are high. The NGO MYRADA, in south India, in fact catalyses what it terms 'self-help affinity groups' formed initially to fulfil social needs and then moving into savings-and-credit when the groups so decide.[13] The groups are constituted of people likely to develop mutual trust due to shared geographic origins (e.g. the same ancestral village), common livelihood sources, shared gender bonds, or some combination of these. These 'affinities' enhance solidarity and discourage free riding. A fair percentage of SHGs are formed of poor and socially disadvantaged women. An all-India survey of 2,750 women-only SHGs in 16 states, for example, found that in 41 per cent of

[9] There is a growing literature on SHGs. See e.g. EDA (2006), Tankha (2002), Nair (2005), APMAS (2007), Reddy and Manak (2005), Ramesh (2007), Fernandez (2005), NCAER (2008), and Deininger and Liu (2009), among others. Most of the major NGOs promoting SHGs have women-only groups, and one had 87 per cent women-only groups in 2001 (Tankha 2002: 20).

[10] The bank assesses SHG functioning in terms of its savings, regularity of meetings, internal lending, repayment record, book keeping, etc. I understand that this SHG-bank link-up is a uniquely Indian innovation (Ramesh 2007). By March 2001, 90 per cent of SHG members who had got bank loans through this linkage were women (Tankha 2002: 15).

[11] See also Ramesh (2007), Harper (2002), Fernandez (2005), and Kalpana (2005).

[12] Typically structured on Bangladesh's Grameen Bank model.

[13] Established in 1968, MYRADA works with poor and socially disadvantaged communities in three southern states of India—Andhra Pradesh, Karnataka, and Tamilnadu. Increasingly it has focused on women-only groups (Fernandez 2001: 142).

the groups the majority of members came from low-caste or tribal households; and in 42 per cent the majority came from landless families (Nirantar 2007). Half the members of the 214 women's SHGs surveyed by EDA (2006) across four states were below the poverty line, and 55 per cent belonged to the lowest castes or tribes. In NCAER's (2008) study of 961 SHGs (of various gender compositions) in six states, 60 per cent of the members were below the poverty line. NGOs such as MYRADA make special efforts to include the poor when promoting SHGs (Fenandez 2001). CFI alliances with women's SHGs would thus help bring not only more women into community forestry but also more economically and socially disadvantaged women.

Many of the women's SHGs have overcome the constraints of social norms and claimed gendered village spaces. When women attend SHG meetings regularly it creates a socially legitimate meeting space for them. With a growing scarcity of spaces that traditionally gave women some social privacy, such as watering points or wells outside the village, 'the privacy and security of an SHG meeting is a godsend', as Fernandez (2001: 142) from MYRADA puts it. He also notes that women fiercely guard this space and sometimes even impose a fine on the men who interrupt their meetings (Fernandez 2006).

A large proportion of women's SHGs have become advocacy groups. Some 30 per cent of those surveyed by EDA (2006) had worked for community betterment (improving the water supply, schools, health care and roads, and protecting natural resources), especially by putting pressure on village councils to complete long-standing projects.[14] Many groups have transcended class and caste divides and reached out to non-members and the poor (see Nair and Shah 2007, NCAER 2008, TARU 2007). And in several cases women SHG members have successfully won village council elections. Reddy and Manak (2005) note: 'SHGs not only empower its members but also wield a powerful political role as a group. At local village meetings, leaders of SHGs are often invited to attend and speak.'

In other words, a considerable proportion of women's SHGs today have exactly the features we need for strengthening women's hands in community forestry groups. In turn, such an alliance would benefit SHGs in several ways. Most are, as noted, involved in individual or family-based micro-enterprises and seldom deal with other aspects of women's needs, such as their access to local forests. A strategic linkage with CFIs would broaden the scope of collective activity among SHGs in women's interest, while simultaneously making CFIs more women inclusive. Such a link could thus empower poor women in both institutions.

In fact, already a few (albeit very few) NGOs have successfully established such links between SHGs and CFIs and created a critical mass of female presence in mixed-gender CFIs, thus influencing forestry decisions in women's favour. When I visited rural Karnataka (India) in 1998, for instance, the India Development Services (IDS) was encouraging women's savings groups to collect CFI

[14] See also Fernandez (2005), on similar achievements by MYRADA.

membership dues and join the CFIs in its sites. In some cases women had gone from house to house to persuade other women to join. As a result, in several of the villages where IDS worked, 80–90 per cent of the women in the savings groups were in the CFI general bodies and were quite vocal in mixed-gender meetings. Indeed some women who were not SHG members had also joined. As women in one of the villages told me, 'without SHG membership we would have received no information about village forest committees. We are now united as women as well.' MYRADA has gone even further in linking SHGs and forestry groups. In Karnataka's Uttara Kannada region, the NGO specifically formed SHGs of poor women in forest communities to increase women's involvement in CFIs. Initially involving 176 villages and later expanding to over 500, these SHGs not only participated in forest protection and decision-making, they also infused new life into the forest protection committees and enhanced their bargaining power vis-à-vis the forest department (see Box 10.2). The IDS and MYRADA experiences indicate that linking CFIs and SHGs can work. Of course, for wider geographic impact we need to go beyond experiments to a much more systematic expansion of such linkages.

Nepal does not have an exact equivalent to India's spreading SHG network, but it has women's groups founded around credit, as well as multipurpose amma samuhs and other types of rural women's associations promoted by NGOs, donors, and sometimes by women themselves, which go beyond credit. The Women's Empowerment Programme, for example, includes literacy and micro-enterprise development and during 1999–2001, 6,500 groups were formed under this initiative, each with 20 members on average (Ashe and Parrott 2001). An evaluation of the programme indicated that 45 per cent of the women were poor, but through group formation had gained access to credit as well as to literacy, in addition to having a greater say in family decisions (Ashe and Parrott 2001). Hence in Nepal too there is scope for strategic alliances between women's associations and CFIs.

In my survey, 68 per cent of the Gujarat villages and 91 per cent of Nepal's CFI sites have various types of women's associations, such as mahila mandals, amma samuhs, and savings groups.[15] These could potentially forge alliances with CFIs. Many have enhanced women's self-confidence and sense of group identity, improved male perceptions about women's capabilities (within the community and family), and weakened conservative social norms that earlier defined only the domestic as legitimate female space. Women's descriptions, cited below, are fairly typical:

> Initially men objected to our going to meetings. But our amma samuh helped men understand better. When we women became united in the amma samuh, men saw we were doing good work. That also helped. (Women to author in Tallo Goundonda CFI, Kaski district, Nepal, 1998)

[15] In Nepal, 60 per cent of the CFIs had amma samuhs, and a fair proportion of the others had some form of women's savings group.

Box 10.2. Linking SHGs and VFCs: the MYRADA experience

Narrated to author by Mr B. R. Bhat, then project officer, Uttara Kannada forestry project

* * *

Around 1993–94 we found that the village forest committees (VFCs) in Uttara Kannada had few active women. Although in nominal terms 3 out of 11 members in the VFC managing committee (MC) had to be women, they seldom came to MC meetings or spoke up. In fact the meetings themselves were irregular and poorly attended. Also the VFCs did not include the very poor who were dependent on the forest for their livelihoods, such as selling firewood and NWFPs. The forest department (FD) gave out rights to collect NWFPs to private contractors. The forester and male members of the VFC managing committees basically ran the whole show.

MYRADA felt a solution lay in linking women's SHGs to the VFCs. Initially the FD resisted the idea, saying that involving SHG members in VFCs would dilute the goals of forest conservation and degrade the forest if SHG members begin to use them for livelihoods. MYRADA finally convinced the FD that this would not happen and the linkage would benefit the forest. There were some good officers in the FD who finally agreed to fund a pilot project for trying this out.

MYRADA then made SHGs of poor landless women in the villages that had VFCs. SHG women had to become members of VFCs. They were also encouraged to attend the MC meetings which were open to all general body members. This led to several positive results: It helped regularize VFC meetings. SHG women would come and wait to attend for the monthly meeting to begin. This forced the VFCs to hold the meetings. A proper agenda began to be set for the meetings and minutes kept. Women who sold firewood from the forest insisted that they be called 'headloaders' and not 'thieves'. It provided feedback to the forest department on what was happening with the forest resources. The villagers also helped the FD fight forest fires on several occasions. Using their greater bargaining power, the VFCs were able to renegotiate the terms of forest use with the FD, from a 50–50 division of the timber extracted to 25% (for the FD) and 75% (for the villagers), in return for the protection work done by the community. The FD also agreed to stop contracting out NWFP collection in villages which had a VFC–SHG linkage and to provide training to SHG workers in bamboo weaving (since bamboo was a local forest product). Around 1994–95 the project was working in 176 villages. Each village had one VFC and around 4–5 SHGs. Each SHG had about 18–20 women. Now we cover over 500 villages in terms of the SHG–VFC linkage.

The SHGs and VFCs also have federations which are autonomous of one another but have worked together on occasion, such as in fighting forest fires and preventing the commercial cutting of trees.

Men used to shut us up and say we shouldn't speak. Women learned to speak up in a *sangathan* (group). Earlier we couldn't speak up even at home. Now we can be more assertive and also go out. I am able to help other women gain confidence as well. (Woman leader of savings group to author, Vejpur village, Sabarkantha, Gujarat, 1999)

There were one or two men who objected to their wives attending our meetings and said you can't go. But when our women's association came to their aid, the men let their wives go. (Women to author in Almavadi village, Bharuch, Gujarat, 1998)

Women used to hide from us initially, but now they have so much confidence they feel they can even teach the new workers in our organization. (Male NGO activist to author, Uttarakhand hills, 1998)

These experiences echo those of many rural women's groups across South Asia, namely that women's collective strength and visible contributions, along with external agent support, can loosen restrictive gender norms, alter male perceptions about women's abilities, and increase social acceptance of women in public roles (see also Agarwal 1994, 1997c).[16] What has been little tried, however, and what I am suggesting here, is linking such all-women collectivities and mixed-gender CFIs.

Since these women's associations and CFIs are both village based, the membership may overlap to some extent. For a *strategic* alliance, however, we would need to establish a more formal link between the two institutional forms, and not just between women in their individual capacities. A strategic alliance between CFIs and SHGs/women's associations could also bridge the deepening gender divide which I found during my fieldwork in India—women's savings groups were widely seen as 'women's groups' and forestry groups as 'men's groups', by both men and women in the village, even though forests are a community resource.

2.3 Group Identities and Public Deliberation

Strategically linking SHGs/women's associations and CFIs could prove to be a foundational step for increasing women's numbers and voice in CFIs and bringing the energy of SHGs into CFI functioning. To gain effective voice as a group and not just as individuals, however, CFI women representatives need to move beyond numbers and personal opinion or interest. Indeed, in recent years, a notable body of feminist political theory has emphasized the importance of a deliberative process for identifying women's interests, and sorting out differences arising from heterogeneity within groups.[17] But for this we require forums for

[16] Of course, these approaches can loosen only certain social norms, so that women are accepted as members of public decision-making forums and even in leadership positions. But some norms, such as the gender division of domestic work, may still remain largely inflexible. Similarly, women's effective participation could be obstructed by historically entrenched structural and cultural inequalities of caste and class, and not only of gender. And women's greater participation in CFIs alone is unlikely to notably improve theirs or their family's personal endowment position. More wide-ranging measures will be needed for bringing this about, as discussed in Agarwal (1994, 2003). Moreover, norms and perceptions are also shaped by institutions beyond the village, including educational and religious bodies and the media.

[17] See e.g. Fraser (2005), Young (2000), and Mansbridge (1990), among others. There is also a substantial literature on deliberative democracy: see e.g. Elster (1998), Dryzek (2002), Benhabib (1996), Young (2000), Fishkin and Laslett (2003), among others, and references therein. Young (1997a, 2000), however, broadens the idea of deliberative democracy to what she terms 'communicative democracy', placing particular emphasis on communication as a means of bridging differences. Also see Sen (2009) on public reasoning. As Sen points out (2009: 331), India has had a long tradition of public deliberation going back to the sixth century BC. See also the discussion on gram sabhas in Chapter 11.

deliberation in which information can be shared, conflicts resolved, priorities arrived at, strategies outlined, and solidarity forged.

What form can such a forum take? One could be as a sub-group consisting only of women EC members constituted within mixed-CFIs. Such a subgroup could first meet separately to discuss women's forest-related concerns, and then strategically place those concerns in the full EC meeting. This could also enable female EC members to better represent women's interests within the CFI. This is somewhat similar to the function that a women's caucus serves in parliament, for instance. A village sub-group could go further, however, by also holding consultative meetings with non-EC women members to identify their concerns. Another way forward could be for SHGs linked to CFIs to set up such discussion forums, both with village women and among themselves. In both forms there could be many gains from deliberation.

First, EC women need such a forum for sharing with other village women information about discussions and decisions taken within the EC. At present, such information is mostly conveyed informally and incidentally, when women happen to meet each other in the fields or near the village well, or on a social visit. The forum can also become a channel by which village women, and especially the poor, convey to the EC women the difficulties they face due to firewood or fodder shortages, or lack of livelihood options. Such sharing or 'communication across difference' (Young 2000: 108) could lead to 'understanding across difference' (Young 1997a: 52), and so enhance the chances of the better-off women EC members being persuaded to take up the cause of the poor. Even where people are already aware of each other's circumstances (since rather little remains hidden in a village), if poor women explicitly express their problems they are more likely to bring moral and social pressure on the better-off EC members to prioritize poor women's needs.

Second, through deliberation EC women can sort out differences among themselves, such as differences between women from landed households who, although they have a strong interest in forest products, can live with relatively strict rules of forest closure, and women from landless households who lack the private resources for alleviating their daily shortages of firewood and fodder.[18] An open discussion could have several beneficial outcomes. The most positive would be if the better-off women become convinced enough to take up the cause of the landless, or, as Young (1997a: 61) puts it, if the better endowed 'transform their preferences according to public-minded ends' or '[discover] answers that integrate the interests of minorities'.[19] My conversation in 1998 with two CFI women

[18] Public deliberation could thus help communities overcome the divisiveness of hierarchical heterogeneity and move toward a shared understanding of their collective interests. Here the idea is that communities can *arrive* at this understanding; they are not presumed to have prior common interest, as is embedded in the idea of 'community-as-shared-understanding' that Agrawal (1999b: 101) correctly criticizes.

[19] See also Sunstein (1991), Mansbridge (1990), Young (1993), and Sen (2009).

who were also members of a woman's self-help group in Malwadi village, Karnataka, is illustrative:

> We discussed how benefits should be shared, whether we should differentiate between rich, poor, and middle-income households. We are poor. The poor often have no employment, so they need other sources of income, such as forest products for making leaf plates and pickle. They also extract gum. We have enough firewood and agricultural wage employment for now, but what about later? We have to discuss all this, and seek to resolve our differences.

However, even if the outcome of deliberation goes against the immediate needs of some and in favour of others (since deliberation does not imply that everyone will agree with the decisions taken), the very fact of deliberation—of being able to express one's views—could make it easier for those losing out to reconcile with the decision. The process of open discussion would also give greater legitimacy to the final outcome, making for better overall cooperation and institutional sustainability. Although no doubt there are limits to the extent to which deliberation can bridge the chasm of social and economic inequalities and associated power differentials, at the very least it can make these differences more transparent and help identify potential spaces for strategic cooperation among women.

Third, without prior interaction the views women express in EC meetings tend to reflect a mix of personal and general concerns. A forum for deliberation can help women representatives form a collective view and arrive at *group* priorities about what forest products they want extracted, the timing of forest opening days, which species to plant, and related matters. It would also help the group work out an agreed strategy on how collective interests and priorities would be expressed outside the group, and who would be the group's spokesperson(s) and representative(s). EC women would be more effective in mixed-gender CFIs when speaking in a unified voice than if speaking as individuals without prior consultation. Over time, forums of deliberation could also help the women build solidarity and a sense of collective identity that can benefit them on other counts, including in dealing with government institutions.

Fourth, the process of open discussion can help village women feel self-confident enough to express their needs in public where they might have hesitated otherwise, or simply 'adapted' their preferences to what they thought was possible,[20] or failed to state their real preferences in public to protect themselves from criticism if those preferences went against the popular grain (what Kuran 1995 calls 'preference falsification').[21] Discussion within women's groups to arrive at common concerns and priorities can help overcome preference adaptation or

[20] See also Sen (1984) and Nussbaum (2000) on adapted preferences, and Sunstein (1993) on how people's preferences are shaped by existing endowments.

[21] This can misdirect public policies, if policy makers assume that what people state in public is what they really want or think.

preference falsification, which women in disadvantaged positions may especially be prone to in male-dominated forums.

Can high social or economic inequality within the group restrict deliberation itself? There is substantial discussion within political theory on whether deliberation is possible among unequals. Some authors hold that equality is a necessary condition for deliberative (or communicative) democracy to work.[22] Fraser (1990: 65), for example, argues that '. . . it is a necessary condition for participatory parity that systemic social inequalities be eliminated. This does not mean that everyone must have exactly the same income, but it does require the sort of rough equality that is inconsistent with systemically-generated relations of dominance and subordination.' Socio-economic equality would no doubt help, but it is debatable whether it is a *necessary* condition for meaningful deliberation. To begin with, social and economic hierarchy does not fully overlap. As I had noted earlier, poor, low-caste rural women in South Asia are often less bound by tradition, especially if they form a group, and are more able to (and more compelled to) break the bounds of 'appropriate' feminine behaviour that tends to bind middle-class, upper-caste rural women.[23] External agent support can empower the disadvantaged as well, and give them voice, despite inequality. Most importantly, however, individual vulnerabilities can be overcome if the disadvantaged form a group. There are many examples where a group of socio-economically disadvantaged people, *acting collectively* in their own interest, have been able to overcome individual disadvantage and make an impact, despite hierarchical socio-economic contexts.[24]

Even as they currently operate, CFIs do occasionally use public deliberation to resolve conflicts of interest between the poor and better-off households, or settle disputes between villages, or arrive at more consensual rules that women might accept. There are cases in my survey, for instance, where rules have been made more lenient after discussion, for pragmatic reasons: 'If we don't adapt the rules the poor will steal anyway.' There are also villages (albeit rare ones) in the survey where deliberation led the economically better-off EC members to make exceptions for poor households, such as allowing them to graze their goats on the far side of a protected hill, while banning such grazing for the better-off villagers, or letting the poor pay a lower price for grass. Similarly, there are cases where a forested village has allowed a forestless one to join its CFI, when the latter discussed its problems. Some inter-village conflicts have also been resolved through discussion, for instance where people living in neighbouring villages in Gujarat stopped stealing from each others' protected forest, after holding a joint

22 See, among others, Fraser (1990), Young (1993), and some contributors in the volume edited by Benhabib (1996).

23 See also Prasad and Haranath (2004), who found that dalit (lower-caste) women who were village council chairpersons in Andhra Pradesh had more interrelationships with their office bearers, other officials, and villagers, than did upper-caste women chairpersons.

24 See also Sunstein (1991) and Young (1993, 2000). Young (1993) recognizes that 'group representation increases the chances of achieving just decisions [for the poor]'.

gram sabha—a meeting of villagers from both villages. And, in earlier chapters we have noted instances where, when men consulted village women, or when women spoke up during public discussions, the decisions changed: for instance more consensual forest use rules emerged; or men ended up accepting women's suggestions about when to extract firewood or fodder, or what distribution method (equal bundles, plot auctions, etc.) to follow. At the same time, these cases of conflict resolution are occasional, and not the result of a systematic institutional mechanism set in place for listening to the voices of the poor or of women. If women were to emerge as a unified force through deliberations first conducted outside the context of EC meetings, they would have more bargaining power within the EC, and their voices would carry more weight. It would also help them better represent village women and strengthen their links with women in SHGs (or equivalent women's associations).

These processes of deliberation have been discussed thus far in the context of alliances between CFIs and women's associations, conceptualized as horizontal links within villages or clusters of villages. But women's bargaining power would be enhanced to much greater extent if they had vertical reach beyond the village. An innovative institutional form for providing such reach to non-governmental village-level institutions is through a federation, constituted of a network of community-based organizations.

3. EXTENDING VERTICAL REACH: FEDERATIONS

Broadly, a federation is an association of organizations, formed to realize economies of scale and to provide strength as an interest group, while retaining the advantages of remaining autonomous (Nair 2005). In South Asia, federations of self-help groups and forestry groups have become an important way of building links, bottom up.[25] Typically federations link the same form of institution—horizontally and vertically. For instance, SHG federations connect SHGs while forestry federations connect CFIs. As discussed further below, however, single focus federations could be substantially strengthened if they established strategic links with federations which had a different focus.

3.1 SHG Federations

There are an estimated 69,000 SHG federations, 89 per cent in southern India, constituted variously at the village, panchayat, or district level, with one at the state level—that in Andhra Pradesh (APMAS 2007). The federations vary in size from 10–40 SHGs to a few thousand, including one with 33,000 SHGs

[25] On federations of SHGs, see especially APMAS (2007), Tankha (2002), Nair (2005), Heijden (2006), EDA (2006), Reddy and Manak (2005), and WINROCK (2006).

(APMAS 2007). A typical SHG federation is multi-tiered—the lowest tier being a cluster of village-level SHGs forming a village organization. Several clusters/ village organizations, with one or two representatives from each SHG, may then come together to form an apex body. Federating provides SHGs with bargaining power vis-à-vis the government and the market, as well as the capacity to sustain.

Typically, SHG federations have been promoted by NGOs, a process which began in the early 1990s, aimed variously at building a more just society, reducing poverty, empowering poor women, and moving toward more self-reliant village communities (Tankha 2002). Apart from financial benefits, many SHGs focus on women's social and political empowerment, and have been effective as pressure groups, especially within the community. A rare study by Heijden (2006), which systematically compared a sample of federated and non-federated SHGs in eastern Uttar Pradesh (India), found that members of federated SHGs were more economically, politically, and socially empowered than those in non-federated SHGs. A larger percentage of federated SHG members, for instance, knew about bank loan services and government schemes; had participated in family and community decision-making; had information on and access to Panchayati Raj schemes and services; knew when village-level meetings were held and attended them; and had brought collective pressure on government officials for village infrastructure development and implementing welfare schemes (such as widows' benefits).[26] Notably, though, greater awareness and access to various public schemes and events among federated SHGs was a result of discussion, information-sharing, and strategizing in federation meetings, that is, it was a result of public deliberation.

Another striking feature of many women's SHG federations has been their ability to reach across class. Even when constituted of the less than poor, women's SHG federations, especially in south India, are helping very poor women in various ways. In 7,000 villages of Andhra Pradesh, for instance, they have been buying foodgrains in bulk and selling them to poor members at a nominal price or on short-term loan (Nair and Shah 2007). Many SHGs also purchase other necessities in bulk at low cost and loan them to poor women to tide them over income troughs and so enable income-smoothing.[27] A recent study found gains in consumption and nutrition across classes, even among the poorest households.[28] Women's SHG federations further empower women by the sheer strength of numbers. As some groups in Andhra Pradesh told me in 1999: 'when we turn up a thousand strong at a local fair, we don't have to say a word. Our strength is there for all to see.' However, barring a few initiatives, such as

[26] On this see also APMAS (2007) and EDA (2006).

[27] Personal observation in Andhra Pradesh and Karnataka in 1998–99. See also TARU (2007).

[28] Deininger and Liu (2009), based on an analysis of two rounds of panel data for 2400 households in Andhra Pradesh, find that households which had been SHG members for 2.5 to 3 years gained in consumption, nutritional intake, and asset accumulation; and even the poorest households benefited on these counts.

those taken by IDS and MYRADA in Karnataka state, SHG federations do not focus on natural resources such as forests,[29] which have their own federations.

3.2 CFI Federations

In contrast to federations of SHGs, those of community forestry groups in India are fewer and less geographically widespread (they are found only in a few states). Typically catalysed by NGOs in India,[30] some of them are constituted for advocacy, and others for marketing non-wood forest products directly, by removing middle men and helping members obtain better prices.[31] Some CFI federations are formally registered, others are informal bodies. The same is true of the CFIs that are members of federations—some have registered as JFM groups, others not.[32] In my study area in Gujarat, both AKRSP(I) and VIKSAT have formed federations which are formally registered and constituted of CFIs that have also typically registered (or are seeking registration) as JFM societies, while SARTHI's federation—Panchmahals Van Parishad—is unregistered and informal.[33]

Most forest federations in India, like most SHG federations, are confined to village clusters or to blocks; only some grow to district-level. State-level federations are rare although market linkages for the sale of forest products can extend to the whole state, as with the Orissa Jungle Manch (SIDA 2004: 8). But unlike SHG federations which by their very composition involve women, forest federations can reproduce the gender exclusions of the CFIs of which they are constituted. Some mandate women's inclusion to limited extent: for instance, a JFM federation in the Jhadol district of Rajasthan state (India) requires that 3 out of 15 members be women, making up one-fifth of the membership (Bose et al. 2006). An NGO in Orissa requires the inclusion of two women in the Executive Committee of each federation. Federations promoting gender-equal membership, such as SAKSHAM in Gujarat, are recent and uncommon. This is a network of 12 block-level federations, in which half of the 24 members representing the 12 federations in the network have to be women (VIKSAT 2007).

Nepal's federation of community forest users (FECOFUN), formed in 1995,[34] is a striking contrast to the varied and relatively small-scale CFI federations in India. FECOFUN is unusual in its scale (it is national-level), its democratic

[29] These two NGOs have promoted women's participation in forest management through SHGs.

[30] See Underwood (1997) and VIKSAT (2007) for CFI federations formed in Gujarat by AKRSP(I) and VIKSAT (2007) respectively; SIDA (2004) for Orissa; Hobley and Sheilds (2000) for Karnataka; and Bose et al. (2006) for forest federations in several states.

[31] See e.g. SIDA (2004) for Orissa, and Singh et al. (2005) for all-India examples.

[32] In Gujarat, even self-initiated groups are often registered under JFM, but this is less common in other states. A federation of self-initiated forest protection groups in Orissa state—the Orissa Jungle Manch—for instance, has remained autonomous of government linkages (SIDA 2004).

[33] Personal communication, Dhansingh Bhai Rathore, SARTHI, 2009.

[34] I draw especially from Britt (1997, 2002) for the description of FECOFUN's organizational structure, and Ojha et al. (2007a) and Bhattarai (2007) for its activities and advocacy.

structure (representatives are elected), and in its attempt at gender inclusiveness (its constitution, as noted, mandates gender parity in committee membership and office bearing). About 13,500 of Nepal's 14,700 CFIs today are members of FECOFUN, representing some nine million forest users and making it the largest civil society organization in the country, covering almost one-third of its population (Bhola Bhattarai, FECOFUN, personal communication, 2010). Its objective is to link forest user groups country-wide and so strengthen their role and voice in forest policy (Britt 2007). Within each district, individual CFIs are linked to district-level committees, and elected representatives from each district then form a national council and executive body. It provides an institutional structure for horizontal and vertical linkages and a means by which local organizations can increase their bargaining power, especially vis-à-vis the government.

The idea of forming such a federation emerged in 1993 at a national workshop in Kathmandu, in which 41 representatives from 40 forest user groups (CFIs) in 28 districts participated. Following the workshop's success, the participants floated the idea of a national-level organization. FECOFUN is backed both financially and strategically by many international organizations and NGOs. This support and its grassroots reach have given it considerable clout with the forest department. In this sense it is both a bottom-up and a top-down network. Its first general assembly, held in Kathmandu in March 1996, was described vividly by Charla Britt (1997:1), who attended it:

> During three intensive days, 94 men and 74 women from 38 districts, and nine observers from seven further districts, worked to amend and ratify the FECOFUN constitution, select a national executive committee, and plan future activities. Sessions went late into the night. Men spoke, women spoke, and babies cried. At times the floor gave way to complete chaos. It was crowded, it was hot, it was noisy, it was messy. I was engrossed by the interactions—the speaking of minds and sharing of ideas.

After extensive debate, and helped by the unified voice of the women attending the meeting for drafting the organization's constitution, it was decided to include 50 per cent women at all levels of the federation, including on all its committees, with half of the four main office bearers (president, vice president, secretary, treasurer) also being women (Britt 2002: 251–3).

The organization represents the interests of forest users to the forest bureaucracy and even parliament; familiarizes the users with their rights and responsibilities toward forest resources; mediates disputes among CFIs, and between them and the forest department or with multinational companies interested in forest resources; and promotes an understanding of democratic functioning. It has negotiated with the government on forest policy, and (on occasion) successfully resisted government attempts to restrict the rights of CFI members by skilfully using memorandums, mass demonstrations, and the media. In the recent past, FECOFUN was also a significant participant in Nepal's democracy movement (Bhattarai 2007, Britt 2007). FECOFUN's experience provides important lessons and scope for optimism about the potential of forming large-scale federations in India and many other countries.

On gender, however, the outcomes are mixed. On the one hand, the emphasis on women's inclusion in FECOFUN decision-making, even nominally, has helped propagate the idea that women can be office bearers. As we had noted, this is one of the likely reasons why in Nepal many CFIs have female office bearers while Gujarat's CFIs have virtually none. FECOFUN also has links with and has, on occasion, collaborated with HIMAWANTI, which was formed around the same time to enhance women's voice in community forestry, and which today has a Nepal chapter (with 200 all-women CFIs as members across 25 districts) and a regional chapter covering four other South Asian countries.[35] On the other hand, the concerns expressed by Britt (1997: 18) that 'serious questions remain about how to adequately negotiate differences—especially in terms of class, caste and gender'—suggest that even in FECOFUN women have to emerge from being a nominal presence to effective participants.[36] As my study shows, on the ground women's participation in Nepal's CFIs is only occasionally empowered.

Forest federations in India and Nepal are important examples of institutional alliances within green governance, which provide rural populations with representation beyond the village, and bargaining power vis-à-vis the State and the market (for forest products). FECOFUN, in particular, has features both unique to it and in common with other forest federations in South Asia. Uniquely, its national character gives it substantial clout with the forest bureaucracy and political representatives, and its focus on a single resource—forests—concentrates its energies to good effect. In India, forest-related federations rarely extend beyond the district, have limited clout with the forest department, and do not mandate gender parity. Indeed, both FECOFUN in Nepal and forest federations in India need to find ways of incorporating women's interests more effectively. Both countries have different strengths on this count.

India, in my view, has enormous potential for forging alliances between women's SHG federations and forest federations, to broaden the scope of both. The country has strong SHG federations in several states, but rather weak forest federations. The latter would clearly gain by an alliance with SHG federations in at least two significant ways: first, forest federations would become more gender inclusive, and second they would expand in membership and reach, and so be able to lobby more effectively with the forest bureaucracy. In turn, women's SHG federations would gain by improving village women's access to a resource that is critical for their lives and livelihoods. Since the alliance is conceptualized as a *strategic* one, rather than one of institutional merger, there need be no diluting of the agendas of either SHGs or CFIs as a result. Figure 10.1 illustrates potential links.

Linkages between SHG federations and CFI federations have been attempted in a limited way by some NGOs in Karnataka. SHG federations and forest

[35] HIMAWANTI and FECOFUN have done advocacy together on certain issues relating to forest users' rights as well as Nepal's democracy movement (information gleaned from ICIMOD staff and meetings with HIMAWANTI's office bearers, but see also Bhatia 2001).

[36] See also Ojha et al. (2007b) on the need for strengthening local accountability within FECOFUN.

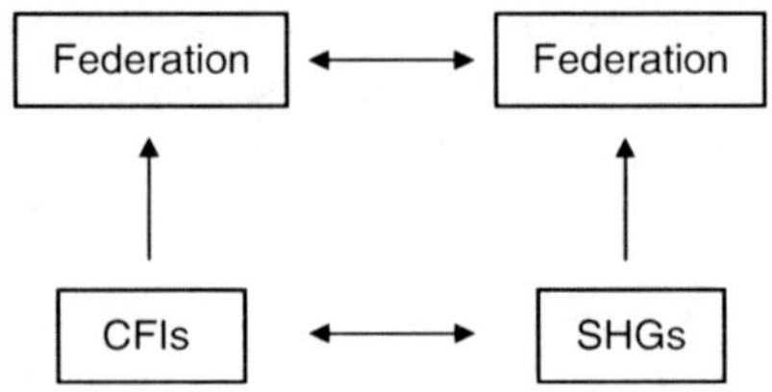

Figure 10.1. A schema of lateral and vertical alliances

federations constituted by MYRADA, for instance, have collaborated on several occasions for tackling forest fires, river flooding, and commercial logging. Similarly, the federation of voluntary organizations for rural development in Uttara Kannada (Karnataka)—a network of 21 NGOs—works closely with SHG and forest federations at the district level.[37] Nepal, by contrast, has in FECOFUN a strong CFI federation, but it has nothing quite equivalent to India's SHG federations. There is scope, however, for village women's associations, such as amma samuhs, to be constituted into federations and to strengthen links with FECOFUN. HIMAWANTI's association with FECOFUN could also be strengthened.

A successful linkage of federations with different strengths would not only enhance their institutional effectiveness as civil society organizations, but could also prove to be an effective means of lobbing the upper echelons of the government to address the issues of domestic energy, the marketing of non-wood forest products, and related concerns of village communities in general, and poor women in particular.

4. CONCLUDING COMMENTS

Associative connections and strategic alliances between local civil society groups can go a long way to enhance women's effective numbers, voice, and influence in decision-making within CFIs, and within the community. In this chapter we have seen many encouraging examples of such alliances. At the same time, just as comprehensive solutions for many local problems cannot be found locally, so solutions for many local problems cannot be found solely within the purview of civil society organizations. For instance, although village women, by their greater presence in CFI decision-making, can negotiate some changes—such as persuading CFIs to extract more firewood—they are less able to shift the common perception that cooking energy is mainly woman's concern to a recognition that it is a community concern. Strategic alliances between women in CFIs and

[37] Personal communication, Mr B. R. Bhat, project officer, MYRADA. Another organizational form being tried by MYRADA is that of Resource Centres which provide a range of services. SHGs and other community-based organizations can become members (Fernandez 2004).

women in SHGs could well bring about such a recognition, but it may not lead to an effective practical response if the community has inadequate material means to implement potential solutions. To establish firewood plantations, for instance, requires community control over land that can be so used.[38] To make clean fuel, such as biogas, available and affordable for the poor, requires technical and financial investment in designing suitable models and their promotion. More sophisticated technology shifts, such as to solar cookers, would require even more substantial investments in design, dissemination, and maintenance. Some of this may be possible through local government such as village councils, but much of it would depend on support from higher levels of government. To develop clean fuel technologies that can be used by households at the bottom of the pyramid, for instance, research institutions must be funded adequately by government departments and planning commissions. Similarly, expertise from beyond the local would be needed to provide the wide range of technical and economic information that impinges on long-term forest management, such as information on the resilience of forest ecosystems, ways of increasing biodiversity, assessing how much biomass can be extracted sustainably, and so on. There are also issues which impact locally but whose resolution requires extra-local government interactions. The membership criteria for CFI general bodies and ECs, for instance, are not formulated locally but at the state-level in India and the national-level in Nepal. Environmental and energy policy priorities are similarly established at higher echelons of government and bureaucracy, again at the state and national levels.

How can village women engage with these different levels of government? Weaving a web of strategic alliances that connect local village organizations which have similar goals is a bottom-up measure for effective engagement with government. Federations, for example, provide some rungs of the ladder by which civil society organizations, inclusive of village women, can reach and influence the upper levels of government. But are government institutions prepared for such an engagement? If not, what additional rungs need to be built to enhance governmental responsiveness and accountability? For addressing these questions we now turn to the concluding chapter.

[38] A case in point is Prosipos Juliflora, which grows fast even in semi-arid climates and provides firewood, but has thorns so that animals don't eat the new leaves. This has been planted selectively and successfully in parts of Rajasthan and Gujarat in north-west India and has done much to reduce firewood shortages. But growing it requires setting aside land such that it does not damage the region's ecology.

APPENDIX 10.1

Summary of Siginificant Gender Results

Appendix 10.1: Summary of significant gender results[a]

Dependent variable	Gujarat	Nepal
Participation (Chapter 5)		
Percentage EC meetings with no women (as a measure of the likelihood of at least one EC woman attending meetings)	*All districts*: 25–<33% W relative to <25% W ⇒ greater likelihood of at least one woman attending EC meetings. There is a 36-point difference in the % of meetings with no women between ECs with <25% W and 25–<33% W	*All districts*: 25–<33% W relative to <25% W ⇒ greater likelihood of at least one woman attending EC meetings. There is a 37-point difference in the % of meetings with no women between ECs with <25% W and 25–33% W
Female attendance rate (average attendance rate of EC women per meeting)	*All districts*: 25–<33% W relative to <25% W ⇒ higher female attendance rate. Attendance rate with 25–<33% W is significantly higher than with <25% W by 0.35. Threshold effect not clear, but critical mass could lie between ≥25% and <33% W.	*All districts*: 25–<33% W relative to <25% W ⇒ higher female attendance rate. Attendance rate with 25–<33% W is significantly higher than with <25% W by 0.23. Threshold effect clear, and critical mass lies between ≥25% and <33% W.
EC women speaking up in EC meetings	*All districts*: higher the % W ⇒ women more likely to speak up at meetings. Also with ≥33% W relative to <33% W ⇒ women more likely to speak up	*All districts*: higher the % W ⇒ women more likely to speak up at meetings Also with ≥33% W relative to <33% W ⇒ women more likely to speak up
EC women holding office (likelihood of each EC woman being office bearer)	Too few cases of female office bearers, hence not tested	*All districts*: higher the % W ⇒ women more likely to be office bearers. Threshold effect clear: critical mass lies near 25% W, but likelihood of women holding office continues to increase till the EC reaches gender parity
EC men holding office (likelihood of each EC man being office bearer)		*All districts*: Gender composition of EC has no impact.
Percentage current female EC members who have been office bearers		*All districts*: ≥33% W relative to <33% W ⇒ EC more likely to have had female office bearers

(continued)

Appendix 10.1: Summary of significant gender results (Continued)

Dependent variable	Gujarat	Nepal
Gender gap in office bearing: % male EC members who have held office minus % female EC members who have held office		*All districts*: $\geq$33% W relative to <33% W $\Rightarrow$ less gender gap in office bearing
Forest use rules (Chapter 6)		
Aggregate strictness index	*All districts*: gender composition not significant *Narmada/Bharuch*: >2 W relative to $\leq$2 W $\Rightarrow$ stricter rules	*All districts*: All-W vs. Other $\Rightarrow$ stricter rules *Gorkha/Dhading*: All-W vs. Other $\Rightarrow$ stricter rules
	Panchmahals: >2 W relative to $\leq$2 W $\Rightarrow$ less strict rules *Sabarkantha*: >2 W relative to $\leq$2 W $\Rightarrow$ stricter rules	*Baglung/Parbat*: gender composition not significant
Product-wise strictness of rules	*All districts*: Twigs collection: gender composition not significant Drywood cutting: >2 W relative to $\leq$2 W $\Rightarrow$ stricter rules	*All districts*: Twigs collection: gender composition not significant Grass cutting: All-W vs. Other $\Rightarrow$ stricter rules
	Grass cutting: gender composition not significant	Tree fodder: gender composition not significant Grazing: All-W vs. Other $\Rightarrow$ stricter rules
	Panchmahals: grazing: >2 W relative to $\leq$2 W $\Rightarrow$ less strict rules[b]	
Rule violations (Chapter 7)		
Total no. of violations per year of CFI protection	*All districts*: gender composition not significant	*All districts*: All-W vs. Other $\Rightarrow$ fewer violations per year of CFI functioning
% violations by women	*All districts:* decreasing with increase in CFI years; gender composition not significant	None of the explanatory variables were significant
% violations by men	*All districts*: increasing with increase in CFI years; gender composition not significant	None of the explanatory variables were significant

Forest condition (Chapter 8)		
Indicators of forest condition and improvement in condition	*All districts*: Researcher's index: >2 W relative to ≤2 W ⇒ better forest condition Forest canopy: gender composition not significant.	*All districts*: Forest regeneration: All-W vs. Other ⇒ greater likelihood of very good forest regeneration Forest canopy: All-W vs. Other ⇒ greater likelihood of improvement in forest canopy or maintaining thick canopy cover.
	% forest area degraded: higher % W ⇒ less % area degraded Forest condition change: >2 W relative to ≤2 W ⇒ greater likelihood of some or substantial improvement in category. Result only indicative, since marginal effect is not significant.	
	Panchmahals: >2 W relative to ≤2 W ⇒ higher researcher's index, better forest canopy, lower % area degraded, and greater likelihood of some or substantial category improvement in forest condition. Gender composition is thus significant for all indicators.	
Firewood and fodder shortages (Chapter 9)		
Firewood shortages	*All districts*: ≥33% W relative to <33% W ⇒ less likelihood of shortages	*All districts*: Gender composition not significant
Fodder shortages	*All districts*: higher the % W ⇒ less the likelihood of shortages	*All districts*: Gender composition not significant

Notes: W = women. % W = percentage of women in the EC. < means less than; > means more than, and ⇒ means leads to or implies
≤2 W means two women or less in the EC; >2 W means more than 2 women in the EC.
<25% W means less than 25% women in the EC; 25–<33% W means between 25% or more to less than 33% EC women; and ≥33% W means 33% or more women in the EC.

[a] Results for aspects of gender, other than the EC's gender composition, are also significant in some cases, but they are not summarized here, such as results relating to the percentage of EC women who are landless, EC women's average age, and the presence of a women's association in the village or community (for details see the relevant chapters).

[b] The equation is not reproduced in the book.

11

Engaging with Government

Extending the Web

Where was the village *adhyaksha* (chairperson) when the forest department evicted us? Where was the collector? Where was the MLA?

(Tribal women displaced from forest land to the author, Karnataka, 1998)[1]

The outcry of these tribal women, evicted from the forest which had been their home for generations, underlines two failed aspects of government–citizen relations. The first is the failure of a government to be the paternalistic father figure that many in developing countries expected it to be in the immediate aftermath of independence from colonialism.[2] The second is the failure of a government to re-establish with its most disadvantaged citizens the kind of connection that is embedded in the idea of a modern democratic state—a connection based on interaction and interdependence rather than on paternalistic largesse toward dependants. Village women, as we have seen, are already stepping out from under the paternal cloak and seeking engagement with and accountability from government. But is the government able to so engage, to face such interrogation and become accountable? How can linkages be established between the government and representatives of poor rural women? What kinds of strategic alliances do we need in order to move from paternalism to partnership? Without claiming to provide definitive answers, this concluding chapter explores some of the complexities involved in addressing these questions and offers reflections on possible ways of moving forward.[3] Our focus remains on environmental issues, although both the questions and the answers could apply to many aspects of policy-making and implementation.

[1] The collector in India is the main administrative representative of the government at the district level; an MLA is the member of the legislative assembly.

[2] In South Asia, the notion of the state as the *mai-bap*—the mother and father of citizen's welfare—is also widespread.

[3] Some of the lessons of this chapter and the previous one would also be relevant for other local associations. In relation to village watershed committees, for instance, Baumann (2000) raises similar concerns about the need for mechanisms that would lead the government to respond.

1. WHY IS ENGAGEMENT WITH GOVERNMENT IMPORTANT?

To address the interrelated concerns of rural women and green governance, of equity and efficiency, the role of civil society organizations and their interlinked web of networks is critical, but not enough. In large part, civil society groups are the takers and not the makers of public policies that affect their constituencies. The makers are usually institutions of government—elected local bodies, the bureaucracy, and the legislature. Engaging with government is thus of central importance since the policies that affect rural women (and men) are complex and framed at many different levels, far away from their villages.[4]

Consider, for instance, energy and forest policies. Framing an energy policy and provisioning for energy sufficiency (including cooking energy sufficiency) can involve numerous ministries of the government. In India it involves the ministries of coal, power, new and renewable energy, petroleum and natural gas, environment and forests, and finance, among others. Even for providing cooking energy security to the rural poor, several ministries must participate to deliver the required basket of diverse energy sources, such as firewood, natural gas, biogas, kerosene, LPG, and electricity. The suggestions of different ministries must then be integrated by the Planning Commission of India for framing an energy policy for the country.[5] After this, the cabinet has to ratify the policy and the Ministry of Finance has to underwrite the costs. A similar coordination between ministries is required for implementing the policy. To establish tree plantations for increasing firewood availability, for instance, land must be allocated—this could come from the forest department, or the ministry of rural development, or the village council, or all of them in some measure. Similarly, for designing biogas plants and energy-efficient cooking stoves that are adapted to the needs of different regions, different climates, and differently endowed households, not only would inputs be needed from the Ministry of Science and Technology, but also from the Ministries of Rural Development and Panchayati Raj for testing and shaping the technologies to user needs. Without such administrative, technical and financial coordination and community outreach, an effective delivery of rural energy to women is unlikely.

A comparison of China's highly successful National Improved Stove Programme launched in the 1980s, with India's rather poorly performing one, initiated around the same time, illustrates this well. The Chinese Programme aimed to provide rural households with more efficient biomass stoves and (later) coal stoves, for cooking and heating. The programme covered

[4] Engagement with government does not imply agreeing with government. Challenging inappropriate government policies and negotiating for alternatives would be critical elements of such engagement.

[5] The Planning Commission of India is the country-level nodal body. Individual states also have state-level planning commissions or boards.

research and development, training stove builders, raising public awareness on the health hazards of indoor air pollution, promoting user understanding of the design aspects of improved stoves, regular monitoring, and good post-installation maintenance (Smith et al. 1993, Jonathan et al. 2004). Administratively, the stove diffusion process stretched from the Department of Saving and Integrated Use of Resources and the State Planning Commission at the top, to the Bureau of Environmental Protection and Energy and the Ministry of Agriculture further below, down to the county offices of rural energy, and finally to the villages and users, along a well-coordinated pathway. Between 1980 and 1992, China installed about 129 million improved stoves, covering 50 per cent of rural households. By 1992 the majority of these households were using such stoves.[6] Over roughly the same period (1983–92) India installed 12.5 million improved stoves under its National Programme of Improved Cook Stoves. In 1992, only an estimated 8.8 million were in use, effectively covering 8 per cent of rural households (Kishore and Ramana 2002: 50).[7] India's low coverage can be traced especially to indequate administrative and technical coordination across ministries and states; top-down methods of dissemination, with little effort to familiarize women users with basic design features and maintenance or to involve them in design adaptation; poor monitoring and evaluation; and intra-household gender bias, wherein improvement in women's kitchens comes very low in household priorities.[8] Of course, improved biomass stoves alone are not an answer to clean domestic energy, and even China has a long way to go in that respect, but the stove programme demonstrates the complexity of coordination involved in effective delivery of cooking energy to rural areas.[9] Indeed, comparisons of improved stove programmes across countries, and across states within India, all point to this complexity, and to the need for close interaction between stove designers, stove builders, and women users.[10]

Similarly, forest policy formulation and implementation involve several government departments and ministries, in addition to those directly concerned with the environment and forests.[11] In India, in the late 1970s, for instance, the National Commission of Agriculture under the Ministry of Agriculture was principally involved in formulating forest policy since forests came under its purview. By the late 1980s, however, the Union Ministry of Environment and Forests (MoEF) had been constituted and the Joint Forest Management

[6] See, Smith et al. (1993: 941, 958) and Jonathan et al. (2004).

[7] Household coverage was calculated using the 1991 population census of rural households.

[8] See also Agarwal (1986a) and Parikh et al. (1999). The culture of top-down dissemination has changed rather little since the 1980s, and the use of improved stoves remains low.

[9] These lessons would also be relevant for other cooking energy technologies that are now being discussed in India, including solar cookers.

[10] See e.g. Agarwal (1986a), Barnes et al. (1994), Barnes and Kumar (2002), and Parikh et al. (1999).

[11] There is a considerable literature on forest policy, some of which was discussed in Chapter 3. I also draw on my conversation with N. C. Saxena (former secretary, Ministry of Rural Development), in 2009.

programme was initiated under its purview. In relation to the more recent Forest Rights Act of 2006, both the Ministry of Tribal affairs and the MoEF played key roles, since the legislation involved the rights of tribal communities over forest land, and for it to become law the approval of the cabinet and the parliament was also needed.

In other words, solving what appears to be a very local, very micro problem, namely of ensuring cooking energy security for a poor rural woman in a remote village in India or Nepal, could require attention from all arms of government—starting with the bureaucracy (the ministries and planning commissions), extending upwards to the cabinet for policy approval, or parliament for legislation, and downward to the village council for implementation. This underlines how imperative it is for rural women or their civil society representatives to engage with government and elicit an effective response. It also underlines the need for government to engage with civil society for solving community problems, given the long-demonstrated ineffectiveness of top-down approaches to policy formulation and implementation. Hence, for solving the problem of clean domestic energy, a strategic partnership between the government and civil society institutions representing rural women would be in the interests of both.

To what extent are government representatives at different levels willing or able to establish such a partnership? Do they see the connections between the interests of poor rural women and the national objectives of protecting the environment or providing energy security to every household? Are even *women* representatives in the government interested in taking up these concerns? True, women representatives are also responsible to the general constituency; and women constituents, as citizens, have a right to be represented by either sex. Nevertheless there is an expectation that *at least* women will focus on women's concerns. That is also the expectation (however implicit) of women's groups promoting women's quotas in village councils or parliament.

2. DISENGAGED GOVERNMENT

Evidence for South Asia and especially India indicates that at present we cannot assume that women in government will be willing to take up women's concerns, let alone prioritize *poor* women's concerns. And cooking energy security or forest conservation remain rather distant from their everyday agendas. Consider three levels of government institutions in India: village councils, the bureaucracy, and the parliament.[12]

[12] I draw most of my examples from India because of the paucity of equivalent material for Nepal, but the arguments have broader relevance.

2.1 Village Councils

The Indian government's policy of reserving seats for women in Panchayati Raj Institutions brought a million women into village councils (GoI 2006a: 29). Unlike CFIs in which representatives are usually selected through a broad consensus and typically cover one village, village councils are formally elected, cover one to several villages, depending on population size, and are institutionally distinct from CFIs, although in some states a council representative is a part of the CFI executive. Moreover, the CFIs focus on a single public resource, while village councils cover a range of public goods. As with CFIs, however, decisions made by the village council are local enough to potentially affect the councillors in direct ways. Hence a decision to invest in a fuelwood plantation would affect not just the villagers but also the council members, and it could affect different members differently, depending on which village and where in the village such a plantation is located (e.g. near a high-caste hamlet or a low-caste one).[13] But here the commonalities between forestry groups and village councils largely end, since the councillors are formal arms of local government and subject to a range of pressures and constraints. To what extent are women councillors willing and able to focus on women's needs?

Since lobbying by women's organizations played an important part in pushing for gender quotas in local government,[14] we might have expected that the women elected would have a special interest in representing women or promoting 'women's issues' (even given the fuzziness in identifying these).[15] In practice this is far from being the case. This is partly due to the external constraints the councillor faces and partly from choice. The 73rd and 74th constitutional amendments in India, for example, specify a list of subjects that village councils can take up, and individual states choose among these when passing their 'Conformity Acts' which give effect to the amendments (Singh et al. 1997). Less than a handful of states have included women and child development in their listed subjects; and although 62 per cent mention forestry, only 40 per cent mention fuel, fodder, or non-conventional energy. The list of subjects is only meant to be indicative (other subjects can also be taken up), but it still flags the issues that the government considers important and will translate into schemes. In general, decentralized natural resource management is not on the priority list of most elected PRI representatives.[16] Another, even more basic, constraint is the tied nature of funds that village councils receive—in some cases, 90 per cent or

[13] See also Chattopadhyay and Duflo (2004) who found that the personal preferences of pradhans (village council chairpersons) played an important role in prioritizing and locating infrastructure. For instance, scheduled caste (SC) pradhans invested a larger share of public goods to SC hamlets than did non-SC pradhans.

[14] See Chapter 3 in this volume, and Rai (1997).

[15] Of course, many of the village women elected are probably unaware of the role played by women's groups in the reservation campaign.

[16] See also TERI's (2004) evaluation of four states on this count.

more of the funds are tied to particular central government projects, and the possibility of raising additional funds is usually limited.[17] This financial restriction curtails the freedom that councillors have in setting priorities, and limits the potential for any substantial gender differences in priority setting (World Bank 2004: 12).[18] Of course, women councillors could still use their official positions and financial allocations in innovative ways to promote women's welfare and green concerns under already approved subjects, such as social forestry and non-conventional energy. But many women councillors lack the information, finances, or institutional support for exercising such agency.[19]

These are the external constraints. There are also internal ones. Elected women often *choose* not to focus on issues that might be seen as 'women's issues'.[20] In Karnataka, Vijaylakshmi (2003: 21, 24) found that the women councillors belonging to different political parties or castes felt that 'their bargaining power would be considerably reduced if they took up gender-specific issues which were not supported by other members or political functionaries' and that 'since gender interests were not an electoral issue in politics . . . the representatives did not . . . act for women. A small section (3 per cent) of women who were more open to the idea of addressing women-specific interests, expressed their inability to do so.' Overall, women councillors were more concerned with strengthening their political position by taking up general constituency interests. In Buch's (1999) survey of three districts in north India, covering 843 elected women councillors at all three levels (village, block, and district) of India's Panchayati Raj Institutions, the issues women raised in meetings were predominantly general ones of rural development, drinking water, and construction. Even in Kerala, the only state where local bodies are advised to set aside a 10 per cent grant-in-aid in the budget for a women's component plan, 70 per cent of the sampled women council heads said they did not deal with women's issues (Radha and Chowdhury 2002). In Calcutta, urban municipal councillors elected to reserved seats felt the same: 'Most women councillors . . . do not want to advocate women's interests within the House, because they do not consider them, or they *do not want to appear* as if they considered them, a major issue' (Lama-Rewal 2001: 36, my emphasis).[21]

Not only do women councillors not see themselves as representing women, many do not even want to be seen as addressing issues that directly or mainly

[17] See World Bank (2004). Also personal communication by researchers Vijaylakshmi for Karnataka and Nirmala Buch for Madhya Pradesh. The number of schemes—sometimes running into a hundred or more—are also too many to coordinate effectively (World Bank 2004: 12).

[18] Studies that point to gender differences in priority setting typically fail to mention what degree of financial freedom the councillors have in this respect.

[19] There is a substantial and growing literature on the constraints women councillors face: see, among others, Andersson and Bohman (2001), Athreya and Rajeshwari (1998), Buch (1999), Manikyamba (1989), Pal (2004), and Radha and Chowdhury (2002).

[20] See Vijaylakshmi (2003), Radha and Chowdhury (2002), and Lama-Rewal (2001).

[21] See also John (2007) who similarly found urban councillors in Delhi and Bangalore reluctant to advance women's issues or interests.

benefit women. Hence the local interpretation of an issue as a 'woman's issue' can become a barrier to a women councillor taking it up, if she feels it can adversely affect her image within the larger constituency. This is not unlike men in predominantly male CFI meetings shying away from raising the problem of firewood shortages that their wives are facing, because it is not considered the done thing for men to raise women's concerns. What can matter therefore is not the issue itself but how it is framed. Hence although in objective terms the schemes women councillors prioritize may fulfil women's needs more than men's, such benefit would be incidental and not a result of women-directed choices.

Within this disappointing picture there are some exceptions, such as all-women panchayats,[22] or village councils in some states such as Himachal Pradesh (north-west India) which have favourable structural and social features. In this predominantly hill state, for instance, women council heads are found more willing to take up women's concerns and are more empowered than in neighbouring Haryana, both socially and institutionally.[23] Socially, Himachali women are not subject to seclusion practices, and have high literacy rates and a substantial role in farming, especially due to male outmigration. Some local NGOs have also conducted women's empowerment programmes here for long years. Institutionally, women councillors have jural authority to settle cases, which gives them more independence than in states where councillors lack this power.[24] Kerala, again, with its special budget allocation for women and inputs from women's organizations, has the potential for taking up more women-focused programmes.

In the above examples, there are several points of note. Most councillors (male or female) stay within the list of 'subjects' formally identified in the Conformity Acts. They are also restricted by the tied nature of funding they receive. *Women* councillors, in particular, are usually found to be more comfortable with schemes seen to be of general benefit rather than specifically for women's benefit, and typically fail to use general schemes for addressing women's needs. Under the rubric of social forestry, for example, they could establish plantations of firewood species, and under the subject of non-conventional energy they could promote clean fuel technologies such as biogas plants, or even solar cookers on an experimental basis, but few have shown an interest in doing so. The gender label on cooking fuel, seen as a 'women's issue' in rural India, could also be a factor constraining women councillors from taking it up. Even Himachali women

[22] In these occasional all-women panchayats, catalysed by women's groups in some states such as Maharashtra, women councillors focused on strategic gender concerns, including on women's land rights (Gala 1990).

[23] Based on the initial results of an ongoing study by Pareena Lawrence (Morris University, USA) and Kavita Chakravarty (Rohtak University, India).

[24] Giving village councillors jural authority in other states could prove similarly empowering, and the Ministry of Panchayati Raj is now planning to introduce a bill in parliament for establishing gram panchayat level judicial councils in all the states (personal communication in 2008 by Mani Shankar Iyer, then cabinet minister for Panchayati Raj).

councillors did not mention firewood shortages or access to forest resources as critical concerns, in the ongoing study cited above. In general, green issues have not entered either the general or the gender category as essential elements of well-being, or become part of the popular mandate.

2.2 The Bureaucracy

What is the approach of a higher level of government—the middle rung of the bureaucracy—toward women's concerns and green issues? In particular, how do women's ministries or departments (established in many countries), which are mandated to focus on policies for women, respond? India, for instance, has a Department of Woman and Child Development initially set up within the Ministry of Human Resource Development in 1985 and upgraded to the rank of a ministry in 2006.[25] Nepal has a similar Ministry of Women, Children, and Social Welfare established in 1995. There is rather little research on how these ministries prioritize and promote particular issues, but to my knowledge they have no clear mechanism for consulting rural women or their representatives about women's needs, or for translating identified needs into policy.[26]

Energy policy, as noted, is framed in India by the Planning Commission of India in interaction with and integrating the inputs from several government ministries, but this is done without mandatory inputs from the Department of Women and Child Development. According to a senior adviser to the Ministry of New and Renewable Energy (MNER), this Department 'is not sensitized enough on gender and energy issues, [its] focus is more on women [and] violence than on their economic position'.[27] Be that as it may, the MNER itself has few mechanisms in place for consulting the Department of Women and Child Development. Nor have the (typically women) bureaucrats in the latter department initiated any processes, or set in place any institutional mechanisms, to solicit information on rural women's needs and priorities, either directly, or through civil society groups who might have these links.[28] In recent years, it is civil society activists themselves who have, from time to time, sought the intervention of women bureaucrats in these departments, both on gender issues per se and on interrelated gender and green issues, such as women's access to forests or contribution to biodiversity.

[25] The persistent conflation of women's issues with social welfare, and the linking of women with children, remains a point of disquiet among women's groups in India who have repeatedly pointed out to policy-makers that women's interests and rights are not confined to their reproductive roles.

[26] Indeed, this is a common feature across many developing countries which have set up women's ministries or departments. As Goetz (2003) observes, after reviewing the experience of several countries, women bureaucrats cannot be assumed automatically to work in women's interests; and their class position also distances them from the concerns of poor women.

[27] Comment made at a gender workshop on national energy policies in 2008 (IRADe-ENERGIA 2009: 70).

[28] This is the general pattern, although an occasional individual may transcend it.

Typically, however, they have received rather uncertain responses.[29] Decentralization of both planning and implementation, if done in a participative way, can enhance local accountability. But local communities are not part of the plan formulation process, nor is there any inbuilt mechanism for community feedback.[30]

Indeed this has been a standing limitation of the planning process. In her analysis of several decades of plan formulation in India, C. P. Sujaya, a retired senior government bureaucrat who worked for long years on gender issues within the government, emphasizes the persistence of top-down planning within both central and state governments. Drawing on her experience, she argues (2002: 17):

> There was no effort to evolve a system of representation that would enable the vast majority of women in the country to feel satisfied that their views were being heard. The millions of poor rural and urban women had no agency in the planning process and no legal and effective first hand representation in the discourse.

Even when women's groups, community-based agencies, and other members of civil society were consulted, Sujaya (2002: 16–17) argues, 'it was more to fulfill an obligation . . . to institute participatory processes or to get feed back from the field, and less to have serious policy dialogues on the planning paradigms and processes'. These discussions, she notes, 'were held at [the government's] instance, time and location'. 'These interactions did not directly involve poor women—urban or rural. Their needs and voices were heard at second-hand through women's groups.' Sujaya's comments make clear that the bureaucracy has set up no formal mechanisms through which poor women can express their views directly and expect to be heard. Even where such direct dialogue is difficult to organize, a regular and two-way discussion—rather than an occasional and top-down one—with gender-progressive organizations that have significant grassroots links, would be an important step forward.

2.3 Legislatures

Finally, to what extent do women members of parliament (MPs) see themselves as representing women's interests or as responsible for environmental concerns? And do they have any mechanisms for soliciting information about women's needs, especially poor women's needs. Again, a lack of detailed research on this for South Asia precludes definitive answers, but there are pointers which suggest a changing picture over time. If we go far back, say to the 1930s and 1940s, Indian

[29] This is based on my own observations, as well as those of my peers, of long years of interaction with the Indian bureaucracy, including members of the Indian Planning Commission and officials of the Ministry of Women and Child Development.

[30] On the positive side, there is now an emerging sensitivity on this count. For instance, a GOI (2008) manual for integrated district planning emphasizes participative consultations with citizens, including women.

women involved in politics had close links with women's organizations, and worked relentlessly for gender-progressive laws and gender equality in the framing of the Indian Constitution (see Chapter 3 and Agarwal 1994). In the 1990s, however, we find a relative disengagement of women MPs from women's issues. Singer (2007: 227, my emphasis), for instance, found that 'many prominent women politicians eschewed the label of *woman politician*, both during elections and in office'. Women MPs also participated rather little in introducing bills or in parliamentary debates. In the fourth Lok Sabha, for instance, none of the 35 bills that were introduced was moved by a woman (Kumari and Dubey 1994: 82). In the eighth Lok Sabha (1985–89) when 8.1 per cent of all MPs were women (the largest percentage until 1999), women MPs spoke up in less than 5 per cent of the short-duration discussions, and in less than 10 per cent of the longer ones (Kumari and Dubey 1994: 82). Typically, the same few women spoke each time. None of the women MPs moved a single private member's resolution, or a government resolution, and none raised issues specifically concerning women. Voting tended to be along party lines, even if the position taken by the party was retrogressive for women, and even if a woman MP might have personally disagreed with that position. Kumari and Dubey attribute women MPs' limited engagement in parliament to their small numbers and to the need to vote with their parties,[31] but we might still ask: to what extent were the MPs even interested in taking up women's concerns and standing up for them within their parties?

Rai (1997, and personal communication in 2006) does address this question. Her detailed interviews with many past and present Indian women parliamentarians indicate that none saw herself as representing women or their particular interests. Typically they felt bound by their party's agendas and priorities. Few had any stated links with the autonomous women's organizations (although they may have known some feminist activists in a personal capacity), and none had come into political life through the women's movement, although, Rai (1997: 117) notes, women MPs '[had] benefited from the growing strength of the women's movement which [had] put the issue of women's empowerment and participation in politics on the national agenda'. The MPs she interviewed did have access to the women's wings of their political parties, but the impact of this depended on how active those women's wings were. Most were by their own admission relatively inactive but, in my observation, a few had grown in strength and leadership, such as the All India Democratic Women's Association (AIDWA) linked with the Communist party (Marxist) (CPM) (see also Ghosh and Lama-Rewal 2005). Over the years, AIDWA has taken up, sometimes in collaboration with non-party women's groups, a number of issues that concern women, including violence against women and women's inheritance rights.[32] The organization has also maintained grassroots contact with rural women through its local

[31] In many other developing countries also, women's position in parties tends to determine their access to political office (Goetz 2009). Both intra-party democracy and overall democratic political systems can affect women's opportunities for political engagement (see Goetz 2009 and Basu 2009).

[32] See also Karat (2005) for an insider's description of AIDWA's role and approach.

cadres, although, despite this, some issues of critical importance to this constituency, such as adequate and clean cooking fuel and access to forest resources for subsistence, appear to have received little attention (except where, in line with the CPM, they have supported issues such as the forest rights of tribal communities). In addition, some women MPs of various parties are committed to gender equality, or have contacts with women's organizations, or are in touch with the women in their constituencies.

In recent years, the one issue on which Indian women parliamentarians have come together across party lines is the Women's Reservation Bill which seeks to reserve one-third seats for women in parliament—for which women MPs have lobbied in various ways, including through the women's caucus and public rallies. This holds the promise but no certainty that other gender-related concerns, especially those with implications for ordinary women's lives, will be similarly embraced. As yet, as with the bureaucracy, there is no *systematic institutional mechanism* through which women MPs might keep themselves informed about rural women's interests, needs, and priorities, even if an occasional MP might seek such information from her own constituency.

It is notable also that green issues in general have received rather little attention from India's main political parties. The 2004 and 2009 election manifestos of the major parties and coalitions are indicative.[33] In 2004 the manifestos touched upon green issues selectively and in only two forms: (i) the need to promote non-conventional energy to reduce fossil fuel use (mentioned by the National Democratic Alliance (NDA) and the Bhartiya Janata party), and (ii) the need to enhance the access of tribal communities to forests for livelihoods, and promote social forestry for creating employment (mentioned by the CPM, the NDA, and the Indian National Congress). None mentioned clean cooking fuel for reducing women's drudgery in gathering firewood or improving their health; or the importance of increasing women's access to non-wood forest products; or even the need for conserving indigenous knowledge systems or the environment, to which women could make a special contribution.

The 2009 election manifestos are equally sparse on gender and green concerns. The Indian National Congress—the largest single party re-elected with strength in 2009 and which has now formed the government—mentions 'the need to supply energy to poor families at affordable prices' but does not link this to *women's* health or drudgery. The manifestos of the BJP and CPM also fail to discuss the energy needs of the poor and women. It is a rare manifesto—that of the Janata Dal (United) (a regional party present mainly in Bihar)—which mentions the dangers to women and children's health from cooking with unprocessed biofuels.

Moreover, even the limited briefs on green issues found in these manifestos have not been followed up by most MPs, including women MPs, although

[33] These manifestos relate respectively to the 14th and 15th Lok Sabha (lower house of parliament) elections in India.

subjects such as non-conventional energy or tribal rights to forests could easily be oriented to promote rural women's interests. Certainly, in terms of political engagement with green issues, South Asia is a long way away from Europe, where green parties have emerged in national governments, and some are explicitly seeking ways of bringing a gender balance within their parties.[34]

Simply increasing the number of women within parliament will not bring such issues to centre stage. In the lively debate on gender quotas in the Indian parliament, there has been rather little focus on what difference the elected women might make, and whether the women who come into power will promote women's interests.[35] This is notwithstanding the fact that the demand for increasing women's numbers in parliament is supported by numerous women's rights activists and organizations. Although the activists differ on whether the most effective way to increase women's political presence is to reserve seats in parliament, or to have quotas within parties, or to follow some other route,[36] there is widespread consensus that women's presence should be increased on grounds of gender equality and setting right a historical injustice. While gender-equal representation is an important argument, we still need to ask what policy priorities the women will bring to parliament. Without such a discussion, there is no obvious reason to expect that the women who come to power will further women's cause or address interrelated green issues any more than those already in power have done.

There are thus lacunae at all levels—from village to parliament—in the mechanisms for bringing the concerns and priorities of rural women into public policy. How can the bureaucracy's and parliament's interest in and accountability to women constituents be enhanced?

3. ENGAGING THE GOVERNMENT

> Changing inequities in social and economic power will require not just the increased representation of women within the state, but also the increased and assertive representation of *poor* women within the state, as well as a strong feminist movement outside the state (Hassim 2005: 8).

Overall we need three levels of engagement from the government: the lowest level is interaction between CFIs/SHGs and village councils. In the context of green governance, the purpose here would be to encourage village councils to

[34] See Muller-Rommel and Poguntke (2002), especially chapter 5 on Germany.

[35] There has also been little discussion on the portfolios that women MPs tend to receive. In India and globally, women rarely have charge of the so-called powerful ministries, such as finance, commerce, defence, or foreign affairs, the exceptions being few and recent in some countries, such as Chile, Spain, and Rwanda (Goetz 2009; see also Staudt 1996 for an earlier period).

[36] See e.g. a summary of the discussion and various viewpoints in Singer (2007). See also Kishwar (1996) and Menon (2000).

proactively seek out schemes that further a green agenda, and to ensure women-inclusive and poor-inclusive implementation of any existing schemes relating to forests and clean cooking energy over which the councillors have control. The second level of interaction needs to be between representatives of CFIs/SHGs and upper-level bureaucrats, especially those involved in framing energy and environmental policies, drawing up guidelines for policy implementation, allocating funds, monitoring, and so on. And the third level needs to be engagement by women legislators with issues concerning the country's resources, such as its land, forests, and water. In other words, engagement is needed to project not only a gender perspective but also a green perspective, and the interrelationship between the two. There are no blueprints on how this could be done, but I present some broad reflections here.

3.1 Engaging with Village Councillors

For village women to engage effectively with village councils, a key starting point will be strengthening women's bargaining power locally. In Chapter 10, I had highlighted the advocacy role that many women's SHGs in India have been playing within communities and how a strategic linkage between SHGs and CFIs could benefit both. Such strategic linkages could also prove effective in dealings with village councils. Some SHG federations, for instance, are already rejuvenating gram sabhas (meetings of all villagers) by their active presence. Gram sabhas are potentially important forums of public deliberation at the lowest level of government in India, and are meant to help village councils solicit villagers' opinions on policies and priorities. If villagers accross class, caste and gender were to attend gram sabhas, interactive discussion between diverse groups and local government could provide the latter with substantial information on differences in the needs and priorities of different segments of the population. Understanding these differences appears necessary for establishing priorities in the use of public goods such as forests. Although such consultation is important at all levels of government it is especially needed at the local level. Deliberation in gram sabhas can also enhance accountability, especially financial.

Village councils are mandated to hold gram sabha meetings at least once a year, and in some states twice a year or more. In practice, the meetings are often irregular and poorly attended, especially by women, although there can be regional differences. In a study of 290 randomly selected gram sabhas held in four south Indian states, only 83 people attended on average (out of village populations ranging between 2,000 and 10,000) and in some cases as few as 7 persons came (Rao and Sanyal 2009: 17–18). However, a third of the attendees on average were women and in about 68 per cent of the gram sabhas at least one woman spoke, albeit briefly. In many other parts of the country women's attendance is much poorer, and to facilitate women's participation some Indian states have tried to make it mandatory for gram sabha meetings to have one-third women to reach a quorum.[37] Some other states have made informal efforts to institute a mahila sabha (a meeting of women villagers) prior to the gram sabha, so that women can strategize and express their views more freely than they do in a mixed-gender forum. In practice, such noteworthy institutional innovations often remain ineffective. Women's self-help groups could give them life.

Pant (2007), for example, examined a sample of women's SHGs initiated by NGOs in three states of northern and central India and found that many SHG members had begun attending gram sabha meetings and had also successfully persuaded non-SHG women to attend. By doing so they created a substantial female presence at meetings; enabled the meetings to reach a quorum; helped change meeting timings to women's convenience; and used their bargaining power to push for the completion of village projects that would benefit women and the community. Most importantly, as a result, male councillors have begun to see SHG women as a potential vote bank, thus giving women substantial bargaining power within the community. Pant does not distinguish between village councils with male or female chairpersons, but if women are seen as a constituency for winning elections, this would encourage councillors of both sexes to address gender concerns. Certainly it could make women councillors less hesitant in taking up so-called 'women's issues' for fear of alienating the general constituency. Developing such links between SHGs and village councils can thus empower women in both institutions. And, if prior alliances have been established between SHGs and community forestry groups, then women in CFIs would also be empowered in their interactions with village councils.

In taking this process forward, the role of local civil society organizations can be critical both in terms of promoting strategic linkages between SHGs and CFIs and in the interaction of such groups with village councils. But these organizations need not be women's organizations. Indeed we need to go beyond women's groups, since a vast range of NGOs which are not specifically women's organizations have played significant roles in promoting women's interests, and especially poor women's interests in South Asia. Many have worked long years in supporting the right to livelihood of poor communities, including their rights of access to forests, and recognized the particularity of gender disadvantage in these communities. The three Gujarat NGOs of my study sites are all of this ilk. MYRADA, similarly, although not specifically a women's organization, has paid substantial attention to the empowerment of poor rural women as well as to green issues. In fact, in many ways, gender-progressive grassroots organizations in rural South Asia have connected gender interests with green issues more successfully than have solely women's organizations. Their work also undercuts the arguments of

[37] See, for instance, the Madhya Pradesh Act 23 of 2001, sub-section (2) which mandated that establishing a quorum would require the presence of one-fifth of the gram sabha members of which one-third had to be women, plus representatives of Scheduled Castes and Scheduled Tribes in proportion to their population in the gram sabha. Unfortunately, the provision for women was subsequently deleted under the Madhya Pradesh Act 20 of 2005 (personal communication from Nirmala Buch).

some scholars that civil society representation—termed by them 'the new politics'—is less effective for the poor than standard channels of political parties.[38] There are in fact numerous examples from India and Nepal in recent years of shifts in environmental policies as a result of pressure from civil society activists and intellectuals.

Civil society organizations can also play a bigger role in enabling women councillors to overcome the financial and attitudinal barriers to their focusing on policies benefiting women. In India, one such step could be to seek a 10 per cent or more allocation in the panchayat budget for a women's component plan in all states (similar to Kerala's). Another step could be the strengthening of existing efforts at raising the gender-awareness of councillors, by collaborating with planners and researchers, and by constituting networks of women chairpersons where they can discuss problems and their solutions.[39] In the various capacity-building programmes ongoing in India and elsewhere in South Asia, however, much more clarity is needed on how the councillors should identify issues of importance for women's well-being and social well-being, including green issues.

3.2 Engaging with Bureaucracy

The second level of necessary engagement is with bureaucrats. Here again, civil society organizations, including women's groups as well as individuals, have played important bridging roles, serving as mediators in raising the concerns of rural women with femocrats (women bureaucrats) in women and development departments/ministries, and elaborating a gender perspective for policy-makers, through a variety of methods. These range from direct participation in policy-making by joining various committees and commissions of the government, to indirect means, such as participating in forums for policy deliberation, providing informal inputs to policymakers, interacting via the media and internet, and lobbying.

Of these diverse routes, perhaps the one that has so far been especially effective in getting government to engage with gender concerns has been through what I term 'lateral entry', namely the formal and informal inputs and influence exercised by gender-sensitive individuals with professional acumen and personal contacts. A case in point is the government of India's *Integrated Energy Policy* (GoI 2008) drafted under the tenure of the United Progressive Alliance (UPA) government of which the Congress party was a central part.[40] The policy emphasizes the

[38] Harriss (2007), for instance, drawing on his work in Chennai city argues that 'the principal possibility for the urban poor to obtain representation for themselves is still through political parties'. This position is contestable even for the urban poor, but especially for poor rural women who lack the visibility and connections with political parties that urban groups, and men in general, are more likely to have.

[39] This is being tried in some states (Everett 2009).

[40] In understanding the process of energy policy formulation, my conversations in 2009 with Kirith Parikh (then member Planning Commission and chairman of the committee for formulating India's energy policy) were especially useful, as was material provided by Jyoti Parikh.

importance of clean cooking energy and ensuring energy security for the rural poor, especially on account of the negative health effects of smoky biofuels on women and children. *The Report of the Expert Committee on Integrated Energy Policy* (henceforth called the *IEP Report*), on which the energy policy document is based, also emphasizes 'energy security for the poor' which goes 'beyond providing energy for subsistence' (GoI 2006b: 99). It calls for an approach that would increase their livelihood opportunities and incomes so that eventually they can afford clean and convenient energy sources on their own. It recommends a range of measures for providing cooking energy security, such as setting up fuelwood plantations within one kilometre of settlements to increase firewood supply, establishing commercially run community biogas plants,[41] and enhancing supplies of kerosene and LPG, apart from solar lamps and electricity from wood gasification for lighting.

Earlier fuel policy committees, set up by the government of India from time to time since the early 1970s, had at best paid lip service to women's cooking energy needs, emphasizing biogas and improved cooking stoves as solutions, but without linking clean energy to women's health, or making cooking energy a significant element of the national energy policy. The *Integrated Energy Policy* (GOI 2008) document and the *IEP Report* are an important shift. They pay particular attention not only to environmental concerns but also women's concerns. This shift, however, was not, to my knowledge, a result either of efforts by women's organizations or civil society groups, nor even of inputs by the Ministry of Women and Child Development. Rather, three factors appear to have been especially important. First, since the 1980s, a growing body of research (global and local) has highlighted the health ill-effects of unprocessed biofuels, and worldwide attention is now being paid to these effects by international agencies, especially the World Health Organization. Second, Kirit Parikh, the chairman of the committee that framed the *IEP Report* and energy policy, had a long-standing interest in clean cooking fuels, especially via biogas plants.[42] Third, in a clear example of 'lateral entry', recommendations were incorporated into the IEP based on a large-scale study of renewable energy from a gender perspective undertaken by a team headed by Jyoti Parikh, the executive director of IRADe, and the gender analysis of some renewable energy projects also undertaken by this team.[43] Similar examples of lateral influence exerted by women researchers and practitioners in bringing a gender perspective into government policy, and influencing especially the Indian Planning Commission in its drafting of

[41] This is a shift from the earlier unsuccessful approach of government agencies promoting biogas plants to individual families: for instance, a government evaluation in 2002 found that only 7 per cent of households in a sample survey of 133 villages in 19 states were using biogas, and often only as a supplementary source (GoI 2002: pp. i–iii).

[42] He wrote his 1963 MIT master's thesis in economics on biogas plants (personal communication, June 2009).

[43] See IRADe-ENERGIA (2009) for the recommendations. IRADe stands for Integrated Research and Action for Development, and ENERGIA is an international network on gender and sustainable energy.

the country's Five Year Plans, can be found in several arenas, including agriculture, employment, forests, and women's development.[44]

At the same time, lateral entry, although effective in influencing policy in women's favour in particular contexts, cannot substitute for efforts to establish wider and more systematic linkages between government and village women's representatives. Without such links the process remains susceptible to ad hoc inputs by gender-sensitive individuals or groups who may not always get it right, even with the best of intentions. Systematic linkages are also necessary for better policy implementation and for setting in place mechanisms by which rural women make informed choices from the basket of energy sources recommended in the policy. If fuelwood plantations are to be established, for instance, several aspects will need to be addressed, such as: who will provide the land for establishing them? Who will protect and manage the plantations? How will the wood that gets generated be distributed? Would it be done through community forestry institutions or in some other way? Similar questions arise in relation to biogas plants or other solutions to cooking energy poverty (including solar)—none of which might work if imposed top-down, as India's experience with fuel-efficient cooking stoves already shows.[45]

It is perhaps unrealistic to hold mainly women and development departments or ministries responsible for bringing gender perspectives into the policies of different ministries, or for shifting gender concerns into the general domain. An alternative, more integrative framework would be for each ministry to have a gender cell or gender advisory body that could bring such a perspective to bear on that department's or ministry's work. A similar overarching body in the Planning Commission of India could integrate diverse aspects of policies that impact women across departments. In other words, the metaphor of a spider's web, evoked in Chapter 10, would be relevant here as well.

3.3 Engaging with Legislators

Finally, we come to the third level of government—the legislators. Here the links with women's organizations and other civil society groups appear to be especially weak in South Asia. Can they be strengthened by building alliances with women's wings of political parties and with women MPs? In the past, such alliances,

[44] For India's 11th Five Year Plan, members of the Committee of Feminist Economists, constituted by the Planning Commission, played important roles, both collectively and in their individual capacities. See also WINROCK (2006) for examples of the role of experts and individuals in shaping forest policy.

[45] Even with commercially run community bio-gas plants (one of the recommendations of India's *IEP Report*), where an entrepreneur would produce and sell the gas to villagers, user-interactive approaches for dissemination would be necessary, to orient women and families to new forms of investment, stove designs, and related aspects. As already noted, biogas plants for individual families have had little success. See also Denton's (2002) emphasis in the African context on 'cooperation and coordination between women's groups and equipment designers' for the better adoption of new technologies.

cutting across ideological spectrums, have been forged on several occasions between autonomous women's groups and women's wings of political parties. A case in point is the campaign against dowry in India in the early 1980s when a diversity of women's groups and women's wings of political parties came together strategically, to demand legal reform and its implementation (see also Karat 2005). In establishing strategic links, women's wings and women's caucuses within the legislature could help connect civil society groups with mainstream political parties (although more direct connections might also be sought for effectiveness). An opportunity for this exists in the campaign for gender quotas in parliament which is supported in India by women parliamentarians across a wide political spectrum and from the outside by many women's groups. This campaign provides a context for women's groups to focus not just on enhancing female presence in parliament, but also on bringing into public office women who would be willing to take up poor village women's concerns, such as their access to fuel, forests, and livelihoods.

Countries that have proactively engaged with a gender perspective at all levels of government have tended to be those with close links between women's movements, women legislators, and/or women bureaucrats. This includes countries as diverse as the USA, Australia, and South Africa. In the USA, Carroll (2003) found, for instance, that many of the women state senators and state representatives whom she interviewed in 2001 described themselves as feminists and had been members of women's organizations. They were part of women's caucuses or informal groups that met not only within party lines but also across parties. These two-way links between the legislators and women's organizations, she argues, provided the former with ongoing access to a perspective on women's interests and made them more accountable toward those interests.[46] In Australia, similarly, links between femocrats and the women's movement were very important in shaping government policy to take account of women's interests (Eisenstein 1995). Here the support provided by women's organizations to the Labor Party election campaign paid off in terms of many women being appointed as advisers and bureaucrats in the government in the 1970s. That activists who joined the bureaucracy came from working-class backgrounds also helped focus more attention on poor women. In South Africa, again, the role played by women's organizations in the anti-apartheid struggle and their associated bargaining power led to the induction into government of many women activists, who helped establish institutional mechanisms for promoting gender equality.

[46] Some scholars, such as Weldon (2002), are sceptical about the reliability of women legislators in carrying forward women's concerns, and give substantial weight instead to women bureaucrats and autonomous women's movements. Weldon (2002: 1161) defines the latter as movements that are 'devoted to promoting women's status and well-being, independently of political parties and other associations that do not make the status of women their main concern'. Given the diversity of international experience, however, this dominant emphasis on femocrats and narrowly-defined women's movements, for promoting women's interests in government, appears to be somewhat misplaced.

These experiences all point to the importance of women representatives in government having a gender perspective and links with women's organizations, if they are to represent women's interests effectively. In South Asia, such links between members of the women's movement and the bureaucracy and legislature are, thus far, largely tenuous, and need strengthening.

In this context, a promising development has been the formation of WomenPowerConnect (WPC) in 2004, by a group of NGOs and development professionals. This is a national-level organization of women's groups and individuals that aims at influencing legislators and policy-makers to frame gender-friendly policies. So far it has 800 individual and institutional members across the country and seeks to work actively with (male and female) members of parliament for legislative coordination to promote women's interests.[47] The five priority issues, however, that WomenPowerConnect lists on its website—sexual harassment, female adverse sex ratios, gender-responsive budgeting, the women's reservation bill, and implementing the domestic violence act—while all important, are not necessarily based on participative feedback from rural women.[48] Green issues and livelihood questions, for instance, do not figure in the list, although the forum would probably be open to enlarging its scope.

Another promising network that has been formed recently is SADED (South Asian Dialogues on Ecological Democracy) which emphasizes the need to broaden the concept of democracy to include environmental sustainability and gender equality, among other social concerns, and plans 'to connect with the representatives of diverse political streams in various elected bodies at different levels in South Asia' to develop a form of 'engaged advocacy' (Pratap and Rovaniemi 2006: 14).

In fact, the project of promoting rural women's interests, and more generally a gender perspective in policies, needs to be conceptualized much more broadly than has been done so far, namely in terms of partnerships that extend substantially beyond what may be defined as 'the women's movement', as well as beyond standard political channels. It would need, in particular, active engagement between government, gender-progressive NGOs working at the grassroots, and emerging federations of organizations of the poor.

4. TACKLING COMPLEXITIES

4.1 Heterogeneity

Although women's organizations and other civil society groups can play, and many have played, a crucial role in representing gender perspectives to the government, they also embody limitations on several counts. First, in most

[47] Personal communication, Ranjana Kumari, founding member and current president of WomenPowerConnect.

[48] See http://www.womenpowerconnect.org.

countries, women's movements and other civil society groups (including environmental groups) are heterogeneous, constituted of diverse organizations and initiatives, with varying ideologies, priorities, and constituencies.[49] Moreover, the assumption that civil society organizations are necessarily egalitarian or democratic in their functioning has long been questioned. But even if many have these internal features, on aggregate they vary in their approaches and focus. This diversity can generate opposing pulls and pressures and neutralize their effectiveness. Even in the South African experience, the persistence of a diversity of perspectives and the lack of a unified approach within the women's movement are argued to have weakened the movement's efforts (Hassim 2003). Instituting mechanisms for arriving at common understandings could thus prove crucial for effectively bargaining with the state.

Second, women (like men) can have many identities, apart from their gender identity, such as those stemming from their caste, class, religion, ethnicity or race. Which identity prevails can vary by context, and there is no guarantee that women's gender identity will prevail over their other identities, even within an organization.[50] As noted in Chapter 1, a group of women—'women in themselves' (as a biological category)—need not imply that they are also 'women for themselves' as a collective entity. Even if gender emerges as a significant identity it could still remain one of several identities. We see this at all levels of elected polity in South Asia—village councils, state legislatures, and parliament—where allegiances of caste and religion often supersede those of gender.

Third, even the myriad organizations constituting a women's movement, and civil society more generally, can sometimes fail to recognize some critical gender needs, in the absence of institutional or other mechanisms for identifying them. I was first struck by this while researching the issue of women's rights in land and property in the mid-1980s and early 1990s, when I found rather little focus on this issue within the women's movement across South Asian countries.[51] Barring the rare exception,[52] NGOs concerned with women's economic position were concentrating on wage employment, non-land related income-generating schemes, or micro-credit. Yet, for rural women themselves, I found that access to land was of critical importance not only as a security against poverty but also for dignity and voice within the home and community. A more macro-perspective on poverty, livelihoods, and agrarian change also pointed to the key importance of women's access to land and other immovable assets. This was somehow missed

[49] Carroll (2003), Eisenstein (1995), and Britton (2002, 2006), writing in the context of the USA, Australia, and South Africa respectively, do not delve into this heterogeneity. Hassim (2003) does, but limitedly. See also Siedman (2003) for South Africa.

[50] See e.g. Chhachhi (1991), Sen (2005), and Menon (2000), among others. Also, as Baumann et al. (2003: 23) point out, individuals can be 'caught up in overlapping circles of relationships'.

[51] See the discussion in Agarwal (1994: Chapter 1, and 2003).

[52] The exceptions include the Bodhgaya movement in Bihar (India) catalysed by the Chatra Yuva Sangharsh Vahini in 1978, the Shetkari Sangathana's movement for farmer's rights launched in Maharashtra in 1980, and the work of the Deccan Development Society in Andhra Pradesh (India): see Agarwal (1994, 2003).

by many grassroots groups. And even today, although a focus on women's land rights has become integral to State policies for rural women's empowerment and poverty alleviation in many countries and among international agencies, it is less well integrated into the programmes of civil society groups.[53]

Similarly, and of central importance for our current discussion, although South Asia has seen environmental movements such as the Chipko movement in the Uttarakhand hills in which women have been major actors, forest governance, and more generally green issues, have not become a cause for significant mobilization in the women's movement. And although some women's organizations have supported tribal access to forests through the Forest Rights Act 2006, the support has been framed largely as a general concern for the livelihoods of the poor, rather than from a gender perspective. Notably, green issues, such as those concerning cooking energy poverty, or women's access to forest resources, or the possible impact of climate change on poor rural women, have not received the attention they deserve either from women's organizations or from the environmental movement more generally, even though, as we have seen in this book, these are issues of central importance to millions of women and their families, and some of them have been highlighted by several writers since the 1970s and 1980s.[54]

For civil society organizations to effectively serve as mediators with government on behalf of rural women and take on the mantle of representing their concerns, we need mechanisms for tackling these complexities, for identifying rural women's needs, and for arriving at a more unified perspective on priorities. Priorities can be both context-specific and cross-context, and they can change over time. Identifying what is in the interest of poor rural women would involve a mix of methods, of which systematic interaction and listening to what women themselves have to say are clearly the most essential. Although many rural groups already facilitate such interactions, there can be issues of regularity and whether the forums enable women to voice their views without hesitation. Also insofar as women in disadvantaged positions adapt their preferences to what appears feasible rather than to what they may objectively need, or lack information on less-visible ill-effects, such as the health ill-effects of unprocessed biofuels or the potential dangers of climate change, village-level discussions for identifying priorities would not be enough. A macro-perspective on changes in the national and global economy and taking account of emergent research findings also appears necessary. I believe that if such processes had been in place, cooking energy shortages would have surfaced in civil society discussions as a critical basic need a long time ago.

Overcoming divisiveness to arrive at a unified view is an equally compelling problem. In principle, divisiveness based on differences in contexts, approaches,

[53] For a brief history of how the issue came into prominence, including the catalytic effect of *A Field of One's Own*, see Agarwal (2003).

[54] See e.g. Eckholm (1976), Agarwal (1986a), Smith et al. (1993), and Sarin (1998), among others.

or identities need not become a defining factor, if alliances are conceptualized flexibly as *strategic*, as a way of focusing on particular issues, while accepting the potential for disagreement on other issues.[55] But, again, making such linkages and forging common platforms requires deliberation, be it through long-tested face-to-face discussions, or by using the new opportunities opened up by the internet, or both. Although this is already happening to a limited extent, it could be taken further in more strategic ways.

In the longer term, however, the promotion of a gendered understanding and a green perspective will require more than interventions on particular issues; it will require an impact on ways of thinking. Indeed, even to weave a web of alliances based on strategic interests, women need to intervene in the arena of ideas and not just in the theatre of presence.

4.2 The Promise of Ideas

> The biggest mistake is to set up ideas as the opposite of political presence: to treat ideas as totally separate from the people who carry them; or worry exclusively about the people without giving a thought to their policies and ideas. (Phillips 1998: 491)

Ideas can be the cement for establishing common cause despite material and cultural difference. At least three types of ideas are critical here: ideas about gender equality and women's potential contribution to governance; ideas about the need to transcend economic and social difference; and ideas about environmental conservation.

If village men recognized, for instance, the considerable contribution women can make to forest management and the disproportionate cost women bear from a lack of adequate and clean cooking energy, we would not need to depend mainly on women for pursuing gender-inclusive governance practices. Informed solutions about affordable clean fuels would emerge through participative processes even with limited female presence. Similarly, if the rich held stronger other-regarding preferences, or if there was a generalized social preference for equality and justice, then principles of accessing forest resources and distributing forest products would be more need-based, rather than predominantly contribution-based.[56] At the same time, there are still enough examples in South Asia and globally, of movements that have emerged around public causes which cut across gender, class, and community, drawing on shared ideas and visions that highlight the possibility of transcending hierarchy and difference. These common

[55] Cases in point are the earlier-mentioned campaigns in India against dowry in the early 1980s and for women's quotas in parliament in the more recent period.

[56] Some scholars argue, in fact, that the process of deliberation can itself produce other-regarding preferences among the privileged (see e.g. Sunstein 1991, Young 1993, 2000, and Sen 2009). Sen (2009: 337) also emphasizes the role of public discussion in producing tolerant values, and argues: 'If [as a result] the majority is ready to support the rights of minorities, and even of dissenting and discordant individuals, then liberty can be guaranteed without having to restrain majority rule.'

understandings constitute the threads not only for weaving strategic alliances, but for weaving alliances that transcend strategic considerations.

Although ideas alone cannot substitute for women's presence in green governance, they can make that presence more effective if ways of thinking could rise above class, caste, and gender previleges. Indeed we would expect a dialectical relationship between ideas and presence. For women to shape thinking, they first need access to deliberative space since, as Phillips (1995: 151) argues, 'if certain groups have been permanently excluded, the process of deliberation cannot even begin.' But, equally, acceptance of the *idea* that women should be represented in public decision-making bodies would enhance the prospects of their inclusion in such bodies.

In this context, it is also time for gender-progressive organizations to focus not merely on increasing women's numbers in public forums, but on where women and men in public stand in relation to questions of gender justice and the environment, among other matters. A link with ideas is similarly essential if grassroots groups working on rural livelihoods are to engage with green issues; if autonomous women's groups are to focus on environmental concerns; and if alliances between CFIs and SHGs are to transform into something bigger, such as a women's green movement. Environ-mentality—the mentality that saving the environment is everyone's concern—is a key idea beyond material self-interest, one which, when it catches the popular imagination, weaves into a community's folk songs and way of life: 'van vavo jeevan bachavo' (plant trees, save lives),[57] and 'whenever you see a vacant space plant trees—fodder trees, oak trees, broad-leafed trees . . . ' (Garwali folk song used in the Chipko movement).

The transformation of ways of thinking is a complex, interactive, long-term process constituting the interplay of diverse ideologies and influences. There are likely to be no short cuts to this process of ideological contestation which will be, as Fraser (1990) correctly emphasizes, 'a site for struggle'.[58] Ideas and values are constituted and contested in many arenas, in particular within the family, within communities, within educational, religious, and legislative institutions, through the media, and now, increasingly, over the internet. Public deliberation is one means of bridging ideational differences between individuals and arriving at a set of group-defined priorities or understandings. And even if individual differences persist, the process holds the promise of a group reaching agreement. Technological advances over the past few decades—in particular TV and the internet—have enormously enlarged the space for deliberation.[59] Although the old-fashioned

[57] Male villagers, Bharuch CFI, Gujarat, author's survey, 2000–01.

[58] A first step is to bring what the French sociologist Pierre Bourdieu (1977: 167–70) terms 'doxa'—the 'undiscussed, unnamed, admitted without argument or scrutiny' into the arena of contestation, the 'field of opinion, of that which is explicitly questioned'.

[59] Sunstein (2006) in an enticingly titled book—*Infotopia*—discusses at length both the virtues and the pitfalls of using the internet as a deliberative space; and how sometimes groups, lacking information, may reach incorrect decisions. This, in my view, strengthens the case for bringing outside information to bear on any process of deliberation. See also Sen (2009) on the role of a well-functioning media in facilitating public reasoning.

radio is still important for reaching remote villages—in Nepal many rural women told me that they had learnt about women's role in community forestry through radio programmes—it is TV and the internet which now form the new threads of the spider's web. In South Asia some elements of the media are already playing an important role in giving voice to the disadvantaged. There are also lively debates over the internet among development NGOs on the effectiveness of their policies and interventions.[60] The influence of ideas is both local and global. And the potential for change is as enormous as the imperative for change.

4.3 Redistribution, Representation, and Empowerment

Finally, let me turn to a key issue—the link between furthering green agendas and women's empowerment. This book has presented many instrumental and intrinsic reasons for enhancing women's participation in institutions of green governance. Such participation is linked with women's social and political empowerment. But here I want to touch briefly on women's economic empowerment.

In *A Field of One's Own* I had argued that women's command over property is the single most important factor in women's economic empowerment, and had advocated measures to increase gender equality in property, focusing mainly on private property, especially agricultural land. Conceptually, however, as I had elaborated, the link between women's command over property and their empowerment lies not only in the ownership of property but also in *control* over it; and not only in private property but also in public property. Hence redistribution of property would imply something much more complex than simply property transfer into individual hands. It would imply the transfer of control over that property in diverse ways. In some contexts such control could go along with a transfer of ownership and in other contexts merely with a transfer of decision-making authority over property. And in some contexts the ownership and/or control could go into individual hands and in other contexts into community hands. At the heart of women's economic empowerment lies increasing their command over both private property resources and common pool resources. Closing the gender gap in command over private property would constitute one critical piece of this; closing the gender gap in command over public resources, such as forests, would constitute another critical piece.

The empowerment potential of command over property, however, lies not only in the end result—namely, achieving actual ownership or control—but also in the process by which that result is achieved. The focus of the present book has been centrally on that process, through the representation of women in public

[60] Cases in point are several open internet discussions in recent years, among NGOs in India working with the rural poor, on the most effective programmes for reducing poverty and empowering their constituents. Some of these exchanges have been facilitated by the UN initiative 'Solution Exchange' (see www.solutionexchange-un.net.in).

decision-making institutions for controlling a critical component of public property and social wealth—forests. We need to conceptualize both processes—that of resource redistribution and that of achieving representation and voice—as ongoing, interactive, and parallel, without insisting that the one or the other be a precondition.[61] Both, however, need to be seen as *intrinsic* elements of women's empowerment and not only as instrumental, each in relation to the other.

Against this background, we might also question the sharpness of the a priori division of women's needs into 'practical' and 'strategic' that has gained substantial popularity in gender analysis and policy advocacy.[62] The argument is that focusing on practical gender needs—the needs of basic subsistence—does not help challenge women's unequal position within the gender division of labour, or a given distribution of property or political power, which constitute strategic gender needs. Examined through the lens of *process*, however, the apparent neatness of this analytical distinction gets blurred. Even meeting subsistence needs often requires challenging existing social and political structures, so that action in pursuit of 'practical' needs can easily turn into action to meet 'strategic' needs. For instance, for poor women, firewood is a practical need, but it can become strategic since persuading a male-dominated CFI committee to extract more forest produce requires enhancing women's voice within the institution. This, in turn, might need collective action by women. Similarly, it may be as necessary for poor women to organize into groups and forge alliances with other groups for effectively participating in forest management, as for effectively campaigning for their land rights. Indeed, as we have noted, for women to even participate in group meetings often requires them to overcome the constraints of social norms and social perceptions, to face the disapproval of their families, to negotiate the domestic division of labour and childcare with family members, and so on.

In several respects, therefore, the process of fulfilling 'practical' gender needs can be quite similar to that of fulfilling 'strategic' gender needs, and this process can be empowering. In other respects, undeniably, the processes may diverge notably, especially where fulfilling strategic gender needs involves establishing greater control over economic resources, such as land or forests, and is likely to meet much greater resistance. Representation in decision-making may enhance women's voice and control over common pool resources, but given the high and growing inequalities of private income and wealth in South Asia (and globally), voice alone may not be enough for bringing about asset redistribution. Hence although representation and the formation of collectivities of the poor is a step forward, the journey toward economic empowerment is likely to be a long one. In efforts to achieve representation by quotas or other means we should not lose sight of the importance of going beyond representation to achieving a better deal for

[61] There is in fact a long-standing debate between political theorists on the issue of recognition vs. redistribution: see Fraser (1995, 1997), Young (1997b), and Phillips (1997).

[62] I draw primarily on Moser's (1989) elaboration which is the most widely used, although the distinction was first made by Molyneux (1985).

women, especially in the distribution of economic resources. 'The newer politics around the recognition of difference' should not, as Phillips (1997: 153) reminds us, 'displace the older politics around economic inequality'.

5. IN CONCLUSION

> Come plant new trees, new forests, decorate the earth.
> Let us free the land of this crisis. Come, all join together.
>
> (Garhwali folk song sung by Chipko activists)

Many conclusions can be drawn from the findings of this book, both as regards green governance from a gender perspective, and as regards gender and governance. I leave the reader to follow particular trails, and conclude with a few points of emphasis.

Effective and democratic institutions of governance require the representation of all segments of the population. In particular, they require the inclusion of women, whose participation would lead to both more efficient and more equitable outcomes. Institutions of local green governance warrant such participatory inclusion to an even greater extent than institutions of government, given the interrelatedness of two important goals—conservation and providing local subsistence. We have seen the many ways in which women's inclusion in institutions of green governance can prove central to the achievement of both goals. But to be effective, women need more than nominal inclusion—they need substantial presence.

There are many obstacles to women attaining such presence in institutions of green governance in South Asia: a long history of exclusion from public space, patriarchal cultural norms, biased perceptions about women's capabilities, women's limited clout as a political constituency, the weak support or attention given to such institutions by the government at all levels, and so on. Yet there is scope for optimism in the rich and diverse base of pro-poor pro-women civil society organizations that have emerged in the region, especially over the past two decades. Nepal has a national-level forest federation with a mandate for including women. In India, we see the emergence of thousands of women's self-help groups and their federations: here a web of strategic alliances—woven horizontally and vertically—between these institutions of civil society and green institutions of governance, can benefit both types of organizations in many ways. They can strengthen women's voice and influence in the latter and broaden the base of environmental awareness in the former. In both regions, such federations and alliances can also provide a means of resisting the multiple pressures on forest resources from competing demands for land and from powerful commercial lobbies that play on the vulnerability of local communities. Most crucially, such alliances, if they include gender-progressive organizations and individuals with national-level reach, could strengthen women's bargaining power with the government at all levels—from village councils to parliament. In doing so, they could both promote rural women's interests and enhance the sustainability of local institutions of green governance.

Long-term environmental sustainability, however, will depend on the access of village households to alternative sources of fuel, building materials, and livelihoods which are less forest dependent. To facilitate this, institutions of government need to be much more interactively and democratically engaged with local institutions of civil society, than they are at present. Moreover, although today the dependence of village communities on forests serves as the basis for community collective action, in the long run the answer lies precisely in reducing that dependence, both for enhancing community welfare and for stemming global warming and preserving biodiversity.

The kinds of strategic alliances and public engagement I have discussed in these two concluding chapters can also prove to be significant allies in the shift out of such dependency. Habits of cooperation, forms of deliberation, social networks, and community connections can all survive their original contexts and carry over into new domains—economic, social, and political. So can that other welcome by-product of gender-inclusive green governance—women's empowerment. These would constitute the foundations on which other canopies of green development could be built.

Definitions of Variables and Descriptive Statistics

Table AE.1. Gujarat: definitions and descriptive statistics for dependent variables (all districts)

Definition	Descriptive statistics				
	N	Mean	CV	Min	Max
I. Participation (mixed-gender CFIs only): Chapter 5					
% EC meetings with no EC women (in all years of CFI functioning)	32	29.1	1.24	0	100
Female attendance rate (in all years of CFI functioning)	32	0.5	0.62	0	1
Do women speak up in EC meetings: dummy (if some or most women spoke up in at least one of the last 3 meetings=1; if none spoke up = 0)	36	23	n.a.	0	1
II. Rules (all CFIs): Chapter 6					
Strictness index: sum of six strictness scores (aggregate of scores for twigs collection, drywood cutting, grass fodder cutting, grazing, cutting timber species for firewood and cutting timber poles for house building). Weights: open always =1; open occasionally = 2.5; partial ban, or given on request for special need or natural disaster = 2.75; full ban = 3. *(All products are subject to the same weight structure. Range of values: 6 to18.)* See text for method used to calculate the index.	65	13.9	0.18	9.8	17.5
Twigs collection rules 1: dummy (if full ban, or partial ban/given on request, or open occasionally = 1; if open always = 0)	65	27	n.a.	0	1
Drywood cutting rules: dummy (if full ban, partial ban/given on request, or open occasionally = 1; if open always = 0)	65	48	n.a.	0	1
Grass fodder cutting rules: dummy (if full ban, partial ban/ given on request, or open occasionally = 1; if open always = 0)	65	33	n.a.	0	1
III. Violations (all CFIs): Chapter 7					
Total no. of violations per year of CFI functioning	44	0.5	0.81	0.11	2
Percentage violations by men per CFI	44	58.0	0.74	0	100
Percentage violations by women per CFI	44	19.7	1.62	0	100
Percentage violations for timber per CFI	44	54.4	0.73	0	100
Percentage violations for firewood per CFI	44	26.6	1.41	0	100

(continued)

Table AE.1. (Continued)

Definition	Descriptive statistics				
	N	Mean	CV	Min	Max
IV. Forest condition (all CFIs): Chapter 8					
Researcher's index: forest quality assessed by forest specialist/ researcher, graded on a scale of 1 to 5, at intervals of 0.25	63	3.5	0.23	1.5	4.8
Forest canopy: dummy: canopy of protected natural forest and plantation (villagers' assessment) (if thick or medium density =1; if thin or patchy = 0)	63	37	n.a.	0	1
Geer: % degraded forest: % forest area with degraded canopy in 1999, assessed by Geer Institute based on satellite data	63	32.6	0.48	0	74.6
Forest condition change: Change in natural forest and plantation condition since protection began (villagers' assessment) (some or substantial improvement in category =1; no improvement in category = 0)	64	53	n.a.	0	1
V. Shortages (all CFIs): Chapter 9					
Firewood shortage: dummy (if most have firewood shortages = 1; if few or none have firewood shortages = 0)	61	45	n.a.	0	1
Fodder shortage: dummy (if most have fodder shortages = 1; if few or none have fodder shortages = 0)	61	42	n.a.	0	1

Notes: Here and in the appendix tables that follow: (1) For dummy variables the means give the number of positive values. (2) For other variables the means are calculated here by first computing the value for each CFI and then averaging it over the number of cases in the whole sample (all districts) or the district subsample, as relevant. The means in Chapter 4, however, are calculated for the sample (or district) as a whole. The differences between the two averages are rather slight.

n.a. = not applicable.

Table AE.2. Gujarat: definitions and descriptive statistics for dependent variables (district-wise)

Districts	Narmada/Bharuch					Panchmahals					Sabarkantha				
Definition	Descriptive statistics														
	N	Mean	CV	Min	Max	N	Mean	CV	Min	Max	N	Mean	CV	Min	Max
I. Rules (all CFIs): Chapter 6															
Strictness index: definition same as for Gujarat (all districts) (see Table AE.1)	16	14.7	0.16	10	17.5	21	13.2	0.21	9.8	17	28	14.0	0.17	10	17.5
II. Forest condition (all CFIs): Chapter 8															
Researcher's index: forest quality assessed by forest specialist/ researcher, graded on a scale of 1 to 5, at intervals of 0.25						19	3.4	0.20	2.5	4.8					
Forest canopy: dummy: canopy of protected natural forest and plantation (villagers' assessment) if thick or medium density =1; if thin or patchy = 0)						19	9	n.a.	0	1					
Geer: % degraded forest: % forest area with degraded canopy in 1999, assessed by Geer Institute based on satellite data						19	29.6	0.52	0	56.0					
Forest condition change: change in natural forest and plantation condition since protection began (villagers' assessment) (some or substantial improvement in category =1; no improvement in category = 0)						20	13	n.a.	0	1					

Table AE.3. Gujarat: definition and descriptive statistics for explanatory variables (all districts)

Definitions (all chapters)	Descriptive statistics				
	N	Mean	CV	Min	Max
GenComp1: dummy (if EC has >2 women=1; if EC has ≤2 women = 0)	65	34	n.a.	0	1
GenComp2: % women in the EC	65	27.3	0.72	0	100
GenComp3: dummy (if EC has <25% women=1) (reference category)	65	33	n.a.	0	1
GenComp4: dummy (if EC has ≥25–<33% women=1; other ECs = 0)	65	13	n.a.	0	1
GenComp5: dummy (if EC has ≥33% women = 1; other ECs = 0)	65	19	n.a.	0	1
Women's association in village: dummy (if association exists=1; if not =0)	65	44	n.a.	0	1
Average age of women EC members, 2000–01	59	40.9	0.16	23	59.5
Average age of all EC members, 2000–01	64	43.6	0.14	28.1	55.6
Average land owned by all EC members (ha)	64	1.2	0.55	0.4	4.2
% EC women from landless households	59	21.3	1.86	0	100
% all EC members from landless households	64	7.4	1.65	0	55.6
Gini coefficient for land owned by the EC	64	0.3	0.37	0.1	0.7
% illiterate EC women	59	53.4	0.66	0	100
Who initiated the CFI: dummy (if villagers =1; if forest department or NGO = 0)	65	32	n.a.	0	1
CFI formation period: dummy (post-1995 =1)	65	30	n.a.	0	1
CFI years of functioning	65	5.7	0.35	2	10
Protection method: dummy (if protected by guard = 1; if protected by patrol group or informally = 0)	65	22	n.a.	0	1
Twigs collection rules 2: dummy (if full ban =1; if partial ban/given on request, or open occasionally, or open always = 0)	65	12	n.a.	0	1
Grazing rules: dummy (if full ban, or partial ban, or open occasionally = 1; if open always = 0)	65	39	n.a.	0	1
Forest area protected (ha)	65	164.9	1.3	15	1536.8
No. of forest segments (viz. non-contiguous parts of protected forest)	65	1.9	0.61	1	6
Gap-filled plus plantation area (ha)	65	15.6	1.65	0	120

Total households in village	65	183.4	0.70	36	758
No. of hamlets in village	65	6.0	0.47	2	13
Average land owned by village households (ha)	65	0.9	0.34	0.3	1.7
Gini coefficient for land owned by villagers (among those owning land)	65	0.32	0.27	0.1	0.5
% landless households in village	65	7.5	1.60	0	40.6
% village households with migrant males	64	12.7	1.33	0	59.5
Use of another local forest to firewood: dummy (if used =1; if not = 0)	58	17	n.a.	0	1
Use of another local forest to fodder: dummy (if used =1; if not = 0)	59	15	n.a.	0	1
Distance of village from road (km)	65	1.9	1.34	0	14
Distance of village from nearest town (km)	65	11.0	0.64	1	32
District1: dummy (Narmada/Bharuch = 1) (reference category)	65	16	n.a.	0	1
District2: dummy (Panchmahals =1; if other districts = 0)	65	21	n.a.	0	1
District3: dummy (Sabarkantha =1; if other districts = 0)	65	28	n.a.	0	1
Firewood shortage: dummy (if most have firewood shortages = 1; if few or none have shortages = 0)	61	45	n.a.	0	1

Table AE.4. Gujarat: definition and descriptive statistics for explanatory variables (district-wise)

Districts	Narmada/Bharuch					Panchmahals					Sabarkantha				
Definition						Descriptive statistics									
	N	Mean	CV	Min	Max	N	Mean	CV	Min	Max	N	Mean	CV	Min	Max
GenComp1: dummy (if EC has >2 women =1; if EC has ≤2 women = 0)	16	8	n.a.	0	1	21	10	n.a.	0	1	28	16	n.a.	0	1
Women's association in village: dummy (if association exists=1; if not = 0)						21	12	n.a.	0	1	28	18	n.a.	0	1
Average age of women EC members, 2000–01						20	41.8	0.14	23	54					
% EC women from landless households						20	57.5	0.86	0	100					
% all EC members from landless households	16	10.0	1.59	0	55.6	20	13.8	0.95	0	36.4					
Gini coefficient for land owned by the EC	16	0.4	0.39	0.1	0.70	20	0.3	0.35	0.1	0.5	28	0.3	0.32	0.1	0.5
Protection method: dummy: (if protected by guard = 1; if without guard but using other methods = 0)						21	6	n.a.	0	1					
Forest area protected (ha)	16	57.9	0.65	20	120	21	224.6	0.72	15.3	546	28	181.4	1.54	15	1536.8
No. of forest segments: number of non-contiguous parts of protected forest	16	1.8	0.46	1	4	21	2.7	0.52	1	6	28	1.3	0.46	1	3
Gap-filled plus plantation area (ha)	16	46.9	0.67	20	120	21	5.1	1.79	0	25	28	5.5	2.52	0	50
Total households in village	16	168.7	0.57	51	353	21	184.3	0.82	55	758	28	191	0.69	36	654
% landless households in village	16	20.8	0.67	2.4	40.6	21	2.0	1.86	0	12.4	28	4.0	2.22	0	33.9
Infrastructure index: this aggregates village facilities (where they exist) for four levels of education, two levels of health care, and village electrification. Each type of facility gets equal weight.						21	3.3	0.27	2	5					

Table AE.5. Nepal: definition and descriptive statistics for dependent variables (all districts and district-wise)

Region	All districts					Gorkha/Dhading					Baglung/Parbat				
Definition						Descriptive statistics									
	N	Mean	CV	Min	Max	N	Mean	CV	Min	Max	N	Mean	CV	Min	Max
I. Participation (mixed gender CFIs only): Chapter 5															
% EC meetings with no EC women (in all years of CFI functioning)	38	18.6	1.42	0	100										
Female attendance rate (in all years of CFI functioning)	38	0.5	0.52	0	1										
Do women speak up in EC meetings (if most spoke up in at least one of the last 3 meetings=1; if some spoke up = 0)	37	28	n.a.	0	1										
% current women EC members who are office bearers	38	13.4	1.36	0	66.7										
Gender gap in office bearing (% male minus % female office bearers)	38	36.3	0.76	-33.3	80										
Characteristic of individual EC members: variable below used only for office bearer analysis **(Table 5.10)**															
Current female EC member who is or has been an office bearer	137	31	n.a	0	1										
Current male EC member who is or has been an office bearer	301	148	n.a	0	1										

(continued)

Table AE.5. Nepal: (Continued)

Region	All districts					Gorkha/Dhading					Baglung/Parbat				
Definition						Descriptive statistics									
	N	Mean	CV	Min	Max	N	Mean	CV	Min	Max	N	Mean	CV	Min	Max
II. Rules (all CFIs): Chapter 6															
Strictness index: sum of 7 scores (aggregate for twigs, drywood, tree fodder, grass fodder, grazing, timber, and leaf litter). Weights are the same as for Gujarat (see Table AE.1)	70	16.4	0.16	11.8	20	36	15.0	0.18	11.8	20	34	17.8	0.09	12.8	20
Twigs collection rules: dummy (if full ban or partial ban/given on request or open occasionally = 1; open always = 0)	70	38	n.a.	0	1										
Grass cutting rules: dummy (if full ban or partial ban/given on request or open occasionally = 1; open always = 0)	70	41	n.a.	0	1										
Tree fodder cutting rules: dummy (if full ban = 1; if partial ban/given on request or open occasionally = 0)	70	42	n.a.	0	1										
Grazing rules: dummy (if full ban or partial ban/given on request or open occasionally = 1; if open always = 0)	70	51	n.a.	0	1										

III. Violations (all CFIs): Chapter 7					
Total no. of violations per year of CFI functioning	49	1.1	1.5	0	11
IV. Forest condition (all CFIs): Chapter 8					
Forest regeneration (villager assessment at time of survey) (poor=1; good=2; very good = 3)	70	10/44/16	n.a.	1	3
Change in forest canopy: dummy: forest department assessment at two points in time (if improvement or thick canopy maintained =1; if no change in canopy (remains thin, patchy, or medium) or worsening canopy = 0)	58	39	n.a.	0	1
V. Shortages (all CFIs): Chapter 9					
Firewood shortage: dummy (if most have firewood shortage = 1; if few or none have shortage = 0)	62	39	n.a.	0	1
Fodder shortage: dummy (if most have fodder shortage =1; if few or none have shortage = 0	60	39	n.a.	0	1

Table AE.6. Nepal: definition and descriptive statistics for explanatory variables (all districts and district-wise)

Region	All districts					Gorkha/Dhading					Baglung/Parbat				
Definition						Descriptive statistics									
	N	Mean	CV	Min	Max	N	Mean	CV	Min	Max	N	Mean	CV	Min	Max
GenComp: dummy (all-women ECs = 1; other ECs = 0)	70	27	n.a.	0	1	36	16	n.a.	0	1	34	11	n.a.	0	1
GenComp2: % EC women	70	55.1	0.69	0	100										
GenComp4: dummy (if EC has ≥25-<33% women =1; other ECs = 0)	70	9	n.a.	0	1										
GenComp5: dummy (if EC has ≥33% women = 1; other ECs = 0)	70	43	n.a.	0	1										
Women's association: dummy (if association exists = 1; if not = 0)	70	42	n.a.	0	1	36	21	n.a.	0	1	34	21	n.a.	0	1
Average age of all EC members in 2000–01	70	41.5	0.12	30.4	54.5	36	39.5	0.11	30.4	49.3	34	43.6	0.12	35.8	54.5
Average land owned by EC members (ha)	67	0.8	0.52	0.19	2.0	35	0.96	0.41	0.39	2.0	32	0.65	0.61	0.19	1.96
Gini coefficient for land owned by EC	67	0.3	0.30	0.1	0.5	35	0.3	0.29	0.1	0.4	32	0.32	0.31	0.14	0.5
% illiterate EC women members	65	43.1	0.83	0	100										
% illiterate all EC members	70	34.3	0.82	0	100										

Gender gap in illiteracy (% illiterate female EC minus % illiterate male EC)	38	22.8	1.63	-35.7	100										
% Brahmins in EC	70	48.6	0.77	0	100	36	43.2	0.80	0	100	34	54.3	0.74	0	100
80% single caste: dummy (if ≥80% of EC members are from a single caste =1; if not = 0)	70	40	n.a.	0	1										
Member of another CFI: dummy (if member =1; if not = 0)	70	53	n.a.	0	1	36	27	n.a.	0	1	34	26	n.a.	0	1
Who made forest use rules: dummy (if rules made without FD help =1; if made with FD help = 0)	70	25	n.a.	0	1	36	20	n.a.	0	1	34	5	n.a.	0	1
CFI formation period: dummy (post-1996 =1)	69	31	n.a.	0	1										
CFI years of functioning	69	5.4	0.45	1	11										
% member households with migrant males	70	17.08	0.84	0	66.67										
Protection method: dummy (protection by guard = 1; protection by patrol group or informally = 0)	70	22	n.a.	0	1										

(continued)

Table AE.6. Nepal: (Continued)

Region	All districts					Gorkha/Dhading					Baglung/Parbat				
Definition	Descriptive statistics														
	N	Mean	CV	Min	Max	N	Mean	CV	Min	Max	N	Mean	CV	Min	Max
Twigs collection rules: dummy (if full ban, partial ban/given on request, or open occasionally = 1; open always= 0)	70	38	n.a.	0	1										
Tree fodder cutting rules: dummy (if full ban = 1; if partial ban/given on request, or open occasionally = 0)	70	42	n.a.	0	1										
Forest area protected (ha)	70	33.6	0.89	3.9	160	36	33.1	1.00	3.9	160	34	34.1	0.78	4.9	105.2
Interactive term 1: forest area with GenComp	70	8.0	1.89	0	75.2	36	8.4	1.83	0	75.2	34	7.6	2.0	0	57
Interactive term 2: forest area with GenComp2	70	1448.4	1.0	0	7525										
Forest canopy at time of handover: dummy (if thick or medium canopy =1; if thin canopy = 0)	60	14	n.a.	0	1										
Forest canopy at time of survey: dummy (if dense = 1; if thin = 0)	70	59	n.a.	0	1										

Forest age: dummy (if medium or old = 1; if young = 0)	70	31	n.a.	0	1	36	18	n.a.	0	1	34	13	n.a.	0	1
No. of toles in CFIs	70	5.2	0.47	1	13	36	5.1	0.43	2	11	34	5.2	0.52	1	13
District: dummy (Baglung/Parbat =1; Gorkha/Dhading = 0)	70	34	n.a.	0	1										
Firewood shortage: dummy (if most have shortages =1; if few or some have shortages = 0)	62	39	n.a.	0	1										
Characteristics of individual EC members: variables below used only for office bearer analysis (Table 5.10)															
Number of EC members	438	12	0.19	7	17										
If EC member has been on the EC before =1	438	165	n.a	0	1										
EC member's age	438	43.4	0.26	17	79										
EC member's marital status: dummy (if currently married =1; if unmarried, divorced, separated, or widowed = 0)	438	416	n.a.	0	1										
Land owned by EC member's household (ha)	433	0.8	0.79	0	3.6										
EC member's literacy: dummy (if literate =1; if not = 0)	438	318	n.a.	0	1										
EC member's caste: dummy (if upper-caste Hindu =1; if other caste or ethnic = 0)	438	226	n.a.	0	1										

References

Acharya, M., and Bennett, L. (1981), *An Aggregate Analysis and Summary of Village Studies: The Status of Women in Nepal, II, Part 9* (Kathmandu: CEDA, Tribhuvan University).

——(1982), 'Women and the Subsistence Sector in Nepal', World Bank Staff Working Paper No. 526, World Bank, Washington, DC.

Adhikari, N., Yadav, G., Ray, S. B., and Kumar, S. (1991), 'Process Documentation of Women's Involvement in Forest Management at Maheshpur, Ranchi', in R. Singh (ed.), *Managing the Village Commons: Proceedings of the National Workshop*, 15–16 Dec. (Bhopal: Indian Institute of Forest Management), 118–23.

Agarwal, A. (1983), 'The Cooking Energy System: Problems and Opportunities', Discussion Paper, Center for Science and Environment, Delhi.

——and Narain, S. (1989), *Towards Green Villages: A Strategy for Environmentally Sound and Participatory Rural Development* (New Delhi: Centre for Science and Environment).

Agarwal, B. (1984), 'Rural Women and the HYV Rice Technology in India', *Economic and Political Weekly*, Review of Agriculture, 19(13): A39–A52.

——(1986a), *Cold Hearths and Barren Slopes: The Woodfuel Crisis in the Third World* (London: Zed Books).

——(1986b), 'Women, Poverty and Agricultural Growth in India', *Journal of Peasant Studies*, 13(4): 165–220.

——(1986c), 'Is Bharatpur for Birds Only?', *Hinduston Times*, Sunday magazine, 7 Dec.

——(1990), 'Social Security and the Family: Coping with Seasonality and Calamity in Rural India', *Journal of Peasant Studies*, 17(3): 341–412.

——(1992), 'The Gender and Environment Debate: Lessons from India', *Feminist Studies*, 18(1): 119–58.

——(1994), *A Field of one's Own: Gender and Land Rights in South Asia* (Cambridge: Cambridge University Press).

——(1997a), 'Environmental Action, Gender Equity, and Women's Participation', *Development and Change*, 28(1): 1–44.

——(1997b), 'Gender, Environment, and Poverty Interlinks: Regional Variations and Temporal Shifts in Rural India, 1971–91', *World Development*, 25(1): 23–52.

——(1997c), '"Bargaining" and Gender Relations: Within and Beyond the Household', *Feminist Economics*, 3(1): 1–51.

——(1998a), 'Environmental Management, Equity, and Ecofeminism: Debating India's Experience', *Journal of Peasant Studies*, 25(4): 55–95.

——(1998b), 'Disinherited Peasants, Disadvantaged Workers: A Gender Perspective on Land and Livelihood', *Economic and Political Weekly*, Review of Agriculture, 33(13): A2–A14.

——(2000a), 'Group Functioning and Community Forestry in South Asia: A Gender Analysis and Conceptual Framework', UNU/WIDER, Working Paper No. 172, Helsinki: World Institute for Development Economic Research.

——(2000b), 'Conceptualizing Environmental Collective Action: Why Gender Matters', *Cambridge Journal of Economics*, 24(3): 283–310.

——(2001), 'Participatory Exclusions, Community Forestry and Gender: An Analysis for South Asia and a Conceptual Framework', *World Development*, 29(10): 1623–48.

Agarwal, B. (2002), 'Bargaining and Legal Change: Gender Equality and Inheritance Laws in India', Discussion Paper No. 165, Institute of Development Studies, Sussex.

——(2003), 'Gender and Land Rights Revisited: Exploring New Prospects via the State, Family and Market', *Journal of Agrarian Change*, 3(1 and 2): 184–224.

——(2006), 'Gender Inequality, Cooperation and Environmental Sustainability', in J. M. Baland, S. Bowles, and P. Bardhan (eds.), *Inequality, Cooperation, and Environmental Sustainability* (Princeton: Princeton University Press), 274–313.

——(2009a), 'Rule Making in Community Forestry Institutions: The Difference Women Make', *Ecological Economics*, 68: 2296–308.

——(2009b), 'Gender and Forest Conservation: The Impact of Women's Participation in Community Forest Governance', *Ecological Economics*, 68(11): 2785–99.

——(2010), 'Does Women's Proportional Strength Affect their Participation? Governing Local Forests in South Asia', *World Development*, 38(1): 98–112.

——and Vercelli, A. (2005), *Psychology, Rationality and Economic Behaviour: Challenging Standard Assumptions* (London: Palgrave).

Agrawal, A. (1997), 'Rules, Rule Making and Rule Breaking: Examining the Fit between Rule Systems and Resource Use', in E. Ostrom, R. Gardner, and J. Walker (eds.), *Rules, Games and Common-Pool Resources* (Ann Arbor: University of Michigan Press), 267–82.

——(1999a), *Decentralization in Nepal: A Comparative Analysis* (Oakland, CA: Institute for Contemporary Studies Press).

——(1999b), 'Community-in-Conservation: Tracing the Outlines of an Enchanting Concept', in R. Jeffery and N. Sundar, *A New Moral Economy for India's Forests? Discourses of Community and Participation* (New Delhi: Sage Publications), 92–108.

——(2001), 'The Decentralizing State: Nature and Origins of Changing Environmental Policies in Africa and Latin America, 1980–2000', paper presented at the American Political Science Association Meeting, Aug.–Sept.

——(2005), *Environmentality: Technologies of Government and the Making of Subjects* (Durham, NC: Duke University Press).

——and Chhatre A. (2006), 'Explaining Success on the Commons: Community Forest Governance in the Indian Himalayas', *World Development*, 34(1): 149–66.

——and Gibson, C. (2001), *Communities and the Environment* (New Brunswick, NJ: Rutgers University Press).

——Yadama, G., Andrade, R., and Bhattacharya, A. (2006), 'Decentralization and Environmental Conservation: Gender Effects from Participation in Joint Forest Management', CAPRI Working Paper No. 53, International Food Policy Research Institute, Washington, DC.

Aguilar, F. V. Jr. (1982), 'Social Forestry for Upland Development: Lessons from Four Case Studies', Institute of Philippine Culture, Ateneo de Manila University, Quezon City, Philippines.

Ahmed, A. S. (1986), *Pakistan Society: Islam, Ethnicity and Leadership in South Asia* (Karachi: Oxford University Press).

Ahmed, S. (1994), 'The Rhetoric and Reality of Women's Participation in Joint Forest Management: The Case of an NGO in Western India', paper presented for an International Seminar on Women, Poverty, and Demographic Change, Oaxaca, Mexico, Oct.

Aiyar, C. R. C. (1883), *Manual of Malabar Law* (Madras: Vest and Company).

Akram-Lodhi, A. H. (1996), 'You are not Excused from Cooking: Peasants and the Gender Division of Labour in Pakistan', *Feminist Economics*, 2(2): 87–105.

Allen, B. C., Gait, E. A., Allen, C. G. H., and Howard, H. F. ([1905] 1993), *Gazetteer of Bengal and North East India* (New Delhi: Mittal Publications).

Anand, S., Knack, S., Lee, Y., and Azfar, O. (2001), 'Gender and Corruption', *Journal of Development Economics,* 64(1): 25–55.

Andersen, K. (1975), 'Working Women and Political Participation: 1952–1972', *American Journal of Political Science,* 19: 439–53.

Anderson, E. (2006), 'Sen, Ethics, and Democracy', in B. Agarwal, I. Robeyns, and J. Humphries (eds.), *Capability, Freedom and Equality: Amartya Sen's Work from a Gender Perspective* (Delhi: Oxford University Press), 233–57.

Anderson, P. N. (2000), 'Commodification, Conservation and Community: An Analysis and a Case Study in South India' Edinburgh Papers in South Asian Studies No. 15, University of Edinburgh.

Andersson, S., and Bohman, S. (2001), 'Women's Political Participation in Kerala, South India', Field Study for a BA thesis in Development Studies, Peace and Development Research Institute, Gothenburg University.

APMAS (2007), *SHG Federations in India: A Perspective* (New Delhi: Access Development Services).

Arat, Y. (1983), 'Women in Turkish Politics' unpublished Ph.D. dissertation in Political Science, Princeton University.

Archer, W. G. ([1946] 1984), *Tribal Law and Justice: A Report on the Santal* (New Delhi: Concept Publishing Company).

Arens, J., and Beurden, J. Van (1977), *Jhagrapur: Poor Peasants and Women in a Village in Bangladesh* (Amsterdam: Third World Publications).

Arnold, J. E. M., and Campbell, J. G. (1986), 'Collective Management of Hill Forests in Nepal', in National Research Council, *Proceedings of the Conference on Common Property Resource Management* (Washington, DC: National Academy Press), 425–54.

Ashe, J., and Parrott, L. (2001), *PACT's Women Empowerment Programme in Nepal: A Savings and Literacy Led Alternative to Financial Institutional Building,* Impact Evaluation (Heller School: Brandeis University).

Athreya, V. B., and Rajeshwari, K. S. (1998), 'Women's Participation in Panchayati Raj: A Case Study from Tamil Nadu', working paper, M. S. Swaminathan Research Foundation, Chennai.

Baden-Powell, B. H. ([1896] 1957), *The Indian Village Community* (New Haven: HRAF Press).

Bagadion, B. U., and Korten, F. F. (1991), 'Developing Irrigator's Organisations: A Learning Process Approach', in M. M. Cernea (ed.), *Putting People First: Sociological Variables in Rural Development* (New York: Oxford University Press), 73–112.

Bahuguna, S. (1984), 'Women's Non-violent Power in the Chipko Movement', in M. Kishwar and R. Vanita (eds.), *In Search of Answers: Indian Women's Voices from Manushi* (London: Zed Books), 149–52.

Bahuguna, V. K. (2004), 'Root to Canopy: An Overview', in V. K. Bahuguna, K. Mitra, D. Capistrano, and S. Saigal (eds.), *Root to Canopy* (New Delhi: Commonwealth Forestry Association and Winrock International), 15–24.

Bailey, F. G. (1957), *Caste and the Economic Frontier: A Village in Highland Orissa* (Manchester: Manchester University Press).

Balakrishnan, P. V. (1981), *Matrilineal System in Malabar* (Cannanore, Kerala: Satyavani Prakashan).

Baland, J. M., and Platteau, J. P. (1996), *Halting Degradation of Natural Resources: Is there a Role for Rural Communities?* (Oxford: Clarendon Press).

Baland, J. M., and Platteau, J. P. (1999), 'The Ambiguous Impact of Inequality on Local Resource Management', *World Development*, 27(5): 773–88.

——Bowles, S., and Bardhan, P. (eds.) (2006), *Inequality, Collective Action and Environmental Sustainability* (Princeton: Princeton University Press).

Ban, R., and Rao, V. (2008), 'Tokenism or Agency? The Impact of Women's Reservations on Village Democracies in South India', *Economic Development and Cultural Change*, 56 (1): 501–30.

Bardhan, K. (1977), 'Rural Employment, Wages and Labour Markets in India: A Survey of Research', *Economic and Political Weekly*, 12(26): A34–A48; 12(27): 1062–74; and 12(28): 1101–18.

Bardhan, P. (1993), 'Analytics of the Institutions of Informal Cooperation in Rural Development', *World Development*, 21(4): 633–9.

——(2001), 'Water Community: An Empirical Analysis of Cooperation on Irrigation in South India', in M. Aoki and Y. Hayami (eds.), *Community and Market in Economic Development* (Oxford: Oxford University Press), 247–64.

——(2006), 'Inequality and the Governance of Water Resources in Mexico and South India', in J. M. Baland, P. Bardhan, and S. Bowles (eds.), *Inequality, Cooperation, and Environmental Sustainability* (Princeton: Princeton University Press), 97–130.

Barnes, D. and Kumar, P. (2002), 'Success Factors in Improved Stoves Programmes: Lessons from Six States in India', *Journal of Environmental Study and Policy*, 5(2): 99–112.

Barnes, D.F., Openshaw, K., Smith, K. R., and Van der Plas, R. (1994), 'What Makes People Cook with Improved Biomass Stoves? A Comparative International Review of Stove Programs', World Bank Technical Paper 242, Energy Series, The World Bank, Washington, DC, May.

Barry, A. M. (1990), 'Women, Politics and Participation: A Study of Women and the Labour Party, 1979–1985', unpublished Ph.D. dissertation, University of York.

Basu, A. (2009), 'Women, Political Parties and Social Movements in South Asia', in A. M. Goetz (ed.), *Governing Women: Women's Political Effectiveness in Contexts of Democratization and Governance Reform* (Geneva: UNRISD), 87–111.

Basu, S. (1999), *She Comes to Take her Rights: Indian Women, Property, and Propriety* (Albany, NY: State University of New York Press).

Batliwala, S. (1983), 'Woman and Cooking Energy', *Economic and Political Weekly*, 18(52 and 53): 24–31.

Baumann, P. (2000), 'Sustainable Livelihoods and Political Capital: Arguments and Evidence from Decentralized and Natural Resource Management in India', Working Paper No. 136, Overseas Development Institute, London.

——and Farrington, J. (2003), 'Decentralizing Natural Resource Management: Lessons from Local Government Reform in India', *Natural Resource Perspectives*, 86 (June): 1–4.

——Ramakrishnan, R., Dubey, M., Raman, R. K., and Farrington, J. (2003), 'Institutionalised National Resource Management in India', Working Paper No. 230, Overseas Development Institute, London.

Baviskar, B. S., and Matthew, G. (2009), *Inclusion and Exclusion in Local Governance: Field Studies from Rural India* (New Delhi: Sage Publications Ltd.).

Beaman, L., Chattopadhyay, R., Duflo, E., Pande, R., and Tapalova, P. (2008), 'Powerful Women: Does Exposure Reduce Bias?', Working Paper No. RWP08-037, John F. Kennedy School of Government, Harvard University.

Becker, G., and Mulligan, C. (1997), 'The Endogenous Determination of Time Preference', *Quarterly Journal of Economics*, 112(3): 729–58.

Behar, A., and Kumar, Y. (2002), 'Decentralisation in Madhya Pradesh, India: From Panchayati Raj to Gram Swaraj (1995 to 2001)', Working Paper No. 170, Overseas Development Institute, London.

Behera, B. (2006), 'Who Forms Local Institutions? Levels of Household Participation in India's Joint Forest Management Program', mimeo, Center for Development Research, University of Bonn.

Beneria, L., and Roldan, M. (1987), *The Crosslands of Class and Gender* (Chicago: University of Chicago Press).

Benhabib, S. (ed.) (1996), *Democracy and Difference: Contesting the Boundaries of the Political* (Princeton: Princeton University Press).

Bennett, L., and Gujurel, K. (2006), 'Negotiating Social Change: Gender, Caste and Ethnic Dimensions of Empowerment and Social Inclusion in Rural Nepal', in R. Alsop, M. F. Bertelsen, and J. Holand (eds.), *Empowerment in Practice: From Analysis to Implementation* (Washington, DC: The World Bank), 193–218.

Bergqvist, C. (2004), 'On the Road to Equal Democracy? Women and Parliamentary Representation in the Nordic Countries', in M. Tremblay (ed.), *Women and Parliamentary Representation Around the World* (Montreal: Remue-Menge).

Berkes, F., Davidson-Hunt, I., and Davidson-Hunt, K. (1998), 'Diversity of Common Property Resource Use and Diversity of Social Interests in the Western Indian Himalaya', *Mountain Research and Development*, 18(1): 19–33.

Berkman, M., and O'Connor, R. (1993), 'Do Women Legislators Matter? Female Legislators and State Abortion Policy', *American Politics Quarterly*, 21(1): 102–24.

Bhaduri, T., and Surin, V. (1980), 'Community Forestry and Women Headloaders', in *Community Forestry and People's Participation Seminar Report* (Ranchi: Consortium for Community Forestry), 20–2 Nov.

Bhanji, Z. (1996), 'Emergence of Community Based Experiences, Panchmahals, Gujarat (India)', mimeo, SARTHI and Integrated Development Management, Agha Khan Foundation, Canada.

Bhargava, B. S. (1949), *The Criminal Tribes: A Socio-economic Study of the Principal Criminal Tribes and Castes in Northern India* (United Provinces: Universal Publishers).

Bhatia, A. (2001), *HIMAWANTI: Women of the Hindu Kush-Himalayas* (Kathmandu: International Center for Integrated Mountain Development (ICIMOD)).

Bhattacharya, N. (1992), 'Colonial State and Agrarian Society', in B. Stein (ed.), *The Making of Agrarian Policy in British India 1770–1900* (Delhi: Oxford University Press), 113–49.

Bhattacharya, U. (1985), 'Syiemship', in S. K. Chattopadhyay (ed.), *Tribal Institutions of Meghalaya* (Guwahati: Spectrum Publications), 51–68.

Bhattarai, B. (2007), 'Enhancing Inequality between Terai and Hill Farmers in Nepal: The Implications of the New Forest Policy 2000', draft paper, FECOFUN, Kathmandu.

Biehl, J. (1991), *Rethinking Ecofeminist Politics* (Boston: South End Press).

Bingeman, K. (2001), 'Policy, Gender and Institutions: A Journey through Forest Management Issues in the Kullu Valley, Himachal Pradesh, India', unpublished MA dissertation in Natural Resource Management, University of Manitoba, Winnipeg.

Binswanger, H. P., and Deininger, K. (1997), 'Explaining Agricultural and Agrarian Policies in Developing Countries', *Journal of Economic Literature*, 35(4): 1958–2005.

Biswas, H. (2009), 'Analysis of Biofuel Use in Northern India: Characteristics, Health Impacts and Policy Implications', unpublished Ph.D. dissertation, Indira Gandhi Institute of Development Research, Mumbai.

Bonder, G., and Nari, M. (1995), 'The 30 Percent Quota Law: A Turning Point for Women's Political Participation in Argentina', in A. Brill (ed.), *A Rising Public Voice: Women in Politics Worldwide* (New York: The Feminist Press), 183–93.

Bose, S., Lal, P., Pareek, P. S., Verma, M., and Saigal, S. (2006), 'Forest Based Associations in India: An Overview', Winrock International India and International Institute for Environment and Development, IIED, London.

Bourdieu, P. (1977), *An Outline of the Theory of Practice* (Cambridge: Cambridge University Press).

Bracho, C. (1998), 'La voluntad del ámbar', translated from the Spanish by Poetry Translation, see http://www.poetrytranslation.org/poems/single/83/Thread_in_a_Spider's_Web.

Brara, R. (1987), 'Shifting Sands: A Study of Right in Common Pastures', Report, Institute of Development Studies, Jaipur.

Bratton, K. A. (2005), 'Critical Mass Theory Revisited: The Behavior and Success of Token Women in State Legislatures', *Politics & Gender*, 1(1): 97–125.

——and Haynie, K. L. (1999), 'Agenda Setting and Legislative Success in State Legislatures: The Effects of Gender and Race', *Journal of Politics*, 61(3): 658–79.

——and Ray, L. P. (2002), 'Descriptive Representation, Policy Outcomes, and Municipal Day-Care Coverage in Norway', *American Journal of Political Science*, 46(2): 428–37.

Brill, A. (ed.) (1995), *A Rising Tide: Women in Politics Worldwide* (New York: Feminist Press).

Britt, C. (1993), *Out of the Wood? Local Institutions and Community Forest Management in Two Central Himalayan Villages*, draft monograph, Cornell University, Ithaca, NY.

——(1997), 'Federation Building and Networking: FECOFUN and Experiences from User Groups Nepal', Discussion Papers, Ford Foundation, New Delhi.

——(2002), 'Changing the Boundaries of Forest Politics: Community Forestry, Social Mobilization and Federation Building in Nepal', unpublished Ph.D. dissertation in Sociology, Cornell University.

——(2007), 'FECOFUN'S Role in the Loktantra Andolan (2005–2006), Forest Users Support for Community Forestry and Democracy in Nepal', Final Report to Ford Foundation, New Delhi, 26 May.

Britton, H. E. (2002), 'Coalition Building, Election Rules, and Party Politics: South African Women's Path to Parliament', *Africa Today*, 49(4): 33–67.

——(2006), 'South Africa: Mainstreaming Gender in a New Democracy', in G. Bauerand and H. E. Britton (eds.), *Women in African Parliaments* (London: Lynne Rienner Publishers).

Bromley, D. W., and Chapagain, D. P. (1984), 'The Village against the Center: Resource Depletion in South Asia', *American Journal of Agricultural Economics*, 66: 868–73.

Bromley, D. W. (1986), 'On Common Property Regimes in International Development', paper prepared for AKRSP/ICIMOD/EAPI Workshop on Institutional Development for Local Management of Rural Resources, Gilgit, Pakistan.

——(ed.) (1992), *Making the Commons Work: Theory, Practice, and Policy* (San Francisco: Institute for Contemporary Studies Press).

Brown, J. (1994), *Modern India: The Origins of an Asian Democracy* (Oxford: Oxford University Press).

Brundtland, G. (1987), *Our Common Future: The World Commission on Environment and Development* (Oxford: Oxford University Press).

Buch, N. (1999), 'From Oppression to Assertion: A Study of Panchayats and Women in M.P., Rajasthan and U.P. Report', Centre for Women's Development Studies, New Delhi.

——(2000), 'Panchayats and Women', in *Status of Panchayat Raj in the States and Union Territories of India* (Delhi: Institute of Social Studies and Concept Publishing Co.).

Buchanan, F. (1807), *A Journey from Madras through the Countries of Mysore, Canara and Malabar*, Vol. II (London: Cadell and Davis).

Buchy, M., and Rai, B. (2008), 'Do Women-Only Approaches to Natural Resource Management Help Women? The Case of Community Forestry in Nepal', in B. P. Resurreccion and R. Elmhirst (eds.), *Gender and Natural Resource Management: Livelihoods, Mobility and Interventions* (London: Earthscan, IDRC), 127–49.

——and Subba, S. (2003), 'Why is Community Forestry a Social and Gender-Blind Technology? The Case of Nepal', *Gender, Technology and Development*, 7(3): 313–32.

Buckingham, S. (2004), 'Ecofeminism in the Twenty-first Century', *The Geographic Journal*, 170 (2): 146–54.

Burling, R. (1963), *Rengsanggri: Family and Kinship in a Garo Village* (Philadelphia: University of Pennsylvania Press).

——(1997), *The Strong Women of Modhupur* (Dhaka: The University Press Limited).

CARE (2000), *Final Evaluation Report Phase II, Remote Area Basic Needs Project, Gorkha* (Nepal: CARE).

Cargan, L. (2007), *Doing Social Research* (Lanham, Md.: Rowman and Littlefield Inc.).

Carroll, S. J. (2001), 'Representing Women: Women State Legislators as Agents of Policy-Related Change', in S. J. Carroll (ed.), *The Impact of Women in Public Office* (Bloomington, Ind.: Indiana University Press), 3–21.

——(2003), 'Are US Women State Legislators Accountable to Women? The Complementary Roles of Feminist Identity and Women's Organizations', paper prepared for presentation at the Gender and Social Capital Conference, St John's College, University of Manitoba, Winnipeg, 2–3 May.

——(2008), 'Committee Assignments: Discrimination or Choice?', in B. Reingold (ed.), *Legislative Women: Getting Elected, Getting Ahead* (Boulder, Colo.: Lynne Rienner Publishers), 135–56.

——and Taylor, E. (1989), 'Gender Differences in Policy Priorities of US State Legislators', paper presented at the American Political Science Association, Atlanta, Aug.–Sept.

Carruthers, I., and Stone, R. (1981), 'Economic Aspects and Policy Issues in Groundwater Development', World Bank Staff Working Paper No. 496, World Bank, Washington, DC.

Carter, E. J. (1992), 'Tree Cultivation on Private Land in the Middle Hills of Nepal: Lessons from Some Villagers of Dolakha District', *Mountain Research and Development*, 12(3): 241–55.

Cernea, M. (1981), 'Land Tenure Systems and Social Implications of Forestry Development Programmes', World Bank Staff Working Paper No. 452, April, World Bank, Washington, DC.

——(1991), *Putting People First: Sociological Variables in Rural Development* (New York: Oxford University Press).

Chaki-Sircar, M. (1984), *Feminism in a Traditional Society: Women of the Manipur Valley* (Delhi: Vikas Publishing House).

Chakravartty, A. (2009), 'Villagers, Foresters Team up to Save Grasslands from Fire in Central Gujarat', *Indian Express*, posted on-line 6 Apr., http://www.indianexpress.com/news/villagers-foresters-team-up-to-save-grasslands-from-fire-in-central-gujarat/443548/0.

Chakravarty-Kaul, M. (1996), *Common Lands and Customary Law: Institutional Change in North India over the Past Two Centuries* (Delhi: Oxford University Press).

Champion, H. G., and Seth, S. K. (1968), *A Revised Survey of Forest Types in India* (New Delhi: Government of India Press).

Chand, M., and Bezboruah, R. (1980), 'Employment Opportunities for Women in Forestry', in *Community Forestry and People's Participation: Seminar Report* (Ranchi: Consortium for Community Forestry, Ranchi, Bihar), 20–2 Nov.

Chattopadhyay, R., and Duflo, E. (2004), 'Women as Policy Makers: Evidence from an India-wide Randomized Policy Experiment', *Econometrica*, 72(5): 1409–43.

Chaudhuri, B. B. (1993), 'Tribal Society in Transition: Eastern India, 1757–1920', in M. Hasan and N. Gupta (eds.), *India's Colonial Encounter: Essays in Memory of Eric Stokes* (Delhi: Manohar), 79–80.

Chaudhuri, S. (2007), 'What Difference Does a Constitutional Amendment Make? The 1994 Panchayati Raj Act and the Attempt to Revitalize Rural Local Government in India', in P. Bardhan and D. Mookerjee (eds.), *Decentralization and Local Governance in Developing Countries* (Delhi: Oxford University Press), 153–202.

——and Pfaff, A. S. P. (2003), 'Fuel-Choice and Indoor Air Quality: A Household-level Perspective on Economic Growth and the Environment', mimeo, Dept. of Economics and School of International and Public Affairs, Columbia University.

Chen, M. (1993), 'Women and Wasteland Development in India: An Issue Paper', in A. Singh and N. Burra (eds.), *Women and Wasteland Development in India* (Delhi: Sage Publishers), 21–90.

Chhachhi, A. (1991), 'Forced Identities: The State, Communalism, Fundamentalism and Women in India', in D. Kandiyoti (ed.), *Women, Islam and the State* (London: Macmillan Press), 144–75.

Chopra, K., Kadekodi, G. K., and Murty, M. N. (1990), *Participatory Development: People and Common Property Resources* (New Delhi: Sage Publications).

Chopra, N., Singh, S., Gupta, S., Narain, U., and Veld, K. V. (2007), 'Who Collect Resources in Degraded Environment? A Case Study from Jhabua District, India', South Asian Network for Development and Environmental Economics, Working Paper No. 23-07.

Chowdhry, P. (2007), *Contentious Marriages, Eloping Couples: Gender, Caste, and Patriarchy in Northern India* (Delhi: Oxford University Press).

Cockburn, C. (1987), *Women, Trade Unions and Political Parties*, Fabian Research Series (London: Fabian Society).

Cohen, J. M., and Uphoff, N. (1977), *Rural Development Participation: Concepts and Measures for Project Design, Implementation and Evaluation* (Ithaca, NY: Rural Development Committee, Cornell University).

Cohn, B. S. (1965), 'Anthropological Notes on Disputes and Law in India', *American Anthropologist*, 67(5–6): 82–122.

Corbridge, C., and Jewitt, S. (1997), 'From Forest Struggles to Forest Citizens? Joint Forest Management in the Unquiet Woods of India, Jharkhand', *Environment and Planning*, 29 (12): 2145–64.

Corcoran-Nantes, Y. (1988), 'Women in Grass Roots Protest Movements in Sao Paulo, Brazil', unpublished Ph.D. dissertation in Latin American Studies, University of Liverpool.

Correa, M. (1997), *Gender and Joint Forest Planning and Management: A Research Study in Uttara Kannada District, Karnataka* (Dharwad: India Development Service).

Crooke, W. ([1896] 1974), *The Tribes and Castes of the North Western India I– IV* (Delhi: Cosmo Publications).

Croson, R., Marks, M., and Snyder, J. (2008), 'Groups Work for Women: Gender and Group Identity in Social Dilemmas', *Negotiation Journal*, 24 (4): 411–27.

CSE (2001), 'Biomass: A Smoky Problem', *Health and Environment Newsletter*, Center for Science and Environment, Delhi, 1 (1): 6.

Custers, P. (1987), *Women in the Tebhaga Uprising: Rural Poor Women and Revolutionary Leadership: 1946–47* (Calcutta: Naya Prokash).

Dahal, D. R. (1994), *A Review of Forest User Groups: Case Studies from Eastern Nepal* (Kathmandu: ICIMOD).

Dahlerup, D. (1988), 'From a Small to a Large Majority: Women in Scandinavian Politics', *Scandinavian Political Studies*, 11 (4): 275–98.

Damodaran, V. (1998), 'Famine in a Forest Tract: Ecological Change and the Causes of the 1897 Famine in Chota Nagpur, Northern India', in R. Grove, V. Damodaran, and S. Sangwan (eds.), *Nature and the Orient: The Environmental History of South and Southeast Asia* (Delhi: Oxford University Press), 853–90.

——(2002), 'Gender, Forests and Famine in 19th Century Chotanagpur, India', *Indian Journal of Gender Studies*, 9(2): 133–63.

Daniggelis, E. K. (1997), 'The Jangal's Hidden Wealth: A Survival Strategy by Foraging Farmers in the Upper Arun Valley, Eastern Nepal', unpublished Ph.D. dissertation, Dept. of Anthropology, University of Hawaii.

Darcy, R., Welch, S., and Clark, J. (1994), *Women, Elections and Representation* (Lincoln, Nebr.: University of Nebraska Press).

Dasgupta, S. (1986), *Caste, Kinship and Community: Social System of a Bengal Caste* (Madras: University Press).

Davidson-Hunt, K. (1995), 'Engendering the Commons: A Case Study in Gender Difference and Common Property in Himachal Pradesh, India', unpublished MA dissertation, Dept. of Anthropology, University of Manitoba.

——(1997), 'Gender, Class and the Commons in the Indian Himalaya', in F. Berkes and J. Gardner (eds.), *Sustainability of Mountain Environments in India and Canada* (Winnipeg: Natural Resources Institute, University of Manitoba).

Davion, V. (1994), 'Is Feminism Feminist?', in K. J. Warren (ed.), *Ecological Feminism* (London: Routledge), 8–28.

Deaton, A. (1997), *The Analysis of Household Surveys: A Microeconometeric Approach to Developement Policy* (Washington, DC: World Bank).

Deininger, K., and Liu, Y. (2009), 'Longer-Term Economic Impacts of Self-Help Groups in India', World Bank Policy Research Working Paper No. 4886, World Bank, Washington, DC.

Denton, F. (2002), *Gender: The Missing Link to Energy for Sustainable Development*, Enda Tiers Monde Energy Program, Senegal.

Development Alternatives (1998), *DAINET NGO Directory* (Delhi: Development Alternatives).

Diamond, I., and Hartsock, N. (1981), 'Beyond Interest in Politics: A Comment on Virginia Sapiro's "When Are Interests Interesting?" The Problem of Political Representation of Women', *American Journal of Political Science Review*, 75(3): 701–16.

Dodson, D. L. (2006), *The Impact of Women in Congress* (New York: Oxford University Press).

Dreber, A., and Johannesson, M. (2008), 'Gender Differences in Deception', *Economics Letters*, 99(1): 197–9.

Dryzek, J. S. (2002), *Deliberative Democracy and Beyond: Liberals, Critics, and Contestations* (New York: Oxford University Press).

Dube, S. C. (1955), *Indian Village* (London: Routledge and Kegan Paul).

Duflo, E., and Topalova, P. (2004), 'Unappreciated Service: Performance, Perceptions, and Women Leaders in India', draft paper, MIT, Cambridge, Mass.

Dufwenberg, M., and Muren, A. (2006), 'Gender Composition in Teams', *Journal of Economic Behavior & Organization*, 61: 50–4.

Duraisamy, P., and Malathy, R. (1991), 'Impact of Public Programs on Fertility and Gender Specific Investment in Human Capital of Children in Rural India: Cross Sectional and Time Series Analyses', in T. Schultz (ed.), *Research in Population Economics*, 7: 157–87.

Dwyer, D., and Bruce, J. (eds.) (1988), *A Home Divided: Women and Income Control in the Third World* (Stanford, Calif.: Stanford University Press).

Eaton, H. and Lorentzen, L.A. (eds.) (2003), *Ecofeminism and Globalization: Exploring Culture, Context and Religion* (Maryland: Rowman and Littlefeld Publishers, Inc.).

Eckel, C. (2008), 'Gender Differences (Experimental Evidence)', in S. Durlauf and L. Blume (eds.), *The New Palgrave Dictionary of Economics* (Basingstoke: Palgrave Macmillan, 2nd edn.), 3: 578–81.

——de Oliveira, A. C. M., and Grossman, P. J. (2008), 'Gender and Negotiation in the Small: Are Women (Perceived to Be) More Cooperative than Men?', *Negotiation Journal*, 24(4): 429–45.

——and Grossman, P. J. (1998), 'Are Women Less Selfish than Men? Evidence from Dictator Experiments', *Economic Journal*, 108: 726–35.

Eckholm, E. P. (1975), 'The Other Energy Crisis', World Watch Paper No. 1, World Watch Institute, Washington, DC., Sept.

——(1976), *Losing Ground: Environmental Stress and World Food Prospects* (Washington, DC: World Watch Institute).

——(1979), 'Planting for the Future: Forestry for Human Needs', World Watch Paper No. 26, World Watch Institute, Washington, DC, Feb.

EDA (2006), *Self Help Groups in India: A Study of Lights and Shades* (Gurgaon: EDA Rural Systems Private Ltd.).

Ehrenfeld, D. W. (1972), *Conserving Life on Earth* (Oxford: Oxford University Press).

Eisenstein, H. (1995), 'The Australian Femocratic Experiment: A Feminist Case for Bureaucracy', in M. M. Ferre and P. Y. Martin (eds.), *Feminist Organizations: Harvest of the New Women's Movement* (Philadelphia: Temple University Press), 69–83.

Elgar, Z. (1960), *A Punjabi Village in Pakistan* (New York: Colombia University Press).

Elster, J. (ed.) (1998), *Deliberative Democracy* (Cambridge: Cambridge University Press).

Elwin, V. ([1939] 2007), *The Baiga* (New Delhi: Gyan Publishing House).

Enslin, E. M. W. (1990), 'The Dynamics of Gender, Class and Caste in a Women's Movement in Rural Nepal', unpublished Ph.D. dissertation, Dept. of Anthropology, Stanford University.

Enthoven, R. E. ([1920] 1975), *The Tribes and Castes of Bombay* (Delhi: Cosmo Publications).

EPA (2000), 'Greenhouse Gases from Small-Scale Combustion Devices in Developing Countries: Phase IIA. Household Stoves in India', EPA/600/R-00/052, Office of Research and Development, National Risk Management Research Laboratory, Environmental Protection Agency, Washington, DC.

Epstein, S. (1962), *Economic Development and Social Change in South Asia* (Manchester: Manchester University Press).

Everett, J. M. (1979), *Women and Social Change in India* (New York: St Martin's Press).

——(2009), 'Women in Local Government in India', in A. M. Goetz (ed.), *Governing Women: Women's Political Effectiveness in Contexts of Democratization and Governance Reform* (Geneva: UNRISD), 196–215.

Falk, I., and Stark, O. (2001), 'Dynasties and Destiny: On the Roles of Altruism and Impatience in the Evolution of Consumption and Bequests', *Economica*, 68(272): 505–18.

Fernandes, W., and Kulkarni, S. (1983), *Toward a New Forest Policy: People's Rights and Environmental Needs* (New Delhi: Indian Social Institute).

——and Menon, G. (1987), *Tribal Women and Forest Economy, Deforestation, Exploitation and Status Change* (Delhi: Indian Social Institute).

Fernandez, A. P. (2001), *The Myrada Experience: Putting Institutions First Even in Micro Finance* (Bangalore: MYRADA).

——(2004), 'Resource Centres or ????', RMAS Paper No 38, MYRADA, Bangalore, 10 May.

——(2005), 'Self Help Affinity Groups (SAGs): Their Role in Poverty Reduction and Financial Sector Development', paper presented at International Conference on Microfinance in the Global Strategy for Meeting the Millennium Development Goals, Concern Worldwide, Dublin, Ireland.

——(2006), 'The History and Spread of the Self-Help Affinity Group (SHG or SAG) Movement in India', Rural Management Systems Series Paper No. 44, MYRADA, Bangalore.

Fierlback, K. (1997), 'Getting Representation Right for Women in Development: Accountability, Consent and the Articulation of Women's Interests', in A. M. Goetz (ed.), *Getting Institutions Right for Women in Development* (London: Zed Books), 31–43.

Fishkin, J. S., and Laslett, P. (ed.) (2003), *Debating Deliberative Democracy* (Oxford: Blackwell Publishing).

Flammang, J. (1985), 'Female Officials in the Feminist Capital: The Case of Santa Clara County', *Western Political Quarterly*, 34: 94–118.

Folger, B., and Dewan, M. (1983), 'Kumaon Hills Reclamation: End of Year Site Visit', mimeo, Oxfam America, Delhi.

Forbes, G. (1979), 'Votes for Women: The Demand for Women's Franchise in India, 1917–1937', in V. Mazumdar (ed.), *Symbols of Power: Studies on the Political Status of Women in India* (Bombay: Allied publishers), 3–23.

——(1981), 'The Indian Women's Movement: A Struggle for Women's Rights or National Liberation?', in G. Minault (ed.), *The Extended Family: Women and Political Participation in India and Pakistan* (New Delhi: Chanakya Publications), 49–82.

——(2000), *Women in Modern India*, The New Cambridge History of India (Cambridge: Cambridge University Press, 2nd repr.).

Franceschet, S. (2001), 'Women in Politics in Post-transitional Democracies', *International Feminist Journal of Politics*, 3(2): 207–36.

Frankel, F. (1978), *India's Political Economy, 1947–77: The Gradual Revolution* (Princeton: Princeton University Press).

Fraser, N. (1989), *Unruly Practices: Power, Discourse and Gender in Contemporary Social Theory* (Minnesota: University of Minnesota Press).

——(1990), 'Rethinking the Public Sphere: A Contribution to the Critique of Actually Existing Democracy', *Social Text*, 25/26: 56–80.

——(1995), 'Recognition or Redistribution? A Critical Reading of Iris Young's Justice and the Politics of Difference', *Journal of Political Philosophy*, 3(2): 166–80.

——(1997), 'A Rejoinder to Iris Young', *New Left Review*, 223: 126–9.

——(2005), 'Reframing Justice in a Globalizing World', *New Left Review*, 36: 69–88.

Fuller, J. E. (2000), 'Village Voices: Gender and Action in Community Politics', unpublished Ph.D. dissertation in sociology, University of Virginia, USA.

Furer-Haimendorf, C. V. ([1939] 1976), *The Return of the Naked Nagas: An Anthropologist's View of Nagaland 1936–1970* (Delhi: Vikas Publishing House).
——(1985), *Tribes of India: The Struggle for Survival* (Delhi: Oxford University Press).
——and Furer-Haimendorf, E. (1979), *The Gonds of Andhra Pradesh* (Boston: George Allen and Unwin).
Gaiha, R., Kaushik, P. D., and Kulkarni, V. (2000), 'Participation and Empowerment of the Rural Poor: The Case of the Panchayats in India', in V. Damodaran and M. Unnithan-Kumar (eds.), *Postcolonial India: History, Politics and Culture* (Delhi: Manohar), 203–42.
Gala, C. (1990), 'Trying to Give Women their Due: The Story of Vitner Village', *Manushi*, 59: 29–32.
Gandhi, N., and Shah, N. (1991), *The Issues at Stake: Theory and Practice in the Contemporary Women's Movement in India* (Delhi: Kali for Women).
Gaul, K. K. (1994), 'Negotiated Positions and Shifting Terrains: Apprehension of Forest Resources in the Western Himalaya', unpublished Ph.D. dissertation, Dept. of Anthropology, University of Massachusetts, Amherst.
GEER (2005), 'Joint Forest Management Programme: Gujarat State', report prepared by the Geer Ecological Education and Research Foundation, Gandhinagar, for the Gujarat Forest Department.
Ghimire-Bastakoti, K., and Bastakoti, R. R. (2006), 'Social Exclusion in Community Forestry: Why Women are Frequently Excluded from Decision-Making and Leadership in Nepal', in *Proceedings of the Women's Global Connection Conference on Affirming Diversity: Women Making a Difference* (San Antonio, Tex.: University of the Incarnate Word), 18–20 May.
Ghosh, A., and Lama-Rewal, S. T. (2005), *Democratization in Progress: Women and Local Politics in Urban India* (Delhi: Tulika Books).
Gilmour, D. A., and Fisher, R. J. (1991), *Villagers, Forest and Foresters: The Philosophy, Process and Practice of Community Forestry in Nepal* (Kathmandu: Sahayogi Press).
Goetz, A. M. (2003), 'National Women's Machinery: State-Based Institutions to Advocate for Gender Equality', in S. Rai (ed.), *Mainstreaming Gender, Democratizing the State? Institutional Mechanisms for the Advancement of Women* (Manchester: Manchester University Press), 69–95.
——(ed.) (2008), *Governing Women: Women's Political Effectiveness in Contexts of Democratization and Governance Reform* (London: Routledge).
——(2009), 'Governing Women: Will New Public Space for Some Women make a Difference for All Women?', in A. M. Goetz (ed.), *Governing Women: Women's Political Effectiveness in Contexts of Democratization and Governance Reform* (Geneva: UNRISD), 3–21.
GoI (1957), Report of the Team for the Study of Community Projects and National Extension Service, chaired by Balwantray Mehta, Vol. I, Committee on Plan Projects, Government of India (GoI), New Delhi.
——(1965), Report of the Committee on Panchayat Raj Elections, chaired by K. Santhanam, Ministry of Community Development and Cooperation, GoI, New Delhi.
——(1974), *Towards Equality: Report of the Committee on the Status of Women in India* (New Delhi: Ministry of Education & Social Welfare, Dept. of Social Welfare, GoI).
——(1978), Report of the Committee on Panchayat Raj Institutions, chaired by Asoka Mehta, Department of Rural Development, Ministry of Agriculture and Irrigation, GoI, New Delhi.
——(1988), *National Perspective Plan for Women, 1988–2000* (New Delhi: Ministry of Human Resource Development, GoI).

——(1996), *The State of Forests Report 1995* (Dehradun: Forest Survey of India, GoI).
——(1998), *Report on Women and Forestry* (New Delhi: Ministry of Environment and Forests, GoI).
——(1999a), *National Forestry Action Plan* (New Delhi: MoEF, Government of India).
——(1999b), *Common Property Resources in India, 54th Round* (January 1998–June 1998), Report No. 452 (54/31/4) (Delhi: National Sample Survey of India, GoI).
——(2000a), *Report of the Pilot Time Use Survey 1998–99*, Department of Statistics, Central Statistical Office, Delhi.
——(2000b), 'Joint Forest Management Guidelines 2000', Ministry of Environment and Forests (Forest Protection Division), No. 22-8/2000-JFM (FPD). http://www.iifm.ac.in/databank/jfm/jfmcell.html#No.22-8/2000-JFM%20(FPD).
——(2000c), *Ninth Five Year Plan: 1997–2002* (New Delhi: Planning Commission).
——(2001), *Report of the Forest Survey of India 2001* (Dehradun: Forest Survey of India, GoI).
——(2002), *Evaluation Study on National Project on Biogas Development* (New Delhi: Project Evaluation Organization, Planning Commission, Government of India).
——(2003), *Report of the Forest Survey of India 2003* (Dehradun: Forest Survey of India, GoI).
——(2006a), *The State of the Panchayats: A Mid-Term Review and Appraisal* (New Delhi: Ministry of Panchayat Raj, Government of India).
——(2006b), *Integrated Energy Policy: Report of the Expert Committee* (Planning Commission, GoI).
——(2008), *Integrated Energy Policy* (New Delhi: Planning Commission, GoI).
Gold, A. G., and Gujar, B. R. (1997), 'Wild Pigs and Kings: Remembered Landscapes in Rajasthan', *American Anthropologist*, 99(1): 70–84.
————(2002), *In the Time of Trees and Sorrows: Nature, Power and Memory in Rajasthan* (Durham, NC: Duke University Press).
Goldemberg, J., Johansson, T. B., Reddy, A. K. N., and Williams, R. H. (2004), 'A Global Clean Cooking Fuel Initiative', *Energy for Sustainable Development*, 8(3): 5–12.
GoM ([1883] 2006), *Gazetteers of the Bombay Presidency* (Bombay: Gazetteer, Government of Maharashtra), Ebook: http://raigad.nic.in/DG/1883/pro_minerals.html#3.
GoN (1995), 'Forest Act 2049 (1993) and Forest Regulation 2051 (1995)', official translation, Law Books Management Board/HMGN, Ministry of Forest and Soil Conservation, Forestry Development Project, HMGN/USAID, Government of Nepal (GoN), Kathmandu.
——(1999), 'Forest Resources of Nepal (1987–1998)', Publication No. 74, Nov., Kathmandu Nepal: Department of Forest Research and Survey (DFRS), Ministry of Forests and Soil Conservation, HMG Nepal, and Forest Resource Information System Project (FRIS), Government of Finland.
——(2000), 'FUG Database', Community and Private Forestry Division, Dept. of Forests, Government of Nepal, Kathmandu.
——(2001), *Census of Nepal, 2001*, National Planning Commission (Kathmandu: CBS and GON).
——(2001–02), 'Nepal Sample Census of Agriculture 2001–02: District Level' (Kathmandu: CBS and GoN).
——(2004), *Nepal Living Standards Survey 2003–04, Statistical Report* (Kathmandu: CBS, National Planning Commission Secretariat, GoN).
——(2009), *Community Forestry Guidelines, 2009* (Kathmandu: Ministry of Forests and Soil Conservation, GoN).

Gough, K. (1961), 'Nayar: Central Kerala', 'Nayar: North Kerala', 'Tiyyar: North Kerala', 'Mappilla: North Kerala', in D. M. Schneider and K. Gough (eds.), *Matrilineal Kinship* (Berkeley and Los Angeles: University of California Press), 298–442.

Grove, R. H. (1995), *Green Imperialism: Colonial Expansion, Tropical Island Edens and the Origins of Environmentalism, 1600–1860* (Cambridge: Cambridge University Press).

——Damodaran, V., and Sangwan, S. (1998), *Nature and the Orient: The Environmental History of South and Southeast Asia* (Delhi: Oxford University Press).

Guha, R. (1989), *The Unquiet Woods: Ecological Change and Peasant Resistance in the Himalaya* (Delhi: Oxford University Press).

Guha, S. (1999), *Environment and Ethnicity in India, 1200–1991* (Cambridge: Cambridge University Press).

Guhathakurta, P., and Bhatia, K. S. (1992), 'A Case Study on Gender and Forest Resources in West Bengal', World Bank, Delhi, 16 June.

Gurdon, P. R. T. ([1907] 1981), *The Khasis* (New Delhi: Cosmo Publications).

Gururani, S. (1996), 'Fuel, Fodder and Forests: Politics of Forest Use and Abuse in Uttarakhand Himalaya, India', unpublished Ph.D. dissertation in cultural anthropology, Syracuse University.

Hardin, G. (1968), 'The Tragedy of the Commons', *Science*, 162: 1243–8.

Harper, M. (2002), 'Grameen Bank Groups and Self-Help Groups: What are the Differences?', ITDG London, case study.

Harriss, J. (2007), 'Antimonies of Empowerment: Observations on Civil Society, Politics and Urban Governance in India', draft paper for the Berkeley CSAS Conference on Local Governance and Empowerment, May.

Hart, G. (1991), 'Engendering Everyday Resistance: Gender, Patronage and Production Politics in Rural Malaysia', *Journal of Peasant Studies*, 19(1): 93–121.

Hassim, S. (2003), 'The Gender Pact and Democratic Consolidation: Institutionalizing Gender Equality in the South African State', *Feminist Studies*, 29(3): 505–28.

——(2005), 'Terms of Engagement: South African Challenges', feature article, *Feminist Africa*, 4: 1–11.

Heath, R. M., Schwindt-Bayer, L. A., and Taylor-Robinson, M. M. (2005),'Women on the Sidelines: Women's Representation on Committees in Latin American Legislatures', *American Journal of Political Science*, 49(2): 420–36.

Heijden, J. Van Der (2006), 'Sustainability and Empowerment through SHG Federations: A Study in East Uttar Pradesh, India', unpublished MA dissertation in development studies, University of Amsterdam.

Heilbroner, R. L. (1974), *An Inquiry into the Human Prospect* (New York: W. W. Norton).

High-Pippert, A., and Comer, J. (1998), 'Female Empowerment: The Influence of Women Representing Women', *Women and Politics*, 19(4): 53–66.

Hobley, M. (1990), 'Social Reality, Social Forestry: The Case of Two Nepalese Panchayats', unpublished Ph.D. dissertation, Dept. of Forestry, Australian National University.

——(1996), *Participatory Forestry: The Process of Change in India and Nepal*, Rural Development Forestry Study Guide 3 (London: Overseas Development Institute).

——and Sheilds, D. (2000), 'The Reality of Trying to Transform Structures and Processes: Forestry in Rural Livelihoods', Working Paper No. 12, Overseas Development Institute, London.

——Campbell, J. Y., and Bhatia, A. (1996), 'Community Forestry in India and Nepal', Discussion Paper Series No. MNR 96/3, ICIMOD, Kathmandu.

Hoque, K. S. (1987), 'Agrarian Structure, Resource Distribution and Production Conditions in a Bangladesh Village', unpublished Ph.D. dissertation, Dept. of Sociology and Anthropology, Purdue University.

Hoskins, M. W. (1979a), 'Women in Forestry for Local Community Development: A Programming Guide', paper prepared for the Office of Women in Development, AID, Washington, DC.

——(1979b), 'Community Participation in African Fuelwood Production, Transformation and Utilization', discussion paper prepared for a Workshop on Fuelwood and Other Renewable Fuels in Africa, Paris, Overseas Development Council, AID, 29–30 Nov.

Howard, P. L. (ed.) (2003), *Women and Plants: Gender Relations in Biodiversity Management and Conservation* (London: Zed Books).

Howes, M., and Jabbar, M. A. (1986), 'Rural Fuel Shortages in Bangladesh: The Evidence from Four Villages', Discussion Paper No. 213, Institute of Development Studies, Sussex.

Htun, M. N. (2002), 'Women in Political Power in Latin America', International IDEA: Women in Parliament, Stockholm: http://www.idea.int.

Humphries, J. (1990), 'Enclosures, Common Rights, and Women: The Proletarianization of Families in the Late Eighteenth and Early Nineteenth Centuries', *Journal of Economic History*, 50: 17–42.

ICIMOD and CBS (2003), *Districts of Nepal: Indicators of Development Update*, Mapping Nepal Census Indicators 2001 and Trends (Kathmandu: ICIMOD and CBS).

IEA (2004), 'Energy and Development', *World Energy Outlook*, International Energy Agency, (Paris: OECD), chapter 10.

Indian Express (2008a), '50 pc Reservation for Women in PRIs, Local Bodies', 9 Apr.

——(2008b), 'Uttarakhand Reserves 50 pc Seats for Women in Panchayats', 13 Mar.

Innocenti, A., and Pazienza, M. G. (2006), 'Altruism and Gender in the Trust Game', working paper, Department of Economics, University of Siena.

IRADe and ENERGIA (2009), 'Gender Analysis of Renewable Energy In India: Present Status, Issues, Approaches and New Initiatives', report submitted to the Ministry of New and Renewable Energy, Government of India, New Delhi.

Isham, J., Narayan, D., and Pitchett, L. (1995), 'Does Participation Improve Performance: Establishing Causality with Subjective Data', *World Bank Economic Review*, 9(2): 175–200.

ISO/Swedforest (1993), *Forests, People and Protection: Case Studies of Voluntary Forest Protection by Communities in Orissa* (Delhi: Swedish International Development Agency).

Iyer, L. K. A. ([1912] 1981), *The Tribes and Castes of Cochin* (Delhi: Cosmo Publications).

Jackson, C. (1993), 'Women/Nature or Gender/History? A Critique of Ecofeminist "Development"', *Journal of Peasant Studies*, 20(3): 389–419.

Jahangir, B. K. (1979), *Differentiation, Polarisation and Confrontation in Rural Bangladesh* (Dhaka: Center for Social Studies).

Jain, L. C. (2007), 'Fate of Gandhi's Economic Thinking', in S. Bhattacharya (ed.), *Development of Modern Indian Thought and the Social Sciences*, Vol. X, Part V (Delhi: Oxford University Press), 19–66.

Jain, S. (1984), 'Women and People's Ecological Movement: A Case Study of Women's Role in the Chipko Movement in Uttar Pradesh', *Economic and Political Weekly*, 19(41): 1788–94.

——and Reddy, V. K. (1979), *Role of Women in Rural Development: A Study of Mahila Mandals* (Hyderabad: National Institute of Rural Development).

Jansen, E. G. (1983), *Rural Bangladesh: Competition for Scarce Resources* (Oslo: Norwegian University Press).

Jewitt, S. (2002), *Environment, Knowledge and Gender: Local Development in India, Jharkhand*, (Burlington: Ashgate Publishing Limited).

Jodha, N. S. (1986), 'Common Property Resources and the Rural Poor', *Economic and Political Weekly*, 21(27): 1169–81.

John, M. (2007), 'Women in Power? Gender, Caste and the Politics of Local Urban Governance', *Economic and Political Weekly*, 29 Sept., 42(39): 3986–93.

Johnson, N., Lilja, N., Ashby, J. A., and Garcia, J. A. (2004), 'The Practice of Participatory Research and Gender Analysis in Natural Resource Management', *Natural Resources Forum*, 28: 189–200.

Jonasdottir, A. G. (1988), 'On the Concept of Interest, Women's Interests, and the Limitation of Interest Theory', in K. B. Jones and A. G. Jonasdottir (eds.), *The Political Interests of Gender: Developing Theory and Research with a Feminist Face* (London: Sage Publications), 33–65.

Jonathan, E. S., Smith, K. R., Peabody, J. W., Yaping, L., Xiliang, Z., Edwards, R., and Quan, G. (2004), 'An Assessment of Programs to Promote Improved Household Stoves in China', *Energy for Sustainable Development*, 8(3): 33–52.

Joshi, A. (2000), 'Roots of Change: Front-Line Workers and Forest Policy Change in West Bengal', unpublished Ph.D. dissertation in public policy, MIT, Cambridge, Mass.

Kaiser, P. S. (2001), 'Strategic Predictors of Women's Parliamentary Participation: A Comparative Study of Twenty-Three Democracies', unpublished Ph.D. dissertation, University of California, Los Angeles.

Kalpana, K. (2005), 'Micro-credit Wins Nobel: A Stocktaking', *Economic and Political Weekly*, 41(50): 5110–12.

Kamas, L., Preston, A., and Baum, S. (2008), 'Altruism in Individual and Joint-Giving Decisions: What's Gender Got to Do With It?', *Feminist Economics*, 14(3): 23–50.

Kant, S., Singh, N. M., and Singh, K. K. (1991), *Community-Based Forest Management Systems: Case Studies from Orissa*, ISO/Swedforest (New Delhi: SIDA).

Kanter, R. M. (1977a), 'Numbers: Minorities and Majorities', in R. M. Kanter (ed.), *Men and Women of the Corporation* (New York: Basic Books), 206–44.

——(1977b), 'Some Effects of Proportions on Group Life: Skewed Sex Ratios and Responses to Token Women', *American Journal of Sociology*, 82(5): 965–90.

Kar, P. C. (1982), *Garos in Transition* (New Delhi: Cosmo Publications).

Karat, B. (2005), *Survival and Emancipation: Notes from Indian Women's Struggles* (New Delhi: Three Essays Collective).

Kaushik, S. (1993), *Women and Panchayat Raj* (New Delhi: Har-Anand Publications).

Kelkar, G., and Nathan, D. (1991), *Women, Land and Forests: A Study of the Jharkhand Adivasis* (London: Zed Books).

Khawar, M. (2005), 'Women's Representation, Effectiveness and Leadership in South Asia', paper presented at the Fifth South Asian Ministerial Conference Celebrating Beijing Plus Ten, Islamabad, Pakistan, 3–5 May.

Kishore, V. V. N., and Ramana, P. V. (2002), 'Improved Cookstoves in Rural India: How Improved are They? A Critique of the Perceived Benefits from the National Programme on Improved Chullas', *Energy*, 27: 47–63.

Kishwar, M. (1996), 'Women and Politics: Beyond Quotas', *Economic and Political Weekly*, 26 Oct., 31(43): 2867–74.

Koolwal, G. B. (2004), 'Is Group Heterogeneity Better? A Study of Women's Community Networks in India', Job Market Paper, Dept. of Economics, Cornell University.

Krieger, L. H. (1995), 'The Content of our Categories: A Cognitive Bias Approach to Discrimination and Equal Employment Opportunity', *Stanford Law Review*, 47(6): 1161–248.

Kumar, S. K., and Hotchkiss, D. (1988), 'Consequences of Direction for Women's Time Allocation, Agricultural Production and Nutrition in Hill Areas of Nepal', Research Report 69, International Food Policy Research Institute, Washington, DC.

Kumari, R., and Dubey, A. (1994), *Women Parliamentarians* (New Delhi: Har-Anand Publications).

Kuran, T. (1995), *Private Truths, Public Lies: The Social Consequences of Preference Falsification* (Cambridge, Mass.: Harvard University Press).

Kymlicka, W. (1995), *Multicultural Citizenship: A Liberal Theory of Minority Rights* (Oxford: Clarendon Press).

Lalita, K., Kannabiran, V., and Melkote, R. (1989), *We Were Making History: Life Stories of Women in the Telangana People's Struggle* (Delhi: Kali for Women).

Lam, W. F. (1998), *Governing Irrigation Systems in Nepal: Institutions, Infrastructure and Collective Action* (Oakland, Calif.: Institute for Contemporary Studies).

Lama, A., and Buchy, M. (2002), 'Gender, Class, Caste and Participation: The Case of Community Forestry in Nepal', *Indian Journal of Gender Studies*, 9(1): 27–41.

Lama-Rewal, S. T. (2001), 'Women in the Calcutta Municipal Corporation: A Study in the Context of the Debate on the Women's Reservation Bill', CSH Occasional Paper No. 2, Publication of the French Research Institutes in India, Delhi.

Laxmi, V., Parikh, J., Karmakar, S., and Dabrase, P. (2003), 'Household Energy, Women's Hardship and Health Impacts in Rural Rajasthan, India: Need for Sustainable Energy Solutions', *Energy and Sustainable Development*, 7(1): 50–68.

Lele, S. (1994), 'Sustainable Use of Biomass Resources: A Note on Definition, Criteria and Practical Applications', *Energy for Sustainable Development*, 1(4): 42–6.

——Rajashekhar, G., Hegde, V. R., Prevish Kumar, G., Sarvanakumar, P. (1998), 'Meso-scale Analysis of Forest Condition and its Determinants: A Case Study from the Western Ghats Region, India', *Current Science*, 75(3): 256–63.

Lewis, O. (1958), *Village Life in Northern India: Studies in a Delhi Village* (Urbana, Ill.: University of Illinois Press).

LFP (2007), 'LFP's Animation and Social Mobilization', Livelihoods and Forestry Programme, DFID-Nepal and GoN, Kathmandu, Nepal.

Li, H.-L. (1993), 'A Cross-Cultural Critique of Ecofeminism', in G. Gaard (ed.), *Ecofeminism: Women, Animals, Nature* (Philadelphia: Temple University Press), 272–94.

Lindholm, C. (1982), *Generosity and Jealousy: The Swat Pukhtun of Northern Pakistan* (New York: Columbia University Press).

Lloyd, W. F. ([1833] 1977), 'On the Checks to Population', in G. Hardinn and J. Beden (eds.), *Managing the Commons* (San Fransicso: W. H. Freeman and Co.), 8–15.

Lorey, D. E. (2002), *Global Environmental Challenges of the Twenty-First Century: Resources, Consumption and Sustainable Solutions* (Washington, DC: Rowman and Littlefield).

Lovenduski, J. (1997), 'Gender Politics: A Breakthrough for Women?', *Parliamentary Affairs*, 50: 708–19.

Lukács, G. (1971), *History and Class Consciousness: Studies in Marxist Dialectics*, trans. Rodney Livingstone (Cambridge, Mass.: MIT Press).

Luschinsky, M. S. (1962), 'The Life of Women in a Village of North India: A Study of Roles and Status', unpublished Ph.D. dissertation, Dept. of Anthropology, Cornell University.

McKean, M. A. (1986), 'Management of Traditional Common Lands (Iriaichi) in Japan', in National Research Council, *Proceedings of the Conference on Common Property Resource Management* (Washington, DC: National Academy Press), 533–89.

Majumdar, D. N. (1978), *Culture Change in Two Garo Villages* (Calcutta: Anthropological Survey of India).

Malhotra, K. C., Chandra, N. S., Vasulu, T. S., Majumdar, L., Basu, S., Adhikari, M., and Yadav, G. (1990), 'Joint Management of Forest Lands in West Bengal: A Case Study of Jamboni Range in Midnapore District', Technical Paper No. 2, IBRAD, Calcutta.

Mandelbaum, D. G. (1970), *Society in India* (Berkeley and Los Angeles: University of California Press).

Manikyamba, P. (1989), *Women in Panchayati Raj Structures* (New Delhi: Gyan Publishing House).

Mann, R. S. (1993), *Culture and Integration of Indian Tribes* (Delhi: MD Publications Pvt. Ltd.).

Manor, J. (1999), *The Political Economy of Democratic Decentralization* (Washington, DC: World Bank).

Mansbridge, J. (1980), *Beyond Adversary Democracy* (New York: Basic Books).

——(1990), 'Feminism and Democracy', *American Prospect*, 1 (Spring).

——(2003), 'Rethinking Representation', *American Political Science Review*, 97(4): 515–28.

Mansingh, O. (1991), 'Community Organization and Ecological Restoration: An Analysis of Strategic Options for NGOs in Central Himalaya, with Particular Reference to the Community Forestry Programme of the NGO Chirag', unpublished MA dissertation in rural development, AFRAS, University of Sussex.

Marriott, M. (1955), 'Little Communities in an Indigenous Civilization', in M. Marriott (ed.), *Village India: Studies in the Little Community* (Chicago: University of Chicago Press), 171–222.

Marwell, G., and Oliver, P. E. (1988), 'Social Networks and Collective Action: A Theory of the Critical Mass. III', *American Journal of Sociology*, 94(3): 502–34.

Mathur, K. S. (1964), *Caste and Ritual in a Malwa Village* (Bombay: Asia Publishing House).

Mayer, A. C. (1960), *Caste and Kinship in Central India: A Village and its Region* (Berkeley, Calif.: University of Berkeley).

Mazhar, F., Buckles, D., Satheesh, P. V., and Akhter, F. (2007), *Food Sovereignty and Uncultivated Biodiversity in South Asia: Essays on the Poverty of Food Policy and Wealth of the Social Landscape* (Ottawa: IDRC).

Mencher, J. (1989), 'Women's Work and Poverty: Women's Contribution to Household Maintenance in Two Regions of South India', in D. Dwyer and J. Bruce (eds.), *A Home Divided: Women and Income Control in the Third World* (Stanford, Calif.: Stanford University Press), 99–119.

Menon, N. (2000), 'Elusive "Woman": Feminism and Women's Reservation Bill', *Economic and Political Weekly*, 35(43–4): 3835–44.

Merchant, C. (1980), *The Death of the Nature: Women, Ecology and the Scientific Revolution* (San Francisco, Calif.: Harper and Row).

——(1990), 'Ecofeminism and Feminist Theory', in I. Diamond and G. F. Orenstein (eds.), *Reweaving the World: The Emergence of Ecofeminism* (San Francisco: Sierra Club Books), 100–5.

Michener, V. J. (1998), 'The Participatory Approach: Contradiction and Cooption in Burkina Faso', *World Development*, 26(12): 2105–18.

Minturn, L. (1993), *Sita's Daughters: Coming out of Purdah* (New York: Oxford University Press).

——and Hitchcock, J. T. (1966), *The Rajputs of Khalapur* (New York: John Wiley).

Misra, V., Retherford, R. D., and Smith, K. R. (2005a), 'Cooking Smoke and Tobacco Smoke as Risk Factors for Stillbirth', *International Journal of Environmental Health Research*, 15(6): 397–410.

——Smith, K. R., and Retherford, R. D. (2005b), 'Effects of Cooking Smoke and Environmental Tobacco Smoke on Acute Respiratory Infections in Young Indian Children', *Population and Environment*, 26(5): 375–96.

Modi, V., McDade, S., Lallement, D., and Saghir, J. (2005), *Energy Services for the Millenium Development Goals* (Washington, DC: UNDP, World Bank, ESMAP).

Moffatt, M. (1998), 'A Gender Analysis of Community Forestry and Community Leasehold Forestry in Nepal with a Macro-Meso-Micro Framework', unpublished MA dissertation in development policy analysis, Dept. of Economics and Social Studies, University of Manchester.

Mohapatra, P. P. (1991), 'Class Conflict and Agrarian Regimes in Chotanagpur, 1860–1950' *Indian Economic and Social History Review*, 8(1): 1–42.

Molinas, J. (1998), 'The Impact of Inequality, Gender, External Assistance and Social Capital on Local-Level Cooperation', *World Development*, 26(3): 413–31.

Molyneux, M. (1985), 'Mobilization without Emancipation? Women's Interests, the State, and Revolution in Nicaragua', *Feminist Studies*, 11(2): 227–54.

Moore, M. A. (1983), 'Taravad: House, Land and Relationship in a Matrilineal Hindu Society', unpublished Ph.D. dissertation, Dept. of Anthropology, University of Chicago at Illinois.

Moser, C. O. (1989), 'Gender Planning in the Third World: Meeting Practical and Strategic Gender Needs', *World Development*, 17(11): 1799–825.

Mukerjee, R., and Roy, S. B. (1993), 'Influence of Social Institutions on Women's Participation in JFM: A Case Study from Sarugarh, North Bengal', Working Paper No. 17, IBRAD, Calcutta.

Muller-Rommel, F., and Poguntke, T. (eds.) (2002), *Green Parties in National Governments* (London: Frank Cass).

Nagbrahman, D., and Sambrani, S. (1983), 'Women's Drudgery in Firewood Collection', *Economic and Political Weekly*, 18(1–2): 33–8.

Nair, A. (2005), 'Sustainability of Microfinance Self-Help Groups in India: Would Federating Help?', World Bank Policy Research Working Paper, 3516.

——and Shah, P. (2007), 'Self-Help Works', *Times of India*, 27 Dec.

Nanda, M. (1991), 'Is Modern Science a Western Patriarchal Myth? A Critique of the Populist Orthodoxy', *South Asia Bulletin*, 11(1–2): 32–61.

Nanjundayya, H. V., and Iyer, L. K. A. ([1928] 1975), *The Mysore Tribes and Castes*, vol. ii (Mysore: Mysore University).

Narain, U. (1994), 'Women's Involvement in Joint Forest Management: Analyzing the Issues', draft paper, Ford Foundation, New Delhi, 6 May.

——and SARTHI (1998), 'Why Do Villagers Cooperate to Manage Forests?' mimeo, SARTHI, Panchmahals, Gujarat.

——Gupta, S., and Veld, K. V. (2005), 'Poverty and the Environment: Exploring the Relationship between Household Incomes, Private Assets and Natural Assets', Discussion Paper 05-18, Resources for the Future, Washington, DC.

Narayan, D. (1996), 'The Contribution of People's Participation: Evidence from 21 Rural Water Supply Projects', Occasional Paper Series No. 1, Environmentally Sustainable Development, World Bank, Washington, DC.

Natarajan, I. (1995), 'Trends in Firewood Consumption in Rural India', *Margin*, 28(1): 41–5.

NCAER (2001–02), *Evaluation Survey of the National Programme on Improved Chulha* (New Delhi: National Council of Applied Economic Research).
——(2008), *Impact and Sustainability of SHG Bank Linkage Programme* (New Delhi: National Council of Applied Economic Research).
NDII (2006), *Nepal District Profile* (Kathmandu: National Development Information Institute).
Neruda, P. ([1947] 1975), 'Tercera Residencia', trans. from the Spanish by Nathaniel Tarn, in N. Tarn (ed.), *Pablo Neruda; Selected Poems. A Bi-lingual Edition* (Harmondsworth: Penguin Books).
Newell, W. H. (1962), 'The Submerged Descent Line among the Gaddi People of North India', *Journal of the Royal Anthropological Institute*, 92, Part I, Jan.–June, 13–22.
Nirantar (2007), *Examining Literacy and Power within Self-Help Groups: A Quantitative Analysis* (Delhi: Nirantar).
Noponen, H. (1991), 'The Dynamics of Work and Survival for Urban Poor: A Gender Analysis of Panel Data from Madras', *Development and Change*, 22(2): 233–60.
——, ——(2001), 'Cultural Obstacles to Equal Representation', *Journal of Democracy*, 12 (3): 126–40.
——and Lovenduski, J. (1989), 'Women Candidates for Parliament: Transforming the Agenda?', *British Journal of Political Science*, 19(1): 106–15.
——, ——(1995), *Political Recruitment: Gender, Race and Class in the British Parliament* (Cambridge: Cambridge University Press).
Nussbaum, M. C. (2000), *Women and Human Development: The Capabilities Approach* (Cambridge: Cambridge University Press).
——(2006), 'Capabilities as Fundamental Entitlements: Sen and Social Justice', in B. Agarwal, I. Robeyns, and J. Humphries (eds.), *Capability, Freedom and Equality: Amartya Sen's Work from a Gender Perspective* (Delhi: Oxford University Press), 39–69.
Ojha, J. (2005), 'Annexe: Mainstreaming IRAP Tool in Nepal', in *Intergrated Approach to Local Level Planning* DoLIDAR (Kathdmandu: Ministry of Local Development, GoN).
——Sharma, H., Khanal, D. R., Dhungana, H., Pathak, B., Pandey, G., Bhattarai, B., Sharma, N., and Pokharel, B. (2007a), 'Citizen Federation in Democratizing Forest Governance: Lessons from Community Forestry Users' Federation of Nepal', paper presented at a Conference on Forest Management, Bangkok.
——Timsina, N., and Khanal, D. (2007b), 'How are Forest Policy Decisions Made in Nepal?', *Journal of Forest and Livelihood*, 6(1): 1–17.
Olson, M. (1965), *The Logic of Collective Action* (Cambridge, Mass.: Harvard University Press).
Ostrom, E. (1990), *Governing the Commons* (Cambridge: Cambridge University Press).
——and Schlager, E. (1996), 'The Formation of Property Rights', in S. Hanna, C. Folke, and K.-G. Maler (eds.), *Rights to Nature* (Washington, DC: Island Press), 127–56.
——Gardner, R., and Walker, J. (eds.) (1997), *Rules, Games and Common-Pool Resources* (Ann Arbor: University of Michigan Press).
Owen, A. L, Videras, J., and Willemsen, C. (2008), 'Democracy, Participation and Life Satisfaction', *Social Science Quarterly*, 89(4): 987–1005.
Padel, F. (1998), 'Forest Knowledge: Tribal People, their Environment and the Structure of Power', in R. Grove, V. Damodaran, and S. Sangwan (eds.), *Nature and the Orient: The Environmental History of South and Southeast Asia* (Delhi: Oxford University Press), 891–917.

Pal, M. (2004), 'Caste and Patriarchy in Panchayats', *Economic and Political Weekly*, 7 Aug., 39(32): 3581–3.

Pandey, S. (1990), 'Women in Hattidunde Forest Management in Dhading District, Nepal', MPE Series No. 9, ICIMOD, Kathmandu.

Pant, M. (2007), 'SHGs as Change Agents in Enhancing the Political Participation of Local Self-Governance', in S. Krishnan (ed.), *Women's Livelihood Rights: Recasting Citizenship for Development* (New Delhi: Sage Publications), 318–44.

Parikh, J., Smith, K., and Laxmi, V. (1999), 'Indoor Air Pollution: A Reflection on Gender Bias', *Economic and Political Weekly*, 34(9): 539–44.

Parker, A. R., Lozano, I., and Messner, L. A. (1995), *Gender Relations Analysis: A Guide for Trainers* (Westport, Conn.: Save the Children).

Parry, J. P. (1979), *Caste and Kinship in Kangra* (Delhi: Vikas Publishing House).

Pathan, R. S., Arul, M. J., and Poffenberger, M. (1991), 'Forest Management Initiatives in Gujarat', Working Paper No. 7, Ford Foundation, New Delhi.

Paul, S. (1987), 'Community Participation in Development Projects: The World Bank Experience', Discussion Paper No. 6. World Bank, Washington, DC.

Paxton, P., and Kunovich, S. (2003), 'Women's Political Representation: The Importance of Ideology', *Social Forces*, 82(1): 87–114.

Pedhazur, E. J., and Schmelkin, L. P. (1991), *Measurement, Design, and Analysis: An Integrated Approach* (Hillsdale, NJ: Lawrence Erlbaum Associates).

Per-Lee, D. A. (1981), 'Employment, Ingenuity and Family Life: Rajasthani Women in Delhi, India', unpublished Ph.D. dissertation, Dept. of Anthropology, American University.

Phillip, K. (2003), *Civilizing Natures: Race, Resources and Modernity in Colonial South India* (Delhi: Orient Longman).

Phillips, A. (1995), *The Politics of Presence: The Political Representation of Gender, Ethnicity and Race* (Oxford: Oxford University Press).

——(1997), 'From Inequality to Difference: A Severe Case of Displacement', Comment, *New Left Review*, 224 (July/Aug.): 143–53.

——(1998), 'Dealing with Difference: A Politics of Ideas or a Politics of Presence?' in J. B. Landes (ed.), *Feminism, the Public and the Private* (Oxford: Oxford University Press), 475–95.

Pitkin, H. F. (1967), *The Concept of Representation* (Berkeley and Los Angeles: University of California Press).

Pitt, M. M., Rosenzweig, M. R., and Hasan, M. N. (2005), 'Sharing the Burden of Disease: Gender, the Household Division of Labor and the Health Effects of Indoor Air Pollution', CID Working Paper No. 119, Harvard Environmental Economics Program, Harvard University, Mar.

Poffenberger, M., and McGean, B. (eds.) (1996), *Village Voices, Forest Choices: Joint Forest Management in India* (Delhi: Oxford University Press).

————and Khare, A. (1996), 'Communities Sustaining India's Forests in the Twenty-First Century', in M. Poffenberger and B. McGean (eds.), *Village Voices, Forest Choices: Joint Forest Management in India* (Delhi: Oxford University Press), 17–55.

Pokharel, B. K. (1998), 'Foresters and Villagers in Contention and Compact: The Case of Community Forestry in Nepal', unpublished Ph.D. dissertation, School of Development Studies, University of East Anglia.

Pokhrel, A. K., Smith, K. R., Khalakdina, A., Deuja, A., and Bates, M. N. (2005), 'Case-Control Study of Indoor Cooking Smoke Exposure and Cataract in Nepal and India', *International Journal of Epidemiology*, 34(3): 702–8.

Prasad, A. (2003), *Against Ecological Romanticism: Verrier Elwin and the Making of an Anti-Modern Tribal Identity* (New Delhi: Three Essays Press).

Prasad, D. B., and Haranath, S. (2004), 'Participation of Women and Dalits in Gram Panchayat', *Journal of Rural Development*, 23(3): 297–318.

Pratap, V., and Rovaniemi, S. (2006), 'South-Asian Dialogues on Ecological Democracy', SIEMENPUU Discussion papers.

Pretty, J. N. (1995), 'Participatory Learning for Sustainable Agriculture', *World Development*, 23(8): 1247–63.

Prokopy, L. S. (2004), 'Women's Participation in Rural Water Supply Projects in India: Is it Moving beyond Tokenism and Does it Matter?', *Water Policy*, 6: 103–16.

Quddus, M. A., Showkat, A. B., Anwar, Z. S. J., and Biswas, T. K. (2001), *Participation of Women in Local Government Institution, Kotbari* (Comilla: Bangladesh Academy for Rural Development).

Radha, S., and Chowdhury, B. (2002), 'Women in Local Bodies', Discussion Paper No. 40, Kerala Research Programme on Local Level Development, Center for Development Studies, Trivandrum.

Rai, S. M. (1997), 'Gender and Representation: Women MPs in the Indian Parliament: 1991–96', in A. M. Goetz (ed.), *Getting Institutions Right for Women in Development* (London: Zed Books), 104–20.

——(2005), 'Reserved Seats in South Asia: A Regional Perspective', in A. Karam (ed.), *Women in Parliament: Beyond Numbers*, Handbook Series (Stockholm: International Institute for Democracy and Electoral Assistance), 174–84.

Raju, S. M. (1997), *Seeking Niches in Forest Canopy: An Enquiry into Women's Participation Report* (New Delhi: Ford Foundation).

Ramesh, J. (2007), 'The SHG Revolution: What Next', Keynote Address, Society for Promotion of Wastelands Development (SPWD), Delhi.

Rao, V. V. (1985), 'The Khasi Political System: The Syiemship', in S. K. Chattopadhyay (ed.), *Tribal Institutions of Meghalaya* (Guwahati: Spectrum publications), 31–50.

——and Sanyal, P. (2009), 'Dignity through Discourse: Poverty and the Culture of Deliberation in Indian Village Democracies', Policy Research Working Paper No. 4924, World Bank, Washington, DC.

Rathore, D. S. (1996), 'Sarthi's Experience and Forest Protection Groups', mimeo, SARTHI, Panchmahals, Gujarat.

Ravindranath, N. H., Murali, K. S., and Malhotra, K. C. (2000), *Joint Forest Management and Community Forestry in India: An Ecological and Institutional Assessment* (New Delhi: Oxford and IBH Publishing Co.).

Ray, B., and Basu, A. (eds.) (1999), *From Independence toward Freedom: Indian Women Since 1947* (Delhi: Oxford University Press).

Ray, S. (1992), 'Participation of Women in Gram Panchayats: A Case Study of Haryana', Working paper, Centre for Women's Development Studies, Delhi.

RCDC (2005), *Statistical Profile of Forest Protection Groups in Orisssa* (Bhubaneshwar, Orissa: Regional Center for Development Cooperation).

Reddy, C. S., and Manak, S. (2005), 'Self-Help Groups: A Keystone of Microfinance in India—Women's Empowerment and Social Security', mimeo, Mahilka Abhivruddhi Society, Andhra Pradesh (APMAS), Hyderabad.

Regmi, S. C. (1989), 'Female Participation in Forest Resource Management. A Case Study of a Women's Forest Committee in a Nepalese Village', unpublished M.Sc. dissertation in social development, Graduate School of the Ateneo de Manila University.

Reingold, B. (2008), 'Women as Officeholders: Linking Descriptive and Substantive Representation', in C. Wolbrecht, K. Beckwith, and L. Baldez (eds.), *Political Women and American Democracy: Critical Perspectives on Women and Politics Research* (New York: Cambridge University Press), 128–47.

Risley, H. H. ([1891] 1981), *The Tribes and Castes of West Bengal* (Calcutta: Bengal Secretariat Press).

Robb, P. G. (1976), *The Government of India and Reform: Policies towards Politics and the Constitution, 1916–1921* (Delhi: Heritage Publishers).

Roy, S. B., Mukerjee, R., and Chatterjee, M. (*c*.1992), 'Endogenous Development and Gender Roles in Participatory Forest Management', IBRAD, Calcutta.

——— Roy, D. S., Bhattacharya, P., and Bhadra, R. K. (1993), 'Profile of Joint Forest Protection Committee at Sarugarh Range, West Bengal', Working Paper No. 16, IBRAD, Calcutta.

Roy, S. C. ([1912] 1970), *The Mundas and their Country* (Bombay: Asia Publishing House).

Russell, R. V., and Hiralal, R. B. ([1916] 1975), *Tribes and Castes of the Central Provinces, Nagpur* (Delhi: Cosmo Publications).

Rusten, E. P. and Gold, M. A. (1991), 'Understanding an Indigenous Knowledge System for Tree Fodder via a Multi-method On-Farm Research Approach', *Agroforestry Systems*, 15 (2 and 3): 139–65.

Ryan, J. G., and Ghodake, R. D. (1980), 'Labour Market Behaviour in Rural Villages of South India: Effects of Season, Sex and Socio-economic Status', Progress Report of the Economic Program No. 15, Indian Crop Research Institute for Semi-Arid Tropics (ICRISAT), Hyderabad.

Sachchidananda (1968), *The Tribal Village in Bihar: A Study of Unity and Extension* (Delhi: Munshiram Manoharlal).

Saint-Germain, M. A. (1989), 'Does their Difference Make a Difference? The Impact of Women on Public Policy in the Arizona Legislature', *Social Science Quarterly*, 70(4): 956–68.

Saldanha, I. M. (1998), 'Colonial Forest Regulations and Collective Resistance: Nineteenth-Century Thana District', in R. Grove, V. Damodaran, and S. Sangwan (eds.), *Nature and the Orient: The Environmental History of South and Southeast Asia* (Delhi: Oxford University Press), 708–33.

Salleh, A. K. (1984), 'Deeper than Deep Ecology. The Eco-feminist Connection', Discussion Paper, *Environmental Ethics*, 6 (Winter): 339–45.

Sapiro, V. (1981), 'Research Frontier Essay: When are Interests Interesting? The Problem of Political Representation of Women', *American Journal of Political Science Review*, 75(3): 701–16.

Sarin, M. (1995a), 'Regenerating India's Forest: Reconciling Gender Equity and Joint Forest Management', *IDS Bulletin*, 26(1): 83–91.

—— (1995b), 'Delving Beneath the Surface: Latent Gender Based Conflicts in Community Forestry Institutions', mimeo, SARTHI, Panchmahals, Gujarat.

—— (1996), *Joint Forest Management: The Haryana Experience* (Ahmedabad: Center for Environmental Education).

—— (1998), *Who is Gaining? Who is Losing? Gender and Equality Concerns in Joint Forest Management* (New Delhi: SPWD).

—— and Khanna, R. (1993), 'Women Organize for Wasteland Development: A Case Study of SARTHI in Gujarat', in A. Singh and N. Burra (eds.), *Women and Wasteland Development in India* (Delhi: Sage publications), 129–69.

Sarin, M., Singh, N. M, Sundar, N., and Bhogal, R. K. (2003), 'Devolution as a Threat to Democratic Decision-Making in Forestry? Findings from Three States in India', Working Paper 197, Overseas Development Institute, London.

SARTHI (1997–98), *Annual Report*, SARTHI, Panchmahals, Gujarat.

Saxena, N. C. (1995), 'Towards Sustainable Forestry in the U.P. Hills', Centre for Sustainable Development, LBS, National Academy of Administration, Mussoorie.

Schlager, E., and Ostrom, E. (1992), 'Property Rights and Natural Resources: A Conceptual Analysis', *Land Economics*, 68(3): 249–62.

Schott, R. G. (2001), 'The Role of Race in Law Enforcement: Racial Profiling or Legitimate Use?, *The FBI Law Enforcement Bulletin*, 70(11): 24–32.

Schwindt-Bayer, L. A. (2006), 'Still Supermadres? Gender and the Policy Priorities of Latin American Legislatures', *American Journal of Political Science*, 50(3): 570–85.

——and Mishler, W. (2005), 'An Integrated Model of Women's Representation', *Journal of Politics*, 67(2): 407–28.

Scott, J. (1985), *Weapons of the Weak: Everyday Forms of Peasant Resistance* (New Haven: Yale University Press).

Seabright, P. (1997a), 'Is Cooperation Habit-Forming?', in P. Dasgupta and K.-G. Maler (eds.), *The Environment and Emerging Development Issues* (Oxford: Clarendon Press), 283–307.

——(1997b), 'The Effect of Inequality on Collective Action', draft paper, Dept. of Applied Economics, University of Cambridge.

Seeley, J. (1996), 'Who benefits from Participatory Forest Management', *Banko Janakari*, 6 (1): 38–9.

Seiz, J. (2000), 'Game Theory and Bargaining Models', in J. Peterson and M. Lewis (ed.), *Elgar Companion to Feminist Economics* (Cheltenham: Elgar Publishing House), 379–90.

Sell, J. (1997), 'Gender, Strategies and Contributions to Public Goods', *Social Psychology Quarterly*, 60(3): 252–65.

Sen, A. K. (1984), *Resources, Values and Development* (Oxford: Clarendon Press).

——(1985), 'Well-Being, Agency and Freedom: The Dewey Lectures 1984', *Journal of Philosophy*, 82(4): 169–221.

——(1990), 'Gender and Cooperative Conflicts', in I. Tinker (ed.), *Persistent Inequalities: Women and World Development* (New York: Oxford University Press), 123–49.

——(2005), 'Human Rights and Capabilities', *Journal of Human Development*, 6(2): 151–66.

——(2006), 'Capabilities, Lists, and Public Reason: Continuing the Conversation', in B. Agarwal, I. Robeyns, and J. Humphries (eds.), *Capability, Freedom and Equality: Amartya Sen's Work from a Gender Perspective* (Delhi: Oxford University Press), 362–5.

——(2009), *The Idea of Justice* (London: Penguin Books).

Sen, I. (1988), 'Class and Gender in Work Time Allocation', *Economic and Political Weekly*, 23(33): 1702–6.

Shah, M. K., and Shah, P. (1995), 'Gender, Environment and Livelihood Security: An Alternative Viewpoint from India', *IDS Bulletin*, 26(1): 75–82.

Shamim, I., and Kumari, R. (2002), *Gender and Local Governance: A New Discourse in Development* (Islamabad: South Asia Network of Economic Research Institutes).

Sharma, A., and Sinha, A. (1993), 'A Study of the Common Property Resources in the Project Area of the Central Himalaya Rural Action Group', Report, Indian Institute of Forest Management, Bhopal, Madhya Pradesh.

Sharma, C. (1995), 'Community Initiatives in Forest Management: Issues of Class and Gender. A Case Study of Panchmahals District, Gujarat', unpublished MA dissertation, Jawaharlal Nehru University, Delhi.

Sharma, K., Nautiyal, K., and Pandey, B. (1987), 'Women in Struggle: Role and Participation of Women in the Chipko Movement in Uttarakhand Region of Uttar Pradesh', Occasional Monograph, Center for Women's Development Studies, Delhi.
Sharma, U. (1980), *Women, Work and Property in North-West India* (London: Tavistock).
Sherring, M. A. ([1881] 1975), *The Tribes and Castes of Rajasthan* (Delhi: Cosmo Publications).
Shiva, V. (1988), *Staying Alive: Women, Ecology and Survival* (London: Zed Books).
SIDA (2004), *Capacity Building in a Forest Project, India* (Stockholm: Environment Policy Division).
Siedman, G. (2003), 'Institutional Dilemmas: Representation vs Mobilisation in the South African Gender Commission', *Feminist Studies*, 29(3): 541–63.
Sikri, S. L. (1960), *A Constitutional History of India* (Jullundur: S. Nagin and Co.).
Singer, W. (2007), *A Constituency Suitable for Ladies: And Other Social Histories of Indian Elections* (Delhi: Oxford University Press).
Singh, A., and Burra, N. (eds.) (1993), *Women and Wasteland Development in India* (New Delhi: Sage Publications).
Singh, K. D., Sinha, B., Mukerji, S. D. (2005), 'Exploring Options for Joint Forest Management in India', Forestry Policy and Institutions Working Paper, FAO, Rome.
Singh, N. M. (1993), 'Regional Workshop of Forest Department on Joint Forest Management at Keonjhar', in Proceedings of the Workshop, Bhubaneshwar, Orissa, 28–9 May.
——and Kumar, K. (1993), 'Community Initiatives to Protect and Manage Forests in Balangir and Sambalpur Districts', Report, SIDA, New Delhi.
Singh, S. S., Misra, S., and Pratap. S. (1997), *Legislative Status of Panchayati Raj in India* (Delhi: Indian Institute of Public Administration).
Sinha, S., Gururani, S., and Greenberg, B. (1997), 'The "New Traditionalist" Discourse of Indian Environmentalism', *Journal of Peasant Studies*, 24(3): 65–99.
Sivaramakrishnan, K. (1999), *Modern Forests: State Making and Environmental Change in Colonial Eastern India* (Stanford, Calif.: Stanford University Press).
——(2000), 'Crafting the Public Sphere in the Forests of West Bengal: Democracy, Development, and Political Action', *American Ethnologist*, 27(2): 431–61.
Smith, K. R., Shuhua, G., Kun, H., and Daxiong, Q. (1993), 'One Hundred Million Improved Cookstoves in China: How was it Done?', *World Development*, 21(6): 941–61.
——Uma, R., Kishore, V. V. N., Zhang, J., Joshi, V., and Khalil, M. A. K. (2000), 'Greenhouse Implications of Household Stoves: An Analysis for India', *Annual Review of Energy Environment*, 25: 741–63.
Somanathan, E., Prabhakar, R., and Mehta, B. S. (2008), 'Decentralizatiion for Cost-Effective Conservation', *PNAS* early edition (http://www.pnas.org/cg/doi/10.1073/pnas.0810049106).
Somers, G. E. (1977), *The Dynamics of Santal Traditions in a Peasant Society* (New Delhi: Abhinav Publications).
Soulliere, A. K. (1996), 'Poor Women's Activities and Politics in Urban Brazil', unpublished MA dissertation submitted to the University of Windsor, Canada.
Springate-Baginski, O., and Blaikie, P. (eds.) (2007), *Forests, People and Power: The Political Ecology of Reform in South Asia* (London: Earthscan).
SPWD (1993), *Joint Forest Management Update 1993* (New Delhi: SPWD).
——(1998), *Joint Forest Management Update 1997* (New Delhi: SPWD).
Srinivas, M. N. (ed.) (1955), *India's Villages* (Bombay: Asia Publishing House).
Stark, O. (1995), *Altruism and Beyond: An Economic Analysis of Transfers and Exchanges within Families and Groups* (Cambridge: Cambridge University Press).

Staudt, K. (1996), 'Political Representation: Engendering Politics', Background Papers, *Human Development Report 1995*, UNDP, New York.
Steenhof, B., Pokharel, B. K., and Stadtmueller, T. (2007), 'Nepal Swiss Community Forestry Project, Phase II', Internal Review Report, Kathmandu, Nepal.
Stevenson, L. S. (1999), 'Gender Politics in the Mexican Democratization Process', in J. Dominquez and A. Poire (eds.), *Toward Mexico's Democratization: Parties, Campaigns, Elections and Public Opinion* (New York: Routledge), 57–87.
Stewart, F. (1996), 'Groups for Good or Ill', *Oxford Development Studies*, 24 (1): 9–25.
Stockard, J., Van de Kragt, A. J. C., and Dodge, P. J. (1988), 'Gender Roles and Behaviour in Social Dilemmas: Are There Sex Differences in Cooperation and in its Justification?', *Social Psychology Quarterly*, 51(12): 154–63.
Studlar, D., and McAllister, J. (2002), 'Does a Critical Mass Exist? A Comparative Analysis of Women's Legislative Representation since 1950', *European Journal of Political Research*, 41(2): 233–53.
Stuntz, W. J. (2006), 'Political Constitution of Criminal Justice', *Harvard Law Review*, 119: 780–851.
Sujaya, C. P. (2002), 'Development Planning, Resource Allocation and Women: Can the Women's Component Plan Help to Ensure Planning for and by Women? A Critique', mimeo, Delhi.
Sundar, N., Roger J., and Thin, N. (2001), *Branching Out: Joint Forest Management in India* (Delhi: Oxford University Press).
Sunstein, C. R. (1991), 'Preferences and Politics', *Philosophy and Public Affairs*, 20(1): 3–34.
——(1993), *The Partial Constitution* (Cambridge, Mass.: Harvard University Press).
——(2006), *Infotopia: How Many Minds Produce Knowledge* (Cambridge, Mass.: Harvard University Press).
Swaminathan, M. (1984), 'Eight Hours a Day for Fuel Collection' *Manushi (India)*, Mar.–Apr.
Swers, M. (2001), 'Understanding the Policy Impact of Electing Women: Evidence from Research on Congress and State Legislatures', *Political Science and Politics*, 34(2): 217–20.
Tankha, A. (2002), 'Self-Help Groups as Financial Intermediaries in India: Cost of Promotion, Sustainability and Impact', A Study Prepared for ICCO and Cordaid, the Netherlands.
TARU (2007), *Assessing the Impact of Andhra Pradesh Rural Livelihoods Programme on Poverty: End Term Assessment, Final Report* (Hyderabad: TARU Leading Edge Pvt. Ltd.)
TERI (1995), 'Community Participation in Van Panchayats of Kumaon Region of Uttar Pradesh', Paper No. 1, Part I, Tata Energy Research Institute, Delhi.
——(2004), 'The Role of Panchayati Raj Institutions in Natural Resource Management-Institutional Issues and Future Strategies', Project Report No. 2004 RE21, The Energy and Resources Institute, Delhi.
Thomas, D. (1990), 'Intra-household Resource Allocation: An Inferential Approach', *Journal of Human Resources*, 25(4): 635–63.
Thomas, S. (1994), *How Women Legislate* (Oxford: Oxford University Press).
——and Welch, S. (2001), 'The Impact of Women in State Legislatures: Numerical and Organizational Strength' in S. J. Carroll (ed.), *The Impact of Women in Public Office* (Bloomington, Ind.: Indiana University Press), 166–82.
Thurston, E., and Rangachari, K. ([1909] 1975), *Castes and Tribes of Southern India* (Delhi: Cosmo Publications).
Tolkien, J. R. R. (1967), *The Lord of the Rings: The Two Towers* (New York: Ballantine Books).

Tucker, R. (1998), 'Non-timber Forest Products Policy in the Western Himalayas under British Rule' in R. Grove, V. Damodaran, and S. Sangwan (eds.), *Nature and the Orient: The Environmental History of South and Southeast Asia* (Delhi: Oxford University Press), 459–83.

Underwood, B. (1997), 'Village Institutions and Federations: An Overview of AKRSP (I)'s Work in the Area of Human Resources Development', Working Paper, Aga Khan Rural Support Programme, India, Ahmedabad, Apr.

Uphoff, N. (1991), 'Fitting Projects to People', in M. M. Cernea (ed.), *Putting People First: Sociological Variables in Rural Development* (New York: Oxford University Press), 467–511.

Vallance, E. (1988), 'Do Women Make a Difference? The Impact of Women MEPs on Community Equality Policy', in M. Buckley and M. Andersen (eds.), *Women, Equality and Europe* (Basingstoke: Macmillan Press), 126–41.

VANI (2000), *Study on Development Organisations* (Delhi: Voluntary Action Network India).

Van Sahyog (2002–03), 'Salient Features of JFM Resolutions', SPWD, Delhi, Dec.–Mar., 4–15.

Vatuk, S. (1981), 'Sharing, Giving and Exchanging of Foods in South Asian Societies', mimeo, University of Illinois at Chicago Circle.

Venkateshwaran, S. (1992), *Living on the Edge: Women, Environment and Development* (New Delhi: Friedrich Ebert Stiftun).

Viegas, P., and Menon, G. (1993), 'Bringing Government and People Together: Forest Protection Committees of West Bengal: Role and Participation of Women', in A. Singh and N. Burra (eds.), *Women and Wasteland Development in India* (New Delhi: Sage Publications), 171–210.

Vijaylakshmi, V. (2003), 'Gender, Accountability and Political Representation in Local Government', Working Paper No. 102, Institute for Social and Economic Change, Bangalore.

——(2008), 'Rent Seeking and Gender in Local Governance', *Journal of Development Studies*, 44(9): 1262–88.

VIKSAT (2007), 'SAKSHAM, A Note', mimeo, VIKSAT, Ahemdabad, Gujarat.

Wade, R. (1988), *Village Republics: Economic Conditions for Collective Action in South India* (Cambridge: Cambridge University Press).

Walker, J., Thomas, S., and Ryan, J. G. (1990), *Village and Household Economics in India's Semi-Arid Tropics* (Baltimore: Johns Hopkins University Press).

Wängnerud, L. (2000), 'Testing the Politics of Presence: Women's Representation in the Swedish Riksdag', *Scandinavian Political Studies*, 23(1): 67–91.

Watson, R. T., Noble, I. R., Boliln, B., Ravindranath, N. H., Verardo, D. J., and Dokken, D. J. (eds.) (2000), *Land Use, Land Use Change, and Forestry: A Special Report of the Intergovernmental Panel on Climate Change* (New York: Cambridge University Press).

Weinberger, K. (2000), *Women's Participation: An Economic Analysis in Rural Chad and Pakistan*, Development Economics and Policy Series No. 15. (Europäischer Verlag der Wissenschaften: Peter Lang).

Weldon, S. L. (2002), 'Beyond Bodies: Institutional Sources of Representation for Women in Democratic Policymaking', *Journal of Politics*, 64(4): 1153–74.

Westerman, O., Ashby, J., and Pretty, J. (2005), 'Gender and Social Capital: The Importance of Gender Differences for the Maturity and Effectiveness of Natural Resource Management Groups', *World Development*, 33(11): 1783–99.

White, S. (1996), 'Depoliticising Development: The Uses and Abuses of Participation', *Development in Practice*, 6(1): 6–15.

White, T. A., and Runge, C. F. (1994), 'The Emergence and Evolution of Collective Action: Lessons from Watershed Management in Haiti', draft paper, Center for International Food and Agricultural Policy, University of Minnesota.

WHO (2002), *World Health Report* (Geneva: World Health Organization).

WINROCK (2006), 'Understanding the Role of Networks as Connecters in Bridging the Research Policy Gap in Participatory Forest Policy Development in India', JBICI Discussion Paper No. 12, Japan Bank for International Cooperation, Tokyo.

Witt, L., Paget, K., and Mathews, G. (1995), 'What Difference Does Difference Make?' in L. Witt, K. M. Paget, and G. Mathews (eds.), *Running Like a Woman: Gender and Power in American Politics* (New York: The Free Press), 265–84.

World Bank (1983a), 'Gujarat Community Forest Project: Mid-Term Review Mission Report', The World Bank, New Delhi.

——(1983b), 'Uttar Pradesh Social Forestry Project: Mid-Term Review Mission Report', The World Bank, New Delhi.

——(2004), 'India: Fiscal Decentralisation to Rural Governments', Report No. 26654, Rural Development Unit, South Asia Region, The World Bank, New Delhi.

Yalman, N. (1967), *Under the Bo Tree* (Berkeley, Calif.: University of Berkeley Press).

Yamanaka, M., and Ashworth, A. (2002), 'Differential Workloads of Boys and Girls in Rural Nepal and their Association with Growth', *American Journal of Human Biology*, 14 (3): 356–63.

Yorke, M. (1985), 'The Situation of the Gonds of Asifabad and Lakshetipet Taluks, Adilabad District', in C. V. Furer-Haimendorf (ed.), *Tribes of India: The Struggle for Survival* (Delhi: Oxford University Press), 203–49.

Young, I. M. (1993), 'Justice and Communicative Democracy', in R. Gottlieb (ed.), *Radical Philosophy: Tradition, Counter-Tradition, Politics* (Philadelphia: Temple University Press), 123–43.

——(1997a), *Intersecting Voices: Dilemmas of Gender, Political Philosophy, and Policy* (Princeton: Princeton University Press).

——(1997b), 'Unruly Categories: A Critique of Nancy Fraser's Dual Systems Theory', *New Left Review*, 222 (Mar.–Apr.): 147–60.

——(2000), *Inclusion and Democracy* (New York: Oxford University Press).

Zimmerman, M. E. (1987), 'Feminism, Deep Ecology and Environmental Ethics', *Environmental Ethics*, 9: 21–44.

Author Index

Subject Index